AF361495

The Saints in Old Norse
and Early Modern Icelandic Poetry

The Saints in Old Norse and Early Modern Icelandic Poetry is a complementary volume to *The Legends of the Saints in Old Norse–Icelandic Prose* (UTP 2013). While its predecessor dealt primarily with medieval prose texts about the saints, this volume not only focuses on medieval poems about saints but also on Icelandic devotional poetry created during the early modern period. The handlist organizes saints' names, manuscripts, and editions of individual poems with references to approximate dates of the manuscripts, as well as modern Icelandic editions and translations. Each entry concludes with secondary literature about the poem in question. These features combine to make *The Saints in Old Norse and Early Modern Icelandic Poetry* an invaluable resource for scholars and students in the field.

(Toronto Old Norse and Icelandic Series)

KIRSTEN WOLF is Kim Nilsson Professor, Torger Thompson Chair, and Associate Chair in the Department of German, Nordic, and Slavic at the University of Wisconsin-Madison.

NATALIE M. VAN DEUSEN is Assistant Professor and Henry Cabot and Linnea Lodge Professor of Scandinavian Studies in the Department of Modern Languages and Cultural Studies at the University of Alberta.

The Saints in Old Norse and Early Modern Icelandic Poetry

Kirsten Wolf and Natalie M. Van Deusen

UNIVERSITY OF TORONTO PRESS
Toronto Buffalo London

ISBN 978-1-4875-0074-0 (cloth)

Printed on acid-free paper.

Library and Archives Canada Cataloguing in Publication

Wolf, Kirsten, 1959–, author
The saints in Old Norse and early modern Icelandic poetry / Kirsten Wolf and Natalie M. Van Deusen.

(Toronto Old Norse and Icelandic series ; 10)
Includes bibliographical references and index.
ISBN 978-1-4875-0074-0 (cloth)

1. Old Norse poetry – Bibliography.   2. Religious poetry, Old Norse – Bibliography.
3. Icelandic poetry – Early modern, 1500–1700 – Bibliography.   4. Christian saints –
Poetry – Early works to 1800 – Bibliography.   5. Christian saints in literature –
Bibliography. I. Van Deusen, Natalie M., 1983–, author II. Title. III. Series:
Toronto Old Norse and Icelandic series ; 10

Z2556.W685 2017   016.839'610080382   C2016-902985-9

University of Toronto Press gratefully acknowledges the financial assistance of the
Centre for Medieval Studies, University of Toronto in the publication of this book.

University of Toronto Press acknowledges the financial assistance to its publishing
program of the Canada Council for the Arts and the Ontario Arts Council, an agency
of the Government of Ontario.

Contents

Preface

The Saints in Old Norse and Early Modern Icelandic Poetry is intended as a sequel to *The Legends of the Saints in Old Norse–Icelandic Prose*, which was published by the University of Toronto Press in 2013. In some respects, however, *The Saints in Old Norse and Early Modern Icelandic Poetry* differs from *The Legends of the Saints in Old Norse–Icelandic Prose*, in which the corpus of prose texts examined was limited to the Middle Ages. This book includes poetic texts also from the early modern period, since some of these poems appear to have their origin in the Middle Ages. Moreover, while *The Legends of the Saints in Old Norse–Icelandic Prose* had a model in the form of Hans Bekker-Nielsen, Ole Widding, and L.K. Shook's index, "The Lives of the Saints in Old Norse Prose: A Handlist" (*Mediaeval Studies* 25 [1963]), and built on the work of the three scholars, the present book has no antecedent.

The medieval poems about the saints have received a fair amount of attention over the years from literary scholars and especially editors of Old Norse–Icelandic poetry, notably Hugo Rydberg (1907), Hans Sperber (1911), Finnur Jónsson (1912–15), Ernst Albin Kock (1923–4), and last, but not least, Margaret Clunies Ross and Diana Whaley, who served as general editors of *Poetry on Christian Subjects* (2007) and *Poetry from the Kings' Sagas* (2012), respectively.

In contrast, the extensive body of Icelandic devotional poetry from the period around and following the Reformation (officially 1550 in Iceland) has received modest scholarly attention, and much of it has never been edited. Jón Þorkelsson did the field a favour with his *Om Digtningen på Island i det 15. og 16. Århundrede* (1888), which serves as an inventory of poetic texts and manuscripts from the time, and later with his *Kvæðasafn eftir nafngreinda íslenzka menn frá miðöldum* (1922–7), which provides editions of a number of poems, including poems about saints. Later, Jón Helgason published two fascicles of *Íslenzk miðaldakvæði: Islandske digte fra senmiddelalderen* (1936 and 1938);

the original plan was a three-volume edition of the late medieval devotional poems, but unfortunately the plan did not materialize. While going through catalogues of manuscripts, we were astonished by the number of post-Reformation manuscripts containing poems about saints.

We have done our best to be comprehensive, but we do not in any way presume to have been exhaustive. Our primary aim is twofold: on the one hand to celebrate the work on the poems that has been done, and, on the other, to draw attention to the work that remains to be done.

The book is arranged according to the following principles:

1 Saints are listed alphabetically according to name, with their feast days indicated in each case.
2 Arabic numerals followed by a title denote a different poem about the same saint. Where possible, the poems are listed in chronological order. For consistency, early modern poems follow the dates in *Bragi-óðfræðivefur* (http://bragi.info/), an online index of late medieval and early modern Icelandic poetry published by Stofnun Árna Magnússonar í íslenskum fræðum og Óðfræðifélagið Boðn, both edited by Kristján Eiríksson. When only a few stanzas of a poem are devoted to a saint, these poems are listed at the end of an entry, and cross-referenced to the main entry for that poem. We have not included each and every mention of the Virgin Mary and Saint Olav of Norway, since this would have added pages to this already substantial volume and caused quite some repetition. We cannot guarantee that we have covered each and every mention of a saint, especially a popular and/or biblical one, or one who is briefly mentioned in a poem such as *Lilja*, which has been edited and translated numerous times. Also, with regard to poems dealing with Saint Olav, only devotional poems have been included. Those late medieval poems about the Virgin Mary without proper titles are denoted by their incipits, as they are in Jón Helgason's edition.
3 Incipits for individual poems are generally presented in a normalized form. Skaldic poems are normalized to Old Norse–Icelandic spelling, and late medieval and early modern Icelandic devotional poetry is normalized to modern Icelandic spelling.
4 Manuscripts are listed in alphabetical order according to their call number.
5 Editions of the individual lives are listed in alphabetical order followed by references to modern Icelandic language editions, though obviously not in the case of the later poems, and translations.
6 The bibliographical material does not presume to be exhaustive, but we hope that most books and mainstream journals within the field of Old Norse and early modern Icelandic language and literature have been

covered. Icelandic names are alphabetized by given and not patronymic names. The cut-off date for publications is January 2015, when the manuscript was submitted to the University of Toronto Press. For practical reasons, we have not generally included references to Bernhard Kahle's *Die Sprache der Skalden auf Grund der Binnen- und Endreime* (1892), Gerd Kreutzer's *Die Dichtungslehre der Skalden: Poetologische Terminologie und Autorenkommentare als Grundlage einer Gattungspoetik* (1977), and Rudolf Meissner's *Die Kenningar der Skalden: Ein Beitrag zur skaldischen Poetik* (1921), since this would have greatly expanded the volume.

The list of poems about the saints is prefaced by a table of abbreviations and symbols used, a list of relevant published catalogues and bibliographies, a list of some of the main editions and collections of Old Norse and early modern Icelandic poems about the saints, and a list of frequently cited general works.

Many of the manuscripts in which the poems are preserved are available in digital form at the archival site Handrit.is. In addition, a number of the out-of-print and rare books and periodicals are digitally accessible on such sites as Bækur.is and Early European Books (eeb.chadwyck.co.uk/).

Our work on the volume was in the main conducted during the spring of 2013 and the spring and fall of 2014. Natalie is grateful to the University of Alberta Killam Research Fund, which enabled her to do fieldwork in Iceland. Kirsten is grateful to the Graduate School of the University of Wisconsin for funding to involve her eminently able research assistants, Susanne Arthur and Lauren Poyer, in the project. In addition, we would like to thank Kari Ellen Gade, Gísli Þór Ólafsson, Guðrún Nordal, Halldóra Kristjánsdóttir, Kristján Eiríksson, Lára Ágústa Ólafsdóttir, Margrét Eggertsdóttir, Katelin Parsons, Sigríður Hjördís Jörundsdóttir, Soffía Guðný Guðmundsdóttir, Svanhildur Óskarsdóttir, and Diana Whaley, who kindly answered questions along the way. Finally, we wish to thank the three anonymous readers of the manuscript for their very useful suggestions and the University of Toronto Press for our pleasant collaboration. We are particularly grateful to Barbara Porter, Suzanne Rancourt, and Judy Williams.

Abbreviations and Symbols

ANF	*Arkiv för nordisk filologi*
APS	*Acta Philologica Scandinavica*
CCI	Corpus Codicum Islandicorum Medii Aevi
CCN	Corpus Codicum Norvegicorum Medii Aevi
EIM	Early Icelandic Manuscripts in Facsimile
JEGP	*Journal of English and Germanic Philology*
KLNM	*Kulturhistorisk leksikon for nordisk middelalder*
Mm	*Maal og minne*
Saga-Book	*Saga-Book of the Viking Society*
STUAGNL	Samfund til Udgivelse af gammel nordisk Litteratur
*	Designated item not examined by the compilers
>>	Designated item's full bibliographical information can be found in "Editions and Collections" or "General Works."

The Saints in Old Norse
and Early Modern Icelandic Poetry

I. Catalogues and Bibliographies

Arnamagnæanske Kommission, Den. *Ordbog over det norrøne prosasprog.
Registre* (Odense: AiO, 1989).
Bekker-Nielsen, Hans, Ole Widding, and L.K. Shook, "The Lives of the
Saints in Old Norse Prose: A Handlist." *Mediaeval Studies* 25 (1963):
294–337.
British Library, The. *Catalogue of Additions to the Manuscripts 1756–1782.
Additional Manuscripts 4101–5017* (London: British Museum Publications
for the British Library Board, 1973).
Grímur M. Helgason and Lárus H. Blöndal. *Handritasafn Landsbókasafns.*
III. *Aukabindi* (Reykjavík: Landsbókasafn Íslands, 1970).
Gödel, Vilhelm. *Katalog öfver Kongl. Bibliotekets fornisländska och
fornnorska handskrifter* (Stockholm: Norstedt and Söner, 1897–1900).
Hollander, Lee M. *A Bibliography of Skaldic Studies* (Copenhagen: Ejnar
Munksgaard, 1958).
Kålund, Kr. *Katalog over Den arnamagnæanske Håndskriftsamling.* 2 vols.
(Copenhagen: Gyldendal, 1889–94).
– *Katalog over de oldnorsk-islandske Håndskrifter i Det store kongelige
Bibliotek og i Universitetsbiblioteket (udenfor Den arnamagnæanske
Samling samt den arnamagnæanske Samlings Tilvækst 1894–99)*
(Copenhagen: Gyldendal, 1900).
Lárus H. Blöndal. *Handritasafn Landsbókasafns. II. Aukabindi. Viðauki.
Skrá um skinnblöð í Landsbókasafni Íslands eftir Jakob Benediktsson*
(Reykjavík: Félagsprintsmiðjan, 1959).
Páll Eggert Ólason. *Skrá um Handritasöfn Landsbókasafnsins.* 3 vols.
(Reykjavík: Gutenberg, 1918–37).
– *Handritasafn Landsbókasafns. I. Aukabindi* (Reykjavík: Félagsprentsmiðjan,
1947).

II. Editions and Collections

Bjarni Aðalbjarnarson, ed. *Snorri Sturluson. Heimskringla*. 3 vols. Íslenzk
   fornrit 26–8 (Reykjavík: Hið íslenzka fornritafélag, 1979).
   Erfidrápa Óláfs helga, Geisli, Glælognskviða, and *Róðudrápa*.
Eeden, Willem van, Jr, ed. *De Codex Trajectinus van de Snorra Edda*
   (Leiden: Eduard Ijdo, 1913).
   Erfidrápa Óláfs helga, Geisli, and *Michaelskvæði*.
Faulkes, Anthony, ed. *Codex Trajectinus: The Utrecht Manuscript of the
   Prose Edda*. EIM 15 (Copenhagen: Rosenkilde and Bagger, 1985).
   Erfidrápa Óláfs helga, Geisli, and *Michaelskvæði*.
Finnur Jónsson, ed. *Heimskringla. Nóregs konunga sǫgur*. 4 vols. STUAGNL
   23 (Copenhagen: Møller, 1893–1900).
   Erfidrápa Óláfs helga, Geisli, Glælognskviða, and *Róðudrápa*.
– ed. *Snorri Sturluson: Heimskringla. Nóregs konunga sǫgur* (Copenhagen:
   Gad, 1911; rpt. Oslo: Universitetsforlaget, 1966).
   Erfidrápa Óláfs helga, Geisli, Glælognskviða, and *Róðudrápa*.
– ed. *Den norsk-islandske skjaldedigtning*. Vols AI, AII (tekst efter
   håndskrifterne) and BI, BII (rettet tekst) (Copenhagen: Gyldendal, 1912–15).
   *Allra postola minnisvísur, Andréasdrápa, Drápa af Máríugrát, Erfidrápa
   Óláfs helga, Geisli, Glælognskviða, Guðmundardrápa* (Arngrímr), *Guð-
   mundardrápa* (Árni Jónsson), *Guðmundarkvæði* (Arngrímr), *Guðmundarkvæði*
   (Einarr Gilsson), *Gyðingsvísur, Harmsól, Heilagra manna drápa, Heilagra
   meyja drápa, Jónsdrápa, Jónsdrápa postola, Jónsvísur, Kátrínardrápa,
   Lausavísur* (Kolbeinn Tumason), *Líknarbraut, Lilja, Máríudrápa,
   Máríuflokkr, Máríuvísur I–III, Michaelskvæði, Nikulásdrápa, Pétrsdrápa,
   Plácítusdrápa, Róðudrápa, Selkolluvísur, Thómasdrápa, Vísur um
   Guðmund biskup*, and *Vitnisvísur af Máríu*.

– ed. *Jón Arasons religiøse digte*. Historisk-filologiske Meddelelser II, 2 (Copenhagen: Høst and Søn, 1918).
  Krossvísur I, Ljómur, Niðurstigningsvísur, and *Píslargrátur*.
– ed. *Edda Snorra Sturlusonar: Codex Wormianus AM 242 fol.* (Copenhagen and Kristiania [Oslo]: Gyldendal, 1924).
  Erfidrápa Óláfs helga, Geisli, Máríuflokkr, Michaelskvæði, and *Nikulásdrápa*.
– ed. *Flateyjarbók (Codex Flateyensis): MS. No. 1005 fol. in the Old Royal Collection in the Royal Library of Copenhagen*. CCI 1 (Copenhagen: Levin and Munksgaard, 1930).
  Erfidrápa Óláfs helga, Geisli, Glælognskviða, Óláfs ríma Haraldssonar, and *Róðudrápa*.
Finnur Sigmundsson. *Rímnatal*. 2 vols. (Reykjavík: Rímnafélagið, 1966). Vol. 1.
  Margrétar rímur, Óláfs ríma Haraldssonar, Óláfs rímur, Rímur af Agnesi píslarvotti, Rímur af Margrétu píslarvotti, Rímur af Páli postula, and *Rímur af sjö sofendum*.
Guðbrandur Þorláksson, ed. *Ein ny wiisna bok med mörgum andlegum viisum og kuædum, psalmum, lof sønguum og rijmum, teknum wr Heilagre Ritningu* (Hólar, 1612).
  Ein ágæt minning herrans Jesú Kristí pínu, Heilags anda höllin glæst, Huggunarvísur fyrir þá sem syrgja eftir ástmenn sína, María móðirin skæra, Máríuvísur, Máríuævi eða Lífssaga helgustu Guðs móðir, Píslargrátur, Píslarminning, and *Vísur um sanna iðran og ávöxtu hennar*.
Guðbrandr Vigfússon and C.R. Unger, ed. *Flateyjarbók: En Samling af norske Konge-Sagaer med indskudte mindre Fortællinger om Begivenheder i og udenfor Norge samt Annaler*. 3 vols. (Christiania [Oslo]: Malling, 1860–8).
  Erfidrápa Óláfs helga, Geisli, Glælognskviða, Óláfs ríma Haraldssonar, and *Róðudrápa*.
Guðni Jónsson, ed. *Byskupa sögur*. 3 vols. (Reykjavík: Íslendingasagnaútgáfan; Haukadalsútgáfan, 1948). Vol. 3.
  Guðmundardrápa (Arngrímr), *Guðmundarkvæði* (Einarr Gilsson), and *Vísur um Guðmund biskup* (Einarr Gilsson).
Heimir Pálsson, ed. *Snorri Sturluson. The Uppsala Edda. DG 11 4to*. Trans. Anthony Faulkes (University College London: Viking Society for Northern Research, 2012).
  Erfidrápa Óláfs helga, Geisli, and *Michaelskvæði*.
Johnsen, Oscar Albert, and Jón Helgason, ed. *Saga Óláfs konungs hins helga: Den store saga om Olav den hellige efter pergamenthåndskrift i Kungliga*

biblioteket i Stockholm nr. 2 4o med varianter fra andre håndskrifter.
2 vols. Det norske historiske kildeskriftfond skrifter 53 (Oslo: Dybwad,
1941).
Erfidrápa Óláfs helga, Geisli, Glælognskviða, and *Róðudrápa.*
Jón Helgason, ed. *Íslenzk miðaldakvæði: Islandske digte fra
senmiddelalderen.* 1.2 (Copenhagen: Levin and Munksgaard and Ejnar
Munksgaard, 1936); 2 (Copenhagen: Ejnar Munksgaard, 1938).
*Agnesardiktur, Ágæt vil ég þér óðinn færa, Allra kærasta jungfrú mín,
Andréasdiktur I–III, Barbörudiktur, Barthólómeusdiktur, Bjóða vil ég þér
bragsins smíð, Blómarós, Boðunarvísur, Brúðkaupsvísur, Cecilíudiktur,
Christeforusvísur, Dórótheudiktur, Dýrðarlegast dygða blóm, Ég vil
lofa eina þá, Enginn heyrði og enginn sá, Eptirdæmið eitt ég sá, Fljóðið
ekki finnast má, Fyrirlát mér jungfrúin hreina, Fýsir mig að fremja dikt,
Gimsteinn, Gjörði í einu, Græðarinn lýðs og landa, Guð sinn mundi,
Gyðingsdiktur, Heiðra vilda ég helgan Krist, Heilags anda höllin glæst,
Helgan kross að heiðra má, Heyr mig bjartast blómsturið mæta, Heyr mig
dýrust drottins frú, Heyr mig himins og láða, Heyr skínandi skærust frú,
Heyr þú hinn hæsti hjálpari minn, Heyrðu hjálpin skæra, Hugarraun, Hvað
skal mig þann sálugi mann, Hæstur heilagur andi, Jakobsdiktur, Jesús
móðirin jungfrú skær, Jóhannesdiktur, Jǫfur gefi upphaf, Kristsbálkur,
Krosskvæði, Krossrímur, Krossþulur, Krossvísur I–II, Kvæði um sankti
Hallvarð, Lárentíusdiktur, Ljómur, Magnúsdiktur, Margrétarvísur, María
drottins liljan guðs og ljómi, María gef mér mælsku til, María heyr mig
háleit víf, María meyjan skæra, María móðirin skæra, María mærin svinna,
María vil ég þig móðir guðs, Máríu nafn með gleði og prís, Máríublóm,
Máríugrátr, Máríulykill, Máríutíðir, Máríuvísur, Máríuævi eða Lífssaga
helgustu Guðs móðir, Milska, Náð, Niðurstigningsvísur, Nikulásdiktur,
Nikulásdrápa, Nikulásvísur I–II, Óláfsvísur I–IV, Pálsdiktur, Pálsvísur,
Pétursdiktur, Pétursvísur, Píslardrápa, Píslargrátur, Rósa, Salutatio
Mariæ, Sankta María móðir mild, Suptungs vilda ég bjórinn blanda, Sælust
sjóvar stjarna, Thómasdiktur, Thómas diktur erkibiskups, Tólf postula
kvæði, Um heiðurs mey vil ég hefja, Út í löndum ég hefi spurt, Vegsemd
alra vífa, Vísur af Máríu Magdalene I–II,* and *Vísur Cecilíu.*
– ed. *Byskupa sǫgur. MS Perg. fol. No. 5 in the Royal Library of Stockholm.*
CCI 19 (Copenhagen: Ejnar Munksgaard, 1950).
Guðmundardrápa (Arngrímr), *Guðmundarkvæði* (Arngrímr), *Guðmundar-
kvæði* (Einarr Gilsson), *Vísur um Guðmund biskup* (Einarr Gilsson),
and *Selkolluvísur* (Einarr Gilsson).
– ed. *Kvæðabók úr Vigur: AM 148, 8vo.* Íslenzk Rit Síðara Alda, 2. flokkur IA
(Copenhagen: Hið íslenzka fræðafélag, 1955).

Gimsteinn, Gyðingsdiktur, Eptirdæmið eitt ég sá, Hugarraun, Iðrunardiktur,
Krosskvæði, Ljómur, Niðurstigningsvísur, Óláfsvísur IV, and *Sethskvæði.*
Jón Sigurðsson et al. *Edda Snorra Sturlusonar: Edda Snorronis Sturlaei.*
3 vols. (Copenhagen: Legatum Arnamagnaeanum, 1848–87; rpt. Osnabrück:
Zeller, 1966).
Erfidrápa Óláfs helga, Máríuflokkr, Michaelskvæði, Nikulásdrápa,
and *Thómasdrápa.*
[Jón Sigurðsson and Guðbrandur Vigfússon, ed.] *Biskupa sögur.* 2 vols.
(Copenhagen: Møller, 1858–78).
Guðmundardrápa, Guðmundarkvæði (Arngrímr), *Guðmundarkvæði*
(Einarr Gilsson), *Krossvísur I* (Jón Arason), *Ljómur* (Jón Arason), *María*
heyr mig háleit víf (Jón Arason), *María meyjan skæra* (Jón Arason),
María móðirin skæra (Jón Arason), *Máríugrátur, Niðurstigningsvísur*
(Jón Arason), *Píslargrátur* (Jón Arason), and *Vísur um Guðmund biskup*
(Einarr Gilsson).
Jón Torfason and Kristján Eiríksson, ed. *Vísnabók Guðbrands* (Reykjavík:
Bókmenntafræðistofnun Háskóla Íslands, 2000).
Ein ágæt minning herrans Jesú Kristi pínu, Heilags anda höllin glæst,
Huggunarvísur fyrir þá sem syrgja eftir ástmenn sína, María móðirin
skæra, Máríuvísur, Máríuævi eða Lífssaga helgustu guðs móður,
Píslargrátur, Píslarminning, and *Vísur um sanna iðran og ávöxtu hennar.*
Jón Þorkelsson, ed. *Kvæðasafn eptir nafngreinda íslenzka menn frá miðöld*
(Reykjavík: Ísafold, 1922–7).
Eptirdæmið eitt ég sá, Gimsteinn, María heyr mig háleit víf, María meyjan
skæra, María móðirin skæra, Máríublóm, Máríulykill, Michaelsflokkur,
Náð, Nikulásdrápa, Óláfsvísur IV, Rósa, Sankta María móðir mild,
and *Sælust sjóvar stjarna.*
Kahle, Bernhard, ed. *Isländische geistliche Dichtungen des ausgehenden*
Mittelalters (Heidelberg: Winter, 1898).
Drápa af Máríugrát, Heilagra manna drápa, Kátrínardrápa, Máríuvísur
I–III, Pétrsdrápa, and *Vitnisvísur af Máríu.*
Kock, Ernst Albin. *Notationes Norrænæ: Anteckningar till Edda och skalde-*
diktning. Lunds Universitets årsskrift. New series, sec. 1 (Lund: Gleerup,
1923–44).
– ed. *Den norsk-isländska skaldediktningen.* 2 vols. (Lund: Gleerup, 1946–50).
Allra postola minnisvísur, Andréasdrápa, Drápa af Máríugrát, Erfidrápa
Óláfs helga, Geisli, Glælognskviða, Guðmundardrápa (Arngrímr),
Guðmundardrápa (Árni Jónsson), *Guðmundarkvæði* (Arngrímr),
Guðmundarkvæði (Einarr Gilsson), *Gyðingsvísur, Harmsól, Heilagra*
manna drápa, Heilagra meyja drápa, Jónsdrápa, Jónsdrápa postola,

Jónsvísur, *Kátrínardrápa*, *Lausavísur* (Kolbeinn Tumason), *Líknarbraut*, *Lilja*, *Máríudrápa*, *Máríuflokkr*, *Máríuvísur I–III*, *Michaelskvæði*, *Nikulásdrápa*, *Pétrsdrápa*, *Plácítusdrápa*, *Róðudrápa*, *Selkolluvísur*, *Thómasdrápa*, *Vísur um Guðmund biskup*, and *Vitnisvísur af Máríu*.

Konráð Gíslason, ed. *Fire og fyrretyve for en stor Deel forhen utrykte Prøver af oldnordisk Sprog og Literatur* (Copenhagen: Gyldendal, 1860). *Andréasdrápa*, *Cecilíudiktur*, *Máríudrápa*, and *Pétrsdrápa*.

Lindblad, Gustaf, ed. *Bergsbók. Perg. Fol. Nr. 1, Royal Library, Stockholm.* EIM (Copenhagen: Rosenkilde and Bagger, 1963). *Erfidrápa Óláfs helga*, *Geisli*, *Glælognskviða*, *Óláfsvísur II*, and *Róðudrápa*.

Loth, Agnete, ed. *Thomasskinna. Gl. Kgl. Saml. 1008 fol. in The Royal Library, Copenhagen.* EIM 6 (Copenhagen: Rosenkilde and Bagger, 1964). *Erfidrápa Óláfs helga*, *Geisli*, *Glælognskviða*, and *Róðudrápa*.

Overgaard, Mariane, ed. *The History of the Cross-Tree Down to Christ's Passion: Icelandic Legend Versions.* Editiones Arnamagnæanæ, Ser. B, vol. 26 (Copenhagen: Munksgaard, 1968). *Krossrímur* and *Krosskvæði*.

Peringskiöld, J.F., ed. *Fragmentum runicopapisticum* (Stockholm, 1721). *Krosskvæði*, *Krossvísur I*, and *Sankta María móðir mild*.

Poetry from the Kings' Sagas 1. Ed. Diana Whaley. 2 vols. *Skaldic Poetry of the Scandinavian Middle Ages*, vol. 1. (Turnhout: Brepols, 2012). *Erfidrápa Óláfs helga*, *Glælognskviða*, and *Róðudrápa*.

Poetry on Christian Subjects. Ed. Margaret Clunies Ross. 2 vols. *Skaldic Poetry of the Scandinavian Middle Ages*, vol. 7 (Turnhout: Brepols, 2007). *Allra postola minnisvísur*, *Andréasdrápa*, *Brúðkaupsvísur*, *Drápa af Máríugrát*, *Geisli*, *Gyðingsvísur*, *Harmsól*, *Heilagra manna drápa*, *Heilagra meyja drápa*, *Jónsdrápa*, *Jónsdrápa postola*, *Jónsvísur*, *Kátrínardrápa*, *Líknarbraut*, *Lilja*, *Máríudrápa*, *Máríuvísur I–III*, *Pétrsdrápa*, *Plácítusdrápa*, and *Vitnisvísur af Máríu*.

Rydberg, Hugo, ed. *Die geistlichen Drápur und Dróttkvættfragmente des Cod. AM 757 4to* (Copenhagen: Møller, 1907). *Gyðingsvísur*, *Harmsól*, *Líknarbraut*, and *Máríudrápa*.

Sigurður Nordal, ed. *Codex Wormianus (The Younger Edda). MS. No. 242 fol. in The Arnamagnean Collection in the University Library of Copenhagen.* CCI 2 (Copenhagen: Levin and Munksgaard, 1931). *Erfidrápa Óláfs helga*, *Máríuflokkr*, *Michaelskvæði*, *Nikulásdrápa*, and *Thómasdrápa*.

Sperber, Hans, ed. *Sechs isländische Gedichte legendarischen Inhalts.* Uppsala Universitets årsskrift, filosofi, språkvetenskap och historiska vetenskaper 2 (Uppsala: Akademische Buchdruckerei Edv. Berling, 1911).

Drápa af Máríugrát, *Kátrínardrápa*, *Máríuvísur I–III*, and *Vitnisvísur af Máríu*.

Unger, C.R., ed. *Postola sögur: Legendariske fortællinger om apostlernes liv, deres kamp for kristendommens udbredelse samt deres martyrdød* (Christiania [Oslo]: Bentzen, 1874).
Jónsdrápa, *Jónsdrápa postola*, and *Jónsvísur* (Kolbeinn Tumason).

Wolf, Kirsten, ed. *Saga heilagrar Önnu* (Reykjavík: Stofnun Árna Magnússonar, 2001).

– ed. *Heilagra meyja sögur*. Íslensk trúarit 1 (Reykjavík: Bókmenntafræðistofnun Háskóla Íslands, 2003).

– ed. *A Female Legendary from Iceland: "Kirkjubæjarbók" (AM 429 12mo) in the Arnamagnæan Collection, Copenhagen)*. Manuscripta Nordica: Early Nordic Manuscripts in Digital Facsimile 3 (Copenhagen: Museum Tusculanum Press, 2011).
Cecilíudiktur and *Dórótheudiktur*.

Wrightson, Kellinde, ed. *Fourteenth-Century Icelandic Verse on the Virgin Mary. Drápa af Maríugrát. Vitnisvísur af Maríu. Maríuvísur I–III*. Viking Society for Northern Research Text Series 14 (University College London: Viking Society for Northern Research, 2001).
Drápa af Máríugrát, *Máríuvísur I–III*, and *Vitnisvísur af Máríu*.

III. General Works

Bekker-Nielsen, Hans, Thorkil Damsgaard Olsen, and Ole Widding. *Norrøn fortællekunst. Kapitler af den norsk-islandske middelalderlitteraturs historie* ([Copenhagen]: Akademisk forlag, 1965).

Chase, Martin, ed. *Eddic, Skaldic, and Beyond: Poetic Variety in Medieval Iceland and Norway* (New York: Fordham University Press, 2014).

Clunies Ross, Margaret. *A History of Old Norse Poetry and Poetics* (Cambridge: D.S. Brewer, 2005).

Cormack, Margaret. *The Saints in Iceland: Their Veneration from the Conversion to 1400.* Subsidia Hagiographica 78 (Brussels: Société des Bollandistes, 1994).

Finnur Jónsson. *Bókmentasaga Íslendinga fram undir siðabót* (Copenhagen: Möller, 1904–5).

– *Den oldnorske og oldislandske Litteraturs Historie.* 2nd ed. 3 vols. (Copenhagen: Gad, 1920–4).

Holm-Olsen, Ludvig, and Kjell Heggelund. *Norges Litteratur Historie: Fra Runene til Norske Selskab.* Ed. Edvard Beyer (Oslo: Cappelen, 1974).

Íslensk Bókmenntasaga 1. Ed. Guðrún Nordal, Sverrir Tómasson, and Vésteinn Ólason (Reykjavík: Mál og menning, 1992).

Íslensk Bókmenntasaga 2. Ed. Böðvar Guðmundsson, Sverrir Tómasson, Torfi H. Tulinius, and Vésteinn Ólason (Reykjavík: Mál og menning, 1993).

Jakob Benediktsson. "Helgikvæði." In *Hugtök og heiti í bókmenntafræði* (Reykjavík: Bókmenntafræðistofnun Háskóla Íslands, Mál og menning, 1983). Pp. 115–17.

Jón Helgason. *Norrøn Litteraturhistorie* (Copenhagen: Levin and Munksgaard, 1934).

– "Norges og Islands digtning." In *Litteraturhistorie B: Norge og Island.* Ed. Sigurður Nordal. Nordisk kultur VIII: B (Stockholm: Bonnier; Oslo: Aschehoug; Copenhagen: Schultz, 1953). Pp. 3–179.

Jón Þorkelsson. *Om Digtningen på Island i det 15. og 16. Århundrede* (Copenhagen: Høst, 1888).

Jónas Kristjánsson. *Eddas and Sagas: Iceland's Medieval Literature.* Trans. Peter Foote (Reykjavík: Hið íslenska bókmenntafélag, 1988).

KLNM = Kulturhistorisk leksikon for nordisk middelalder fra vikingetid til reformationstid. 22 vols. (Copenhagen: Rosenkilde and Bagger, 1956–78).

Lange, Wolfgang. *Studien zur christlichen Dichtung der Nordgermanen 1000–1200.* Palaestra 222 (Göttingen: Vandenhoeck and Ruprecht, 1958).

McTurk, Rory, ed. *A Companion to Old Norse–Icelandic Literature and Culture.* (Oxford: Blackwell, 2005).

Medieval Scandinavia: An Encyclopedia. Ed. Phillip Pulsiano and Kirsten Wolf with Paul Acker and Donald K. Fry (New York and London: Garland, 1993).

Mogk, Eugen. *Geschichte der norwegisch-isländischen Literatur* (Strassburg: Trübner, 1904).

Paasche, Fredrik. *Kristendom og kvad: En studie i norrøn middelalder* (Kristiania [Oslo]: Aschehoug, 1914).

– *Norges og Islands litteratur inntil utgangen av middelalderen.* Rev. ed. by Anne Holtsmark (Oslo: Aschehoug, 1947).

Schottmann, Hans. *Die isländische Mariendichtung. Untersuchungen zur volkssprachigen Mariendichtung des Mittelalters.* Münchner Germanistische Beiträge 9 (Munich: Wilhelm Fink, 1973).

Stefán Einarsson. *Íslensk bókmenntasaga 874–1960* (Reykjavík: Oddi, 1961).

Til heiðurs og hugbótar: Greinar um trúarkveðskap fyrri alda. Ed. Svanhildur Óskarsdóttir and Anna Guðmundsdóttir. Snorrastofa, Rit 1 (Reykholt: Snorrastofa, 2003).

Turville-Petre, G. *Origins of Icelandic Literature* (Oxford: Clarendon Press, 1967).

Vries, Jan de. *Altnordische Literaturgeschichte.* 2 vols. 2nd ed. (Berlin: de Gruyter, 1964–7).

IV. Individual Saints

AGATHA   February 5

Heilagra meyja drápa

A fourteenth-century poem about holy maidens. Stz. 26–8 treat Saint Agatha.
Incipit: "Heyrðu ómælds himna veldis herra guð."

Manuscripts:
AM 713 4to (ca. 1500–50), AM 721 4to (ca. 1500–50), Lbs 444 4to (ca. 1820–
50; stz. 1–2 only), and Lbs 2166 4to (ca. 1885–1920; stz. 1 and 60 only).
Editions:
Finnur Jónsson, ed. >> *Den norsk-islandske skjaldedigtning* (1912–15).
Vol. AII, p. 532 and vol. BII, pp. 588–9.
Edition of AM 721 4to with variants from AM 713 4to.
Kock, Ernst Albin, ed. >> *Notationes Norrœnæ* (1923–44). §1843.
– ed. >> *Den norsk-islandske skaldediktningen* (1946–50). Vol. 2, pp. 325–6.
Wolf, Kirsten, ed. "Anonymous, *Heilagra meyja drápa* 'Drápa about Holy
Maidens'." In >> *Poetry on Christian Subjects* (2007). Vol. 2, pp. 908–9.
Edition of AM 721 4to with variants from AM 713 4to.
Danish translation:
Finnur Jónsson, ed. >> *Den norsk-islandske skjaldedigtning* (1912–15).
Vol. BII, pp. 588–9.
English translation:
Wolf, Kirsten, ed. "Anonymous, *Heilagra meyja drápa* 'Drápa about Holy
Maidens'." In >> *Poetry on Christian Subjects* (2007). Vol. 2, pp. 908–9.
Literature:
Clunies Ross, Margaret. >> *A History of Old Norse Poetry and Poetics* (2005).
P. 214.

Cormack, Margaret. >> *The Saints in Iceland* (1994). P. 41n60.

Finnur Jónsson. >> *Den oldnorske og oldislandske Litteraturs Historie* (1920–4). Vol. 3, p. 18.

Guðrún Nordal. "Handrit, prentaðar bækur og pápísk kvæði á siðskiptaöld." In >> *Til heiðurs og hugbótar* (2003). Pp. 131–43, esp. pp. 139–40.

Jakob Benediktsson. "Helgendigte." *KLNM* 6 (1961). Cols. 318–21, esp. col. 320.

– "Helgener." *KLNM* 21 (1977). Cols. 194–5, esp. col. 194.

– >> "Helgikvæði." In *Hugtök og heiti í bókmenntafræði* (1983). Pp. 115–17, esp. p. 116.

Jón Helgason. "Nokkur íslenzk handrit frá 16. öld." *Skírnir* 106 (1932): 143–68.

– >> "Norges og Islands digtning." In *Litteraturhistorie B: Norge og Island* (1953). Pp. 3–179, esp. p. 163.

Schottmann, Hans. >> *Die isländische Mariendichtung* (1973). Pp. 68n10, 206, and 255.

Soffía Ófeigsdóttir. "*Veroníkukvæði.*" BA thesis. University of Iceland, 1986. P. 66.

Stéfan Einarsson. "Íslenzk helgikvæði á miðöldum." *Tímarit Þjóðræknisfélags Íslendinga* 36 (1955): 43–63, esp. p. 49.

Vésteinn Ólason. "Kveðskapur frá síðmiðöldum" In >> *Íslensk Bókmenntasaga* 2 (1993). Pp. 285–378, esp. p. 299.

Vries, Jan de. >> *Altnordische Literaturgeschichte* (1964–7). Vol. 2, p. 523.

Wolf, Kirsten, ed. >> *Heilagra meyja sögur* (2003). Pp. liii–lv.

NOTE:

The poem contains material about Saints Agatha, Anastasia, Anne, Barbara, Brigid of Kildare, Catherine, Cecilia, Christina, Clare, Constancia, Eufemia, Felicity, Fides, Spes, and Caritas, Mary the Blessed Virgin, Mary of Egypt, Mary Magdalen, Juliana, Lucy of Rome, Lucy of Sicily, Margaret, Petronilla, Praxis, Prisca, Pusina, Putentiana, Sabina, Scholastica, Sunniva and Companions, and Ursula and Companions. See the entries for the individual saints.

AGNES   January 21

1. Agnesardiktur

A poem relating part of the legend of Saint Agnes and omitting her actual martyrdom. According to Jón Helgason, several verses are missing after stz. 12. It was probably composed between 1300 and 1550.

Incipit: "Hæstur guð með heiðri skapti."

Manuscripts:

BLAdd 4892 (ca. 1700–1800), BLAdd 11.179 (ca. 1700–1800), JS 260 4to
(1796), JS 265 4to (ca. 1860), JS 284 8vo (ca. 1850), JS 487 8vo (ca. 1675–
1900), JS 514 8vo (ca. 1675–1900), Lbs 936 4to (ca. 1880, stz. 1 only),
Lbs 953 4to (ca. 1760), Lbs 1326 4to (ca. 1890), Lbs 2166 4to (ca. 1885–
1920), Lbs 201 8vo (ca. 1850–70), and Lbs 754 8vo (ca. 1700–1900, stz.
1 only).

Editions:

Jón Helgason, ed. >> *Íslenzk miðaldakvæði* (1936–8). Vol. 2, pp. 326–30.
Based on JS 260 4to with variants from BLAdd 4892, BLAdd 11.179,
JS 487 8vo, Lbs 953 4to, Lbs 1326 4to, and Lbs 2166 4to.

Jón Þorkelsson. >> *Om Digtningen på Island* (1888). P. 92 (stz. 1).
Based on JS 260 4to and Lbs 201 8vo.

Literature:

Anon. "Den Oldnordisk-islandske Afdeling." Annual Report for 1846.
Antiquarisk Tidsskrift 1846–8 (Copenhagen: Sally B. Salomon, 1847).
Pp. 39–49, esp. p. 40.

– "Den Oldnordisk-islandske Afdeling." Annual Report for 1847. *Antiquarisk
Tidsskrift* 1846–8 (Copenhagen: Sally B. Salomon, 1847). Pp. 154–72,
esp. p. 165.

Finnur Jónsson. >> *Den oldnorske og oldislandske Litteraturs Historie*
(1920–4). Vol. 3, p. 126.

Foote, Peter, ed. *Lives of Saints. Perg. fol. nr. 2 in the Royal Library,
Stockholm.* EIM 4 (Copenhagen: Rosenkilde and Bagger, 1962). P. 28.

Hálfdan Einarsson. *Sciagraphia historiæ literariæ islandicæ* (Copenhagen:
Sander and Schröder, 1777). P. 58.

Jakob Benediktsson. "Helgendigte." *KLNM* 6 (1961). Cols. 318–21, esp.
col. 320.

Järvelä, Tuomas, and Jón Gunnar Jörgensen. "*Agnesarkvæði.*" In *Fimm
kvæði um heilaga menn: Agnesarkvæði, Dórotheukvæði, Laurentíuskvæði,
Margrétarkvæði, Úrsulúkvæði.* Unpublished manuscript at Landsbókasafn,
1981. Pp. 6–8.

Jón Helgason. >> "Norges og Islands digtning." In *Litteraturhistorie B:
Norge og Island* (1953). Pp. 3–179, esp. pp. 163–4.

Jón Torfason and Kristján Eiríksson, ed. >> *Vísnabók Guðbrands* (2000).
P. xxxix.

Jón Þorkelsson. "Islandske håndskrifter i England og Skotland." *ANF* 8
(1892): 199–237, esp. pp. 206–7.

Mogk, Eugen. >> *Geschichte der norwegisch-isländischen Literatur* (1904).
P. 719.

Soffía Ófeigsdóttir "*Veroníkukvæði*." BA thesis. University of Iceland, 1986. P. 66.
Stefán Einarsson. "Íslenzk helgikvæði á miðöldum." *Tímarit Þjóðræknisfélags Íslendinga* 36 (1955): 43–63, esp. p. 56.
– *Íslensk bókmenntasaga 874–1960* (Reykjavík: Oddi, 1961). P. 92.
Vésteinn Ólason. "Kveðskapur frá síðmiðöldum." In >> *Íslensk Bókmenntasaga* 2 (1993). Pp. 283–378, esp. p. 316.
Wolf, Kirsten, ed. >> *Heilagra meyja sögur* (2003). P. lv.

2. Rímur af Agnesi píslarvotti

A set of four *rímur* about the life and martyrdom of Saint Agnes. The *rímur*, which were apparently based on *Agnesar saga* with some additional material, were composed by Eiríkur Hallsson í Höfða (1614–98) for Hólmfríður Benediktsdóttir.
Incipit: "Hefði ég lag sem hyggnir menn."

Manuscript:
Lbs 705 4to (ca. 1825–34).
Editions:
Finnur Sigmundsson, ed. >> *Rímnatal*. 2 vols. (1966). Vol. 1, p. 8 (I.1 and 13; IV.52).
Järvelä, Tuomas, and Jón Gunnar Jörgensen. "*Agnesarkvæði*." In *Fimm kvæði um heilaga menn: Agnesarkvæði, Dórotheukvæði, Laurentíuskvæði, Margrétarkvæði, Úrsulúkvæði*. Unpublished manuscript at Landsbókasafn, 1981. Pp. 8–11 (I.13–14 and 62$^{1-2}$, IV. 47, 49, and 52^{1}) and 27–8 (I.13, 21^{1}, 33, III. 28, 38, and IV.25).
Literature:
Þórunn Sigurðardóttir. *Heiður og huggun. Erfiljóð, harmljóð og huggunarkvæði á 17. öld* (Reykjavík: Háskóli Íslands, 2015). P. 355.

3. Agnesarkvæði

A poetic rendering of the life and martyrdom of Saint Agnes. The poem, which was probably composed ca. 1725, is attributed to Þorvaldur Magnússon (d. 1747).
Incipit: "Í þann tíma ríkti í Róm" (variants: "Á þann tíma ríkti í Róm," "Forðum tíma ríkti í Róm," and "Áður fyrri ríkti í Róm").

Manuscripts:
Eink 1-5 (1850–1950), Eink 210-23 (ca. 1855), Eink 330-34 (ca. 1865–1931), Eink 379-10 (ca. 1657–1705), G-13/29 (ca. 1800–1900), G-32/5 (ca. 1892–

1971), G-63/10 (ca. 1889), HSk 2484 4to (ca. 1800–1900), ÍB 49 4to
(ca. 1820–30), ÍB 183 4to (ca. 1750), ÍB 29 8vo (ca. 1800–1900), ÍB 33
8vo (ca. 1800–1900), ÍB 49 8vo (ca. 1800 and later), ÍB 136 8vo (1797),
ÍB 278a 8vo (ca. 1700–1900), ÍB 310 8vo (ca. 1700–1900), ÍB 816 8vo
(ca. 1600–1900), ÍBR 32 8vo (ca. 1700–1850), ÍBR 42 8vo (ca. 1800–
1900), ÍBR 113 8vo (ca. 1700–1800), JS 201 4to (ca. 1837–50), JS 265 4to
(ca. 1860), JS 286 4to (ca. 1800–50), JS 582 4to (ca. 1600–1900), JS 588
4to (ca. 1800–1900), JS 43 8vo (1835), JS 237 8vo (ca. 1700–1900), JS
244 8vo (ca. 1800–20), JS 259 8vo (ca. 1800–50), JS 284 8vo (ca. 1850),
JS 389 8vo (ca. 1775–1825), JS 471 8vo (ca. 1675–1900), JS 473 8vo
(ca. 1675–1900), JS 481 8vo (ca. 1675–1900), JS 492 8vo (ca. 1675–1900),
JS 495 8vo (ca. 1675–1900), JS 499 8vo (ca. 1675–1900), JS 508 8vo
(ca. 1675–1900), JS 510 8vo (ca. 1675–1900), JS 511 8vo (ca. 1675–1900),
JS 513 8vo (ca. 1675–1800), JS 514 8vo (ca. 1675–1900), JS 518 8vo
(ca. 1675–1900), Kvennasögusafn Íslands box 27 (ca. 1980), Lbs 480 fol.
(ca. 1800–2000), Lbs 565 4to (ca. 1860), Lbs 953 4to (ca. 1760), Lbs 1275
4to (ca. 1862–70), Lbs 1293 4to (ca. 1845–57), Lbs 1326 4to (ca. 1890),
Lbs 2125 4to (1865–1912), Lbs 2259–2260 4to (1886–97), Lbs 2286 4to
(1879–1905), Lbs 2344 4to (1871–3), Lbs 4174 4to (ca. 1800–2000), Lbs
201 8vo (ca. 1850–70), Lbs 270 8vo (ca. 1850–70), Lbs 448 8vo (ca. 1850),
Lbs 655 8vo (ca. 1800), Lbs 676 8vo (1842), Lbs 987 8vo (ca. 1780), Lbs
1014 8vo (1821–3), Lbs 1108 8vo (ca. 1800–50), Lbs 1157 8vo (ca. 1777),
Lbs 1262 8vo (ca. 1600–1825), Lbs 1405 8vo (1895–1900), Lbs 1545 8vo
(ca. 1850), Lbs 1571 8vo (ca. 1780 and ca. 1810), Lbs 1600 8vo (ca. 1700–
1850), Lbs 1633 8vo (ca. 1700–1900), Lbs 1718 8vo (ca. 1700–1850), Lbs
1730 8vo (ca. 1830), Lbs 1779 8vo (ca. 1700–1900), Lbs 1877 8vo (1888–
99), Lbs 2166 8vo (ca. 1860 and 1897), Lbs 2393 8vo (ca. 1700–1900),
Lbs 2510 8vo (ca. 1800–1900), Lbs 2681 8vo (1819–20 and 1931), Lbs
2859 8vo (1870–1904), Lbs 2930 8vo (1788), Lbs 2937 8vo (ca. 1800–
2000), Lbs 2941 8vo (1884–6), Lbs 3170 8vo (ca. 1800), Lbs 3241 8vo
(ca. 1800–2000), Lbs 3391 8vo (1803), Lbs 3436 8vo (ca. 1800–1900), Lbs
3566 8vo (ca. 1800–1900), Lbs 3673 8vo (ca. 1800–2000), Lbs 3714 8vo
(ca. 1800–50), Lbs 3909 8vo (ca. 1800–1900), Lbs 3982 8vo (ca. 1800–50),
Lbs 4041 8vo (1882, 1885, and 1904), Lbs 4089 8vo (ca. 1850–1900), Lbs
4156 8vo (ca. 1800–1900), Lbs 4254 8vo (ca. 1800–1900), Lbs 4255 8vo
(ca. 1850–1900), Musikafd. 180 C II (ca. 1846–7), SÁM 85/101 EF (1968),
SÁM 85/114 EF (1969), SÁM 85/121 EF (1969), SÁM 85/161 EF (1969),
SÁM 85/192 EF (1969), SÁM 85/233 EF (1966), SÁM 85/300A EF
(1965), SÁM 85/301 EF (1969), SÁM 85/351 EF (1969), SÁM 85/354 EF
(1969), SÁM 85/409 EF (1970), SÁM 85/416 EF (1970), SÁM 85/541 EF

(1970), SÁM 86/644 EF (1971), SÁM 86/700 EF (1973), SÁM 87/1136 EF
(1970), SÁM 88/1540 EF (1967), SÁM 88/1608 EF (1967), SÁM 89/1741
EF (1967), SÁM 90/2294 EF (1970), and SÁM 92/3171 EF (1964).

Editions:

Agnesarkvæði. In *Hlín: Ársrit Íslenzkra kvenna.* Ed. Halldóra Bjarnadóttir.
Vol. 34. (Akureyri: Prentverk Odds Björnssonar, 1952). Pp. 137–40.
Written according to the memory of Sigurleif Sigurðardóttir frá
Lýtingsstöðum í Holtum in Rangárvallasýsla.

Anna Sigurðardóttir. *Allt hafði annan róm áður í páfadóm: Nunnuklaustrin
tvö á Íslandi á miðöldum og brot úr kristnisögu* (Reykjavík: Kvennasögusafn
Íslands, 1988). Pp. 343–7.
Edition of Sigríður Einarsdóttir's (1901–1989) handwritten copy in
Kvennasögusafn Íslands box 27.

Benedikt Ásgrímsson. *Tvö systkini* (Reykjavík: Gutenberg, 1907). Pp. 57–64.
Edition of Eink 379-10.

Bjarni Halldórsson. "*Agnesarkvæði.*" *Lesbók Morgunblaðsins.* Vol. 45.
December 24, 1967. P. 31.
Edition of unnamed nineteenth-century manuscript.

Bjarni Þorsteinsson, ed. *Íslenzk þjóðlög* (Copenhagen: Møller, 1960–9).
P. 597 (stz. 1).
Edition based on oral tradition from Sigurveig Árnadóttir í Lundi in
Fnjóskadalur with musical annotation.

Jón Árnason and Ólafur Davíðsson, ed. *Íslenzkar gátur, skemtanir, vikivakar
og þulur.* 4 vols. (Copenhagen: Møller, 1887–1903). Vol. 2, p. 252 (stz. 24,
with notation).
Edition of ÍB 310 8vo.

Jón Þorkelsson. >> *Om Digtningen på Island* (1888). P. 93 (stz. 1).
Based on ÍB 183 4to, ÍB 29 8vo, ÍB 33 8vo, ÍB 49 8vo, ÍB 136 8vo, ÍB 278
8vo, ÍB 310 8vo, ÍBR 42 8vo, ÍBR 113 8vo, and Lbs 201 8vo.

Jón Þórarinsson. *Íslensk tónlistarsaga 1000–1800* (Reykjavík: Tónlistarsafn
Íslands, 2012). P. 370 (stz. 1).
Edition of two variants of stz. 1. One, with the incipit "Í þann tíð sem ríkti
í Róm," is based on Pétur Guðmundsson's transcription in Musikafd. 180
C II, and the other, with the incipit "Forðum tíma ríkti í Róm," is based on
Bjarni Þorsteinsson's transcription in *Íslenzk þjóðlög.*

Järvelä, Tuomas, and Jón Gunnar Jörgensen. "*Agnesarkvæði.*" In *Fimm
kvæði um heilaga menn: Agnesarkvæði, Dórotheukvæði, Laurentíuskvæði,
Margrétarkvæði, Úrsulúkvæði.* Unpublished manuscript at Landsbókasafn,
1981. Pp. 18–28.
Based on Lbs 1600 8vo with variants from ÍB 183 4to and edition of stz.
1^{1-3}, 3^{1-2}, 4^{6-9}, 16^{6-9}, 17^{6-9}, and 24^{1-2} based on JS 492 8vo. Common variants

among manuscript groupings (p. 33) to stz. 1, 4, 6–9, 11–12, 15, 21, and 23–5 are listed on pp. 34–5.

Literature:

Anon. "Den Oldnordisk-islandske Afdeling." Annual Report for 1847. *Antiquarisk Tidsskrift* 1846–8 (Copenhagen: Sally B. Salomon, 1847). Pp. 154–72, esp. p. 165.

Finnur Jónsson. >> *Den oldnorske og oldislandske Litteraturs Historie* (1920–4). Vol. 3, p. 126.

Hálfdan Einarsson. *Sciagraphia historiæ literariæ islandicæ* (Copenhagen: Sander and Schröder, 1777). P. 58.

Soffía Ófeigsdóttir. "*Veroníkukvæði.*" BA thesis. University of Iceland, 1986. P. 66.

Stefán Einarsson. "Íslenzk helgikvæði á miðöldum." *Tímarit Þjóðræknisfélags Íslendinga* 36 (1955): 43–63, esp. pp. 55–6.

– *Íslensk bókmenntasaga 874–1960* (Reykjavík: Oddi, 1961). P. 92.

Vésteinn Ólason. "Kveðskapur frá síðmiðöldum." In >> *Íslensk bókmenntasaga* 2 (1993). Pp. 285–378, esp. p. 316.

4. Heilagra meyja drápa

A fourteenth-century poem about holy maidens. Stz. 30–2 treat Saint Agnes. Incipit: "Heyrðu ómælds himna veldis herra guð."

Manuscripts:
See Agatha note (p. 13).

Editions:

Finnur Jónsson, ed. >> *Den norsk-islandske skjaldedigtning* (1912–15). Vol. AII, pp. 532–3 and vol. BII, pp. 589–90.

Kock, Ernst Albin, ed. >> *Notationes Norrœnæ* (1923–44). §§1844, 1845, and 2971A.

– ed. >> *Den norsk-islandske skaldedigtningen* (1946–50). Vol. 2, p. 326.

Wolf, Kirsten, ed. "Anonymous, *Heilagra meyja drápa* 'Drápa about Holy Maidens'." In >> *Poetry on Christian Subjects* (2007). Vol. 2, pp. 910–11.

Danish translation:

Finnur Jónsson, ed. >> *Den norsk-islandske skjaldedigtning* (1912–15). Vol. BII, pp. 589–90.

English translation:

Wolf, Kirsten, ed. "Anonymous, *Heilagra meyja drápa* 'Drápa about Holy Maidens'." In >> *Poetry on Christian Subjects* (2007). Vol. 2, pp. 910–11.

AMBROSE   December 7

Michaelsflokkur

An early sixteenth-century poem about Saint Michael ascribed to the priest
Hallur Ögmundarson (d. ca. 1540). Saint Ambrose is mentioned in stz. 48.
   Incipit: "Óðar gef þú upphaf."
Manuscripts:
See Michael the Archangel 2 note (p. 256).
Edition:
Jón Þorkelsson, ed. >> *Kvæðasafn* (1922–7). P. 381.

AMICUS AND AMELIUS   October 12

Amíkuss ok Amilíuss rímur

A poetic rendering of the tale of Saints Amicus and Amelius that stems ulti-
mately from a Latin *vita* of the type edited by Kölbing (1884).
   Incipit: "Semja ætla ég Suptungs smíð."

Manuscript:
AM 609c 4to (ca. 1600–1700).
Edition:
Kölbing, Eugen, ed. *Amis and Amiloun. Zugleich mit der altfranzösichen
   Quelle. Nebst einer Beilage: Amícus ok Amilíus Rímur.* Altenglische
   Bibliothek 2 (Heilbronn: Henninger, 1884). Pp. 189–229.
Literature:
Björn K. Þórólfsson. *Rímur fyrir 1600.* Safn Fræðafjelagsins um Ísland og
   Íslendinga 9 (Copenhagen: Møller, 1934). Pp. 481–2.
Finnur Sigmundsson. >> *Rímnatal* (1966). Vol. 1, p. 29.
Henning, Sam. "Amicus och Amelius." *KLNM* 1 (1956). Cols. 127–9, esp.
   col. 128.
Hume, Kathryn. "Structure and Perspective: Romance and Hagiographic
   Features in the Amicus and Amelius Story." *JEGP* 69 (1970): 89–107,
   esp. pp. 89n2, 90, 94–6, and 100–7.
Kölbing, Eugen. "Zur Ueberlieferung der Sage von Amicus und Amelius."
   Beiträge zur Geschichte der deutschen Sprache und Literatur (1877):
   271–314, esp. pp. 275–9.

Leach, MacEdward, ed. *Amis and Amiloun*. Early English Text Society,
    Original Series 203 (London: Oxford University Press, 1937). P. xiii.
Mogk, Eugen. >> *Geschichte der norwegisch-isländischen Literatur* (1904).
    P. 729.
Wolf, Kirsten, "Amicus and Amileus." In >> *Medieval Scandinavia:
    An Encyclopedia* (1993). Pp. 13–14.

ANANIAS   January 25

Postularaun

A poem in praise of all the apostles composed by Guðmundur Bergþórsson
(1657–1705). Stz. 80 mentions Saint Ananias.
    Incipit: "Hér skal eina hróðar grein."

Manuscripts:
ÍB 105 4to (1758–68), JS 267 4to (ca. 1700–1900), Lbs 625 4to (ca. 1800–10),
    Lbs 2289 4to (1879–1905), and Lbs 1117 8vo (ca. 1850).
Literature:
Jón Þorkelsson. >> *Om Digtningen på Island* (1888). P. 63.
NOTE:
The poem contains material about Saints Andrew, Bartholomew, James the
Greater, James the Less, John the Evangelist, John the Baptist, Jude, Matthew,
Matthias, Paul, Peter, Philip, Simon, Thomas, and Zachariah. See the entries
for the individual saints.

ANASTASIA   December 25

Heilagra meyja drápa

A fourteenth-century poem about holy maidens. Stz. 42–3 treat Saint Anastasia.
    Incipit: "Heyrðu ómælds himna veldis herra guð."

Manuscripts:
See Agatha note (p. 13).
Editions:
Finnur Jónsson, ed. >> *Den norsk-islandske skjaldedigtning* (1912–15).
    Vol. AII, p. 535 and vol. BII, pp. 592–3.

Kock, Ernst Albin, ed. >> *Den norsk-islandske skaldediktningen* (1946–50).
   Vol. 2, p. 328.
Wolf, Kirsten, ed. "Anonymous, *Heilagra meyja drápa* 'Drápa about Holy
   Maidens'." In >> *Poetry on Christian Subjects* (2007). Vol. 2, pp. 917–18.
Danish translation:
Finnur Jónsson, ed. >> *Den norsk-islandske skjaldedigtning* (1912–15).
   Vol. BII, pp. 592–3.
English translation:
Wolf, Kirsten, ed. "Anonymous, *Heilagra meyja drápa* 'Drápa about Holy
   Maidens'." In >> *Poetry on Christian Subjects* (2007). Vol. 2, pp. 917–18.

ANDREW THE APOSTLE   November 30

1. Andréasdrápa

A fragment of a fourteenth-century poem in honour of Saint Andrew.
   Incipit: "Enn kom elsku þinnar annarr drottins manna."

Manuscripts:
AM 669c 4to (ca. 1700–25), AM 194 8vo (1387), and NKS 1598 4to
   (ca.1750–1800).
Editions:
Finnur Jónsson, ed. >> *Den norsk-islandske skjaldedigtning* (1912–15).
   Vol. AII, pp. 508–9 and vol. BII, pp. 558–9.
   Edition of AM 194 8vo.
Jón Þorkelsson. >> *Om Digtningen på Island* (1888). P. 65 (stz. 1^{1-2}).
   Edition of AM 669c 4to, AM 194 8vo, and NKS 1598 4to.
Kock, Ernst Albin, ed. >> *Notationes Norrœna* (1923–44). §§1756, 1757,
   2296, and 2886.
– ed. >> *Den norsk-isländska skaldediktningen* (1946–50). Vol. 2, pp. 305–6.
Konráð Gíslason, ed. *Fire og fyrretyve for en stor deel forhen utrykte prøver
   af oldnordisk sprog og literatur* (Copenhagen: Gyldendal, 1860). P. 558
   (extract only).
   Edition of AM 194 8vo.
McDougall, Ian, ed. "Anonymous, *Andréasdrápa* 'Drápa about S. Andrew'."
   In >> *Poetry on Christian Subjects* (2007). Vol. 2, pp. 845–51.
   Edition of AM 194 8vo with variants from AM 669c 4to.
Danish translation:
Finnur Jónsson, ed. >> *Den norsk-islandske skjaldedigtning* (1912–15).
   Vol. BII, pp. 558–9.

English translation:
McDougall, Ian, ed. "Anonymous, *Andréasdrápa* '*Drápa* about S. Andrew'."
   In >> *Poetry on Christian Subjects* (2007). Vol. 2, pp. 845–51.
Literature:
Cormack, Margaret. >> *The Saints in Iceland* (1994). Pp. 41n60 and 42.
Finnur Jónsson. >> *Den oldnorske og oldislandske Litteraturs Historie*
   (1920–4). Vol. 3, p. 18.
Jakob Benediktsson. "Helgendigte." *KLNM* 6 (1961). Cols. 318–21, esp.
   col. 320.
Jón Þorkelsson. >> *Om Digtningen på Island* (1888). P. 65.
Mogk, Eugen. >> *Geschichte der norwegisch-isländischen Literatur* (1904).
   P. 718.
Stéfan Einarsson. "Íslenzk helgikvæði á miðöldum." *Tímarit*
   Þjóðræknisfélags Íslendinga 36 (1955): 43–63, esp. p. 49.
– *Íslensk bókmenntasaga 874–1960* (Reykjavík: Oddi, 1961). P. 86.
Vésteinn Ólason. "Kveðskapur frá síðmiðöldum." In >> *Íslensk*
   Bókmenntasaga 2 (1993). Pp. 285–378, esp. p. 315.
– "Old Icelandic Poetry." In *A History of Icelandic Literature*. Ed. Daisy
   Neijmann. Histories of Scandinavian Literature 5 (Lincoln: University
   of Nebraska Press, 2006). Pp. 1–64, esp. p. 48.

2. Andréasdiktur I

A poem about the life and martyrdom of Saint Andrew probably composed ca.
1400–1550.
   Incipit: "Miskun þín hinn mildi guð."

Manuscripts:
AM 713 4to (ca. 1500–50) and Lbs 2166 4to (ca. 1885–1920).
Editions:
Jón Helgason, ed. >> *Íslenzk miðaldakvæði* (1936–8). Vol. 2, pp. 292–6.
   Edition of AM 713 4to with additions from C.R. Unger >> *Postola sögur*
   (1874).
Jón Þorkelsson. >> *Om Digtningen på Island* (1888). P. 65 (stz. 1).
   Edition of AM 713 4to.
Literature:
Finnur Jónsson. >> *Bókmentasaga Íslendinga fram undir siðabót* (1904–5).
   P. 461.
Guðrún Nordal. "Handrit, prentaðar bækur og pápísk kvæði á siðskiptaöld."
   In >> *Til heiðurs og hugbótar* (2003). Pp. 131–43, esp. pp. 139–40.

Jakob Benediktsson. "Helgendigte." *KLNM* 6 (1961). Cols. 318–21, esp.
   col. 320.
Jón Helgason. "Nokkur íslenzk handrit frá 16. öld." *Skírnir* 106 (1932):
   143–68.
Kock, E.A. "Anteckningar till Íslenzk Miðaldakvæði." *ANF* 61 (1946): 1–125,
   esp. pp. 81–4.
Schottmann, Hans. >> *Die isländische Mariendichtung* (1973). P. 24n10.
Stéfan Einarsson. "Íslenzk helgikvæði á miðöldum." *Tímarit Þjóðræknisfélags
   Íslendinga* 36 (1955): 43–63, esp. p. 54.
– *Íslensk bókmenntasaga 874–1960* (Reykjavík: Oddi, 1961). P. 91.
Vésteinn Ólason. "Kveðskapur frá síðmiðöldum." In >> *Íslensk
   Bókmenntasaga* 2 (1993). Pp. 285–378, esp. p. 315.
NOTE:
The poem contains material about Saints John the Baptist and Peter. See the
entries for the two saints.

3. Andréasdiktur II

A late medieval (ca. 1400–1550) poem about the life of Saint Andrew based on
oral tradition.
   Incipit: "Timens veit ég tíma rýra (að skýra)."

Manuscripts:
A: AM 713 4to (ca. 1500–50) and Lbs 2166 4to (ca. 1885–1920);
B: AM 717a 4to (ca. 1700–25) and AM 150 8vo (ca. 1650–1700).

Editions:
Jón Helgason, ed. >> *Íslenzk miðaldakvæði* (1936–8). Vol. 2, pp. 298–301.
   Edition of AM 713 4to with variants from AM 717a 4to, AM 150 8vo, and
   Lbs 2166 4to and notes from C.R. Unger >> *Postola sögur* (1874).
Jón Þorkelsson. >> *Om Digtningen på Island* (1888). P. 66 (stz. 1).
   Based on AM 713 4to, AM 717a 4to, and AM 150 8vo.
Literature:
Finnur Jónsson. >> *Bókmentasaga Íslendinga fram undir siðabót* (1904–5).
   P. 461.
Guðrún Nordal. "Handrit, prentaðar bækur og pápísk kvæði á siðskiptaöld."
   In >> *Til heiðurs og hugbótar* (2003). Pp. 131–43, esp. pp. 139–40.
Jakob Benediktsson. "Helgendigte." *KLNM* 6 (1961). Cols. 318–21, esp.
   col. 320.
Jón Helgason. "Nokkur íslenzk handrit frá 16. öld." *Skírnir* 106 (1932):
   143–68.

Kock, E.A. "Anteckningar till Íslenzk Miðaldakvæði." *ANF* 61 (1946): 1–125, esp. pp. 53 and 85.

Schottmann, Hans. >> *Die isländische Mariendichtung* (1973). Pp. 24n10 and 52n16.

Stéfan Einarsson. "Íslenzk helgikvæði á miðöldum." *Tímarit Þjóðræknisfélags Íslendinga* 36 (1955): 43–63, esp. p. 54.

– *Íslensk bókmenntasaga 874–1960* (Reykjavík: Oddi, 1961). P. 91.

Vésteinn Ólason. "Kveðskapur frá síðmiðöldum." In >> *Íslensk Bókmenntasaga* 2 (1993). Pp. 285–378, esp. p. 315.

NOTE:

The poem contains material about Saints John the Baptist, Matthias, and Peter. See the entries for the individual saints.

4. Andréasdiktur III

A late medieval (ca. 1400–1550) poem based on a legend about a bishop who was saved from temptation by Saint Andrew (cf. C.R. Unger, ed., *Heilagra manna søgur: Fortællinger og legender om hellige mænd og kvinder*, 2 vols. [Christiania (Oslo): Bentzen, 1877], vol. 1, pp. 383–9 and 400–3, and Hugo Gering, ed., *Islendzk ævintyri: Isländische Legenden Novellen und Märchen*, 2 vols. [Halle a. S: Waisenhaus, 1882–4), vol. 1, pp. 95–100, and vol. 2, pp. 77–81).

Incipit: "María drottning mild og blíð."

Manuscripts:
AM 711a 4to (ca. 1700–25), AM 713 4to (ca. 1500–50), JS 399a–b 4to (ca. 1700–1900), and Lbs 2166 4to (ca. 1885–1920).

Editions:
Jón Helgason, ed. >> *Íslenzk miðaldakvæði* (1936–8). Vol. 2, pp. 303–8. Based on AM 713 4to with variants from AM 711a 4to, JS 399a–b 4to, Lbs 2166 4to, and Jón Þorkelsson's edition (1888).

Jón Þorkelsson. >> *Om Digtningen på Island* (1888). P. 53 (stz. 1, 3, 47, and 51). Based on AM 711a 4to and AM 713 4to.

Literature:
Finnur Jónsson. >> *Bókmentasaga Íslendinga fram undir siðabót* (1904–5). P. 461.

– >> *Den oldnorske og oldislandske Litteraturs Historie* (1920–4). Vol. 3, pp. 124–5.

Guðrún Nordal. "Handrit, prentaðar bækur og pápísk kvæði á siðskiptaöld." In >> *Til heiðurs og hugbótar* (2003). Pp. 131–43, esp. pp. 139–40.

Jakob Benediktsson. "Helgendigte." *KLNM* 6 (1961). Cols. 318–21, esp. col. 320.

Kock, E.A. "Anteckningar till Íslenzk Miðaldakvæði." *ANF* 61 (1946): 1–125, esp. pp. 86–7.

Stéfan Einarsson. "Íslenzk helgikvæði á miðöldum." *Tímarit Þjóðræknisfélags Íslendinga* 36 (1955): 43–63, esp. p. 54.

– *Íslensk bókmenntasaga 874–1960* (Reykjavík: Oddi, 1961). P. 91.

Vésteinn Ólason. "Kveðskapur frá síðmiðöldum." In >> *Íslensk Bókmenntasaga* 2 (1993). Pp. 283–378, esp. p. 315.

5. Máríuvísur I

A fourteenth-century poem about a miracle of Mary the Blessed Virgin in which a woman who had her son-in-law killed is burned alive but emerges unscathed from the fire. Saint Andrew is mentioned in stz. 2.

Incipit: "Mér gefi hljóð, sá er heyrir hjarta mitt."

Manuscripts:
See Mary the Blessed Virgin 5 note (p. 168).

Editions:
Finnur Jónsson, ed. >> *Den norsk-islandske skjaldedigtning* (1912–15). Vol. AII, p. 487 and vol. BII, p. 526.

Gade, Kari Ellen, ed. "Anonymous, *Máríuvísur I* 'Vísur about Mary I'." In >> *Poetry on Christian Subjects* (2007). Vol. 2, p. 679.

Kahle, Bernhard, ed. >> *Isländische geistliche Dichtungen des ausgehenden Mittelalters* (1898). P. 31.

Kock, Ernst Albin, ed. >> *Notationes Norrœna* (1923–44). §1679.

– ed. >> *Den norsk-isländska skaldediktningen* (1946–50). Vol. 2, p. 288.

Sperber, Hans, ed. >> *Sechs isländische Gedichte legendarischen Inhalts* (1911). P. 1.

Wrightson, Kellinde, ed. >> *Fourteenth-Century Icelandic Verse on the Virgin Mary* (2001). P. 40.

Danish translation:
Finnur Jónsson, ed. >> *Den norsk-islandske skjaldedigtning* (1912–15). Vol. BII, p. 526.

English translations:
Gade, Kari Ellen, ed. "Anonymous, *Máríuvísur I* 'Vísur about Mary I'." In >> *Poetry on Christian Subjects* (2007). Vol. 2, p. 679.

Wrightson, Kellinde, ed. >> *Fourteenth-Century Icelandic Verse on the Virgin Mary* (2001). P. 40.

6. Máríuvísur II

A fourteenth-century poem about a miracle of Mary the Blessed Virgin in which a woman's dead son is revived. Saint Andrew is mentioned in stz. 2.
  Incipit: "Dýrðar, gef þú, dóms vörðr."

Manuscripts:
See Mary the Blessed Virgin 6 note (p. 170).
Editions:
Finnur Jónsson, ed. >> *Den norsk-islandske skjaldedigtning* (1912–15). Vol. AII, p. 492 and vol. BII, p. 532.
Gade, Kari Ellen, ed. "Anonymous, *Máríuvísur II* 'Vísur about Mary II'." In >>*Poetry on Christian Subjects* (2007). Vol. 2, p. 703.
Kahle, Bernhard, ed. >> *Isländische geistliche Dichtungen des ausgehenden Mittelalters* (1898). P. 38.
Kock, Ernst Albin, ed. >> *Den norsk-isländska skaldediktningen* (1946–50). Vol. 2, p. 292.
Sperber, Hans, ed. >> *Sechs isländische Gedichte legendarischen Inhalts* (1911). P. 9.
Wrightson, Kellinde, ed. >> *Fourteenth-Century Icelandic Verse on the Virgin Mary* (2001). P. 55.
Danish translation:
Finnur Jónsson, ed. >> *Den norsk-islandske skjaldedigtning* (1912–15). Vol. BII, p. 532.
English translations:
Gade, Kari Ellen, ed. "Anonymous, *Máríuvísur II* 'Vísur about Mary II'." In >> *Poetry on Christian Subjects* (2007). Vol. 2, p. 703.
Wrightson, Kellinde, ed. >> *Fourteenth-Century Icelandic Verse on the Virgin Mary* (2001). P. 55.

7. Máríuvísur III

A fourteenth-century poem about a miracle of Mary the Blessed Virgin known variously as "The Drowned Sacristan" or "Ave on the Tongue." Saint Andrew is mentioned in stz. 2.
  Incipit: "Dróttinn, gef þú mér mátt, máttugr, bragarhátt."

Manuscripts:
See Mary the Blessed Virgin 7 note (p. 172).

Editions:
Finnur Jónsson, ed. >> *Den norsk-islandske skjaldedigtning* (1912–15).
  Vol. AII, p. 496. and vol. BII, p. 538.
Gade, Kari Ellen, ed. "Anonymous, *Máríuvísur III* '*Vísur* about Mary III'."
  In >> *Poetry on Christian Subjects* (2007). Vol. 2, p. 719.
Kahle, Bernhard, ed. >> *Isländische geistliche Dichtungen des ausgehenden*
  Mittelalters (1898). P. 43
Kock, Ernst Albin, ed. >> *Notationes Norrœna* (1923–44). §2871.
– ed. >> *Den norsk-isländska skaldediktningen* (1946–50). Vol. 2, p. 295.
Sperber, Hans, ed. >> *Sechs isländische Gedichte legendarischen Inhalts*
  (1911). P. 15.
Wrightson, Kellinde, ed. >> *Fourteenth-Century Icelandic Verse on the Virgin*
  Mary (2001). P. 67.
Danish translation:
Finnur Jónsson, ed. >> *Den norsk-islandske skjaldedigtning* (1912–15).
  Vol. BII, p. 538.
English translations:
Gade, Kari Ellen, ed. "Anonymous, *Máríuvísur III* '*Vísur* about Mary III'."
  In >> *Poetry on Christian Subjects* (2007). Vol. 2, p. 719.
Wrightson, Kellinde, ed. >> *Fourteenth-Century Icelandic Verse on the Virgin*
  Mary (2001). P. 67.

8. Vitnisvísur af Máríu

A fourteenth-century poem about a miracle of Mary the Blessed Virgin variously
referred to as "Faithless Lover" or "Jilted Fiancée." Saint Andrew is mentioned
in stz. 2.
  Incipit: "Heyrðu til upphafsorða, allsvinnandi minna."

Manuscripts:
See Mary the Blessed Virgin 8 note (p. 174).
Editions:
Finnur Jónsson, ed. >> *Den norsk-islandske skjaldedigtning* (1912–15).
  Vol. AII, pp. 483 and vol. BII, p. 520.
Gade, Kari Ellen, ed. "Anonymous, *Vitnisvísur af Máríu* 'Testimonial *Vísur*
  about Mary'." In >> *Poetry on Christian Subjects* (2007). Vol. 2, p. 741.
Kahle, Bernhard, ed. >> *Isländische geistliche Dichtungen des ausgehenden*
  Mittelalters (1898). P. 50.
Kock, Ernst Albin, ed. >> *Notationes Norrœna* (1923–44). §1674.
– ed. >> *Den norsk-isländska skaldediktningen* (1946–50). Vol. 2, p. 285.

Sperber, Hans, ed. >> *Sechs isländische Gedichte legendarischen Inhalts*
(1911). P. 23.
Wrightson, Kellinde, ed. >> *Fourteenth-Century Icelandic Verse on the Virgin
Mary* (2001). P. 27.
Danish translation:
Finnur Jónsson, ed. >> *Den norsk-islandske skjaldedigtning* (1912–15).
Vol. BII, p. 520.
English translations:
Gade, Kari Ellen, ed. "Anonymous, *Vitnisvísur af Máríu* 'Testimonial *Vísur*
about Mary'." In >> *Poetry on Christian Subjects* (2007). Vol. 2, p. 741.
Wrightson, Kellinde. "The Jilted Fiancée: The Old Icelandic Miracle Poem
Vitnisvísur af Maríu and Its Modern English Translation." *Parergon* 15
(1997): 117–136, esp. p. 132.
– >> *Fourteenth-Century Icelandic Verse on the Virgin Mary* (2001). P. 27.

9. Pétrsdrápa

A fourteenth-century poem in honour of Saint Peter. Stz. 11 mentions Saint
Andrew.
Incipit: "Orð satt upphafs gjörði eitt næst stafi hæsta."

Manuscripts:
See Peter the Apostle 1 note (p. 318).
Editions:
Finnur Jónsson, ed. >> *Den norsk-islandske skjaldedigtning* (1912–15).
Vol. AII, p. 502 and vol. BII, p. 547–8.
Kahle, Bernhard, ed. >> *Isländische geistliche Dichtungen des ausgehenden
Mittelalters* (1898). P. 80.
Kock, Ernst Albin, ed. >> *Den norsk-isländska skaldediktningen* (1946–50).
Vol. 2, p. 300.
McDougall, David, ed. "Anonymous, *Pétrsdrápa* '*Drápa* about S. Peter'."
In >> *Poetry on Christian Subjects* (2007). Vol. 2, p. 805.
Danish translation:
Finnur Jónsson, ed. >> *Den norsk-islandske skjaldedigtning* (1912–15).
Vol. BII, p. 547.
English translation:
McDougall, David, ed. "Anonymous, *Pétrsdrápa* '*Drápa* about S. Peter'."
In >> *Poetry on Christian Subjects* (2007). Vol. 2, p. 805.

10. Allra postola minnisvísur

A fourteenth-century poem about all the apostles. Saint Andrew is treated in stz. 3.

Incipit: "Pétr er páfi drottins prísaðr gleðivísum."

Manuscript:
AM 721 4to (ca. 1500–50).

Editions:
Finnur Jónsson, ed. >> *Den norsk-islandske skjaldedigtning* (1912–15).
   Vol. AII, pp. 509–10 and vol. BII, pp. 559–60.
Jón Þorkelsson. >> *Om Digtningen på Island* (1888). P. 62 (stz. 1^2, 2^1, 3^1, 4^1,
   and 5^1).
Kock, Ernst Albin, ed. >> *Den norsk-isländska skaldediktningen* (1946–50).
   Vol. 2, p. 306.
McDougall, Ian, ed. "Anonymous, *Allra postula minnisvísur* 'Celebratory
   Vísur about All the Apostles'." In >> *Poetry on Christian Subjects* (2007).
   Vol. 2, p. 856.

Danish translation:
Finnur Jónsson, ed. >> *Den norsk-islandske skjaldedigtning* (1912–15).
   Vol. BII, p. 559.

English translation:
McDougall, Ian, ed. "Anonymous, *Allra postula minnisvísur* 'Celebratory
   Vísur about All the Apostles'." In >> *Poetry on Christian Subjects* (2007).
   Vol. 2, p. 856.

Literature:
Cormack, Margaret. >> *The Saints in Iceland* (1994). P. 41n60.
Finnur Jónsson. >> *Den oldnorske og oldislandske Litteraturs Historie*
   (1920–4). Vol. 3, p. 19.
Jakob Benediktsson. "Helgendigte." *KLNM* 6 (1961). Cols. 318–21, esp.
   col. 319.
– ed. >> "Helgikvæði." In *Hugtök og heiti í bókmenntafræði* (1983).
   Pp. 115–17, esp. p. 116.
Jón Helgason. >> "Norges og Islands digtning." In *Litteraturhistorie B:*
   Norge og Island (1953). Pp. 3–179, esp. p. 163.
Lange, Wolfgang. >> *Studien zur christlichen Dichtung der Nordgermanen*
   1000–1200 (1958). Pp. 86 and 96.
Stéfan Einarsson. "Íslenzk helgikvæði á miðöldum." *Tímarit Þjóðræknisfélags*
   Íslendinga 36 (1955): 43–63, esp. p. 49.
– *Íslensk bókmenntasaga 874–1960* (Reykjavík: Oddi, 1961). P. 86.

Vésteinn Ólason. "Kveðskapur frá síðmiðöldum." In >> *Íslensk Bókmenntasaga* 2 (1993). Pp. 283–378, esp. p. 315.

NOTE:

The poem contains material about Saints Bartholomew, James the Greater, James the Less, John the Evangelist, Jude, Matthias, Paul, Peter, Philip, Simon, and Thomas. See the entries for the individual saints.

11. Tólf postula kvæði

A late medieval (ca. 1400–1550) celebratory poem about all the apostles. Saint Andrew is treated in stz. 3.

Incipit: "Sankti Pétur sannur páfi í Róma."

Manuscripts:
AM 713 4to (ca. 1500–50) and Lbs 2166 4to (ca. 1885–1920).
Edition:
Jón Helgason, ed. >> *Íslenzk miðaldakvæði* (1936–8). Vol. 2, p. 275.
Based on AM 713 4to with notes from Jón Helgason's edition of *Pálsvísur* in >> *Íslenzk miðaldakvæði*, vol. 2 (1938) and C.R. Unger, ed. >> *Postola sögur* (1874).
Literature:
Deutsche Islandsforschung: 1930. Veröffentlichungen der Schleswig-Holsteinischen Universitätsgesellschaft 28 (Breslau: Ferdinand Hirt, 1930). Vol. 1, p. 233.
Finnur Jónsson. >> *Bókmentasaga Íslendinga fram undir siðabót* (1904–5). P. 461.
– >> *Den oldnorske og oldislandske Litteraturs Historie* (1920–4). Vol. 3, p. 126.
Hálfdan Einarsson. *Sciagraphia historiæ literariæ islandicæ* (Copenhagen: Sander and Schröder, 1777). P. 58.
Jakob Benediktsson. "Helgendigte." *KLNM* 6 (1961). Cols. 318–21, esp. pp. 319–20.
Jakob Benediktsson, ed. >> "Helgikvæði." In *Hugtök og heiti í Bókmenntafræði* (1983). Pp. 115–17, esp. p. 116.
Jón Helgason. >> "Norges og Islands digtning." In *Litteraturhistorie B: Norge og Island* (1953). Pp. 3–179, esp. p. 163.
Jón Þorkelsson. >> *Om Digtningen på Island* (1888). Pp. 62–3.
Kock, E.A. "Anteckningar till Íslenzk Miðaldakvæði." *ANF* 61 (1946): 1–125, esp. pp. 76–8 and 107.

Stéfan Einarsson. "Íslenzk helgikvæði á miðöldum." *Tímarit Þjóðræknisfélags Íslendinga* 36 (1955): 43–63, esp. p. 54.
– *Íslensk bókmenntasaga 874–1960* (Reykjavík: Oddi, 1961). P. 91.
NOTE:
The poem contains material about Saints Bartholomew, James the Greater, James the Less, John the Evangelist, Jude, Matthew, Matthias, Paul, Peter, Philip, Simon, and Thomas. See the entries for the individual saints.

12. Rósa

An early sixteenth-century cosmological poem with an emphasis on the life of Mary the Blessed Virgin attributed to Sigurður blindur. Stz. 6 mentions Saint Andrew.
Incipit: "Faðir og son á hæstum hæðum."

Manuscripts:
See Mary the Blessed Virgin 48 note (p. 212).
Editions:
Jón Helgason, ed. >> *Íslenzk miðaldakvæði* (1936–8). Vol. 1.2, p. 7.
Jón Þorkelsson, ed. >> *Kvæðasafn* (1922–7). P. 264.
Norwegian translation:
Orgland, Ivar, trans. and Anne-Lise Knoff, illus. *Rósa. Sigurður blindi í Fagradal* (Oslo: Solum, 1989). P. 20.

13. Milska

An early sixteenth-century poem about the life of Mary the Blessed Virgin. Stz. 4 mentions Saint Andrew.
Incipit: "Faðir vor Kristur friður hinn hæsti."

Manuscripts:
See Mary the Blessed Virgin 49 note (p. 214).
Edition:
Jón Helgason, ed. >> *Íslenzk miðaldakvæði* (1936–8). Vol. 1.2, p. 39.
Modern Icelandic language edition:
Jón Sigurðsson, ed. *Milska* (Reykjavík: Listahátíð í Reykjavík, 1994). P. [2].
Norwegian translations:
Orgland, Ivar, trans. *Milska* (Reykjavík: Listahátíð í Reykjavík, 1994). P. [2].
Orgland, Ivar, trans. and Anne-Lise Knoff, illus. *Milska: Eit Maria-kvad frå islandsk seinmellomalder* (Oslo: Solum, 1993). P. 22.

Literature:
Schottmann, Hans. >> *Die isländische Mariendichtung* (1973). P. 26.

14. Postulavísur

A poem about all the apostles composed in 1629 by Guðmundur Erlendsson í Felli (1595–1670). Stz. 8–9 and 29 concern Saint Andrew.
   Incipit: "Herrans hér postula."

Manuscripts:
ÍB 379 8vo (ca. 1700–1900), ÍB 633 8vo (ca. 1764–75), ÍBR 109 8vo (1829), JS 256 4to (1840–5), JS 399a–b 4to (ca. 1700–1900), Lbs 541 fol. (ca. 1850–1900), Lbs 399 4to (ca. 1680–1700), Lbs 1529 4to (ca. 1600–1700), Lbs 192 8vo (ca. 1700–1900), Lbs 499 8vo (1680), and Lbs 3170 8vo (ca. 1800)

Literature:
Jón Þorkelsson. >> *Om Digtningen på Island* (1888). P. 63.
NOTE:
The poem contains material about Saints Bartholomew, James the Greater, James the Less, John the Evangelist, Jude, Matthew, Matthias, Paul, Peter, Philip, Simon, and Thomas. See the entries for the individual saints.

15. Postularaun

A poem in praise of all the apostles composed by Guðmundur Bergþórsson (1657–1705). Stz. 15 and 22–39 concern Saint Andrew.
   Incipit: "Hér skal eina hróðar grein."

Manuscripts:
See Ananias note (p. 20).

ANNE   July 26

1. Náð

An early sixteenth-century poem in honour of Saint Anne and her daughter Mary the Blessed Virgin ascribed to the priest Hallur Ögmundarson (d. ca. 1540).
   Incipit: "Heyr mildingur allra alda."

Manuscripts:
AM 622 4to (ca. 1549), AM 715e 4to (ca. 1700–25), JS 399a–b 4to
   (ca. 1700–1900), and Lbs 444 4to (ca. 1820–50).
Editions:
Carpenter, William H., ed. *Nikolásdrápa Halls prests: An Icelandic Poem
   from circa A.D. 1400* (Halle: Karras, 1881). P. 6 (stz. 1).
   Edition of AM 622 4to.
Jón Helgason, ed. >> *Íslenzk miðaldakvæði* (1936–8). Vol. 2, pp. 4–26.
   Edition of AM 622 4to with variants from AM 715e 4to, JS 399a–b 4to,
   Lbs 444 4to, C.R. Unger, ed., *Mariu saga: Legender om Jomfru Maria og
   hendes jertegn* (Christiania [Oslo]: Brögger and Christie, 1871), and Jón
   Þorkelsson's (1922–7) edition.
Jón Þorkelsson. >> *Om Digtningen på Island* (1888). Pp. 54 (stz. 1^{1-2}) and
   320 (stz. 1, 103, and 107^{7-8}).
   Based on AM 622 4to and AM 715e 4to.
Jón Þorkelsson, ed. >> *Kvæðasafn* (1922–7). Pp. 327–53.
   Based on JS 399a–b 4to with variants from AM 622 4to and Lbs 444 4to.
Literature:
Ármann Jakobsson. "The Homer of the North, or: Who Was Sigurður the
   Blind?" *European Journal of Scandinavian Studies* 44 (2014): 4–19, esp.
   p. 5.
Bekker-Nielsen, Hans. "Mariadigtning." *KLNM* 11 (1966). Cols. 379–80, esp.
   col. 379.
Björn K. Þórólfsson. "Kvantitetsomvæltningen i islandsk." *ANF* 45 (1929):
   35–81, esp. pp. 42–5.
Björn Þorsteinsson and Guðrún Ása Grímsdóttir. "Kirkjan og þjóðlífið."
   In *Saga Íslands* 5. Ed. Sigurður Líndal (Reykjavík: Hið íslenzka
   bókmenntafélag, Sögufélagið, 1900). Pp. 141–79, esp. p. 168.
Finnur Jónsson. >> *Bókmentasaga Íslendinga fram undir siðabót* (1904–5).
   P. 463.
– >> *Den oldnorske og oldislandske Litteraturs Historie* (1920–4). Vol. 3,
   pp. 127–8.
Guðrún Nordal. "Á mörkum tveggja tíma: Kaþólskt kvæðahandrit með hendi
   siðbótarmanns, Gísla biskups Jónssonar." *Gripla* 16 (2005): 209–28, esp.
   pp. 219–20.
– "Helgubók." In *Góssið hans Árna: Minningar heimsins í íslenskum
   handritum*. Ed. Jóhanna Katrín Friðriksdóttir (Reykjavík: Stofnun Árna
   Magnússonar í íslenskum fræðum, 2014). Pp. 21–5, esp. p. 30.
Jón Helgason. *Gamall kveðskapur* (Copenhagen: Hið íslenzka fræðafélag,
   1979). P. 12.

- >> "Norges og Islands digtning." In *Litteraturhistorie B: Norge og Island* (1953). Pp. 3–179, esp. pp. 162 and 164.

Kock, E.A. "Anteckningar till Íslenzk Miðaldakvæði." *ANF* 61 (1946): 1–125, esp. pp. 10, 17, 31–5, and 85.

Mogk, Eugen. >> *Geschichte der norwegisch-isländischen Literatur* (1904). P. 719.

Schottmann, Hans. >> *Die isländische Mariendichtung* (1973). Pp. 33, 46, 54n18, 57n25, 57n26, 60, 62, 71, 84–6, 98, 102, 126, 130, 277–313, 324, 481, 485, 549, 552, and 554.

Stéfan Einarsson. "Íslenzk helgikvæði á miðöldum." *Tímarit Þjóðræknisfélags Íslendinga* 36 (1955): 43–63, esp. pp. 53–5.

- *Íslensk bókmenntasaga 874–1960* (Reykjavík: Oddi, 1961). Pp. 90–1.

Vésteinn Ólason. "Kveðskapur frá síðmiðöldum." In >> *Íslensk Bókmenntasaga* 2 (1993). Pp. 283–387, esp. pp. 301, 306, and 310–11.

- "Old Icelandic Poetry." In *A History of Icelandic Literature*. Ed. Daisy Neijmann. Histories of Scandinavian Literature 5 (Lincoln: University of Nebraska Press, 2006). Pp. 1–64, esp. pp. 51–2.

Wolf, Kirsten, ed. >> *Saga heilagrar Önnu* (2001). P. xliii.

NOTE:

The poem contains material about other saints, especially Mary the Blessed Virgin, but also James the Greater, James the Less, Joachim, John the Evangelist, Joseph, Jude, Peter, and Simon. See the entries for the individual saints.

2. Heilagra meyja drápa

A fourteenth-century poem about holy maidens. Stz. 1–10 treat Mary the Blessed Virgin, her mother Saint Anne, and the Virgin's half-sisters, Mary, wife of Alphaeus, and Mary, wife of Zebedee.

Incipit: "Heyrðu ómælds himna veldis herra guð."

Manuscripts:
See Agatha note (p. 13).
Editions:
Finnur Jónsson, ed. >> *Den norsk-islandske skjaldedigtning* (1912–15). Vol. AII, pp. 526–8 and vol. BII, pp. 582–5.

Jón Þorkelsson. >> *Om Digtingen på Island* (1888). P. 87 (stz. 1 only).

Kock, Ernst Albin, ed. >> *Notationes Norrænæ* (1923–44). §§1838, 1839, 1840, 2970A, 2970B, 2971A, 2972, 3389A, 3389B, 3389C, and 3390.

– ed. >> *Den norsk-islandske skaldediktningen* (1946–50). Vol. 2, pp. 321–3.
Wolf, Kirsten, ed. "Anonymous, *Heilagra meyja drápa* 'Drápa about Holy
   Maidens'." In >> *Poetry on Christian Subjects* (2007). Vol. 2, pp. 892–8.
Danish translation:
Finnur Jónsson, ed. >> *Den norsk-islandske skjaldedigtning* (1912–15).
   Vol. BII, pp. 582–5.
English translation:
Wolf, Kirsten, ed. "Anonymous, *Heilagra meyja drápa* 'Drápa about Holy
   Maidens'." In >> *Poetry on Christian Subjects* (2007). Vol. 2, pp. 892–8.

3. Græðarinn lýðs og landa

A Marian miracle poem from ca. 1300–1550 about the repentence of two
brothers (cf. C.R. Unger, ed., *Mariu saga: Legender om Jomfru Maria og hen-
des jertegn* [Christiania (Oslo): Brögger and Christie, 1871], pp. 608–22. Stz.
4 mentions Saint Anne.
   Incipit: "Græðarinn lýðs og landa."

Manuscripts:
See Mary the Blessed Virgin 15 note (p. 180).
Edition:
Jón Helgason, ed. >> *Íslenzk miðaldakvæði* (1936–8). Vol. 2, p. 181.

4. Boðunarvísur

A poem in honour of Mary the Blessed Virgin composed ca. 1300–1550. Stz.
12 mentions Saint Anne.
   Incipit: "Ave dýrust drósa."

Manuscripts:
See Mary the Blessed Virgin 19 note (p. 184).
Edition:
Jón Helgason, ed. >> *Íslenzk miðaldakvæði* (1936–8). Vol. 2, p. 30.

5. Vísur af Máríu Magdalene I

A late medieval (ca. 1400–1550) poem in praise of Saint Mary Magdalen. Stz.
20 mentions Saint Anne.
   Incipit: "Vil ég þér vísur vanda."

Manuscripts:
See Mary Magdalen 2 note (p. 242).
Edition:
Jón Helgason, ed. >> *Íslenzk miðaldakvæði* (1936–8). Vol. 2, p. 389.

6. Kristsbálkur

A late medieval (ca. 1400–1550) poem in praise of Jesus Christ based on oral
tradition. Stz. 18 mentions Saint Anne.
   Incipit: "Hæstur drottinn heiðri þig loptinn."

Manuscripts:
AM 717f α 4to (1670), AM 717f β1 4to (ca. 1700), AM 717f β2 4to (ca. 1700),
   JS 399a–b 4to (ca. 1700–1900), and Lbs 2166 4to (ca. 1885–1920).
Edition:
Jón Helgason, ed. >> *Íslenzk miðaldakvæði* (1936–8). Vol. 1, p. 146.
   Based on AM 717f β2 4to with variants from AM 717f α 4to, AM 717f β1
   4to, JS 399a–b 4to, and Lbs 2166 4to.
Literature:
Hálfdan Einarsson. *Sciagraphia historiæ literariæ islandicæ* (Copenhagen:
   Sander and Schröder, 1777). P. 58.
Jón Þorkelsson. >> *Om Digtningen på Island* (1888). P. 94.
Vésteinn Ólason. "Kveðskapur frá síðmiðöldum." In >> *Íslensk Bókmenntasaga*
   2 (1993). Pp. 283–378, esp. p. 303.
Wolf, Kirsten, ed. >> *Saga heilagrar Önnu* (2001). Pp. xliii–xliv.
NOTE:
The poem contains material about other saints, especially Mary the Blessed
Virgin but also Saint John the Evangelist. See the entries for the two saints.

7. Pálsdiktur

A late medieval (ca. 1400–1550) poem in honour of Saint Paul. Stz. 25 men-
tions Saint Anne.
   Incipit: "Bið ég að styrki málsnilld mína."

Manuscripts:
See Paul the Apostle 2 note (p. 312).
Edition:
Jón Helgason, ed. >> *Íslenzk miðaldakvæði* (1936–8). Vol. 2, p. 291.

8. Salutatio Mariæ

A poem in praise of Mary the Blessed Virgin composed ca. 1400–1550 and extant in three redactions. Stz. 9 of the A redaction and stz. 16 of the B redaction mention Saint Anne.

Incipits: A and C: "Ave ágæt Máriá"; B: "María melli plena."

Manuscripts:
See Mary the Blessed Virgin 29 note (p. 194).
Edition:
Jón Helgason, ed. >> *Íslenzk miðaldakvæði* (1936–8). Vol. 2, pp. 231 and 232.

9. Máríulykill

A poem in praise of Mary the Blessed Virgin composed ca. 1425. The first half of the poem is possibly by Jón Pálsson Máríuskáld (ca. 1390–1471). It has also been attributed to Bishop Jón Arason (1484–1550), though the approximate date of composition makes this unlikely. Stz. 19 mentions Saint Anne.

Incipit: "Drottning æðsta dýr af ættum."

Manuscripts:
See Mary the Blessed Virgin 44 note (p. 207).
Editions:
Jón Helgason, ed. >> *Íslenzk miðaldakvæði* (1936–8). Vol. 2, p. 216.
– "Nokkur íslenzk miðaldakvæði." *ANF* 40 (1924): 285–313, esp. pp. 304–9.
Jón Þorkelsson, ed. >> *Kvæðasafn* (1922–7). P. 129.
– >> *Om Digtningen på Island* (1888). P. 258.

10. Heyr mig himins og láða

A fragmentary poem from ca. 1500 about the events surrounding Christ's birth and childhood. Stz. 12 mentions Saint Anne.

Incipit: "Heyr mig himins og láða."

Manuscript:
JS 413 8vo (ca. 1700–1900).
Edition:
Jón Helgason, ed. >> *Íslenzk miðaldakvæði* (1926–8). Vol. 1.2, p. 187.

Literature:
Kock, E.A. "Anteckningar till Íslenzk miðaldakvæði." *ANF* 61 (1946): 1–125,
    esp. p. 28.
Schottmann, Hans. >> *Die isländische Mariendichtung* (1973). P. 314n1.
NOTE:
The poem contains material about Saints Joseph, Mary the Blessed Virgin, and
Simeon the Righteous. See the entries for the individual saints.

11. Rósa

An early sixteenth-century cosmological poem with an emphasis on the life of
Mary the Blessed Virgin attributed to Sigurður blindur. Stz. 39–47 concern
Saint Anne, and she is mentioned in stz. 50.
    Incipit: "Faðir og son á hæstum hæðum."

Manuscripts:
See Mary the Blessed Virgin 48 note (p. 212).
Editions:
Jón Helgason, ed. >> *Íslenzk miðaldakvæði* (1936–8). Vol. 1, pp. 14–18.
Jón Þorkelsson, ed. >> *Kvæðasafn* (1922–7). Pp. 271–5.
Norwegian translation:
Orgland, Ivar, trans. and Anne-Lise Knoff, illus. *Rósa. Sigurður blindi í
    Fagradal* (Oslo: Solum, 1989). Pp. 34 and 36.

12. Ljómur

A Christian history of the world composed ca. 1525 and ascribed to Bishop Jón
Arason (1484–1550). Stz. 8 mentions Saint Anne.
    Incipit: "Hæstur heilagur andi."

Manuscripts:
A: AM 713 4to (ca. 1500–50) and AM 1032 4to (ca. 1700–25);
B: AM 104 8vo (ca. 1680), Lbs 1276 4to (1862–70), and Lbs 1197 8vo (1773);
C: AM 695a 4to (ca. 1650–1700), AM 716i 4to (ca. 1600–1700), AM 148 8vo
    (ca. 1650–1700), BLAdd 4892 (ca. 1700–1800), BLAdd 11.179 (ca. 1700–
    1800), JS 260 4to (1796), JS 284 8vo (ca. 1850), JS 473 8vo (ca. 1675–
    1900), JS 487 8vo (ca. 1675–1900), JS 494 8vo (ca. 1675–1900), Lbs 953
    4to (ca. 1760), Lbs 201 8vo (ca. 1850–70), Lbs 754 8vo (ca. 1700–1900),
    Lbs 1197 8vo (1773; stz. 1–7 only), and NKS 1955 4to (ca. 1800);
D: AM 716h 4to (ca. 1650–1800);

E: JS 583 4to (ca. 1690);

F: JS 244 8vo (ca. 1800–20), JS 475 8vo (ca. 1675–1900), JS 509 8vo
  (ca. 1675–1900), Lbs 201 8vo (ca. 1850–70), and Lbs 1014 8vo (1821–3);

G (the Faroese tradition): GKS 2894 4to (ca. 1775–1800), NKS 1955 4to
  (ca. 1800), and Rask 113 (ca. 1800–25).[1]

Editions:

Finnur Jónsson, ed. >> *Jón Arasons religiøse digte* (1918). Pp. 40–1 and
  46–7.
  Based on AM 713 4to with variants from AM 695a 4to and the so-called
  Faroese text (G).

Jón Helgason, ed. >> *Íslenzk miðaldakvæði* (1936–8). Vol. 1.2, p. 125.
  Based on A (AM 713 4to) with variants from AM 695a 4to, AM 716h 4to,
  AM 716i 4to, AM 104 8vo, AM 148 8vo, BLAdd 11.179, BLAdd 4892,
  GKS 2894 4to, JS 583 4to, JS 260 4to, JS 244 8vo, JS 509 8vo, Lbs 953
  4to, Lbs 1197 8vo, and NKS 1955 4to.

– ed. >> *Kvæðabók úr Vigur: AM 148, 8vo* (1955). Fol. 301r–305r
  Facsimile of AM 148 8vo.

[Jón Sigurðsson and Guðbrandur Vigfússon, ed.] >> *Biskupa sögur* (1858–
  78). Vol. 2, pp. 524–5.
  Normalized edition based on AM 713 4to.

Norwegian translation:

Næss, Leonhard, trans. "Ljomur av Jón Arason." *Norsk aarsbok* (1930). P. 74.

Literature:

Anon. "Den Oldnordisk-islandske Afdeling." Annual Report for 1846.
  Antiquarisk Tidsskrift 1846–8 (Copenhagen: Sally B. Salomon, 1847).
  Pp. 39–49, esp. p. 41.

Bjarni Þorsteinsson, ed. *Íslenzk þjóðlög* (Copenhagen: Møller, 1906–9).
  P. 635.

Debes, Lucas Jacobsøn. *Færoæ et Færoa reserata* (Copenhagen: Matthias
  Jørgensen, 1673). Pp. 307–8.

Einar Sigurbjörnsson. "Maríukveðskapur á mótum kaþólsku og lúthersku."
  In >> *Til heiðurs og hugbótar* (2003). Pp. 113–29, esp. p. 115.

Einar Ól. Sveinsson, Páll Eggert Ólason, and Arnór Sigurjónsson, ed. *Íslands
  þúsund ár: Kvæðasafn.* 3 vols. (Reykjavík: Helgafell, 1947). Vol. 3,
  pp. 150–2.

---

1 This book is concerned with Icelandic poetry on saints. Accordingly, editions of and literature
  on the G redaction of *Ljómur* (the so-called Faroese tradition) have not been included.
  For information on the subject, see Jón Helgason, "Færøiske Studier," *Mm* (1924): 29–48
  (*Ljómur* ed., pp. 37–47).

Finnur Jónsson. >> *Bókmentasaga Íslendinga fram undir siðabót* (1904–5).
Pp. 461 and 464–5.
- >> *Den oldnorske og oldislandske Litteraturs Historie* (1920–4). Vol. 3,
p. 129.
Jakob Benediktsson. >> "Helgikvæði." In *Hugtök og heiti í bókmenntafræði*
(1983). Pp. 115–17, esp. p. 116.
Jensen, R. *Aarbøger for nordisk Oldkyndighed og Historie* (1869). Pp. 335–6.
Jón Helgason. >> "Norges og Islands digtning." In *Litteraturshistorie B:
Norge og Island* (1953). Pp. 3–179, esp. pp. 162–3.
Jón Torfason and Kristján Eiríksson, ed. >> *Vísnabók Guðbrands* (2000). P. xl.
Jón Þorkelsson. >> *Om Digtningen på Island* (1888). Pp. 94, 185, and 327.
- "Islandske håndskrifter i England og Skotland." *ANF* 8 (1892): 199–237,
esp. p. 205.
Jónas Kristjánsson. >> *Eddas and Sagas: Iceland's Medieval Literature*
(1988). Pp. 388 and 390.
Kock, E.A. "Liljukvistur." *Studia Neophilologica* 15 (1942): 141–56, esp. p. 143.
- "Anteckningar till Íslenzk Miðaldakvæði." *ANF* 61 (1946): 1–125, esp.
pp. 13–16, and 28.
Mogk, Eugen. >> *Geschichte der norwegisch-isländischen Literatur* (1904).
Pp. 719–20.
Myrvoll, Klaus Johan, and Trygve Skomedal. "Tonelagsskilnad i islendsk i
Tridje grammatiske avhandling." *Mm* (2010): 68–97, esp. pp. 72–3.
Orgland, Ivar, trans. *Islandske dikt. Frå Solarljóð til opplysningstid (13.
hundreåret–1835)* (Reykjavík: Fonna, 1977). Pp. 237–8.
Páll Eggert Ólason. *Menn og menntir siðskiptaaldarinnar á Íslandi.* Vol. 1
(Reykjavík: Guðm. Gamalíelsson, 1919). Pp. 416–17 and 438.
Pétur Sigurðsson. "Vísnabók Guðbrands biskups." In *Iðunn: Tímarit til
skemtunar, nytsemdar og fróðleiks.* Vol. 8. Ed. Magnús Jónsson (Reykjavík:
Gutenberg, 1923–4). Pp. 61–87, esp. p. 63.
Schottmann, Hans. >> *Die isländische Mariendichtung* (1973). Pp. 292,
314–16, and 554.
Sigurður Nordal, ed. *Íslenzk lestrarbók 1400–1900* (Reykjavík: Sigfús
Eymundsson, 1924). Pp. 22–6.
Stéfan Einarsson. "Íslenzk helgikvæði á miðöldum." *Tímarit
Þjóðræknisfélags Íslendinga* 36 (1954): 43–63, esp. pp. 53, 57, and 60–2.
- *Íslensk bókmenntasaga 874–1960* (Reykjavík: Oddi, 1961). Pp. 90, 93–4,
98–9, 219, 329, and 342.
Vésteinn Ólason. "Kveðskapur frá síðmiðöldum." In >> *Íslensk Bókmenntasaga*
2 (1993). Pp. 283–387, esp. pp. 300–3, 307, 373, and 375.

– "Old Icelandic Poetry." In *A History of Icelandic Literature*. Ed. Daisy
  Neijmann. Histories of Scandinavian Literature 5 (Lincoln: University
  of Nebraska Press, 2006). Pp. 1–64, esp. pp. 51–3.
Wolf, Kirsten. "The Influence of the *Evangelium Nicodemi* on Norse
  Literature: A Survey." In *The Medieval* Gospel of Nicodemus: *Texts,
  Intertexts, and Contexts in Western Europe*. Ed. Zbigniew Izydorczyk
  (Tempe, AZ; Medieval and Renaissance Texts and Studies, 1997).
  Pp. 261–86, esp. p. 278.
Wolf, Kirsten, ed. >> *Saga heilagrar Önnu* (2001). Pp. xliii–xliv.
NOTE:
The poem contains material about Saint John the Evangelist. See his entry.

13. Niðurstigningsvísur

A poetic rendering of the story of Christ's descent to hell composed ca. 1525
by Bishop Jón Arason (1484–1550). Saint Anne is mentioned in an additional
stz. found only in AM 104 8vo, JS 265 8vo, Lbs 953 4to, and Lbs 1197 8vo.
  Incipit: "Djarflig er mér diktan."

Manuscripts:
A: AM 710c 4to (ca. 1700–25), AM 713 4to (ca. 1500–50), JS 581 4to
  (ca. 1600–1900), and Lbs 201 8vo (ca. 1850–70);
B: AM 714 4to (ca. 1600);
C: AM 720b 4to (ca. 1600);
D: AM 766a 4to (ca. 1600–1700);
E: AM 695a 4to (ca. 1650–1700), AM 695f 4to (ca. 1700), AM 716d 4to
  (ca. 1600–1700), and AM 148 8vo (ca. 1650–1700);
F: AM 716e 4to (ca. 1700–25), AM 716f 4to (1673), and Stock. Papp. fol.
  no. 64 (ca. 1650–1700);
G: AM 716g 4to (ca. 1675–1700);
H: AM 716e 4to (ca. 1700–25), AM 104 8vo (ca. 1680), JS 589 4to (1841),
  JS 265 8vo (ca. 1760–6), Lbs 953 4to (ca. 1760), Lbs 1276 4to (1862–70),
  Lbs 201 8vo (ca. 1850–70), Lbs 1197 8vo (1773),
  and Stock. Papp. fol. no. 64 (ca. 1650–1700);
I: Lbs 201 8vo (ca. 1850–70).
Editions:
Finnur Jónsson, ed. >> *Jón Arasons religiøse digte* (1918). Pp. 58–69.
  Based on AM 713 4to with variants from AM 695a 4to and AM 720b 4to.
  The additional stz. mentioning Saint Anne is not included in this edition,

but the entry has been listed here for purposes of cross-referencing from
subsequent entries.

Jón Helgason, ed. >> *Íslenzk miðaldakvæði* (1936–8). Vol. 1.2, pp. 237–8.
Based on AM 713 4to with variants from AM 695a 4to, AM 714 4to, AM
716d 4to, AM 716e 4to, AM 716f 4to, AM 716g 4to, AM 720b 4to, AM
104 8vo, AM 148 8vo, JS 265 8vo, Lbs 953 4to, Lbs 201 8vo, Lbs 1197
8vo, and Stock. Papp. fol. no. 64. The additional stz. on pp. 237–8 are
edited as follows: stz. 1 is based on E3 with variants from E1–2 and F; stz.
2 is based on F; stz. 3 is based on H3 with variants from H1–2 and 4–6;
stz. 4 is based on H3 with variants from H1–2 and 4–6; stz. 5 is based
on F with variants from G and H3–4.

– ed. >> *Kvæðabók úr Vigur: AM 148, 8vo* (1955). Fol. 297r–301r.
Facsimile of AM 148 8vo.

[Jón Sigurðsson and Guðbrandur Vigfússon, ed.] >> *Biskupa sögur* (1858–78).
Vol. 2, p. 548.
Based on AM 713 4to with variants from AM 714 4to, AM 716d 4to, AM
716e 4to, AM 716f 4to, AM 716g 4to, AM 720b 4to, and AM 104 8vo.

Literature:

Chase, Martin. "Leviathan and the *Miðgardsormr* in Old Norse Christian
Texts: An Attempt to Diabolize the World-Serpent?" In *The Devil in
Society in Premodern Europe*. Ed. Richard Raiswell and Peter Dendle.
Essays and Studies (Toronto: Centre for Reformation and Renaissance
Studies, 2012). Pp. 109–35.

Einar Ó. Sveinsson, Páll Eggert Ólason, and Arnór Sigurjónsson, ed.
Íslands þúsund ár: Kvæðasafn. 3 vols. (Reykjavík: Helgafell, 1947).
Vol. 3, p. 150.

Finnur Jónsson. >> *Bókmentasaga Íslendinga fram undir siðabót* (1904–5).
P. 465.

– >> *Den oldnorske og oldislandske Litteraturs Historie* (1920–4). Vol. 3,
p. 129.

Guðrún Ingólfsdóttir. "Elínarbók: AM 67 8vo, AM 716f 4to, AM 717c
4to, AM 717f α 4to og AM 717g 4to." In *Handritasyrpa: Rit til
heiðurs Sigurgeiri Steingrímssyni sjötugum, 2. október 2013*. Ed. Rósa
Þorsteinsdóttir (Reykjavík: Stofnun Árna Magnússonar, 2014). Pp. 103–20,
esp. p. 109.

Jakob Benediktsson. "Kristdigte." *KLNM* 9 (1964). Cols. 292–4, esp.
col. 293.

Jón Helgason. >> "Norges og Islands digtning." In *Litteraturhistorie B:
Norge og Island* (1953). Pp. 3–179, esp. pp. 162–3.

Jón Þorkelsson. >> *Om Digtningen på Island* (1888). Pp. 94, 328, and 334.

Mogk, Eugen. >> *Geschichte der norwegisch-isländischen Literatur* (1904).
   P. 720.
Páll Eggert Ólason. *Menn og menntir siðskiptaaldarinmar á Íslandi.* Vol. 1
   (Reykjavík: Guðm. Gamalíelsson, 1919). Pp. 419, 422, and 438.
Pétur Sigurðsson. "Vísnabók Guðbrands biskups." In *Iðunn: Tímarit til
   skemtuna, nytsemdar og fróðleiks.* Vol. 8. Ed. Magnús Jónsson (Reykjavík:
   Gutenberg, 1923–4). Pp. 61–87, esp. p. 63.
Schottmann, Hans. >> *Die isländishe Mariendichtung* (1973). P. 32n29.
Stéfan Einarsson. "Íslenzk helgikvæði á miðöldum." *Tímarit Þjóðræknisfélags
   Íslendinga* 36 (1955): 43–63, esp. pp. 53 and 62.
– *Íslensk bókmenntasaga 874–1960* (Reykjavík: Oddi, 1961). Pp. 90
   and 98.
Vésteinn Ólason. "Kveðskapur frá síðmiðöldum." In >> *Íslensk Bókmenntasaga*
   2 (1993). Pp. 283–387, esp. pp. 307, 320, and 375.
– "Old Icelandic Poetry." In *A History of Icelandic Literature.* Ed. Daisy
   Neijmann. Histories of Scandinavian Literature 5 (Lincoln: University of
   Nebraska Press, 2006). Pp. 1–64, esp. pp. 52–3.
Wolf, Kirsten. "The Influence of the *Evangelium Nicodemi* on Norse
   Literature: A Survey." In *The Medieval* Gospel of Nicodemus: *Texts,
   Intertexts, and Contexts in Western Europe.* Ed. Zbigniew Izydorczyk
   (Tempe, AZ; Medieval and Renaissance Texts and Studies, 1997).
   Pp. 261–86, esp. pp. 274–7 and 286.
Wolf, Kirsten, ed. >> *Saga heilagrar Önnu* (2001). P. xliv.
NOTE:
The poem contains material about Saints Joachim, John the Evangelist, Joseph,
Lazarus, Nicodemus, and Peter. See the entries for the individual saints.

AUGUSTINE   August 28

1. Drápa af Máríugrát

A fourteenth-century poem about Mary the Blessed Virgin's lament to Saint
Augustine about her sorrows and her enumeration to a monk of her five joys.
Stz. 4–5 and 8–10 concern Saint Augustine.
   Incipit: "Orðin gief þú mjög til mærðar, minn lausnari, skáldi þínu."

Manuscripts:
See Mary the Blessed Virgin 9 note (p. 176).

Editions:
Finnur Jónsson, ed. >> *Den norsk-islandske skjaldedigtning* (1912–15).
  Vol. AII, pp. 473–4 and vol. BII, pp. 506–8.
Gade, Kari Ellen, ed. "Anonymous, *Drápa af Máríugrát* 'Drápa about the
  Lament of Mary'." In >> *Poetry on Christian Subjects* (2007). Vol. 2,
  pp. 762 and 765–7.
Kahle, Bernhard, ed. >> *Isländische geistliche Dichtungen des ausgehenden
  Mittelalters* (1898). Pp. 56–7.
Kock, Ernst Albin, ed. >> *Notationes Norrœna* (1923–44). §§1663, 1664D,
  1666, 2680A, 2683, and 3354B.
– ed. >> *Den norsk-isländska skaldediktningen* (1946–50). Vol. 2, pp. 276–8.
Sperber, Hans, ed. >> *Sechs isländische Gedichte legendarischen Inhalts*
  (1911). Pp. 31–2.
Wrightson, Kellinde, ed. >> *Fourteenth-Century Icelandic Verse on the Virgin
  Mary* (2001). Pp. 2–5.
Danish translation:
Finnur Jónsson, ed. >> *Den norsk-islandske skjaldedigtning* (1912–15).
  Vol. BII, pp. 506–8.
English translations:
Gade, Kari Ellen, ed. "Anonymous, *Drápa af Máríugrát* 'Drápa about the
  Lament of Mary'." In >> *Poetry on Christian Subjects* (2007). Vol. 2, pp.
  762–3 and 765–7.
Wrightson, Kellinde, ed. >> *Fourteenth-Century Icelandic Verse on the Virgin
  Mary* (2001). Pp. 2–5.

2. Michaelsflokkur

An early sixteenth-century poem about Saint Michael ascribed to the priest
Hallur Ögmundarson (d. ca. 1540). Saint Augustine is mentioned in stz. 30.
  Incipit: "Óðar gef þú upphaf."

Manuscripts:
See Michael the Archangel 2 note (p. 256).
Edition:
Jón Þorkelsson, ed. >> *Kvæðasafn* (1922–7). P. 377.

3. Nikulásdrápa

An early sixteenth-century poem in honour of Saint Nicholas ascribed to the
priest Hallur Ögmundarson (d. ca. 1540). Stz. 2 mentions Saint Augustine.
  Incipit: "Í nafni guðs vil ég upphaf efna."

Manuscripts:
See Nicholas 5 note (p. 262).
Editions:
Carpenter, William H., ed. *Nikolásdrápa Halls prests: An Icelandic Poem from circa A.D. 1400* (Halle: Karras, 1881). P. 13.
Jón Helgason, ed. >> *Íslenzk miðaldakvæði* (1936–8). Vol. 2, p. 417.
Jón Þorkelsson, ed. >> *Kvæðasafn* (1922–7). P. 386.

BARBARA   December 4

1. Barbörudiktur (-kvæði, -vísur)

A late medieval (ca. 1400–1550) poetic rendering of the legend of Saint Barbara.

Incipits: A: "Fyrir Distal réði drengur heiðinn"; B: "Herra guð sem hæðstan um stýrir."

Manuscripts:
A: BLAdd 4892 (ca. 1700–1800), BLAdd 11.179 (ca. 1700–1800), JS 260 4to (1796), JS 265 4to (ca. 1860), JS 284 8vo (ca. 1850), JS 487 8vo (ca. 1675–1900), JS 494 8vo (ca. 1675–1900), JS 514 8vo (ca. 1675–1900), Lbs 936 4to (ca. 1880; stz. 1 only), Lbs 953 4to (ca. 1760), Lbs 1326 4to (ca. 1890), Lbs 2166 4to (ca. 1885–1920), Lbs 201 8vo (ca. 1850–70), and Lbs 754 8vo (ca. 1700–1900, stz. 1 only);
B: G-32/5 (ca. 1892–1971), Eink 1-5 (ca. 1850–1950), Eink 210-23 (ca. 1885), JS 201 4to (ca. 1837–50), Lbs 2127 4to (ca. 1873), Lbs 2222 8vo (ca. 1800–1900), SÁM 85/348 EF (1969), and SÁM 85/354 EF (1969).
Editions:
Jón Helgason, ed. >> *Íslenzk miðaldakvæði* (1936–8). Vol. 2, pp. 332–5 (A) and 336–41 (B).
   Redaction A based on BLAdd 4892 with variants from BLAdd 11.179, JS 260 4to, JS 284 8vo, JS 487 8vo, Lbs 953 4to, and Lbs 2166 4to; redaction B based on JS 201 4to with variants from Lbs 2127 4to and Lbs 2222 8vo.
Jón Þorkelsson. >> *Om Digtningen på Island* (1888). P. 93 (stz. 1).
   Based on JS 260 4to and Lbs 201 8vo.
Literature:
Anon. "Den Oldnordisk-islandske Afdeling." Annual Report for 1846.
   Antiquarisk Tidsskrift 1846–8 (Copenhagen: Sally B. Salomon, 1847).
   Pp. 39–49, esp. pp. 40–1.

– "Den Oldnordisk-islandske Afdeling." Annual Report for 1847. *Antiquarisk Tidsskrift* 1846–8 (Copenhagen: Sally B. Salomon, 1847). Pp. 154–72, esp. p. 165.

Foote, Peter, ed. *Lives of Saints. Perg. fol. nr. 2 in the Royal Library, Stockholm.* EIM 4 (Copenhagen: Rosenkilde and Bagger, 1962). P. 26.

Jakob Benediktsson. "Helgendigte." *KLNM* 6 (1961). Cols. 318–21, esp. col. 320.

– "Nödhjälparna." *KLNM* 21 (1977). Cols. 289–90, esp. col. 289.

Jón Helgason. >> "Norges og Islands digtning." In *Litteraturhistorie B: Norge og Island* (1953). Pp. 3–179, esp. pp. 163–4.

Jón Þorkelsson. "Islandske håndskrifter i England og Skotland." *ANF* 8 (1892): 199–237, esp. pp. 206–7.

Kock, E.A. "Anteckningar till Íslenzk Miðaldakvæði." *ANF* 61 (1946): 1–125, esp. pp. 42–3 and 90–1.

Mogk, Eugen. >> *Geschichte der norwegisch-isländischen Literatur* (1904). P. 719.

Soffía Ófeigsdóttir. "*Veroníkukvæði.*" BA thesis. University of Iceland, 1986. P. 66.

Stéfan Einarsson. "Íslenzk helgikvæði á miðöldum." *Tímarit Þjóðræknisfélags Íslendinga* 36 (1955): 43–63, esp. p. 55.

– *Íslensk bókmenntasaga 874–1960* (Reykjavík: Oddi, 1961). P. 92.

Vésteinn Ólason. "Kveðskapur frá síðmiðöldum." In >> *Íslensk Bókmenntasaga* 2 (1993). Pp. 283–378, esp. p. 316.

Wolf, Kirsten, ed. *The Old Norse–Icelandic Legend of Saint Barbara.* Studies and Texts 134 (Toronto: Pontifical Institute of Mediaeval Studies, 2000). Pp. 73–7.

– ed. >> *Heilagra meyja sögur* (2003). P. lv.

2. Heilagra meyja drápa

A fourteenth-century poem about holy maidens. Stz. 52 treats Saint Barbara. Incipit: "Heyrðu ómælds himna veldis herra guð."

Manuscripts:
See Agatha note (p. 13).
Editions:
Finnur Jónsson, ed. >> *Den norsk-islandske skjaldedigtning* (1912–15). Vol. AII, p. 537 and vol. BII, p. 595.

Kock, Ernst Albin, ed. >> *Notationes Norrœnæ* (1923–44). §§91 and 2970B.

– ed. >> *Den norsk-islandske skaldedigtningen* (1946–50). Vol. 2, p. 329.

Wolf, Kirsten, ed. "Anonymous, *Heilagra meyja drápa 'Drápa* about Holy
Maidens'." In >> *Poetry on Christian Subjects* (2007). Vol. 2, p. 923.
Danish translation:
Finnur Jónsson, ed. >> *Den norsk-islandske skjaldedigtning* (1912–15).
Vol. BII, p. 595.
English translation:
Wolf, Kirsten, ed. "Anonymous, *Heilagra meyja drápa 'Drápa* about Holy
Maidens'." In >> *Poetry on Christian Subjects* (2007). Vol. 2, p. 923.

BARNABAS   June 11

Rósa

An early sixteenth-century cosmological poem with an emphasis on the life of
Mary the Blessed Virgin attributed to Sigurður blindur. Stz. 6 mentions Saint
Barnabas.
   Incipit: "Faðir og son á hæstum hæðum."

Manuscripts:
See Mary the Blessed Virgin 48 note (p. 212).
Editions:
Jón Helgason, ed. >> *Íslenzk miðaldakvæði* (1936–8). Vol. 1, p. 7.
Jón Þorkelsson, ed. >> *Kvæðasafn* (1922–7). P. 264.
Norwegian translation:
Orgland, Ivar, trans. and Anne-Lise Koff, illus. *Rósa. Sigurður blindi í Fagradal*
(Oslo: Solum, 1989). P. 20.

BARTHOLOMEW   August 24

1. Barthólómeusdiktur

A fragmentary poem in honour of Saint Bartholomew composed ca.
1300–1550.
   Incipit: "Drottinn gef þú að dikturinn mætur."

Manuscripts:
AM 720c 4to (ca. 1700–25), AM 721 4to (ca. 1500–50), and Lbs 2166 4to
(ca. 1885–1920).

Editions:
Jón Helgason, ed. >> *Íslenzk miðaldakvæði* (1936–8). Vol. 2, pp. 319–24.
  Based on AM 721 4to with variants from AM 720c 4to.
Jón Þorkelsson. >> *Om Digtningen på Island* (1888). P. 67 (stz. 1).
  Based on AM 720c 4to and AM 721 4to.

Literature:
Hálfdan Einarsson. *Sciagraphia historiæ literariæ islandicæ* (Copenhagen:
  Sander and Schröder, 1777). P. 58.
Jakob Benediktsson. "Helgendigte." *KLNM* 6 (1961). Cols. 318–21, esp. col. 320.
Kock, E.A. "Anteckningar till Íslenzk Miðaldakvæði." *ANF* 61 (1946): 1–125,
  esp. p. 89.
Schottmann, Hans. >> *Die isländische Mariendichtung* (1973). P. 24n10.
Stéfan Einarsson. "Íslenzk helgikvæði á miðöldum." *Tímarit Þjóðræknisfélags
  Íslendinga* 36 (1955): 43–63, esp. p. 54.
– *Íslensk bókmenntasaga 874–1960* (Reykjavík: Oddi, 1961). P. 91.
Vésteinn Ólason. "Kveðskapur frá síðmiðöldum." In >> *Íslensk Bókmenntasaga*
  2 (1993). Pp. 283–378, esp. p. 315.

2. Allra postola minnisvísur

A fourteenth-century poem about all the apostles. Saint Bartholomew is treated
in stz. 9.
  Incipit: "Pétr er páfi drottins prísaðr gleðivísum."

Manuscript:
See Andrew the Apostle 10 note (p. 30).
Editions:
Finnur Jónsson, ed. >> *Den norsk-islandske skjaldedigtning* (1912–15).
  Vol. AII, pp. 510–11 and vol. BII, p. 561.
Kock, Ernst Albin, ed. >> *Notationes Norrœnæ* (1923–44). §1760.
– ed. >> *Den norsk-isländska skaldediktningen* (1946–50). Vol. 2, p. 307.
McDougall, Ian, ed. "Anonymous, *Allra postula minnisvísur* 'Celebratory
  Vísur about All the Apostles'." In >> *Poetry on Christian Subjects* (2007).
  Vol. 2, p. 864.
Danish translation:
Finnur Jónsson, ed. >> *Den norsk-islandske skjaldedigtning* (1912–15).
  Vol. BII, p. 561.
English translation:
McDougall, Ian, ed. "Anonymous, *Allra postula minnisvísur* 'Celebratory
  Vísur about All the Apostles'." In >> *Poetry on Christian Subjects* (2007).
  Vol. 2, p. 864.

3. Tólf postula kvæði

A late medieval (ca. 1400–1550) celebratory poem about all the apostles. Saint Bartholomew is treated in stz. 6.

Incipit: "Sankti Pétur sannur páfi í Róma."

Manuscripts:
See Andrew the Apostle 11 note (p. 31).
Edition:
Jón Helgason, ed. >> *Íslenzk miðaldakvæði* (1936–8). Vol. 2, p. 276.

4. Rósa

An early sixteenth-century cosmological poem with an emphasis on the life of Mary the Blessed Virgin attributed to Sigurður blindur. Stz. 6 mentions Saint Bartholomew.

Incipit: "Faðir og son á hæstum hæðum."

Manuscripts:
See Mary the Blessed Virgin 48 note (p. 212).
Editions:
Jón Helgason, ed. >> *Íslenzk miðaldakvæði* (1936–8). Vol. 1, p. 7.
Jón Þorkelsson, ed. >> *Kvæðasafn* (1922–7). P. 264.
Norwegian translation:
Orgland, Ivar, trans. and Anne-Lise Knoff, illus. *Rósa. Sigurður blindur í Fagradal* (Oslo: Solum, 1989). P. 20.

5. Postulavísur

A poem about all the apostles composed in 1629 by Guðmundur Erlendsson í Felli (1595–1670). Stz. 16–17 and 25 concern Saint Bartholomew.

Incipit: "Herrans hér postula."

Manuscripts:
See Andrew the Apostle 14 note (p. 32).

6. Postularaun

A poem in praise of all the apostles composed by Guðmundur Bergþórsson (1657–1705). Stz. 15 and 39–43 concern Saint Bartholomew.

Incipit: "Hér skal eina hróðar grein."

Manuscripts:
See Ananias note (p. 20).

BERNARD OF CLAIRVAUX   August 20

Máríublóm

An early sixteenth-century poem in praise of Jesus Christ attributed to the priest
Hallur Ögmundarson (d. ca. 1540). Stz. 4 mentions Saint Bernard of Clairvaux.
   Incipit: "Heyr mig Jesús hjálparinn mætur."

Manuscripts:
A: AM 622 4to (1549) and Lbs 1327 4to (ca. 1890);
B: Adv 21.8.10 (1712) and Lbs 1327 4to (ca. 1890);
C: AM 714 4to (ca. 1600).

Editions:
Jón Helgason, ed. >> *Íslenzk miðaldakvæði* (1936–8). Vol. 1.2, p. 173.
   Based on AM 622 4to with variants from Adv 21.8.10, Lbs 1327 4to, AM
   714 4to, and Jón Þorkelsson's edition (1922–7).
Jón Þorkelsson, ed. >> *Kvæðasafn* (1922–7). P. 354.
   Based on AM 622 4to with variants from Adv 21.8.10 and AM 714 4to.

Literature:
Ármann Jakobsson. "The Homer of the North, or: Who Was Sigurður the
   Blind?" *European Journal of Scandinavian Studies* 44 (2014): 4–19, esp. p. 5.
Björn Þorleifsson. "Kvantitetsomvæltningen i islandsk." *ANF* 45 (1929):
   35–81, esp. pp. 48–50.
Carpenter, William H., ed. *Nikolásdrápa Halls prests: An Icelandic Poem
   from circa A.D. 1400* (Halle: Karras, 1881). Pp. 3–4.
Finnur Jónsson. >> *Bókmentasaga Íslendinga fram undir siðabót* (1904–5).
   P. 463.
– >> *Den oldnorske og oldislandske Litteraturs Historie* (1920–4). Vol. 3,
   p. 128.
Guðrún Nordal. "Á mörkum tveggja tíma: Kaþólskt kvæðahandrit með hendi
   siðbótarmanns, Gísla biskups Jónssonar." *Gripla* 16 (2005): 209–28,
   esp. pp. 219–20 and 223.
– "Helgubók." In *Góssið hans Árna: Minningar heimsins í íslenskum
   handritum.* Ed. Jóhanna Katrín Friðriksdóttir (Reykjavík: Stofnun Árna
   Magnússonar í íslenskum fræðum, 2014). Pp. 21–35, esp. p. 30.
Jakob Benediktsson. "Kristdigte." *KLNM* 9 (1964). Cols. 292–4, esp. col. 293.

Jón Þorkelsson. >> *Om Digtningen på Island* (1888). Pp. 54 and 320–1.

Kock, E.A. "Liljukvistur." *Studia Neophilologica* 15 (1942): 141–56, esp. p. 143.

– "Anteckningar till Íslenzk Miðaldakvæði." *ANF* 61 (1946): 1–125, esp. pp. 19–20 and 28.

Mogk, Eugen. >> *Geschichte der norwegisch-isländischen Literatur* (1904). P. 718.

Schottmann, Hans. >> *Die isländische Mariendichtung* (1973). P. 32.

Stefán Einarsson. "Íslenzk helgikvæði frá miðöldum." *Tímarit Þjóðræknisfélags Íslendinga* 36 (1954): 43–62, esp. p. 53.

– *Íslensk bókmenntasaga 874–1960* (Reykjavík: Oddi, 1961). P. 90.

Vésteinn Ólason. "Kveðskapur frá síðmiðöldum." In >> *Íslensk Bókmenntasaga* 2 (1993). Pp. 283–378, esp. pp. 305–6.

NOTE:

The poem contains material about Mary the Blessed Virgin. See her entry.

BLASE February 3

Heilagra manna drápa

A fourteenth-century poem about holy men. Stz. 15–19 treat Saint Blase. Incipit: "... mildings f ... um dyrnar þustu ... særa."

Manuscripts:
AM 720a 4to VI (ca. 1400–1500) and JS 399a–b 4to (ca. 1700–1900).

Editions:
Finnur Jónsson, ed. >> *Den norsk-islandske skjaldedigtning* (1912–15). Vol. AII, pp. 514–15 and vol. BII, pp. 566–7.
Edition of AM 720a 4to VI.

Kahle, Bernhard, ed. >> *Isländische geistliche Dichtungen des ausgehenden Mittelalters* (1898). Pp. 93–4.
Edition of AM 720a 4to VI.

Kock, Ernst Albin, ed. >> *Notationes Norrœnæ* (1923–44). §§1767, 1771, 2156Anm, 2889, and 2891.

– ed. >> *Den norsk-islandske skaldediktningen* (1946–50). Vol. 2, pp. 310–11.

Wolf, Kirsten, ed. "Anonymous, *Heilagra manna drápa* 'Drápa about Holy Men'." In >> *Poetry on Christian Subjects* (2007). Vol. 2, pp. 883–6.
Edition of AM 720a 4to VI with variants from JS 399a–b 4to.

Danish translation:
Finnur Jónsson, ed. >> *Den norsk-islandske skjaldedigtning* (1912–15).
   Vol. BII, pp. 566–7.
English translation:
Wolf, Kirsten, ed. "Anonymous, *Heilagra manna drápa* 'Drápa about Holy
   Men'." In >> *Poetry on Christian Subjects* (2007). Vol. 2, pp. 883–6.
Literature:
Cormack, Margaret. >> *The Saints in Iceland* (1994). P. 41n60.

Finnur Jónsson. >> *Den oldnorske og oldislandske Litteraturs Historie*
   (1920–4). Vol. 3, p. 18.

Jakob Benediktsson. "Helgendigte." *KLNM* 6 (1961). Cols. 318–21, esp. col. 320.

– "Nödhjälparna." *KLNM* 21 (1977). Cols. 289–90, esp. col. 289.

– >> "Helgikvæði." In *Hugtök og heiti í Bókmenntafræði* (1983). Pp. 115–17,
   esp. p. 116.

Jón Helgason. >> "Norges og Islands digtning." In *Litteraturhistorie B:
   Norge og Island* (1953). Pp. 3–179, esp. p. 163.

Kahle, Bernhard. "Das Christentum in der altwestnordischen Dichtung." *ANF*
   13 (1901): 1–40 and 97–160, esp. pp. 31, 100, 116, and 122.

Mogk, Eugen. >> *Geschichte der norwegisch-isländischen Literatur* (1904).
   P. 718.

Poole, R.G. *Viking Poems on War and Peace: A Study in Skaldic Narrative*
   (Toronto: University of Toronto Press, 1991). P. 32.

Stéfan Einarsson. "Íslenzk helgikvæði á miðöldum." *Tímarit
   Þjóðræknisfélags Íslendinga* 36 (1955): 43–63, esp. p. 49.

– *Íslensk bókmenntasaga 874–1960* (Reykjavík: Oddi, 1961). P. 86.

Vésteinn Ólason. "Kveðskapur frá síðmiðöldum." In >> *Íslensk
   Bókmenntasaga* 2 (1993). Pp. 283–378, esp. p. 299.

Vries, Jan de. >> *Altnordische Literaturgeschichte* (1964–7). Vol. 2, p. 523.

NOTE:
The poem contains material about Saints Canute of Denmark, Dionysius,
Edmund, Hallvard, Maurice, and Thomas Becket. See the entries for the indi-
vidual saints.

BRIGID OF KILDARE   February 1

Heilagra meyja drápa

A fourteenth-century poem about holy maidens. Stz. 50–1 treat Saint Brigid.
   Incipit: "Heyrðu ómælds himna veldis herra guð."

Manuscripts:
See Agatha note (p. 13).
Editions:
Finnur Jónsson, ed. >> *Den norsk-islandske skjaldedigtning* (1912–15).
   Vol. AII, pp. 536–7 and vol. BII, pp. 594–5.
Kock, Ernst Albin, ed. >> *Notationes Norrœnæ* (1923–44). §§1848 and 2978.
– ed. >> *Den norsk-islandske skaldediktningen* (1946–50). Vol. 2, p. 329.
Wolf, Kirsten, ed. "Anonymous, *Heilagra meyja drápa* '*Drápa* about Holy
   Maidens'." In >> *Poetry on Christian Subjects* (2007). Vol. 2, pp. 922–3.
Danish translation:
Finnur Jónsson, ed. >> *Den norsk-islandske skjaldedigtning* (1912–15).
   Vol. BII, pp. 594–5.
English translation:
Wolf, Kirsten, ed. "Anonymous, *Heilagra meyja drápa* '*Drápa* about Holy
   Maidens'." In >> *Poetry on Christian Subjects* (2007). Vol. 2, pp. 922–3.

CANUTE OF DENMARK   January 19

Heilagra manna drápa

A fourteenth-century poem about holy men. Stz. 20–1 treat Saint Canute of
Denmark and his brother Benedikt.
   Incipit: "... mildings f ... um dyrnar þustu ... særa."

Manuscripts:
See Blase note (p. 52).
Editions:
Finnur Jónsson, ed. >> *Den norsk-islandske skjaldedigtning* (1912–15).
   Vol. AII, p. 515 and vol. BII, pp. 567–8.
Kahle, Bernhard, ed. >> *Isländische geistliche Dichtungen des ausgehenden
   Mittelalters* (1898). P. 95.
Kock, Ernst Albin, ed. >> *Notationes Norrœnæ* (1923–44). §§1763, 1772,
   2680B, 2892, 2983, 3378B, 3379, and 3380.
– ed. >> *Den norsk-islandske skaldediktningen* (1946–50). Vol. 2, p. 311.
Wolf, Kirsten, ed. "Anonymous, *Heilagra manna drápa* '*Drápa* about Holy
   Men'." In >> *Poetry on Christian Subjects* (2007). Vol. 2, pp. 886–7.
Danish translation:
Finnur Jónsson, ed. >> *Den norsk-islandske skjaldedigtning* (1912–15).
   Vol. BII, pp. 567–8.

English translation:
Wolf, Kirsten, ed. "Anonymous, *Heilagra manna drápa* 'Drápa about Holy
  Men." In >> *Poetry on Christian Subjects* (2007). Vol. 2, pp. 886–7.

CATHERINE OF ALEXANDRIA   November 25

1. Kátrínardrápa

A fourteenth-century poem in honour of Saint Catherine presumably com-
posed by Kálfr Hallsson.
  Incipit: "Drottinn, gef þú, dýrr, að ek mætta."

Manuscripts:
AM 713 4to (ca. 1500–50), AM 920 4to (ca. 1800–1900), JS 399a–b 4to
  (ca. 1700–1900), Lbs 444 4to (ca. 1820–50, stz. 1–2 only), and Lbs 2166
  4to (ca. 1885–1920, line 1 of stz. 1 only).
Editions:
Finnur Jónsson, ed. >> *Den norsk-islandske skjaldedigtning* (1912–15).
  Vol. AII, pp. 516–26 and vol. BII, pp. 569–82.
  Edition of AM 713 4to.
Kahle, Bernhard, ed. >> *Isländische geistliche Dichtungen des ausgehenden
  Mittelalters* (1898). Pp. 67–78.
  Edition of AM 713 4to.
Kock, Ernst Albin, ed. >> *Notationes Norrœna* (1923–44). §§1774, 1775,
  1776, 1777, 2764, 2958, 2958A–E, 2959, 2960, 2961, 2962, 2963, 2964,
  2965, 2966, 2967, 2968, 2969, 3384, 3385, 3386A–D, 3387, 3388, and
  3397M.
– ed. >> *Den norsk-isländska skaldediktningen* (1946–50). Vol. 2, pp.
  312–21.
Sperber, Hans, ed. >> *Sechs isländische Gedichte legendarischen Inhalts*
  (1911). Pp. 43–55.
  Edition of AM 713 4to.
Wolf, Kirsten, ed. "Kálfr Hallsson, *Kátrínardrápa* 'Drápa about S.
  Catharine'." In >> *Poetry on Christian Subjects* (2007). Vol. 2, pp. 931–64.
  Based on AM 713 4to with variants from AM 920 4to, JS 399a–b 4to, and
  Lbs 444 4to.
Danish translation:
Finnur Jónsson, ed. >> *Den norsk-islandske skjaldedigtning* (1912–15).
  Vol. BII, pp. 569–82.

English translation:
Wolf, Kirsten, ed. "Kálfr Hallsson, *Kátrínardrápa* '*Drápa* about S. Catharine'."
In >> *Poetry on Christian Subjects* (2007). Vol. 2, pp. 931–64.
Literature:
Attwood, Katrina. "Intertextual Aspects of the Twelfth-Century Christian
    Drápur." *Saga-Book* 24 (1996): 221–39, esp. pp. 226 and 229.
– "Leiðarvísan and the 'Sunday Letter' Tradition in Scandinavia." In >>
    Til heiðurs og hugbótar (2003). Pp. 53–78, esp. p. 56.
*Bjarni Ólafsson. "*Katrínar saga*." MA dissertation, University of Iceland,
    1972.
Björn Þórólfsson. *Rímur fyrir 1600*. Safn fræðafjelagsins 9 (Copenhagen:
    Møller, 1934). Pp. 49 and 305.
Clunies Ross, Margaret. >> *A History of Old Norse Poetry and Poetics*
    (2005). P. 33.
Cormack, Margaret. >> *The Saints in Iceland* (1994). Pp. 42 and 87.
Finnur Jónsson. >> *Den oldnorske og oldislandske Litteraturs Historie*
    (1920–4). Vol. 3, p. 18.
Foote, Peter, ed. *Lives of Saints. Perg. fol. nr 2 in the Royal Library,*
    Stockholm. EIM 4 (Copenhagen: Rosenkilde and Bagger, 1962). P. 26.
Gad, Tue. "Katarina af Alexandria." *KLNM* 8 (1963). Cols. 335–8, esp.
    col. 337.
Guðrún Nordal. *Tools of Literacy: The Role of Skaldic Verse in Icelandic*
    Textual Culture of the Twelfth and Thirteenth Centuries (Toronto:
    University of Toronto Press, 2001). Pp. 89, 329, 332, 376n11, 378n23,
    383n49, and 386nn64 and 66.
– "Handrit, prentaðar bækur og pápísk kvæði á siðskiptaöld." In >> *Til*
    heiðurs og hugbótar (2003). Pp. 131–43, esp. pp. 139–40.
Jakob Benediktsson. "Helgendigte." *KLNM* 6 (1961). Cols. 318–21, esp.
    cols.319–20.
Jón Helgason. >> "Norges og Islands digtning." In *Litteraturhistorie B:*
    Norge og Island (1953). Pp. 3–179, esp. pp. 164 and 171.
Jón Þorkelsson. >> *Om Digtningen på Island* (1888). P. 89 and 235–7.
Kahle, Bernhard. "Das Christentum in der altwestnordischen Dichtung."
    ANF 13 (1901): 1–40 and 97–160, esp. pp. 9–10, 28, 98, 108–9, 121,
    and 131–6.
Kock, E.A. "Anteckningar till Íslenzk Miðaldakvæði." *ANF* 54 (1939):
    94–107, esp. p. 94.
Lange, Wolfgang. >> *Studien zur christlichen Dichtung der Nordgermanen*
    1000–1200 (1958). Pp. 32 and 71.

Mogk, Eugen. >> *Geschichte der norwegisch-isländischen Literatur* (1904).
P. 719.

Poole, R.G. *Viking Poems on War and Peace: A Study in Skaldic Narrative*
(Toronto: University of Toronto Press, 1991). P. 31.

Schottmann, Hans. >> *Die isländische Mariendichtung* (1973). Pp. 255, 399,
and 553.

Stefán Einarsson. *Íslensk bókmenntasaga 874–1960* (Reykjavík: Oddi, 1961).
P. 86.

Vésteinn Ólason. "Kveðskapur frá síðmiðöldum." In >> *Íslensk
Bókmenntasaga* 2 (1993). Pp. 283–378, esp. pp. 299 and 315–16.

– "Old Icelandic Poetry." In *A History of Icelandic Literature*. Ed. Daisy
Neijmann. Histories of Scandinavian Literature 5 (Lincoln: University
of Nebraska Press, 2006). Pp. 1–64, esp. p. 48.

Vries, Jan de. >> *Altnordische Literaturgeschichte* (1964–7). Vol. 1, p. 201
and vol. 2, p. 523.

Wolf, Kirsten, ed. >> *Heilagra meyja sögur* (2003). P. lv.

2. Heilagra meyja drápa

A fourteenth-century poem about holy maidens. Stz. 22–4 treat Saint Catherine.
Incipit: "Heyrðu ómælds himna veldis herra guð."

Manuscripts:
See Agatha note (p. 13).
Editions:
Finnur Jónsson, ed. >> *Den norsk-islandske skjaldedigtning* (1912–15).
Vol. AII, p. 531 and vol. BII, pp. 587–8.

Kock, Ernst Albin, ed. >> *Notationes Norrœnæ* (1923–44). §§1841, 2975,
and 3391B.

– ed. >> *Den norsk-islandske skaldediktningen* (1946–50). Vol. 2, pp. 324–5.

Wolf, Kirsten, ed. "Anonymous, *Heilagra meyja drápa* 'Drápa about Holy
Maidens'." In >> *Poetry on Christian Subjects* (2007). Vol. 2, pp. 905–7.
Danish translation:
Finnur Jónsson, ed. >> *Den norsk-islandske skjaldedigtning* (1912–15).
Vol. BII, pp. 587–8.
English translation:
Wolf, Kirsten, ed. "Anonymous, *Heilagra meyja drápa* 'Drápa about Holy
Maidens'." In >> *Poetry on Christian Subjects* (2007). Vol. 2, pp. 905–7.

CECILIA   November 22

1. Vísur Cecilíu

A poetic legend of Saint Cecilia composed ca. 1300–1550.
  Incipit: "Holdsins girndir hrinda mér."

Manuscripts:
AM 713 4to (ca. 1500–50), AM 920 4to (ca. 1800–1900), and Lbs 2166 4to
  (ca. 1885–1920).
Editions:
Jón Helgason, ed. >> *Íslenzk miðaldakvæði* (1936–8). Vol. 2, pp. 347–8.
  Based on AM 713 4to with variants from AM 920 4to.
Jón Þorkelsson. >> *Om Digtningen på Island* (1888). P. 89 (stz. 1).
  Based on AM 713 4to and AM 920 4to.
Literature:
Finnur Jónsson. >> *Den oldnorske og oldislandske Litteraturs Historie*
  (1920–4). Vol. 3, p. 126.
Guðrún Nordal. "Handrit, prentaðar bækur og pápísk kvæði á siðskiptaöld."
  In >> *Til heiðurs og hugbótar* (2003). Pp. 131–43, esp. pp. 139–40.
Hálfdan Einarsson. *Sciagraphia historiæ literariæ islandicæ* (Copenhagen:
  Sander and Schröder, 1777). P. 58.
Jakob Benediktsson. "Helgendigte." *KLNM* 6 (1961). Cols. 318–21, esp.
  col. 320.
– "Helgener." *KLNM* 21 (1977). Cols. 194–5, esp. col. 194.
Jón Helgason. "Nokkur íslenzk handrit frá 16. öld." *Skírnir* 106 (1932): 143–68.
– >> "Norges og Islands digtning." In *Litteraturhistorie B: Norge og Island*
  (1953). Pp. 3–179, esp. pp. 163–4.
Schottmann, Hans. >> *Die isländische Mariendichtung* (1973). P. 61n41.
Soffía Ófeigsdóttir. *"Veroníkukvæði."* BA thesis. University of Iceland, 1986.
  P. 66.
Stéfan Einarsson. "Íslenzk helgikvæði á miðöldum." *Tímarit Þjóðræknisfélags
  Íslendinga* 36 (1954): 43–63, esp. p. 55.
– *Íslensk bókmenntasaga 874–1960* (Reykjavík: Oddi, 1961). P. 92.
Wolf, Kirsten, ed. >> *Heilagra meyja sögur* (2003). P. lv.

2. Cecilíudiktur

A late medieval (ca. 1400–1550) poem in honour of Saint Cecilia.
  Incipit: "Guð minn sæti blíðki og bæti."

Manuscripts:
AM 721 4to (ca. 1500–50), AM 429 12mo (ca. 1500), JS 399a–b 4to
(ca. 1700–1900), JS 112 8vo (ca. 1700–1800), Lbs 848 4to (ca. 1700–
1900), Lbs 936 4to (ca. 1880), Lbs 2166 4to (ca. 1885–1920), and Lbs 201
8vo (ca. 1850–70).

Editions:
Jón Helgason, ed. >> *Íslenzk miðaldakvæði* (1936–8). Vol. 2, pp. 342–6.
Based on AM 721 4to with variants from AM 429 12mo.
Jón Þorkelsson. >> *Om Digtningen på Island* (1888). Pp. 88–9 (stz. 1
and 31).
Based on AM 721 4to and AM 429 12mo.
Konráð Gíslason, ed. *Fire og fyrretyve for en stor deel forhen utrykte prøver
af oldnordisk sprog og litteratur* (Copenhagen: Gyldendal, 1860).
Pp. 559–60.
Edition of AM 429 12mo.
Wolf, Kirsten, ed. >> *A Female Legendary from Iceland: "Kirkjubæjarbók"
(AM 429 12mo) in the Arnamagnæan Collection, Copenhagen)* (2011).
Pp. 108–10.
Facsimile and text edition of AM 429 12mo.

Literature:
Bjarni Þorsteinsson. *Íslenzk þjóðlög* (Copenhagen: Møller, 1906–9). P. 34.
Cormack, Margaret. "Poetry, Paganism and the Sagas of Icelandic Bishops."
In >> *Til heiðurs og hugbótar* (2003). Pp. 33–51, esp. p. 51.
Finnur Jónsson. >> *Den oldnorske og oldislandske Litteraturs Historie*
(1920–4). Vol. 3, p. 126.
Jakob Benediktsson. "Helgendigte." *KLNM* 6 (1961). Cols. 318–21, esp.
col. 320.
– "Helgener." *KLNM* 21 (1977). Cols. 194–5, esp. col. 194.
Jón Helgason. >> "Norges og Islands digtning." In *Litteraturhistorie B:
Norge og Island* (1953). Pp. 3–179, esp. pp. 163–4.
Kock, E.A. "Anteckningar till Íslenzk Miðaldakvæði." *ANF* 61 (1946): 1–125,
esp. p. 91.
Meissner, Rudolf. "Minnetrinken in Island und in der Auvergne." In
Deutsche Islandsforschung 1930: I: Kultur. Ed. Walther Heinrich Vogt.
Veröffentlichungen der Schleswig-Holsteinischen Universitätsgesellschaft
Nr. 28.1 (Breslau, 1930). P. 235.
Mogk, Eugen. >> *Geschichte der norwegisch-isländischen Literatur* (1904).
P. 719.
Soffía Ófeigsdóttir. "*Veroníkukvæði*." BA thesis. University of Iceland, 1986.
P. 66.

Stéfan Einarsson. "Íslenzk helgikvæði á miðöldum." *Tímarit Þjóðræknisfélags Íslendinga* 36 (1954): 43–63, esp. p. 55.
– *Íslensk bókmenntasaga 874–1960* (Reykjavík: Oddi, 1961). P. 92.
Vésteinn Ólason. "Kveðskapur frá síðmiðöldum." In >> *Íslensk Bókmenntasaga* 2 (1993). Pp. 283–378, esp. pp. 299 and 315–16.
Wolf, Kirsten, ed. >> *Heilagra meyja sögur* (2003). (2003). Pp. lii and lv.
– ed. "Female Scribes at Work? A Consideration of Kirkjubæjarbók (Codex AM 429 12mo)." In *Beatus Vir: Studies in Early English and Norse Manuscripts in Memory of Phillip Pulsiano*. Ed. A.N. Doane and Kirsten Wolf (Tempe, AZ: ACMRS, 2006). Pp. 265–95, esp. pp. 270 and 277–8.

3. Heilagra meyja drápa

A fourteenth-century poem about holy maidens. Stz. 18–21 treat Saint Cecilia. Incipit: "Heyrðu ómælds himna veldis herra guð."

Manuscripts:
See Agatha note (p. 13).
Editions:
Finnur Jónsson, ed. >> *Den norsk-islandske skjaldedigtning* (1912–15). Vol. AII, pp. 530–1 and vol. BII, pp. 586–7.
Kock, Ernst Albin, ed. >> *Notationes Norrænæ* (1923–44). §§2970D, 1070F, 2971C, and 2974.
– ed. >> *Den norsk-islandske skaldediktningen* (1946–50). Vol. 2, p. 324.
Wolf, Kirsten, ed. "Anonymous, *Heilagra meyja drápa* 'Drápa about Holy Maidens'." In >> *Poetry on Christian Subjects* (2007). Vol. 2, pp. 903–5.
Danish translation:
Finnur Jónsson, ed. >> *Den norsk-islandske skjaldedigtning* (1912–15). Vol. BII, pp. 586–7.
English translation:
Wolf, Kirsten, ed. "Anonymous, *Heilagra meyja drápa* 'Drápa about Holy Maidens'." In >> *Poetry on Christian Subjects* (2007). Vol. 2, pp. 903–5.

CHRISTINA   July 24

Heilagra meyja drápa

A fourteenth-century poem about holy maidens. Stz. 48–9 treat Saint Christina. Incipit: "Heyrðu ómælds himna veldis herra guð."

Manuscripts:
See Agatha note (p. 13).
Editions:
Finnur Jónsson, ed. >> *Den norsk-islandske skjaldedigtning* (1912–15).
    Vol. AII, p. 536 and vol. BII, p. 594.
Kock, Ernst Albin, ed. >> *Den norsk-islandske skaldediktningen* (1946–50).
    Vol. 2, p. 329.
Wolf, Kirsten, ed. "Anonymous, *Heilagra meyja drápa* '*Drápa* about Holy
    Maidens'." In >> *Poetry on Christian Subjects* (2007). Vol. 2, pp. 920–1.
Danish translation:
Finnur Jónsson, ed. >> *Den norsk-islandske skjaldedigtning* (1912–15).
    Vol. BII, p. 594.
English translation:
Wolf, Kirsten, ed. "Anonymous, *Heilagra meyja drápa* '*Drápa* about Holy
    Maidens'." In >> *Poetry on Christian Subjects* (2007). Vol. 2, p. 921.

CHRISTOPHER   July 25

Christeforusvísur

A late medieval (ca. 1400–1550) poem in honour of Saint Christopher. In terms
of content, it is closely related to the legend in Jacobus de Voragine's *Legenda
aurea*.
    Incipit: "Hæstur guð ég heiti á þig."

Manuscripts:
AM 710b 4to (ca. 1700–25), AM 713 4to (ca. 1500–50), JS 531 4to
    (ca. 1700–1900), Lbs 2166 4to (ca. 1885–1920), and Lbs 1907 8vo
    (ca. 1860–70).
Stz. 39 is found also in Finni Johannæi *Historia ecclesiastica Islandiæ* II
    (1774), ÍB 69 4to (ca. 1820–30), Jón Árnason's *Íslenzkar þjóðsögur* II
    (1864), Bor 6 (20647) (ca. 1700–1800), JS 260 4to (1796), JS 284 8vo
    (ca. 1850), JS 514 8vo (ca. 1675–1900), Lbs 512 4to (ca. 1700–50), Lbs 966
    4to (ca. 1750–1800), and Lbs 201 8vo (ca. 1850–70). See Jón Helgason,
    ed., *Íslenzk miðaldakvæði* (1936–8), p. 358.
Editions:
Jón Helgason, ed. >> *Íslenzk miðaldakvæði* (1936–8). Vol. 2, pp. 350–9.
    Based on AM 713 4to with variants from AM 710b 4to and JS 531 4to.

Jón Þorkelsson. >> *Om Digtningen på Island* (1888). P. 84 (stz. 1 and 40).
Based on AM 710b 4to and AM 713 4to.

Literature:

Bjarni Þorsteinsson. *Íslenzk þjóðlög* (Copenhagen: Møller, 1906–9). P. 276.

Finnur Jónsson. >> *Den oldnorske og oldislandske Litteraturs Historie*
(1920–4). Vol. 3, p. 126.

Gad, Tue. "Kristoffer." *KLNM* 9 (1964). Cols. 356–63, esp. col. 359.

Guðrún Nordal. "Handrit, prentaðar bækur og pápísk kvæði á siðskiptaöld."
In >> *Til heiðurs og hugbótar* (2003). Pp. 131–43, esp. pp. 139–40.

Hálfdan Einarsson. *Sciagraphia historiæ literariæ islandicæ* (Copenhagen:
Sander and Schröder, 1777). P. 58.

Jakob Benediktsson. "Helgendigte." *KLNM* 6 (1961). Cols. 318–21, esp.
col. 320.

Jón Helgason. "Nokkur íslenzk handrit frá 16. öld." *Skírnir* 106 (1932):
143–68.

– >> "Norges og Islands digtning." In *Litteraturhistorie B: Norge og Island*
(1953). Pp. 3–179, esp. pp. 163–4.

Kalinke, Marianne E. *The Book of Reykjahólar: The Last of the Great
Medieval Legendaries* (Toronto: University of Toronto Press, 1996). P.
280n9.

Kock, E.A. "Anteckningar till Íslenzk Miðaldakvæði." *ANF* 61 (1946): 1–125,
esp. pp. 52, 87, and 93.

Mogk, Eugen. >> *Geschichte der norwegisch-isländischen Literatur* (1904).
P. 719.

Stéfan Einarsson. "Íslenzk helgikvæði á miðöldum." *Tímarit Þjóðræknisfélags
Íslendinga* 36 (1955): 43–63, esp. p. 55.

– *Íslensk bókmenntasaga 874–1960* (Reykjavík: Oddi, 1961). P. 92.

Vésteinn Ólason. "Kveðskapur frá síðmiðöldum." In >> *Íslensk Bókmenntasaga*
2 (1993). Pp. 283–378, esp. p. 317.

CLARE   August 11

Heilagra meyja drápa

A fourteenth-century poem about holy maidens. Stz. 57 mentions Saint Clare.
Incipit: "Heyrðu ómælds himna veldis herra guð."

Manuscripts:
See Agatha note (p. 13).

Editions:

Finnur Jónsson, ed. >> *Den norsk-islandske skjaldedigtning* (1912–15).
   Vol. AII, p. 538 and vol. BII, p. 596.

Kock, Ernst Albin, ed. >> *Notationes Norrænæ* (1923–44). §§2970B and
   2971B.

– ed. >> *Den norsk-islandske skaldediktningen* (1946–50). Vol. 2, p. 330.

Wolf, Kirsten, ed. "Anonymous, *Heilagra meyja drápa* '*Drápa* about Holy
   Maidens'." In >> *Poetry on Christian Subjects* (2007). Vol. 2, p. 927.

Danish translation:

Finnur Jónsson, ed. >> *Den norsk-islandske skjaldedigtning* (1912–15).
   Vol. BII, p. 596.

English translation:

Wolf, Kirsten, ed. "Anonymous, *Heilagra meyja drápa* '*Drápa* about Holy
   Maidens'." In >> *Poetry on Christian Subjects* (2007). Vol. 2, p. 927.

CONSTANCIA   February 25

Heilagra meyja drápa

A fourteenth-century poem about holy maidens. Stz. 57 mentions Saint
Constancia.
   Incipit: "Heyrðu ómælds himna veldis herra guð."

Manuscripts:

See Agatha note (p. 13).

Editions:

Finnur Jónsson, ed. >> *Den norsk-islandske skjaldedigtning* (1912–15).
   Vol. AII, p. 538 and vol. BII, p. 596.

Kock, Ernst Albin, ed. >> *Notationes Norrænæ* (1923–44). §§2970B and
   2971B.

– ed. >> *Den norsk-islandske skaldediktningen* (1946–50). Vol. 2, p. 330.

Wolf, Kirsten, ed. "Anonymous, *Heilagra meyja drápa* '*Drápa* about Holy
   Maidens'." In >> *Poetry on Christian Subjects* (2007). Vol. 2, p. 927.

Danish translation:

Finnur Jónsson, ed. >> *Den norsk-islandske skjaldedigtning* (1912–15).
   Vol. BII, p. 596.

English translation:

Wolf, Kirsten, ed. "Anonymous, *Heilagra meyja drápa* '*Drápa* about Holy
   Maidens'." In >> *Poetry on Christian Subjects* (2007). Vol. 2, p. 927.

CROSS, THE HOLY   May 3 / September 14

1. Líknarbraut

A poem on the Cross probably composed in the late thirteenth century.
Incipit: "Einn, lúk upp, sem ek bæni."

Manuscripts:
AM 757a 4to (ca. 1400), JS 399a–b 4to (ca. 1700–1900), and Lbs 444 4to
(ca. 1820–50).

Editions:
*Attwood, Katrina. "The Poems of MS AM 757 a 4to: An Edition and
Contextual Study." PhD dissertation, University of Leeds, 1996.

Finnur Jónsson, ed. >> *Den norsk-islandske skjaldedigtning* (1912–15).
Vol. AII, pp. 150–9 and vol. BII, pp. 160–74.
Edition of AM 757a 4to with restorations from Sveinbjörn Egilsson's
edition (1844).

Kock, Ernst Albin, ed. >> *Notationes Norrœnæ* (1923–44). §§30, 1197,
1385, 1386, 1387, 1388, 1389, 1390, 1391, 1392, 1393, 1394, 1395, 1396,
1398, 1399, 1400, 1401, 1956, 2113, 2327, 2328, 2329, 2331, 2332, 2333,
2448A, 2584, 2710A, 3040, 3277B, 3278, and 3279.

– ed. >> *Den norsk-islandske skaldediktningen* (1946–50). Vol. 2, pp. 85–91.

Kock, Ernst Albin, and R. Meissner, ed. *Skaldisches Lesebuch.* 2 vols.
Rheinische Beiträge und Hilfsbücher zur germanischen Philologie und
Volkskunde 17 (Halle am S.: Max Niemeyer, 1931). Vol. 1, p. 91 (extract
only).

Rydberg, Hugo, ed. >> *Die geistlichen Drápur und Dróttkvættfragmente
des Cod. AM 757 4to* (1907). Pp. 47–53.
Edition of AM 757a 4to.

Sveinbjörn Egilsson, ed. *Fjøgur gømul kvæði. Boðsrit til að hlusta á þá
opinberu yfirheyrslu í Bessastaða Skóla þann 22–29 mai 1844*
(Viðeyjarklaustur: Helgi Helgason, 1844). Pp. 35–51.
Edition of AM 757a 4to.

Tate, George. "*Líknarbraut*: A Skaldic *drápa* on the Cross." PhD dissertation,
Cornell University, 1974. Pp. 46–97.
Based on AM 757a 4to with restorations from JS 399a–b 4to, Hugo
Rydberg's edition (1907), and Finnur Jónsson's edition (1912–15).

Tate, George, ed. "Anonymous, *Líknarbraut* 'Way of Grace'." In >> *Poetry
on Christian Subjects* (2007). Vol. 1, pp. 230–86.

Based on AM 757a 4to with variant readings from JS 399a–b 4to, Hugo
Rydberg's edition (1907), and Finnur Jónsson's edition (1912–15).
Modern Icelandic language edition:
Einar Ól. Sveinsson, Páll Eggert Ólason, and Arnór Sigurjónsson, ed. *Íslands
þúsund ár: Kvæðasafn.* 3 vols. (Reykjavík: Helgafell, 1947). Vol. 1,
pp. 529–32 (stz. 1, 4, 14–16, 18, 26–8, and 31 only).
Danish translation:
Finnur Jónsson, ed. >> *Den norsk-islandske skjaldedigtning* (1912–15).
Vol. BII, pp. 160–74.
English translations:
Barwell, Graham, and John Kennedy, ed. "Two Icelandic Medieval Passion-
Poems." In *Old Norse Studies in the New World: A Collection of Essays
to Celebrate the Jubilee of the Teaching of Old Norse at the University
of Sydney 1943–1993.* Ed. Geraldine Barnes, Margaret Clunies Ross, and
Judy Quinn (Sydney: Department of English, University of Sydney, 1994).
Pp. 46–70, esp. pp. 50–9.
Edition of Charles Venn Pilcher's (1879–1961) translation.
Tate, George. ed. "Anonymous, *Líknarbraut* 'Way of Grace'." In >> *Poetry
on Christian Subjects* (2007). Vol. 1, pp. 230–86.
Norwegian translation:
Røkke, Olav, trans. "*Líknarbraut.*" In *Norrøne kristenkvæde.* Ed. Olaf
Hanssen (Oslo: Det norske samlaget, 1928). Pp. 38–45.
Literature:
Ásdís Egilsdóttir, Gunnar Harðarson, and Svanhildur Óskarsdóttir, ed.
Maríukver: Sögur og kvæði af heilagri guðsmóður frá fyrri tíð (Reykjavík:
Hið íslenska bókmenntafélag, 1996). P. xxxv.
Attwood, Katrina. "Christian Poetry." In *A Companion to Old Norse–
Icelandic Literature and Culture.* Ed. Rory McTurk (Oxford: Blackwell,
2005). Pp. 43–63, esp. pp. 57–8.
Chase, Martin. "*Concatenatio* as a Structural Element in the Christian
Drápur." In *The Sixth International Saga Conference 28/7–2/8 1985.
Workshop Papers.* 2 vols. ([Copenhagen]: Det arnamagnæanske Institut,
1985). Vol. 1, pp. 115–29, esp. pp. 118–20 and 124–5.
– "Christian Poetry: West Norse." In >> *Medieval Scandinavia: An
Encyclopedia* (1993). Pp. 73–7, esp. p. 75.
Clunies Ross, Margaret. >> *A History of Old Norse Poetry and Poetics*
(2005). Pp. 33, 133, 209, and 219.
Cormack, Margaret. >> *The Saints in Iceland* (1994). Pp. 42 and 104.
Finnur Jónsson. >> *Den oldnorske og oldislandske Litteraturs Historie*
(1920–4). Vol. 2, pp. 120–1 and 126.

Guðrún Nordal. *Tools of Literacy: The Role of Skaldic Verse in Icelandic Textual Culture of the Twelfth and Thirteenth Centuries* (Toronto: University of Toronto Press, 2001). Pp. 64, 66, 71, 82–3, 90, 141, 250–1, 256, 258, 260–1, 284, 289, 292–4, 300–1, 381n37, 384n53, and 385nn54 and 56.

Haugen, Odd Einar. "Nicodemus, Gospel of." In >> *Medieval Scandinavia: An Encyclopedia* (1993). Pp. 430–2, esp. p. 431.

Holtsmark, Anne. "Líknarbraut." *KLNM* 10 (1965). Cols. 553–4, esp. col. 554.

Jakob Benediktsson. "Kristdigte." *KLNM* 9 (1964). Cols. 292–4, esp. col. 293.

Jón Helgason. *Norrøn Litteraturhistorie* (Copenhagen: Levin and Munksgaard, 1934). P. 88.

– >> "Norges og Islands digtning." In *Litteraturhistorie B: Norge og Island* (1953). Pp. 3–179, esp. pp. 156 and 161.

Jónas Kristjánsson. "Bókmenntasaga." In *Saga Íslands* 2. Ed. Sigurður Líndal (Reykjavík: Hið íslenzka bókmenntafélag, Sögufélagið, 1975). Pp. 147–258, esp. pp. 208–9.

– >> *Eddas and Sagas: Iceland's Medieval Literature* (1988). P. 113.

Kahle, Bernhard. "Das Christentum in der altwestnordischen Dichtung." *ANF* 13 (1901): 1–40 and 97–160, esp. pp. 27–8, 31–2, 99–100, 108, 129, 130, 133–40, 144–7, and 151–6.

Konráð Gíslason. "Om helrim i förste og tredje linie af regelmæssigt 'drottkvætt' og 'hrynhenda'." *Indbydelsesskrift til Kjøbenhavns Universitets Aarsfest til Erindring om Kirkens Reformation* (Copenhagen: Schultz, 1877). Pp. 1–60, esp. pp. 17, 21, 23, 26–7, 46, and 52.

Lange, Wolfgang. >> *Studien zur christlichen Dichtung der Nordgermanen 1000–1200* (1958). Pp. 69, 90, and 263.

Lindow, John. "Narrative and the Nature of Skaldic Poetry." *ANF* 97 (1982): 94–121, esp. p. 100n23.

Mogk, Eugen. >> *Geschichte der norwegisch-isländischen Literatur* (1904). P. 712

Møller, Arne. *Islands Lovsang gennem Tusind Aar* (Copenhagen: Gyldendal, 1923). Pp. 18–25.

Noreen, Erik. *Studier i fornvästnordisk diktning* 2. Uppsala Universitets Årsskrift 1922 (Uppsala: Akademiska bokhandeln, 1922). P. 30.

Paasche, Fredrik. >> *Kristendom og kvad* (1914). Pp. 65, 71, 117–18, 125–34, 137, 162, and 173.

– *Norges og Islands litteratur inntil utgangen av middelalderen*. Rev. ed. by Anne Holtsmark (Oslo: Aschehoug, 1947). Pp. 430–1 and 534.

Schottmann, Hans. >> *Die isländische Mariendichtung* (1973). Pp. 82, 133, 208, 214, 242n14, 247, and 552–3.

Stefán Einarsson. *Íslensk bókmenntasaga 874–1960* (Reykjavík: Oddi, 1961). P. 81.

Tate, George S. "Good Friday Liturgy and the Structure of *Líknarbraut.*" *Scandinavian Studies* 50 (1978): 31–8.

– "The Cross as Ladder: *Geisli* 5–16 and *Líknarbraut* 34." *Mediaeval Scandinavia* 11 (1978–9): 258–64.

Vésteinn Ólason. "Kristileg trúarkvæði til loka 13. aldar." In >> *Íslensk Bókmenntasaga* 1 (1992). Pp. 481–515, esp. pp. 492, 497–9, and 512.

– "Kveðskapur frá síðmiðöldum." In >> *Íslensk Bókmenntasaga* 2 (1993). Pp. 283–378, esp. pp. 288, 298, and 309.

– "Old Icelandic Poetry." In *A History of Icelandic Literature.* Ed. Daisy Neijmann. Histories of Scandinavian Literature 5 (Lincoln: University of Nebraska Press, 2006). Pp. 1–64, esp. p. 45.

Viðar Pálsson. "Pagan Mythology in Christian Society." *Gripla* 19 (2008): 123–58, esp. p. 141.

Vries, Jan de. >> *Altnordische Literaturgeschichte* (1964–7). Vol. 2, pp. 76–9.

Wolf, Kirsten. "The Influence of the *Evangelium Nicodemi* on Norse Literature: A Survey." In *The Medieval* Gospel of Nicodemus: *Texts, Intertexts, and Contexts in Western Europe.* Ed. Zbigniew Izydorczyk (Tempe, AZ; Medieval and Renaissance Texts and Studies, 1997). Pp. 261–86, esp. p. 277.

NOTE:
The poem contains material about Mary the Blessed Virgin. See her entry.

2. Krossvísur II

A poem about Christ and the Holy Cross composed between 1300 and 1550. Incipit: "Sannan guð með sætri grein."

Manuscripts:
A: AM 710g 4to (ca. 1700–25), AM 713 4to (ca. 1500–50), JS 581 4to (ca. 1600–1900), Lbs 2166 4to (ca. 1885–1920), and Lbs 201 8vo (ca. 1850–70);
B: AM 714 4to (ca. 1600) and Lbs 2166 4to (ca. 1885–1920).

Editions:
Guðbrandur Þorláksson, ed. >> *Ein ny wiisna bok* (1612). Pp. 262–3.
Jón Helgason, ed. >> *Íslenzk miðaldakvæði* (1936–8). Vol. 1.2, pp. 262–6.

Based on AM 713 4to with variants from AM 714 4to, *Ein ny wiisna bok* (1612), and Lbs 201 8vo.

Jón Torfason and Kristján Eiríksson, ed. >> *Vísnabók Guðbrands* (2000). Pp. 295–6.

Based on *Ein ny wiisna bok* (1612). The stz. are ordered differently here than in redaction A and the B redaction preserved in AM 714 4to.

Literature:

Finnur Jónsson. >> *Bókmentasaga Íslendinga fram undir siðabót* (1904–5). P. 461.

Kock, E.A. "Anteckningar till Íslenzk Miðaldakvæði." *ANF* 61 (1946): 1–125, esp. p. 17.

Pétur Sigurðsson. "Vísnabók Guðbrands biskups." In *Iðunn: Tímarit til skemtunar, nytsemdar og fróðleiks.* Vol. 8. Ed. Magnús Jónsson (Reykjavík: Gutenberg, 1923–4). Pp. 61–87, esp. p. 84.

Stéfan Einarsson. "Íslenzk helgikvæði á miðöldum." *Tímarit Þjóðræknisfélags Íslendinga* 36 (1955): 43–63, esp. p. 60.

– *Íslensk bókmenntasaga 874–1960* (Reykjavík: Oddi, 1961). P. 97.

3. Krossþulur

A poem about Christ and the Holy Cross composed ca. 1400–1550.
Incipit: "Það er upphaflegt."

Manuscripts:

A: AM 710g 4to (ca. 1700–25), AM 713 4to (ca. 1500–50), JS 399a–b 4to (ca. 1700–1900), JS 581 4to (ca. 1600–1900), Lbs 444 4to (ca. 1820–50), Lbs 2166 4to (ca. 1885–1920), and Lbs 201 8vo (ca. 1850–70);

B: AM 716a 4to (ca. 1650–1700).

Editions:

Jón Helgason, ed. >> *Íslenzk miðaldakvæði* (1936–8). Vol. 1.2, pp. 239–46.
Based on AM 713 4to with variants from AM 710a 4to, AM 716a 4to, JS 581 4to, Lbs 444 4to, Lbs 2166 4to, and Lbs 201 8vo.

Jón Þorkelsson. >> *Om Digtningen på Island* (1888). P. 77 (stz. 1).
Based on AM 710a 4to, AM 713 4to, AM 716a 4to, and Lbs 201 8vo.

Literature:

Chase, Martin. "Devotional Poetry at the End of the Middle Ages in Iceland." In >> *Eddic, Skaldic, and Beyond: Poetic Variety in Medieval Iceland.* Ed. Martin Chase (2014). Pp. 136–49, esp. p. 139.

Finnur Jónsson. >> *Bókmentasaga Íslendinga fram undir siðabót* (1904–5). P. 461.

– >> *Den oldnorske og oldislandske Litteraturs Historie* (1920–4). Vol. 3, p. 126.

Jakob Benediktsson. "Kristdigte." *KLNM* 9 (1964). Cols. 292–4, esp. col. 293.

Jón Helgason. >> "Norges og Islands digtning." In *Litteraturhistorie B: Norge og Island* (1953). Pp. 3–179, esp. pp. 162–3.

Kock, E.A. "Anteckningar till Íslenzk Miðaldakvæði." *ANF* 61 (1946): 1–125, esp. pp. 24–7.

Stéfan Einarsson. "Íslenzk helgikvæði á miðöldum." *Tímarit Þjóðræknisfélags Íslendinga* 36 (1955): 43–63, esp. p. 55.

– *Íslensk bókmenntasaga 874–1960* (Reykjavík: Odddi, 1961). P. 92.

Vésteinn Ólason. "Kveðskapur frá síðmiðöldum." In >> *Íslensk Bókmenntasaga* 2 (1993). Pp. 285–378, esp. p. 308.

NOTE:
The poem contains material about Saint Mary Magdalen. See her entry.

4. Helgan kross að heiðra má

A four-stz. poem about the Holy Cross composed ca. 1400–1550.
   Incipit: "Helgan kross að heiðra má."

Manuscripts:
AM 710a 4to (ca. 1700–25) and AM 721 4to (ca. 1500–50).
Editions:
Jón Helgason, ed. >> *Íslenzk miðaldakvæði* (1936–8). Vol. 1.2, p. 267.
   Based on AM 721 4to with variants from Jón Þorkelsson's edition (1888).
Jón Þorkelsson. >> *Om Digtningen på Island* (1888). P. 77.
   Based on AM 710a 4to and AM 721 4to.
Literature:
Finnur Jónsson. >> *Bókmentasaga Íslendinga fram undir siðabót* (1904–5). P. 461.
Jón Helgason. "Jófreys kvæði." *Fróðskaparrit* 13 (1964): 140–57, esp. p. 145.

5. Krosskvæði

A poetic rendering of the legend of the cross-tree from ca. 1400–1550.
   Incipit: "Guð himnanna, græðari manna."

Manuscripts:
A: AM 721 4to (ca. 1500–50) and Lbs 2166 4to (ca. 1885–1920);

B: AM 710g 4to (ca. 1700–25), AM 713 4to (ca. 1500–50), JS 399a–b 4to
(ca. 1700–1900), JS 581 4to (ca. 1600–1900), Lbs 2166 4to (ca. 1885–
1920), and Lbs 201 8vo (ca. 1850–70);
C: AM 920 4to (ca. 1800–1900), AM 1033 4to (ca. 1700–25), AM 148 8vo
(ca. 1650–1700), and JS 399a–b 4to (ca. 1700–1900);
D: AM 717g 4to (1673);
E: AM 716b 4to (ca. 1600–1700), JS 399a–b 4to (ca. 1700–1900), and Lbs
2166 4to (ca. 1885–1920);
F: AM 717a 4to (ca. 1700–25) AM 717h 4to (ca. 1650–1700), AM 150 8vo
(ca. 1650–1700), BLAdd 4892 (ca. 1700–1800), BLAdd 11.179 (ca. 1700–
1800), Bor 6 (20647) (ca. 1700–1800), JS 256 4to (1840–5), JS 260 4to
(1796), JS 648 4to (ca. 1800), JS 112 8vo (ca. 1700–1800), JS 487 8vo
(ca. 1675–1900), JS 494 8vo (ca. 1675–1900), Lbs 512 4to (ca. 1700–50),
Lbs 953 4to (ca. 1760), Lbs 1630 4to (ca. 1800–1900), Lbs 754 8vo
(ca. 1700–1900), Lbs 1571 8vo (ca. 1780 and ca. 1810), Lbs 2345 8vo
(ca. 1775–1800), and Stock. Papp. fol. no. 64 (ca. 1650–1700);
G: Adv 21.8.14 (ca. 1750–75).

Editions:

Jón Helgason, ed. >> *Íslenzk miðaldakvæði* (1936–8). Vol. 1.2, pp. 278
and 280–1.
   Based on AM 721 4to with variants from Adv 21.8.14, AM 713 4to, AM
   716b 4to, AM 717g 4to, AM 717h 4to, AM 148 8vo, and AM 150 8vo.
– ed. >> *Kvæðabók úr Vigur: AM 148, 8vo* (1955). Fol. 213v–215v.
   Facsimile of AM 148 8vo.
Jón Þorkelsson. >> *Om Digtningen på Island* (1888). P. 76 (stz. 1–2 and
additional stz. 1.).
   Based on AM 710g 4to, AM 713 4to, AM 716b 4to, AM 717a 4to, AM
   717g 4to, AM 717h 4to, AM 920 4to, AM 1033 4to, AM 148 8vo, AM 150
   8vo, JS 260 4to, Lbs 201 8vo, and Stock. Papp. fol. no. 64.
*Peringskiöld, J.F. >> *Fragmentum runicopapisticum* (1721). Pp. 16–20.
   Facsimile edition of Stock. Papp. fol. no. 64 (351r–353r).

Literature:

Anon. "Den Oldnordisk-islandske Afdeling." Annual Report for 1846.
   Antiquarisk Tidsskrift 1846–8 (Copenhagen: Sally B. Salomon, 1847).
   Pp. 39–49, esp. p. 40.
Bjarni Þorsteinsson, ed. *Íslenzk þjóðlög* (Copenhagen: Møller, 1906–9). P. 32.
Finnur Jónsson. >> *Bókmentasaga Íslendinga fram undir siðabót* (1904–5).
   P. 461.
Guðrún Ingólfsdóttir. "Elínarbók: AM 67 8vo, AM 716f 4to, AM 717c 4to,
   AM 717f α 4to og AM 717g 4to." *Handritasyrpa: Rit til heiðurs Sigurgeiri*

Steingrímssyni sjötugum, 2. október 2013. Ed. Rósa Þorsteinsdóttir (Reykjavík: Stofnun Árna Magnússonar, 2014). Pp. 103–20, esp. p. 109.

Guðrún Nordal. "Handrit, prentaðar bækur og pápísk kvæði á siðskiptaöld." In >> *Til heiðurs og hugbótar* (2003). Pp. 131–43, esp. pp. 139–40.

Jón Helgason. "Nokkur íslenzk handrit frá 16. öld." *Skírnir* 106 (1932): 143–68.

Jón Þorkelsson. "Islandske håndskrifter i England og Skotland." *ANF* 8 (1892): 199–237, esp. pp. 205–6.

Kock, E.A. "Anteckningar till Íslenzk Miðaldakvæði." *ANF* 61 (1946): 1–125, esp. pp. 17, 29, and 42.

Mogk, Eugen. >> *Geschichte der norwegisch-isländischen Literatur* (1904). P. 718.

Overgaard, Mariane, ed. *The History of the Cross-Tree Down to Christ's Passion: Icelandic Legend Versions*. Editiones Arnamagnæanæ, Ser. B, vol. 26 (Copenhagen: Munksgaard, 1968). Pp. xx, cxl, cxlii–cxliv, and clxx.

Páll Eggert Ólason. *Menn og menntir siðskiptaaldarinnar á Íslandi*. Vol. 1 (Reykjavík: Guðm. Gamalíelsson, 1919). P. 410n1.

Wolf, Kirsten, "The Influence of the *Evangelium Nicodemi* on Norse Literature: A Survey." In *The Medieval* Gospel of Nicodemus: *Texts, Intertexts, and Contexts in Western Europe*. Ed. Zbigniew Izydorczyk (Tempe, AZ; Medieval and Renaissance Texts and Studies, 1997). Pp. 261–86, esp. p. 278.

NOTE:
The poem contains material about Saint Helena. See her entry.

6. Fyrirlát mér jungfrúin hreina

A poem about Christ and the Holy Cross probably composed in Norway ca. 1400–1550.

Incipit: "Fyrirlát mér jungfrúin hreina."

Manuscripts:
AM 710g 4to (ca. 1700–25), AM 713 4to (ca. 1500–50), JS 581 4to (ca. 1600–1900), Lbs 2166 4to (ca. 1885–1920), and Lbs 201 8vo (ca. 1850–70).

Editions:
Jón Helgason, ed. >> *Íslenzk miðaldakvæði* (1936–8). Vol. 1.2, pp. 269–72. Based on AM 713 4to with variants from AM 710g 4to and Lbs 201 8vo.

Jón Þorkelsson. >> *Om Digtningen på Island* (1888). P. 78 (stz. 1). Based on AM 710g 4to, AM 713 4to, and Lbs 201 8vo.

Literature:
Finnur Jónsson. >> *Bókmentasaga Íslendinga fram undir siðabót* (1904–5).
   P. 461.
Kock, E.A. "Anteckningar till Íslenzk Miðaldakvæði." *ANF* 61 (1946): 1–125,
   esp. p. 28.
NOTE:
The poem contains material about Saints Elizabeth, John the Baptist, and
Stephen. See the entries for the three saints.

7. Gimsteinn

An early sixteenth-century poem about the cross-tree ascribed to the priest
Hallur Ögmundarson (d. ca. 1540).
   Incipit: "Heyr mig ilmanda hjartans yndi."

Manuscripts:
A: Adv 21.8.10 (1712), AM 622 4to (ca. 1549), AM 708 4to (ca. 1700–25),
   AM 709 4to (ca. 1700–25), AM 714 4to (ca. 1600), AM 719a 4to
   (ca. 1700), AM 148 8vo (ca. 1650–1700), BLAdd 11.179 (1700–1800),
   ÍBR 74 8vo (1852), ÍBR 113 8vo (ca. 1700–1800), JS 399a–b 4to
   (ca. 1700–1900), JS 413 8vo (ca. 1700–1900), JS 444 8vo (ca. 1700–
   1800), Lbs 444 4to (ca. 1820–50), Lbs 201 8vo (ca. 1850–70), Lbs 1571
   8vo (ca. 1780 and ca. 1810), Lbs 2290 8vo (1823–4), Lbs 2293 8vo
   (ca. 1700), and Trinity L.2.3 (ca. 1700–1800);
B: AM 695a 4to (ca. 1650–1700), AM 719b 4to (ca. 1700), AM 960 4to
   (ca. 1850), AM 104 8vo (ca. 1680), ÍB 105 4to (1758–68), JS 260 4to
   (1796), JS 399a–b 4to (ca. 1700–1900), JS 473 8vo (ca. 1675–1900), JS
   284 8vo (ca. 1850), JS 481 8vo (ca. 1675–1900), JS 491 8vo (1675–1900),
   Lbs 966 4to (ca. 1750–1800), Lbs 2289 4to (1879–1905), Lbs 201 8vo
   (ca. 1850–70), Lbs 1059 8vo (1793), Lbs 1671 8vo (1767), Lbs 1847 8vo
   (1855), and NKS 1898 4to (ca. 1775–1800).
Editions:
Anon. "Det historisk-archaeologiske archiv, islandske Afdeling." Annual
   Report for 1851. *Antiquarisk Tidsskrift* 1849–51 (Copenhagen: Berling,
   1852). Pp. 218–66, esp. p. 257 (stz. 1 and 124[7-8]).
   Based on AM 622 4to.
Carpenter, William H., ed. *Nikolásdrápa Halls Prests: An Icelandic Poem
   from Circa A.D. 1400* (Halle: Karras, 1881). P. 5 (stz. 1).
   Edition of AM 622 4to.

Einar Ól. Sveinsson, Páll Eggert Ólason, and Arnór Sigurjónsson, ed. *Íslands
   þúsund ár: Kvæðasafn*. 3 vols. (Reykjavík: Helgafell, 1947). Vol. 2, pp.
   139–40 (stz. 110–12).
Jón Helgason, ed. >> *Íslenzk miðaldakvæði* (1936–8). Vol. 1.2, pp. 305–32.
   Edition of AM 622 4to with variants from AM 695a 4to, AM 714 4to,
   AM 719a 4to, AM 719b 4to, AM 148 8vo, JS 413 8vo (and occasionally
   BLAdd 11.179, Adv 21.8.10, ÍBR 113 8vo, JS 399a–b 4to, JS 444 8vo,
   Lbs 1571 8vo, Lbs 2290 8vo, and Lbs 2293 8vo).
 – ed. >> *Kvæðabók úr Vigur: AM 148, 8vo* (1955). Fol. 185r–213r.
   Facsimile of AM 148 8vo.
Jón Þorkelsson, ed. >> *Om Digtningen på Island* (1888). Pp. 318 (stz. 1 and
   124[7–8]).
   Based on AM 622 4to and AM 714a 4to.
 – ed. >> *Kvæðasafn* (1922–7). Pp. 298–326.
   Based on AM 622 4to with variants from AM 714 4to and ÍB 105 4to.
Literature:
Ármann Jakobsson. "The Homer of the North, or: Who Was Sigurður the
   Blind?" *European Journal of Scandinavian Studies* 44 (2014): 4–19,
   esp. p. 5.
Björn Þorleifsson. "Kvantitetsomvæltningen i islandsk." *ANF* 45 (1929):
   35–81, esp. p. 41.
Finnur Jónsson. >> *Bókmentasaga Íslendinga fram undir siðabót* (1904–5).
   Pp. 461 and 563.
 – >> *Den oldnorske og oldislandske Litteraturs Historie* (1920–4). Vol. 3,
   p. 127.
Guðrún Nordal. "Handrit, prentaðar bækur og pápísk kvæði á siðskiptaöld."
   In >> *Til heiðurs og hugbótar* (2003). Pp. 131–43, esp. pp. 140–1.
 – "Á mörkum tveggja tíma: Kaþólskt kvæðahandrit með hendi
   siðbótarmanns, Gísla biskups Jónssonar." *Gripla* 16 (2005): 209–28, esp.
   pp. 219–20.
 – "Helgubók." In *Góssið hans Árna: Minningar heimsins í íslenskum
   handritum*. Ed. Jóhanna Katrín Friðriksdóttir (Reykjavík: Stofnun Árna
   Magnússonar í íslenskum fræðum, 2014). Pp. 21–35, esp. p. 30.
Jakob Benediktsson. "Kristdigte." *KLNM* 9 (1964). Cols. 292–4, esp.
   col. 293.
Jón Helgason. >> "Norges og Islands digtning." In *Litteraturhistorie B:
   Norge og Island* (1953). Pp. 3–179, esp. pp. 162–3.
 – *Gamall kveðskapur* (Copenhagen: Hið íslenzka fræðafélag, 1979). P. 54n1.
Jón Þorkelsson. "Islandske håndskrifter i England og Skotland." *ANF* 8
   (1892): 199–237, esp. p. 206.

Jónas Kristjánsson. >> *Eddas and Sagas: Iceland's Medieval Literature* (1988). P. 388.

Kock, E.A. "Liljukvistur." *Studia Neophilologica* 15 (1942): 141–56, esp. p. 143.

– "Anteckningar till Íslenzk Miðaldakvæði." *ANF* 61 (1946): 1–125, esp. pp. 19, 23, 26–7, 29–31, and 57.

Mogk, Eugen. >> *Geschichte der norwegisch-isländischen Literatur* (1904). P. 719.

Overgaard, Mariane, ed. *The History of the Cross-Tree Down to Christ's Passion: Icelandic Legend Versions*. Editiones Arnamagnæanæ, Ser. B, vol. 26 (Copenhagen: Munksgaard, 1968). Pp. xx, cxl, cxlii–cxliv, and clxx.

Páll Eggert Ólason. *Menn og menntir siðskiptaaldarinnar á Íslandi*. Vol. 4 (Reykjavík: Ársæll Árnason, 1926). P. 627.

Schottmann, Hans. >> *Die isländische Mariendichtung* (1973). Pp. 83–4, 207, 510, and 512.

Stefán Einarsson. "Íslenzk helgikvæði á miðöldum." *Tímarit Þjóðræknisfélags Íslendinga* 36 (1955): 43–63, esp. p. 53.

– *Íslensk bókmenntasaga 874–1960* (Reykjavík: Oddi, 1961). P. 90.

Vésteinn Ólason. "Kveðskapur frá síðmiðöldum." In >> *Íslensk Bókmenntasaga* 2 (1993). Pp. 283–378, esp. pp. 301, 304–6, and 311.

NOTE:
The poem contains material about Saints Helena, John the Evangelist, Joseph of Arimathea, Mary Magdalen, Nicodemus, Peter, and Stephen. See the entries for the individual saints.

8. Krossvísur I

A poem about Christ and the Holy Cross composed ca. 1525 by Bishop Jón Arason (1484–1550).

Incipit: "Dýrðarfullur drottinn minn."

Manuscripts:
A: AM 710g 4to (ca. 1700–25), AM 713 4to (ca. 1500–50), JS 581 4to (ca. 1600–1900), and Lbs 201 8vo (ca. 1850–70);
B: AM 721 4to (ca. 1500–50) and AM 1032 4to (ca. 1700–25);
C: AM 717a 4to (ca. 1700–25), AM 717h 4to (ca. 1650–1700), AM 150 8vo (ca. 1650–1700), BLAdd 4892 (ca. 1700–1800), BLAdd 11.179 (ca. 1700–1800), ÍBR 109 8vo (1829), JS 256 4to (1840–5), JS 260 4to (1796), JS 112 8vo (ca. 1700–1800), JS 487 8vo (ca. 1675–1900), JS 494

8vo (ca. 1675–1900), Lbs 512 4to (ca. 1700–50), Lbs 953 4to (ca. 1760),
Lbs 1630 4to (ca. 1800–1900), Lbs 201 8vo (ca. 1850–70), Lbs 754 8vo
(ca. 1700–1900), and Stock. Papp. fol. no. 64 (ca. 1650–1700).

Editions:

Einar Ól. Sveinsson, Páll Eggert Ólason, and Arnór Sigurjónsson, ed. *Íslands
þúsund ár: Kvæðasafn.* 3 vols. (Reykjavík: Helgafell, 1947). Vol. 3,
pp. 156–7 (stz. 20–2, 37, 39, and 41).

Finnur Jónsson, ed. >> *Jón Arasons religiøse digte* (1918). Pp. 69–77.
Based on AM 713 4to with variants from AM 721 4to.

Jón Helgason, ed. >> *Íslenzk miðaldakvæði* (1936–8). Vol. 1.2, pp. 253–60.
Based on AM 713 4to with variants from AM 717a 4to, AM 717h 4to, AM
721 4to, and AM 150 8vo.

[Jón Sigurðsson and Guðbrandur Vigfússon, ed.] >> *Biskupa sögur* (1858–
78). Vol. 2, pp. 558–67.
Based primarily on AM 710g 4to and AM 713 4to and to a lesser extent on
AM 721 4to, BLAdd 4892, and Peringskiöld's edition (1721).

Jón Þorkelsson. >> *Om Digtningen på Island* (1888). P. 78 (stz. 1^{1-2}) and 328
(stz. 1–2, 30^{1-2}).
Based on *Biskupa sögur* (1858–78) and Peringskiöld's edition (1721).

*Peringskiöld, J.F. >> *Fragmentum runicopapisticum* (1721). Pp. 16–20.
Facsimile edition of Stock. Papp. fol. no. 64 (353v–356v).

Literature:

Anon. "Den Oldnordisk-islandske Afdeling." Annual Report for 1846.
Antiquarisk Tidsskrift 1846–8 (Copenhagen: Sally B. Salomon, 1847).
Pp. 39–49, esp. p. 40.

Bjarni Þorsteinsson, ed. *Íslenzk þjóðlög* (Copenhagen: Møller, 1906–9). P. 33.

Finnur Jónsson. >> *Bókmentasaga Íslendinga fram undir siðabót* (1904–5).
Pp. 461 and 465.

– >> *Den oldnorske og oldislandske Litteraturs Historie* (1920–4). Vol. 3,
p. 129.

Jakob Benediktsson. "Kristdigte." *KLNM* 9 (1964). Cols. 292–4, esp. col. 293.

Jón Helgason. >> "Norges og Islands digtning." In *Litteraturhistorie B:
Norge og Island* (1953). Pp. 3–179, esp. p. 162.

Jón Þorkelsson. "Islandske håndskrifter i England og Skotland." *ANF* 8
(1892): 199–237, esp. pp. 205–6.

Kock, E.A. "Anteckningar till Íslenzk Miðaldakvæði." *ANF* 61 (1946): 1–125,
esp. pp. 17 and 26–8.

Mogk, Eugen. >> *Geschichte der norwegisch-isländischen Literatur* (1904).
P. 720.

Páll Eggert Ólason. *Menn og menntir siðskiptaaldarinnar á Íslandi.* Vol. 1
(Reykjavík: Guðm. Gamalíelsson, 1919). Pp. 419, 423, and 438.

Pétur Sigurðsson. "Vísnabók Guðbrands biskups." In *Iðunn: Tímarit til skemtunar, nytsemdar og fróðleiks*. Vol. 8. Ed. Magnús Jónsson (Reykjavík: Gutenberg, 1923–4). Pp. 61–87, esp. p. 63.

Stéfan Einarsson. "Íslenzk helgikvæði á miðöldum." *Tímarit Þjóðræknisfélags Íslendinga* 36 (1954): 43–63, esp. p. 53.

– *Íslensk bókmenntasaga 874–1960* (Reykjavík: Oddi, 1961). Pp. 90 and 98.

Vésteinn Ólason. "Kveðskapur frá síðmiðöldum." In >> *Íslensk Bókmenntasaga* 2 (1993). Pp. 285–378, esp. p. 308.

Wolf, Kirsten, "The Influence of the *Evangelium Nicodemi* on Norse Literature: A Survey." In *The Medieval* Gospel of Nicodemus: *Texts, Intertexts, and Contexts in Western Europe*. Ed. Zbigniew Izydorczyk (Tempe, AZ; Medieval and Renaissance Texts and Studies, 1997). Pp. 261–86, esp. p. 278.

NOTE:

The poem contains material about Saints John the Evangelist, Lazarus, and Peter. See the entries for the three saints.

9. Sethskvæði

A poetic rendering by Jón Pétursson from ca. 1600 of the legend of the cross-tree.

Incipit: "Ótti dróttins upphaf er."

Manuscripts:
AM 100 8vo (ca. 1700–25), AM 148 8vo (ca. 1650–1700), G-40/270 (ca. 1700–1900), ÍB 105 4to (1758–68) ÍB 50 8vo (ca. 1800–1900), ÍB 379 8vo (ca. 1700–1900), ÍB 387 8vo (ca. 1700–1900), ÍB 521 8vo (ca. 1700–1800), ÍB 745 8vo (ca. 1800–50), ÍB 816 8vo (ca. 1600–1900), ÍBR 74 8vo (1852), ÍBR 109 8vo (1829), JS 258 4to (1840–5), JS 267 4to (ca. 1700–1900), JS 588 4to (ca. 1800–1900), JS 284 8vo (ca. 1850), JS 480 8vo (ca. 1675–1900), JS 481 8vo (ca. 1675–1900), JS 492 8vo (ca. 1675–1900), JS 499 8vo (ca. 1675–1900), JS 508 8vo (ca. 1675–1900), JS 510 8vo (ca. 1675–1900), JS 515 8vo (ca. 1675–1900), Kall 614 4to (ca. 1700–1800), Lbs 480 fol. (ca. 1800–2000), Lbs 625 4to (ca. 1800–10), Lbs 1221 4to (ca. 1860–70), Lbs 1662 4to (ca. 1800), Lbs 1756 4to (ca. 1800–25), Lbs 2133 4to (1865–1912), Lbs 2290 4to (1879–1905), Lbs 201 8vo (ca. 1850–70), Lbs 605 8vo (ca. 1600–1800), Lbs 709 8vo (ca. 1700–1800), Lbs 907 8vo (ca. 1700–1900), Lbs 1059 8vo (1793), Lbs 1156 8vo (ca. 1775–1825), Lbs 1222 8vo (ca. 1700–1825), Lbs 1389 8vo (1775–1900), Lbs 1405 8vo (1895–1900), Lbs 1571 8vo (ca. 1780 and ca. 1810), Lbs 1715 8vo (ca. 1820), Lbs 1730 8vo (ca. 1830), Lbs 1766 8vo (ca. 1800–50), Lbs 1868 8vo (1892–8), Lbs 1975 8vo (ca. 1850),

Lbs 2144 8vo (1838), Lbs 2157 8vo (ca. 1770), Lbs 2473 8vo (ca. 1750–1850), Lbs 2915 8vo (1861), Lbs 2941 8vo (ca. 1884–6), Lbs 3013 8vo (ca. 1750–1825), Lbs 3234 8vo (1843–5), Lbs 3630 8vo (ca. 1750–1850), Lbs 3668 8vo (ca. 1800–2000), Lbs 3714 8vo (ca. 1800–50), Lbs 3920 8vo (ca. 1900), Lbs 4104 8vo (ca. 1800–1900), Lbs 4156 8vo (ca. 1800–1900), NKS 1139 fol. (ca. 1750–1800), and Thott 514 8vo (ca. 1700–50).

Editions:

Jón Helgason, ed. >> *Kvæðabók úr Vigur: AM 148, 8vo* (1955). Fol. 116v–121v. Facsimile of AM 148 8vo.

Jón Þorkelsson. >> *Om Digtningen på Island* (1888). P. 335 (stz. 1 and 44). Based on AM 100 8vo, AM 148 8vo, ÍB 521 8vo, ÍBR 109 8vo, and Lbs 201 8vo.

Literature:

Bjarni Þorsteinsson, ed. *Íslenzk þjóðlög* (Copenhagen: Møller, 1906–9). P. 596.

Finnur Jónsson. >> *Bókmentasaga Íslendinga fram undir siðabót* (1904–5). P. 461.

Overgaard, Mariane, ed. *The History of the Cross-Tree Down to Christ's Passion: Icelandic Legend Versions.* Editiones Arnamagnæanæ, Ser. B, vol. 26 (Copenhagen: Munksgaard, 1968). Pp. xx, cxl–cxli, cxliii, cxlv, and clxx.

Páll Eggert Ólason. *Menn og menntir siðskiptaaldarinnar á Íslandi.* Vol. 4 (Reykjavík: Ársæll Árnason, 1926). Pp. 622–5.

10. Krossrímur

A set of five *rímur* composed on the subject of the cross-tree by the minister Sigurður Jónsson (d. 1661). The source is a now-lost text of *Origo Crucis.* Incipit: "Út skal leida yggjar skeið."

Manuscripts:

A: JS 214 8vo (1768), JS 515 8vo (ca. 1675–1900), Lbs 9 8vo (1796), Lbs 187 8vo (ca. 1850–70), and Lbs 2682 8vo (ca. 1775–1900);

B: Bor 118 (20759) (ca. 1800);

C: AM 276 8vo (ca. 1800–75), ÍB 865 8vo (ca. 1800–1900), JS 329 8vo (ca. 1700–1900), Lbs 2324 4to (1882–93), and Lbs 1049 8vo (ca. 1850);

D: ÍB 183 4to (ca. 1750), ÍBR 109 8vo (1829), and Lbs 2173 4to (ca. 1840);

E: ÍB 847 8vo (ca. 1775–1800);

F: ÍB 651 8vo (1863), JS 510 8vo (ca. 1675–1900), and Lbs 2965 8vo (1864);

G: ÍB 374 8vo (ca. 1800–25), JS 477 8vo (ca. 1675–1900), and Þjms MS 8vo in Ásbúð Collection (ca. 1800);

H: ÍB 974 8vo (ca. 1800–1900), Lbs 705 4to (ca. 1825–34), Lbs 1192 4to
   (ca. 1700–1800), and Þjms. MS 8vo in Ásbúð Collection (ca. 1800);
I: Lbs 1458 4to (ca. 1700–1900);
J: G-6/4 (ca. 1800–1900).

Edition:

Overgaard, Mariane, ed. *The History of the Cross-Tree Down to Christ's
   Passion: Icelandic Legend Versions.* Editiones Arnamagnæanæ, Ser. B,
   vol. 26 (Copenhagen: Munksgaard, 1968). Pp. 93–137.
   Based on JS 214 8vo with emendations and variants from Bor 118, ÍB 183
   4to, ÍB 651 8vo, ÍB 847 8vo, ÍB 865 8vo, ÍB 974 8vo, ÍBR 109 8vo, JS 329
   8vo, JS 477 8vo, JS 510 8vo, JS 515 8vo, Lbs 705 4to, Lbs 1192 4to, Lbs
   1458 4to, Lbs 2173 4to, Lbs 2324 4to, Lbs 9 8vo, Lbs 2682 8vo, Lbs 2965
   8vo, and Þjms. MS 8vo in Ásbúð Collection.

Literature:

Björn K. Þórólfsson. *Rímur fyrir 1600.* Safn Fræðafjelagsins um Ísland og
   Íslendinga 9 (Copenhagen: Møller, 1934). P. 322.

11. Krossrímur

A paraphrase of the fourth and fifth *rímur* in *Krossrímur.*
   Incipit: "Valla fagur fjórði bragur fram skal gá."

Manuscripts:
ÍB 651 8vo (1863) and Lbs 2965 8vo (1864).

Edition:
Overgaard, Mariane, ed. *The History of the Cross-Tree Down to Christ's
   Passion: Icelandic Legend Versions.* Editiones Arnamagnæanæ, Ser. B,
   vol. 26 (Copenhagen: Munksgaard, 1968). Pp. 138–47.
   Edition of Lbs 2965 8vo with variants from ÍB 651 8vo.

DIONYSIUS   October 9

Heilagra manna drápa

A fourteenth-century poem about holy men. Stz. 10–14 treat Saint Dionysius
and his associates, Rusticus and Elutherius.
   Incipit: "... mildings f ... um dyrnar þustu ... særa."

Manuscripts:
See Blase note (p. 52).

Editions:

Finnur Jónsson, ed. >> *Den norsk-islandske skjaldedigtning* (1912–15). Vol. AII, pp. 513–14 and vol. BII, pp. 565–6.

Kahle, Bernhard, ed. >> *Isländische geistliche Dichtungen des ausgehenden Mittelalters* (1898). Pp. 92–3.

Kock, Ernst Albin, ed. >> *Notationes Norrœnæ* (1923–44). §§1763, 1767, 1770, 2889, and 2983.

– ed. >> *Den norsk-islandske skaldediktningen* (1946–50). Vol. 2, pp. 309–10.

Wolf, Kirsten, ed. "Anonymous, *Heilagra manna drápa* 'Drápa about Holy Men'." In >> *Poetry on Christian Subjects* (2007). Vol. 2, pp. 879–82.

Danish translation:

Finnur Jónsson, ed. >> *Den norsk-islandske skjaldedigtning* (1912–15). Vol. BII, pp. 565–6.

English translation:

Wolf, Kirsten, ed. "Anonymous, *Heilagra manna drápa* 'Drápa about Holy Men'." In >> *Poetry on Christian Subjects* (2007). Vol. 2, pp. 879–82.

DOROTHY   February 6

1. Dórótheudiktur

A late medieval (ca. 1400–1550) poem in honour of Saint Dorothy based on oral tradition.

Incipit: "Hjálparinn himins og landa."

Manuscripts:

AM 920 4to (ca. 1800–1900), AM 429 12mo (ca. 1500), JS 399a–b 4to (ca. 1700–1900, stz. 1 only), and Lbs 2166 4to (ca. 1885–1920).

Editions:

Jón Helgason, ed. >> *Íslenzk miðaldakvæði* (1936–8). Vol. 2, pp. 359–63. Edition of AM 429 12mo.

Jón Þorkelsson. >> *Om Digtningen på Island i det 15. og 16. Århundrede* (1888). Pp. 91–2 (stz. 1).

Based on AM 920 4to and AM 429 12mo.

Wolf, Kirsten, ed. >> *A Female Legendary from Iceland: "Kirkjubæjarbók" (AM 429 12mo) in the Arnamagnæan Collection, Copenhagen)* (2011). Pp. 119–21.

Facsimile and edition of AM 429 12mo.

Literature:
Cormack, Margaret. "Poetry, Paganism and the Sagas of Icelandic Bishops."
    In >> *Til heiðurs og hugbótar* (2003). Pp. 33–51, esp. p. 51.
Finnur Jónsson. >> *Den oldnorske og oldislandske Litteraturs Historie*
    (1920–4). Vol. 3, p. 126.
Jakob Benediktsson. "Helgendigte." *KLNM* 6 (1961). Cols. 318–21, esp. col. 320.
– "Nödhjälparna." *KLNM* 21 (1977). Cols. 289–90, esp. col. 289.
Jón Hallur Stefánsson. "Dórótheukvæði, uppruni þess og afdrif. Tvær
    uppskriftir að Dórótheukvæði, auk umfjöllunar þar um." In *Fimm kvæði
    um heilaga menn: Agnesarkvæði, Dórotheukvæði, Laurentíuskvæði,
    Margrétarkvæði, Úrsúlukvæði*. Unpublished manuscript at Landsbókasafn,
    1981. Pp. 2 and 6–7.
Jón Helgason. >> "Norges og Islands digtning." In *Litteraturhistorie B:
    Norge og Island* (1953). Pp. 3–179, esp. pp. 163–4.
Jón Þórarinsson. *Íslensk tónlistarsaga 1000–1800* (Reykjavík: Tónlistarsafn
    Íslands, 2012). P. 368.
Mogk, Eugen. >> *Geschichte der norwegisch-isländischen Literatur* (1904).
    P. 719.
Soffía Ófeigsdóttir. "*Veroníkukvæði.*" BA thesis. University of Iceland, 1986.
    P. 66.
Stéfan Einarsson. "Íslenzk helgikvæði á miðöldum." *Tímarit Þjóðræknisfélags
    Íslendinga* 36 (1955): 43–63, esp. p. 55.
– *Íslensk bókmenntasaga 874–1960* (Reykjavík: Oddi, 1961). P. 92.
Vésteinn Ólason. "Kveðskapur frá síðmiðöldum." In >> *Íslensk Bókmenntasaga*
    2 (1993). Pp. 283–378, esp. pp. 299 and 316.
Wolf, Kirsten. "The Legend of Saint Dorothy: Medieval Vernacular
    Renderings and Their Latin Source." *Analecta Bollandiana* 114 (1996):
    41–72, esp. pp. 64–6.
– "Female Scribes at Work? A Consideration of Kirkjubæjarbók (Codex
    AM 429 12mo)." In *Beatus Vir: Studies in Early English and Norse
    Manuscripts in Memory of Phillip Pulsiano*. Ed. A.N. Doane and Kirsten
    Wolf (Tempe, AZ: ACMRS, 2006). Pp. 265–95, esp. pp. 270 and 275.
Wolf, Kirsten, ed. *The Icelandic Legend of Saint Dorothy*. Studies and Texts
    130 (Toronto: Pontifical Institute of Mediaeval Studies, 1997). Pp. 60–2.
– ed. >> *Heilagra meyja sögur* (2003). P. lv.

2. Dórótheukvæði I

A poetic rendering of the legend of Saint Dorothy ascribed to Ólafur Jónsson á
Söndum (1560–1672).
    Incipit: "Eitt sinn með öðrum kristnum."

Manuscripts:

AM 240 8vo I (ca. 1700–25), G-63/10 (ca. 1889), ÍB 70 4to (1693), JS 133
   8vo (ca. 1600–1800), JS 244 8vo (ca. 1800–20), JS 510 8vo (ca. 1675–
   1900), Lbs 201 8vo (ca. 1850–70), Lbs 1205 4to (1687), Lbs 1516 4to
   (1689), Lbs 2157 8vo (ca. 1770), and Lbs 3170 8vo (ca. 1800).

Edition:

Jón Þorkelsson. >> *Om Digtningen på Island* (1888). Pp. 92 (stz. 1^{1-4}).
   Based on Lbs 201 8vo.

Literature:

Finnur Jónsson. >> *Den oldnorske og oldislandske Litteraturs Historie*
   (1920–4). Vol. 3, p. 126.

Jón Hallur Stefánsson. "Dórótheukvæði, uppruni þess og afdrif. Tvær
   uppskriftir að Dórótheukvæði, auk umfjöllunar þar um." In *Fimm kvæði
   um heilaga menn: Agnesarkvæði, Dórotheukvæði, Laurentíuskvæði,
   Margrétarkvæði, Úrsúlukvæði.* Unpublished manuscript at Landsbókasafn,
   1981. Pp. 2–4 and 6–7.

Soffía Ófeigsdóttir. "*Veroníkukvæði.*" BA thesis. University of Iceland, 1986.
   P. 66.

Stéfan Einarsson. "Íslenzk helgikvæði á miðöldum." *Tímarit Þjóðræknisfélags
   Íslendinga* 36 (1955): 43–63, esp. p. 55.

– *Íslensk bókmenntasaga 874–1960* (Reykjavík: Oddi, 1961). P. 92.

Vésteinn Ólason. "Kveðskapur frá síðmiðöldum." In >> *Íslensk Bókmenntasaga*
   2 (1993). Pp. 283–378, esp. p. 316.

Wolf, Kirsten, ed. *The Icelandic Legend of Saint Dorothy.* Studies and Texts
   130 (Toronto: Pontifical Institute of Mediaeval Studies, 1997). Pp. 62–3.

3. Dórótheukvæði II

A seventeenth-century paraphrase of the Danish ballad *Den hellige Dorothea.*
Incipit: "Hef ég mér sett að herrans ráði."

Manuscripts:

A: JS 255 4to (1841), JS 589 4to (1841), JS 323 8vo (ca. 1800–50), Lbs 201
   8vo (ca. 1850–70), and Lbs 665 8vo (1755–60);

B: Lbs 2125 4to (1865–1912), Lbs 2166 8vo (ca. 1860 and 1897), SÁM
   85/354 EF (1969), and SÁM 85/357 EF (1969).

Editions:

Jón Hallur Stefánsson. "Dórótheukvæði, uppruni þess og afdrif. Tvær
   uppskriftir að Dórótheukvæði, auk umfjöllunar þar um." In *Fimm kvæði
   um heilaga menn: Agnesarkvæði, Dórotheukvæði, Laurentíuskvæði,*

Margrétarkvæði, Úrsúlukvæði. Unpublished manuscript at Landsbókasafn, 1981. Edition not paginated (inserted between pp. 4 and 5)
Editions of A (based on Lbs 665 8vo) and B (based on Lbs 2125 4to).
Jón Þorkelsson. >> *Om Digtningen på Island* (1888). Pp. 92 (stz. 1). Based on Lbs 201 8vo.

Literature:
Finnur Jónsson. >> *Den oldnorske og oldislandske Litteraturs Historie* (1920–4). Vol. 3, p. 126.
Soffía Ófeigsdóttir. *"Veroníkukvæði."* BA thesis. University of Iceland, 1986. P. 66.
Stéfan Einarsson. "Íslenzk helgikvæði á miðöldum." *Tímarit Þjóðræknisfélags Íslendinga* 36 (1955): 43–63, esp. p. 55.
– *Íslensk bókmenntasaga 874–1960* (Reykjavík: Oddi, 1961). P. 92.
Vésteinn Ólason. "Kveðskapur frá síðmiðöldum." In >> *Íslensk Bókmenntasaga* 2 (1993). Pp. 283–378, esp. p. 316.
Wolf, Kirsten, ed. *The Icelandic Legend of Saint Dorothy.* Studies and Texts 130 (Toronto: Pontifical Institute of Mediaeval Studies, 1997). Pp. 62–3.

EDMUND   November 20

Heilagra manna drápa

A fourteenth-century poem about holy men. Stz. 5–8 treat King Edmund of East Anglia.
Incipit: "... mildings f ... um dyrnar þustu ... særa."

Manuscripts:
See Blase note (p. 52).
Editions:
Finnur Jónsson, ed. >> *Den norsk-islandske skjaldedigtning* (1912–15). Vol. AII, pp. 512–13 and vol. BII, pp. 563–4.
Kahle, Bernhard, ed. >> *Isländische geistliche Dichtungen des ausgehenden Mittelalters* (1898). Pp. 91–2.
Kock, Ernst Albin, ed. >> *Notationes Norrænæ* (1923–44). §§1767, 1768, 1769, 2807A, 2889, and 3378A.
– ed. >> *Den norsk-islandske skaldediktningen* (1946–50). Vol. 2, p. 309.
Wolf, Kirsten, ed. "Anonymous, *Heilagra manna drápa* 'Drápa about Holy Men'." In >> *Poetry on Christian Subjects* (2007). Vol. 2, pp. 876–9.

Danish translation:
Finnur Jónsson, ed. >> *Den norsk-islandske skjaldedigtning* (1912–15).
   Vol. BII, pp. 563–4.
English translation:
Wolf, Kirsten, ed. "Anonymous, *Heilagra manna drápa* '*Drápa* about Holy
   Men'." In >> *Poetry on Christian Subjects* (2007). Vol. 2, pp. 876–8.

ELIZABETH   November 5

1. Gjörði í einu

A poetic rendering of biblical stories composed between 1400 and 1550. The
poem is also known as *Liljukvistur*. Stz. 18 mentions Saint Elizabeth, mother
of John the Baptist.
   Incipit: "Gjörði í einu orði hreinu."

Manuscripts:
AM 621 4to (ca. 1450–1500), JS 399a–b 4to (ca. 1700–1900), and Lbs 2166
   4to (ca. 1885–1920).
Edition:
Jón Helgason, ed. >> *Íslenzk miðaldakvæði* (1936–8). Vol. 1.2, p. 161.
   Based on AM 621 4to with variants from JS 399a–b 4to and Lbs 2166 4to.
Literature:
Cormack, Margaret. "Poetry, Paganism and the Sagas of Icelandic Bishops."
   In >> *Til heiðurs og hugbótar* (2003). Pp. 33–51, esp. p. 50.
Finnur Jónsson. >> *Bókmentasaga Íslendinga fram undir siðabót* (1904–5).
   P. 461.
– >> *Den oldnorske og oldislandske Litteraturs Historie* (1920–4). Vol. 3,
   pp. 124–5.
Jón Þorkelsson. >> *Om Digtningen på Island* (1888). P. 41.
Kock, E.A. "Anteckningar till Íslenzk Miðaldakvæði." *ANF* 61 (1946): 1–125,
   esp. pp. 19, 37, and 85.
– "Liljukvistur." *Studia Neophilologica* 15 (1942): 141–156, esp. p. 147.
Schottmann, Hans. >> *Die isländische Mariendichtung* (1973). Pp. 61–2,
   70n19, 224–5, 234, 318–36, 509, and 556.
Sverrir Tómasson. "'Nikulám skulu vér heiðra hér …'." In >> *Til heiðurs og
   hugbótar* (2003). Pp. 79–92, esp. p. 89.
NOTE:
The poem contains material about other saints, especially Mary the Blessed
Virgin, but also Joachim, John the Baptist, John the Evangelist, Joseph,

Lazarus, Martha, Mary Magdalen, and Simeon the Righteous. See the entries for the individual saints.

2. María móðirin skæra

A poem in honour of Mary the Blessed Virgin dated to ca. 1400–1550 and attributed alternatively to Loptur ríki Guttormsson (d. 1432), Jón Pálsson Máríuskáld (ca. 1390–1471), and Bishop Jón Arason (1484–1550). Stz. 12 mentions Saint Elizabeth.
   Incipit: "María móðirin skæra."

Manuscripts:
See Mary the Blessed Virgin 21 note (p. 186).
Editions:
Jón Helgason, ed. >> *Íslenzk miðaldakvæði* (1936–8). Vol. 2, pp. 50–1.
Jón Þorkelsson, ed. >> *Kvæðasafn* (1922–7). P. 144.

3. Fyrirlát mér jungfrúin hreina

A poem about Christ and the Holy Cross probably composed in Norway ca. 1400–1550. Stz. 3 concerns Saint Elizabeth.
   Incipit: "Fyrirlát mér jungfrúin hreina."

Manuscripts:
See Cross, the Holy 6 note (p. 71).
Edition:
Jón Helgason, ed. >> *Íslenzk miðaldakvæði* (1936–8). Vol. 1.2, p. 269.

4. Bjóða vil ég þér bragsins smíð

A poem in praise of Mary the Blessed Virgin from ca. 1400–1550. The text is probably based on oral tradition. Stz. 3–10 concern Saint Elizabeth.
   Incipit: "Bjóða vil ég þér bragsins smíð."

Manuscripts:
See Mary the Blessed Virgin 36 note (p. 199).
Edition:
Jón Helgason, ed. >> *Íslenzk miðaldakvæði* (1936–8). Vol. 2, p. 54.

5. Nikulásdrápa

An early sixteenth-century poem in honour of Saint Nicholas ascribed to the priest Hallur Ögmundarson (d. ca. 1540). Stz. 16 mentions Saint Elizabeth.
   Incipit: "Í nafni guðs vil ég upphaf efna."

Manuscripts:
See Nicholas 5 note (p. 262).
Editions:
Carpenter, William H., ed. *Nikolásdrápa Halls prests: An Icelandic Poem from circa A.D. 1400* (Halle: Karras, 1881). P. 16.
Jón Helgason, ed. >> *Íslenzk miðaldakvæði* (1936–8). Vol. 2, p. 420.
Jón Þorkelsson, ed. >> *Kvæðasafn* (1922–7). P. 389.

6. Blómarós

A poem praising Jesus Christ and relating various biblical stories composed ca. 1400–1550. Jón Helgason argues that it is probably from 1550 or the first decade thereafter during the transition from Catholicism to Protestantism. Stz. 82–3 concern Saint Elizabeth.
   Incipit: "Heyr guð faðir á himna hæðum."

Manuscripts:
A: AM 704 4to (ca. 1500–1600) and AM 710f 4to (ca. 1700–25);
B: Adv 21.8.10 (1712), Lbs 1327 4to (ca. 1890), and Lbs 2166 4to (ca. 1885–1920).
Edition:
Jón Helgason, ed. >> *Íslenzk miðaldakvæði* (1936–8). Vol. 1.2, p. 79.
   Based on AM 704 4to with variants from Adv 21.8.10, AM 710f 4to, and Lbs 1327 4to.
Literature:
Chase, Martin. "Devotional Poetry at the End of the Middle Ages in Iceland." In >> *Eddic, Skaldic, and Beyond: Poetic Variety in Medieval Iceland.* Ed. Martin Chase (2014). Pp. 136–49, esp. p. 142.
Finnur Jónsson. >> *Bókmentasaga Íslendinga fram undir siðabót* (1904–5). P. 461.
– >> *Den oldnorske og oldislandske Litteraturs Historie* (1920–4). Vol. 3, pp. 124–5.
Hálfdan Einarsson. *Sciagraphia historiæ literariæ islandicæ* (Copenhagen: Sander and Schröder, 1777). P. 58.
Jakob Benediktsson. >> "Helgikvæði." In *Hugtök og heiti í bókmenntafræði* (1983). Pp. 115–17, esp. p. 116.

Jón Helgason. *Gamall kveðskapur* (Copenhagen: Hið íslenzka fræðafélag, 1979). P. 54n1.

Jón Þorkelsson. >> *Om Digtningen på Island* (1888). Pp. 43–4.

Kock, E.A. "Liljukvistur." *Studia Neophilologica* 15 (1942): 141–56, esp. p. 143.

– "Anteckningar till Íslenzk Miðaldakvæði." *ANF* 61 (1946): 1–125, esp. pp. 5–12, 26, 36, 52, and 61.

Schottmann, Hans. >> *Die isländische Mariendichtung* (1973). Pp. 32, 89n26, 206, 220n20, 300n3, and 315n5.

Vésteinn Ólason. "Kveðskapur frá síðmiðöldum." In >> *Íslensk Bókmenntasaga* 2 (1993). Pp. 283–378, esp. p. 301.

Wolf, Kirsten, "The Influence of the *Evangelium Nicodemi* on Norse Literature: A Survey." In *The Medieval* Gospel of Nicodemus: *Texts, Intertexts, and Contexts in Western Europe*. Ed. Zbigniew Izydorczyk (Tempe, AZ; Medieval and Renaissance Texts and Studies, 1997). Pp. 261–86, esp. p. 278.

NOTE:

The poem contains material about other saints, especially Mary the Blessed Virgin, but also John the Baptist, Joseph, Joseph of Arimathea, Lazarus, Mary Magdalen, Simeon the Righteous, and Thomas. See the entries for the individual saints.

7. Máríuvísur

A poem in praise of Mary the Blessed Virgin composed ca. 1600 by Einar Sigurðsson í Eydölum (1539–1626). Stz. 18 and 20–1 mention Saint Elizabeth.
   Incipit: "Mjúkast vilda ég mærðarvers."

Manuscripts:
See Mary the Blessed Virgin 55 note (p. 220).
Editions:
Guðbrandur Þorláksson, ed. >> *Ein ny wiisna bok* (1612). Pp. 95.
Jón Torfason and Kristján Eiríksson, ed. >> *Vísnabók Guðbrands* (2000). P. 111.

8. Máríuævi eða Lífssaga helgustu guðs móður

A poem about the life of Mary the Blessed Virgin composed ca. 1600 by the priest Ólafur Guðmundsson (ca. 1537–1609). Stz. 22 mentions Saint Elizabeth.

Manuscript:
See Mary the Blessed Virgin 57 note (p. 221).
   Incipit: "Ég vil jómfrú eina."

Editions:
Guðbrandur Þorláksson, ed. >> *Ein ny wiisna bok* (1612). Pp. 302.
Jón Torfason and Kristján Eiríksson, ed. >> *Vísnabók Guðbrands* (2000).
   P. 341.

EUFEMIA   September 16

Heilagra meyja drápa

A fourteenth-century poem about holy maidens. Stz. 46–7 treat Saint Eufemia.
   Incipit: "Heyrðu ómælds himna veldis herra guð."

Manuscripts:
See Agatha note (p. 13).
Editions:
Finnur Jónsson, ed. >> *Den norsk-islandske skjaldedigtning* (1912–15).
   Vol. AII, p. 536 and vol. BII, pp. 593–4.
Kock, Ernst Albin, ed. >> *Notationes Norrœnæ* (1923–44). §2971C.
– ed. >> *Den norsk-islandske skaldediktningen* (1946–50). Vol. 2, pp. 328–9.
Wolf, Kirsten, ed. "Anonymous, *Heilagra meyja drápa* '*Drápa* about Holy
   Maidens'." In >> *Poetry on Christian Subjects* (2007). Vol. 2, pp. 919–20.
Danish translation:
Finnur Jónsson, ed. >> *Den norsk-islandske skjaldedigtning* (1912–15).
   Vol. BII, pp. 593–4.
English translation:
Wolf, Kirsten, ed. "Anonymous, *Heilagra meyja drápa* '*Drápa* about Holy
   Maidens'." In >> *Poetry on Christian Subjects* (2007). Vol. 2, pp. 919–20.

EUGENIA   December 25

Nikulásdrápa

An early sixteenth-century poem in honour of Saint Nicholas ascribed to the
priest Hallur Ögmundarson (d. ca. 1540). Stz. 58 mentions Saint Eugenia.
   Incipit: "Í nafni guðs vil ég upphaf efna."

Manuscripts:
See Nicholas 5 note (p. 262).

Editions:
Carpenter, William H., ed. *Nikolásdrápa Halls prests: An Icelandic Poem from circa A.D. 1400* (Halle: Karras, 1881). P. 26.
Jón Helgason, ed. >> *Íslenzk miðaldakvæði* (1936–18). Vol. 2, p. 428.
Jón Þorkelsson, ed. >> *Kvæðasafn* (1922–7). P. 399.
Literature:
Björn K. Þórólfsson. "Kvantitetsomvæltningen i islandsk" *ANF* 45 (1929): 35–81, esp. p. 42.

EUSTACE   September 20

Plácítusdrápa

A twelfth-century poem in honour of Saint Eustace.
    Incipit: "... gengit, fjǫrnis valdr kvað foldar."

Manuscript:
AM 673b 4to (ca. 1200).
Editions:
Finnur Jónsson, ed. "Plácítusdrápa efter håndskriftet no 673 B 4. i den Arna-Magn. saml." *Opuscula Philologica. Mindre Afhandlinger udgivne af Det philologisk-historiske Samfund* (Copenhagen: Cohen, 1887). Pp. 210–64, esp. pp. 214–22.
– ed. >> *Den norsk-islandske skjaldedigtning* (1912–15). Vol. AI, pp. 607–18 and vol. BI, pp. 606–22.
Hreinn Benediktsson. *Early Icelandic Script as Illustrated in Vernacular Texts from theTwelfth and Thirteenth Centuries.* Íslenzk handrit: Icelandic Manuscripts, Series in Folio 2 (Reykjavík: Manuscript Institute of Iceland, 1965). Plate 5 and pp. v–vi. Facsimile and edition of fol. 2v.
Jón Helgason. "Til Skjaldediktningen." *APS* 7 (1932–3): 150–68. (Parts of stz. 3, 4, 9, 14–15, 20, 23, 27, 33, 38, 40, 45, 47, 49, 51–3, and 56–8 only.)
Kock, Ernst Albin, ed. >> *Notationes Norrœna* (1923–44). §§1243, 1244, 1245, 1246, 1247, 1248, 1249, 1250, 1252, 1255, 1256, 1793, 1797, 2131, 2132, 2133, 2134, 2135A, 2136, 2137, 2138, 2139, 2247B, 2315Anm, 2315B, 2318, 2369, 2490, 2491, 2492, 2493A, 2553, 2554, 2555, 2556, 2811, 2812, 2991C, 3133B, 3134, 3135, 3136, 3247, and 3396X.
– ed. >> *Den norsk-isländska skaldediktningen* (1946–50). Vol. 1, pp. 295–302.

Louis-Jensen, Jonna, ed. In *Plácidus saga. With an Edition of* Plácitus drápa *by Jonna Louis-Jensen*. Ed. John Tucker. Editiones Arnamagnæanæ, Ser. B, vol. 31 (Copenhagen: Reitzel, 1998). Pp. 93–123.

Louis-Jensen, Jonna, and Tarrin Wills, ed. "Anonymous, *Plácitusdrápa* 'Drápa about Plácitus'." In >> *Poetry on Christian Subjects* (2007). Vol. 1, pp. 182–220.

Sveinbjörn Egilsson, ed. *Brot af Placidus-drápu* (Viðeyjarklaustur: Helgi Helgason, 1833).

Danish translation:

Finnur Jónsson, ed. >> *Den norsk-islandske skjaldedigtning* (1912–15). Vol. BI, pp. 606–22.

English translations:

Louis-Jensen, Jonna, ed. In *Plácidus saga. With an Edition of* Plácitus drápa *by Jonna Louis-Jensen*. Ed. John Tucker. Editiones Arnamagnæanæ, Ser. B, vol. 31 (Copenhagen: Reitzel, 1998). Pp. 93–123.

Louis-Jensen, Jonna, and Tarrin Wills. "Anonymous, *Plácitusdrápa* 'Drápa about Plácitus'." In >> *Poetry on Christian Subjects* (2007). Vol. 1, pp. 182–220.

Literature:

Abram, Christopher. "Einarr Skúlason, Snorri Sturluson, and the Post-Pagan Mythological Kennings." In >> *Eddic, Skaldic, and Beyond: Poetic Variety in Medieval Iceland*. Ed. Martin Chase (2014). Pp. 44–61, esp. p. 55.

Attwood, Katrina. "Intertextual Aspects of the Twelfth-Century Christian *Drápur*." *Saga-Book* 24 (1996): 221–39.

– "Leiðarvísan and the 'Sunday Letter' Tradition in Scandinavia." In >> *Til heiðurs og hugbótar* (2003). Pp. 53–78, esp. p. 54.

– "Christian Poetry." In *A Companion to Old Norse–Icelandic Literature and Culture*. Ed. Rory McTurk (Oxford: Blackwell, 2005). Pp. 43–63, esp. pp. 50, 52–3, and 56.

Bekker-Nielsen, Hans. "Et par ord om de ældste norrøne helgensager." In *Eyvindarbók: Festskrift til Eyvind Fjeld Halvorsen 4. mai 1992*. Ed. Finn Hødnebø et al. (Oslo: Drammen Grafisk AS, 1992). Pp. 29–33, esp. p. 32.

Bekker-Nielsen, Hans, Thorkil Damsgaard Olsen, and Ole Widding. >> *Norrøn fortællekunst* (1965). P. 123.

Chase, Martin. "*Concatenatio* as a Structural Element in the Christian *Drápur*." In *The Sixth International Saga Conference 28/7–2/8 1985. Workshop Papers*. 2 vols. ([Copenhagen]: Det arnamagnæanske Institut, 1985). Vol. 1, pp. 115–29, esp. pp. 118–19 and 124–5.

– "Christian Poetry: West Norse." In >> *Medieval Scandinavia: An Encyclopedia* (1993). Pp. 73–7, esp. p. 75.

– "Devotional Poetry at the End of the Middle Ages in Iceland." In >> *Eddic, Skaldic, and Beyond: Poetic Variety in Medieval Iceland*. Ed. Martin Chase (2014). Pp. 136–49, esp. p. 138.

Clunies Ross, Margaret. >> *A History of Old Norse Poetry and Poetics* (2005). Pp. 131–2, 134, 137–9, and 230.

Cormack, Margaret. >> *The Saints in Iceland* (1994). P. 41.

– "Sagas of Saints." In *Old Icelandic Literature and Society*. Ed. Margaret Clunies Ross (Cambridge: Cambridge University Press, 2000). Pp. 302–25, esp. pp. 311–12.

– "Poetry, Paganism and the Sagas of Icelandic Bishops." In >> *Til heiðurs og hugbótar* (2003). Pp. 33–51, esp. pp. 33–4 and 44.

Edwards, Diana. "Christian and Pagan References in Eleventh-Century Norse Poetry: The Case of Arnórr Jarlaskáld." *Saga-Book* 21 (1982–3): 34–53, esp. p. 45.

Finnur Jónsson. >> *Den oldnorske og oldislandske Litteraturs Historie* (1920–4). Vol. 2, pp. 117–18 and 125.

Frank, Roberta. *Old Norse Court Poetry: The* Dróttkvætt *Stanza*. Islandica 42 (Ithaca: Cornell University Press, 1998). P. 99.

Guðrún Nordal. *Tools of Literacy: The Role of Skaldic Verse in Icelandic Textual Culture of the Twelfth and Thirteenth Centuries* (Toronto: University of Toronto Press, 2001). Pp. 40, 89–90, 141, 341, 367n33, 377nn19 and 22, 382n46, and 383n49.

Hammerich, Fr. *De Episk-kristelige Oldkvad hos de gotiske Folk* (Copenhagen: Gyldendal, 1875). P. 140.

Jakob Benediktsson. "Helgendigte." *KLNM* 6 (1961). Cols. 318–21, esp. col. 318.

– "Plácítusdrápa." *KLNM* 13 (1968). Cols. 326–7.

– "Religiøs digtning." *KLNM* 14 (1969). Cols. 37–40, esp. col. 38.

– "*Hafgerðingadrápa*." In *Specvlvm Norroenvm: Norse Studies in Memory of Gabriel Turville-Petre*. Ed. Ursula Dronke, Guðrún P. Helgadóttir, Gerd Wolfgang Weber, and Hans Bekker-Nielsen (Odense: Odense University Press, 1981). Pp. 27–32, esp. p. 31.

Jón Helgason. *Norrøn Litteraturhistorie* (Copenhagen: Levin and Munksgaard, 1934). P. 88.

– >> "Norges og Islands digtning." In *Litteraturhistorie B: Norge og Island* (1953). Pp. 3–179, esp. pp. 103, 155, and 232.

Jónas Kristjánsson. "Bókmenntasaga." In *Saga Íslands* 2. Ed. Sigurður Líndal (Reykjavík: Hið íslenzka bókmenntafélag, Sögufélagið, 1975). Pp. 147–258, esp. p. 208.

– >> *Eddas and Sagas: Iceland's Medieval Literature* (1988). Pp. 112 and 142.

Jørgensen, Jørgen Højgaard. "Hagiography and the Icelandic Bishop Sagas."
    Peritia 1 (1982): 1–16, esp. p. 3.
Kahle, Bernhard. *Die Sprache der Skalden auf Grund der Binnen- und
    Endreime* (Strassburg: Karl J. Trübner, 1892).
– "Das Christentum in der altwestnordischen Dichtung." *ANF* 13 (1901):
    1–40 and 97–160, esp. pp. 7, 18, 28, 30–1, 98, 107, 11, 114–15, 117,
    123–9, 134–5, 138, and 152.
Konráð Gíslason. "Om helrim i förste og tredje linie af regelmæssigt
    'drottkvætt' og 'hrynhenda'." *Indbydelsesskrift til Kjøbenhavns Universitets
    Aarsfest til Erindring om Kirkens Reformation* (Copenhagen: Schultz,
    1877). Pp. 1–60, esp. pp. 12, 17, 24, 27–31, and 41.
Kuhn, Hans. *Das Dróttkvætt* (Heidelberg: Carl Winter Universitätsverlag,
    1983). P. 255.
Lange, Wolfgang. >> *Studien zur christlichen Dichtung der Nordgermanen
    1000–1200* (1958). Pp. 98, 100–10, and 213.
Lindow, John. "Narrative and the Nature of Skaldic Poetry." *ANF* 97 (1982):
    94–121, esp. pp. 102, 114–17, and 120n107.
Lindquist, Ivar. "En fornisländsk sjöterm *skokkr.*" *Festskrift til Finnur Jónsson
    29. maj 1928.* Ed. Johs. Brøndum-Nielsen et al. (Copenhagen: Levin and
    Munksgaard, 1928). Pp. 385–94, esp. pp. 392–4.
Marold, Edith. "Das Gottesbild der christlichen Skaldik." In *The Sixth
    International Saga Conference 28/7–2/8 1985. Workshop Papers.* 2 vols.
    ([Copenhagen]: Det arnamagnæanske Institut, 1985). Vol. 2, pp. 717–49,
    esp. pp. 731, 736, and 744–6.
Mogk, Eugen. >> *Geschichte der norwegisch-isländischen Literatur* (1904).
    P. 712
Noreen, Erik. *Studier i fornvästnordisk diktning* 2. Uppsala Universitets
    Årsskrift 1922 (Uppsala: Akademiska bokhandeln, 1922). P. 27.
Paasche, Fredrik. >> *Kristendom og kvad* (1914). Pp. 32, 85–91, 106, 108,
    118, 131, and 151.
– *Norges og Islands litteratur inntil utgangen av middelalderen.* Rev. ed.
    by Anne Holtsmark (Oslo: Aschehoug, 1947). Pp. 313 and 335.
Schottmann, Hans. >> *Die isländische Mariendichtung* (1973). Pp. 205–6,
    208–9, 302n7, and 395.
Seip, Didrik Arup. "Plácítúsdrápa." *Studier i nordisk filologi* 39 (1949):
    20–4. Rpt. in Didrik Arup Seip. *Nye studier i norsk språkhistorie* (Oslo:
    Aschehoug, 1954). Pp. 100–4.
Skard, Vemund. "Harmsól, Plácítusdrápa og Leiðarvísan." *ANF* 68 (1953):
    97–108.
Stéfan Einarsson. "Íslenzk helgikvæði á miðöldum." *Tímarit Þjóðræknisfélags
    Íslendinga* 36 (1955): 43–63, esp. pp. 43 and 45–6.

– *Íslensk bókmenntasaga 874–1960* (Reykjavík: Oddi, 1961). Pp. 81–3 and 86–9.

*Tucker, John. "A Study of the *Plácitus Saga*, Including an Edition, and of Its Relation to the *Plácitus Drápa*." BLitt thesis, University of Oxford, 1974.

Tucker, John. "St. Eustace in Iceland: On the Origins, Structure, and Possible Influence of the *Plácítus saga*." In *Les Sagas de Chevaliers (Riddarasögur). Actes de la Ve Conférence Internationale sur les Sagas (Toulon, Juillet 1982)*. Civilisations 10. Ed. Régis Boyer (Paris: Presses de l'Université Paris-Sorbonne, 1985). Pp. 327–39.

– "The Relation of the Plácítus drápa to the Plácítus saga." In *The Sixth International Saga Conference 28/7–2/8 1985. Workshop Papers*. 2 vols. ([Copenhagen]: Det arnamagnæanske Institut, 1985). Vol. 2, pp. 1057–66.

– "Plácítus saga." In >> *Medieval Scandinavia: An Encyclopedia* (1993). Pp. 504–5, esp. p. 505.

Turville-Petre, G. *Origins of Icelandic Literature* (Oxford: Clarendon Press, 1967). P. 131.

Þórhallur Þorgilsson. "Um þýðingar og endursagnir úr ítölskum miðaldaritum." *Landsbókasafn Íslands. Árbók* 1946–7 (1948): 212–24, esp. p. 222.

Vésteinn Ólason. "Eddukvæði." In >> *Íslensk Bókmenntasaga* 1 (1992). Pp. 75–187, esp. p. 142.

– "Kristileg trúarkvæði til loka 13. aldar." In >> *Íslensk Bókmenntasaga* 1 (1992). Pp. 483–515, esp. pp. 488, 492, 501, and 514.

– "Kveðskapur frá síðmiðöldum." In >> *Íslensk Bókmenntasaga* 2 (1993). Pp. 283–378, esp. p. 315.

– "Old Icelandic Poetry." In *A History of Icelandic Literature*. Ed. Daisy Neijmann. Histories of Scandinavian Literature 5 (Lincoln: University of Nebraska Press, 2006). Pp. 1–64, esp. p. 44.

Viðar Pálsson. "Pagan Mythology in Christian Society." *Gripla* 19 (2008): 123–58, esp. p. 140.

Vries, Jan de. >> *Altnordische Literaturgeschichte* (1964–7). Vol. 1, pp. 148, 196, 198, and vol. 2, pp. 56–8, 61, 78, 94, 160, and 184.

FELICITY   November 23

Heilagra meyja drápa

A fourteenth-century poem about holy maidens. Stz. 57 briefly mentions Saint Felicity.

Incipit: "Heyrðu ómælds himna veldis herra guð."

Manuscripts:
See Agatha note (p. 13).
Editions:
Finnur Jónsson, ed. >> *Den norsk-islandske skjaldedigtning* (1912–15).
  Vol. AII, p. 538 and vol. BII, p. 596.
Kock, Ernst Albin, ed. >> *Notationes Norrœnæ* (1923–44). §§2970B and
  2971B.
– ed. >> *Den norsk-islandske skaldediktningen* (1946–50). Vol. 2, p. 330.
Wolf, Kirsten, ed. "Anonymous, *Heilagra meyja drápa* '*Drápa* about Holy
  Maidens'." In >> *Poetry on Christian Subjects* (2007). Vol. 2, p. 927.
Danish translation:
Finnur Jónsson, ed. >> *Den norsk-islandske skjaldedigtning* (1912–15).
  Vol. BII, p. 596.
English translation:
Wolf, Kirsten, ed. "Anonymous, *Heilagra meyja drápa* '*Drápa* about Holy
  Maidens'." In >> *Poetry on Christian Subjects* (2007). Vol. 2, p. 927.

FIDES, SPES, AND CARITAS   August 1

Heilagra meyja drápa

A fourteenth-century poem about holy maidens. Stz. 58 mentions Saints Fides,
Spes, and Caritas.
   Incipit: "Heyrðu ómælds himna veldis herra guð."

Manuscripts:
See Agatha note (p. 13).
Editions:
Finnur Jónsson, ed. >> *Den norsk-islandske skjaldedigtning* (1912–15).
  Vol. AII, p. 538 and vol. BII, p. 596.
Kock, Ernst Albin, ed. >> *Notationes Norrœnæ* (1923–44). §§2970B, 2971B,
  and 3391C.
– ed. >> *Den norsk-islandske skaldediktningen* (1946–50). Vol. 2, p. 330.
Wolf, Kirsten, ed. "Anonymous, *Heilagra meyja drápa* '*Drápa* about Holy
  Maidens'." In >> *Poetry on Christian Subjects* (2007). Vol. 2, p. 928.
Danish translation:
Finnur Jónsson, ed. >> *Den norsk-islandske skjaldedigtning* (1912–15).
  Vol. BII, p. 596.

English translation:
Wolf, Kirsten, ed. "Anonymous, *Heilagra meyja drápa* '*Drápa* about Holy
   Maidens'." In >> *Poetry on Christian Subjects* (2007). Vol. 2, p. 928.

GREGORY THE GREAT   April 23

Michaelsflokkur

An early sixteenth-century poem about Saint Michael ascribed to the priest
Hallur Ögmundarson (d. ca. 1540). Saint Gregory is mentioned in stz. 48.
   Incipit: "Óðar gef þú upphaf."

Manuscripts:
See Michael the Archangel 2 note (p. 256).
Edition:
Jón Þorkelsson, ed. >> *Kvæðasafn* (1922–7). P. 381.

GUÐMUNDR THE GOOD   March 16

1. Guðmundarkvæði

A poem in praise of Bishop Guðmundr Arason by Arngrímr (Brandsson?)
(d. 1361 or 1362).
   Incipit: "Ræsi heiðra ek lopt ins ljósa."

Manuscripts:
Stock. Perg. fol. no. 5 (ca. 1350–65).
Editions:
Finnur Jónsson, ed. >> *Den norsk-islandske skjaldedigtning* (1912–15).
   Vol. AII, pp. 348–62 and vol. BII, pp. 371–89.
   In the edition, 6 stz. (*lausavísur* by Arngrímr) are added to the *drápa*
   (despite the manuscript evidence).
Isberg, Arvid, ed. *Kvæði Guðmundar byskups efter skinnboken N:o 5
   fol. å Kongl. Biblioteket i Stockholm* (Lund: Berling, 1877). Pp. 26–40
   (transcribed text), 41–9 (normalized text).
Jón Helgason, ed. *Byskupa sǫgur. MS Perg. fol. No. 5 in the Royal Library of
   Stockholm.* CCI 19 (Copenhagen: Ejnar Munksgaard, 1950).

[Jón Sigurðsson and Guðbrandur Vigfússon, ed.] >> *Biskupa sögur* (1858–78). Vol. 2, pp. 187–201.

In the edition, the *drápa* is printed in accordance with the manuscript evidence, that is, as a poem with 60 stz.

Kock, Ernst Albin, ed. >> *Notationes Norrœna* (1923–44). §§1489, 1490, 1491A, 1491B, 1491C, 1491D, 1492, 1493, 1494, 1495, 1496A, 1496B, 1497, 1509A, 1510, 1511, 1512, 2207, 2622B, 2622C, 2622D, 2622E, 2623, 2624, 2625, 2626, 2627, 2628, 2622A, 2841, 2842, 2843, 2995B, 3301, 3302, 3303, 3304, 3305, 3306, 3307, and 3397E.

– ed. >> *Den norsk-isländska skaldediktningen* (1946–50). Vol. 2, pp. 200–11.

Sveinbjörn Egilsson, ed. *Fjǫgur gǫmul kvæði. Boðsrit til að hlusta á þá opinberu yfirheyrslu í Bessastaða Skóla þann 22–29 mai 1844* (Viðeyjarklaustur: Helgi Helgason, 1844). Pp. VIII–IX and XI (stz. 2 and 43 only).

Modern Icelandic language edition:

Einar Ól. Sveinsson, Páll Eggert Ólason, and Arnór Sigurjónsson, ed. *Íslands þúsund ár: Kvæðasafn.* 3 vols. (Reykjavík: Helgafell, 1947). Vol. 2, pp. 11–12 (stz. 1–2).

Danish translation:

Finnur Jónsson, ed. >> *Den norsk-islandske skjaldedigtning* (1912–15). Vol. BII, pp. 372–89.

Swedish translation:

Isberg, Arvid, ed. *Kvæði Guðmundar byskups efter skinnboken N:o 5 fol. å Kongl. Biblioteket i Stockholm* (Lund: Berling, 1877). Pp. 50–81.

Literature:

Björn Sigfússon. "Guðmundar saga biskups Arasonar." *KLNM* 5 (1960). Cols. 542–3, esp. col. 543.

Chase, Martin. "Christian Poetry: West Norse." In >> *Medieval Scandinavia: An Encyclopedia* (1993). Pp. 73–7, esp. pp. 75–6.

Clunies Ross, Margaret. >> *A History of Old Norse Poetry and Poetics* (2005). P. 230.

Cormack, Margaret. >> *The Saints in Iceland* (1994). Pp. 42, 99, and 101.

– "Poetry, Paganism and the Sagas of Icelandic Bishops." In >> *Til heiðurs og hugbótar* (2003). Pp. 33–51, esp. pp. 48–50.

– "Christian Biography." In *A Companion to Old Norse–Icelandic Literature and Culture.* Ed. Rory McTurk (Oxford: Blackwell, 2005). Pp. 27–42, esp. pp. 38–9.

Faulkes, Anthony. "Edda." *Gripla* 2 (1977): 32–9, esp. p. 34n11.

Finnur Jónsson. >> *Den oldnorske og oldislandske Litteraturs Historie* (1920–4). Vol. 3, pp. 8–9.

Foote, Peter. "Latin Rhetoric and Icelandic Poetry: Some Contacts." In
    Aurvandilstá: Norse Studies. Ed. Michael Barnes, Hans Bekker-Nielsen,
    and Gerd Wolfgang Weber. Viking Collection 2 (Odense: Odense
    University Press, 1984). Pp. 249–70, esp. p. 265n42.
Guðrún Nordal. *Tools of Literacy: The Role of Skaldic Verse in Icelandic
    Textual Culture of the Twelfth and Thirteenth Centuries* (Toronto: University
    of Toronto Press, 2001). Pp. 100, 108, 299, and 377nn18 and 20.
Holtsmark, Anne. "Lovkvad." *KLNM* 10 (1965). Cols. 700–4, esp. col. 702.
Jakob Benediktsson. "Helgendigte." *KLNM* 6 (1961). Cols. 318–21, esp.
    col. 319.
– >> "Helgikvæði." In *Hugtök og heiti í Bókmenntafræði* (1983). Pp. 115–17,
    esp. p. 116.
Jón Helgason. >> "Norges og Islands digtning." In *Litteraturhistorie B:
    Norge og Island* (1953). Pp. 3–179, esp. p. 161.
Jón Þórarinsson. *Íslensk tónlistarsaga 1000–1800* (Reykjavík: Tónlistarsafn
    Íslands, 2012). P. 146.
Jón Þorkelsson. >> *Om Digtningen på Island* (1888). P. 27.
Kahle, Bernhard. "Das Christentum in der altwestnordischen Dichtung."
    ANF 13 (1901): 1–40 and 97–160, esp. pp. 10, 20, 32, 98–102, 104–5,
    107, 109, 111, 113–18, 121–5, 127–32, 135, 137–40, 147, 150–1, 153,
    and 155–6.
Konráð Gíslason. "Om helrim i förste og tredje linie af regelmæssigt
    'drottkvætt' og 'hrynhenda'." *Indbydelsesskrift til Kjøbenhavns
    Universitets Aarsfest til Erindring om Kirkens Reformation* (Copenhagen:
    Schultz, 1877). Pp. 1–60, esp. pp. 2–4, 16, 25, 28, and 43.
Kuhn, Hans. *Das Dróttkvætt* (Heidelberg: Carl Winter Universitätsverlag,
    1983). P. 330.
Lange, Wolfgang. >> *Studien zur christlichen Dichtung der Nordgermanen
    1000–1200* (1958). Pp. 228 and 274–5.
Lindow, John. "Narrative and the Nature of Skaldic Poetry." *ANF* 97 (1982):
    94–121, esp. pp. 102 and 118–19.
Mogk, Eugen. >> *Geschichte der norwegisch-isländischen Literatur* (1904).
    P. 715.
Ólafur Lárusson. "Guðmundur góði í þjóðtrú Íslendinga." *Skírnir* 116 (1942):
    113–39, esp. p. 117.
Schottmann, Hans. >> *Die isländische Mariendichtung* (1973). Pp. 53, 82,
    190, 205, 238–9, 248, 252–3, 256, 306, and 552.
Skórzewska, Joanna A. *Constructing a Cult: The Life and Veneration of
    Guðmundr Arason (1161–1237) in the Icelandic Written Sources* (Leiden:
    Brill, 2011). Pp. 26, 263, and 266.

Stéfan Einarsson. "Íslenzk helgikvæði á miðöldum." *Tímarit Þjóðræknisfélags Íslendinga* 36 (1955): 43–63, esp. pp. 49–50.
– *Íslensk bókmenntasaga 874–1960* (Reykjavík: Oddi, 1961). P. 87.
Stefán Karlsson. "Guðmundar sögur biskups: Authorial Viewpoints and Methods." In *The Sixth International Saga Conference 28/7–2/8 1985. Workshop Papers*. 2 vols. ([Copenhagen]: Det arnamagnæanske Institut, 1985). Vol. 2, pp. 983–1005, esp. p. 999.
– "Guðmundar sögur biskups." In >> *Medieval Scandinavia: An Encyclopedia* (1993). Pp. 245–6, esp. p. 246.
Thorkelsson, J. "Bemærkninger til nogle Steder i Versene i Guðmundar saga ved Abbed Arngrim." *Oversigt over det Kongelige Danske Videnskabs Selskabs Forhandlinger* 2 (1883): 93–104, esp. pp. 101–4.
Vésteinn Ólason. "Kveðskapur frá síðmiðöldum." In >> *Íslensk Bókmenntasaga* 2 (1993). Pp. 283–378, esp. pp. 289, 299, and 315.
"Old Icelandic Poetry." In *A History of Icelandic Literature*. Ed. Daisy Neijmann. Histories of Scandinavian Literature 5 (Lincoln: University of Nebraska Press, 2006). Pp. 1–64, esp. p. 47.
Viðar Pálsson. "Pagan Mythology in Christian Society." *Gripla* 19 (2008): 123–58, esp. pp. 139–40.

2. Guðmundardrápa

A fragment of a poem in praise of Bishop Guðmundr Arason by Arngrímr (Brandsson?) (d. 1361 or 1362).

Incipit: "Leysti, lýð sá er fǫstur lætr jafnan vel gæta."

Manuscript:
Stock. Perg. fol. no. 5 (ca. 1350–65).

Editions:
Finnur Jónsson, ed. >> *Den norsk-islandske skjaldedigtning* (1912–15). Vol. AII, pp. 362–3 and vol. BII, pp. 389–90.
Guðni Jónsson, ed. >> *Byskupa sögur* (1948). Vol. 3, pp. 231–2, 243, and 473–4.
Based on *Biskupa sögur* (1858–78).
Jón Helgason, ed. *Byskupa sǫgur. MS Perg. fol. No. 5 in the Royal Library of Stockholm.* CCI 19 (Copenhagen: Ejnar Munksgaard, 1950).
[Jón Sigurðsson and Guðbrandur Vigfússon, ed.] >> *Biskupa sögur* (1858–78). Vol. 2, pp. 43, 49–50, and 172–3.
Kock, Ernst Albin, ed. >> *Den norsk-isländska skaldediktningen* (1946–50). Vol. 2, pp. 211–12.

Danish translation:
Finnur Jónsson, ed. >> *Den norsk-islandske skjaldedigtning* (1912–15).
  Vol. BII, pp. 371–89.
Literature:
Björn Sigfússon. "Guðmundar saga biskups Arasonar." *KLNM* 5 (1960).
  Cols. 542–3, esp. col. 543.
Cormack, Margaret. >> *The Saints in Iceland* (1994). Pp. 42 and 99.
– "Poetry, Paganism and the Sagas of Icelandic Bishops." In >> *Til heiðurs
  og hugbótar* (2003). Pp. 33–51, esp. pp. 48–9.
Finnur Jónsson. >> *Den oldnorske og oldislandske Litteraturs Historie*
  (1920–4). Vol. 3, pp. 8–9.
Guðbrandur Jónsson. "Arngrímur ábóti Brandsson og bróðir Eysteinn
  Ásgrímsson." *Saga* 1 (1949–53): 394–469, esp. pp. 455–6.
Holtsmark, Anne. "Lovkvad." *KLNM* 10 (1965). Cols. 700–4, esp. col. 702.
Jakob Benediktsson. "Helgendigte." *KLNM* 6 (1961). Cols. 318–21, esp.
  col. 319.
– >> "Helgikvæði." In *Hugtök og heiti í bókmenntafræði* (1983). Pp. 115–17,
  esp. p. 116.
Jón Þórarinsson. *Íslensk tónlistarsaga 1000–1800* (Reykjavík: Tónlistarsafn
  Íslands, 2012). P. 146.
Kahle, Bernhard. "Das Christentum in der altwestnordischen Dichtung." *ANF*
  13 (1901): 1–40 and 97–160, esp. p. 18.
Orgland, Ivar, trans. *Islandske Dikt. Frå Sólarljóð til opplysningstid (13.
  hundreåret–1835)* (Reykjavík: Fonna, 1977). Pp. 26 and 35–6.
Skórzewska, Joanna A. *Constructing a Cult: The Life and Veneration of
  Guðmundr Arason (1161–1237) in the Icelandic Written Sources* (Leiden:
  Brill, 2011). P. 264.
Stéfan Einarsson. "Íslenzk helgikvæði á miðöldum." *Tímarit Þjóðræknisfélags
  Íslendinga* 36 (1955): 43–63, esp. pp. 49–50.
– *Íslensk bókmenntasaga 874–1960* (Reykjavík: Oddi, 1961). P. 87.
Thorkelsson, J. "Bemærkninger til nogle Steder i Versene i Guðmundar saga
  ved Abbed Arngrim." *Oversigt over det Kongelige Danske Videnskabs
  Selskabs Forhandlinger* 2 (1883): 93–104, esp. pp. 96 and 99.
Vésteinn Ólason. "Kveðskapur frá síðmiðöldum." In >> *Íslensk
  Bókmenntasaga* 2 (1993). Pp. 283–378, esp. pp. 261, 289, and 299.
– "Old Icelandic Poetry." In *A History of Icelandic Literature*. Ed. Daisy
  Neijmann. Histories of Scandinavian Literature 5 (Lincoln: University
  of Nebraska Press, 2006). Pp. 1–64, esp. pp. 47 and 51.
Viðar Pálsson. "Pagan Mythology in Christian Society." *Gripla* 19 (2008):
  123–58, esp. pp. 139–40.

3. Guðmundarkvæði

A fourteenth-century poem in praise of Bishop Guðmundr Arason by Einarr
Gilsson (d. 1369).

Manuscripts:
AM 396 4to (ca. 1350–1400) and Stock. Perg. fol. no. 5 (ca. 1350–65).
  Incipit: "Fæddr var ǫlr, sá er eyddi alnýtr fira lýtum."
Editions:
Finnur Jónsson, ed. >> *Den norsk-islandske skjaldedigtning* (1912–15).
  Vol. AII, pp. 397–404 and vol. BII, pp. 418–29.
  Stz. 1–2 and 4^{2-8} based on AM 396 4to; stz. 3, 4^1; stz. 4^{2-8} and 5–40 based
  on Stock. Perg. fol. no. 5 with variants from AM 396 4to to stz. 4^{2-8}–13 and
  23–31.
Guðni Jónsson, ed. >> *Byskupa sögur* (1948). Vol. 3, pp. 164, 174–9, 182–4,
  186–9, 404–5, 469–71, and 476–8.
  Based on *Biskupa sögur* (1858–78).
Jón Helgason, ed. *Byskupa sǫgur. MS Perg. fol. No. 5 in the Royal Library
  of Stockholm.* CCI 19 (Copenhagen: Ejnar Munksgaard, 1950).
  Facsimile of Stock. Perg. fol. no. 5.
[Jón Sigurðsson and Guðbrandur Vigfússon, ed.] >> *Biskupa sögur* (1858–
  78). Vol. 2, pp. 7, 12–15, 17–20, 22, 127–8, 135–6, 170–1, and 174–6.
  Based on AM 396 4to and Stock. Perg. fol. no. 5.
Kock, Ernst Albin, ed. >> *Notationes Norrœna* (1923–44). §§893, 1497,
  1535, 1536, 1537, 1538, 1539, 1540, 1541, 1542, 1543, 1544, 2496, 2497,
  2529, 2622C, 2635, 2636, 2637, 2638, 2995D, 3277B, 3320, 3321, 3322,
  and 3323.
– ed. >> *Den norsk-isländska skaldediktningen* (1946–50). Vol. 2, pp. 229–34.
Wolf, Kirsten, ed. "Einarr Gilsson, *Guðmundarkvæði* 'Poem about
  Guðmundr'." In *Poetry on Icelandic History.* Ed. Guðrún Nordal. *Scaldic
  Poetry of the Middle Ages* (Turnhout: Brepols). [Forthcoming.]
  Stz. 1–2 and 4^{2-8} based on AM 396 4to; stz. 3, 4^1; stz. 4^{2-8} and 5–40 based
  on Stock. Perg. fol. no. 5 with variants from AM 396 4to to stz. 4^{2-8}–13 and
  23–31.
Danish translation:
Finnur Jónsson, ed. >> *Den norsk-islandske skjaldedigtningz* (1912–15).
  Vol. BII, pp. 418–29.
English translation:
Wolf, Kirsten, ed. "Einarr Gilsson, *Guðmundarkvæði* 'Poem about
  Guðmundr'." In *Poetry on Icelandic History.* Ed. Guðrún Nordal. *Scaldic
  Poetry of the Middle Ages* (Turnhout: Brepols). [Forthcoming.]

Literature:

Chase, Martin. "Christian Poetry: West Norse." In >> *Medieval Scandinavia: An Encyclopedia* (1993). Pp. 73–7, esp. p. 76.

Clunies Ross, Margaret. "Christian Skaldic Rhetoric in Einarr Gilsson's *Selkolluvísur*." In *Scandinavian and Christian Europe in the Middle Ages. Papers of the 12th International Saga Conference. Bonn/Germany, 28th July–2nd August 2003*. Ed. Rudolf Simek and Judith Meurer (Bonn: Hausdruckerei der Universität Bonn, 2003). Pp. 90–8, esp. p. 90.

Cormack, Margaret. >> *The Saints in Iceland* (1994). Pp. 42, 99, and 142.

– "Poetry, Paganism and the Sagas of Icelandic Bishops." In >> *Til heiðurs og hugbótar* (2003). Pp. 33–51, esp. p. 48.

– "Christian Biography." In *A Companion to Old Norse–Icelandic Literature and Culture*. Ed. Rory McTurk (Oxford: Blackwell, 2005). Pp. 27–42, esp. pp. 38–9.

Finnur Jónsson. >> *Den oldnorske og oldislandske Litteraturs Historie* (1920–4). Vol. 3, p. 13.

Guðrún Nordal. *Tools of Literacy: The Role of Skaldic Verse in Icelandic Textual Culture of the Twelfth and Thirteenth Centuries* (Toronto: University of Toronto Press, 2001). Pp. 101, 108, 292, 331, 377n18, and 382n46.

Holtsmark, Anne. "Lovkvad." *KLNM* 10 (1965). Cols. 700–70, esp. col. 702.

Jakob Benediktsson. "Helgendigte." *KLNM* 6 (1961). Cols. 318–21, esp. cols. 319–20.

– >> "Helgikvæði." In *Hugtök og heiti í bókmenntafræði* (1983). Pp. 115–17, esp. p. 116.

Jón Helgason. >> "Norges og Islands digtning." In *Litteraturhistorie B: Norge og Island* (1953). Pp. 3–179, esp. p. 161.

Jón Þorkelsson. >> *Om digtningen på Island* (1888). P. 27.

Kahle, Bernhard. "Das Christentum in der altwestnordischen Dichtung." *ANF* 13 (1901): 1–40 and 97–160, esp. p. 8.

Mogk, Eugen. >> *Geschichte der norwegisch-isländischen Literatur* (1904). Pp. 715 and 794.

Ólafur Lárusson. "Guðmundur góði í þjóðtrú Íslendinga." *Skírnir* 116 (1942): 113–39, esp. pp. 117 and 124–5.

Poole, R.G. *Viking Poems on War and Peace: A Study in Skaldic Narrative* (Toronto: University of Toronto Press, 1991). P. 30.

Schottmann, Hans. >> *Die isländische Mariendichtung* (1973). Pp. 252 and 256.

Skórzewska, Joanna A. *Constructing a Cult: The Life and Veneration of Guðmundr Arason (1161–1237) in the Icelandic Written Sources* (Leiden: Brill, 2011). Pp. 57, 145, 263, and 265–6.

Stéfan Einarsson. "Íslenzk helgikvæði á miðöldum." *Tímarit Þjóðræknisfélags Íslendinga* 36 (1955): 43–63, esp. p. 49.

Stefán Karlsson. "Guðmundar sögur biskups." In >> *Medieval Scandinavia: An Encyclopedia* (1993). Pp. 245–6, esp. p. 246.

Thorkelsson, J. "Bemærkninger til nogle Steder i Versene i Guðmundar saga ved Abbed Arngrim." *Oversigt over det Kongelige Danske Videnskabs Selskabs Forhandlinger* 2 (1883): 93–104, esp. pp. 93–4, 97–9, and 100.

Vésteinn Ólason. "Kveðskapur frá síðmiðöldum: Trúarkvæði." In >> *Íslensk Bókmenntasaga* 2 (1993). Pp. 283–378, esp. pp. 299 and 315.

– "Old Icelandic Poetry." In *A History of Icelandic Literature*. Ed. Daisy Neijmann. Histories of Scandinavian Literature 5 (Lincoln: University of Nebraska Press, 2006). Pp. 1–64, esp. pp. 47 and 56.

Viðar Pálsson. "Pagan Mythology in Christian Society." *Gripla* 19 (2008): 123–58, esp. pp. 139–40.

Vries, Jan de. >> *Altnordische Literaturgeschichte* (1964–7). Vol. 1, p. 201n240 and vol. 2, p. 522.

4. Vísur um Guðmund biskup

A fourteenth-century poem in praise of Bishop Guðmundr Arason by Einarr Gilsson (d. 1369).

Incipit: "Frétt hefir ǫld, at sækir sótti sóttalaus at vilja dróttins."

Manuscripts:
AM 396 4to (ca. 1350–1400) and Stock. Perg. fol. no. 5 (ca. 1350–65).

Editions:
Finnur Jónsson, ed. >> *Den norsk-islandske skjaldedigtning* (1912–15). Vol. AII, pp. 404–8 and vol. BII, pp. 429–34.
Edition of AM 396 4to.

Guðni Jónsson, ed. >> *Byskupa sögur* (1948). Vol. 3, pp. 335–43.
Based on *Biskupa sögur* (1858–78).

Jón Helgason, ed. *Byskupa sǫgur. MS Perg. fol. No. 5 in the Royal Library of Stockholm*. CCI 19 (Copenhagen: Ejnar Munksgaard, 1950).
Facsimile of Stock. Perg. fol. no. 5.

[Jón Sigurðsson and Guðbrandur Vigfússon, ed.] >> *Biskupa sögur* (1858–78). Vol. 2, pp. 99–103.
Edition of AM 396 4to.

Kock, Ernst Albin, ed. >> *Notationes Norrœna* (1923–44). §§1513, 1545B, 1546, 1547, 1548, 1549, 2639, 2639Anm, 2640, 2641, 2845, 2995D, 3097H, 3324, 3326, 3327.

– ed. >> *Den norsk-isländska skaldediktningen* (1946–50). Vol. 2, pp. 234–7.
Wolf, Kirsten, ed. "Einarr Gilsson, *Guðmundarkvæði* 'Poem about
   Guðmundr'." In *Poetry on Icelandic History*. Ed. Guðrún Nordal. *Scaldic
   Poetry of the Middle Ages* (Turnhout: Brepols). [Forthcoming.]
   Based on Stock. Perg. fol. no. 5 with variants from AM 396 4to.
Danish translation:
Finnur Jónsson, ed. >> *Den norsk-islandske skjaldedigtning* (1912–15).
   Vol. BII, pp. 429–34.
English translation:
Wolf, Kirsten, ed. "Einarr Gilsson, *Guðmundarkvæði* 'Poem about
   Guðmundr'." In *Poetry on Icelandic History*. Ed. Guðrún Nordal. *Scaldic
   Poetry of the Middle Ages* (Turnhout: Brepols). [Forthcoming.]
Literature:
Chase, Martin. "Christian Poetry: West Norse." In >> *Medieval Scandinavia:
   An Encyclopedia* (1993). Pp. 73–7, esp. p. 76.
Clunies Ross, Margaret. "Christian Skaldic Rhetoric in Einarr Gilsson's
   Selkolluvísur." In *Scandinavian and Christian Europe in the Middle
   Ages. Papers of the 12th International Saga Conference. Bonn/Germany,
   28th July–2nd August 2003*. Ed. Rudolf Simek and Judith Meurer (Bonn:
   Hausdruckerei der Universität Bonn, 2003). Pp. 90–8, esp. p. 90.
Cormack, Margaret. >> *The Saints in Iceland* (1994). Pp. 42, 99, and 142.
– "Poetry, Paganism and the Sagas of Icelandic Bishops." In >> *Til heiðurs
   og hugbótar* (2003). Pp. 33–51, esp. p. 48.
– "Christian Biography." In *A Companion to Old Norse–Icelandic Literature
   and Culture*. Ed. Rory McTurk (Oxford: Blackwell, 2005). Pp. 27–42, esp.
   pp. 38–9.
Finnur Jónsson. >> *Den oldnorske og oldislandske Litteraturs Historie*
   (1920–4). Vol. 3, p. 13.
Holtsmark, Anne. "Lovkvad." *KLNM* 10 (1965). Cols. 700–4, esp. col. 702.
Jakob Benediktsson. "Helgendigte." *KLNM* 6 (1961). Cols. 318–21, esp. cols.
   319–20.
– >> "Helgikvæði." In *Hugtök og heiti í bókmenntafræði* (1983). Pp. 115–17,
   esp. p. 116.
Jón Helgason. >> "Norges og Islands digtning." In *Litteraturhistorie B:
   Norge og Island* (1953). Pp. 3–179, esp. p. 161.
Jón Þorkelsson. >> *Om digtningen på Island* (1888). P. 27.
Konráð Gíslason. "Om helrim i förste og tredje linie af regelmæssigt
   'drottkvætt' og 'hrynhenda'." *Indbydelsesskrift til Kjøbenhavns
   Universitets Aarsfest til Erindring om Kirkens Reformation* (Copenhagen:
   Schultz, 1877). Pp. 1–60, esp. p. 3.

Mogk, Eugen. >> *Geschichte der norwegisch-isländischen Literatur* (1904).
Pp. 715 and 794.

Poole, R.G. *Viking Poems on War and Peace: A Study in Skaldic Narrative*
(Toronto: University of Toronto Press, 1991). P. 30.

Schottmann, Hans. >> *Die isländische Mariendichtung* (1973). P. 252 and
256.

Skórzewska, Joanna A. *Constructing a Cult: The Life and Veneration of
Guðmundr Arason (1161–1237) in the Icelandic Written Sources* (Leiden:
Brill, 2011). Pp. 265–6.

Stéfan Einarsson. "Íslenzk helgikvæði á miðöldum." *Tímarit Þjóðræknisfélags
Íslendinga* 36 (1955): 43–63, esp. p. 49.

Stefán Karlsson. "Guðmundar sögur biskups." In >> *Medieval Scandinavia:
An Encyclopedia* (1993). Pp. 245–6, esp. p. 246.

Vésteinn Ólason. "Kveðskapur frá síðmiðöldum." In >> *Íslensk
Bókmenntasaga* 2 (1993). Pp. 283–378, esp. pp. 299 and 315.

– "Old Icelandic Poetry." In *A History of Icelandic Literature*. Ed. Daisy
Neijmann. Histories of Scandinavian Literature 5 (Lincoln: University
of Nebraska Press, 2006). Pp. 1–64, esp. p. 47.

Viðar Pálsson. "Pagan Mythology in Christian Society." *Gripla* 19 (2008):
123–58, esp. pp. 139–40.

Vries, Jan de. >> *Altnordische Literaturgeschichte* (1964–7). Vol. 2, p. 522.

5. Selkolluvísur

A fourteenth-century poem by Einarr Gilsson (d. 1369) narrating one of Bishop
Guðmundr Arason's miracles.

Incipit: "Askr fór éls ok Rǫskva ósvinn dalar tvinna."

Manuscripts:
AM 396 4to (ca. 1350–1400) and Stock. Perg. fol. no. 5 (ca. 1350–65).
Editions:
Finnur Jónsson, ed. >> *Den norsk-islandske skjaldedigtning* (1912–15).
Vol. AII, pp. 408–11 and vol. BII, pp. 434–40.
Edition of Stock. Perg. fol. no. 5 with variants from AM 396 4to.

Jón Helgason, ed. *Byskupa sǫgur. MS Perg. fol. No. 5 in the Royal Library
of Stockholm.* CCI 19 (Copenhagen: Ejnar Munksgaard, 1950).
Facsimile of Stock. Perg. fol. no. 5.

Kock, Ernst Albin, ed. >> *Notationes Norrœna* (1923–44). §§188, 1533,
1550, 1551, 1552, 1554, 1555, 1556, 1557, 2642, 2643, 2644, 2645, 2764,
2995D, 3014C, 3313, 3328, 3329, and 3397G.

– ed. >> *Den norsk-isländska skaldediktningen* (1946–50). Vol. 2, pp. 237–40.

Danish translation:
Finnur Jónsson, ed. >> *Den norsk-islandske skjaldedigtning* (1912–15). Vol. BII, pp. 434–40.

English translation:
Clunies Ross, Margaret. "Christian Skaldic Rhetoric in Einarr Gilsson's *Selkolluvísur*." In *Scandinavian and Christian Europe in the Middle Ages. Papers of the 12th International Saga Conference. Bonn/Germany, 28th July–2nd August 2003*. Ed. Rudolf Simek and Judith Meurer (Bonn: Hausdruckerei der Universität Bonn, 2003). Pp. 90–8, esp. pp. 92–3 (extract only).

Literature:
Chase, Martin. "Christian Poetry: West Norse." In >> *Medieval Scandinavia: An Encyclopedia* (1993). Pp. 73–7, esp. p. 76.

Clunies Ross, Margaret. >> *A History of Old Norse Poetry and Poetics* (2005). P. 213.

Cormack, Margaret. >> *The Saints in Iceland* (1994). Pp. 42 and 99.

– "Poetry, Paganism and the Sagas of Icelandic Bishops." In >> *Til heiðurs og hugbótar* (2003). Pp. 33–51, esp. p. 48.

Falk, Hjalmar. "Skjaldesprogets Kjenninger." *ANF* 39 (1923): 59–89, esp. p. 80.

Finnur Jónsson. >> *Den oldnorske og oldislandske Litteraturs Historie* (1920–4). Vol. 3, p. 13.

Guðrún Nordal. *Tools of Literacy: The Role of Skaldic Verse in Icelandic Textual Culture of the Twelfth and Thirteenth Centuries* (Toronto: University of Toronto Press, 2001). P. 386n66.

Holtsmark, Anne. "Lovkvad." *KLNM* 10 (1965). Cols. 700–4, esp. col. 702.

Jakob Benediktsson. "Helgendigte." *KLNM* 6 (1961). Cols. 318–21, esp. col. 319.

– >> "Helgikvæði." In *Hugtök og heiti í bókmenntafræði* (1983). Pp. 115–17, esp. p. 116.

Kahle, Bernhard. "Das Christentum in der altwestnordischen Dichtung." *ANF* 13 (1901): 1–40 and 97–160, esp. pp. 108, 111, 114, 117, and 146.

Mogk, Eugen. >> *Geschichte der norwegisch-isländischen Literatur* (1904). P. 715.

Skórzewska, Joanna A. *Constructing a Cult: The Life and Veneration of Guðmundr Arason (1161–1237) in the Icelandic Written Sources* (Leiden: Brill, 2011). Pp. 265–6.

Vries, Jan de. >> *Altnordische Literaturgeschichte* (1964–7). Vol. 2, p. 522.

6. Guðmundardrápa

A poem in praise of Bishop Guðmundr Arason by Abbot Árni Jónsson (alive in 1379).

Incipit: "Almáttugr sé dýrðar drottinn, dyggr ok bjartr í mínu hjarta."

Manuscripts:
AM 398 4to (ca. 1600–1700), AM 713 4to (ca. 1500–50), and AM 721 4to (ca. 1500–50).

Editions:
Finnur Jónsson, ed. >> *Den norsk-islandske skjaldedigtning* (1912–15). Vol. AII, pp. 412–30 and vol. BII, pp. 440–61.
Edition of AM 398 4to with variants from AM 713 4to and AM 721 4to.

[Jón Sigurðsson and Guðbrandur Vigfússon, ed.] >> *Biskupa sögur* (1858–78). Vol. 2, pp. 202–20.
Based on AM 398 4to, AM 713 4to, and AM 721 4to.

Kock, Ernst Albin, ed. >> *Notationes Norrœna* (1923–44). §§1558, 1559, 1560, 1562, 1562, 1563, 1564, 1565, 1969E, 2622, 2622C, 2631, 2646, 2647, 2648, 2649, 2724, 2764, 2843, 2846, 2847, 2849, 2972, 2995E, 3330, 3331, 3332, 3333, 3334, 3335, 3336, and 3337.

– ed. >> *Den norsk-isländska skaldediktningen* (1946–50). Vol. 2, pp. 240–54.

Sveinbjörn Egilsson, ed. *Fjøgur gømul kvæði. Boðsrit til að hlusta á þá opinberu yfirheyrslu í Bessastaða Skóla þann 22–29 mai 1844* (Viðeyjarklaustur: Helgi Helgason, 1844). Pp. IX.
Edition of AM 713 4to.

Danish translation:
Finnur Jónsson, ed. >> *Den norsk-islandske skjaldedigtning* (1912–15). Vol. BII, pp. 440–61.

Literature:
Chase, Martin. "Christian Poetry: West Norse." In >> *Medieval Scandinavia: An Encyclopedia* (1993). Pp. 73–7, esp. p. 76.

Clunies Ross, Margaret. >> *A History of Old Norse Poetry and Poetics* (2005). Pp. 230–1.

Cormack, Margaret. >> *The Saints in Iceland* (1994). Pp. 42 and 99.

– "Poetry, Paganism and the Sagas of Icelandic Bishops." In >> *Til heiðurs og hugbótar* (2003). Pp. 33–51, esp. pp. 48–50.

– "Christian Biography." In *A Companion to Old Norse–Icelandic Literature and Culture*. Ed. Rory McTurk (Oxford: Blackwell, 2005). Pp. 27–42, esp. pp. 38–9.

Faulkes, Anthony. "Edda." *Gripla* 2 (1977): 32–9, esp. p. 34n11.

Finnur Jónsson. >> *Den oldnorske og oldislandske Litteraturs Historie* (1920–4). Vol. 3, pp. 14–15.

Foote, Peter. "Latin Rhetoric and Icelandic Poetry: Some Contacts." In *Aurvandilstá: Norse Studies*. Ed. Michael Barnes, Hans Bekker-Nielsen, and Gerd Wolfgang Weber. Viking Collection 2 (Odense: Odense University Press, 1984). Pp. 249–70, esp. p. 265n42.

Gade, Kari Ellen. *The Structure of Old Norse Dróttkvætt Poetry*. Islandica 49 (Ithaca and London: Cornell University Press, 1995). P. 245.

Guðrún Nordal. *Tools of Literacy: The Role of Skaldic Verse in Icelandic Textual Culture of the Twelfth and Thirteenth Centuries* (Toronto: University of Toronto Press, 2001). Pp. 108 and 377n16.

Holtsmark, Anne. "Lovkvad." *KLNM* 10 (1965). Cols. 700–4, esp. col. 702.

Jakob Benediktsson. "Helgendigte." *KLNM* 6 (1961). Cols. 318–21, esp. cols. 319–20.

– >> "Helgikvæði." In *Hugtök og heiti í bókmenntafræði* (1983). Pp. 115–17, esp. p. 116.

Jón Helgason. "Nokkur íslenzk handrit frá 16. öld." *Skírnir* 106 (1932): 143–68.

– >> "Norges og Islands digtning." In *Litteraturhistorie B: Norge og Island* (1953). Pp. 3–179, esp. p. 161.

Jón Þorkelsson. >> *Om digtningen på Island* (1888). P. 27.

Kahle, Bernhard. "Das Christentum in der altwestnordischen Dichtung." *ANF* 13 (1901): 1–40 and 97–160, esp. pp. 11, 18, 20, 27, 30–1, 98–100, 103, 105–8, 110–18, 121–4, 126–9, 137, 148, and 150–2.

Konráð Gíslason. "Om helrim i förste og tredje linie af regelmæssigt 'drottkvætt' og 'hrynhenda'." *Indbydelsesskrift til Kjøbenhavns Universitets Aarsfest til Erindring om Kirkens Reformation* (Copenhagen: Schultz, 1877). Pp. 1–60, esp. pp. 25, 28, 30, and 52.

Kuhn, Hans. *Das Dróttkvætt* (Heidelberg: Carl Winter Universitätsverlag, 1983). P. 330.

Lange, Wolfgang. >> *Studien zur christlichen Dichtung der Nordgermanen 1000–1200* (1958). Pp. 228, 263, and 273–4.

Lie, Hallvard. "Skaldestil-studier." *Mm* (1952): 1–92, esp. pp. 78–9.

Lindow, John. "Narrative and the Nature of Skaldic Poetry." *ANF* 97 (1982): 94–121, esp. pp. 102 and 117–18.

Mogk, Eugen. >> *Geschichte der norwegisch-isländischen Literatur* (1904). Pp. 715 and 719.

Ólafur Lárusson. "Guðmundur góði í þjóðtrú Íslendinga." *Skírnir* 116 (1942): 113–39, esp. pp. 117 and 128–9.

Orgland, Ivar, trans. *Islandske Dikt. Frå Sólarljóð til opplysningstid (13. hundreåret–1835)* (Reykjavík: Fonna, 1977). P. 35.

Schottmann, Hans. >> *Die isländische Mariendichtung* (1973). Pp. 42, 49n8, 54n19, 59, 68–9, 82–3, 206n18, 238–9, 253–6, 306, and 552.

Skórzewska, Joanna A. *Constructing a Cult: The Life and Veneration of Guðmundr Arason (1161–1237) in the Icelandic Written Sources* (Leiden: Brill, 2011). Pp. 263–4 and 266.

Stéfan Einarsson. "Íslenzk helgikvæði á miðöldum." *Tímarit Þjóðræknisfélags Íslendinga* 36 (1955): 43–63, esp. p. 49.

Vésteinn Ólason. "Kveðskapur frá síðmiðöldum." In >> *Íslensk Bókmenntasaga* 2 (1993). Pp. 283–378, esp. pp. 299 and 315.

– "Old Icelandic Poetry." In *A History of Icelandic Literature*. Ed. Daisy Neijmann. Histories of Scandinavian Literature 5 (Lincoln: University of Nebraska Press, 2006). Pp. 1–64, esp. pp. 47 and 51.

Viðar Pálsson. "Pagan Mythology in Christian Society." *Gripla* 19 (2008): 123–58, esp. pp. 139–40.

Vries, Jan de. >> *Altnordische Literaturgeschichte* (1964–7). Vol. 2, p. 522.

7. Lausavísur

Stz. 1, 4, and 6 of Kolbeinn Tumasson's *lausavísur* (1173–1208) mention Bishop Guðmundr Arason.

Manuscripts:
These include: AM 114 fol. (ca. 1640), AM 122a fol. (*Króksfjarðarbók*) (ca. 1350–70), AM 396 4to (ca. 1350–1400), AM 399 4to (ca. 1300–50), AM 440 4to (ca. 1650), AM 657c 4to (ca. 1350–1400), NKS 1234 fol. (ca. 1700–50), Stock. Papp. fol. no. 8 (ca. 1650), and Stock. Perg. fol. no. 5 (ca. 1350–65).

Editions:
Finnur Jónsson, ed. >> *Den norsk-islandske skjaldedigtning* (1912–15). Vol. AII, pp. 38–9 and vol. BII, pp. 47–8.
Stz. based on AM 122a fol. with variants from AM 114 fol., AM 440 4to, NKS 1234 fol., and Stock Papp. fol. no. 8; stz. 2 based on AM 122a fol. with variants from AM 114 fol., AM 440 4to, NKS 1234 fol., and Stock. Papp. fol. no. 8; stz. 3 based on AM 396 4to with variants from AM 657c 4to and Stock. Papp. fol. no. 5.

Kock, Ernst Albin, ed. >> *Notationes Norrœna* (1923–44). §1285.

– ed. >> *Den norsk-isländska skaldediktningen* (1946–50). Vol. 2, pp. 29–30.

Kock, Ernst Albin, and R. Meissner, ed. *Skaldisches Lesebuch*. 2 vols.
Rheinische Beiträge und Hilfbücher zur germanischen Philologie und
Volkskunde 17 (Halle am S: Max Niemeyer, 1931). Vol. 1, p. 82.
Jón Sigurðsson and Guðbrandur Vigfússon, ed. >> *Biskupa sögur* (1858–78).
Vol. 1, pp. 490–1; vol. 2, pp. 62–3.
Danish translation:
Finnur Jónsson, ed. >> *Den norsk-islandske skjaldedigtning* (1912–15).
Vol. BII, pp. 47–8.
Literature:
Chase, Martin. "Christian Poetry: West Norse." In >> *Medieval Scandinavia:
An Encyclopedia* (1993). Pp. 73–7, esp. p. 76.

HALLVARD   May 14

1. Kvæði um sankti Hallvarð

A poem, possibly fragmentary, in honour of Saint Hallvard probably composed
ca. 1400–1550 and then recorded from oral tradition during Árni Magnússon's
time.
Incipit: "Vébjörn nefni ég bónda þann."

Manuscripts:
AM 670l 4to (ca. 1700–25), Lbs 848 4to (ca. 1700–1900), Lbs 936 4to
(ca. 1880), Lbs 2166 4to (ca. 1885–1920), and Lbs 201 8vo (ca. 1850–70).
Editions:
Jón Helgason, ed. >> *Íslenzk miðaldakvæði* (1936–8). Vol. 2, pp. 364–6.
Edition of AM 670l 4to.
Jón Þorkelsson. >> *Om Digtningen på Island* (1888). Pp. 31–3.
Edition of AM 670l 4to.
Vésteinn Ólason, ed. *Sagnadansar*. Íslensk rit gefin út af Rannsóknarstofnun
í bókmenntafræði við Háskóla Íslands (Reykjavík: Prentsmiðja
Hafnarfjarðar,1979). Pp. 302–5.
Literature:
Bjarni Þorsteinsson, ed. *Íslenzk þjóðlög* (Copenhagen: Møller, 1960–9).
P. 119.
Finnur Jónsson. >> *Den oldnorske og oldislandske Litteraturs Historie*
(1920–4). Vol. 3, p. 126.
Gjerløw, Lilli. "Hallvard." *KLNM* 6 (1961). Cols. 63–6, esp. col. 65.

Jakob Benediktsson. "Helgendigte." *KLNM* 6 (1961). Cols. 318–21, esp.
col. 320.

Jón Helgason. >> "Norges og Islands digtning." In *Litteraturhistorie B:
Norge og Island* (1953). Pp. 3–179, esp. pp. 163–4.

Kock, E.A. "Anteckningar till Íslenzk Miðaldakvæði." *ANF* 61 (1946): 1–125,
esp. pp. 85 and 95.

Mogk, Eugen. >> *Geschichte der norwegisch-isländischen Literatur* (1904).
P. 718.

Stéfan Einarsson. "Íslenzk helgikvæði á miðöldum." *Tímarit Þjóðræknisfélags
Íslendinga* 36 (1955): 43–63, esp. p. 55.

– *Íslenzk bókmenntasaga 874–1960* (Reykjavík: Oddi, 1961). Pp. 92–3
and 117.

Vésteinn Ólason. *The Traditional Ballads of Iceland* (Reykjavík: Stofnun
Árna Magnússonar, 1982). Pp. 373–5.

– "Kveðskapur frá síðmiðöldum." In >> *Íslensk Bókmenntasaga* 2 (1993).
Pp. 283–378, esp. p. 317.

2. Heilagra manna drápa

A fourteenth-century poem about holy men. Stz. 22–3 treat Saint Hallvard.
Incipit: "... mildings f ... um dyrnar þustu ... særa."

Manuscripts:
See Blase note (p. 52).
Editions:
Finnur Jónsson, ed. >> *Den norsk-islandske skjaldedigtning* (1912–15).
Vol. AII, pp. 515–16 and vol. BII, p. 568.

Kahle, Bernhard, ed. >> *Isländische geistliche Dichtungen des ausgehenden
Mittelalters* (1898). P. 95.

Kock, Ernst Albin, ed. >> *Notationes Norrænæ* (1923–44). §§3379 and 3381.
– ed. >> *Den norsk-islandske skaldediktningen* (1946–50). Vol. 2, pp. 311–12.

Wolf, Kirsten, ed. "Anonymous, *Heilagra manna drápa* 'Drápa about Holy
Men'." In >> *Poetry on Christian Subjects* (2007). Vol. 2, pp. 887–8.
Danish translation:
Finnur Jónsson, ed. >> *Den norsk-islandske skjaldedigtning* (1912–15).
Vol. BII, p. 568.
English translation:
Wolf, Kirsten, ed. "Anonymous, *Heilagra manna drápa* 'Drápa about Holy
Men'." In >> *Poetry on Christian Subjects* (2007). Vol. 2, pp. 887–8.

HELENA   August 18

1. Helenukvæði

A sixteenth-century poem in honour of Constantine the Great and his mother, Saint Helena.

Incipit: "Konstantínus keisarinn eini."

Manuscripts:
ÍB 183 4to (ca. 1750), ÍB 816 8vo (ca. 1600–1900), ÍBR 74 4to (1782), JS
258 4to (ca. 1840–5), JS 588 4to (ca. 1800–1900), JS 473 8vo (ca. 1675–
1900), JS 515 8vo (ca. 1675–1900), Lbs 3128 4to (ca. 1700–2000), Lbs
201 8vo (ca. 1850–70), Lbs 1228 8vo (ca. 1780), Lbs 1368 8vo (ca. 1750–
1900), Lbs 1730 8vo (ca. 1830), and SÁM 12 (1848).

Edition:
Jón Þorkelsson. >> *Om Digtningen på Island* (1888). P. 85 (stz. 1).

Literature:
Finnur Jónsson. >> *Bókmentasaga Íslendinga fram undir siðabót* (1904–5).
P. 461.

Mogk, Eugen. >> *Geschichte der norwegisch-isländischen Literatur* (1904).
P. 719.

2. Krosskvæði

A poetic rendering of the legend of the cross-tree from ca. 1400–1550. Stz. 31–4
concern Saint Helena.

Incipit: "Guð himnanna græðari manna."

Manuscripts:
See Cross, the Holy 5 note (p. 70).

Editions:
Jón Helgason, ed. >> *Íslenzk miðaldakvæði* (1936–8). Vol. 1.2, pp. 282–3.
*Peringskiöld, J.F. >> *Fragmentum runicopapisticum* (1721).

3. Gimsteinn

An early sixteenth-century poem about the cross-tree ascribed to the priest
Hallur Ögmundarson (d. ca. 1540). Stz. 88–96 concern Saint Helena.

Incipit: "Heyr mig ilmanda hjartans yndi."

Manuscripts:
See Cross, the Holy 7 note (p. 73).
Editions:
Jón Helgason, ed. >> *Íslenzk miðaldakvæði* (1936–8). Vol. 1.2, pp. 318–20.
Jón Þorkelsson, ed. >> *Kvæðasafn* (1922–7). Pp. 318–20.

IGNATIUS OF ANTIOCH   October 17

Ignatíuskvæði píslvarvotts

A sixteenth-century poem about Saint Ignatius of Antioch by a certain Ólafur.
   Incipit: "Heyrðu mig góða hugarins traust."

Manuscripts:
ÍB 633 8vo (ca. 1764–75), Lbs 2166 4to (ca. 1885–1920), Lbs 201 8vo
   (ca. 1850–70), and Lbs 1988 8vo (1790 and later).
Edition:
Jón Þorkelsson. >> *Om Digtningen på Island* (1888). P. 85 (stz. 1, 14^{6-8}, and 15).
   Based on ÍB 633 8vo and Lbs 201 8vo.

ISIDORE OF SEVILLE   April 4

Michaelsflokkur

An early sixteenth-century poem about Saint Michael ascribed to the priest Hallur
Ögmundarson (d. ca. 1540). Saint Isidore of Seville is mentioned in stz. 48.
   Incipit: "Óðar gef þú upphaf."

Manuscripts:
See Michael the Archangel 2 note (p. 256).
Edition:
Jón Þorkelsson, ed. >> *Kvæðasafn* (1922–7). P. 381.

JAMES THE GREATER   July 25

1. Jakobsdiktur

A late medieval (ca. 1400–1550) poem in honour of Saint James the Greater.

Incipit: "Prísa vildag prúðan dikt."

Manuscripts:
AM 721 4to (ca. 1500–50), AM 1032 4to (ca. 1700–25), and Lbs 2166 4to
 (ca. 1885–1920).
Editions:
Jón Helgason, ed. >> *Íslenzk miðaldakvæði* (1936–8). Vol. 2, pp. 313–16.
 Based on AM 721 4to with variants from AM 1032 4to.
Jón Þorkelsson. >> *Om Digtningen på Island* (1888). Pp. 66–7 (stz. 1).
 Based on AM 721 4to and AM 1032 4to.
Literature:
Finnur Jónsson. >> *Bókmentasaga Íslendinga fram undir siðabót* (1904–5).
 P. 461.
– >> *Den oldnorske og oldislandske Litteraturs Historie* (1920–4). Vol. 3,
 p. 126.
Jakob Benediktsson. "Helgendigte." *KLNM* 6 (1961). Cols. 318–21, esp.
 col. 320.
Stéfan Einarsson. "Íslenzk helgikvæði á miðöldum." *Tímarit Þjóðræknisfélags
 Íslendinga* 36 (1955): 43–63, esp. p. 54.
– *Íslensk bókmenntasaga 874–1960* (Reykjavík: Oddi, 1961). P. 91.
NOTE:
The poem contains material about Saint John the Evangelist. See his entry.

2. Allra postola minnisvísur

A fourteenth-century poem about all the apostles. Saint James the Greater is
treated in stz. 5.
 Incipit: "Pétr er páfi drottins prísaðr gleðivísum."

Manuscript:
See Andrew the Apostle 10 note (p. 30).
Editions:
Finnur Jónsson, ed. >> *Den norsk-islandske skjaldedigtning* (1912–15).
 Vol. AII, p. 510 and vol. BII, p. 560.
Jón Þorkelsson. >> *Om Digtningen på Island* (1888). P. 62 (stz. 1^2, 2^1, 3^1, 4^1,
 and 5^1).
Kock, Ernst Albin, ed. >> *Den norsk-isländska skaldediktningen* (1946–50).
 Vol. 2, p. 307.
McDougall, Ian, ed. "Anonymous, *Allra postula minnisvísur* 'Celebratory
 Vísur about All the Apostles'." In >> *Poetry on Christian Subjects* (2007).
 Vol. 2, p. 859.

Danish translation:
Finnur Jónsson, ed. >> *Den norsk-islandske skjaldedigtning* (1912–15).
  Vol. BII, p. 560.
English translation:
McDougall, Ian, ed. "Anonymous, *Allra postula minnisvísur* 'Celebratory
  Vísur about All the Apostles'." In >> *Poetry on Christian Subjects* (2007).
  Vol. 2, p. 859.

3. Tólf postula kvæði

A late medieval (ca. 1400–1550) celebratory poem about all the apostles. Saint
James the Greater is treated in stz. 9.
  Incipit: "Sankti Pétur sannur páfi í Róma."

Manuscripts:
See Andrew the Apostle 11 note (p. 31).
Edition:
Jón Helgason, ed. >> *Íslenzk miðaldakvæði* (1936–8). Vol. 2, p. 276.

4. Jóhannesdiktur

A late medieval (ca. 1400–1550) poem in honour of Saint John the Evangelist.
Stz. 2 mentions Saint James the Greater.
  Incipit: "Bið ég nú einvald engla kong."

Manuscripts:
See John the Evangelist 4 note (p. 130).
Edition:
Jón Helgason, ed. >> *Íslenzk miðaldakvæði* (1936–8). Vol. 2, p. 309.

5. Rósa

An early sixteenth-century cosmological poem with an emphasis on the life of
Mary the Blessed Virgin attributed to Sigurður blindur. Stz. 6 mentions Saint
James the Greater.
  Incipit: "Faðir og son á hæstum hæðum."

Manuscripts:
See Mary the Blessed Virgin 48 note (p. 212).

Editions:
Jón Helgason, ed. >> *Íslenzk miðaldakvæði* (1936–8). Vol. 1.2, p. 7.
Jón Þorkelsson, ed. >> *Kvæðasafn* (1922–7). P. 264.
Norwegian translation:
Orgland, Ivar, trans. and Anne-Lise Knoff, illus. *Rósa. Sigurður blindi í Fagradal* (Oslo: Solum, 1989). P. 20.

6. Náð

An early sixteenth-century poem in honour of Saint Anne and her daughter Mary the Blessed Virgin ascribed to the priest Hallur Ögmundarson (d. ca. 1540). Stz. 79 mentions Saint James the Greater.
   Incipit: "Heyr mildingur allra alda."

Manuscripts:
See Anne 1 note (p. 34).
Editions:
Jón Helgason, ed. >> *Íslenzk miðaldakvæði* (1936–8). Vol. 2, pp. 19–20.
Jón Þorkelsson, ed. >> *Kvæðasafn* (1922–7). P. 346.

7. Postulavísur

A poem about all the apostles composed in 1629 by Guðmundur Erlendsson í Felli (1595–1670). Stz. 10–11 and 29 concern Saint James the Greater.
   Incipit: "Herrans hér postula."

Manuscripts:
See Andrew the Apostle 14 note (p. 32).

8. Postularaun

A poem in praise of all the apostles composed by Guðmundur Bergþórsson (1657–1705). Stz. 15 and 30–2 concern Saint James the Greater.
   Incipit: "Hér skal eina hróðar grein."

Manuscripts:
See Ananias note (p. 20).

JAMES THE LESS   May 1

1. Allra postola minnisvísur

A fourteenth-century poem about all the apostles. Saint James the Less is treat-
ed in stz. 8.

Incipit: "Pétr er páfi drottins prísaðr gleðivísum."

Manuscript:
See Andrew the Apostle 10 note (p. 30).
Editions:
Finnur Jónsson, ed. >> *Den norsk-islandske skjaldedigtning* (1912–15).
Vol. AII, p. 510 and vol. BII, p. 561.
Kock, Ernst Albin, ed. >> *Notationes Norrœnæ* (1923–44). §§1758, 1759,
and 2887.
– ed. >> *Den norsk-isländska skaldediktningen* (1946–50). Vol. 2, p. 307.
McDougall, Ian, ed. "Anonymous, *Allra postula minnisvísur* 'Celebratory
Vísur about All the Apostles'." In >> *Poetry on Christian Subjects* (2007).
Vol. 2, p. 863.
Danish translation:
Finnur Jónsson, ed. >> *Den norsk-islandske skjaldedigtning* (1912–15).
Vol. BII, p. 561.
English translation:
McDougall, Ian, ed. "Anonymous, *Allra postula minnisvísur* 'Celebratory
Vísur about All the Apostles'." In >> *Poetry on Christian Subjects* (2007).
Vol. 2, p. 863.

2. Tólf postula kvæði

A late medieval (ca. 1400–1550) celebratory poem about all the apostles. Saint
James the Less is treated in stz. 8.

Incipit: "Sankti Pétur sannur páfi í Róma."

Manuscripts:
See Andrew the Apostle 11 note (p. 31).
Edition:
Jón Helgason, ed. >> *Íslenzk miðaldakvæði* (1936–8). Vol. 2, p. 276.

3. Rósa

An early sixteenth-century cosmological poem with an emphasis on the life of
Mary the Blessed Virgin attributed to Sigurður blindur. Stz. 6 mentions Saint
James the Less.
   Incipit: "Faðir og son á hæstum hæðum."

Manuscripts:
See Mary the Blessed Virgin 48 note (p. 212).
Editions:
Jón Helgason, ed. >> *Íslenzk miðaldakvæði* (1936–8). Vol. 1.2, p. 7.
Jón Þorkelsson, ed. >> *Kvæðasafn* (1922–7). P. 264.
Norwegian translation:
Orgland, Ivar, trans. and Anne-Lise Knoff, illus. *Rósa. Sigurður blindi í
   Fagradal* (Oslo: Solum, 1989). P. 20.

4. Náð

An early sixteenth-century poem in honour of Saint Anne and her daughter
Mary the Blessed Virgin ascribed to the priest Hallur Ögmundarson (d. ca.
1540). Stz. 76 mentions Saint James the Less.
   Incipit: "Heyr mildingur allra alda."

Manuscripts:
See Anne 1 note (p. 34).
Editions:
Jón Helgason, ed. >> *Íslenzk miðaldakvæði* (1936–8). Vol. 2, p. 19.
Jón Þorkelsson, ed. >> *Kvæðasafn* (1922–7). P. 345.

5. Postulavísur

A poem about all the apostles composed in 1629 by Guðmundur Erlendsson í
Felli (1595–1670). Stz. 23, 25, and 32 concern Saint James the Less.
   Incipit: "Herrans hér postula."

Manuscripts:
See Andrew the Apostle 14 note (p. 32).

6. Postularaun

A poem in praise of all the apostles composed by Guðmundur Bergþórsson (1657–1705). Stz. 56–61 concern Saint James the Less.
Incipit: "Hér skal eina hróðar grein."

Manuscripts:
See Ananias note (p. 20).

JOACHIM   July 26

1. Boðunarvísur

A poem in honour of Mary the Blessed Virgin composed ca. 1300–1550. Stz. 12 mentions Saint Joachim, her father.
Incipit: "Ave dýrust drósa."

Manuscripts:
See Mary the Blessed Virgin 19 note (p. 184).
Edition:
Jón Helgason, ed. >> *Íslenzk miðaldakvæði* (1936–8). Vol. 2, p. 30.

2. Gjörði í einu

A poetic rendering of biblical stories composed between 1400 and 1550. The poem is also known as *Liljukvistur*. Stz. 14 mentions Saint Joachim.
Incipit: "Gjörði í einu orði hreinu."

Manuscripts:
See Elizabeth 1 note (p. 82).
Edition:
Jón Helgason, ed. >> *Íslenzk miðaldakvæði* (1936–8). Vol. 1.2, p. 160.
German translation:
Kock, E.A. "Liljukvistur." *Studia Neophilologica* 15 (1942): 141–56, esp.
p. 145.

3. Salutatio Mariæ

A poem in praise of Mary the Blessed Virgin composed ca. 1400–1550 and extant in three versions. Stz. 9 of the A redaction and stz. 16 of the B redaction mention Saint Joachim.

Incipits: A and C: "Ave ágæt Máriá"; B: "María melle plena."

Manuscripts:
See Mary the Blessed Virgin 29 note (p. 194).
Edition:
Jón Helgason, ed. >> *Íslenzk miðaldakvæði* (1936–8). Vol. 2, pp. 231–2.

4. Rósa

An early sixteenth-century cosmological poem with an emphasis on the life of Mary the Blessed Virgin attributed to Sigurður blindur. Saint Joachim is treated in stz. 39–47 and mentioned in stz. 59.

Incipit: "Faðir og son á hæstum hæðum."

Manuscripts:
See Mary the Blessed Virgin 48 note (p. 212).
Editions:
Jón Helgason, ed. >> *Íslenzk miðaldakvæði* (1936–8). Vol. 1.2, pp. 14–17 and
   19.
Jón Þorkelsson, ed. >> *Kvæðasafn* (1922–7). Pp. 271–4 and 276.
Norwegian translation:
Orgland, Ivar, trans. and Anne-Lise Knoff, illus. *Rósa. Sigurður blindi í*
   Fagdaral (Oslo: Solum, 1989). Pp. 34, 36, and 38.

5. Náð

An early sixteenth-century poem in honour of Saint Anne and her daughter Mary the Blessed Virgin ascribed to the priest Hallur Ögmundarson (d. ca. 1540). Stz. 29–75 concern Saint Joachim.

Incipit: "Heyr mildingur allra alda."

Manuscripts:
See Anne 1 note (p. 34).

Editions:
Jón Helgason, ed. >> *Íslenzk miðaldakvæði* (1936–8). Vol. 2, pp. 9–19.
Jón Þorkelsson, ed. >> *Kvæðasafn* (1922–7). Pp. 334–5.

6. Niðurstigningsvísur

A poetic rendering of the story of Christ's descent to hell composed ca. 1525 by Bishop Jón Arason (1484–1550). Saint Joachim is mentioned in an additional stz. found only in AM 104 8vo, JS 265 8vo, Lbs 953 4to, and Lbs 1187 8vo.
   Incipit: "Djarflig er mér diktan."

Manuscripts:
See Anne 13 note (p. 43).
Editions:
Jón Helgason, ed. >> *Íslenzk miðaldakvæði* (1936–8). Vol. 1.2, pp. 237–8.
[Jón Sigurðsson and Guðbrandur Vigfússon, ed.] >> *Biskupa sögur* (1858–78). Vol. 2, p. 548.

JOHN THE BAPTIST   June 24

1. Sankt Jóhannesvísur

An Icelandic translation of a summer/morning hymn to "Saint John" (probably Saint John the Baptist, with the association of the feast of his birthday, June 24, with midsummer).
   Incipit: "Nú er sú hin myrka nátt í burt liðin."

Manuscripts:
AM 717d α 4to (ca. 1700), Lbs 1740 4to (ca. 1850–1910), and Lbs 2166 4to (ca. 1885–1920).
Editions:
*Brix, Hans. "Den Signede Dag." *Edda* 3 (1915): 177–96.
*– *Verse fra gamle Dage: Studier i middelalderens Digtekunst* (Copenhagen, 1918). Pp. 166–8.
Jón Þorkelsson. >> *Om Digtningen på Island* (1888). Pp. 64–5 (st. 1^{1-2}, 5, 8, and 9^{1-3}).
   Edition of AM 717d α 4to.
Literature:
Bruun, Henry. *Den middelalderlige dagvise.* Studier fra Sprog- og Oldtidsforskning, 257 (Copenhagen: Gad, 1965).

Chase, Martin. "Devotional Poetry at the End of the Middle Ages in Iceland."
In >> *Eddic, Skaldic, and Beyond: Poetic Variety in Medieval Iceland*. Ed.
Martin Chase (2014). Pp. 136–49, esp. p. 149.
Finnur Jónsson. >> *Bókmentasaga Íslendinga fram undir siðabót* (1904–5).
P. 461.
– >> *Den oldnorske og oldislandske Litteraturs Historie* (1920–4). Vol. 3,
p. 126.

2. Gjörði í einu

A poetic rendering of biblical stories composed between 1400 and 1550. The
poem is also known as *Liljukvistur*. Stz. 19 mentions Saint John the Baptist.
Incipit: "Gjörði í einu orði hreinu."

Manuscripts:
See Elizabeth 1 note (p. 82).
Edition:
Jón Helgason, ed. >> *Íslenzk miðaldakvæði* (1936–8). Vol. 1.2, pp. 162–3.
German translation:
Kock, E.A. "Liljukvistur." *Studia Neophilologica* 15 (1942): 141–56, esp.
p. 149.

3. Andréasdiktur I

A poem about the life and martyrdom of Saint Andrew the Apostle probably
composed ca. 1400–1550. Saint John the Baptist is mentioned in stz. 2.
Incipit: "Miskun þín hinn mildi guð."

Manuscripts:
See Andrew the Apostle 2 note (p. 23).
Editions:
Jón Helgason, ed. >> *Íslenzk miðaldakvæði* (1936–8). Vol. 2, p. 292.

4. Andréasdiktur II

A late medieval (ca. 1400–1550) poem about the life of Saint Andrew the
Apostle based on oral tradition. Stz. 2 mentions Saint John the Baptist.
Incipit: "Timens veit ég tíma rýra (að skýra)."

Manuscripts:
See Andrew the Apostle 3 note (p. 24).
Editions:
Jón Helgason, ed. >> *Íslenzk miðaldakvæði* (1936–8). Vol. 2, p. 298.

5. Fyrirlát mér jungfrúin hreina

A poem about Christ and the Holy Cross probably composed in Norway ca. 1400–1550. Stz. 3 and 15–16 concern Saint John the Baptist.
   Incipit: "Fyrirlát mér jungfrúin hreina."

Manuscripts:
See Cross, the Holy 6 note (p. 71).
Edition:
Jón Helgason, ed. >> *Íslenzk miðaldakvæði* (1936–8). Vol. 1.2, pp. 270–1.

6. Bjóða vil ég þér bragsins smíð

A poem in praise of Mary the Blessed Virgin from ca. 1400–1550. The text is probably based on oral tradition. Stz. 3–14 concern Saint John the Baptist.
   Incipit: "Bjóða vil ég þér bragsins smíð."

Manuscripts:
See Mary the Blessed Virgin 36 note (p. 199).
Edition:
Jón Helgason, ed. >> *Íslenzk miðaldakvæði* (1936–8). Vol. 2, pp. 54–5.

7. Rósa

An early sixteenth-century cosmological poem with an emphasis on the life of Mary the Blessed Virgin attributed to Sigurður blindur. Stz. 4 and 82 concern Saint John the Baptist.
   Incipit: "Faðir og son á hæstum hæðum."

Manuscripts:
See Mary the Blessed Virgin 48 note (p. 212).
Editions:
Jón Helgason, ed. >> *Íslenzk miðaldakvæði* (1936–8). Vol. 1.2, pp. 17 and 24.
Jón Þorkelsson, ed. >> *Kvæðasafn* (1922–7). Pp. 263 and 281.

Norwegian translation:
Orgland, Ivar, trans. and Anne-Lise Knoff, illus. *Rósa. Sigurður blindi í
  Fagradal* (Oslo: Solum, 1989). Pp. 20 and 48.

8. Milska

An early sixteenth-century poem about the life of Mary the Blessed Virgin.
Stz. 38 mentions Saint John the Baptist.
   Incipit: "Faðir vor Kristur friður hinn hæsti."

Manuscripts:
See Mary the Blessed Virgin 49 note (p. 214).
Edition:
Jón Helgason, ed. >> *Íslenzk miðaldakvæði* (1936–8). Vol. 1.2, p. 47.
Modern Icelandic language edition:
Jón Sigurðsson, ed. *Milska* (Reykjavík: Listahátíð í Reykjavík, 1994). P. [13].
Norwegian translations:
Orgland, Ivar. *Milska* (Reykjavík: Listahátíð í Reykjavík, 1994). P. [13].
Orgland, Ivar, trans. and Anne-Lise Knoff, illus. *Milska: Eit Maria-kvad frå
  islandsk seinmellomalder* (Oslo: Solum, 1993). P. 40.

9. Michaelsflokkur

An early sixteenth-century poem about Saint Michael ascribed to the priest
Hallur Ögmundarson (d. ca. 1540). Saint John the Baptist is mentioned in stz.
33 and 40.
   Incipit: "Óðar gef þú upphaf."

Manuscripts:
See Michael the Archangel 2 note (p. 256).
Edition:
Jón Þorkelsson, ed. >> *Kvæðasafn* (1922–7). Pp. 377 and 379.

10. Nikulásdrápa

An early sixteenth-century poem in honour of Saint Nicholas ascribed to the
priest Hallur Ögmundarson (d. ca. 1540). Stz. 14 and 17 mention Saint John
the Baptist.
   Incipit: "Í nafni guðs vil ég upphaf efna."

Manuscripts:
See Nicholas 5 note (p. 262).
Editions:
Carpenter, William H., ed. *Nikolásdrápa Halls prests: An Icelandic Poem from circa A.D. 1400* (Halle: Karras, 1881). Pp. 16–17.
Jón Helgason, ed. >> *Íslenzk miðaldakvæði* (1936–8). Vol. 2, p. 420.
Jón Þorkelsson, ed. >> *Kvæðasafn* (1922–7). Pp. 388–9.

11. Blómarós

A poem praising Jesus Christ and relating various biblical stories composed ca. 1400–1550. Jón Helgason argues that it is probably from 1550 or the first decade thereafter, during the transition from Catholicism to Protestantism. Stz. 99 concerns Saint John the Baptist.

Incipit: "Heyr guð faðir á himna hæðum."

Manuscripts:
See Elizabeth 6 note (p. 85).
Edition:
Jón Helgason, ed. >> *Íslenzk miðaldakvæði* (1936–8). Vol. 1.2, p. 80.

12. Máríuævi eða Lífssaga helgustu guðs móður

A poem about the life of Mary the Blessed Virgin composed ca. 1600 by the priest Ólafur Guðmundsson (ca. 1537–1609). Stz. 11 and 47 mention Saint John the Baptist.

Manuscript:
See Mary the Blessed Virgin 57 note (p. 221).
Incipit: "Ég vil jómfrú eina."
Editions:
Guðbrandur Þorláksson, ed. >> *Ein ny wiisna bok* (1612). Pp. 302 and 306.
Jón Torfason and Kristján Eiríksson, ed. >> *Vísnabók Guðbrands* (2000). P. 341.
Edition of *Ein ny wiisna bok* (1612).

13. Postularaun

A poem in praise of all the apostles composed by Guðmundur Bergþórsson (1657–1705). Stz. 6–7 concern Saint John the Baptist
Incipit: "Hér skal eina hróðar grein."

Manuscripts:
See Ananias note (p. 20).

JOHN THE EVANGELIST   December 27

1. Jónsdrápa postola

A fragment of a poem in honour of Saint John the Evangelist composed by
Níkulás Bergsson (d. 1159).
  Incipit: "Unni allra manna."

Manuscript:
AM 649a 4to (ca. 1350–1400).
Editions:
Bugge, Sophus, ed. "Anmærkninger ved de til Jons saga IV henhørende viser."
  In C.R. Unger, ed. >> *Postola sögur* (1874). Pp. 932–6, esp. pp. 932–3.
Finnur Jónsson, ed. >> *Den norsk-islandske skjaldedigtning* (1912–15).
  Vol. AI, pp. 560 and vol. BI, p. 546.
Kock, Ernst Albin, ed. >> *Den norsk-isländska skaldediktningen* (1946–50).
  Vol. 1, p. 265.
La Farge, Beatrice, ed. "Níkulás Bergsson, *Jónsdrápa* 'Drápa about S.
  John'." In >> *Poetry on Christian Subjects* (2007). Vol. 1, pp. 67–8.
Lange, Wolfgang. >> *Studien zur christlichen Dichtung der Nordgermanen
  1000–1200* (1958). Pp. 78–9 and 101–2.
Unger, C.R., ed. >> *Postola sögur* (1874). Pp. 509–10.
Danish translation:
Finnur Jónsson, ed. >> *Den norsk-islandske skjaldedigtning* (1912–15).
  Vol. BI, p. 546.
English translation:
La Farge, Beatrice, ed. "Níkulás Bergsson, *Jónsdrápa* 'Drápa about S.
  John'." In >> *Poetry on Christian Subjects* (2007). Vol. 1, pp. 67–9.
German translation:
Lange, Wolfgang. *Christliche Skaldendichtung* (Göttingen: Vandenhoeck and
  Ruprecht, 1958). P. 17 (extract only).
Literature:
Attwood, Katrina. "Intertextual Aspects of the Twelfth-Century Christian
  Drápur." *Saga-Book* 24 (1996): 221–39, esp. p. 225.
– "Leiðarvísan and the 'Sunday Letter' Tradition in Scandinavia." In >> *Til
  heiðurs og hugbótar* (2003). Pp. 53–78, esp. p. 66.

Clunies Ross, Margaret. >> *A History of Old Norse Poetry and Poetics* (2005). P. 211.

Cormack, Margaret. >> *The Saints in Iceland* (1994). Pp. 41 and 114.

– "Poetry, Paganism and the Sagas of Icelandic Bishops." In >> *Til heiðurs og hugbótar* (2003). Pp. 33–51, esp. p. 50.

Finnur Jónsson. >> *Den oldnorske og oldislandske Litteraturs Historie* (1920–4). Vol. 2, pp. 114 and 125.

Foote, Peter. "Postulatal." In *Minjar og menntir: Afmælisrit helgað Kristjáni Eldjárn 6 desember 1976.* Ed. Guðni Kolbeinsson (Reykjavík: Menningarsjóður, 1976). Pp. 152–73, esp. p. 161.

Guðrún Nordal. *Tools of Literacy: The Role of Skaldic Verse in Icelandic Textual Culture of the Twelfth and Thirteenth Centuries* (Toronto: University of Toronto Press, 2001). Pp. 76, 89, 101, 114, 141, and 388n22.

Jakob Benediktsson. "Helgendigte." *KLNM* 6 (1961). Cols. 318–21, esp. col. 318.

Jakob Benediktsson, ed. >> "Helgikvæði." In *Hugtök og heiti í bókmenntafræði* (1983). Pp. 115–17, esp. p. 116.

Jón Helgason. >> "Norges og Islands digtning." In *Litteraturhistorie B: Norge og Island* (1953). Pp. 3–179, esp. pp. 154–5.

Kahle, Bernhard. "Das Christentum in der altwestnordischen Dichtung." *ANF* 13 (1901): 1–40 and 97–160, esp. pp. 114 and 135.

Konráð Gíslason. "Om helrim i förste og tredje linie af regelmæssigt 'drottkvætt' og 'hrynhenda'." *Indbydelsesskrift til Kjøbenhavns Universitets Aarsfest til Erindring om Kirkens Reformation* (Copenhagen: Schultz, 1877). Pp. 1–60, esp. pp. 17, 26, 30, and 44.

Marold, Edith. "Das Gottesbild der christlichen Skaldik." In *The Sixth International Saga Conference 28/7–2/8 1985. Workshop Papers.* 2 vols. ([Copenhagen]: Det arnamagnæanske Institut, 1985). Vol. 2, pp. 717–49, esp. pp. 731–2.

Mogk, Eugen. >> *Geschichte der norwegisch-isländischen Literatur* (1904). Pp. 712 and 888.

Lange, Wolfgang. >> *Studien zur christlichen Dichtung der Nordgermanen 1000–1200* (1958). Pp. 76–81, 225, and 262n2.

Marchand, James W. "Two Christian Skaldic Fragments." *ANF* 91 (1976): 138–52, esp. p. 152.

Paasche, Fredrik. >> *Kristendom og kvad* (1914). Pp. 96–8, 120, and 122.

– *Norges og Islands litteratur inntil utgangen av middelalderen.* Rev. ed. by Anne Holtsmark (Oslo: Aschehoug, 1947). P. 316.

Schottmann, Hans. >> *Die isländische Mariendichtung* (1973). Pp. 78 and 227–8.

Stéfan Einarsson. "Íslenzk helgikvæði á miðöldum." *Tímarit Þjóðræknisfélags Íslendinga* 36 (1955): 43–63, esp. p. 45.

– *Íslensk bókmenntasaga 874–1960* (Reykjavík: Oddi, 1961). P. 82.

Sverrir Tómasson. "Kristnar trúarbókmenntir í óbundnu máli." In >> *Íslensk Bókmenntasaga* 1 (1992). Pp. 419–79, esp. p. 446.

Turville-Petre, G. *Origins of Icelandic Literature* (Oxford: Clarendon Press, 1967). P. 161.

Vesteinn Ólason. "Old Icelandic Poetry." In *A History of Icelandic Literature.* Ed. Daisy Neijmann. Histories of Scandinavian Literature 5 (Lincoln: University of Nebraska Press, 2006). Pp. 1–64, esp. p. 48.

Viðar Pálsson. "Pagan Mythology in Christian Society." *Gripla* 19 (2008): 123–58, esp. p. 140.

Vries, Jan de. >> *Altnordische Literaturgeschichte* (1964–7). Vol. 2, p. 53.

2. Jónsdrápa

A twelfth-century poem in honour of Saint John the Evangelist composed by Gamli.

Incipit: "Tígnar frák þik upphaf eignask."

Manuscript:
AM 649a 4to (ca. 1350–1400).

Editions:
Bugge, Sophus, ed. "Anmærkninger ved de til Jons saga IV henhørende viser." In C.R. Unger, ed. >> *Postola sögur* (1874). Pp. 932–6, esp. pp. 933–4.

Finnur Jónsson, ed. >> *Den norsk-islandske skjaldedigtning* (1912–15). Vol. AI, pp. 561 and vol. BI, pp. 547–8.

Kock, Ernst Albin, ed. >> *Notationes Norrœna* (1923–44). §3124.

– ed. >> *Den norsk-isländska skaldediktningen* (1946–50). Vol. 1, pp. 265–6.

La Farge, Beatrice, ed. "Gamli kanóki, *Jónsdrápa* 'Drápa about S. John'." In >> *Poetry on Christian Subjects* (2007). Vol. 1, pp. 133–6.

Lange, Wolfgang. >> *Studien zur christlichen Dichtung der Nordgermanen 1000–1200* (1958). Pp. 81–6 and 101–2.

Unger, C.R., ed. >> *Postola sögur* (1874). Pp. 510–11.

Danish translation:
Finnur Jónsson, ed. >> *Den norsk-islandske skjaldedigtning* (1912–15). Vol. BI, pp. 547–8.

English translation:
La Farge, Beatrice, ed. "Gamli kanóki, *Jónsdrápa* 'Drápa about S. John'." In >> *Poetry on Christian Subjects* (2007). Vol. 1, pp. 133–6.

German translation:
Lange, Wolfgang. *Christliche Skaldendichtung* (Göttingen: Vandenhoeck and
   Ruprecht, 1958). P. 17 (extract only).

Literature:
Attwood, Katrina. "Intertextual Aspects of the Twelfth-Century Christian
   Drápur." *Saga-Book* 24 (1996): 221–39, esp. p. 225.
– "Christian Poetry." In *A Companion to Old Norse–Icelandic Literature
   and Culture.* Ed. Rory McTurk (Oxford: Blackwell, 2005). Pp. 43–63, esp.
   pp. 49 and 53.
Clunies Ross, Margaret. >> *A History of Old Norse Poetry and Poetics*
   (2005). Pp. 132 and 211.
Cormack, Margaret. >> *The Saints in Iceland* (1994). Pp. 41 and 114.
Fidjestøl, Bjarne. "Gamli kanóki." In >> *Medieval Scandinavia: An
   Encyclopedia* (1993). Pp. 223–4.
Finnur Jónsson. >> *Den oldnorske og oldislandske Litteraturs Historie*
   (1920–4). Vol. 2, pp. 114 and 125.
Guðrún Nordal. *Tools of Literacy: The Role of Skaldic Verse in Icelandic
   Textual Culture of the Twelfth and Thirteenth Centuries* (Toronto:
   University of Toronto Press, 2001). Pp. 76, 89, 101, 114, and 141.
Jakob Benediktsson. "Helgendigte." *KLNM* 6 (1961). Cols. 318–21, esp. cols.
   318–19.
– "*Hafgerðingadrápa.*" In *Specvlvm Norroenvm: Norse Studies in Memory
   of Gabriel Turville-Petre.* Ed. Ursula Dronke, Guðrún P. Helgadóttir, Gerd
   Wolfgang Weber, and Hans Bekker-Nielsen (Odense: Odense University
   Press, 1981). Pp. 27–32, esp. p. 31.
– "Helgendigte." *KLNM* 6 (1961). Cols. 318–21, esp. col. 319.
– >> "Helgikvæði." In *Hugtök og heiti í bókmenntafræði* (1983). Pp. 115–17,
   esp. p. 116.
Jón Helgason. >> "Norges og Islands digtning." In *Litteraturhistorie B:
   Norge og Island* (1953). Pp. 3–179, esp. p. 155.
Kahle, Bernhard. "Das Christentum in der altwestnordischen Dichtung." *ANF*
   13 (1901): 1–40 and 97–160, esp. pp. 106, 111, 114, 124–9, and 137–9.
Konráð Gíslason. "Om helrim i förste og tredje linie af regelmæssigt
   'drottkvætt' og 'hrynhenda'." *Indbydelsesskrift til Kjøbenhavns
   Universitets Aarsfest til Erindring om Kirkens Reformation* (Copenhagen:
   Schultz, 1877). Pp. 1–60, esp. p. 28.
Kuhn, Hans. *Das Dróttkvætt* (Heidelberg: Carl Winter Universitätsverlag,
   1983). P. 322.
Lie, Hallvard. "Skaldestil-studier." *Mm* (1952): 1–92, esp. p. 88.

Marold, Edith. "Das Gottesbild der christlichen Skaldik." In *The Sixth International Saga Conference 28/7–2/8 1985. Workshop Papers*. 2 vols. ([Copenhagen]: Det arnamagnæanske Institut, 1985). Vol. 2, pp. 717–49, esp. pp. 732, 736, and 747.

Mogk, Eugen. >> *Geschichte der norwegisch-isländischen Literatur* (1904). Pp. 712 and 888.

Paasche, Fredrik. >> *Kristendom og kvad* (1914). Pp. 108–9, 120, and 122.

Schottman, Hans. >> *Die isländische Mariendichtung* (1973). Pp. 227–8.

Skard, Vemund. "Harmsól, Plácítusdrápa og Leiðarvísan." *ANF* 68 (1953): 97–108, esp. pp. 102–3.

Stefán Einarsson. *Íslensk bókmenntasaga 874–1960* (Reykjavík: Oddi, 1961). P. 83.

Turville-Petre, G. *Origins of Icelandic Literature* (Oxford: Clarendon Press, 1967). Pp. 161–2.

Vésteinn Ólason, "Kristileg trúarkvæði til loka 13. aldar." In >> *Íslensk Bókmenntasaga* 1 (1992). Pp. 481–515, esp. pp. 492 and 494.

– "Old Icelandic Poetry." In *A History of Icelandic Literature*. Ed. Daisy Neijmann. Histories of Scandinavian Literature 5 (Lincoln: University of Nebraska Press, 2006). Pp. 1–64, esp. p. 48.

Viðar Pálsson. "Pagan Mythology in Christian Society." *Gripla* 19 (2008): 123–58, esp. p. 140.

Vries, Jan de. >> *Altnordische Literaturgeschichte* (1964–7). Vol. 2, p. 54.

3. Jónsvísur

A fragment of a poem in honour of Saint John the Evangelist composed by Kolbeinn Tumason (d. 1208).

Incipit: "Angrfellir, vast ǫllum einn postolum hreinni."

Manuscript:
AM 649a 4to (ca. 1350–1400).
Editions:
Bugge, Sophus, ed. "Anmærkninger ved de til Jons saga IV henhørende viser." In C.R. Unger, ed. >> *Postola sögur* (1874). Pp. 932–6, esp. pp. 935–6.

Finnur Jónsson, ed. >> *Den norsk-islandske skjaldedigtning* (1912–15). Vol. AII, p. 37 and vol. BII, pp. 45–6.

[Jón Sigurðsson and Guðbrandur Vigfússon, ed.] >> *Biskupa sögur* (1858–78). Vol. 1, pp. 570–1n1.

Kock, Ernst Albin, ed. >> *Notationes Norrœna* (1923–44). §§2160 and 2165.
– ed. >> *Den norsk-isländska skaldediktningen* (1946–50). Vol. 2, pp. 28–9.
Kock, Ernst Albin, and R. Meissner, ed. *Skaldisches Lesebuch.* 2 vols.
   Rheinische Beiträge und Hilfsbücher zur germanischen Philologie und
   Volkskunde 17 (Halle am S.: Max Niemeyer, 1931). Vol. 1, p. 82.
La Farge, Beatrice, ed. "Kolbeinn Tumason, *Jónsvísur* 'Vísur about S. John'."
   In >> *Poetry on Christian Subjects* (2007). Vol. 1, pp. 224–7.
Unger, C.R., ed. >> *Postola sögur* (1874). Pp. 511–12.

Danish translation:
Finnur Jónsson, ed. >> *Den norsk-islandske skjaldedigtning* (1912–15).
   Vol. BII, pp. 45–6.

English translation:
La Farge, Beatrice, ed. "Kolbeinn Tumason, *Jónsvísur* 'Vísur about S. John'."
   In >> *Poetry on Christian Subjects* (2007). Vol. 1, pp. 224–6.

German translation:
Lange, Wolfgang. *Christliche Skaldendichtung* (Göttingen: Vandenhoeck and
   Ruprecht, 1958). P. 19 (extract only).

Literature:
Attwood, Katrina. "Intertextual Aspects of the Twelfth-Century Christian
   Drápur." *Saga-Book* 24 (1996): 221–39, esp. p. 225.
Clunies Ross, Margaret. >> *A History of Old Norse Poetry and Poetics*
   (2005). P. 211.
Cormack, Margaret. >> *The Saints in Iceland* (1994). Pp. 41 and 114.
Finnur Jónsson. >> *Den oldnorske og oldislandske Litteraturs Historie*
   (1920–4). Vol. 2, pp. 114, 116, and 125.
Guðrún Nordal. *Tools of Literacy: The Role of Skaldic Verse in Icelandic
   Textual Culture of the Twelfth and Thirteenth Centuries* (Toronto:
   University of Toronto Press, 2001). Pp. 89, 101, 175–6 and 294.
Jakob Benediktsson. "Helgendigte." *KLNM* 6 (1961). Cols. 318–21, esp.
   col. 318.
– >> "Helgikvæði." In *Hugtök og heiti í bókmenntafræði* (1983). Pp. 115–17,
   esp. p. 116.
Jón Helgason. >> "Norges og Islands digtning." In *Litteraturhistorie B:
   Norge og Island* (1953). Pp. 3–179, esp. pp. 155–8.
Kahle, Bernhard. "Das Christentum in der altwestnordischen Dichtung." *ANF*
   13 (1901): 1–40 and 97–160, esp. pp. 99, 105, 132–5, and 144.
Konráð Gíslason. "Om helrim i förste og tredje linie af regelmæssigt
   'dróttkvætt' og 'hrynhenda'." *Indbydelsesskrift til Kjøbenhavns
   Universitets Aarsfest til Erindringom Kirkens Reformation* (Copenhagen:
   Schultz, 1877). Pp. 1–60, esp. pp. 11–12, 20–1, and 31–3.

Lange, Wolfgang. >> *Studien zur christlichen Dichtung der Nordgermanen 1000–1200* (1958). Pp. 81 and 84.

Lindow, John. "Narrative and the Nature of Skaldic Poetry." *ANF* 97 (1982): 94–121, esp. p. 102n30.

Mogk, Eugen. >> *Geschichte der norwegisch-isländischen Literatur* (1904). Pp. 713 and 888.

Paasche, Fredrik. >> *Kristendom og kvad* (1914). Pp. 109, 119–20, and 122.

– *Norges og Islands litteratur inntil utgangen av middelalderen*. Rev. ed. by Anne Holtsmark (Oslo: Aschehoug, 1947). P. 400.

Schottman, Hans. >> *Die isländische Mariendichtung* (1973). Pp. 227–8.

Sigurður Nordal. "Icelandic Notes." *APS* 6 (1931–2): 144–50, esp. p. 146.

Skórzewska, Joanna A. *Constructing a Cult: The Life and Veneration of Guðmundr Arason (1161–1237) in the Icelandic Written Sources* (Leiden: Brill, 2011). P. 116.

Stéfan Einarsson. "Íslenzk helgikvæði á miðöldum." *Tímarit Þjóðræknisfélags Íslendinga* 36 (1955): 43–63, esp. p. 46.

– *Íslensk bókmenntasaga 874–1960* (Reykjavík: Oddi, 1961). P. 83.

Sverrir Tómasson. "Kristnar trúarbókmenntir í óbundnu máli." In >> *Íslensk Bókmenntasaga* 1 (1992). Pp. 419–79, esp. p. 446.

Vésteinn Ólason, "Kristileg trúarkvæði til loka 13. aldar." In >> *Íslensk Bókmenntasaga* 1 (1992). Pp. 481–515, esp. pp. 494 and 496.

– "Old Icelandic Poetry." In *A History of Icelandic Literature*. Ed. Daisy Neijmann. Histories of Scandinavian Literature 5 (Lincoln: University of Nebraska Press, 2006). Pp. 1–64, esp. p. 48.

Viðar Pálsson. "Pagan Mythology in Christian Society." *Gripla* 19 (2008): 123–58, esp. p. 140.

Vries, Jan de. >> *Altnordische Literaturgeschichte* (1964–7). Vol. 2, pp. 54 and 62.

4. Jóhannesdiktur

A late medieval (ca. 1400–1550) poem in honour of Saint John the Evangelist. Incipit: "Bið ég nú einvald engla kong."

Manuscripts:
AM 717a 4to (ca. 1700–25), AM 150 8vo (ca. 1650–1700), and Lbs 2166 4to (ca. 1885–1920).

Editions:
Jón Helgason, ed. >> *Íslenzk miðaldakvæði* (1936–8). Vol. 2, pp. 309–13. Based on AM 150 8vo with variants from AM 717a 4to.

Jón Þorkelsson. >> *Om Digtningen på Island* (1888). P. 64 (stz. 1 and 22^2)
Based on AM 717 4to and AM 150 8vo.
Literature:
Jakob Benediktsson. "Helgendigte." *KLNM* 6 (1961). Cols. 318–21, esp.
col. 320.
Finnur Jónsson. >> *Bókmentasaga Íslendinga fram undir siðabót* (1904–5).
P. 461.
– >> *Den oldnorske og oldislandske Litteraturs Historie* (1920–4). Vol. 3,
p. 126.
Hálfdan Einarsson. *Sciagraphia historiæ literariæ islandicæ* (Copenhagen:
Sander and Schröder, 1777). P. 58.
Stéfan Einarsson. "Íslenzk helgikvæði á miðöldum." *Tímarit Þjóðræknisfélags
Íslendinga* 36 (1955): 43–63, esp. p. 54.
– *Íslensk bókmenntasaga 874–1960* (Reykjavík: Oddi, 1961). P. 91.
Vésteinn Ólason. "Kveðskapur frá síðmiðöldum." In >> *Íslensk
Bókmenntasaga* 2 (1993). Pp. 283–378, esp. p. 315.
NOTE:
The poem contains material about Saint James the Greater. See his entry.

5. Drápa af Máríugrát

A fourteenth-century poem about Mary the Blessed Virgin's lament to Saint
Augustine about her sorrows and her enumeration to a monk of her five joys.
Stz. 26 mentions Saint John the Evangelist.

Incipit: "Orðin gef þú mjög til mærðar, minn lausnari, skáldi þínu."

Manuscripts:
See Mary the Blessed Virgin 9 note (p. 176).
Editions:
Finnur Jónsson, ed. >> *Den norsk-islandske skjaldedigtning* (1912–15).
Vol. AII, pp. 477 and vol. BII, p. 512.
Gade, Kari Ellen, ed. "Anonymous, *Drápa af Máríugrát* 'Drápa about the
Lament of Mary'." In >> *Poetry on Christian Subjects* (2007). Vol. 2, p. 778.
Kahle, Bernhard, ed. >> *Isländische geistliche Dichtungen des ausgehenden
Mittelalters* (1898). P. 61.
Kock, Ernst Albin, ed. >> *Den norsk-isländska skaldediktningen* (1946–50).
Vol. 2, p. 280.

Sperber, Hans, ed. >> *Sechs isländische Gedichte legendarischen Inhalts* (1911). P. 36.

Wrightson, Kellinde, ed. >> *Fourteenth-Century Icelandic Verse on the Virgin Mary* (2001). P. 13.

Danish translation:

Finnur Jónsson, ed. >> *Den norsk-islandske skjaldedigtning* (1912–15). Vol. BII, p. 512.

English translations:

Gade, Kari Ellen, ed. "Anonymous, *Drápa af Máríugrát* 'Drápa about the Lament of Mary'." In >> *Poetry on Christian Subjects* (2007). Vol. 2, p. 778.

Wrightson, Kellinde, ed. >> *Fourteenth-Century Icelandic Verse on the Virgin Mary* (2001). P. 13.

6. Allra postola minnisvísur

A fourteenth-century poem about all the apostles. Saint John the Evangelist is treated in stz. 4.

Incipit: "Pétr er páfi drottins prísaðr gleðivísum."

Manuscript:

See Andrew the Apostle 10 note (p. 30).

Editions:

Finnur Jónsson, ed. >> *Den norsk-islandske skjaldedigtning* (1912–15). Vol. AII, p. 510 and vol. BII, p. 560.

Jón Þorkelsson. >> *Om Digtningen på Island* (1888). Pp. 64–5 (stz. 1^2, 2^1, 3^1, 4^1, and 5^1).

Kock, Ernst Albin, ed. >> *Den norsk-isländska skaldediktningen* (1946–50). Vol. 2, pp. 306–7.

McDougall, Ian, ed. "Anonymous, *Allra postula minnisvísur* 'Celebratory Vísur about All the Apostles'." In >> *Poetry on Christian Subjects* (2007). Vol. 2, p. 857.

Danish translation:

Finnur Jónsson, ed. >> *Den norsk-islandske skjaldedigtning* (1912–15). Vol. BII, p. 560.

English translation:

McDougall, Ian, ed. "Anonymous, *Allra postula minnisvísur* 'Celebratory Vísur about All the Apostles'." In >> *Poetry on Christian Subjects* (2007). Vol. 2, p. 857.

7. Tólf postula kvæði

A late medieval (ca. 1400–1550) celebratory poem about all the apostles. Saint John the Evangelist is treated in stz. 4 and 9.
  Incipit: "Sankti Pétur sannur páfi í Róma."

Manuscripts:
See Andrew the Apostle 11 note (p. 31).
Edition:
Jón Helgason, ed. >> *Íslenzk miðaldakvæði* (1936–8). Vol. 2, pp. 275–6.

8. Jakobsdiktur

A late medieval (ca. 1400–1550) poem in honour of Saint James the Greater. Stz. 4 mentions Saint John the Evangelist.
  Incipit: "Prísa vildag prúðan dikt."

Manuscripts:
See James the Greater 1 note (p. 111).
Editions:
Jón Helgason, ed. >> *Íslenzk miðaldakvæði* (1936–8). Vol. 2, p. 314.

9. Gjörði í einu

A poetic rendering of biblical stories composed between 1400 and 1550. The poem is also known as *Liljukvistur*. Stz. 49 concerns Saint John the Evangelist.
  Incipit: "Gjörði í einu orði hreinu."

Manuscripts:
See Elizabeth 1 note (p. 82).
Edition:
Jón Helgason, ed. >> *Íslenzk miðaldakvæði* (1936–8). Vol. 1.2, p. 166.

10. Píslardrápa

A fragmentary passion poem composed ca. 1400–1550. Stz. 10 and 15 mention Saint John the Evangelist.
  Incipit: "Postuli einn með prýði hæsta."

Manuscripts:
AM 720a 4to V (ca. 1500), JS 531 4to (ca. 1700–1900), and Lbs 2166 4to
(ca. 1885–1920).
Edition:
Jón Helgason, ed. >> *Íslenzk miðaldakvæði* (1936–8). Vol. 1.2, p. 60.
Edition of AM 720a 4to V.
Literature:
Jón Þorkelsson. >> *Om Digtningen på Island* (1888). Pp. 95–6.
Wolf, Kirsten. "The Influence of the *Evangelium Nicodemi* on Norse Literature:
A Survey." In *The Medieval* Gospel of Nicodemus: *Texts, Intertexts,
and Contexts in Western Europe.* Ed. Zbigniew Izydorczyk (Tempe, AZ;
Medieval and Renaissance Texts and Studies, 1997). Pp. 261–86, esp. p. 278.
NOTE:
The poem contains material about Mary the Blessed Virgin and Saint Peter. See
the entries for the two saints.

11. Bjóða vil ég þér bragsins smíð

A poem in praise of Mary the Blessed Virgin from ca. 1400–1550. The text is
probably based on oral tradition. Stz. 15–30 treat Saint John the Evangelist.
Incipit: "Bjóða vil ég þér bragsins smíð."

Manuscripts:
See Mary the Blessed Virgin 36 note (p. 199).
Edition:
Jón Helgason, ed. >> *Íslenzk miðaldakvæði* (1936–8). Vol. 1.2, pp. 55–7.

12. Máríugrátur

A poem in honour of Mary the Blessed Virgin from ca. 1400–1550. Stz. 3–4
concern Saint John the Evangelist.
Incipit: "Blómstrið brúda og kvenna."

Manuscripts:
See Mary the Blessed Virgin 37 note (p. 201).
Editions:
Jón Helgason, ed. >> *Íslenzk miðaldakvæði* (1936–8). Vol. 2, p. 61.
[Jón Sigurðsson and Guðbrandur Vigfússon, ed.] >> *Biskupa sögur* (1858–
78). Vol. 2, p. 585 (stz. 1[1] and 3).

Modern Icelandic language edition:
Ásdís Egilsdóttir, Gunnar Harðarson, and Svanhildur Óskarsdóttir, ed.
  Maríukver. Sögur og kvæði af heilagri guðsmóður frá fyrri tíð (Reykjavík:
  Hið íslenska bókmenntafélag, 1996). Pp. 155–6.

13. Kristsbálkur

A poem from ca. 1400–1550 in praise of Jesus Christ based on oral tradition.
Stz. 34 mentions Saint John the Evangelist.
  Incipit: "Hæstur drottinn heiðri þig loptinn."

Manuscripts:
See Anne 6 note (p. 36).
Edition:
Jón Helgason, ed. >> *Íslenzk miðaldakvæði* (1936–8). Vol. 1.2, p. 148.

14. Rósa

An early sixteenth-century cosmological poem with an emphasis on the life of
Mary the Blessed Virgin attributed to Sigurður blindur. Stz. 5 and 107 concern
Saint John the Evangelist.
  Incipit: "Faðir og son á hæstum hæðum."

Manuscripts:
See Mary the Blessed Virgin 48 note (p. 212).
Editions:
Jón Helgason, ed. >> *Íslenzk miðaldakvæði* (1936–8). Vol. 1.2, pp. 7 and 29.
Jón Þorkelsson. >> *Om Digtningen på Island* (1888). Pp. 51 and 282–3 (stz.
  1, 5^{1-2}, 8–9, 46^{5-8}, and 133^{7-8}).
Jón Þorkelsson, ed. >> *Kvæðasafn* (1922–7). Pp. 51, 282–3 (stz. 1, 5^{1-2}, 8–9,
  46^{5-8}, and 133^{7-8}).
Norwegian translation:
Orgland, Ivar, trans. and Anne-Lise Knoff, illus. *Rósa. Sigurður blindi í
  Fagradal* (Oslo: Solum, 1989). Pp. 20 and 56.

15. Milska

An early sixteenth-century poem about the life of Mary the Blessed Virgin. Stz.
48 and 61 concern Saint John the Evangelist.
  Incipit: "Faðir vor Kristur friður hinn hæsti."

Manuscripts:
See Mary the Blessed Virgin 49 note (p. 214).
Edition:
Jón Helgason, ed. >> *Íslenzk miðaldakvæði* (1936–8). Vol. 1.2, pp. 49 and 52.
Modern Icelandic language edition:
Jón Sigurðsson, ed. *Milska* (Reykjavík: Listahátíð í Reykjavík, 1994).
    Pp. [17] and [21].
Norwegian translations:
Orgland, Ivar. *Milska* (Reykjavík: Listahátíð í Reykjavík, 1994). Pp. [17]
    and [21].
Orgland, Ivar, trans. and Anne-Lise Knoff, illus. *Milska: Eit Maria-kvad frå
    islandsk seinemellomalder* (Oslo: Solum, 1993). Pp. 44 and 52.

16. Gimsteinn

An early sixteenth-century poem about the cross-tree ascribed to the priest
Hallur Ögmundarson (d. ca. 1540). Stz. 47, 74, and 78–9 mention Saint John
the Evangelist.
    Incipit: "Heyr mig ilmanda hjartans yndi."

Manuscripts:
See Cross, the Holy 7 note (p. 73).
Editions:
Jón Helgason, ed. >> *Íslenzk miðaldakvæði* (1936–8). Vol. 1.2, pp. 315 and
    320–1.
Jón Þorkelsson. >> *Om Digtningen på Island* (1888). Pp. 318 (stz. 1 and 124[7–8])
Jón Þorkelsson, ed. >> *Kvæðasafn* (1922–7). Pp. 308–9 and 314–16.

17. Náð

An early sixteenth-century poem in honour of Saint Anne and her daughter
Mary the Blessed Virgin, ascribed to the priest Hallur Ögmundarson (d. ca.
1540). Stz. 79 mentions Saint John the Evangelist.
    Incipit: "Heyr mildingur allra alda."

Manuscripts:
See Anne 1 note (p. 34).
Editions:
Jón Helgason, ed. >> *Íslenzk miðaldakvæði* (1936–8). Vol. 2, pp. 19–20.
Jón Þorkelsson, ed. >> *Kvæðasafn* (1922–7). P. 346.

18. Krossvísur I

A poem about Christ and the Holy Cross composed ca. 1525 by Bishop Jón
Arason (1484–1550). Stz. 12 mentions Saint John the Evangelist.
   Incipit: "Dýrðarfullur drottinn minn."

Manuscripts:
See Cross, the Holy 8 note (p. 75).
Editions:
Finnur Jónsson, ed. >> *Jón Arasons religiøse digte* (1918). P. 71.
Jón Helgason, ed. >> *Íslenzk miðaldakvæði* (1936–8). Vol. 1.2, p. 255.
[Jón Sigurðsson and Guðbrandur Vigfússon, ed.] >> *Biskupa sögur* (1858–78).
   Vol. 2, pp. 560–1.
*Peringskiöld, J.F. >> *Fragmentum runicopapisticum* (1721).

19. Ljómur

A Christian history of the world composed ca. 1525 and ascribed to Bishop Jón
Arason (1484–1550). Stz. 12 and 29–31 treat Saint John the Evangelist.
   Incipit: "Hæstur heilagur andi."

Manuscripts:
See Anne 12 note (p. 41).
Editions:
Finnur Jónsson, ed. >> *Jón Arasons religiøse digte* (1918). Pp. 40–1 and 46–7.
Jón Helgason, ed. >> *Íslenzk miðaldakvæði* (1936–8). Vol. 1.2, pp. 127 and
   134–5.
– ed. >> *Kvæðabók úr Vigur: AM 148, 8vo* (1955). Fol. 302v and 304v–305r.
   Facsimile of AM 148 8vo.
[Jón Sigurðsson and Guðbrandur Vigfússon, ed.] >> *Biskupa sögur* (1858–
   78). Vol. 2, pp. 526 and 231–2.
Modern Icelandic language edition:
Einar Ól. Sveinsson, Páll Eggert Ólason, and Arnór Sigurjónsson, ed. *Íslands
   þúsund ár: Kvæðasafn.* 3 vols. (Reykjavík: Helgafell, 1947). Vol. 3, pp.
   151–2 (stz. 30–1).
Norwegian translations:
Næss, Leonhard. "Ljomur av Jón Arason." *Norsk aarbok* (1930). Pp. 75 and
   81–2.
Orgland, Ivar, trans. *Islandske Dikt. Frå Sólarljóð til opplysningstid (13.
   hundreåret–1835)* (Reykjavík: Fonna, 1977). P. 238 (stz. 30–1).

20. Niðurstigningsvísur

A poetic rendering of the story of Christ's descent to hell composed ca. 1525 by Bishop Jón Arason (1484–1550). Stz. 21 mentions Saint John the Evangelist.
   Incipit: "Djarflig er mér diktan."

Manuscripts:
See Anne 13 note (p. 43).
Editions:
Finnur Jónsson, ed. >> *Jón Arasons religiøse digte* (1918). P. 63.
Jón Helgason, ed. >> *Íslenzk miðaldakvæði* (1936–8). Vol. 1.2, p. 228.
[Jón Sigurðsson and Guðbrandur Vigfússon, ed.] >> *Biskupa sögur* (1858–78). Vol. 2, pp. 551–2.

21. Píslargrátur

A poetic rendering of the passion of Christ composed ca. 1525 by Bishop Jón Arason (1484–1550). Stz. 38 mentions Saint John the Evangelist.
   Incipit: "Faðir vor Kristur í friðinum hæsta."

Manuscripts:
A: AM 715c 4to (ca. 1700–25), AM 715d 4to (ca. 1700–25), and AM 99a 8vo (ca. 1500–1600);
B: Adv 21.8.10 (1712), AM 622 4to (ca. 1549), AM 720b 4to (ca. 1600), AM 1032 4to (ca. 1700–25), AM 104 8vo (ca. 1680), ÍB 105 4to (1758–68), JS 413 8vo (ca. 1700–1900), Lbs 315 4to (ca. 1800–1900), Lbs 1276 4to (1862–70), Lbs 201 8vo (ca. 1850–70), Lbs 1157 8vo (ca. 1777), Lbs 1245 8vo (ca. 1700–1800), and Lbs 2293 8vo (ca. 1700).
Editions:
Finnur Jónsson, ed. >> *Jón Arasons religiøse digte* (1918). P. 34.
   Based on AM 622 4to with variants from AM 720b 4to and AM 99a 8vo.
Guðbrandur Þorláksson, ed. >> *Ein ny wiisna bok* (1612). P. 259.
Jón Helgason, ed. >> *Íslenzk miðaldakvæði* (1936–8). Vol. 1.2, p. 204.
   Based on AM 99a 8vo with variants from AM 715d 4to, AM 720b 4to, AM 622 4to, AM 1032 4to, AM 104 8vo, and *Ein ny wiisna bok* (1612).
[Jón Sigurðsson and Guðbrandur Vigfússon, ed.] >> *Biskupa sögur* (1858–78). Vol. 2, p. 518.
   Based on AM 622 4to, AM 99a 8vo, and *Ein ny wiisna bok* (1612) with variants from AM 1032 4to and ÍB 105 4to.

Jón Torfason and Kristján Eiríksson, ed. >> *Vísnabók Guðbrands* (2000).
 P. 292.
Literature:
Ármann Jakobsson. "The Homer of the North, or: Who Was Sigurður the
 Blind?" *European Journal of Scandinavian Studies* 44 (2014): 4–19,
 esp. p. 5.
Bjarni Þorsteinsson, ed. *Íslenzk þjóðlög* (Copenhagen: Møller, 1906–9).
 Pp. 32 and 132.
Carpenter, William H., ed. *Nikolásdrápa Halls prests: An Icelandic Poem
 from circa A.D. 1400* (Halle: Karras, 1881). Pp. 3 and 5.
Einar Ól. Sveinsson, Páll Eggert Ólason, and Arnór Sigurjónsson, ed. *Íslands
 þúsund ár: Kvæðasafn*. 3 vols. (Reykjavík: Helgafell, 1947). Vol. 3, p. 150.
Finnur Jónsson. >> *Bókmentasaga Íslendinga fram undir siðabót* (1904–5).
 P. 464.
– >> *Den oldnorske og oldislandske Litteraturs Historie* (1920–4). Vol. 3,
 pp. 128–9.
Guðrún Nordal. "Helgubók. Kvæðasafn á mörkum kaþólsku og lútersku."
 In *Handrit úr förum Árna Magnússonar*. Ed. Svanhildur Óskarsdóttir,
 Matthew Driscoll, and Sigurður Svavarsson (Copenhagen: Den
 Arnamagnæanske Samling, Nordisk Forkningsinstitut; Reykjavík: Stofnun
 Árna Magnússonar í íslenskum fræðum; and Reykjavík: Bókaútgáfan
 Opna, 2013). P. 127.
– "Helgubók." In *Góssið hans Árna: Minningar heimsins í íslenskum
 handritum*. Ed Jóhanna Katrín Friðriksdóttir (Reykjavík: Stofnun Árna
 Magnússonar í íslenskum fræðum, 2014). Pp. 21–35, esp. p. 27.
Jakob Benediktsson. "Kristdigte." *KLNM* 9 (1964). Cols. 292–4, esp. col. 293.
Jón Helgason. >> "Norges og Islands digtning." In *Litteraturhistorie B:
 Norge og Island* (1953). Pp. 3–179, esp. pp. 162–3.
Jón Þorkelsson. >> *Om Digtningen på Island* (1888). Pp. 77, 94, 283, and 327.
Jónas Kristjánsson. >> *Eddas and Sagas: Iceland's Medieval Literature*
 (1988). P. 388.
Kock, E.A. "Liljukvistur." *Studia Neophilologica* 15 (1942): 141–56, esp.
 p. 143.
– "Anteckningar till Íslenzk Miðaldakvæði." *ANF* 61 (1946): 1–125, esp.
 pp. 5 and 20–1.
Mogk, Eugen. >> *Geschichte der norwegisch-isländischen Literatur* (1904).
 P. 719.
Páll Eggert Ólason. *Menn og menntir siðskiptaaldarinnar á Íslandi*. Vol. 1
 (Reykjavík: Guðm. Gamalíelsson, 1919). Pp. 412, 415, 420, and 424.

Pétur Sigurðsson. "Vísnabók Guðbrands biskups." In *Iðunn: Tímarit til skemtunar, nytsemdar og fróðleiks*. Vol. 8. Ed. Magnús Jónsson (Reykjavík: Gutenberg, 1923–4). Pp. 61–87, esp. pp. 63 and 82.

Schottmann, Hans. >> *Die isländische Mariendichtung* (1973). Pp. 273 and 510.

Stéfan Einarsson. "Íslenzk helgikvæði á miðöldum." *Tímarit Þjóðræknisfélags Íslendinga* 36 (1955): 43–63, esp. pp 53, 55, and 62.

– *Íslensk bókmenntasaga 874–1960* (Reykjavík: Oddi, 1961). Pp. 90 and 98.

Vésteinn Ólason. "Kveðskapur frá síðmiðöldum." In >> *Íslensk Bókmenntasaga* 2 (1993). Pp. 283–378, esp. p. 350.

Wolf, Kirsten, ed. >> *Saga heilagrar Önnu* (2001). P. xliii.
NOTE:
The poem also contains material about Saint Simeon the Righteous. See his entry.

22. Máríuvísur

A poem in praise of Mary the Blessed Virgin composed ca. 1600 by Einar Sigurðsson í Eydölum (1539–1626). Saint John the Evangelist is mentioned in stz. 34.

Incipit: "Mjúkast vilda ég mærðarvers."

Manuscripts:
See Mary the Blessed Virgin 55 note (p. 220).

Editions:
Guðbrandur Þorláksson, ed. >> *Ein ny wiisna bok* (1612). P. 96,
Jón Torfason and Kristján Eiríksson, ed. >> *Vísnabók Guðbrands* (2000). P. 112.

23. Píslarminning

A poem about Christ's passion composed ca. 1600 by Einar Sigurðsson í Eydölum (1539–1626). Saint John the Evangelist is mentioned in stz. 17.
Incipit: "Hinn helgi Paulus hefur það kent."

Manuscripts:
ÍB 105 4to (1758–68), JS 413 8vo (ca. 1700–1900), JS 417 8vo (ca. 1700–1900), Lbs 1157 8vo (ca. 1777), Lbs 1208 8vo (ca. 1800), Lbs 1245 8vo (ca. 1700–1800), Lbs 1847 8vo (1855), Lbs 2290 8vo (1823–4), and Lbs 2293 8vo (ca. 1700).

Editions:
Guðbrandur Þorláksson, ed. >> *Ein ny wiisna bok* (1612). Pp. 91–2.
Jón Torfason and Kristján Eiríksson, ed. >> *Vísnabók Guðbrands* (2000).
  P. 108.
Literature:
Jón Þorkelsson. >> *Om Digtningen på Island* (1888). Pp. 96–7, 442, and 474.
Pétur Sigurðsson. "Vísnabók Guðbrands biskups." In *Iðunn: Tímarit til
  skemtunar, nytsemdar og fróðleiks.* Vol. 8. Ed. Magnús Jónsson (Reykjavík:
  Gutenberg, 1923–4). Pp. 61–87, esp. p. 72.
NOTE:
The poem also contains material about Saint Paul. See his entry.

24. Postulavísur

A poem about all the apostles composed in 1629 by Guðmundur Erlendsson í
Felli (1595–1670). Stz. 10, 12–14, and 30 concern Saint John the Evangelist.
  Incipit: "Herrans hér postula."

Manuscripts:
See Andrew the Apostle 14 note (p. 32).

25. Postularaun

A poem in praise of all the apostles composed by Guðmundur Bergþórsson
(1657–1705). Stz. 22, 30, and 32–6 concern Saint John the Evangelist.
  Incipit: "Hér skal eina hróðar grein."

Manuscripts:
See Ananias note (p. 20).

JOSEPH   March 19

1. Gjörði í einu

A poetic rendering of biblical stories composed between 1400 and 1550. The
poem is also known as *Liljukvistur.* Stz. 14 mentions Saint Joseph.
  Incipit: "Gjörði í einu orði hreinu."

Manuscripts:
See Elizabeth 1 note (p. 82).
Edition:
Jón Helgason, ed. >> *Íslenzk miðaldakvæði* (1936–8). Vol. 1, p. 160.
German translation:
Kock, E.A. "Liljukvistur." *Studia Neophilologica* 15 (1942): 141–56, esp.
  p. 145.

2. Fýsir mig að fremja dikt

A macaronic poem from ca. 1400–1550 in praise of Mary the Blessed Virgin
probably translated from a foreign (possibly Danish) source. Stz. 19 concerns
Saint Joseph.
  Incipit: "Fýsir mig að fremja dikt."

Manuscripts:
See Mary the Blessed Virgin 30 note (p. 195).
Edition:
Jón Helgason, ed. >> *Íslenzk miðaldakvæði* (1936–8). Vol. 2, p. 28.

3. Heyr mig himins og láða

A fragmentary poem from ca. 1500 about the events surrounding Christ's birth
and childhood. Stz. 13–19 concern Saint Joseph.
  Incipit: "Heyr mig himins og láða."

Manuscript:
See Anne 10 note (p. 38).
Edition:
Jón Helgason, ed. >> *Íslenzk miðaldakvæði* (1936–8). Vol. 1.2, pp. 187–8.

4. Rósa

An early sixteenth-century cosmological poem with an emphasis on the life of
Mary the Blessed Virgin attributed to Sigurður blindur. Stz. 54–6, 66–71, and
81 treat Saint Joseph.
  Incipit: "Faðir og son á hæstum hæðum."

Manuscripts:
See Mary the Blessed Virgin 48 note (p. 212).
Editions:
Jón Helgason, ed. >> *Íslenzk miðaldakvæði* (1936–8). Vol. 1.2, pp. 17–18,
    20–1, and 23.
Jón Þorkelsson, ed. >> *Kvæðasafn* (1922–7). Pp. 275, 278–9, and 281.
Norwegian translation:
Orgland, Ivar, trans. and Anne-Lise Knoff, illus. *Rósa. Sigurður blindi í
    Fagradal* (Oslo: Solum, 1989). Pp. 37, 40, 42, 44, and 48.

5. Milska

An early sixteenth-century poem about the life of Mary the Blessed Virgin.
Stz. 26–7 treat Saint Joseph.
    Incipit: "Faðir vor Kristur friður hinn hæsti."

Manuscripts:
See Mary the Blessed Virgin 49 note (p. 214).
Edition:
Jón Helgason, ed. >> *Íslenzk miðaldakvæði* (1936–8). Vol. 1.2, p. 44.
Modern Icelandic language edition:
Jón Sigurðsson, ed. *Milska* (Reykjavík: Listahátíð í Reykjavík, 1994). P. [9].
Norwegian translations:
Orgland, Ivar. *Milska* (Reykjavík: Listahátíð í Reykjavík, 1994). P. [9].
Orgland, Ivar, trans. and Anne-Lise Knoff, illus. *Milska: Eit Maria-kvad frå
    islandsk seinmellomalder* (Oslo: Solum, 1993). P. 25.

6. Náð

An early sixteenth-century poem in honour of Saint Anne and her daughter
Mary the Blessed Virgin ascribed to the priest Hallur Ögmundarson (d. ca.
1540). Stz. 75 and 76 concern Saint Joseph.
    Incipit: "Heyr mildingur allra alda."

Manuscripts:
See Anne 1 note (p. 34).
Editions:
Jón Helgason, ed. >> *Íslenzk miðaldakvæði* (1936–8). Vol. 2, p. 19.
Jón Þorkelsson, ed. >> *Kvæðasafn* (1922–7). P. 345.

7. Niðurstigningsvísur

A poetic rendering of the story of Christ's descent to hell composed ca. 1525
by Bishop Jón Arason (1484–1550). Stz. 7–8 concern Saint Joseph.
   Incipit: "Djarflig er mér diktan."

Manuscripts:
See Anne 13 note (p. 43).
Editions:
Finnur Jónsson, ed. >> *Jón Arasons religiøse digte* (1918). P. 60.
Jón Helgason, ed. >> *Íslenzk miðaldakvæði* (1936–8). Vol. 1.2, pp. 223–4.
[Jón Sigurðsson and Guðbrandur Vigfússon, ed.] >> *Biskupa sögur*. 2 vols.
   (1858–78). Vol. 2, pp. 558–9.

8. Blómarós

A poem praising Jesus Christ and relating various biblical stories composed ca.
1400–1550. Jón Helgason argues that it is probably from 1550 or the first de-
cade thereafter, during the transition from Catholicism to Protestantism. Stz.
107 concerns Saint Joseph.
   Incipit: "Heyr guð faðir á himna hæðum."

Manuscripts:
See Elizabeth 6 note (p. 85).
Edition:
Jón Helgason, ed. >>*Íslenzk miðaldakvæði* (1936–8). Vol. 1.2, p. 82.

9. Máríuvísur

A poem in priase of Mary the Blessed Virgin composed ca. 1600 by Einar
Sigurðsson í Eydölum (1539–1626). Stz. 28 mentions Saint Joseph.
   Incipit: "Mjúkast vilda ég mærðarvers."

Manuscripts:
See Mary the Blessed Virgin 55 note (p. 220).
Editions:
Guðbrandur Þorláksson, ed. >> *Ein ny wiisna bok* (1612). P. 96.
Jón Torfason and Kristján Eiríksson, ed. >> *Vísnabók Guðbrands* (2000). P. 112.

10. Máríuævi eða Lífssaga helgustu guðs móður

A poem about the life of Mary the Blessed Virgin composed ca. 1600 by the priest Ólafur Guðmundsson (ca. 1537–1609). Stz. 4, 12, 26–7, and 35 mention Saint Joseph.

Incipit: "Ég vil jómfrú eina."

Manuscript:
See Mary the Blessed Virgin 57 note (p. 221).
Editions:
Guðbrandur Þorláksson, ed. >> *Ein ny wiisna bok* (1612). Pp. 302 and 304–5.
Jón Torfason and Kristján Eiríksson, ed. >> *Vísnabók Guðbrands* (2000).
  Pp. 343–4.

JOSEPH OF ARIMATHEA   August 31

1. Gimsteinn

An early sixteenth-century poem about the cross-tree ascribed to the priest Hallur Ögmundarson (d. ca. 1540). Stz. 64–5 and 73 mention Saint Joseph of Arimathea.

Incipit: "Heyr mig ilmanda hjartans yndi."

Manuscripts:
See Cross, the Holy 7 note (p. 73).
Editions:
Jón Helgason, ed. >> *Íslenzk miðaldakvæði* (1936–8). Vol. 1.2, pp. 318
  and 320.
Jón Þorkelsson, ed. >> *Kvæðasafn* (1922–7). Pp. 312–14.

2. Blómarós

A poem praising Jesus Christ and relating various biblical stories composed ca. 1400–1550. Jón Helgason argues that it is probably from 1550 or the first decade thereafter, during the transition from Catholicism to Protestantism. Stz. 209 concerns Saint Joseph of Arimathea.

Incipit: "Heyr guð faðir á himna hæðum."

Manuscripts:
See Elizabeth 6 note (p. 85).
Edition:
Jón Helgason, ed. >> *Íslenzk miðaldakvæði* (1936–8). Vol. 1.2, p. 96.

JUDE   October 28

1. Allra postola minnisvísur

A fourteenth-century poem about all the apostles. Saint Jude is treated in stz. 12.
  Incipit: "Pétr er páfi drottins prísaðr gleðivísum."

Manuscript:
See Andrew the Apostle 10 note (p. 30).
Editions:
Finnur Jónsson, ed. >> *Den norsk-islandske skjaldedigtning* (1912–15).
  Vol. AII, p. 511 and vol. BII, p. 562.
Kock, Ernst Albin, ed. >> *Notationes Norrœnæ* (1923–44). §§1762, 2888,
  and 3376C.
– ed. >> *Den norsk-isländska skaldediktningen* (1946–50). Vol. 2, p. 308.
McDougall, Ian, ed. "Anonymous, *Allra postula minnisvísur* 'Celebratory
  Vísur about All the Apostles'." In >> *Poetry on Christian Subjects* (2007).
  Vol. 2, p. 868.
Danish translation:
Finnur Jónsson, ed. >> *Den norsk-islandske skjaldedigtning* (1912–15).
  Vol. BII, p. 562.
English translation:
McDougall, Ian, ed. "Anonymous, *Allra postula minnisvísur* 'Celebratory
  Vísur about All the Apostles'." In >> *Poetry on Christian Subjects* (2007).
  Vol. 2, p. 868.

2. Tólf postula kvæði

A late medieval (ca. 1400–1550) celebratory poem about all the apostles. Saint
Jude is mentioned in stz. 11.
  Incipit: "Sankti Pétur sannr páfi í Róma."

Manuscripts:
See Andrew the Apostle 11 note (p. 31).

Edition:
Jón Helgason, ed. >> *Íslenzk miðaldakvæði* (1936–8). Vol. 2, p. 277.

3. Rósa

An early sixteenth-century cosmological poem with an emphasis on the life of Mary the Blessed Virgin attributed to Sigurður blindur. Stz. 6 mentions Saint Jude.
   Incipit: "Faðir og son á hæstum hæðum."

Manuscripts:
See Mary the Blessed Virgin 48 note (p. 212).
Editions:
Jón Helgason, ed. >> *Íslenzk miðaldakvæði* (1936–8). Vol. 1.2, p. 7.
Jón Þorkelsson, ed. >> *Kvæðasafn* (1922–7). P. 264.
Norwegian translation:
Orgland, Ivar, trans. and Anne-Lise Knoff, illus. *Rósa. Sigurður blindi í Fagradal* (Oslo: Solum, 1989). P. 20.

4. Náð

An early sixteenth-century poem in honour of Saint Anne and her daughter Mary the Blessed Virgin ascribed to the priest Hallur Ögmundarson (d. ca. 1540). Stz. 76 mentions Saint Jude.
   Incipit: "Heyr mildingur allra alda."

Manuscripts:
See Anne 1 note (p. 34).
Editions:
Jón Helgason, ed. >> *Íslenzk miðaldakvæði* (1936–8). Vol. 2, p. 19.
Jón Þorkelsson, ed. >> *Kvæðasafn* (1922–7). P. 345.

5. Postulavísur

A poem about all the apostles composed in 1629 by Guðmundur Erlendsson í Felli (1595–1670). Stz. 25–6 and 32 concern Saint Jude.
   Incipit: "Herrans hér postula."

Manuscripts:
See Andrew the Apostle 14 note (p. 32).

6. Postularaun

A poem in praise of all the apostles composed by Guðmundur Bergþórsson (1657–1705). Stz. 67 mentions Saint Jude (called Thaddeus).
  Incipit: "Hér skal eina hróðar grein."

Manuscripts:
See Ananias note (p. 20).

JULIANA   February 16

Heilagra meyja drápa

A fourteenth-century poem about holy maidens. Stz. 44–5 treat Saint Juliana.
  Incipit: "Heyrðu ómælds himna veldis herra guð."

Manuscripts:
See Agatha note (p. 13).
Editions:
Finnur Jónsson, ed. >> *Den norsk-islandske skjaldedigtning* (1912–15).
  Vol. AII, p. 535 and vol. BII, p. 593.
Kock, Ernst Albin, ed. >> *Notationes Norrænæ* (1923–44). §2971A.
– ed. >> *Den norsk-islandske skaldediktningen* (1946–50). Vol. 2, p. 328.
Wolf, Kirsten, ed. "Anonymous, *Heilagra meyja drápa* '*Drápa* about Holy
  Maidens'." In >> *Poetry on Christian Subjects* (2007). Vol. 2, pp. 918–19.
Danish translation:
Finnur Jónsson, ed. >> *Den norsk-islandske skjaldedigtning* (1912–15).
  Vol. BII, p. 593.
English translation:
Wolf, Kirsten, ed. "Anonymous, *Heilagra meyja drápa* '*Drápa* about Holy
  Maidens'." In >> *Poetry on Christian Subjects* (2007). Vol. 2, pp. 918–19.

LAURENCE OF ROME   August 10

1. Lárentíusdiktur

A poetic rendering of the legend of Saint Laurence composed between 1300 and 1550.
  Incipit: "Heyr þú heilagur andi."

Manuscripts:
AM 713 4to (ca. 1500–50), G-63/10 (ca. 1889), JS 399a–b 4to (ca. 1700–
    1900), Lbs 1750 4to (ca. 1850–65), and Lbs 2166 4to (ca. 1885–1920).
Editions:
Jón Helgason, ed. >> *Íslenzk miðaldakvæði* (1936–8). Vol. 2, pp. 367–75.
    Based on AM 713 4to with variants from JS 399a–b 4to, Lbs 1750 4to,
    and Lbs 2166 4to.
Jón Þorkelsson. >> *Om Digtningen på Island* (1888). Pp. 83–4 (stz. 1 and
    55–7).
    Edition of AM 713 4to.
Literature:
Chase, Martin. "Devotional Poetry at the End of the Middle Ages in Iceland."
    In >> *Eddic, Skaldic, and Beyond: Poetic Variety in Medieval Iceland.*
    Ed. Martin Chase (2014). Pp. 136–49, esp. p. 142.
Foote, Peter, ed. *Lives of Saints. Perg. fol. nr. 2 in the Royal Library,*
    Stockholm. EIM 4 (Copenhagen: Rosenkilde and Bagger, 1962). P. 24.
Guðrún Nordal. "Handrit, prentaðar bækur og pápísk kvæði á siðskiptaöld."
    In >> *Til heiðurs og hugbótar* (2003). Pp. 131–43, esp. pp. 139–40.
Jakob Benediktsson. "Helgendigte." *KLNM* 6 (1961). Cols. 318–21, esp.
    col. 320.
Jón Helgason. >> "Norges og Islands digtning." In *Litteraturhistorie B:*
    Norge og Island (1953). Pp. 3–179, esp. pp. 163–4.
Kock, E.A. "Anteckningar till Íslenzk Miðaldakvæði." *ANF* 61 (1946):
    1–125, esp. p. 5.
Mogk, Eugen. >> *Geschichte der norwegisch-isländischen Literatur* (1904).
    P. 719.
Nína Leósdóttir and Símon Jón Jóhannsson. "Kvæðið af Laurentio Einom
    Drottins pyslarvott." In *Fimm kvæði um heilaga menn: Agnesarkvæði,*
    Dórotheukvæði, Laurentíuskvæði, Margrétarkvæði, Úrsúlukvæði.
    Unpublished manuscript at Landsbókasafn, 1981. Pp. 4 and 6–7.
Stéfan Einarsson. "Íslenzk helgikvæði á miðöldum." *Tímarit Þjóðræknisfélags*
    Íslendinga 36 (1955): 43–63, esp. p. 55.
– *Íslensk bókmenntasaga 874–1960* (Reykjavík: Oddi, 1961). P. 92.
Vésteinn Ólason. "Kveðskapur frá síðmiðöldum." In >> *Íslensk Bókmenntasaga*
    2 (1993). Pp. 283–378, esp. p. 317.

2. Kvæði af Laurentíusi píslarvotti

A late poem about the life and martyrdom of Saint Laurence.
    Incipit: "Filpó nefndist forðum einn."

Manuscripts:
ÍB 183 4to (ca. 1750), ÍB 811 8vo (ca. 1800–1900), ÍBR 100 8vo (ca. 1700–
1800), ÍBR 152 8vo (ca. 1735–6 and later), JS 265 4to (ca. 1860), JS 588
4to (ca. 1800–1900), JS 84 8vo (ca. 1700–1900), JS 284 8vo (ca. 1850),
JS 471 8vo (ca. 1675–1900), JS 510 8vo (ca. 1675–1900), Lbs 2125 4to
(1865–1912), Lbs 201 8vo (ca. 1850–70), Lbs 607 8vo (ca. 1600–1900),
Lbs 1447 8vo (ca. 1800–30), Lbs 1988 8vo (ca. 1790 and later), Lbs 2974
8vo (ca. 1800–1900), Lbs 3668 8vo (ca. 1800–2000), Lbs 3976 8vo
(ca. 1850–1900), and Lbs 3982 8vo (ca. 1800–50).

Editions:
Jón Þorkelsson. >> *Om Digtningen på Island* (1888). P. 84 (stz. 1).
   Based on ÍB 183 4to, ÍBR 152 8vo, and Lbs 201 8vo.
Nína Leósdóttir and Símon Jón Jóhannsson. "Kvæðið af Laurentio Einom
   Drottins pyslarvott." In *Fimm kvæði um heilaga menn: Agnesarkvæði,
   Dórotheukvæði, Laurentíuskvæði, Margrétarkvæði, Úrsúlukvæði.*
   Unpublished manuscript at Landsbókasafn, 1981. Pp. 11–19.
   Edition of JS 84 8vo.

3. Rímur af Lárentíusi píslarvotti

Five *rímur* about Saint Laurence composed by Eiríkur Hallsson á Höfða
(1614–1698).
   Incipit: "Geðjast mér því gefur stund."

Manuscripts:
ÍB 509 4to (1770–1), ÍBR 93 8vo (ca. 1700–1800), and ÍBR 109 8vo (1829).
Edition:
Nína Leósdóttir and Símon Jón Jóhannsson. "Kvæðið af Laurentio Einom
   Drottins pyslarvott." In *Fimm kvæði um heilaga menn: Agnesarkvæði, Dóro-
   theukvæði, Laurentíuskvæði, Margrétarkvæði, Úrsúlukvæði.* Unpublished
   manuscript at Landsbókasafn, 1981. Pp. 7–8 (I.1–2, 53–4 and 61–2).
   Edition of ÍBR 109 8vo.

LAZARUS OF BETHANY   December 17

1. Vísur af Máríu Magdalene II

A poetic rendering composed between 1300 and 1550 of the composite legend
of Saints Mary Magdalen and Martha. Stz. 3 and 37–41 treat Saint Lazarus.
   Incipit: "Ágætt óðar efni."

Manuscripts:
See Mary Magdalen 1 note (p. 241).
Edition:
Jón Helgason, ed. >> *Íslenzk miðaldakvæði* (1936–8). Vol. 2, pp. 391 and 396–7.

2. Vísur af Máríu Magdalene I

A late medieval (ca. 1400–1550) poem in praise of Saint Mary Magdalen. Stz. 11 mentions Saint Lazarus.
  Incipit: "Vil ég þér vísur vanda."

Manuscripts:
See Mary Magdalen 2 note (p. 242).
Edition:
Jón Helgason, ed. >> *Íslenzk miðaldakvæði* (1936–8). Vol. 2, p. 388.

3. Gjörði í einu

A poetic rendering of biblical stories composed between 1400 and 1550. The poem is also known as *Liljukvistur*. Stz. 32 concerns Saint Lazarus.
  Incipit: "Gjörði í einu orði hreinu."

Manuscripts:
See Elizabeth 1 note (p. 83).
Edition:
Jón Helgason, ed. >> *Íslenzk miðaldakvæði* (1936–8). Vol. 1.2, p. 163.
German translation:
Kock, E.A. "Liljukvistur." *Studia Neophilologica* 15 (1942): 141–56, esp.
  p. 150.

4. Rósa

An early sixteenth-century cosmological poem with an emphasis on the life of Mary the Blessed Virgin attributed to Sigurður blindur. Stz. 84 mentions Saint Lazarus.
  Incipit: "Faðir og son á hæstum hæðum."

Manuscripts:
See Mary the Blessed Virgin 48 note (p. 212).
Editions:
Jón Helgason, ed. >> *Íslenzk miðaldakvæði* (1936–8). Vol. 1.2, p. 24.

Jón Þorkelsson, ed. >> *Kvæðasafn* (1922–7). P. 282.
Norwegian translation:
Orgland, Ivar, trans. and Anne-Lise Knoff, illus. *Rósa. Sigurður blindi í Fagradal* (Oslo: Solum, 1989). P. 50.

5. Krossvísur I

A poem about Christ and the Holy Cross composed ca. 1525 by Bishop Jón Arason (1484–1550). Stz. 23 treats Saint Lazarus.
   Incipit: "Dýrðarfullur drottinn minn."

Manuscripts:
See Cross, the Holy 8 note (p. 75).
Editions:
Finnur Jónsson, ed. >> *Jón Arasons religiøse digte* (1918). Pp. 69–77.
Jón Helgason, ed. >> *Íslenzk miðaldakvæði* (1936–8). Vol. 1.2, p. 257.
[Jón Sigurðsson and Guðbrandur Vigfússon, ed.] >> *Biskupa sögur* (1858–78).
   Vol. 2, p. 562.
*Peringskiöld, J.F. >> *Fragmentum runicopapisticum* (1721).

6. Niðurstigningsvísur

A poetic rendering of the story of Christ's descent to hell composed ca. 1525 by Bishop Jón Arason (1484–1550). Stz. 25 mentions Saint Lazarus.
   Incipit: "Djarflig er mér diktan."

Manuscripts:
See Anne 13 note (p. 43).
Editions:
Finnur Jónsson, ed. >> *Jón Arasons religiøse digte* (1918). P. 64.
Jón Helgason, ed. >> *Íslenzk miðaldakvæði* (1936–8). Vol. 1.2, p. 230.
[Jón Sigurðsson and Guðbrandur Vigfússon, ed.] >> *Biskupa sögur* (1858–78).
   Vol. 2, p. 552.

7. Blómarós

A poem praising Jesus Christ and relating various biblical stories composed ca. 1400–1550. Jón Helgason argues that it is probably from 1550 or the first decade thereafter during the transition from Catholicism to Protestantism. Stz. 125 mentions Saint Lazarus.
   Incipit: "Heyr guð faðir á himna hæðum."

Manuscripts:
See Elizabeth 6 note (p. 85).
Edition:
Jón Helgason, ed. >> *Íslenzk miðaldakvæði* (1936–8). Vol. 1.2, p. 85.

LUCY OF ROME   July 6

Heilagra meyja drápa

A fourteenth-century poem about holy maidens. Stz. 40–1 treat Saint Lucy of
Rome.
   Incipit: "Heyrðu ómælds himna veldis herra guð."

Manuscripts:
See Agatha note (p. 13).
Editions:
Finnur Jónsson, ed. >> *Den norsk-islandske skjaldedigtning* (1912–15).
   Vol. AII, pp. 534–5 and vol. BII, p. 592.
Kock, Ernst Albin, ed. >> *Den norsk-islandske skaldediktningen* (1946–50).
   Vol. 2, pp. 327–8.
Wolf, Kirsten, ed. "Anonymous, *Heilagra meyja drápa* '*Drápa* about Holy
   Maidens'." In >> *Poetry on Christian Subjects* (2007). Vol. 2, pp. 916–17.
Danish translation:
Finnur Jónsson, ed. >> *Den norsk-islandske skjaldedigtning* (1912–15).
   Vol. BII, p. 592.
English translation:
Wolf, Kirsten, ed. "Anonymous, *Heilagra meyja drápa* '*Drápa* about Holy
   Maidens'." In >> *Poetry on Christian Subjects* (2007). Vol. 2, pp. 916–917.

LUCY OF SICILY   December 13

Heilagra meyja drápa

A fourteenth-century poem about holy maidens. Stz. 38–9 treat Saint Lucy of
Sicily.
   Incipit: "Heyrðu ómælds himna veldis herra guð."

Manuscripts:
See Agatha note (p. 13).

Editions:
Finnur Jónsson, ed. >> *Den norsk-islandske skjaldedigtning* (1912–15).
   Vol. AII, p. 534 and vol. BII, pp. 591–2.
Kock, Ernst Albin, ed. >> *Notationes Norrœnæ* (1923–44). §§1847, 2970E,
   and 3397N.
– ed. >> *Den norsk-islandske skaldediktningen* (1946–50). Vol. 2, p. 327.
Wolf, Kirsten, ed. "Anonymous, *Heilagra meyja drápa* 'Drápa about Holy
   Maidens'." In >> *Poetry on Christian Subjects* (2007). Vol. 2, p. 915.
Danish translation:
Finnur Jónsson, ed. >> *Den norsk-islandske skjaldedigtning* (1912–15).
   Vol. BII, pp. 591–2.
English translation:
Wolf, Kirsten, ed. "Anonymous, *Heilagra meyja drápa* 'Drápa about Holy
   Maidens'." In >> *Poetry on Christian Subjects* (2007). Vol. 2, pp. 915–16.

MAGNUS   April 6

Magnúsdiktur

A poetic legend about Saint Magnus, Earl of Orkney, composed ca. 1400–
1550.
   Incipit: "Mína bið ég að málsnilld bæti."

Manuscripts:
AM 710k 4to (ca. 1700–25), AM 721 4to (ca. 1500–50), JS 399a–b 4to
   (ca. 1700–1900), Lbs 2033 4to (ca. 1880–1920), and Lbs 2166 4to
   (ca. 1885–1920).
Editions:
Jón Helgason, ed. >> *Íslenzk miðaldakvæði* (1936–8). Vol. 2, pp. 375–83.
   Based on AM 721 4to II with variants from AM 710k 4to, JS 399a–b 4to,
   Lbs 2033 4to, and Lbs 2166 4to.
Jón Þorkelsson. >> *Om Digtningen på Island* (1888). P. 83 (stz. 1).
   Based on AM 710k 4to II and AM 721 4to.
Literature:
Finnur Jónsson. >> *Den oldnorske og oldislandske Litteraturs Historie*
   (1920–4). Vol. 3, p. 126.
Jakob Benediktsson. "Helgendigte." *KLNM* 6 (1961). Cols. 318–21, esp.
   col. 320.
Jón Helgason. >> "Norges og Islands digtning." In *Litteraturhistorie B:
   Norge og Island* (1953). Pp. 3–179, esp. pp. 163–4.

Jón Torfason and Kristján Eiríksson, ed. >> *Vísnabók Guðbrands* (2000). P. xxxix.

Kock, E.A. "Antecknningar till Íslenzk Miðaldakvæði." *ANF* 61 (1946): 1–125, esp. pp. 95–7.

Mogk, Eugen. >> *Geschichte der norwegisch-isländischen Literatur* (1904). P. 719.

Phelpstead, Carl. *Holy Vikings: Saints' Lives in the Old Icelandic Kings' Sagas* (Tempe, AZ: ACMRS, 2007). P. 16.

Stéfan Einarsson. "Íslenzk helgikvæði á miðöldum." *Tímarit Þjóðræknisfélags Íslendinga* 36 (1955): 43–63, esp. p. 55.

– *Íslensk bókmenntasaga 874–1960* (Reykjavík: Oddi, 1961). P. 92.

Vésteinn Ólason. "Kveðskapur frá síðmiðöldum." In >> *Íslensk Bókmenntasaga* 2 (1993). Pp. 283–378, esp. p. 317.

MARGARET OF ANTIOCH   July 20

1. Margrétarvísur

A late medieval (ca. 1400–1550) poetic rendering of the legend of Saint Margaret.

Incipit: "Margrét heitir mærin bjarta."

Manuscripts:
AM 720a 4to II (ca. 1500–1600), AM 920 4to (ca. 1800–1900), and Lbs 2166 4to (ca. 1885–1920).

Editions:
Jón Helgason, ed. >> *Íslenzk miðaldakvæði* (1936–8). Vol. 2, pp. 383–5. Based on AM 720a 4to II with variants from AM 920 4to and Lbs 2166 4to.

Jón Þorkelsson. >> *Om Digtningen på Island* (1888). Pp. 89–90 (stz. 2^{3-4}, 3, and 18). Based on AM 720a 4to II and AM 920 4to.

Literature:
Bekker-Nielsen, Hans. "Margareta (af Antiochia): Norge og Island." *KLNM* 11 (1966). Cols. 347–8, esp. col. 348.

Guðrún Nordal, Halla Kjartansdóttir, and Vilhjálmur Sigurjónsson. "Um Margrétarkvæði píslarvotts." In *Fimm kvæði um heilaga menn: Agnesarkvæði, Dórotheukvæði, Laurentíuskvæði, Margrétarkvæði, Úrsúlukvæði.* Unpublished manuscript at Landsbókasafn, 1981. Pp. 2–3.

Hálfdan Einarsson. *Sciagraphia historiæ literariæ islandicæ* (Copenhagen: Sander and Schröder, 1777). P. 58.

Jakob Benediktsson. "Helgendigte." *KLNM* 6 (1961). Cols. 318–21, esp. col. 320.

Jón Helgason. >> "Norges og Islands digtning." In *Litteraturhistorie B: Norge og Island* (1953). Pp. 3–179, esp. pp. 163–4.

Kock, E.A. "Antecknningar till Íslenzk Miðaldakvæði." *ANF* 61 (1946): 1–125, esp. pp. 97–8.

Mogk, Eugen. >> *Geschichte der norwegisch-isländischen Literatur* (1904). P. 719.

Soffía Ófeigsdóttir. "*Veroníkukvæði.*" BA thesis, University of Iceland, 1986. P. 66.

Stéfan Einarsson. "Íslenzk helgikvæði á miðöldum." *Tímarit Þjóðræknisfélags Íslendinga* 36 (1954): 43–63, esp. p. 55.

– *Íslensk bókmenntasaga 874–1960* (Reykjavík: Oddi, 1961). P. 92.

Vésteinn Ólason. "Kveðskapur frá síðmiðöldum." In >> *Íslensk Bókmenntasaga* 2 (1993). Pp. 283–378, esp. p. 316.

Wolf, Kirsten, ed. >> *Heilagra meyja sögur* (2003). P. lv.

2. Vísa um Sankta Margareta

A four-line verse about Saint Margaret's encounter with Olibrius, dated to the sixteenth century.

Incipit: "Olibríus var óður og ær."

Manuscript:
AM 433d 12mo (ca. 1500–25).

Literature:

Bekker-Nielsen, Hans. "Margareta (af Antiochia): Norge og Island." *KLNM* 11 (1966). Cols. 347–8, esp. col. 348.

Finnur Jónsson. >> *Den oldnorske og oldislandske Litteraturs Historie* (1920–4). Vol. 3, p. 126.

Guðrún Nordal, Halla Kjartansdóttir, and Vilhjálmur Sigurjónsson. "Um Margrétarkvæði píslarvotts." In *Fimm kvæði um heilaga menn: Agnesarkvæði, Dórotheukvæði, Laurentíuskvæði, Margrétarkvæði, Úrsúlukvæði*. Unpublished manuscript at Landsbókasafn, 1981. P. 3.

Jón Þorkelsson. >> *Om Digtningen på Island* (1888). P. 90.

Stéfan Einarsson. "Íslenzk helgikvæði á miðöldum." *Tímarit Þjóðræknisfélags Íslendinga* 36 (1955): 43–63, esp. p. 55.

Vésteinn Ólason. "Kveðskapur frá síðmiðöldum." In >> *Íslensk Bókmenntasaga* 2 (1993). Pp. 283–378, esp. p. 316.

3. Margrétarkvæði

A late poem (ca. 1725) based on the legend of Saint Margaret.
  Incipit: "Svo er skrifað suður í Róm."

Manuscripts:
Eink 74-3 (ca. 1784–1872), G-2/7 (1837 or earlier), G-63/10 (ca. 1889),
  ÍB 205 8vo (ca. 1800–1900), ÍB 278a 8vo (ca. 1700–1900), ÍB 387 8vo
  (ca. 1700–1900), ÍBR 32 8vo (ca. 1700–1850), ÍBR 100 8vo (ca. 1700–
  1800), JS 256 4to (1840–5), JS 265 4to (ca. 1860), JS 580 4to (ca. 1600–
  1900), JS 84 8vo (ca. 1700–1900), JS 241 8vo (ca. 1820), JS 244 8vo
  (ca. 1800–20), JS 259 8vo (ca. 1800–50), JS 284 8vo (ca. 1850), JS 481
  8vo (ca. 1675–1900), JS 492 8vo (ca. 1675–1900), JS 495 8vo (ca. 1675–
  1900), JS 499 8vo (ca. 1675–1900), JS 510 8vo (ca. 1675–1900), JS
  513 8vo (ca. 1675–1900), JS 515 8vo (ca. 1675–1900), Kvennasögusafn
  Íslands box 27 (ca. 1980), Lbs 2125 4to (1865–1912), Lbs 190 8vo
  (ca. 1850–70), Lbs 201 8vo (ca. 1850–70), Lbs 556 8vo (ca. 1700–1900),
  Lbs 567 8vo (ca. 1700–1900), Lbs 833 8vo (ca. 1800), Lbs 1014 8vo
  (1821–3), Lbs 1109 8vo (ca. 1800–1900), Lbs 1160 8vo (ca. 1870), Lbs
  1217 8vo (ca. 1800–1900), Lbs 1317 8vo (ca. 1800–50), Lbs 1404 8vo
  (1895–1900), Lbs 1447 8vo (ca. 1800–30), Lbs 1633 8vo (ca. 1700–1900),
  Lbs 1669 8vo (ca. 1800–60), Lbs 2503 8vo (ca. 1800–2000), Lbs 3668 8vo
  (ca. 1800–2000), Lbs 3714 8vo (ca. 1800–50), Lbs 3982 8vo (ca. 1800–
  50), Lbs 4255 8vo (ca. 1850–1900), Lbs 4411 8vo (1878–9), SÁM 85/190
  EF (1969), SÁM 85/191 EF (1969), SÁM 85/302 EF (1969), SÁM 85/408
  EF (1970), and SÁM 87/1135 EF (1970).

Editions:
Anna Sigurðardóttir. *Allt hafði annan róm áður í páfadóm: Nunnuklaustrin tvö
  á Íslandi á miðöldum og brot úr kristnisögu* (Reykjavík: Kvennasögusafn
  Íslands, 1988). Pp. 348–52.
  Edition of Sigríður Einarsdóttir's (1901–1989) handwritten copy in
  Kvennasögusafn Íslands box 27.
Guðrún Nordal, Halla Kjartansdóttir, and Vilhjálmur Sigurjónsson.
  "Um Margrétarkvæði píslarvotts." In *Fimm kvæði um heilaga menn:
  Agnesarkvæði, Dórotheukvæði, Laurentíuskvæði, Margrétarkvæði,
  Úrsúlukvæði.* Unpublished manuscript at Landsbókasafn, 1981. Pp. 26–
  41.
  Editions of (in order of presentation): ÍBR 32 8vo (complete poem);
  Lbs 1014 8vo (stz. 19–20 and 37); and Lbs 1447 8vo (complete poem).

Jón Þorkelsson. >> *Om Digtningen på Island* (1888). P. 90 (stz. 1)
  Based on ÍB 205 8vo, ÍB 278a 8vo, ÍB 387 8vo, ÍBR 100 8vo, and Lbs 201
  8vo.
Literature:
Finnur Jónsson. >> *Den oldnorske og oldislandske Litteraturs Historie*
  (1920–4). Vol. 3, p. 126.
Hálfdan Einarsson. *Sciagraphia historiæ literariæ islandicæ* (Copenhagen:
  Sander and Schröder, 1777). P. 58.
Jón Þórarinsson. *Íslensk tónlistarsaga 1000–1800* (Reykjavík: Tónlistarsafn
  Íslands, 2012). P. 368.
Soffía Ófeigsdóttir. *"Veroníkukvæði."* BA thesis, University of Iceland, 1986.
  P. 66.
Stéfan Einarsson. "Íslenzk helgikvæði á miðöldum." *Tímarit Þjóðræknisfélags
  Íslendinga* 36 (1955): 43–63, esp. p. 55.
– *Íslensk bókmenntasaga 874–1960* (Reykjavík: Oddi, 1961). P. 92.
Vésteinn Ólason. "Kveðskapur frá síðmiðöldum." In >> *Íslensk Bókmenntasaga*
  2 (1993). Pp. 283–378, esp. p. 316.

4. Margrétar rímur

A fragmentary *ríma* about Saint Margaret by an unknown author.
  Incipit: "Þundar kera drykkju damm."

Manuscript:
JS 477 8vo (ca. 1675–1900).
Edition:
Finnur Sigmundsson, ed. >> *Rímnatal*. 2 vols. (1966). Vol. 1, pp. 339–40
  (I.1 and 17).
Literature:
Guðrún Nordal, Halla Kjartansdóttir, and Vilhjálmur Sigurjónsson.
  "Um Margrétarkvæði píslarvotts." In *Fimm kvæði um heilaga menn:
  Agnesarkvæði, Dórotheukvæði, Laurentíuskvæði, Margrétarkvæði,
  Úrsúlukvæði*. Unpublished manuscript at Landsbókasafn, 1981. P. 3.

5. Rímur af Margrétu píslarvotti

Three *rímur* about Saint Margaret composed by Gunnar Ólafsson frá Selvogi
(1727–95).
  Incipit: "Fuglin Óma flýgur svo."

Manuscripts:
ÍBR 45 8vo (ca. 1850), ÍBR 144 8vo (ca. 1866–71), Lbs 2468 4to (ca. 1883–4), and Lbs 878 8vo (1876).
Editions:
Finnur Sigmundsson, ed. >> *Rímnatal.* 2 vols. (1966). Vol. 1, p. 339 (I.1 and 18).
Guðrún Nordal, Halla Kjartansdóttir, and Vilhjálmur Sigurjónsson. "Um Margrétarkvæði píslarvotts." In *Fimm kvæði um heilaga menn: Agnesarkvæði, Dórotheukvæði, Laurentíuskvæði, Margrétarkvæði, Úrsúlukvæði.* Unpublished manuscript at Landsbókasafn, 1981. P. 3 (I.18 and III.22–3).
Edition of Lbs 878 8vo.

6. Heilagra meyja drápa

A fourteenth-century poem about holy maidens. Stz. 34–6 treat Saint Margaret. Incipit: "Heyrðu ómælds himna veldis herra guð."

Manuscripts:
See Agatha note (p. 13).
Editions:
Finnur Jónsson, ed. >> *Den norsk-islandske skjaldedigtning* (1912–15). Vol. AII, pp. 533–4 and vol. BII, pp. 590–1.
Kock, Ernst Albin, ed. >> *Notationes Norrœnæ* (1923–44). §§1846, 2976A, and 2976B.
– ed. >> *Den norsk-islandske skaldeddiktningen* (1946–50). Vol. 2, pp. 326–7.
Wolf, Kirsten, ed. "Anonymous, *Heilagra meyja drápa* 'Drápa* about Holy Maidens'." In >> *Poetry on Christian Subjects* (2007). Vol. 2, pp. 912–14.
Danish translation:
Finnur Jónsson, ed. >> *Den norsk-islandske skjaldedigtning* (1912–15). Vol. BII, pp. 590–1.
English translation:
Wolf, Kirsten, ed. "Anonymous, *Heilagra meyja drápa* 'Drápa* about Holy Maidens'." In >> *Poetry on Christian Subjects* (2007). Vol. 2, pp. 912–14.

MARTHA OF BETHANY   July 29

1. Vísur af Máríu Magdalene II

A poetic rendering composed between 1300 and 1550 of the composite legend
of Saints Mary Magdalen and Martha. Stz. 3, 10–15, 17, and 46–52 treat Saint
Martha.
   Incipit: "Ágætt óðar efni."

Manuscripts:
See Mary Magdalen 1 note (p. 241).
Edition:
Jón Helgason, ed. >> *Íslenzk miðaldakvæði* (1936–8). Vol. 2, pp. 391–3 and
   397–8.
Literature:
Bekker-Nielsen, Hans. "Maria Magdalena." *KLNM* 11 (1966). Cols. 410–11,
   esp. col. 410.

2. Vísur af Máríu Magdalene I

A late medieval (ca. 1400–1550) poem in praise of Saint Mary Magdalen. Stz.
10–11 concern Saint Martha.
   Incipit: "Vil ég þér vísur vanda."

Manuscripts:
See Mary Magdalen 2 note (p. 242).
Edition:
Jón Helgason, ed. >> *Íslenzk miðaldakvæði* (1936–8). Vol. 2, pp. 387–8.
Literature:
Bekker-Nielsen, Hans. "Maria Magdalena." *KLNM* 11 (1966). Cols. 410–11,
   esp. col. 410.

3. Gjörði í einu

A poetic rendering of biblical stories composed between 1400 and 1550. The
poem is also known as *Liljukvistur*. Stz. 32 mentions Saint Martha.
   Incipit: "Gjörði í einu orði hreinu."

Manuscripts:
See Elizabeth 1 note (p. 83).

Edition:
Jón Helgason, ed. >> *Íslenzk miðaldakvæði* (1936–8). Vol. 1, p. 163.
German translation:
Kock, E.A. "Liljukvistur." *Studia Neophilologica* 15 (1942): 141–56, esp. p. 150.

MARY THE BLESSED VIRGIN   August 15

1. Máríuflokkr

A fragment of a poem in praise of Mary the Blessed Virgin from the twelfth
century.
   Incipit: "Knǫttu mǫrg á mergjar."

Manuscript:
AM 242 fol. (*Codex Wormianus*) (ca. 1350).
Editions:
Finnur Jónsson, ed. >> *Den norsk-islandske skjaldedigtning* (1912–15).
   Vol. AI, p. 627 and vol. BI, p. 634.
– ed. *Edda Snorra Sturlusonar: Codex Wormianus AM 242, fol.* (Copenhagen
   and Kristiania [Oslo]: Gyldendal, 1924). P. 112.
Jón Sigurðsson et al. *Edda Snorra Sturlusonar: Edda Snorronis Sturlaei.* 3
   vols. (Copenhagen: Legatum Arnamagnaeanum, 1848–87; rpt. Osnabrück:
   Zeller, 1966). Vol. 2, p. 500.
Kock, Ernst Albin, ed. >> *Notationes Norrœnæ* (1923–44). §1271.
– ed. >> *Den norsk-isländska skaldediktningen* (1946–50). Vol. 1, p. 308.
Kock, Ernst Albin, and R. Meissner, ed. *Skaldisches Lesebuch.* 2 vols.
   Rheinische Beiträge und Hilfsbücher zur germanischen Philologie und
   Volkskunde 17 (Halle am S.: Max Niemeyer, 1931). Vol. 1, p. 80.
Sigurður Nordal, ed. *Codex Wormianus (The Younger Edda). MS. No. 242 fol.*
   in The Arnamagnean Collection in the University Library of Copenhagen.
   CCI 2 (Copenhagen: Levin and Munksgaard, 1931).
   Facsimile.
Danish translation:
Finnur Jónsson, ed. >> *Den norsk-islandske skjaldedigtning* (1912–15).
   Vol. BI, p. 634.
Literature:
Ásdís Egilsdóttir, Gunnar Harðarson, and Svanhildur Óskarsdóttir, ed.
   Maríukver. Sögur og kvæði af heilagri guðsmóður frá fyrri tíð (Reykjavík:
   Hið íslenska bókmenntafélag, 1996). P. xxxv.

Clunies Ross, Margaret. >> *A History of Old Norse Poetry and Poetics* (2005). Pp. 209 and 214.

Cormack, Margaret. >> *The Saints in Iceland* (1994). P. 128.

Finnur Jónsson. >> *Den oldnorske og oldislandske Litteraturs Historie* (1920–4). Vol. 2, p. 122.

Guðrún Nordal. *Tools of Literacy: The Role of Skaldic Verse in Icelandic Textual Culture of the Twelfth and Thirteenth Centuries* (Toronto: University of Toronto Press, 2001). Pp. 79–80, 290, 375n4, and 381n41.

Jón Helgason. >> "Norges og Islands digtning." In *Litteraturhistorie B: Norge og Island* (1953). Pp. 3–179, esp. p. 156.

Konráð Gíslason. "Om helrim i förste og tredje linie af regelmæssigt 'drottkvætt' og 'hrynhenda'." *Indbydelsesskrift til Kjøbenhavns Universitets Aarsfest til Erindring om Kirkens Reformation* (Copenhagen: Schultz, 1877). Pp. 1–60, esp. p. 44.

Lange, Wolfgang. >> *Studien zur christlichen Dichtung der Nordgermanen 1000–1200* (1958). Pp. 91–5, 145, and 225–6.

Paasche, Fredrik. >> *Kristendom og kvad* (1914). P. 122.

Vésteinn Ólason. "Old Icelandic Poetry." In *A History of Icelandic Literature*. Ed. Daisy Neijmann. Histories of Scandinavian Literature 5 (Lincoln: University of Nebraska Press, 2006). Pp. 1–64, esp. p. 46.

Viðar Pálsson. "Pagan Mythology in Christian Society." *Gripla* 19 (2008): 123–58, esp. p. 141.

Vries, Jan de. >> *Altnordische Literaturgeschichte* (1964–7). Vol. 1, p. 190 and vol. 2, pp. 62–3.

2. Máríudrápa

A fourteenth-century poem in praise of Mary the Blessed Virgin comprising a catalogue of epithets for Mary and prayers for her mediation and mercy.
Incipit: "Heil, gleði og mildi móðir."

Manuscripts:
AM 757a 4to (ca. 1400), JS 399a–b 4to (ca. 1700–1900), and Lbs 444 4to (ca. 1820–50).

Editions:
*Attwood, Katrina. "The Poems of MS 757a 4to: An Edition and Contextual Study." PhD dissertation. University of Leeds, 1996. Pp. 102–15.
Edition of AM 757a 4to.

Attwood, Katrina, ed. "Anonymous, *Máríudrápa* 'Drápa about Mary'." In >> *Poetry on Christian Subjects* (2007). Vol. 2, pp. 478–514.
Edition of AM 757a 4to with variants from JS 399a–b 4to.

Finnur Jónsson, ed. >> *Den norsk-islandske skjaldedigtning* (1912–15).
   Vol. AII, pp. 464–72 and vol. BII, pp. 496–505.
   Edition of AM 757a 4to.
Kock, Ernst Albin, ed. >> *Notationes Norrœna* (1923–44). §§1633, 1634,
   1635, 1636, 1637, 1638, 1639, 1640, 1641, 1642, 1643, 1644, 1645, 1646,
   1647, 1648, 1649, 1650, 1651, 1652, 1653, 1654, 1655, 1657, 1658, 1659,
   1660, 1661, 1662, 1905Anm, 2113, 2492, 2668, 2669A, 2669B, 2670,
   2671, 2672, 2673, 2674, 2675, 2676, 2677, 2678, 2855, 2856, 2983, 2997,
   2997A, 3266B, 3349, 3350, 3351, 3352, and 3353.
– ed. >> *Den norsk-isländska skaldediktningen* (1946–50). Vol. 2, pp. 271–6.
Konráð Gíslason, ed. *Fire og fyrretyve for en stor Deel forhen utrykte Prøver
   af oldnordisk Sprog og Literatur* (Copenhagen: Gyldendal, 1860). Pp. 555–
   6 (extract only).
   Edition of AM 757a 4to.
Rydberg, Hugo, ed. >> *Die geistlichen Drápur und Dróttkvættfragmente des
   Cod. AM. 757 4to* (1907). Pp. 53–8.
   Edition of AM 757a 4to.
Sveinbjörn Egilsson, ed. *Fjøgur gømul kvæði. Boðsrit til að hlusta á
   þá opinberu yfirheyrslu í Bessastaða Skóla þann 22–29 mai 1844*
   (Viðeyjarklaustur: Helgi Helgason, 1844). P. XI (stz. 28 only).
   Edition of AM 757a 4to.
Wisén, Theodor. *Úrval af norrænum fornkvæðum handa hinum bókmennta-
   iðkendum* (Lund: Berling, 1870). Pp. 47–8 (extract only).
Modern Icelandic language edition:
Ásdís Egilsdóttir, Gunnar Harðarson, and Svanhildur Óskarsdóttir, ed.
   Maríukver. Sögur og kvæði af heilagri guðsmóður frá fyrri tíð (Reykjavík:
   Hið íslenska bókmenntafélag, 1996). P. 149 (extract only).
Danish translation:
Finnur Jónsson, ed. >> *Den norsk-islandske skjaldedigtning* (1912–15).
   Vol. BII, pp. 497–505.
English translation:
Atwood, Katrina, ed. "Anonymous, *Máríudrápa* 'Drápa about Mary'." In >>
   Poetry on Christian Subjects (2007). Vol. 2, pp. 478–514.
Literature:
Attwood, Katrina. "Intertextual Aspects of the Twelfth-Century Christian
   Drápur." *Saga-Book* 24 (1996): 221–39, esp. p. 229.
Bekker-Nielsen, Hans. "Mariadigtning." *KLNM* 11 (1966). Cols. 379–80, esp.
   col. 379.

Chase, Martin. "Christian Poetry: West Norse." In >> *Medieval Scandinavia: An Encyclopedia* (1993). Pp. 73–7, esp. p. 75.

Clunies Ross, Margaret. >> *A History of Old Norse Poetry and Poetics* (2005). Pp. 133–4.

– "Love in a Cold Climate – with the Virgin Mary." In *Romance and Love in Late Medieval and Early Modern Iceland: Essays in Honor of Marianne Kalinke*. Ed. Kirsten Wolf and Johanna Denzin. Islandica 54 (Ithaca: Cornell University Library, 2008). Pp. 303–17, esp. p. 304.

Cormack, Margaret. >> *The Saints in Iceland* (1994). P. 41n60.

Finnur Jónsson. >> *Den oldnorske og oldislandske Litteraturs Historie* (1920–4). Vol. 3, pp. 16–17.

Frank, Roberta. *Old Norse Court Poetry: The* Dróttkvætt *Stanza*. Islandica 42. (Ithaca: Cornell University Press, 1998). P. 99.

Guðrún Nordal. *Tools of Literacy: The Role of Skaldic Verse in Icelandic Textual Culture of the Twelfth and Thirteenth Centuries* (Toronto: University of Toronto Press, 2001). Pp. 64, 66, 71, and 82–3.

Kahle, Bernhard. "Das Christentum in der altwestnordischen Dichtung." *ANF* 13 (1901): 1–40 and 97–160, esp. pp. 30, 32, 100–6, 111, 126–7, 129, and 138–9.

Lange, Wolfgang. >> *Studien zur christlichen Dichtung der Nordgermanen 1000–1200* (1958). Pp. 90 and 225.

Paasche, Fredrik. >> *Kristendom og kvad* (1914). P. 77.

Schorn, Brittany. "Divine Semantics: Terminology for the Human and the Divine in Old Norse Poetry." *Scripta Islandica* 64 (2013): 67–97, esp. pp. 87 and 91.

Schottmann, Hans. >> *Die isländische Mariendichtung* (1973). Pp. 34, 43n29, 48–51, 89, 91, 97–8, 108, 488–9, 491, 493, 518–19, 535–6, 538, 548, and 552–3.

Stéfan Einarsson. "Íslenzk helgikvæði á miðöldum." *Tímarit Þjóðræknisfélags Íslendinga* 36 (1955): 43–63, esp. p. 49.

– *Íslensk bókmenntasaga 874–1960* (Reykjavík: Oddi, 1961). P. 86.

Vésteinn Ólason. "Kveðskapur frá síðmiðöldum." In >> *Íslensk Bókmenntasaga* 2 (1993). Pp. 283–378, esp. p. 309.

– "Old Icelandic Poetry." In *A History of Icelandic Literature*. Ed. Daisy Neijmann. Histories of Scandinavian Literature 5 (Lincoln: University of Nebraska Press, 2006). Pp. 1–64, esp. p. 46.

Viðar Pálsson. "Pagan Mythology in Christian Society." *Gripla* 19 (2008): 123–58, esp. p. 141.

Vries, Jan de. >> *Altnordische Literaturgeschichte* (1964–7). Vol. 2, p. 522.

3. Gyðingsvísur

A fourteenth-century poem about miracles of Mary the Blessed Virgin. It is a
versification of a legend in which a generous Christian man asks a Jew for a loan.
Incipit: "Aldýran biðk óra."

Manuscripts:
AM 757a 4to (ca. 1400), JS 399a–b 4to (ca. 1700–1900), and Lbs 444 4to
(ca. 1820–50).

Editions:
*Attwood, Katrina. "The Poems of MS 757a 4to: An Edition and Contextual
Study." PhD dissertation. University of Leeds, 1996. Pp. 346–8.
Edition of AM 757a 4to.

Attwood, Katrina, ed. "Anonymous, *Gyðingsvísur* 'Vísur about a Jew'." In >>
Poetry on Christian Subjects (2007). Vol. 2, pp. 516–25.
Based on AM 757a 4to with variants from JS 399a–b 4to.

Finnur Jónsson, ed. >> *Den norsk-islandske skjaldedigtning* (1912–15).
Vol. AII, pp. 539–41 and vol. BII, pp. 597–9.
Edition of AM 757a 4to.

Kock, Ernst Albin, ed. >> *Notationes Norrœna* (1923–44). §§1850, 2980,
2981, 2982, 3392, 3393, and 3394.

– ed. >> *Den norsk-isländska skaldediktningen* (1946–50). Vol. 2, pp. 331–2.

Rydberg, Hugo, ed. >> *Die geistlichen Drápur und Dróttkvættfragmente des
Cod. AM. 757 4to* (1907). Pp. 59–60.
Edition of AM 757a 4to.

Danish translation:
Finnur Jónsson, ed. >> *Den norsk-islandske skjaldedigtning* (1912–15).
Vol. BII, pp. 597–9.

English translation:
*Attwood, Katrina, ed. "Anonymous, *Gyðingsvísur* 'Vísur about a Jew'."
In >> *Poetry on Christian Subjects* (2007). Vol. 2, pp. 515–26.

Literature:
Chase, Martin. "Christian Poetry: West Norse." In >> *Medieval Scandinavia:
An Encyclopedia* (1993). Pp. 73–7, esp. p. 75.

Clunies Ross, Margaret. >> *A History of Old Norse Poetry and Poetics*
(2005). Pp. 133 and 209.

– "Love in a Cold Climate – with the Virgin Mary." In *Romance and Love in
Late Medieval and Early Modern Iceland: Essays in Honor of Marianne
Kalinke*. Ed. Kirsten Wolf and Johanna Denzin. Islandica 54 (Ithaca:
Cornell University Library, 2008). Pp. 303–17, esp. p. 305.

Cormack, Margaret. >> *The Saints in Iceland* (1994). P. 43.

Frank, Roberta. *Old Norse Court Poetry: The* Dróttkvætt *Stanza*. Islandica 42. (Ithaca: Cornell University Press, 1998). P. 99.

Guðrún Nordal. *Tools of Literacy: The Role of Skaldic Verse in Icelandic Textual Culture of the Twelfth and Thirteenth Centuries* (Toronto: University of Toronto Press, 2001). Pp. 64, 66, 71, 82–3, and 378n22.

Noreen, Erik. *Studier i fornvästnordisk diktning* 2. Uppsala Universitets Årsskrift 1922 (Uppsala: Akademiska bokhandeln, 1922). P. 30.

Schottmann, Hans. >> *Die isländische Mariendichtung* (1973). Pp. 348, 350, 359–60, 386, 394–6, 398, and 548.

Viðar Pálsson. "Pagan Mythology in Christian Society." *Gripla* 19 (2008): 123–58, esp. p. 141.

4. Brúðkaupsvísur

A fourteenth-century poem narrating a miracle of Mary the Blessed Virgin in which a young man calls off a planned wedding to devote himself to a life in service of the Virgin.

Incipit: "Jöfurr gefi upphaf óðar."

Manuscripts:
AM 721 4to (ca. 1500–50), AM 1032 4to (ca. 1700–25), JS 399a–b 4to (ca. 1700–1900), and Lbs 2166 4to (ca. 1885–1920).

Editions:
Jón Helgason, ed. >> *Íslenzk miðaldakvæði* (1936–8) Vol. 2, pp. 129–36. Edition of AM 721 4to with variants from JS 399a–b 4to and Lbs 2166 4to.

Jón Þorkelsson. >> *Om Digtningen på Island* (1888). P. 98 (stz. 1). Edition of AM 721 4to.

Valgerður Erna Þorvaldsdóttir, ed. "Anonymous, *Brúðkaupsvísur* 'Vísur about a Wedding'." In >> *Poetry on Christian Subjects* (2007). Vol. 2, pp. 529–53.
Edition of AM 721 4to with variants from JS 399a–b 4to and Lbs 2166 4to.

English translation:
Valgerður Erna Þorvaldsdóttir, ed. "Anonymous, *Brúðkaupsvísur* 'Vísur about a Wedding'." In >> *Poetry on Christian Subjects* (2007). Vol. 2, pp. 529–53

Literature:
Bekker-Nielsen, Hans. "Mariadigtning." *KLNM* 11 (1966). Cols. 379–80, esp. col. 379.

Clunies Ross, Margaret. "Love in a Cold Climate – with the Virgin Mary." In *Romance and Love in Late Medieval and Early Modern Iceland: Essays in Honor of Marianne Kalinke*. Ed. Kirsten Wolf and Johanna Denzin. Islandica 54 (Ithaca: Cornell University Library, 2008). Pp. 303–17, esp. pp. 305, 307–16.

Finnur Jónsson. >> *Bókmentasaga Íslendinga fram undir siðabót* (1904–5). P. 461.

– >> *Den oldnorske og oldislandske Litteraturs Historie* (1920–4). Vol. 3, p. 18.

Jón Þorkelsson. >> *Om digtningen på Island* (1888). P. 98.

Kock, E.A. "Anteckningar till Íslenzk miðaldakvæði." *ANF* 61 (1946): 1–125, esp. pp. 3 and 44–9.

Schottmann, Hans. >> *Die isländische Mariendichtung* (1973). Pp. 127, 354–9, 386–8, 393–8, 401–2, 477, and 548.

Vésteinn Ólason. "Kveðskapur frá síðmiðöldum." In >> *Íslensk Bókmenntasaga* 2 (1993). Pp. 283–378, esp. p. 310.

Wrightson, Kellinde, ed. *Fourteenth-Century Icelandic Verse on the Virgin Mary. Drápa af Maríugrát. Vitnisvísur af Maríu. Maríuvísur I–III*. Viking Society for Northern Research Text Series 14 (University College London: Viking Society for Northern Research, 2001). Pp. xiv–xv.

5. Máríuvísur I

A fourteenth-century poem about a miracle of Mary the Blessed Virgin in which a woman who had her son-in-law killed is burned alive but emerges unscathed from the fire.

Incipit: "Mér gefi hljóð, sá er heyrir hjarta mitt."

Manuscripts:
AM 721 4to (ca. 1500–50) and AM 1032 4to (ca. 1700–25).
Editions:
Finnur Jónsson, ed. >> *Den norsk-islandske skjaldedigtning* (1912–15). Vol. AII, pp. 487–92 and vol. BII, pp. 526–32.
Edition of AM 721 4to.
Gade, Kari Ellen, ed. "Anonymous, *Máríuvísur I* '*Vísur* about Mary I'." In >> *Poetry on Christian Subjects* (2007). Vol. 2, pp. 679–99.
Edition of AM 721 4to with variants from AM 1032 4to.
Kahle, Bernhard, ed. >> *Isländische geistliche Dichtungen des ausgehenden Mittelalters* (1898). Pp. 31–7.
Edition of AM 721 4to.
Kock, Ernst Albin, ed. >> *Notationes Norrœna* (1923–44). §§1679, 1680B, 1681, 1682, 1683, 1684, 1685, 1686, 1687, 1688, 1689, 1690, 1691, 1692, 2764, 2800, 2863, 2864, 2865, 2866, 2867, 2868, 2869, 2870, 3359, 3360, and 3397K.

– ed. >> *Den norsk-isländska skaldediktningen* (1946–50). Vol. 2, pp. 288–92.
Sperber, Hans, ed. >> *Sechs isländische Gedichte legendarischen Inhalts*
   (1911). Pp. 1–8.
   Edition of AM 721 4to.
Wrightson, Kellinde, ed. >> *Fourteenth-Century Icelandic Verse on the Virgin
   Mary* (2001). Pp. 40–54.
   Edition of AM 721 4to with variants from AM 1032 4to.
Danish translation:
Finnur Jónsson, ed. >> *Den norsk-islandske skjaldedigtning* (1912–15).
   Vol. BII, pp. 526–32.
English translations:
Gade, Kari Ellen, ed. "Anonymous, *Máríuvísur I* '*Vísur* about Mary I'." In >>
   Poetry on Christian Subjects (2007). Vol. 2, pp. 679–99.
Wrightson, Kellinde, ed. >> *Fourteenth-Century Icelandic Verse on the Virgin
   Mary* (2001). Pp. 40–54.
Literature:
Ármann Jakobsson. "The Homer of the North, or: Who Was Sigurður the
   Blind?" *European Journal of Scandinavian Studies* 44 (2014): 4–19, esp.
   p. 5n2.
Bekker-Nielsen, Hans. "Mariadigtning." *KLNM* 11 (1966). Cols. 379–80, esp.
   col. 379.
Clunies Ross, Margaret. "Love in a Cold Climate – with the Virgin Mary."
   In *Romance and Love in Late Medieval and Early Modern Iceland: Essays
   in Honor of Marianne Kalinke*. Ed. Kirsten Wolf and Johanna Denzin.
   Islandica 54 (Ithaca: Cornell University Library, 2008). Pp. 303–17, esp.
   pp. 305–6.
Cormack, Margaret. >> *The Saints in Iceland* (1994). P. 41n60.
Finnur Jónsson. >> *Bókmentasaga Íslendinga fram undir siðabót* (1904–5).
   P. 461.
– >> *Den oldnorske og oldislandske Litteraturs Historie* (1920–4). Vol. 3,
   pp. 16–17.
Guðrún Nordal. *Tools of Literacy: The Role of Skaldic Verse in Icelandic
   Textual Culture of the Twelfth and Thirteenth Centuries* (Toronto:
   University of Toronto Press, 2001). P. 382n46.
Kahle, Bernhard. "Das Christentum in der altwestnordischen Dichtung." *ANF*
   13 (1901): 1–40 and 97–160, esp. pp. 10, 19, and 101.
Jón Þorkelsson. >> *Om digtningen på Island* (1888). P. 41.
Mogk, Eugen. >> *Geschichte der norwegisch-isländischen Literatur* (1904).
   P. 717.
Poole, R.G. *Viking Poems on War and Peace: A Study in Skaldic Narrative*
   (Toronto: University of Toronto Press, 1991). P. 32.

Schottmann, Hans. >> *Die isländische Mariendichtung* (1973). Pp. 127–8,
    351–4, 360–7, 385, and 387.
Vries, Jan de. >> *Altnordische Literaturgeschichte* (1964–7). Vol. 2, p. 522.
Wrightson, Kellinde. "Marian Miracles in Old Icelandic Skaldic Poetry."
    In *Treasures of the Elder Tongue: Fifty Years of Old Norse in Melbourne.
    The Proceedings of the Symposium to Celebrate the Golden Jubilee of
    Old Norse at the University of Melbourne 14th May 1994.* Ed. Katrina
    Burge and John Stanley Martin (Melbourne: Department of Germanic and
    Russian Studies, 1995). Pp. 87–99, esp. pp. 87–9 and 93–4.
– "The Jilted Fiancée: The Old Icelandic Miracle Poem *Vitnisvísur af Maríu*
    and Its Modern English Translation." *Parergon* 15 (1997): 117–36, esp.
    p. 127n23.
NOTE:
The poem contains material about Saint Andrew. See his entry.

6. Máríuvísur II

A fourteenth-century poem about a miracle of Mary the Blessed Virgin in
which a woman's dead son is revived.
    Incipit: "Dýrðar, gef þú, er dóms vörðr."

Manuscripts:
AM 711a 4to (ca. 1700–25), AM 713 4to (ca. 1500–50), and AM 721 4to
    (ca. 1500–50).
Editions:
Finnur Jónsson, ed. >> *Den norsk-islandske skjaldedigtning* (1912–15).
    Vol. AII, pp. 492–6 and vol. BII, pp. 532–8.
    Edition of AM 721 4to with variants from AM 713 4to.
Gade, Kari Ellen, ed. "Anonymous, *Máríuvísur II* '*Vísur* about Mary II'."
    In >> *Poetry on Christian Subjects* (2007). Vol. 2, pp. 702–17.
    Edition of AM 713 4to with variants from AM 721 4to.
Kahle, Bernhard, ed. >> *Isländische geistliche Dichtungen des ausgehenden
    Mittelalters* (1898). Pp. 37–42.
    Edition of AM 721 4to.
Kock, Ernst Albin, ed. >> *Notationes Norrœna* (1923–44). §§1693, 1694,
    1695, 1696, 1697, 2247D, 3266D, 3350, 3361, 3362, 3363, and 3364.
– ed. >> *Den norsk-isländska skaldediktningen* (1946–50). Vol. 2, pp. 292–5.
Sperber, Hans, ed. >> *Sechs isländische Gedichte legendarischen Inhalts*
    (1911). Pp. 9–14.
    Edition of AM 721 4to with variants from AM 713 4to.

Wrightson, Kellinde, ed. >> *Fourteenth-Century Icelandic Verse on the Virgin Mary* (2001). Pp. 55–66.
   Edition of AM 721 4to with variants from AM 713 4to and AM 711a 4to.
Danish translation:
Finnur Jónsson, ed. >> *Den norsk-islandske skjaldedigtning* (1912–15).
   Vol. BII, pp. 533–8.
English translations:
Gade, Kari Ellen, ed. "Anonymous, *Máríuvísur II* 'Vísur about Mary II'."
   In >> *Poetry on Christian Subjects* (2007). Vol. 2, pp. 702–17.
Wrightson, Kellinde, ed. >> *Fourteenth-Century Icelandic Verse on the Virgin Mary* (2001). Pp. 55–66.
Literature:
Bekker-Nielsen, Hans. "Mariadigtning." *KLNM* 11 (1966). Cols. 379–80, esp. col. 379.
Clunies Ross, Margaret. "Love in a Cold Climate – with the Virgin Mary." In *Romance and Love in Late Medieval and Early Modern Iceland: Essays in Honor of Marianne Kalinke.* Ed. Kirsten Wolf and Johanna Denzin. Islandica 54 (Ithaca: Cornell University Library, 2008). Pp. 303–17, esp. pp. 305–6.
Cormack, Margaret. >> *The Saints in Iceland* (1994). P. 41n60.
Finnur Jónsson. >> *Bókmentasaga Íslendinga fram undir siðabót* (1904–5). P. 461.
– >> *Den oldnorske og oldislandske Litteraturs Historie* (1920–4). Vol. 3, pp. 16–17.
Guðrún Nordal. *Tools of Literacy: The Role of Skaldic Verse in Icelandic Textual Culture of the Twelfth and Thirteenth Centuries* (Toronto: University of Toronto Press, 2001). P. 384n50.
– "Handrit, prentaðar bækur og pápísk kvæði á siðskiptaöld." In >> *Til heiðurs og hugbótar* (2003). Pp. 131–43, esp. p. 139–40.
Jón Helgason. "Nokkur íslenzk handrit frá 16. öld." *Skírnir* 106 (1932): 143–68.
– >> "Norges og Islands digtning." In *Litteraturhistorie B: Norge og Island* (1953). Pp. 3–179, esp. p. 162.
Jón Þorkelsson. >> *Om digtningen på Island* (1888). P. 41.
Kahle, Bernhard. "Das Christentum in der altwestnordischen Dichtung." *ANF* 13 (1901): 1–40 and 97–160, esp. pp. 10, 19, 101, and 104–5.
Kock, Ernst Albin. "Ett kapitel nordisk metrik och textkritik." *ANF* 49 (1933): 279–94.
Mogk, Eugen. >> *Geschichte der norwegisch-isländischen Literatur* (1904). P. 717.

Schottmann, Hans. >> *Die isländische Mariendichtung* (1973). Pp. 68, 128,
    352–4, 380–5, 387–8, 393–4, 400, 403, 475–6, 483, and 553.
Vries, Jan de. >> *Altnordische Literaturgeschichte* (1964–7). Vol. 2, p. 522.
Wrightson, Kellinde. "Marian Miracles in Old Icelandic Skaldic Poetry."
    In *Treasures of the Elder Tongue: Fifty Years of Old Norse in Melbourne.*
    The Proceedings of the Symposium to Celebrate the Golden Jubilee of Old
    Norse at the University of Melbourne 14th May 1994. Ed. Katrina Burge
    and John Stanley Martin (Melbourne: Department of Germanic
    and Russian Studies, 1995). Pp. 87–99, esp. pp. 87–90 and 93–4.
NOTE:
The poem contains material about Saint Andrew. See his entry.

7. Máríuvísur III

A fourteenth-century poem about a miracle of Mary the Blessed Virgin known
variously as "The Drowned Sacristan" or "Ave on the Tongue."
    Incipit: "Dróttinn, gef þú mér mátt, máttugr, bragarhátt."

Manuscripts:
AM 721 4to (ca. 1500–50) and AM 1032 4to (ca. 1700–25).
Editions:
Finnur Jónsson, ed. >> *Den norsk-islandske skjaldedigtning* (1912–15).
    Vol. AII, pp. 496–500 and vol. BII, pp. 538–45.
    Edition of AM 721 4to.
Gade, Kari Ellen, ed. "Anonymous, *Máríuvísur III* 'Vísur about Mary III'."
    In >> *Poetry on Christian Subjects* (2007). Vol. 2, pp. 719–38.
    Edition of AM 721 4to with variants from AM 1032 4to.
Kahle, Bernhard, ed. >> *Isländische geistliche Dichtungen des ausgehenden*
    Mittelalters (1898). Pp. 43–9.
    Edition of AM 721 4to.
Kock, Ernst Albin, ed. >> *Notationes Norrœna* (1923–44). §§1698B, 1698C,
    1699, 1700, 1701, 1702, 1703, 1704, 1705, 1706, 2871, 2872, 2873,
    2997B, 3277B, 3357, 3365, 3366, 3367, 3368, and 3370.
– ed. >> *Den norsk-isländska skaldediktningen* (1946–50). Vol. 2, pp. 295–9.
Sperber, Hans, ed. >> *Sechs isländische Gedichte legendarischen Inhalts*
    (1911). Pp. 15–22.
    Edition of AM 721 4to.
Wrightson, Kellinde, ed. >> *Fourteenth-Century Icelandic Verse on the Virgin*
    Mary (2001). Pp. 67–81.
    Edition of AM 721 4to with variants from AM 1032 4to.

Danish translation:
Finnur Jónsson, ed. >> *Den norsk-islandske skjaldedigtning* (1912–15).
Vol. BII, pp. 538–45.
English translations:
Gade, Kari Ellen, ed. "Anonymous, *Máríuvísur III* 'Vísur about Mary III'."
In >> *Poetry on Christian Subjects* (2007). Vol. 2, pp. 719–38.
Wrightson, Kellinde, ed. >> *Fourteenth-Century Icelandic Verse on the Virgin Mary* (2001). Pp. 67–81.
Literature:
Bekker-Nielsen, Hans. "Mariadigtning." *KLNM* 11 (1966). Cols. 379–80, esp. col. 379.
Clunies Ross, Margaret. "Love in a Cold Climate – with the Virgin Mary."
In *Romance and Love in Late Medieval and Early Modern Iceland: Essays in Honor of Marianne Kalinke*. Ed. Kirsten Wolf and Johanna Denzin. Islandica 54 (Ithaca: Cornell University Library, 2008). Pp. 303–17, esp. pp. 305–6.
Cormack, Margaret. >> *The Saints in Iceland* (1994). P. 41n60.
Finnur Jónsson. >> *Bókmentasaga Íslendinga fram undir siðabót* (1904–5). P. 461.
– >> *Den oldnorske og oldislandske Litteraturs Historie* (1920–4). Vol. 3, pp. 16–17.
Jón Helgason. >> "Norges og Islands digtning." In *Litteraturhistorie B: Norge og Island* (1953). Pp. 3–179, esp. p. 162.
Jón Þorkelsson. >> *Om Digtningen på Island* (1888). P. 42.
Kahle, Bernhard. "Das Christentum in der altwestnordischen Dichtung." *ANF* 13 (1901): 1–40 and 97–160, esp. pp. 10, 101, 105, and 151.
Kock, Ernst Albin. "Ett kapitel nordisk metrik och textkritik." *ANF* 49 (1933): 279–94.
Mogk, Eugen. >> *Geschichte der norwegisch-isländischen Literatur* (1904). P. 717.
Poole, R.G. *Viking Poems on War and Peace: A Study in Skaldic Narrative* (Toronto: University of Toronto Press, 1991). P. 32.
Schottmann, Hans. >> *Die isländische Mariendichtung* (1973). Pp. 128, 352–4, 367–74, 385, 387, 389, 391n8, 393–4, and 406.
Vries, Jan de. >> *Altnordische Literaturgeschichte* (1964–7). Vol. 2, p. 522.
Wrightson, Kellinde. "Marian Miracles in Old Icelandic Skaldic Poetry."
In *Treasures of the Elder Tongue: Fifty Years of Old Norse in Melbourne. The Proceedings of the Symposium to Celebrate the Golden Jubilee of Old Norse at the University of Melbourne 14th May 1994*. Ed. Katrina

Burge and John Stanley Martin (Melbourne: Department of Germanic and
Russian Studies, 1995). Pp. 87–99, esp. pp. 87–9 and 91–3.
NOTE:
The poem contains material about Saint Andrew. See his entry.

8. Vitnisvísur af Máríu

A fourteenth-century poem about a miracle of Mary the Blessed Virgin re-
ferred to as "Faithless Lover" or "Jilted Fiancée."
  Incipit: "Heyrðu til upphafsorða, allsvinnandi minna."

Manuscripts:
AM 711a 4to (ca. 1700–25), AM 713 4to (ca. 1500–50), and AM 721 4to
  (ca. 1500–50).
Editions:
Finnur Jónsson, ed. >> *Den norsk-islandske skjaldedigtning* (1912–15).
  Vol. AII, pp. 483–7 and vol. BII, pp. 520–6.
  Edition of AM 713 4to with variants from AM 721 4to.
Gade, Kari Ellen, ed. "Anonymous, *Vitnisvísur af Máríu* 'Testimonial *Vísur*
  about Mary'." In >> *Poetry on Christian Subjects* (2007). Vol. 2, pp.
  740–57.
  Edition of AM 713 4to with variants from AM 721 4to.
Kahle, Bernhard, ed. >> *Isländische geistliche Dichtungen des ausgehenden
  Mittelalters* (1898). Pp. 49–55.
  Edition of AM 713 4to.
Kock, Ernst Albin, ed. >> *Notationes Norrœna* (1923–44). §§1667Anm,
  1674, 1675, 1676, 1677A, 1677B, 1677C, 1678, 2668, 2858, 2859, 2860,
  2861, 2862, 2668, 3266C, 3358, 3358A, and 3358B.
– ed. >> *Den norsk-isländska skaldediktningen* (1946–50). Vol. 2,
  pp. 285–8.
Sperber, Hans, ed. >> *Sechs isländische Gedichte legendarischen Inhalts*
  (1911). Pp. 23–9.
  Edition of AM 721 4to with variants from AM 713 4to.
Wrightson, Kellinde, ed. >> *Fourteenth-Century Icelandic Verse on the Virgin
  Mary* (2001). Pp. 27–39.
  Edition of AM 713 4to with variants from AM 721 4to and AM 711a 4to.
Danish translation:
Finnur Jónsson, ed. >> *Den norsk-islandske skjaldedigtning* (1912–15).
  Vol. BII, pp. 520–6.

English translations:
Gade, Kari Ellen, ed. "Anonymous, *Vitnisvísur af Máríu* 'Testimonial *Vísur* about Mary'." In >> *Poetry on Christian Subjects* (2007). Vol. 2, pp. 741–57.
Wrightson, Kellinde. "The Jilted Fiancée: The Old Icelandic Miracle Poem *Vitnisvísur af Maríu* and Its Modern English Translation." *Parergon* 15 (1997): 117–36, esp. pp. 132–6.
– >> *Fourteenth-Century Icelandic Verse on the Virgin Mary. Drápa af Maríugrát* (2001). Pp. 27–39.
Literature:
Bekker-Nielsen, Hans. "Mariadigtning." *KLNM* 11 (1966). Cols. 379–80, esp. col. 379.
Clunies Ross, Margaret. >> *A History of Old Norse Poetry and Poetics* (2005). P. 214n8.
– "Love in a Cold Climate – with the Virgin Mary." In *Romance and Love in Late Medieval and Early Modern Iceland: Essays in Honor of Marianne Kalinke*. Ed. Kirsten Wolf and Johanna Denzin. Islandica 54 (Ithaca: Cornell University Library, 2008). Pp. 303–17, esp. pp. 305–6 and 311n16.
Cormack, Margaret. >> *The Saints in Iceland* (1994). P. 41n60.
Guðrún Nordal. "Handrit, prentaðar bækur og pápísk kvæði á siðskiptaöld." In >> *Til heiðurs og hugbótar* (2003). Pp. 131–43, esp. pp. 139–40.
Jón Þorkelsson. >> *Om Digtningen på Island* (1888). P. 42.
Mogk, Eugen. >> *Geschichte der norwegisch-isländischen Literatur* (1904). P. 717.
Poole, R.G. *Viking Poems on War and Peace: A Study in Skaldic Narrative* (Toronto: University of Toronto Press, 1991). P. 32.
Schottmann, Hans. >> *Die isländische Mariendichtung* (1973). Pp. 128, 351–4, 374–9, 381, 385–6, 388–90, 399–401, 476, 483, and 553.
Wrightson, Kellinde. "Changing Attitudes to Old Norse Marian Poetry." In *Old Norse Studies in the New World: A Collection of Essays to Celebrate the Jubilee of the Teaching of Old Norse at the University of Sydney 1943–1993*. Ed. Geraldine Barnes, Margaret Clunies Ross, and Judy Quinn (Sydney: Department of English, University of Sydney, 1994). Pp. 138–53, esp. pp. 139–48.
– "Marian Miracles in Old Icelandic Skaldic Poetry." In *Treasures of the Elder Tongue: Fifty Years of Old Norse in Melbourne. The Proceedings of the Symposium to Celebrate the Golden Jubilee of Old Norse at the University of Melbourne 14th May 1994*. Ed. Katrina Burge and John Stanley Martin (Melbourne: Department of Germanic and Russian Studies, 1995). Pp. 87–99, esp. pp. 87–9 and 93.

NOTE:
The poem contains material about Saint Andrew. See his entry.

9. Drápa af Máríugrát

A fourteenth-century poem about Mary the Blessed Virgin's lament to Saint Augustine about her sorrows and her enumeration to a monk of her five joys.
  Incipit: "Orðin gef þú mjög til mærðar, minn lausnari, skáldi þínu."

Manuscripts:
AM 713 4to (ca. 1500–50), AM 920 4to (ca. 1800–1900), and AM 1032 4to (ca. 1700–25).

Editions:
Finnur Jónsson, ed. >> *Den norsk-islandske skjaldedigtning* (1912–15). Vol. AII, pp. 472–82 and vol. BII, pp. 505–19.
  Edition of AM 713 4to and AM 1032 4to.
Gade, Kari Ellen, ed. "Anonymous, *Drápa af Máríugrát* 'Drápa about the Lament of Mary'." In >> *Poetry on Christian Subjects* (2007). Vol. 2, pp. 759–94.
  Based on AM 713 4to, AM 920 4to, and AM 1032 4to.
Kahle, Bernhard, ed. >> *Isländische geistliche Dichtungen des ausgehenden Mittelalters* (1898). Pp. 55–6.
  Edition of AM 713 4to.
Kock, Ernst Albin, ed. >> *Notationes Norrœna* (1923–44). §§1663, 1664A, 1664D, 1665, 1666, 1667, 1668, 1669, 1670, 1671, 1672, 1673, 2663, 2680Anm, 2680AAnm, 2680B, 2680C, 2680D, 2681, 2682, 2683, 2684, 2685, 2686, 2687, 2680B, 2688, 2689, 2690, 2691, 2692, 2693, 2694, 2695, 2696, 2697, 2831, 2857, 2858, 3354A, 3354B, 3355, 3356, and 3357.
– ed. >> *Den norsk-isländska skaldediktningen* (1946–50). Vol. 2, pp. 276–85.
Sperber, Hans, ed. >> *Sechs isländische Gedichte legendarischen Inhalts* (1911). Pp. 30–42.
  Edition of AM 713 4to.
Wrightson, Kellinde, ed. >> *Fourteenth-Century Icelandic Verse on the Virgin Mary* (2001). Pp. 1–26.
  Edition of AM 713 4to with variants from AM 920 4to and AM 1032 4to.
Danish translation:
Finnur Jónsson, ed. >> *Den norsk-islandske skjaldedigtning* (1912–15). Vol. BII, pp. 505–19.

English translations:
Gade, Kari Ellen, ed. "Anonymous, *Drápa af Máríugrát* 'Drápa about the Lament of Mary'." In >> *Poetry on Christian Subjects* (2007). Vol. 2, pp. 759–94.

Wrightson, Kellinde, ed. >> *Fourteenth-Century Icelandic Verse on the Virgin Mary* (2001). Pp. 1–26.

Literature:
Attwood, Katrina. "Intertextual Aspects of the Twelfth-Century Christian *Drápur.*" *Saga-Book* 24 (1996): 221–39, esp. p. 230.

Bekker-Nielsen, Hans. "Mariadigtning." *KLNM* 11 (1966). Cols. 379–80, esp. col. 379.

– "Mariaklager." *KLNM* 11 (1966). Cols. 396–8, esp. col. 397.

Clunies Ross, Margaret. >> *A History of Old Norse Poetry and Poetics* (2005). Pp. 38n15, 214, 215n8, and 219.

– "Love in a Cold Climate – with the Virgin Mary." In *Romance and Love in Late Medieval and Early Modern Iceland: Essays in Honor of Marianne Kalinke*. Ed. Kirsten Wolf and Johanna Denzin. Islandica 54 (Ithaca: Cornell University Library, 2008). Pp. 303–17, esp. p. 304.

Finnur Jónsson. >> *Den oldnorske og oldislandske Litteraturs Historie* (1920–4). Vol. 3, pp. 16–17.

Harris, Joseph. "The Bällsta-Inscriptions and Old Norse Literary History." In *International Scandinavian and Medieval Studies in Memory of Gerd Wolfgang Weber*. Ed. Michael Dallapiazza, Olaf Hansen, Preben Meulengracht Sørensen, and Yvonne S. Bonnetain (Trieste: Edizioni Parnaso, 2000). Pp. 223–39, esp. pp. 225, 228, and 235.

Jón Helgason. "Nokkur íslenzk handrit frá 16. öld." *Skírnir* 106 (1932): 143–68.

– "Bällsta-indskriftens 'i grati'." *ANF* 59 (1944): 159–67.

– >> "Norges og Islands digtning." In *Litteraturhistorie B: Norge og Island* (1953). Pp. 3–179, esp. p. 164.

Jón Þorkelsson. >> *Om Digtningen på Island* (1888). P. 42.

Kahle, Bernhard. "Das Christentum in der altwestnordischen Dichtung." *ANF* 13 (1901): 1–40 and 97–160, esp. pp. 20, 32, 101–3, 106, 117, 131–6, 139, and 144.

Kock, E.A. "Anteckningar till Íslenzk Miðaldakvæði." *ANF* 54 (1939): 94–107, esp. p. 94.

Mogk, Eugen. >> *Geschichte der norwegisch-isländischen Literatur* (1904). Pp. 716–17.

Schorn, Brittany. "Divine Semantics: Terminology for the Human and the Divine in Old Norse Poetry." *Scripta Islandica* 64 (2013): 67–97, esp. p. 87.

Schottmann, Hans. >> *Die isländische Mariendichtung* (1973). Pp. 88–9, 92, 106–8, 125, 205, 306, 490–3, 504–12, 519, 549, and 553.

Stéfan Einarsson. "Íslenzk helgikvæði á miðöldum." *Tímarit Þjóðræknisfélags Íslendinga* 36 (1955): 43–63, esp. p. 49.

– *Íslensk bókmenntasaga 874–1960* (Reykjavík: Oddi, 1961). P. 86.

Vésteinn Ólason. "Kveðskapur frá síðmiðöldum." In >> *Íslensk Bókmenntasaga* 2 (1993). Pp. 283–378, esp. p. 311.

von See, Klaus. "Das Phantom einer altgermanischen Elegiendichtung. Kritische Bemerkungen zu Daniel Sävborg, 'Sorg och elegi i Eddans hjaltediktning'." *Skandinavistik* 28 (1998): 87–100.

Vries, Jan de. >> *Altnordische Literaturgeschichte* (1964–7). Vol. 2, p. 522.

Wrightson, Kellinde. "*Drápa af Maríugrát*, the Joys and Sorrows of the Virgin and Christ, and the Dominican Rosary." *Saga-Book* 24 (1997): 283–92.

– "The *lærðir menn* of the Old Icelandic Marian Lament *drápa af Maríugrát*." In *Sagas and the Norwegian Experience/Sagaene og Noreg. 10th International Saga Conference, Trondheim, 3.–9. August 1977* (Trondheim: NTNU, 1997). Pp. 685–92.

NOTE:
The poem contains material about Saints Augustine, Simeon the Righteous, Mary Magdalen, and John the Evangelist. See the entries for the individual saints.

10. Um heiðurs mey vil ég hefja

A poem from ca. 1300–1550 based on a popular medieval Marian legend about a sacristine nun who left the convent to wed her childhood sweetheart (cf. Robert Guiette, *La légende de la Sacristine* [Paris, 1927] and C.R. Unger, ed., *Mariu saga: Legender om Jomfru Maria og hendes jertegn* [Christiania (Oslo): Brögger and Christie, 1871], pp. 514–20 and 521–7). Only the first six stz. survive.

Incipit: "Um heiðurs mey vil ég hefja."

Manuscripts:
AM 720a 4to I (ca. 1500), AM 920 4to (ca. 1800–1900), and Lbs 2166 4to (ca. 1885–1920).

Editions:
Jón Helgason, ed. >> *Íslenzk miðaldakvæði* (1936–8). Vol. 2, pp. 179–80 Based on AM 720a 4to I with variants from Lbs 2166 4to and notes from C.R. Unger, ed., *Mariu saga: Legender om Jomfru Maria og hendes jertegn* (Christiania [Oslo]: Brögger and Christie, 1871).

Jón Þorkelsson. >> *Om Digtningen på Island* (1888). Pp. 87–8 (stz. 1, 2¹, 3¹, 4¹, 5¹, and 6).

Based on AM 720a 4to I and AM 920 4to.

Literature:

Bekker-Nielsen, Hans. "Mariadigtning." *KLNM* 11 (1966). Cols. 379–80, esp. col. 379.

Finnur Jónsson. >> *Bókmentasaga Íslendinga fram undir siðabót* (1904–5). P. 461.

Kock, E.A. "Anteckningar till Íslenzk Miðaldakvæði." *ANF* 61 (1946): 1–125, esp. p. 63.

Schottmann, Hans. >> *Die isländische Mariendichtung* (1973). Pp. 437–8, 476–7, and 487n20.

11. Pétursdiktur

A Marian miracle poem from ca. 1300–1550 about a monk at Saint Peter's Church in Cologne who fathered a child and died without last rites, but was brought back to life through the aid of Saint Peter and Mary the Blessed Virgin (cf. C.R. Unger, ed., *Mariu saga: Legender om Jomfru Maria og hendes jertegn* [Christiania (Oslo): Brögger and Christie, 1871], pp. 860–2).

Incipit: "María ertu mild og skær."

Manuscripts:

AM 713 4to (ca. 1500–50), AM 715f 4to (ca. 1700–25), and Lbs 2166 4to (ca. 1885–1920).

Editions:

Jón Helgason, ed. >> *Íslenzk miðaldakvæði* (1936–8). Vol. 2, pp. 123–7.
    Based on AM 713 4to with variants from AM 715f 4to and Lbs 2166 4to.

Jón Þorkelsson. >> *Om Digtningen på Island* (1888). P. 49 (stz. 1).
    Based on AM 713 4to and AM 715f 4to.

Literature:

Bekker-Nielsen, Hans. "Mariadigtning." *KLNM* 11 (1966). Cols. 379–80.

Finnur Jónsson. >> *Bókmentasaga Íslendinga fram undir siðabót* (1904–5). P. 461.

– >> *Den oldnorske og oldislandske Litteraturs Historie* (1920–4). Vol. 3, pp. 124–5.

Schottmann, Hans. >> *Die isländische Mariendichtung* (1973). Pp. 432–6 and 543–4.

NOTE:

The poem contains material about Saint Peter. See his entry.

12. María vil ég þig móðir guðs

A Marian miracle poem from ca. 1300–1550 about an abbess who became
pregnant and was aided by Mary the Blessed Virgin (cf. C.R. Unger, ed., *Mariu
saga: Legender om Jomfru Maria og hendes jertegn* [Christiania (Oslo):
Brögger and Christie, 1871], pp. 121–6 and 900–4).
   Incipit: "María vil ég þig móðir guðs."

Manuscripts:
AM 711a 4to (ca. 1700–25), AM 713 4to (ca. 1500–50), AM 920 4to
   (ca. 1800–1900), and Lbs 2166 4to (ca. 1885–1920).
Editions:
Jón Helgason, ed. >> *Íslenzk miðaldakvæði* (1936–8). Vol. 2, pp. 136–41.
   Based on AM 713 4to with variants from AM 711a 4to and AM 920 4to.
Jón Þorkelsson. >> *Om Digtningen på Island* (1888). P. 49 (stz. 1).
   Based on AM 711a 4to, AM 713 4to, and AM 920 4to.
Literature:
Bekker-Nielsen, Hans. "Mariadigtning." *KLNM* 11 (1966). Cols. 379–80.
Finnur Jónsson. >> *Bókmentasaga Íslendinga fram undir siðabót* (1904–5).
   P. 461.
– >> *Den oldnorske og oldislandske Litteraturs Historie* (1920–4). Vol. 3,
   pp. 124–5.
Kock, E.A. "Anteckningar till Íslenzk Miðaldakvæði." *ANF* 61 (1946): 1–125,
   esp. pp. 49–52.
Louis-Jensen, Jonna. "En norsk vagantstrofe." *Opuscula* 5. Bibliotheca
   Arnamagnæana 31 (Copenhagen: Munksgaard, 1975). Pp. 216–18, esp.
   p. 218.
Schottmann, Hans. >> *Die isländische Mariendichtung* (1973). Pp. 406,
   428–32, 454, 478, and 481n7.

13. Út í löndum ég hefi spurt

A Marian miracle poem from ca. 1300–1550 about a man who sold his wife to
the devil (cf. C.R. Unger, ed., *Mariu saga: Legender om Jomfru Maria og hen-
des jertegn* [Christiania (Oslo): Brögger and Christie, 1871], pp. 282–9 and
291–7).
   Incipit: "Út í löndum ég hefi spurt."

Manuscript:
Lbs 1571 8vo (ca. 1780 and ca. 1810).
Edition:
Jón Helgason, ed. >> *Íslenzk miðaldakvæði* (1936–8). Vol. 2, pp. 159–62.
Literature:
Bekker-Nielsen, Hans. "Mariadigtning." *KLNM* 11 (1966). Cols. 379–80, esp.
col. 379.
Finnur Jónsson. >> *Bókmentasaga Íslendinga fram undir siðabót* (1904–5).
P. 461.
Schottmann, Hans. >> *Die isländische Mariendichtung* (1973). Pp. 59n33,
447, 457–64, 476–7, 479, 483, and 486n20.

14. Heyrðu hjálpin skæra

A Marian miracle poem from ca. 1300–1550 about a widow whose imprisoned
son was set free by Mary the Blessed Virgin (cf. C.R. Unger, ed., *Mariu saga:
Legender om Jomfru Maria og hendes jertegn* [Christiania (Oslo): Brögger and
Christie, 1871], pp. 314–17).
Incipit: "Heyrðu hjálpin skæra."

Manuscripts:
A: AM 710a 4to (ca. 1700–25), AM 721 4to (ca. 1500–50), JS 581 4to
(ca. 1600–1900), and Lbs 2166 4to (ca. 1885–1920);
B: JS 470 8vo (ca. 1675–1900) and Lbs 201 8vo (ca. 1850–70).
Editions:
Jón Helgason, ed. >> *Íslenzk miðaldakvæði* (1936–8). Vol. 2, pp. 163–8.
Based on AM 721 4to with variants from AM 710a 4to, JS 470 8vo, Lbs
2166 4to, and Sigurður Nordal (1924).
Jón Þorkelsson. >> *Om Digtningen på Island* (1888). P. 48 (stz. 1).
Based on AM 710a 4to, AM 721 4to, and Lbs 201 8vo.
Sigurður Nordal, ed. *Íslenzk lestrarbók 1400–1900* (Reykjavík: Sigfús
Eymundsson, 1924). Pp. 11–16.
Edition of AM 721 4to.
Literature:
Bekker-Nielsen, Hans. "Mariadigtning." *KLNM* 11 (1966). Cols. 379–80.
Finnur Jónsson. >> *Bókmentasaga Íslendinga fram undir siðabót* (1904–5).
P. 461.
– >> *Den oldnorske og oldislandske Litteraturs Historie* (1920–4). Vol. 3,
p. 124.

Jónas Kristjánsson. >> *Eddas and Sagas: Iceland's Medieval Literature* (1988). P. 390.

Kock, E.A. "Anteckningar till Íslenzk Miðaldakvæði." *ANF* 61 (1946): 1–125, esp. pp. 43 and 60–2.

Schottmann, Hans. >> *Die isländische Mariendichtung* (1973). Pp. 405, 413–17, 475–6, 479, and 487n20.

15. Græðarinn lýðs og landa

A Marian miracle poem from ca. 1300–1550 about the repentence of two brothers (cf. C.R. Unger, ed., *Mariu saga: Legender om Jomfru Maria og hendes jertegn* [Christiania (Oslo): Brögger and Christie, 1871], pp. 608–22).
Incipit: "Græðarinn lýðs og landa."

Manuscripts:
AM 622 4to (ca. 1549), Lbs 1486b 4to (ca. 1860–78), Lbs 2166 4to (ca. 1885–1920), and Trinity L.2.3 (ca. 1700–1800).

Editions:
Jón Helgason, ed. >> *Íslenzk miðaldakvæði* (1936–8). Vol. 2, pp. 181–95. Based on AM 622 4to with variants from Lbs 1486b 4to and Lbs 2166 4to and notes from C.R. Unger, ed., *Mariu saga: Legender om Jomfru Maria og hendes jertegn* (Christiania [Oslo]: Brögger and Christie, 1871).

Jón Þorkelsson. >> *Om Digtningen på Island* (1888). P. 46 (stz. 1). Edition of AM 622 4to.

Literature:
Bekker-Nielsen, Hans. "Mariadigtning." *KLNM* 11 (1966). Cols. 379–80, esp. col. 379.

Carpenter, William H., ed. *Nikolásdrápa Halls prests: An Icelandic Poem from circa A.D. 1400* (Halle: Karras, 1881). P. 3.

Finnur Jónsson. >> *Bókmentasaga Íslendinga fram undir siðabót* (1904–5). P. 462.

– >> *Den oldnorske og oldislandske Litteraturs Historie* (1920–4). Vol. 3, p. 124.

Kock, E.A. "Anteckningar till Íslenzk Miðaldakvæði." *ANF* 61 (1946): 1–125, esp. pp. 53 and 64–5.

Schottmann, Hans. >> *Die isländische Mariendichtung* (1973). Pp. 25, 291, 405–6, 417–20, 475–7, 481, and 487n20.

NOTE:
The poem contains material about Saint Anne. See her entry.

16. María mærin svinna

A three-stz. poem in praise of Mary the Blessed Virgin from ca. 1300–1550.
Incipit: "María mærin svinna."

Manuscripts:
AM 81a fol. (ca. 1400–1500; first four words only, written in a sixteenth-
or seventeenth-century hand), Lbs 953 4to (ca. 1760), Lbs 2166 4to
(ca. 1885–1920), and Lbs 1070 8vo (1748).
Editions:
Jón Helgason, ed. >> *Íslenzk miðaldakvæði* (1936–8). Vol. 2, pp. 270–1.
Based on Lbs 1070 8vo with variants from Lbs 953 4to.
Stefán Einarsson. "Íslenzk helgikvæði á miðöldum." *Tímarit Þjóðræknisfélags
Íslendinga* 36 (1954): 43–62, esp. p. 59.
Based on an unnamed source.
Literature:
Bekker-Nielsen, Hans. "Mariadigtning." *KLNM* 11 (1966). Cols. 379–80, esp.
col. 379.
Finnur Jónsson. >> *Bókmentasaga Íslendinga fram undir siðabót* (1904–5).
P. 461.
Schottmann, Hans. >> *Die isländische Mariendichtung* (1973). Pp. 528 and
544n34.
Stefán Einarsson. *Íslensk bókmenntasaga 874–1960* (Reykjavík: Oddi, 1961).
P. 96.

17. Eptirdæmið eitt ég sá

A Marian miracle poem about a boy who swallowed a piece of iron and was
saved by Mary the Blessed Virgin (cf. C.R. Unger, ed., *Mariu saga: Legender
om Jomfru Maria og hendes jertegn* [Christiania (Oslo): Brögger and Christie,
1871], pp. 280–2). The poem was composed ca. 1300–1550 by a certain
Ásmundur, whose name is encrypted in stz. 12^5.
Incipit: "Eptirdæmið eitt ég sá."

Manuscripts:
A: AM 920 4to (ca. 1800–1900), AM 148 8vo (ca. 1650–1700), JS 399a–b
4to (ca. 1700–1900), and Lbs 2033 4to (ca. 1880–1920);
B: JS 405 4to (1819) and NKS 1141 fol. (ca. 1750–1800).

Editions:

Anon. "Det historisk-archaeologiske archiv, islandske Afdeling." Annual
Report for 1851. *Antiquarisk Tidsskrift* 1849–51 (Copenhagen: Berling,
1852). Pp. 218–66, esp. p. 253 (stz. 1 and 12).
Based on the B redaction.

Jón Helgason, ed. >> *Íslenzk miðaldakvæði* (1936–8). Vol. 2, pp. 156–7.
Based on AM 148 8vo with variants from JS 399a–b 4to, JS 405 4to, Lbs
2033 4to, and NKS 1141 fol.

– ed. >> *Kvæðabók úr Vigur: AM 148, 8vo* (1955). Fol. 226v–227v.
Facsimile of AM 148 8vo.

Jón Þorkelsson. >> *Om Digtningen på Island* (1888). Pp. 53 (stz. 1^{1-2}) and
277 (stz. 1 and 12).
Based on JS 405 4to and NKS 1141 fol.

Jón Þorkelsson, ed. >> *Kvæðasafn* (1922–7). Pp. 233–5.
Based on AM 148 8vo with variants from JS 405 4to.

Literature:

Bekker-Nielsen, Hans. "Mariadigtning." *KLNM* 11 (1966). Cols. 379–80, esp.
col. 379.

Finnur Jónsson. >> *Bókmentasaga Íslendinga fram undir siðabót* (1904–5).
P. 461.

– >> *Den oldnorske og oldislandske Litteraturs Historie* (1920–4). Vol. 3,
pp. 124–5.

Kock, E.A. "Anteckningar till Íslenzk Miðaldakvæði." *ANF* 61 (1946): 1–125,
esp. p. 57.

Schottmann, Hans. >> *Die isländische Mariendichtung* (1973). Pp. 406,
455–6, 476, and 486n20.

18. Hugarraun

A Marian miracle poem composed ca. 1300–1550 about the trials and redemp-
tion of a Roman empress (cf. C.R. Unger, ed., *Mariu saga: Legender om
Jomfru Maria og hendes jertegn* [Christiania (Oslo): Brögger and Christie,
1871], pp. 421–38, 1104–12, and 1112–16).
Incipit: "Það er upphaf dygða."

Manuscripts:

A: AM 148 8vo (ca. 1650–1700), JS 405 4to (1819), and NKS 1141 fol.
(ca. 1750–1800);

B: JS 399a–b 4to (ca. 1700–1900), JS 610 4to (ca. 1700–1900), JS 515
8vo (ca. 1675–1900), Lbs 2166 4to (ca. 1885–1920), and Lbs 201 8vo
(ca. 1850–70).

Editions:

Anon. "Det historisk-archaeologiske archiv, islandske Afdeling." Annual
Report for 1851. *Antiquarisk Tidsskrift* 1849–51 (Copenhagen: Berling,
1852). P. 254 (stz. 1).
Edition of JS 405 4to.

Jón Helgason, ed. >> *Íslenzk miðaldakvæði* (1936–8). Vol. 2, pp. 170–9.
Based on AM 148 8vo with variants from JS 405 4to, JS 610 4to, and NKS
1141 fol.

– ed. >> *Kvæðabók úr Vigur: AM 148, 8vo* (1955). Fol. 215v–219v.
Facsimile of AM 148 8vo.

Jón Þorkelsson. >> *Om Digtningen på Island* (1888). P. 58 (stz. 1).
Edition of JS 405 4to.

Literature:

Bekker-Nielsen, Hans. "Mariadigtning." *KLNM* 11 (1966). Cols. 379–80, esp.
col. 379.

Finnur Jónsson. >> *Bókmentasaga Íslendinga fram undir siðabót* (1904–5).
P. 461.

– >> *Den oldnorske og oldislandske Litteraturs Historie* (1920–4). Vol. 3,
p. 124.

Kock, E.A. "Anteckningar till Íslenzk Miðaldakvæði." *ANF* 61 (1946): 1–125,
esp. pp. 14 and 62–3.

Schottmann, Hans. >> *Die isländische Mariendichtung* (1973). Pp. 464–74,
483, and 487n20.

19. Boðunarvísur

A poem in honour of Mary the Blessed Virgin composed ca. 1300–1550.
Incipit: "Ave dýrust drósa."

Manuscripts:

AM 713 4to (ca. 1500–50), AM 1032 4to (ca. 1700–25), and Lbs 2166 4to
(ca. 1885–1920).

Editions:

Jón Helgason, ed. >> *Íslenzk miðaldakvæði* (1936–8). Vol. 2, pp. 29–33.
Edition of AM 713 4to.

Jón Þorkelsson. >> *Om Digtningen på Island* (1888). P. 44 (stz. 1 and 32$^{5-7}$).
Based on AM 713 4to and AM 1032 4to.

Literature:
Bekker-Nielsen, Hans. "Mariadigtning." *KLNM* 11 (1966). Cols. 379–80, esp.
　　col. 379.
Finnur Jónsson. >> *Bókmentasaga Íslendinga fram undir siðabót* (1904–5).
　　P. 461.
– >> *Den oldnorske og oldislandske Litteraturs Historie* (1920–44). Vol. 3,
　　pp. 124–5.
Kock, E.A. "Anteckningar till Íslenzk Miðaldakvæði." *ANF* 61 (1946): 1–125,
　　esp. pp. 3 and 35–6.
Schottmann, Hans. >> *Die isländische Mariendichtung* (1973). Pp. 490, 499,
　　541–2, and 549.
Wolf, Kirsten, ed. >> *Saga heilagrar Önnu* (2001). P. xliv.
NOTE:
The poem contains material about other saints, especially Anne, Joachim, and
Peter. See the entries for the individual saints.

20. Heyr skínandi skærust frú

A poem composed ca. 1300–1550 in praise of Mary the Blessed Virgin. The
text, which is based on oral tradition, is defective in some places.
　　Incipit: "Heyr skínandi skærust frú."

Manuscripts:
AM 243f fol. (ca. 1500), AM 711b 4to (ca. 1700–25), and Lbs 2166 4to
　　(ca. 1885–1920).
Editions:
Jón Helgason, ed. >> *Íslenzk miðaldakvæði* (1936–8). Vol. 2, pp. 67–70.
　　Based on AM 243f fol. with variants from AM 711b 4to and Lbs 2166 4to.
Jón Þorkelsson. >> *Om Digtningen på Island* (1888). P. 48 (stz. 1–2).
　　Normalized text based on AM 711b 4to.
Jón Þorkelsson, ed. >> *Kvæðasafn* (1922–7). Pp. 366–70.
　　Normalized edition based on AM 243f fol. and AM 711b 4to.
Literature:
Bekker-Nielsen, Hans. "Mariadigtning." *KLNM* 11 (1966). Cols. 379–80, esp.
　　col. 379.
Finnur Jónsson. >> *Bókmentasaga Íslendinga fram undir siðabót* (1904–5).
　　P. 461.
– >> *Den oldnorske og oldislandske Litteraturs Historie* (1920–4). Vol. 3,
　　pp. 124–5.

Kock, E.A. "Anteckningar till Íslenzk Miðaldakvæði." *ANF* 61 (1946): 1–125, esp. pp. 28 and 38–41.

Schottmann, Hans. >> *Die isländische Mariendichtung* (1973). Pp. 489–91.

21. María móðirin skæra

A poem in honour of Mary the Blessed Virgin dated to ca. 1400–1550 and attributed alternatively to Loptur ríki Guttormsson (1375–1432), Jón Pálsson Máríuskáld (ca. 1390–1471), and Bishop Jón Arason (1484–1550).

Incipit: "María móðirin skæra."

Manuscripts:
A: AM 717h 4to (ca. 1650–1900), BLAdd 11.179 (ca. 1700–1800), Bor 6 (20647) (ca. 1700–1800), JS 33 4to (ca. 1730; stz. 17 only), JS 256 4to (1840–5), JS 260 4to (1796), JS 648 4to (ca. 1800), JS 112 8vo (ca. 1700–1800), JS 514 8vo (ca. 1675–1900), Lbs 953 4to (ca. 1760), Lbs 1440 4to (1855 or 1856), Lbs 1750 4to (ca. 1850–65), Lbs 2031 4to (ca. 1880–1920), Lbs 201 8vo (ca. 1850–70), Lbs 558 8vo (ca. 1700–1900; stz. 1 only), Lbs 2160 8vo (1819; stz. 1 only), Lbs 2345 8vo (ca. 1775–1800), and Stock. Papp. fol. no. 64 (ca. 1650–1700);
B: AM 717h 4to (ca. 1650–1700), AM 426 12mo (ca. 1600–1700), and Lbs 498 8vo (1748);
C: Lbs 494 8vo (ca. 1700) and Lbs 1331 8vo (ca. 1700–1900);
D: JS 309 8vo (ca. 1810; stz. 17–21 only), JS 389 8vo (ca. 1775–1825), and Lbs 1119 8vo (ca. 1760; stz. 17–21 only);
E: JS 580 4to (ca. 1600–1900), JS 507 8vo (ca. 1675–1900), Lbs 2178 8vo (ca. 1800–1900), and Lbs 2412 8vo (ca. 1830);
F: JS 154 8vo (ca. 1780).
Editions:
Jón Helgason, ed. >> *Íslenzk miðaldakvæði* (1936–8). Vol. 2, pp. 48–52.
  Based on AM 717h 4to with variants from AM 426 12mo, BLAdd 11.179, JS 260 4to, JS 154 8vo, JS 389 8vo, JS 507 8vo, Lbs 953 4to, Lbs 494 8vo, Lbs 498 8vo, Lbs 1331 8vo, Lbs 2178 8vo, Lbs 2412 8vo.
[Jón Sigurðsson and Guðbrandur Vigfússon, ed.] >> *Biskupa sögur* (1858–78). Vol. 2, p. 583 (stz. 1).
  Normalized edition, possibly based on Stock. Papp. fol. no. 64.
Jón Þorkelsson. >> *Om Digtningen på Island* (1888). Pp. 43 (stz. 1^{1-4}) and 271–2 (stz. 1, 5, 13^{1-2}, 14, 17, 18^{1-4}, 19, 20, 21^{4-9}, and 22).
  Based on Stock. Papp. fol. no. 64 or Lbs 2031 4to.
Jón Þorkelsson, ed. >> *Kvæðasafn* (1922–7). Pp. 144–6.
  Based on AM 426 12mo, JS 389 8vo, Lbs 953 4to, Lbs 494 8vo, and Stock. Papp. fol. no. 64.

Literature:

Bekker-Nielsen, Hans. "Mariadigtning." *KLNM* 11 (1966). Cols. 379–80, esp.
col. 379.

Finnur Jónsson. >> *Den oldnorske og oldislandske Litteraturs Historie*
(1920–4). Vol. 3, p. 124.

Jón Helgason. "Nokkur íslenzk miðaldakvæði." *ANF* 36 (1924): 285–313,
esp. pp. 309–10.

Pétur Sigurðsson. "Vísnabók Guðbrands biskups." In *Iðunn: Tímarit til
skemtunar, nytsemdar og fróðleiks*. Vol. 8. Ed. Magnús Jónsson (Reykjavík:
Gutenberg, 1923–4). Pp. 61–87, esp. p. 62.

Schottmann, Hans. >> *Die isländische Mariendichtung* (1973). Pp. 489,
491n3, 495–7, and 545–6.

NOTE:
The poem contains material about Saint Elizabeth. See her entry.

22. María heyr mig háleit víf

A poem invoking Mary the Blessed Virgin alternatively attributed to Loptur
ríki Guttormsson (1375–1432) and Bishop Jón Arason (1484–1550). It has
been dated to ca. 1400–1550.

Incipit: "María heyr mig háleit víf."

Manuscripts:
A: AM 711a 4to (ca. 1700–25) and AM 713 4to (ca. 1500–50);
B: AM 711b 4to (ca. 1700–25);
C: AM 242 fol. (ca. 1400–1500, later addition to originally blank page);
D: AM 717h 4to (ca. 1650–1700), BLAdd 4892 (ca. 1700–1800), BLAdd
11.179 (ca. 1700–1800), Bor 6 (20647) (ca. 1700–1800), ÍB 37 8vo
(ca. 1840), JS 256 4to (ca. 1840–5), JS 260 4to (1796), JS 580 4to
(ca. 1600–1900), JS 648 4to (ca. 1800), JS 112 8vo (ca. 1700–1800),
JS 494 8vo (ca. 1675–1900), JS 487 8vo (ca. 1675–1900), JS 498 8vo
(ca. 1675–1900), Lbs 512 4to (ca. 1700–50), Lbs 936 4to (ca. 1880), Lbs
953 4to (ca. 1760), Lbs 1750 4to (ca. 1850–65), Lbs 201 8vo (ca. 1850–
70), Lbs 494 8vo (ca. 1700), Lbs 754 8vo (ca. 1700–1900), Lbs 1331 8vo
(ca. 1700–1900), Lbs 2345 8vo (ca. 1775–1800), and Stock. Papp. fol.
no. 64 (ca. 1650–1700).

Editions:
Jón Helgason, ed. >> *Íslenzk miðaldakvæði* (1936–8). Vol. 2, pp. 257–9.
Based on AM 713 4to with variants from AM 242 fol, AM 711a 4to, AM
711b 4to, AM 717h 4to, Lbs 494 8vo, Lbs 1331 8vo, and Jón Þorkelsson's
edition (1888).

[Jón Sigurðsson and Guðbrandur Vigfússon, ed.] >> *Biskupa sögur* (1858–
78). Vol. 2, p. 584 (stz. 1).
  Based on the A redaction.
Jón Þorkelsson. >> *Om Digtningen på Island* (1888). Pp. 43 (stz. 1$^{1-2}$) and
246–8.
  Redaction A based on AM 711a 4to with variants from AM 713 4to and
  AM 242 fol., and redaction B, equivalent to Jón Helgason's D, based on
  Stock. Papp. fol. no. 64.
Jón Þorkelsson, ed. >> *Kvæðasafn* (1922–7). Pp. 105–10.
  Redaction A based on AM 711a 4to with variants from AM 713 4to and
  AM 242 fol., and redaction B based on Stock. Papp. fol. no. 64.

Literature:
Anna Sigurðardóttir. *Allt hafði annan róm áður í páfadóm: Nunnuklaustrin
  tvö á Íslandi á miðöldum og brot úr kristnisögu* (Reykjavík:
  Kvennasögusafn Íslands, 1988). P. 363.
Bekker-Nielsen, Hans. "Mariadigtning." *KLNM* 11 (1966). Cols. 379–80, esp.
  col. 379.
Finnur Jónsson. >> *Bókmentasaga Íslendinga fram undir siðabót* (1904–5).
  P. 461.
– >> *Den oldnorske og oldislandske Litteraturs Historie* (1920–4). Vol. 3,
  p. 124.
Jón Þorkelsson. "Islandske håndskrifter i England og Skotland." *ANF* 8
  (1892): 199–237, esp. p. 206.
Pétur Sigurðsson. "Vísnabók Guðbrands biskups." In *Iðunn: Tímarit til
  skemtunar, nytsemdar og fróðleiks.* Vol. 8. Ed. Magnús Jónsson (Reykjavík:
  Gutenberg, 1923–4). Pp. 61–87, esp. p. 62.
Schottmann, Hans. >> *Die isländische Mariendichtung* (1973). Pp. 488, 490,
  499, 524, 538, and 540–1.

23. Sankta María móðir mild

A poem in praise of Mary the Blessed Virgin composed ca. 1400–1550 and
attributed (questionably) to Jón Pálsson Máríuskáld (ca. 1390–1471).
  Incipit: "Sankta María móðir mild."

Manuscripts:
A: AM 717h 4to (ca. 1650–1800), BLAdd 4892 (ca. 1700–25), BLAdd
  11.179 (ca. 1700–1800), Bor 6 (20647) (ca. 1700–1800), JS 256 4to
  (ca. 1840–5), JS 260 4to (1796), JS 648 4to (ca. 1800), JS 112 8vo
  (ca. 1700–1800), JS 487 8vo (ca. 1675–1900), JS 494 8vo (ca. 1675–

1900), Lbs 512 4to (ca. 1700–50), Lbs 936 4to (ca. 1880), Lbs 953 4to
(ca. 1760), Lbs 1630 4to (ca. 1800–1900), Lbs 2031 4to (ca. 1880–1920),
Lbs 201 8vo (ca. 1850–70), Lbs 754 8vo (ca. 1700–1900), Lbs 2345 8vo
(ca. 1775–1800), and Stock. Papp. fol. no. 64 (ca. 1650–1700);
B: AM 717e 4to (ca. 1700–25);
C: AM 428a 12mo (ca. 1300–1400 and ca. 1600–1800), and Lbs 2031 4to
(1877).

Editions:

Jón Helgason, ed. >> *Íslenzk miðaldakvæði* (1936–8). Vol. 2, pp. 266–7.
Based on AM 717h 4to with variants from AM 717e 4to and AM 428a
12mo.

Jón Þorkelsson. >> *Om Digtningen på Island* (1888). Pp. 43 (stz. 1^{1-2}) and
270.
Based on AM 717e 4to, AM 717h 4to, AM 428a 12mo, and Stock. Papp.
fol. no. 64.

Jón Þorkelsson, ed. >> *Kvæðasafn* (1922–7). Pp. 134–7.
Based on AM 717e 4to, AM 717h 4to, AM 428a 12mo, and Stock. Papp.
fol. no. 64.

*Peringskiöld, J.F., ed. >> *Fragmentum runicopapisticum* (1721). Pp. 20–1.
Facsimile of Stock. Papp. fol. no. 64.

Literature:

Bekker-Nielsen, Hans. "Mariadigtning." *KLNM* 11 (1966). Cols. 379–80, esp.
col. 379.

Finnur Jónsson. >> *Bókmentasaga Íslendinga fram undir siðabót* (1904–5).
P. 461.

– >> *Den oldnorske og oldislandske Litteraturs Historie* (1920–4). Vol. 3,
p. 125.

Jón Helgason. "Nokkur íslenzk miðaldakvæði." *ANF* 36 (1924): 285–313,
esp. pp. 309–10.

Jón Þorkelsson. "Islandske håndskrifter i England og Skotland." *ANF* 8
(1892): 199–237, esp. p. 206.

Kock, E.A. "Anteckningar till Íslenzk Miðaldakvæði." *ANF* 61 (1946): 1–125,
esp. pp. 74–5.

Pétur Sigurðsson. "Vísnabók Guðbrands biskups." In *Iðunn: Tímarit til
skemtunar, nytsemdar og fróðleiks.* Vol. 8. Ed. Magnús Jónsson (Reykjavík:
Gutenberg, 1923–4). Pp. 61–87, esp. p. 62.

Schottmann, Hans. >> *Die isländische Mariendichtung* (1973). Pp. 491n3,
498, 500, 502, and 528.

24. María meyjan skæra

A poem in praise of Mary the Blessed Virgin possibly composed ca. 1400–
1550 by Jón Pálsson Maríuskáld (ca. 1390–1471), or by Bishop Jón Arason
(1484–1550). The poem has also been attributed to Bishop Brynjólfur
Sveinsson (1605–75), although the approximate date of composition makes
this unlikely.

   Incipit: "María meyjan skæra."

Manuscripts:

A: AM 717e 4to (ca. 1700–50) and AM 150 8vo (ca. 1650–1700);
B: AM 426 12mo (ca. 1600–1700);
C: AM 717h 4to (ca. 1650–1700), BLAdd 4892 (ca. 1700–1800), BLAdd
   11.179 (ca. 1700–1800), Bor 6 (20647) (ca. 1700–1800), JS 260 4to
   (1796), JS 580 4to (ca. 1600–1900), JS 648 4to (ca. 1800), JS 487 8vo
   (ca. 1675–1900), JS 494 8vo (ca. 1675–1900), JS 514 8vo (ca. 1675–
   1900), Lbs 936 4to (ca. 1880), Lbs 953 4to (ca. 1760), Lbs 1750 4to
   (ca. 1850–65), Lbs 201 8vo (ca. 1850–70), Lbs 754 8vo (ca. 1700–1900),
   and Stock. Papp. fol. no. 64 (ca. 1650–1700);
D: AM 719c 4to (ca. 1650–1700) and JS 136 8vo (ca. 1770);
E: Lbs 1070 8vo (1748);
F: JS 33 4to (ca. 1730), Lbs 558 8vo (ca. 1700–1900), and Lbs 1091 8vo (ca. 1883);
G: Lbs 1568 8vo (1689);
H: ÍB 37 8vo (ca. 1840), Lbs 494 8vo (ca. 1700), and Lbs 1331 8vo
   (ca. 1700–1900);
I: JS 389 8vo (ca. 1775–1825);
J: JS 309 8vo (ca. 1810);
K: JS 471 8vo (ca. 1675–1900);
L: Lbs 1030 8vo (ca. 1810);
M: Lbs 852 4to (ca. 1750–1800), Lbs 201 8vo (ca. 1850–70), and Lbs 1390
   8vo (ca. 1800–1900);
N: JS 92 8vo (ca. 1750–1800) and JS 154 8vo (ca. 1780);
O: Lbs 1119 8vo (ca. 1760);
P: JS 580 4to (ca. 1600–1900), JS 507 8vo (ca. 1675–1900), Lbs 2160 8vo
   (1819; stz. 1 only), Lbs 2178 8vo (ca. 1800–1900), and Lbs 2412 8vo
   (ca. 1830).

Editions:

Jón Helgason, ed. >> *Íslenzk miðaldakvæði* (1936–8). Vol. 2, pp. 40–1.
   Based on AM 150 8vo with variants from AM 717h 4to, AM 719c 4to, AM
   426 12mo, JS 33 4to, JS 580 4to, JS 154 8vo, JS 309 8vo, JS 389 8vo, JS
   471 8vo, JS 507 8vo, Lbs 852 4to, Lbs 558 8vo, Lbs 494 8vo, Lbs 1030

8vo, Lbs 1070 8vo, Lbs 1119 8vo, Lbs 1331 8vo, Lbs 1390 8vo, Lbs 1568
8vo, Lbs 2178 8vo, and Lbs 2412 8vo.

Jón Þorkelsson. >> *Om Digtningen på Island* (1888). Pp. 43 (stz. 1^{1-4}) and
272–3 (entire poem).
Based on AM 717e 4to, AM 717h 4to, AM 719c 4to, AM 150 8vo, AM 426
12mo, ÍB 37 8vo, and Stock. Papp. fol. no. 64.

Jón Þorkelsson, ed. >> *Kvæðasafn* (1922–17). Pp. 138–40.
Based on AM 719c 4to, JS 33 4to, JS 136 8vo, JS 309 8vo, JS 389 8vo,
Lbs 953 4to, Lbs 494 8vo, and Lbs 1070 8vo.

Literature:

Bekker-Nielsen, Hans. "Mariadigtning." *KLNM* 11 (1966). Cols. 379–80.

Finnur Jónsson. >> *Bókmentasaga Íslendinga fram undir siðabót* (1904–5).
P. 461.

– >> *Den oldnorske og oldislandske Litteraturs Historie* (1920–4). Vol. 3,
p. 124.

Jón Helgason. "Nokkur íslenzk miðaldakvæði." *ANF* 36 (1924): 285–313,
esp. pp. 309–10.

Jón Þorkelsson. "Islandske håndskrifter i England og Skotland." *ANF* 8
(1892): 199–237, esp. p. 206.

Pétur Sigurðsson. "Vísnabók Guðbrands biskups." In *Iðunn: Tímarit til
skemtunar, nytsemdar og fróðleiks*. Vol. 8. Ed. Magnús Jónsson (Reykjavík:
Gutenberg, 1923–4). Pp. 61–87, esp. pp. 62–3.

Schottmann, Hans. >> *Die isländische Mariendichtung* (1973). Pp. 489, 491,
527n10, and 545–6.

Stéfan Einarsson. "Íslenzk helgikvæði á miðöldum." *Tímarit Þjóðræknisfélags
Íslendinga* 36 (1955): 43–63, esp. p. 57.

– *Íslensk bókmenntasaga 874–1960* (Reykjavík: Oddi, 1961). Pp. 93 and 97.

25. Ágæt vil ég þér óðinn færa

A poem from ca. 1400–1550 about the five joys of Mary the Blessed Virgin.
Incipit: "Ágæt vil ég þér óðinn færa."

Manuscripts:

AM 713 4to (ca. 1500–50), AM 1032 4to (ca. 1700–25), and Lbs 2166 4to
(ca. 1885–1920).

Editions:

Jón Helgason, ed. >> *Íslenzk miðaldakvæði* (1936–8). Vol. 2, pp. 73–6.
Edition of AM 713 4to.

Jón Þorkelsson. >> *Om Digtningen på Island* (1888). P. 44 (stz. 1 and 33).
   Based on AM 713 4to and AM 1032 4to.
Literature:
Bekker-Nielsen, Hans. "Mariadigtning." *KLNM* 11 (1966). Cols. 379–80, esp.
   col. 379.
Finnur Jónsson. >> *Bókmentasaga Íslendinga fram undir siðabót* (1904–5).
   P. 461.
– >> *Den oldnorske og oldislandske Litteraturs Historie* (1920–4). Vol. 3,
   pp. 124–5.
Schottmann, Hans. >> *Die isländische Mariendichtung* (1973). Pp. 28, 490,
   and 521–2.
Stéfan Einarsson. "Íslenzk helgikvæði á miðöldum." *Tímarit Þjóðræknisfélags
   Íslendinga* 36 (1955): 43–63, esp. p. 58.
– *Íslensk bókmenntasaga 874–1960* (Reykjavík: Oddi, 1961). P. 95.

26. Heyr mig dýrust drottins frú

A poem in praise of Mary the Blessed Virgin composed ca. 1400–1550.
   Incipit: "Heyr mig dýrust drottins frú."

Manuscripts:
AM 711a 4to (ca. 1700–25), AM 713 4to (ca. 1500–50), AM 920 4to
   (ca. 1800–1900), and Lbs 2166 4to (ca. 1885–1920).
Editions:
Jón Helgason, ed. >> *Íslenzk miðaldakvæði* (1936–8). Vol. 2, pp. 240–2.
   Based on AM 713 4to with variants from AM 920 4to and Lbs 2166 4to.
Jón Þorkelsson. >> *Om Digtningen på Island* (1888). P. 47 (stz. 1).
   Based on AM 711a 4to, AM 713 4to, and AM 920 4to.
Literature:
Bekker-Nielsen, Hans. "Mariadigtning." *KLNM* 11 (1966). Cols. 379–80, esp.
   col. 379.
Finnur Jónsson. >> *Bókmentasaga Íslendinga fram undir siðabót* (1904–5).
   P. 461.
– >> *Den oldnorske og oldislandske Litteraturs Historie* (1920–4). Vol. 3,
   p. 124.
Kock, E.A. "Anteckningar till Íslenzk Miðaldakvæði." *ANF* 61 (1946): 1–125,
   esp. p. 71.
Schottmann, Hans. >> *Die isländische Mariendichtung* (1973). Pp. 490 and
   529–30.

27. Heyr þú hinn hæsti hjálpari minn

A poem from ca. 1400–1550 in praise of Mary the Blessed Virgin.
Incipit: "Heyr þú hinn hæsti hjálpari minn."

Manuscripts:
AM 711a 4to (ca. 1700–25), AM 713 4to (ca. 1500–50), AM 920 4to
(ca. 1800–1900), and Lbs 2166 4to (ca. 1885–1920).

Editions:
Jón Helgason, ed. >> *Íslenzk miðaldakvæði* (1936–8). Vol. 2, pp. 246–8.
Based on AM 713 4to with variants from AM 711a 4to and AM 920 4to.
Jón Þorkelsson. >> *Om Digtningen på Island* (1888). P. 48 (stz. 1 and 13$^{5-7}$).
Based on AM 713 4to, AM 711a 4to, and AM 920 4to.
Literature:
Bekker-Nielsen, Hans. "Mariadigtning." *KLNM* 11 (1966). Cols. 379–80.
Finnur Jónsson. >> *Bókmentasaga Íslendinga fram undir siðabót* (1904–5).
P. 461.
– >> *Den oldnorske og oldislandske Litteraturs Historie* (1920–4). Vol. 3,
p. 124.
Kock, E.A. "Anteckningar till Íslenzk Miðaldakvæði." *ANF* 61 (1946): 1–125,
esp. pp. 68 and 72–3.
Schottmann, Hans. >> *Die isländische Mariendichtung* (1973). Pp. 24, 490,
530, and 541.

28. María gef mér mælsku til

A poem in praise of Mary the Blessed Virgin composed ca. 1400–1550.
Incipit: "María gef mér mælsku til."

Manuscripts:
AM 710a 4to (ca. 1700–25), AM 721 4to (ca. 1500–50), and Lbs 2166 4to
(ca. 1885–1920).
Editions:
Jón Helgason, ed. >> *Íslenzk miðaldakvæði* (1936–8). Vol. 2, pp. 251–4.
Based on AM 721 4to with variants from AM 710a 4to and Lbs 2166 4to.
Jón Þorkelsson. >> *Om Digtningen på Island* (1888). P. 47 (stz. 1).
Based on AM 710a 4to and AM 721 4to.
Literature:
Bekker-Nielsen, Hans. "Mariadigtning." *KLNM* 11 (1966). Cols. 379–80.

Finnur Jónsson. >> *Bókmentasaga Íslendinga fram undir siðabót* (1904–5).
P. 461.

- >> *Den oldnorske og oldislandske Litteraturs Historie* (1920–4). Vol. 3, p. 124.

Kock, E.A. "Anteckningar till Íslenzk Miðaldakvæði." *ANF* 61 (1946): 1–125,
esp. pp. 74 and 78.

Schottmann, Hans. >> *Die isländische Mariendichtung* (1973). Pp. 59n35,
490, 494n10, and 502.

Vésteinn Ólason. "Kveðskapur frá síðmiðöldum." In >> *Íslensk
Bókmenntasaga* 2 (1993). Pp. 283–387, esp. p. 314.

29. Salutatio Mariæ

A poem in praise of Mary the Blessed Virgin composed ca. 1400–1550 and ex-
tant in three redactions.

Incipits: A and C: "Ave ágæt Máriá"; B: "María melle plena."

Manuscripts:
A: AM 713 4to (ca. 1500–50), AM 920 4to (ca. 1800–1900), AM 1032 4to
(ca. 1700–25), and Lbs 2166 4to (ca. 1885–1920);

B: BLAdd 4892 (ca. 1700–1800), BLAdd 11.179 (ca. 1700–1800), JS 260
4to (1796), JS 580 4to (ca. 1600–1900), JS 487 8vo (ca. 1675–1900), JS
494 8vo (ca. 1675–1900), Lbs 936 4to (ca. 1880), Lbs 953 4to (ca. 1760),
Lbs 1326 4to (ca. 1890), Lbs 2166 4to (ca. 1885–1920), Lbs 201 8vo
(ca. 1850–70), and Lbs 754 8vo (ca. 1700–1900; stz. 1 only);

C: AM 242 fol. (ca. 1400–1500, later addition to originally blank page), AM
1032 4to (ca. 1700–25), and Lbs 2166 4to (1885–1920).

Editions:
Jón Helgason, ed. >> *Íslenzk miðaldakvæði* (1936–8). Vol. 2, pp. 230–8.
Redaction A based on AM 713 with variants from redactions B and C;
redaction B based on BLAdd 4892 with variants from BLAdd 11.179,
JS 260 4to, JS 580 4to, Lbs 953 4to, and redactions A and C; redaction C
based on AM 242 fol. with variants from redactions A and B.

Jón Þorkelsson. >> *Om Digtningen på Island* (1888). Pp. 46–7 (stz. 1, 2^{1-2},
and 17^{5-7} of the A redaction, stz. 1–2 and 4–5 of the B redaction, and stz.
12 of the C redaction).

Based on AM 713 4to, AM 920 4to, and AM 1032 4to (A); JS 260 4to and
201 8vo (B); and AM 242 fol. (C).

Literature:
Bekker-Nielsen, Hans. "Mariadigtning." *KLNM* 11 (1966). Cols. 379–80, esp.
col. 379.

Finnur Jónsson. >> *Bókmentasaga Íslendinga fram undir siðabót* (1904–5).
P. 461.

– >> *Den oldnorske og oldislandske Litteraturs Historie* (1920–4). Vol. 3,
pp. 124–5.

Jón Þorkelsson. "Islandske håndskrifter i England og Skotland." *ANF* 8
(1892): 199–237, esp. pp. 206–7.

– >> *Om Digtningen på Island* (1888). Pp. 46–7.

Schottmann, Hans. >> *Die isländishe Mariendichtung* (1973). Pp. 488–90,
494, 499, 502–3, 538–41, 542n31, and 555.

Stéfan Einarsson. "Íslenzk helgikvæði á miðöldum." *Tímarit Þjóðræknisfélags
Íslendinga* 36 (1954): 43–63, esp. p. 54.

– *Íslensk bókmenntasaga 874–1960* (Reykjavík: Oddi, 1961). P. 91

Wolf, Kirsten, ed. >> *Saga heilagrar Önnu* (2001). P. xliv.

NOTE:
The poem contains material about Saints Anne and Joachim. See the entries for
the two saints.

30. Fýsir mig að fremja dikt

A macaronic poem from ca. 1400–1550 in praise of Mary the Blessed Virgin
probably translated from a foreign (possibly Danish) source.

Incipit: "Fýsir mig að fremja dikt."

Manuscripts:
AM 711a 4to (ca. 1700–25), AM 713 4to (ca. 1500–50), and Lbs 2166 4to
(ca. 1885–1920).

Editions:
Jón Helgason, ed. >> *Íslenzk miðaldakvæði* (1936–8). Vol. 2, pp. 26–8.
Based on AM 713 4to with variants from AM 711a 4to.

Jón Þorkelsson. >> *Om Digtningen på Island* (1888). P. 57 (stz. 1, 2, and 21).
Based on AM 711a 4to and AM 713 4to.

Literature:
Bekker-Nielsen, Hans. "Mariadigtning." *KLNM* 11 (1966). Cols. 379–80, esp.
col. 379.

Finnur Jónsson. >> *Bókmentasaga Íslendinga fram undir siðabót* (1904–5).
P. 461.

– >> *Den oldnorske og oldislandske Litteraturs Historie* (1920–4). Vol. 3,
pp. 124–5.

Schottmann, Hans. >> *Die isländische Mariendichtung* (1973). Pp. 489, 498,
and 542.

Stéfan Einarsson. *Íslensk bókmenntasaga 874–1960* (Reykjavík: Oddi, 1961).
P. 96.
NOTE:
The poem contains material about Saint Joseph. See his entry.

31. Heiðra vilda ég helgan Krist

A poem from ca. 1400–1550 based on a Marian miracle about a woman who
had an incestuous relationship with her son (cf. C.R. Unger, ed., *Mariu saga:
Legender om Jomfru Maria og hendes jertegn* [Christiania (Oslo): Brögger and
Christie, 1871], pp. 157–69, 444–53, 1126–33, and 1133–9).
   Incipit: "Heiðra vilda ég helgan Krist."

Manuscripts:
AM 713 4to (ca. 1500–50), AM 715g 4to (ca. 1700–25), and Lbs 2166 4to
   (ca. 1885–1920).
Editions:
Jón Helgason, ed. >> *Íslenzk miðaldakvæði* (1936–8). Vol. 2, pp. 142–8.
   Based on AM 713 4to with variants from AM 715g 4to and Lbs 2166 4to.
Jón Þorkelsson. >> *Om Digtningen på Island* (1888). Pp. 54 (stz. 1^{1-2}) and
   322 (stz. 1 and 35).
   Based on AM 713 4to and AM 715g 4to.
Literature:
Bekker-Nielsen, Hans. "Mariadigtning." *KLNM* 11 (1966). Cols. 379–80, esp.
   col. 379.
Finnur Jónsson. >> *Bókmentasaga Íslendinga fram undir siðabót* (1904–5).
   P. 461.
– >> *Den oldnorske og oldislandske Litteraturs Historie* (1920–4). Vol. 3,
   p. 124.
Kock, E.A. "Anteckningar till Íslenzk Miðaldakvæði." *ANF* 61 (1946): 1–125,
   esp. pp. 39 and 52–5.
Páll Eggert Ólason. *Menn og menntir siðskiptaaldarinnar á Íslandi.* Vol. 1
   (Reykjavík: Guðm. Gamalíelsson, 1919). P. 410.
– *Menn og menntir siðskiptaaldarinnar á Íslandi.* Vol. 4 (Reykjavík: Ársæll
   Árnason, 1926). Pp. 453 and 628.
Schottmann, Hans. >> *Die isländische Mariendichtung* (1973). Pp. 405–7,
   422–8, 453–4, and 478–81.

32. Fljóðið ekki finnast má

A poem from ca. 1400–1550 based on a Marian miracle regarding a wealthy and pious patroness's vision at the altar of Mary the Blessed Virgin (cf. C.R. Unger, ed., *Mariu saga: Legender om Jomfru Maria og hendes jertegn* [Christiania (Oslo): Brögger and Christie, 1871], pp. 207–11).

Incipit: "Fljóðið ekki finnast má."

Manuscripts:
AM 721 4to (ca. 1500–50), AM 1032 4to (ca. 1700–25), and Lbs 2166 4to (ca. 1885–1920).

Editions:
Finnur Jónsson. >> *Bókmentasaga Íslendinga fram undir siðabót* (1904–5). P. 462 (stz. 1).
Normalized edition based on an unnamed manuscript.
Jón Helgason, ed. >> *Íslenzk miðaldakvæði* (1936–8). Vol. 2, pp. 149–55.
Based on AM 721 4to with variants from AM 1032 4to, Lbs 2166 4to, and Jón Þorkelsson's edition (1888).
Jón Þorkelsson. >> *Om Digtningen på Island* (1888). P. 43 (stz. 1).
Based on AM 721 4to and AM 1032 4to.

Literature:
Bekker-Nielsen, Hans. "Mariadigtning." *KLNM* 11 (1966). Cols. 379–80, esp. col. 379.
Finnur Jónsson. >> *Den oldnorske og oldislandske Litteraturs Historie* (1920–4). Vol. 3, p. 124.
Kock, E.A. "Anteckningar till Íslenzk Miðaldakvæði." *ANF* 61 (1946): 1–125, esp. pp. 53–7.
Schottmann, Hans. >> *Die isländische Mariendichtung* (1973). Pp. 405, 407–13, 408, 475–6, 479, 481, and 483.

33. Hæstur heilagur andi

A miracle poem from ca. 1400–1550 about a man for whom a piece of wood was transformed into a golden image of Mary the Blessed Virgin. The source is unknown.

Incipit: "Hæstur heilagur andi."

Manuscripts:
AM 711a 4to (ca. 1700–25), AM 713 4to (ca. 1500–50), and Lbs 2166 4to (ca. 1885–1920).

Editions:
Jón Helgason, ed. >> *Íslenzk miðaldakvæði* (1936–8). Vol. 2, pp. 195–9.
   Based on AM 713 4to with variants from AM 711a 4to and Lbs 2166 4to.
Jón Þorkelsson. >> *Om Digtningen på Island* (1888). P. 53 (stz. 1).
   Based on AM 711a 4to and AM 713 4to.
Literature:
Bekker-Nielsen, Hans. "Mariadigtning." *KLNM* 11 (1966). Cols. 379–80, esp.
   col. 379.
Finnur Jónsson. >> *Bókmentasaga Íslendinga fram undir siðabót* (1904–5).
   P. 461.
– >> *Den oldnorske og oldislandske Litteraturs Historie* (1920–4). Vol. 3,
   pp. 124–5.
Kock, E.A. "Anteckningar till Íslenzk Miðaldakvæði." *ANF* 61 (1946): 1–125,
   esp. pp. 39–40 and 64.
Schottmann, Hans. >> *Die isländische Mariendichtung* (1973). Pp. 406,
   421–2, 476, 479, and 501.
Vésteinn Ólason. "Kveðskapur frá síðmiðöldum." In >> *Íslensk
   Bókmenntasaga* 2 (1993). Pp. 283–387, esp. p. 312.

34. Hvað skal mig þann sálugi mann

A macaronic poem in praise of Mary the Blessed Virgin composed ca. 1400–
1550 and based on a Danish original.
   Incipit: "Hvað skal mig þann sálugi mann."

Manuscript:
AM 622 4to (ca. 1549).
Editions:
Jón Helgason, ed. >> *Íslenzk miðaldakvæði* (1936–8). Vol. 2, pp. 269–70.
   Based on AM 622 4to with variants from the Danish original (AM 76 8vo),
   Kristensen's edition (1933), and Jón Þorkelsson's edition (1888).
Jón Þorkelsson. >> *Om Digtningen på Island* (1888). P. 57 (stz. 1).
Kristensen, Marius. *En klosterbog fra middelalderens slutning. AM 76, 8o*
   (Copenhagen: Jørgensen, 1933). Pp. 217–18.
Literature:
Bekker-Nielsen, Hans. "Mariadigtning." *KLNM* 11 (1966). Cols. 379–80, esp.
   col. 379.
Brandt, Carl J., and Ludvig Helweg. *Den danske psalmedigtning.* Vol. 1
   (Copenhagen: Reitzel, 1847). P. XIII.
Carpenter, William H., ed. *Nikolásdrápa Halls prests: An Icelandic Poem
   from circa A.D. 1400* (Halle: Karras, 1881). P. 1.

Finnur Jónsson. >> *Bókmentasaga Íslendinga fram undir siðabót* (1904–5).
P. 461.

– >> *Den oldnorske og oldislandske Litteraturs Historie* (1920–4). Vol. 3,
pp. 124–5.

Frandsen, Ernst. *Mariaviserne. Den lyriske Madonnadigtning fra Danmarks
Middelalder, belyst gennem Bønnebøgernes Prosatexter* (Copenhagen:
Levin and Munksgaard, 1926). Pp. 33–4.

35. Dýrðarlegast dygða blóm

A macaronic two-stz. poem from ca. 1400–1550 in praise of Mary the Blessed
Virgin and based on a Latin model (cf. Guido Maria Dreves, *Analecta hymnica
medii ævi* XXXII [Leipzig: O.R. Reisland, 1899], p. 166).
   Incipit: "Dýrðarlegast dygða blóm."

Manuscripts:
A: AM 717h 4to (ca. 1650–1700), BLAdd 4892 (ca. 1700–1800), BLAdd
   11.179 (ca. 1700–1800), Bor 6 (20647) (ca. 1800), JS 260 4to (1796),
   JS 580 4to (ca. 1600–1900), JS 648 4to (ca. 1800), JS 112 8vo (ca. 1700–
   1800), JS 487 8vo (ca. 1675–1900), JS 494 8vo (ca. 1675–1900), Lbs
   512 4to (ca. 1700–50), Lbs 936 4to (ca. 1880; stz. 1 only), Lbs 953 4to
   (ca. 1760), Lbs 1750 4to (ca. 1850–65), Lbs 201 8vo (ca. 1850–70), Lbs
   754 8vo (ca. 1700–1900; stz. 1 only), Lbs 2345 8vo (ca. 1775–1800), and
   Stock. Papp. fol. no. 64 (ca. 1650–1700);
B: ÍB 37 8vo (ca. 1840), Lbs 494 8vo (ca. 1700), and Lbs 1331 8vo
   (ca. 1700–1900);
C: Adv 21.8.14 (ca. 1750–75), Bor 102 (20743) (ca. 1800), JS 309 8vo
   (ca. 1810), and Lbs 1091 8vo (ca. 1883);
D: BLAdd 11.179 (ca. 1700–1800) and BLAdd 11.191 (ca. 1750–1800).
Editions:
Jón Helgason, ed. >> *Íslenzk miðaldakvæði* (1936–8). Vol. 2, p. 261.
   Based on AM 717h 4to with variants from Adv 21.8.14, BLAdd 11.191,
   Lbs 494 8vo, and Lbs 1331 8vo.
Jón Þorkelsson. >> *Om Digtningen på Island* (1888). P. 45.
   Based on Stock. Papp. fol. no. 64 with variants from AM 717h 4to, ÍB 37
   8vo, JS 260 4to, and Lbs 201 8vo.
Literature:
Bekker-Nielsen, Hans. "Mariadigtning." *KLNM* 11 (1966). Cols. 379–80, esp.
   col. 379.

Finnur Jónsson. >> *Bókmentasaga Íslendinga fram undir siðabót* (1904–5).
   P. 461.
– >> *Den oldnorske og oldislandske Litteraturs Historie* (1920–4). Vol. 3,
   p. 124.
Jón Þorkelsson. "Islandske håndskrifter i England og Skotland." *ANF* 8
   (1892): 199–237, esp. p. 206.
Schottmann, Hans. >> *Die isländische Mariendichtung* (1973). Pp. 494–5
   and 528.
Stéfan Einarsson. "Íslenzk helgikvæði á miðöldum." *Tímarit Þjóðræknisfélags
   Íslendinga* 36 (1955): 43–63, esp. p. 56.
– *Íslensk bókmenntasaga 874–1960* (Reykjavík: Oddi, 1961). Pp. 93 and 97.

36. Bjóða vil ég þér bragsins smíð

A poem in praise of Mary the Blessed Virgin from ca. 1400–1500. The text is
probably based on oral tradition.
   Incipit: "Bjóða vil ég þér bragsins smíð."

Manuscripts:
AM 711b 4to (ca. 1700–25) and Lbs 2166 4to (ca. 1885–1920).
Editions:
Jón Helgason, ed. >> *Íslenzk miðaldakvæði* (1936–8). Vol. 2, pp. 53–8.
   Edition of AM 711b 4to.
Jón Þorkelsson. >> *Om Digtningen på Island* (1888). P. 45 (stz. 1, 3^{1-2}, and
   44).
   Edition of AM 711b 4to.
Literature:
Bekker-Nielsen, Hans. "Mariadigtning." *KLNM* 11 (1966). Cols. 379–80, esp.
   col. 279.
Finnur Jónsson. >> *Bókmentasaga Íslendinga fram undir siðabót* (1904–5).
   P. 461.
– >> *Den oldnorske og oldislandske Litteraturs Historie* (1920–4). Vol. 3,
   p. 124.
Schottmann, Hans. >> *Die isländische Mariendichtung* (1973). Pp. 129, 489,
   492n6, 499, 516–17, 527–8, and 542.
Stéfan Einarsson. *Íslensk bókmenntasaga 874–1960* (Reykjavík: Oddi, 1961).
   P. 97.
NOTE:
The poem contains material about other saints, especially Elizabeth, John the
Baptist, John the Evangelist, Simeon the Righteous, and Zachariah. See the
entries for the individual saints.

37. Máríugrátur

A poem in honour of Mary the Blessed Virgin from ca. 1400–1550.
  Incipit: "Blómstrið brúða og kvenna."

Manuscripts:
BLAdd 4892 (ca. 1700–1800), BLAdd 11.179 (ca. 1700–1800), JS 260 4to
  (1796), JS 487 8vo (ca. 1675–1900), Lbs 936 4to (ca. 1880), Lbs 953 4to
  (ca. 1760), Lbs 1326 4to (ca. 1890), Lbs 2031 4to (ca. 1880–1920), Lbs 201
  8vo (ca. 1850–70), Lbs 494 8vo (ca. 1700), and Lbs 754 8vo (ca. 1700–1900).

Editions:
Jón Helgason, ed. >> *Íslenzk miðaldakvæði* (1936–8). Vol. 2, pp. 60–3
  Based on BLAdd 4892 with variants from BLAdd 11.179, JS 260 4to, JS
  487 8vo, Lbs 953 4to, and Lbs 201 8vo.
[Jón Sigurðsson and Guðbrandur Vigfússon, ed.] >> *Biskupa sögur* (1858–
  78). Vol. 2, p. 585 (stz. 1^1 and 3).
  Probably based on JS 260 4to.
Jón Þorkelsson. >> *Om Digtningen på Island* (1888). P. 55 (stz. 1).
  Based on BLAdd 4892, JS 260 4to, and Lbs 201 8vo.

Modern Icelandic language edition:
Ásdís Egilsdóttir, Gunnar Harðarson, and Svanhildur Óskarsdóttir, ed.
  Maríukver. Sögur og kvæði af heilagri guðsmóður frá fyrri tíð (Reykjavík:
  Hið íslenska bókmenntafélag, 1996). Pp. 155–8.

Literature:
Anon. "Den oldnordisk-islandske Afdeling." Annual Report for 1847.
  Antiquarisk Tidsskrift 1846–8 (Copenhagen: Sally B. Salomon, 1847). Pp.
  154–72, esp. pp. 40 and 165.
Bekker-Nielsen, Hans. "Mariadigtning." *KLNM* 11 (1966). Cols. 379–80, esp.
  col. 379.
Finnur Jónsson. >> *Bókmentasaga Íslendinga fram undir siðabót* (1904–5).
  P. 461.
– >> *Den oldnorske og oldislandske Litteraturs Historie* (1920–4). Vol. 3,
  p. 125.
Kock, E.A. "Anteckningar till Íslenzk Miðaldakvæði." *ANF* 61 (1946): 1–125,
  esp. p. 38.
Jón Helgason. >> "Norges og Islands digtning." In *Litteraturhistorie B:
  Norge og Island* (1953). Pp. 3–179, esp. p. 164.
Jón Þorkelsson. "Islandske håndskrifter i England og Skotland." *ANF* 8
  (1892): 192–237, esp. pp. 207–8.

Mogk, Eugen. >> *Geschichte der norwegisch-isländischen Literatur* (1904).
Pp. 716–17.

Páll Eggert Ólason. *Menn og menntir siðskiptaaldarinnar á Íslandi.* Vol. 1
(Reykjavík: Guðm. Gamalíelsson, 1919). Pp. 424–5.

Schottmann, Hans. >> *Die isländische Mariendichtung* (1973). Pp. 491, 499,
and 511–12.

Stéfan Einarsson. "Íslenzk helgikvæði á miðöldum." *Tímarit Þjóðræknisfélags
Íslendinga* 36 (1954): 43–63, esp. pp. 49 and 53–4.

– *Íslensk bókmenntasaga 874–1960* (Reykjavík: Oddi, 1961). Pp. 86, 91,
and 254.

Vésteinn Ólason. "Kveðskapur frá síðmiðöldum." In >> *Íslensk
Bókmenntasaga* 2 (1993). Pp. 283–387, esp. pp. 299 and 311.

NOTE:

The poem contains material about Saints John the Evangelist and Simeon the
Righteous. See the entries for the two saints.

38. Suptungs vilda ég bjórinn blanda

A poem from ca. 1400–1550 in praise of Mary the Blessed Virgin.
Incipit: "Suptungs vilda ég bjórinn blanda."

Manuscripts:
BLAdd 4892 (ca. 1700–1800), BLAdd 11.179 (ca. 1700–1800), JS 260 4to
(JS 1796), JS 487 8vo (ca. 1675–1900), JS 494 8vo (ca. 1675–1900), JS
514 8vo (ca. 1675–1900), Lbs 936 4to (ca. 1880), Lbs 953 4to (1760),
Lbs 1326 4to (ca. 1890), Lbs 2166 4to (ca. 1885–1920), Lbs 201 8vo
(ca. 1850–70), and Lbs 754 8vo (ca. 1700–1900).

Editions:
Jón Helgason, ed. >> *Íslenzk miðaldakvæði* (1936–8). Vol. 2, pp. 249–50
Based on BLAdd 4892 with variants from BLAdd 11.179, JS 260 4to, JS
514 8vo, Lbs 953 4to, Lbs 1326 4to, Lbs 2166 4to, and Jón Þorkelsson's
edition (1888).

Jón Þorkelsson. >> *Om Digtningen på Island* (1888). P. 56 (stz. 1 and 16).
Based on JS 260 4to and Lbs 201 8vo.

Literature:
Bekker-Nielsen, Hans. "Mariadigtning." *KLNM* 11 (1966). Cols. 379–80, esp.
col. 379.

Finnur Jónsson. >> *Bókmentasaga Íslendinga fram undir siðabót* (1904–5).
P. 461.

- >> *Den oldnorske og oldislandske Litteraturs Historie* (1920–4). Vol. 3,
  p. 125.
Jón Þorkelsson. "Islandske håndskrifter i England og Skotland." *ANF* 8
  (1892): 199–237, esp. pp. 206–7
Kock, E.A. "Anteckningar till Íslenzk Miðaldakvæði." *ANF* 61 (1946): 1–125,
  esp. pp. 73–4.
Schottmann, Hans. >> *Die isländische Mariendichtung* (1973). Pp. 530 and
  541.

39. María drottins liljan guðs og ljómi

A poem in praise of Mary the Blessed Virgin composed ca. 1400–1550.
  Incipit: "María drottins liljan guðs og ljómi."

Manuscripts:
BLAdd 4892 (ca. 1700–1800), BLAdd 11.179 (ca. 1700–1800), JS 260 4to
  (1796) JS 487 8vo (ca. 1675–1900), JS 494 8vo (ca. 1675–1900), Lbs 953
  4to (ca. 1760), Lbs 1326 4to (ca. 1890), Lbs 2166 4to (ca. 1885–1920), and
  Lbs 201 8vo (ca. 1850–70).
Editions:
Jón Helgason, ed. >> *Íslenzk miðaldakvæði* (1936–8). Vol. 2, pp. 268–9.
  Based on BLAdd 4892 with variants from BLAdd 11.179, JS 260 4to, Lbs
  953 4to, and Lbs 201 8vo.
Jón Þorkelsson. >> *Om Digtningen på Island* (1888). P. 57 (stz. 1).
  Based on JS 260 4to and Lbs 201 8vo.
Literature:
Bekker-Nielsen, Hans. "Mariadigtning." *KLNM* 11 (1966). Cols. 379–80, esp.
  col. 379.
Finnur Jónsson. >> *Bókmentasaga Íslendinga fram undir siðabót* (1904–5).
  P. 461.
- >> *Den oldnorske og oldislandske Litteraturs Historie* (1920–4). Vol. 3,
  pp. 124–5.
Jón Þorkelsson. "Islandske håndskrifter i England og Skotland." *ANF* 8
  (1892): 199–237, esp. pp. 206–7.
Kock, E.A. "Anteckningar till Íslenzk Miðaldakvæði." *ANF* 61 (1946): 1–125,
  esp. pp. 74–5.
Schottmann, Hans. >> *Die isländische Mariendichtung* (1973). P. 511n20.

40. Ég vil lofa eina þá

A poem in praise of Mary the Blessed Virgin composed ca. 1400–1550.
   Incipit: "Ég vil lofa eina þá."

Manuscripts:
JS 389 8vo (ca. 1775–1825), Lbs 2166 4to (ca. 1885–1920), and Lbs 201 8vo
   (ca. 1850–70).
Editions:
Jón Helgason, ed. >> *Íslenzk miðaldakvæði* (1936–8). Vol. 2, pp. 271–2.
   Edition of JS 389 8vo.
Jón Þorkelsson. >> *Om Digtningen på Island* (1888). P. 56 (stz. 1).
   Edition of Lbs 201 8vo.
Literature:
Bekker-Nielsen, Hans. "Mariadigtning." *KLNM* 11 (1966). Cols. 379–80, esp.
   col. 379.
Finnur Jónsson. >> *Bókmentasaga Íslendinga fram undir siðabót* (1904–5).
   P. 461.
– >> *Den oldnorske og oldislandske Litteraturs Historie* (1920–4). Vol. 3,
   pp. 124–5.
Kock, E.A. "Anteckningar till Íslenzk Miðaldakvæði." *ANF* 61 (1946): 1–125,
   esp. p. 76.
Schottmann, Hans. >> *Die isländische Mariendichtung* (1973). Pp. 544–5.

41. Máríutíðir

A poem in praise of Mary the Blessed Virgin from ca. 1400–1550.
   Incipit: "Ave helgasta mey manna."

Manuscript:
ÍB 629 8vo (ca. 1740).
Edition:
Jón Helgason, ed. >> *Íslenzk miðaldakvæði* (1936–8). Vol. 2, pp. 272–3.
Literature:
Bekker-Nielsen, Hans. "Mariadigtning." *KLNM* 11 (1966). Cols. 379–80, esp.
   col. 379.
Finnur Jónsson. >> *Bókmentasaga Íslendinga fram undir siðabót* (1904–5).
   P. 461.
Schottmann, Hans. >> *Die isländische Mariendichtung* (1973). Pp. 498 and
   528–9.

42. Allra kærasta jungfrú mín

A poem in honour of Mary the Blessed Virgin composed ca. 1400–1550.
Incipit: "Allra kærasta jungfrú mín."

Manuscripts:
AM 711b 4to (ca. 1700–25) and Lbs 2166 4to (ca. 1885–1920).
Editions:
Jón Helgason, ed. >> *Íslenzk miðaldakvæði* (1936–8). Vol. 2, pp. 262–4.
Based on AM 711b 4to with variants from Lbs 2166 4to and Jón
Þorkelsson's edition (1888).
Jón Þorkelsson. >> *Om Digtningen på Island* (1888). P. 50 (stz. 1, 5–6, and
15–16).
Based on AM 711b 4to.
Modern Icelandic language edition:
Ásdís Egilsdóttir, Gunnar Harðarson, and Svanhildur Óskarsdóttir, ed.
Maríukver. Sögur og kvæði af heilagri guðsmóður frá fyrri tíð (Reykjavík:
Hið íslenska bókmenntafélag, 1996). Pp. 167–70.
Literature:
Bekker-Nielsen, Hans. "Mariadigtning." *KLNM* 11 (1966). Cols. 379–80, esp.
col. 379.
Finnur Jónsson. >> *Bókmentasaga Íslendinga fram undir siðabót* (1904–5).
P. 461.
– >> *Den oldnorske og oldislandske Litteraturs Historie* (1920–4). Vol. 3,
p. 124.
Schottmann, Hans. >> *Die isländische Mariendichtung* (1973). Pp. 491, 500,
503, 524n3, 527, and 530.
Stéfan Einarsson. *Íslensk bókmenntasaga 874–1960* (Reykjavík: Oddi, 1961).
P. 96.

43. Heilags anda höllin glæst

A poem in praise of Mary the Blessed Virgin composed ca. 1400–1550.
Incipit: "Heilags anda höllin glæst."

Manuscripts:
AM 713 4to (ca. 1500–50), AM 920 4to (ca. 1800–1900), and Lbs 2166 4to
(ca. 1885–1920).
Editions:
Jón Helgason, ed. >> *Íslenzk miðaldakvæði* (1936–8). Vol. 2, pp. 70–3.
Based on AM 713 4to with a variant from Jón Þorkelsson's edition (1888).

Jón Torfason and Kristján Eiríksson, ed. >> *Vísnabók Guðbrands* (2000).
Pp. xxxix–xl (stz. 1).
Based on Jón Helgason's edition (1936–8).
Jón Þorkelsson. >> *Om Digtningen på Island* (1888). Pp. 52–3 (stz. 1, 7^{1-2},
8^{1-2}, 13^{1-3}, and 14^{1-4}).
Literature:
Bekker-Nielsen, Hans. "Mariadigtning." *KLNM* 11 (1966). Cols. 379–80, esp.
col. 379.
Finnur Jónsson. >> *Bókmentasaga Íslendinga fram undir siðabót* (1904–5).
P. 461.
– >> *Den oldnorske og oldislandske Litteraturs Historie* (1920–4). Vol. 3,
pp. 124–5.
Kock, E.A. "Anteckningar till Íslenzk Miðaldakvæði." *ANF* 61 (1946): 1–125,
esp. pp. 41–2.
Schottmann, Hans. >> *Die isländische Mariendichtung* (1973). Pp. 60, 521,
and 541.

44. Máríulykill

A poem in praise of Mary the Blessed Virgin composed ca. 1425. The first half
of the poem is possibly by Jón Pálsson Máríuskáld (ca. 1390–1471). It has also
been attributed to Bishop Jón Arason (1484–1550), though the approximate
date of composition makes this unlikely.
   Incipit: "Drottning æðsta dýr af ættum."

Manuscripts:
A: AM 150 8vo (ca. 1650–1700);
B: AM 719c 4to (ca. 1650–1700);
C: Þor 75 (20716) (ca. 1700–1800), JS 404 4to (ca. 1700–1900), Lbs 201 8vo
   (ca. 1850–70), and Rask 88a (ca. 1700);
D: JS 404 4to (ca. 1700–1900) and JS 112 8vo (ca. 1700–1800);
E: BLAdd 4892 (ca. 1700–1800), BLAdd 11.179 (ca. 1700–1800), ÍB 521
   8vo (ca. 1700–1800), JS 260 4to (1796), JS 404 4to (ca. 1700–1900),
   JS 487 8vo (ca. 1675–1900), JS 494 8vo (ca. 1675–1900), JS 514 8vo
   (ca. 1675–1900), Lbs 269 4to (ca. 1700–1900), Lbs 936 4to (ca. 1880),
   Lbs 953 4to (ca. 1760), Lbs 1276 4to (1862–70), Lbs 2031 4to (ca.
   1880–1920), Lbs 201 8vo (ca. 1850–70), Lbs 328 8vo (1830), Lbs 754
   8vo (ca. 1700–1900), Lbs 1197 8vo (1773), Lbs 2402 8vo (1852 and
   later), and Rask 21a (ca. 1600–1800).

Editions:
Einar Ól. Sveinsson, Páll Eggert Ólason, and Arnór Sigurjónsson, ed. *Íslands þúsund ár: Kvæðasafn.* 3 vols. (Reykjavík: Helgafell, 1947). Vol. 3, pp. 46–7 (stz. 1 and 10).
Jón Helgason, ed. >> *Íslenzk miðaldakvæði* (1936–8). Vol. 2, pp. 212–28. Based on AM 150 8vo with variants and additional stz. from AM 719c 4to, BLAdd 4892, BLAdd 11.179, Bor 75 (20716), JS 260 4to, JS 404 4to, JS 112 8vo, JS 487 8vo, Js 494 8vo, JS 514 8vo, Lbs 953 4to, Lbs 2031 4to, Lbs 1197 8vo, Rask 88a, Jón Helgason's article (1924), and Jón Þorkelsson's (1888) edition.
Jón Þorkelsson. >> *Om Digtningen på Island* (1888). Pp. 43 (stz. 1^{1-2}) and 255–62. Based on AM 150 8vo with variants from AM 719c 4to, JS 404 4to, and Rask 88a.
– >> *Kvæðasafn* (1922–7), Pp. 123–34. Based on AM 150 8vo with variants from AM 719c 4to, JS 404 4to, and Rask 88a.
Norwegian translation:
Orgland, Ivar, trans. *Islandske Dikt. Frå Sólarljóð til opplysningstid (13. hundreåret–1835)* (Reykjavík: Fonna, 1977) P. 176 (stz. 1 and 10).
Literature:
Anna Sigurðardóttir. *Allt hafði annan róm áður í páfadóm: Nunnuklaustrin tvö á Íslandi á miðöldum og brot úr kristnisögu* (Reykjavík: Kvennasögusafn Íslands, 1988). Pp. 364–5.
Anon. "Den Oldnordisk-islandske Afdeling." Annual Report for 1847. *Antiquarisk Tidsskrift* 1846–8 (Copenhagen: Sally B. Salomon, 1847). Pp. 154–72, esp. p. 165.
Bekker-Nielsen, Hans. "Mariadigtning." *KLNM* 11 (1966). Cols. 379–80.
Björn Þorsteinsson and Guðrún Ása Grímsdóttir. "Kirkjan og þjóðlífið." In *Saga Íslands* 5. Ed. Sigurður Líndal (Reykjavík: Hið íslenzka bókmenntafélag, Sögufélagið, 1990). Pp. 141–79, esp. p. 171.
Finnur Jónsson. >> *Bókmentasaga Íslendinga fram undir siðabót* (1904–5). P. 461.
– >> *Den oldnorske og oldislandske Litteraturs Historie* (1920–4). Vol. 3, pp. 15–16 and 124.
Holtsmark, Anne. "Háttalykill." *KLNM* 9 (1964). Cols. 242–3, esp. col. 243.
Jón Helgason. "Nokkur íslenzk miðaldakvæði." *ANF* 40 (1924): 285–313, esp. pp. 304–9.
– >> "Norges og Islands digtning." In *Litteraturhistorie B: Norge og Island* (1953). Pp. 3–179, esp. p. 164.

Kock, E.A. "Anteckningar till Íslenzk Miðaldakvæði." *ANF* 61 (1946): 1–125,
esp. pp. 67–71.

Mogk, Eugen. >> *Geschichte der norwegisch-isländischen Literatur* (1904).
Pp. 716–17.

Pétur Sigurðsson. "Vísnabók Guðbrands biskups." In *Iðunn: Tímarit til
skemtunar, nytsemdar og fróðleiks*. Vol. 8. Ed. Magnús Jónsson (Reykjavík:
Gutenberg, 1923–4). Pp. 61–78, esp. p. 62.

Schottmann, Hans. >> *Die isländische Mariendichtung* (1973). Pp. 490,
491n3, 530–5, 548, and 553.

Stéfan Einarsson. "Íslenzk helgikvæði á miðöldum." *Tímarit Þjóðræknisfélags
Íslendinga* 36 (1954): 43–63, esp. pp. 52 and 54.

– *Íslensk bókmenntasaga 874–1960* (Reykjavík: Oddi, 1961). Pp. 89, 91,
and 119.

Wolf, Kirsten, ed. >> *Saga heilagrar Önnu* (2001). P. xliv.

NOTE:

The poem contains material about Saint Anne. See her entry.

45. Máríu nafn með gleði og prís

A defective Marian miracle poem from ca. 1400–1550 about a man whom
Mary the Blessed Virgin saved from illness and evil spirits. Jón Þorkelsson
proposes that it was composed in the eastern part of Iceland ca. 1500. It ap-
pears to be based on a foreign legend and closely resembles a legend edited by
G.E. Klemming (see *Klosterläsning: Järteckensbok, apostola gerningar, helga
manna lefverne, legender, Nichodemi evangelium* [Stockholm: Norstedt and
Sons, 1877–8], pp. 88–9).

Incipit: "Máríu nafn með gleði og prís."

Manuscripts:
AM 232 fol. (ca. 1350; sixteenth-century marginal entry), AM 127 4to
(ca. 1400–1500), and Lbs 2166 4to (ca. 1885–1920).

Editions:
Jón Helgason, ed. >> *Íslenzk miðaldakvæði* (1936–8). Vol. 2, pp. 200–3.
Based on AM 127 4to with variants from AM 232 fol. and Jón Þorkelsson's
(1888) edition.

Jón Þorkelsson. >> *Om Digtningen på Island* (1888). Pp. 51–2 (stz. 1–2,
9–10, 11$^{4-5}$, and 12–13).
Edition of Lbs 2166 4to.

Literature:
Bekker-Nielsen, Hans. "Mariadigtning." *KLNM* 11 (1966). Cols. 379–80, esp.
col. 379.

Finnur Jónsson. >> *Bókmentasaga Íslendinga fram undir siðabót* (1904–5).
P. 461.

– >> *Den oldnorske og oldislandske Litteraturs Historie* (1920–4). Vol. 3,
pp. 124–5.

Kock, E.A. "Anteckningar till Íslenzk Miðaldakvæði." *ANF* 61 (1946): 1–125,
esp. pp. 65–7.

46. Guð sinn mundi

A fragmentary miracle poem from ca. 1500 based on a legend about a sinful
deacon whose soul was saved by Mary the Blessed Virgin (cf. C.R. Unger, ed.,
Mariu saga: Legender om Jomfru Maria og hendes jertegn [Christiania (Oslo):
Brögger and Christie, 1871], pp. 604–8 and 835–6).
Incipit: "Guð sinn mundi."

Manuscripts:
AM 720a 4to II (ca. 1500–1600), AM 920 4to (ca. 1800–1900), and Lbs 2166
4to (ca. 1885–1920).

Editions:
Jón Helgason, ed. >> *Íslenzk miðaldakvæði* (1936–8). Vol. 2, pp. 120–1.
Based on AM 720a 4to II with variants from AM 920 4to and Lbs 2166
4to.

Jón Þorkelsson. >> *Om Digtningen på Island* (1888). P. 55 (stz. 1–2).
Based on AM 720a 4to II and AM 920 4to.

Literature:
Bekker-Nielsen, Hans. "Mariadigtning." *KLNM* 11 (1966). Cols. 379–80, esp.
col. 379.

Finnur Jónsson. >> *Bókmentasaga Íslendinga fram undir siðabót* (1904–5).
P. 461.

– >> *Den oldnorske og oldislandske Litteraturs Historie* (1920–4). Vol. 3, p. 124.

Kock, E.A. "Anteckningar till Íslenzk Miðaldakvæði." *ANF* 61 (1946): 1–125,
esp. p. 44.

47. Gyðingsdiktur

A Marian miracle poem about a Jewish boy who converted to Christianity (cf.
C.R. Unger, ed., *Mariu saga: Legender om Jomfru Maria og hendes jertegn*
[Christiania (Oslo): Brögger and Christie, 1871], pp. 71–2). The poem was
likely composed ca. 1500 but was not recorded until the seventeenth century
or later.

Incipits: A: "Hér vil ég ágætt ævintýr"; B and F: "Staðurinn einn var stór og ríkur"; H: "Staðurinn heitir stór og ríkur"; C: "Gyðingur nokkur garði í gjörði"; G: "Gyðingur ríkur garði í gjörði"; and I: "Nú skal hefja nýjan óð."

Manuscripts:

A: AM 717a 4to (ca. 1700–25), AM 717d β 4to (ca. 1700–25), AM 150 8vo (ca. 1650–1700), JS 399a–b 4to (ca. 1700–1900), and Lbs 2166 4to (ca. 1885–1920);

B: AM 148 8vo (ca. 1650–1700), JS 405 4to (1819), Lbs 2166 4to (ca. 1885–1920), and NKS 1141 fol. (ca. 1750–1800);

C: JS 588 4to (ca. 1800–1900), Lbs 201 8vo (ca. 1850–70);

D: JS 481 8vo (ca. 1675–1900);

E: JS 510 8vo (ca. 1675–1800), Lbs 201 8vo (ca. 1850–70), and Lbs 685 8vo (ca. 1775–1800);

F: JS 201 4to (ca. 1837–50);

G: Lbs 1988 8vo (ca. 1790 and later);

H: JS 507 8vo (ca. 1675–1900) and Lbs 201 8vo (ca. 1850–70);

I: JS 513 8vo (ca. 1675–1900) and Lbs 201 8vo (ca. 1850–70).

Editions:

Anon. "Det historisk-archaeologiske archiv, islandske Afdeling." Annual Report for 1851. *Antiquarisk Tidsskrift* 1849–51 (Copenhagen: Berling, 1852). Pp. 218–66, esp. p. 253 (B: stz. 1).
    Edition of JS 405 4to.

Jón Helgason, ed. >> *Íslenzk miðaldakvæði* (1936–8). Vol. 2, pp. 90–119.
    A: based on AM 150 8vo with variants from versions B-I; B: based on AM 148 8vo with variants from NKS 1141 fol. and JS 405 4to; C: edition of JS 588 4to; D: edition of JS 481 8vo; E: based on Lbs 685 8vo with variants from JS 510 8vo and versions H and I; F: edition of JS 201 4to; G: edition of Lbs 1988 8vo; H: based on JS 507 8vo with variants from Lbs 201 8vo and versions D, G, and I; I: based on JS 513 8vo with variants from Lbs 201 8vo.

– ed. >> *Kvæðabók úr Vigur: AM 148, 8vo* (1955). Fol. 227v–228v.
    Facsimile of AM 148 8vo.

Jón Þorkelsson. >> *Om Digtningen på Island* (1888). P. 44 (A: stz. 1 and 2^1; B: stz. 1^1; C [= Jón Helgason's I]: stz. 1^{1-2} and 5^1)
    Based on AM 717a 4to, AM 717d β 4to, and AM 150 8vo (A); AM 148 8vo (B); and Lbs 201 8vo (C).

Literature:

Bekker-Nielsen, Hans. "Mariadigtning." *KLNM* 11 (1966). Cols. 379–80.

Finnur Jónsson. >> *Bókmentasaga Íslendinga fram undir siðabót* (1904–5). P. 461.

– >> *Den oldnorske og oldislandske Litteraturs Historie* (1920–4). Vol. 3, p. 124.

Hálfdan Einarsson. *Sciagraphia historiæ literariæ islandicæ* (Copenhagen: Sander and Schröder, 1777). P. 58.

Jón Helgason. >> "Norges og Islands digtning." In *Litteraturhistorie B: Norge og Island* (1953). Pp. 3–179, esp. p. 163.

Kock, E.A. "Anteckningar till Íslenzk Miðaldakvæði." *ANF* 61 (1946): 1–125, esp. pp. 43–4.

Schottmann, Hans. >> *Die isländische Mariendichtung* (1973). Pp. 440–55, 444n12, and 486n20.

48. Rósa

An early sixteenth-century cosmological poem with an emphasis on the life of Mary the Blessed Virgin attributed to Sigurður blindur.

Incipit: "Faðir og son á hæstum hæðum."

Manuscripts:
AM 622 4to (ca. 1549), AM 713 4to (ca. 1500–50), AM 920 4to (ca. 1800–1900), AM 1032 4to (ca. 1700–25), JS 399a–b 4to (ca. 1700–1900), Lbs 444 4to (ca. 1820–50; stz. 1–2 only), Lbs 1486b 4to (ca. 1860–78), and Trinity L.2.3 (ca. 1700–1800).

Editions:
Einar Ól. Sveinsson, Páll Eggert Ólason, and Arnór Sigurjónsson, ed. *Íslands þúsund ár: Kvæðasafn*. 3 vols. (Reykjavík: Helgafell, 1947). Vol. 3, pp. 135–9 (stz. 10, 12, 73, 114–15, and 122–8).

Jón Helgason, ed. >> *Íslenzk miðaldakvæði* (1936–8). Vol. 1.2, pp. 6–35. Based on AM 713 4to with variants from AM 622 4to, AM 920 4to, AM 1032 4to, JS 399a–b 4to, Lbs 1486b 4to, the edition by Jón Þorkelsson (1922–7), and Björn Þorleifsson's article (1929).

Jón Þorkelsson. >> *Om Digtningen på Island* (1888). Pp. 51 (stz. 1^{1-2}) and 282–3 (stz. 1, 8–9, 132^{5-8}, and 133^{7-8}). Based on AM 622 4to, AM 713 4to, and AM 1032 4to.

Jón Þorkelsson, ed. >> *Kvæðasafn* (1922–7). Pp. 262–94. Based on JS 399a–b 4to with variants from AM 622 4to, AM 713 4to, and AM 1032 4to.

Sigurður Nordal, ed. *Íslenzk lestrarbók 1400–1900* (Reykjavík: Sigfús Eymundsson, 1924). Pp. 8–10 (stz. 114–15 and 122–8). Based on Jón Þorkelsson's edition (1922–7).

Norwegian translation:
Orgland, Ivar, trans. and Anne-Lise Knoff, illus. *Rósa. Sigurður blindur í Fagradal* (Oslo: Solum, 1989). Pp. 20–70.

Literature:
Ármann Jakobsson. "The Homer of the North, or: Who Was Sigurður the Blind?" *European Journal of Scandinavian Studies* 44 (2014): 4–19, esp. pp. 4–9, 13, and 15–17.

Björn Þorleifsson. "Kvantitetsomvæltningen i islandsk." *ANF* 45 (1929): 35–81, esp. pp. 36–40.

Björn K. Þórólfsson. *Rímur fyrir 1600.* Safn fræðafjelagsins 9 (Copenhagen: Møller, 1934). Pp. 433–4, 436, and 440.

Carpenter, William H., ed. *Nikolásdrápa Halls prests: An Icelandic Poem from circa A.D. 1400* (Halle: Karras, 1881). P. 3. (The poem is here given the title *Máríuvísur*, and *Milska* is incorrectly titled *Rósa.*)

Finnur Jónsson. >> *Bókmentasaga Íslendinga fram undir siðabót* (1904–5). Pp. 461 and 463.

– >> *Den oldnorske og oldislandske Litteraturs Historie* (1920–4). Vol. 3, pp. 124 and 127.

Guðrún Nordal. "Helgubók. Kvæðasafn á mörkum kaþólsku og lútersku." In *Handrit úr förum Árna Magnússonar.* Ed. Svanhildur Óskarsdóttir, Matthew Driscoll, and Sigurður Svavarsson (Copenhagen: Den Arnamagnæanske Samling, Nordisk Forkningsinstitut; Reykjavík: Stofnun Árna Magnússonar í íslenskum fræðum; and Reykjavík: Bókaútgáfan Opna, 2013). P. 127.

– "Helgubók." In *Góssið hans Árna: Minningar heimsins í íslenskum handritum.* Ed. Jóhanna Katrín Friðriksdóttir (Reykjavík: Stofnun Árna Magnússonar í íslenskum fræðum, 2014). Pp. 21–35, esp. p. 30.

Jakob Benediktsson. >> "Helgikvæði." In *Hugtök og heiti í bókmenntafræði* (1983). Pp. 115–17, esp. p. 116.

Jón Helgason. *Gamall kveðskapur* (Copenhagen: Hið íslenzka fræðafélag, 1979). P. 12.

– >> "Norges og Islands digtning." In *Litteraturhistorie B: Norge og Island* (1953). Pp. 3–179, esp. pp. 162–3.

Jónas Kristjánsson. >> *Eddas and Sagas: Iceland's Medieval Literature* (1988). Pp. 387–8.

Kock, E.A. "Liljukvistur." *Studia Neophilologica* 15 (1942): 141–56, esp. p. 143.

– "Anteckningar till Íslenzk Miðaldakvæði." *ANF* 61 (1946): 1–125, esp. pp. 1–3, 31, 52, 69, 107, and 110.

Mauritzen, Else. "Som den hviteste lijle er den rødeste rose: En analyse av *Lilja* og *Rósa*, med hovedvekt på *Rósa*." *Nordistica Bergensia* 27 (2002): 125–74.

Mogk, Eugen. >> *Geschichte der norwegisch-isländischen Literatur* (1904). P. 718.

Schottmann, Hans. >> *Die isländische Mariendichtung* (1973). Pp. 30–1, 70, 110–11, 124, 134–5, 257–77, 299–313, 485, 518, and 554.

Stéfan Einarsson. "Íslenzk helgikvæði á miðöldum." *Tímarit Þjóðræknisfélags Íslendinga* 36 (1954): 43–63, esp. pp 53 and 55.

– *Íslensk bókmenntasaga 874–1960* (Reykjavík: Oddi, 1961). P. 90.

Vésteinn Ólason. "Kveðskapur frá síðmiðöldum." In >> *Íslensk Bókmenntasaga* 2 (1993). Pp. 283–378, esp. pp. 300–1, 317, and 350.

– "Old Icelandic Poetry." In *A History of Icelandic Literature*. Ed. Daisy Neijmann. Histories of Scandinavian Literature 5 (Lincoln: University of Nebraska Press, 2006). Pp. 1–64, esp. p. 51.

Wolf, Kirsten, ed. >> *Saga heilagrar Önnu* (2001). P. xliii.

NOTE:

The poem contains material about Saints Andrew, Anne, Barnabas, Bartholomew, James the Greater, James the Less, Joachim, John the Baptist, John the Evangelist, Joseph, Jude, Lazarus, Matthew, Paul, Peter, Philip, Simeon the Righteous, Simon, and Thomas. See the entries for the individual saints.

49. Milska

An early sixteenth-century poem about the life of Mary the Blessed Virgin. Incipit: "Faðir vor Kristur friður hinn hæsti."

Manuscripts:
AM 713 4to (ca. 1500–50), AM 622 4to (ca. 1549), AM 721 4to (ca. 1500–50), JS 399a–b 4to (ca. 1700–1900), Lbs 444 4to (ca. 1820–50), Lbs 1486b 4to (ca. 1860–78), Lbs 2166 4to (ca. 1885–1920), and Trinity L.2.3 (ca. 1700–1800).

Editions:
Jón Helgason, ed. >> *Íslenzk miðaldakvæði* (1936–8). Vol. 1.2, pp. 38–58. Based on AM 713 4to with variants from AM 622 4to, AM 721 4to, JS 399a–b 4to, Lbs 444 4to, and Lbs 1486b 4to and notes from C.R. Unger, ed. *Mariu saga: Legender om Jomfru Maria og hendes jertegn* (Christiania [Oslo]: Brögger and Christie, 1871).

Jón Þorkelsson. >> *Om Digtningen på Island* (1888). Pp. 51 (stz. 1^{1-2}) and 283–4 (stz. 1 and 90 and refrains).
Based on AM 622 4to.

Modern Icelandic language edition:
Jón Sigurðsson, ed. *Milska* (Reykjavík: Listahátíð í Reykjavík, 1994).
   Pp. [1]–[31].
Norwegian translations:
Orgland, Ivar. *Milska* (Reykjavík: Listahátíð í Reykjavík, 1994). Pp. [1]–[31].
Orgland, Ivar, and Anne-Lise Knoff, illus. *Milska: Eit Maria-kvad frå
   islandsk seinmellomalder* (Oslo: Solum, 1993). Pp. 20–66.
Literature:
Ármann Jakobsson. "The Homer of the North, or: Who Was Sigurður the
   Blind?" *European Journal of Scandinavian Studies* 44 (2014): 4–19, esp.
   pp. 4–7, 9, and 16–17.
Björn K. Þórólfsson. *Rímur fyrir 1600.* Safn fræðafjelagsins 9 (Copenhagen:
   Møller, 1934). Pp. 433–4.
Carpenter, William H., ed. *Nikolásdrápa Halls prests: An Icelandic Poem
   from circa A.D. 1400* (Halle: Karras, 1881). P. 3. (The poem is here
   incorrectly given the title *Rósa*, and *Rósa* the title *Máríuvísur*.)
Finnur Jónsson. >> *Bókmentasaga Íslendinga fram undir siðabót* (1904–5).
   P. 461.
– >> *Den oldnorske og oldislandske Litteraturs Historie* (1920–4). Vol. 3,
   pp. 124–5.
Guðrún Nordal. "Helgubók. Kvæðasafn á mörkum kaþólsku og lútersku."
   In *Handrit úr förum Árna Magnússonar.* Ed. Svanhildur Óskarsdóttir,
   Matthew Driscoll, and Sigurður Svavarsson (Copenhagen: Den
   Arnamagnæanske Samling, Nordisk Forkningsinstitut; Reykjavík: Stofnun
   Árna Magnússonar í íslenskum fræðum; and Reykjavík: Bókaútgáfan
   Opna, 2013). P. 127.
– "Helgubók." In *Góssið hans Árna: Minningar heimsins í íslenskum
   handritum.* Ed. Jóhanna Katrín Friðriksdóttir (Reykjavík: Stofnun Árna
   Magnússonar í íslenskum fræðum, 2014). Pp. 21–35, esp. pp. 27 and 29.
Jakob Benediktsson. >> "Helgikvæði." In *Hugtök og heiti í bókmenntafræði*
   (1983). Pp. 115–17, esp. p. 116.
Jón Helgason. *Gamall kveðskapur* (Copenhagen: Hið íslenzka fræðafélag,
   1979). P. 12.
– >> "Norges og Islands digtning." In *Litteraturhistorie B: Norge og Island*
   (1953). Pp. 3–179, esp. p. 163.
Jón Þorkelsson, ed. >> *Kvæðasafn* (1922–7). P. 262.
Jónas Kristjánsson. >> *Eddas and Sagas: Iceland's Medieval Literature*
   (1988). P. 387.
Kock, E.A. "Liljukvistur." *Studia Neophilologica* 15 (1942): 141–56, esp.
   p. 143.

– "Anteckningar till Íslenzk Miðaldakvæði." *ANF* 61 (1946): 1–125, esp.
   pp. 3–5 and 31.
Mogk, Eugen. >> *Geschichte der norwegisch-isländischen Literatur* (1904).
   P. 718.
Schottmann, Hans. >> *Die isländische Mariendichtung* (1973). Pp. 111n22,
   200n24, 289–313, and 554.
Vésteinn Ólason. "Kveðskapur frá síðmiðöldum." In >> *Íslensk
   Bókmenntasaga* 2 (1993). Pp. 283–378, esp. pp. 299 and 301.
NOTE:
The poem contains material about Saints Andrew, John the Baptist, John the
Evangelist, Joseph, and Simeon the Righteous. See the entries for the individ-
ual saints.

50. Sælust sjóvar stjarna

An early sixteenth-century poem in praise of Mary the Blessed Virgin attrib-
uted to the priest Hallur Ögmundarson (d. ca. 1540).
   Incipit: "Sælust sjóvar stjarna."

Manuscripts:
AM 622 4to (ca. 1549), AM 711b 4to (ca. 1700–25), JS 399a–b 4to (ca. 1700–
   1900), Lbs 444 4to (ca. 1820–50), and Trinity L.2.3 (ca. 1700–1800).
Editions:
Carpenter, William H., ed. *Nikolásdrápa Halls prests: An Icelandic Poem
   from circa A.D. 1400* (Halle: Karras, 1881). P. 5 (stz. 1).
   Edition of AM 622 4to.
Jón Helgason, ed. >> *Íslenzk miðaldakvæði* (1936–8). Vol. 2, pp. 64–6.
   Based on AM 622 4to with variants from AM 711b 4to, JS 399a–b 4to, and
   Jón Þorkelsson's edition (1922–7).
Jón Þorkelsson. >> *Om Digtningen på Island* (1888). Pp. 54 (stz. 1^{1-2} and 319
   (stz. 1 and 18).
   Based on AM 622 4to and AM 711b 4to.
Jón Þorkelsson, ed. >> *Kvæðasafn* (1922–7). Pp. 366–70.
   Edition of AM 622 4to, AM 711b 4to, JS 399a–b 4to, and Lbs 444 4to.
Literature:
Bekker-Nielsen, Hans. "Mariadigtning." *KLNM* 11 (1966). Cols. 379–80, esp.
   col. 379.
Björn Þorleifsson. "Kvantitetsomvæltningen i Islandsk. " *ANF* 45 (1929):
   35–81, esp. pp. 47–8.

Finnur Jónsson. >> *Bókmentasaga Íslendinga fram undir siðabót* (1904–5).
  Pp. 461 and 463.
– >> *Den oldnorske og oldislandske Litteraturs Historie* (1920–4). Vol. 3,
  p. 128.
Kock, E.A. "Anteckningar till Íslenzk Miðaldakvæði." *ANF* 61 (1946): 1–125,
  esp. pp. 38–9.
Mogk, Eugen. >> *Geschichte der norwegisch-isländischen Literatur* (1904).
  P. 718.
Schottmann, Hans. >> *Die isländische Mariendichtung* (1973). Pp. 490–1,
  493, 502, 518, 527, 541, and 545.
Vésteinn Ólason. "Kveðskapur frá síðmiðöldum." In >> *Íslensk
  Bókmenntasaga* 2 (1993). Pp. 283–387, esp. pp. 306 and 313.
NOTE:
The poem contains material about Simeon the Righteous. See his entry.

51. Jesús móðirin jungfrú skær

A poem in praise of Mary the Blessed Virgin composed ca. 1525.
  Incipit: "Jesús móðirin jungfrú skær."

Manuscripts:
AM 713 4to (ca. 1500–50), AM 920 4to (ca. 1800–1900), AM 1032 4to
  (ca. 1700–25), and Lbs 2166 4to (ca. 1885–1920).
Editions:
Jón Helgason, ed. >> *Íslenzk miðaldakvæði* (1936–8). Vol. 2, pp. 243–5.
  Based on AM 713 4to with variants from AM 920 4to and Lbs 2166 4to.
Jón Þorkelsson. >> *Om Digtningen på Island* (1888). P. 49 (stz. 1 and 16$^{5-6}$).
  Based on AM 713 4to, AM 920 4to, and AM 1032 4to.
Literature:
Bekker-Nielsen, Hans. "Mariadigtning." *KLNM* 11 (1966). Cols. 379–80, esp.
  col. 379.
Finnur Jónsson. >> *Bókmentasaga Íslendinga fram undir siðabót* (1904–5).
  P. 461.
– >> *Den oldnorske og oldislandske Litteraturs Historie* (1920–4). Vol. 3,
  p. 124.
Kock, E.A. "Anteckningar till Íslenzk Miðaldakvæði." *ANF* 61 (1946): 1–125,
  esp. pp. 3 and 72.
Schottmann, Hans. >> *Die isländische Mariendichtung* (1973). Pp. 43n33,
  490, 502, and 520–2.

Vésteinn Ólason. "Kveðskapur frá síðmiðöldum." In >> *Íslensk
Bókmenntasaga* 2 (1993). Pp. 283–387, esp. p. 313.

52. Heyr mig bjartast blómsturið mæta

A poem in praise of Mary the Blessed Virgin composed ca. 1550.
Incipit: "Heyr mig bjartast blómsturið mæta."

Manuscripts:
A: BLAdd 11.242 (ca. 1540–90) and Lbs 1329 4to (ca. 1890).
B: BLAdd 4892 (ca. 1700–1800), BLAdd 11.179 (ca. 1700–1800), BLAdd
11.242 (ca. 1540–90), JS 260 4to (1796), JS 399a–b 4to (ca. 1700–1900),
JS 487 8vo (ca. 1675–1900), JS 494 8vo (ca. 1675–1900), JS 514 8vo
(ca. 1675–1900), Lbs 936 4to (ca. 1880), Lbs 953 4to (ca. 1760), Lbs 1326
4to (ca. 1890), Lbs 1329 4to (ca. 1890), Lbs 2166 4to (ca. 1885–1920),
Lbs 201 8vo (ca. 1850–70), and Lbs 754 8vo (ca. 1700–1900).

Editions:
Jón Helgason, ed. >> *Íslenzk miðaldakvæði* (1936–8). Vol. 2, pp. 78–83.
Based on BLAdd 11.242 with variants from BLAdd 4892, BLAdd 11.179,
JS 260 4to, and Lbs 953 4to.
Jón Þorkelsson. >> *Om Digtningen på Island* (1888). P. 56 (stz. 1 and 37).
Based on JS 260 4to and Lbs 201 8vo.

Modern Icelandic language edition:
Ásdís Egilsdóttir, Gunnar Harðarson, and Svanhildur Óskarsdóttir, ed.
Maríukver. Sögur og kvæði af heilagri guðsmóður frá fyrri tíð (Reykjavík:
Hið íslenska bókmenntafélag, 1996). Pp. 159–66.

Literature:
Bekker-Nielsen, Hans. "Mariadigtning." *KLNM* 11 (1966). Cols. 379–80, esp.
col. 379.
Finnur Jónsson. >> *Bókmentasaga Íslendinga fram undir siðabót* (1904–5).
P. 461.
– >> *Den oldnorske og oldislandske Litteraturs Historie* (1920–4). Vol. 3,
p. 125.
Jón Helgason. *Gamall kveðskapur* (Copenhagen: Hið íslenzka fræðafélag,
1979). P. 10.
Jón Þorkelsson. "Islandske håndskrifter i England og Skotland." *ANF* 8
(1892): 199–237, esp. pp. 206–7.

Kock, E.A. "Anteckningar till Íslenzk Miðaldakvæði." *ANF* 61 (1946): 1–125, esp. pp. 5, 38, and 42.

Schottmann, Hans. >> *Die isländische Mariendichtung* (1973). Pp. 88–9, 92, 106–7, 125n18, 205, 306, and 490–2, 506–12, 519, 549, and 553.

Stéfan Einarsson. "Íslenzk helgikvæði á miðöldum." *Tímarit Þjóðræknisfélags Íslendinga* 36 (1955): 43–63, esp. p. 54.

– *Íslensk bókmenntasaga 874–1960* (Reykjavík: Oddi, 1961). P. 91.

53. Enginn heyrði og enginn sá

A poem in honour of Mary the Blessed Virgin composed ca. 1550.
Incipit: "Enginn heyrði og enginn sá."

Manuscripts:
AM 711a 4to (ca. 1700–25), AM 713 4to (ca. 1500–50), AM 920 4to (ca. 1800–1900), and Lbs 2166 4to (ca. 1885–1920).

Editions:
Jón Helgason, ed. >> *Íslenzk miðaldakvæði* (1936–8). Vol. 2, pp. 239–40. Based on AM 713 4to with variants from AM 711a 4to and AM 920 4to.

Jón Þorkelsson. >> *Om Digtningen på Island* (1888). P. 45 (stz. 1 and 16). Based on AM 713 4to, AM 711a 4to, and AM 920 4to.

Modern Icelandic language edition:
Ásdís Egilsdóttir, Gunnar Harðarson, and Svanhildur Óskarsdóttir, ed. *Maríukver. Sögur og kvæði af heilagri guðsmóður frá fyrri tíð* (Reykjavík: Hið íslenska bókmenntafélag, 1996). Pp. 171–3.

Literature:
Bekker-Nielsen, Hans. "Mariadigtning." *KLNM* 11 (1966). Cols. 379–80, esp. col. 379.

Finnur Jónsson. >> *Bókmentasaga Íslendinga fram undir siðabót* (1904–5). P. 461.

– >> *Den oldnorske og oldislandske Litteraturs Historie* (1920–4). Vol. 3, p. 124.

Kock, E.A. "Anteckningar till Íslenzk Miðaldakvæði." *ANF* 61 (1946): 1–125, esp. pp. 70–1.

Schottmann, Hans. >> *Die isländische Mariendichtung* (1973). Pp. 490, 494, 498n17, 499–500, 503, and 529–30.

54. Máríuvísur

A poem in praise of Mary the Blessed Virgin likely composed around the time of the Reformation.
Incipit: "Máría móðirin skæra."

Manuscripts:
AM 717g 4to (1673), AM 426 12mo (ca. 1600–1700), AM 428a 12mo
(ca. 1300–1400 and ca. 1600–1700), and Lbs 201 8vo (ca. 1850–70).
Edition:
Jón Þorkelsson. >> *Om Digtningen på Island* (1888). P. 54 (stz. 1–3).
Based on AM 717g 4to, AM 426 12mo, AM 428a 12mo, and Lbs 201 8vo.
Literature:
Finnur Jónsson. >> *Bókmentasaga Íslendinga fram undir siðabót* (1904–5).
P. 461.
– >> *Den oldnorske og oldislandske Litteraturs Historie* (1920–4). Vol. 3,
p. 124.
Schottmann, Hans. >> *Die isländische Mariendichtung* (1973). P. 545n35.

55. Máríuvísur

A poem in praise of Mary the Blessed Virgin composed ca. 1600 by Einar
Sigurðsson í Eydölum (1539–1626).
Incipit: "Mjúkast vilda ég mærðarvers."

Manuscripts:
ÍB 37 8vo (ca. 1840), ÍB 629 8vo (ca. 1740), ÍBR 100 8vo (ca. 1700–1800),
JS 33 4to (ca. 1730), JS 256 4to (1840–5), JS 260 4to (1796), JS 399a–b
4to (ca. 1700–1900), JS 580 4to (ca. 1600–1900), JS 648 4to (ca. 1800),
JS 112 8vo (ca. 1700–1800), JS 154 8vo (ca. 1780), JS 309 8vo (ca. 1810),
JS 389 8vo (ca. 1775–1825), JS 471 8vo (ca. 1675–1900), JS 487 8vo
(ca. 1675–1900), JS 494 8vo (ca. 1675–1900), JS 507 8vo (ca. 1675–
1900), JS 514 8vo (ca. 1675–1900), Lbs 399 4to (ca. 1680–1700), Lbs
444 4to (ca. 1820–50), Lbs 512 4to (ca. 1700–50), Lbs 852 4to (ca.
1750–1800), Lbs 953 4to (ca. 1760), Lbs 1293 4to (1845–57), Lbs 1326
4to (1890), Lbs 2031 4to (ca. 1880–1920), Lbs 2166 4to (ca. 1885–1920),
Lbs 201 8vo (ca. 1850–70), Lbs 494 8vo (ca. 1700), Lbs 503 8vo

(ca. 1820–40), Lbs 558 8vo (ca. 1700–1900), Lbs 1030 8vo (ca. 1810), Lbs 1091 8vo (ca. 1883), Lbs 1119 8vo (ca. 1760), Lbs 1331 8vo (ca. 1700–1900), Lbs 2361 8vo (ca. 1700–1900), Lbs 2366 8vo (ca. 1770–90), and Lbs 2412 8vo (ca. 1830).

Editions:

Guðbrandur Þorláksson, ed. >> *Ein ny wiisna bok* (1612). Pp. 93–7.

Jón Torfason and Kristján Eiríksson, ed. >> *Vísnabók Guðbrands* (2000). Pp. 110–13.

Jón Þorkelsson. >> *Om Digtningen på Island* (1888). Pp. 111–12 (stz. 1–8, 42–3, and 442 (stz. 1^{1-2}).

Sigurður Nordal, ed. *Íslenzk lestrarbók 1400–1900* (Reykjavík: Sigfús Eymundsson, 1924). Pp. 32–3 (stz. 1–7).

Modern Icelandic language edition:

Ásdís Egilsdóttir, Gunnar Harðarson, and Svanhildur Óskarsdóttir, ed. *Maríukver. Sögur og kvæði af heilagri guðsmóður frá fyrri tíð* (Reykjavík: Hið íslenska bókmenntafélag, 1996). Pp. 179–88.

Norwegian translation:

Orgland, Ivar, trans. *Islandske Dikt. Frå Sólarljóð til opplysningstid (13. hundreåret–1835)* (Reykjavík: Fonna, 1977). Pp. 251–3 (stz. 1–7).

Literature:

Anna Sigurðardóttir. *Allt hafði annan róm áður í páfadóm: Nunnuklaustrin tvö á Íslandi á miðöldum og brot úr kristnisögu* (Reykjavík: Kvennasögusafn Íslands, 1988). Pp. 364–5.

Bjarni Þorsteinsson, ed. *Íslenzk þjóðlög* (Copenhagen: Møller, 1906–9). P. 378.

Björn Þorleifsson. "Kvantitetsomvæltningen i islandsk." *ANF* 45 (1929): 35–81, esp. p. 55.

Einar Sigurbjörnsson. "Maríukveðskapur á mótum kaþólsku og lúthersku." In >> *Til heiðurs og hugbótar* (2003). Pp. 113–29, esp. pp. 120–4 and 127.

Finnur Jónsson. >> *Bókmentasaga Íslendinga fram undir siðabót* (1904–5). P. 461.

– >> *Den oldnorske og oldislandske Litteraturs Historie* (1920–4). Vol. 3, p. 124.

Páll Eggert Ólason. *Menn og menntir siðskiptaaldarinnar á Íslandi.* Vol. 1 (Reykjavík: Guðm. Gamalíelsson, 1919). Pp. 424–5.

– *Menn og menntir siðskiptaaldarinnar á Íslandi.* Vol. 4 (Reykjavík: Ársæll Árnason, 1926). Pp. 463, 568, and 625.

Pétur Sigurðsson. "Vísnabók Guðbrands biskuups." In *Iðunn: Tímarit til skemtunar, nytsemdar og fróðleiks*. Vol. 8. Ed. Magnús Jónsson (Reykjavík: Gutenberg, 1923–4). Pp. 61–87, esp. pp. 72–4.

NOTE:

The poem contains material about other saints, especially Elizabeth, John the Evangelist, Joseph, and Simeon the Righteous. See the entries for the individual saints.

56. Vegsemd allra vífa

A poem in praise of Mary the Blessed Virgin composed ca. 1600.
   Incipit: "Vegsemd allrú vífa."

Manuscripts:
Bor 113 (20754) (1740), Lbs 1326 4to (ca. 1890), Lbs 2166 4to (ca. 1885–
   1920), Lbs 201 8vo (ca. 1850–70), and Lbs 2366 8vo (ca. 1770–90).
Editions:
Finnur Jónsson. >> *Den oldnorske og oldislandske Litteraturs Historie*
   (1920–4). Vol. 3, p. 123.
   Based on Jón Þorkelsson's edition (1888).
Jón Helgason, ed. >> *Íslenzk miðaldakvæði* (1936–8). Vol. 2, pp. 84–7.
   Based on Bor 113 (20754) with variants from Lbs 2166 4to and Lbs 2366
   8vo.
Jón Þorkelsson. >> *Om Digtningen på Island* (1888). P. 56 (stz. 1).
   Based on Lbs 201 8vo.
Literature:
Bekker-Nielsen, Hans. "Mariadigtning." *KLNM* 11 (1966). Cols. 379–80, esp.
   col. 379.
Finnur Jónsson. >> *Bókmentasaga Íslendinga fram undir siðabót* (1904–5).
   P. 461.
Schottmann, Hans. >> *Die isländische Mariendichtung* (1973). Pp. 87 and
   544–5.

57. Máríuævi eða Lífssaga helgustu guðs móður

A poem about the life of Mary the Blessed Virgin composed ca. 1600 by the priest Ólafur Guðmundsson (ca. 1537–1609).
   Incipit: "Ég vil jómfrú eina."

Editions:
Guðbrandur Þorláksson, ed. >> *Ein ny wiisna bok* (1612). Pp. 302–7.
Jón Torfason and Kristján Eiríksson, ed. >> *Vísnabók Guðbrands* (2000).
   Pp. 340–6.
Literature:
Einar Sigurbjörnsson. "Maríukveðskapur á mótum kaþólsku og lúthersku."
   In >> *Til heiðurs og hugbótar* (2003). Pp. 113–29, esp. pp. 124–7.
NOTE:
The poem contains material about other saints, especially Elizabeth, John the
Baptist, Joseph, and Simeon the Righteous. See the entries for the individual
saints.

58. Máríuvísur

A poorly preserved poem in honour of Mary the Blessed Virgin. The date of
composition is unknown.
   Incipit: "Náðar sæta nafnið þitt."

Manuscript:
AM 720a 4to XI (ca. 1600–1700).
Edition:
Jón Þorkelsson. >> *Om Digtningen på Island* (1888). P. 55 (stz. 1^{1-2}).
Literature:
Finnur Jónsson. >> *Bókmentasaga Íslendinga fram undir siðabót* (1904–5).
   P. 461.
– >> *Den oldnorske og oldislandske Litteraturs Historie* (1920–4). Vol. 3,
   pp. 124–5.

59. Kvæði um herrans móður Máríu

A late poem in praise of Mary the Blessed Virgin attributed to a certain "Síra M."
   Incipit: "Það er öllum þægilegt."

Manuscripts:
ÍBR 28 8vo (ca. 1700–1900) and Lbs 201 8vo (ca. 1850–70).
Edition:
Jón Þorláksson. >> *Om Digtningen på Island* (1888). P. 58 (stz. 1).
Literature:
Finnur Jónsson. >> *Bókmentasaga Íslendinga fram undir siðabót* (1904–5).
   P. 461.
– >> *Den oldnorske og oldislandske Litteraturs Historie* (1920–4). Vol. 3, p. 124.

60. Máríuvers

A short rhyme about Mary the Blessed Virgin. It was first transcribed in the nineteenth century and now exists in several versions.
   Incipit: "María gekk til kirkju."

Manuscripts:
JS 511 8vo (ca. 1675–1900), Lbs 587 4to (ca. 1800–1900), Lbs 176 8vo
   (ca. 1850–70), Lbs 201 8vo (ca. 1850–70), Lbs 421 8vo (ca. 1800–30),
   Lbs 724 8vo (ca. 1800–1900), and Lbs 1420 8vo (1849–54).
Editions:
Einar Ól. Sveinsson, Páll Eggert Ólason, and Arnór Sigurjónsson, ed. *Íslands
   þúsund ár: Kvæðasafn.* 3 vols. (Reykjavík: Helgafell, 1947). Vol. 2, pp. 157–8.
"Gamalt Máríuvers." *Alþýðublaðið* 148 (July 1942). P. 8 [no author listed].
Jón Samsonarson. "Þulan um Maríu." In *Minjar og menntir: Afmælisrit
   helgað Kristjáni Eldjarn 6 desember 1976.* Ed. Guðni Kolbeinsson
   (Reykjavík: Menningarsjóður, 1976). Pp. 260–70, esp. pp. 263–9.
Jón Þorkelsson. >> *Om Digtningen på Island* (1888). Pp. 39–40.
Based on Lbs 2018 8vo.

61. Harmsól

A twelfth-century praise-poem addressed to Christ by Gamli. Stz. 59 and 61 treat Mary the Blessed Virgin.
   Incipit: "Hár stillir, lúk heilli."

Manuscripts:
AM 757a 4to (ca. 1400), JS 399a–b 4to (ca. 1700–1900) Lbs 444 4to
   (ca. 1820–50), and Lbs 1152 8vo (ca. 1800–1900).
Editions:
*Attwood, Katrina, ed. "The Poems of MS AM 757a 4to: An Edition and
   Contextual Study." PhD dissertation, University of Leeds, 1996.
– ed. "Gamli kanóki, *Harmsól* 'Sun of Sorrow'." In >> *Poetry on Christian
   Subjects* (2007). Vol. 1, pp. 126–7.
   Edition of AM 757a 4to with emendations and variants from JS 399a–b 4to,
   Hugo Rydberg's edition (1907), and Sveinbjörn Egilsson's edition (1844).
*Black, Elizabeth L. "*Harmsól*: An Edition." BLitt thesis, University of
   Oxford, 1971.
Finnur Jónsson, ed. >> *Den norsk-islandske skjaldedigtning* (1912–15).
   Vol. AI, p. 571 and vol. BI, pp. 563–4.

Edition of AM 757a 4to with emendations and variants from Sveinbjörn
Egilsson's edition (1844).

– ed. *Carmina scaldica: udvalg af norske og islandske skjaldekvad.* 2nd rev.
ed. (Copenhagen: Gad, 1923). P. 86.
Based on Finnur Jónsson's edition (1912–15).

Jón Helgason. "Til skjaldedigtningen." *APS* 10 (1935–6): 250–64, esp. p. 262.
Edition of AM 757a 4to.

Kempff, Hjalmar, ed. *Kaniken Gamles "Harmsol" (Sol i Sorgen): Isländskt
andligt qväde från medeltiden, öfversättning och förklaringar* (Uppsala:
Edquist and Berglund, 1867). P. 18.
Based on Sveinbjörn Egilsson's edition (1844).

Kock, Ernst Albin, ed. >> *Den norsk-islandske skaldediktningen* (1946–50).
Vol. 1, p. 27.

Rydberg, Hugo, ed. *Die geistlichen Drápur und Dróttkvættfragmente des
Cod. AM 757 4to* (Copenhagen: Møller, 1907). Pp. 30–1.
Edition of AM 757a 4to.

Sveinbjörn Egilsson, ed. *Fjøgur gømul kvæði. Boðsrit til að hlusta á
þá opinberu yfirheyrslu í Bessastaða Skóla þann 22–29 mai 1844*
(Viðeyjarklaustur: Helgi Helgason, 1844). Pp. 32–3.
Edition of AM 757a 4to.

Danish translation:
Finnur Jónsson, ed. >> *Den norsk-islandske skjaldedigtning* (1912–15).
Vol. BI, pp. 563–4.

English translation:
Attwood, Katrina, ed. "Gamli kanóki, *Harmsól* 'Sun of Sorrow'." In >>
Poetry on Christian Subjects (2007). Vol. 1, pp. 126–7.

Norwegian translation:
Audne, Kr., trans. "*Harmsól.*" In *Norrøne kristenkvæde.* Ed. Olaf Hanssen
(Oslo: Detnorske samlaget, 1928). P. 35.

Swedish translation:
Kempff, Hjalmar, ed. *Kaniken Gamles "Harmsol" (Sol i Sorgen): Isländskt
andligt qväde från medeltiden, öfversättning och förklaringar* (Uppsala:
Edquist and Berglund, 1867). P. 18.

Literature:
Ásdís Egilsdóttir, Gunnar Harðarson, and Svanhildur Óskarsdóttir, ed.
Maríukver. Sögur og kvæði af heilagri guðsmóður frá fyrri tíð (Reykjavík:
Hið íslenska bókmenntafélag, 1966). P. xxxv.

Attwood, Katrina. "Leiðarvísan and the 'Sunday Letter' Tradition in
Scandinavia." In >> *Til heiðurs og hugbótar* (2003). Pp. 53–78, esp.
pp. 54 and 77.

Bekker-Nielsen, Hans. "Mariadigtning." *KLNM* 11 (1966). Cols. 379–80, esp. col. 379.

Bjarni Einarsson. "Harmsól." *KLNM* 6 (1961). Cols. 230–1.

Chase, Martin. "*Concatenatio* as a Structural Element in the Christian *Drápur*." In *The Sixth International Saga Conference 28/7–2/8 1985. Workshop Papers*. 2 vols. ([Copenhagen]: Det arnamagnæanske Institut, 1985). Vol. 1, pp. 115–29, esp. pp. 118, 120–1, and 124–5.

Clunies Ross, Margaret. >> *A History of Old Norse Poetry and Poetics* (2005). Pp. 38n15, 131–8, 208–9, 211, 223, and 239.

Edsman, Carl-Martin. "Solsymbolik." *KLNM* 16 (1971). Cols. 421–6, esp. col. 424.

Edwards, Diana. "Christian and Pagan References in Eleventh-Century Norse Poetry: The Case of Arnórr Jarlaskáld." *Saga-Book* 21 (1982–3): 34–53, esp. p. 45.

Finnur Jónsson. >> *Den oldnorske og oldislandske Litteraturs Historie* (1920–4). Vol. 2, pp. 114–15.

Hammerich, Fr. *De Episk-kristelige Oldkvad hos de gotiske Folk* (Copenhagen: Gyldendal, 1875). P. 140.

Holtsmark, Anne. "Líknarbraut." *KLNM* 10 (1965). Cols. 553–4, esp. col. 554.

Jakob Benediktsson. "Helgendigte." *KLNM* 6 (1961). Cols. 318–21, esp. col. 318.

– "Kristdigte." *KLNM* 9 (1964). Cols. 292–4, esp. col. 293.

– "*Hafgerðingadrápa*." In *Specvlvm Norroenvm: Norse Studies in Memory of Gabriel Turville-Petre*. Ed. Ursula Dronke, Guðrún P. Helgadóttir, Gerd Wolfgang Weber, and Hans Bekker-Nielsen (Odense: Odense University Press, 1981). Pp. 27–32, esp. p. 31.

– >> "Helgikvæði." In *Hugtök og heiti í bókmenntafræði* (1983). Pp. 115–17, esp. p. 116.

Jón Helgason. "Til Skjaldedigtningen." *APS* 6 (1931–2): 195–8.

– *Norrøn Litteraturhistorie* (Copenhagen: Levin and Munksgaard, 1934). P. 88.

– >> "Norges og Islands digtning." In *Litteraturhistorie B: Norge og Island* (1953). Pp. 3–179, esp. pp. 110 and 155.

Jónas Kristjánsson. "Bókmenntasaga." In *Saga Íslands* 2. Ed. Sigurður Líndal (Reykjavík: Hið íslenzka bókmenntafélag, Sögufélagið, 1975). Pp. 147–258, esp. p. 208.

– >> *Eddas and Sagas: Iceland's Medieval Literature* (1988). Pp. 112 and 386.

Kahle, Bernhard. "Das Christentum in der altwestnordischen Dichtung." *ANF* 13 (1901): 1–40 and 97–160, esp. pp. 9–11, 20, 28, 31, 99, 101, 105, 108, 114–16, 121–35, 137–40, 144–5, 148, and 150–5.

Konráð Gíslason. "Om helrim i förste og tredje linie af regelmæssigt 'drottkvætt' og 'hrynhenda'." *Indbydelsesskrift til Kjøbenhavns Universitets Aarsfest til Erindring om Kirkens Reformation* (Copenhagen: Schultz, 1877). Pp. 1–60, esp. p. 31.

Kuhn, Hans. "Vor tausend Jahren. Zur Geschichte des skaldischen Innenreims." In *Specvlvm Norroenvm: Norse Studies in Memory of Gabriel Turville-Petre*. Ed. Ursula Dronke, Guðrún P. Helgadóttir, Gerd Wolfgang Weber, and Hans Bekker-Nielsen (Odense: Odense University Press, 1981). Pp. 293–309, esp. p. 297.

– *Das Dróttkvætt* (Heidelberg: Carl Winter Universitätsverlag, 1983). Pp. 321–2.

Lange, Wolfgang. >> *Studien zur christlichen Dichtung der Nordgermanen 1000–1200* (1958). Pp. 81, 95, 98, 143–58, 216, 219, 222, and 224.

Lindow, John. "Narrative and the Nature of Skaldic Poetry." *ANF* 97 (1982): 94–121, esp. pp. 100n23 and 102.

Marold, Edith. "Das Gottesbild der christlichen Skaldik." In *The Sixth International Saga Conference 28/7–2/8 1985. Workshop Papers.* 2 vols. ([Copenhagen]: Det arnamagnæanske Institut, 1985). Vol. 2, pp. 717–49, esp. p. 732.

Mogk, Eugen. >> *Geschichte der norwegisch-isländischen Literatur* (1904). P. 712.

Møller, Arne. *Islands Lovsang gennem Tusind Aar* (Copenhagen: Gyldendal, 1923). Pp. 18–25.

Naumann, Hans-Peter. "Nordische Kreuzzugsdichtung." In *Festschrift für Oskar Bandle: Zum 60. Geburtstag am 11. Januar 1986*. Ed. Hans-Peter Naumann with Magnus von Platen and Stefan Sonderegger. Beiträge zur nordischen Philologie 15 (Basel and Frankfurt am Main: Helbing and Lichtenhahn, 1986), pp. 175–89, esp. p. 188.

Paasche, Fredrik. >> *Kristendom og kvad* (1914). Pp. 39, 71, 106, 108–18, 122, 126–7, 129, 131–2, 136–7, 162, 171, and 173.

– *Norges og Islands litteratur inntil utgangen av middelalderen*. Rev. ed. by Anne Holtsmark (Oslo: Aschehoug, 1947). Pp. 314–15, 335, and 534.

Schottmann, Hans. >> *Die isländische Mariendichtung* (1973). Pp. 103–4, 205, 208, 228, 247, 249, 398, 402, 538, and 551.

Skard, Vemund. "Harmsól, Plácítusdrápa og Leiðarvísan." *ANF* 68 (1953): 97–108.

Stéfan Einarsson. "Íslenzk helgikvæði á miðöldum." *Tímarit Þjóðræknisfélags Íslendinga* 36 (1955): 43–63, esp. pp. 43–5.

– *Íslensk bókmenntasaga 874–1960* (Reykjavík: Oddi, 1961). Pp. 81–2.

Sverrir Tómasson. "Kristnar trúarbókmenntir í óbundnu máli." In >> *Íslensk Bókmenntasaga* 1 (1992). Pp. 421–79, esp. p. 459.

– "Erlendur vísdómur og forn fræði." In >> *Íslensk Bókmenntasaga* 1 (1992). Pp. 519–70, esp. p. 552.

Vésteinn Ólason. "Kristileg trúarkvæði til loka 13. aldar." In >> *Íslensk Bókmenntasaga* 1 (1992). Pp. 483–515, esp. pp. 492–5, 407, 499, 512, and 515.

– "Kveðskapur frá síðmiðöldum: Trúarkvæði." In >> *Íslensk Bókmenntasaga* 2 (1993). Pp. 285–378, esp. pp. 288, 298, and 316.

– "Old Icelandic Poetry." In *A History of Icelandic Literature*. Ed. Daisy Neijmann. Histories of Scandinavian Literature 5 (Lincoln: University of Nebraska Press, 2006). Pp. 1–64, esp. pp. 44–5.

Viðar Pálsson. "Pagan Mythology in Christian Society." *Gripla* 19 (2008): 123–58, esp. pp. 140–1.

Vries, Jan de. >> *Altnordische Literaturgeschichte* (1964–7). Vol. 2, pp. 55–6, 66n131, 61n136, 77, and 112.

NOTE:
The poem contains material about Saints Mary Magdalen and Peter. See their entries.

62. Líknarbraut

A poem on the Cross probably composed in the late thirteenth century. Stz. 18 treats Mary the Blessed Virgin.

Incipit: "Einn, lúk upp, sem ek bæni."

Manuscripts:
See Cross, the Holy 1 note (p. 66).

Editions:

*Attwood, Katrina. "The Poems of MS AM 757 a 4to: An Edition and Contextual Study." PhD dissertation, University of Leeds, 1996.

Finnur Jónsson, ed. >> *Den norsk-islandske skjaldedigtning* (1912–15). Vol. AII, pp. 153–4 and vol. BII, p. 165.

Kock, Ernst Albin, ed. >> *Den norsk-islandske skaldediktningen* (1946–50). Vol. 2, p. 87.

Rydberg, Hugo, ed. >> *Die geistlichen Drápur und Dróttkvættfragmente des Cod. AM 757 4to* (1907). P. 49.

Sveinbjörn Egilsson, ed. *Fjøgur gømul kvæði. Boðsrit til að hlusta á þá opinberu yfirheyrslu í Bessastaða Skóla þann 22–29 mai 1844* (Viðeyjarklaustur: Helgi Helgason, 1844). Pp. 40–1.

Tate, George. "*Líknarbraut*: A Skaldic *drápa* on the Cross." PhD dissertation, Cornell University, 1974. P. 63.

Tate, George, ed. "Anonymous, *Líknarbraut* 'Way of Grace'." In >> *Poetry on Christian Subjects* (2007). Vol. 1, p. 248.

Modern Icelandic language edition:

Einar Ól. Sveinsson, Páll Eggert Ólason, and Arnór Sigurjónsson, ed. *Íslands þúsund ár: Kvæðasafn*. 3 vols. (Reykjavík: Helgafell, 1947). Vol. 1, p. 530.

Danish translation:

Finnur Jónsson, ed. >> *Den norsk-islandske skjaldedigtning* (1912–15). Vol. BII, p. 165.

English translations:

Barwell, Graham, and John Kennedy, ed. "Two Icelandic Medieval Passion-Poems." In *Old Norse Studies in the New World: A Collection of Essays to Celebrate the Jubilee of the Teaching of Old Norse at the University of Sydney 1943–1993*. Ed. Geraldine Barnes, Margaret Clunies Ross, and Judy Quinn (Sydney: Department of English, University of Sydney, 1994). Pp. 46–70, esp. p. 53.

Tate, George. ed. "Anonymous, *Líknarbraut* 'Way of Grace'." In >> *Poetry on Christian Subjects* (2007). Vol. 1, p. 248.

Norwegian translation:

Røkke, Olav, trans. "*Líknarbraut*." In *Norrøne kristenkvæde*. Ed. Olaf Hanssen (Oslo: Det norske samlaget, 1928). P. 40.

63. Lilja

A summary of all Christian history beginning with the Creation by Eysteinn Ásgrímsson (d. 1361). Stz. 28–35 treat Mary the Blessed Virgin.

Incipit: "Almáttigr guð allra stétta."

Manuscripts:

Adv 21.8.10 (1712), AM 136 4to (ca. 1500), AM 622 4to (ca. 1549), AM 695a 4to (ca. 1650–1700), AM 705 4to (ca. 1700–25), AM 706 4to (ca. 1700–25), AM 707 4to (ca. 1700–25), AM 713 4to (ca. 1500–50), AM 714 4to (ca. 1600), AM 715a 4to (ca. 1700–25), AM 715b 4to (ca. 1700–25), AM 717h 4to (ca. 1650–1700), AM 720a 4to VIII (ca. 1400–50), AM 720b 4to (ca. 1600), AM 99a 8vo (ca. 1500–1600), AM 104 8vo (ca. 1680), BLAdd 4892 (ca 1700–1800), BLAdd 11.242 (ca. 1540–90), DKNVSB 41 8vo (1671), ÍB 104 4to (ca. 1700–1800), ÍB 105 4to (1758–68), ÍB 159 8vo (ca. 1820), ÍB 200 8vo (ca. 1700–1900), ÍBR 16 8vo (ca. 1700–1900), ÍBR 74 8vo (1852), JS 260 4to (1796), JS 399a–b 4to (ca. 1700–1900), JS 406

4to (ca. 1800–1900), JS 413 8vo (ca. 1700–1900), Lbs 221 4to (ca. 1760–
70), Lbs 804 4to (1731), Lbs 848 4to (ca. 1700–1900), Lbs 953 4to
(ca. 1760), Lbs 966 4to (ca. 1750–1800), Lbs 1745 4to (ca. 1850–1910),
Lbs 2289 4to (1879–1905), Lbs 2293 8vo (ca. 1700), Stock. Papp. fol. no.
23 (1656), Stock. Papp. fol. no. 64 (ca. 1650–1700), Stock. Perg. fol. no. 1
(*Bergsbók*) (ca. 1400–25), and Oslo UB R 547 4to (ca. 1750–75).

Editions:

Chase, Martin. "Anonymous, *Lilja* 'Lily'." In >> *Poetry on Christian Subjects*
(2007). Vol. 2, pp. 595–604.
Edition of Stock. Perg. fol. no. 1 with variants from AM 705 4to, AM 713
4to, AM 720a 4to VIII, AM 720b 4to, AM 99a 8vo, BLAdd 4892, and
DKNVSB 41 8vo.

de Rivière, Philpin, ed. *Le chantre du Lilja Eystein Ásgrímsson ou le skalde
de la Sainte vierge au quatorzième siècle en Islande avec traduction du
poème en vers francais* (Rome: Sacred Congregation for the Propagation
of the Faith, 1833), pp. 116–20.
Based on Páll Halsson's edition (1858 [1773]).

Eirikr Magnusson, ed. and trans. *Lilja (The Lily): An Icelandic Religious
Poem of the Fourteenth Century* (London and Edinburgh: Williams and
Norgate, 1870). Pp. 28, 30, 32, 34, and 36.
Edition of Stock. Perg. fol. no. 1 with variants and emendations from
BLAdd 4892.

Finnur Jónsson, ed. *Carmina Norrœna: Rettet Tekst* (Copenhagen: Nielsen
and Lydiche, 1893). Pp. 120–2.

– ed. >> *Den norsk-islandske skjaldedigtning* (1912–15). Vol. AII, pp. 372–5
and vol. BII, pp. 398–9.
Edition of Stock. Perg fol. no. 1 with variants from AM 99 4to, AM 622
4to, AM 714 4to, and AM 720a VIII 4to.

– ed. *Carmina scaldica: udvalg af norske og islandske skjaldekvad*
(Copenhagen: Gad, 1923). Pp. 96–7.
Based on Finnur Jónsson's edition (1912–15).

– ed. *Carmina scaldica: udvalg af norske og islandske skjaldekvad*. 2nd rev.
ed. (Copenhagen: Gad, 1929). Pp. 97–9.
Based on Finnur Jónsson's edition (1912–15).

Guðbrandur Þorláksson, ed. >> *Ein ny wiisna bok* (1612). Pp. 140–50.

Jón Torfason and Kristján Eiríksson, ed. *Vísnabók Guðbrands Þorlákssonar
biskups* (Reykjavík: Bókmenntafræðistofnun Háskóla Íslands, 2000).
P. 279.

Kock, Ernst Albin, ed. >> *Notationes Norrœna* (1923–44). §1521.

– ed. >> *Den norsk-isländska skaldediktningen* (1946–50). Vol. 2, pp. 216–18.

[n.e.], *Lilja. Le Lis, poême islandais en l'honneur de la Mère de Dieu par Eystein Ásgrímsson* (Copenhagen: Berling, 1858). Pp. 20, 22, and 24.

Páll Hallsson, ed. and trans. *Eysteins Asgrimssonar Lilia, cum versione latina & lectionibus variantibus edita* (Copenhagen: [n.p.], 1773). Pp. 16, 18, and 20.
Edition of Stock. Perg. fol. no. 1.

Sigurður Nordal, ed. *Bishop Gudbrand's Vísnabók, 1612*. Monumenta typographica Islandica 5 (Copenhagen: Levin and Munksgaard and Ejnar Munksgaard, 1937).
Facsimile.

Taillè, Michel, ed. and trans. *Le Lis: Poème religieux islandais ("Lilja") écrit au XIVe siècle par Frère Eysteinn Asgrimsson. Text original, présentation, traduction et commentaire.* Cahiers du Centre de linguistique et de littérature religieuses 3 (Angers: Université Catholique de l'Ouest, 1989). Pp. 56, 58, 60, 62, 64, 66, 68, and 70.
Edition of Stock. Perg fol. no. 1.

Wisén, Theodor, ed., *Carmina Norrœna. Ex Reliquiis Vestustioris Norrœnæ Poësis. Selecta, Regognita, Commentariis et Glossario Instructa.* 2 vols. (Lund: Ohlsson 1886–9). Vol. 1, pp. 90–1.
Edition of Stock. Perg. fol. no. 1.

Modern Icelandic language editions:

Einar Bragi, ed. *Lilja eftir bróður Eystein Ásgrímsson munk í Helgisetri útgefin á 600. Ártíð skáldsins á langaföstu árið 1961* (Reykjavík: Prentsmiðja Jóns Helgasonar, 1961). Pp. 17–21.

Einar Ól. Sveinsson, Páll Eggert Ólason, and Arnór Sigurjónsson, ed. *Íslands þúsund ár: Kvæðasafn.* 3 vols. (Reykjavík: Helgafell, 1947). Vol. 2, pp. 21–3.

Finnur Jónsson, ed. *Lilja*. Ed. Bogi Melsted. Íslenzk smárit handa alþýðu 1 (Copenhagen: Møller, 1913). Pp. 14–15.

Guðbrandur Jónsson, ed. *Lilja: Krists konungs drápa tíræð eftir bróður Eystein Ásgrímsson* (Reykjavík: Bókverzlun Sig. Kristjánssonar, 1933). Pp. 28–34.

– ed. *Lilja: Krists konungs drápa tíræð eftir bróður Eystein Ásgrímsson* (Reykjavík: Helgafell, 1951). Pp. 75–84.

– ed. *Lilja: Krists konungs drápa tíræð eftir Eystein munk*. Preface by Pétur Már Ólafsson (Reykjavík: Vaka-Helgafell, 1992). Pp. 36–40.

Gunnar Finnbogason, ed. *Lilja*. 2nd rev. ed. (Reykjavík: Stafafell, 1988). Pp. 41–8.

Czech translation:

*Walter, Emil, trans. *Lilja* (Stará Risi: Z skladu Marty Florianove, 1924).

Danish translations:

*Finn Magnusen, trans. *Dana: Poetisk Lommebog for 1820*. Ed. Andreas Peter Liunge (Copenhagen: Chr. Steens Forlag, 1820).

Finnur Jónsson, ed. >> *Den norsk-islandske skjaldedigtning* (1912–15). Vol. BII, pp. 397–9.

Holstein-Rathlou, Viggo J. von, trans. *Lilje: Digtet paa Islandsk c. 1340* (Copenhagen: Gyldendal, 1937). Pp. 14–15.

*Páll Halsson, ed. and trans. *Lilie. Det er Det Gammelt Islandske Rim* (Stock. Papp fol. no. 23, 1656).

Dutch translation:

Winters, J.-M. *Lelie. Der Dellingen en Bloemen des Velds* (Hasselt: St-Quintinus-Drukkerij, 1901). Pp. 54–6.

English translations:

Boucher, Alan, trans. *The Lily and Lay of the Sun: Two Mediaeval Religious Poems*. Parallel Text Series: University of Iceland, Faculty of Arts Language Centre 1 (Reykjavík: Bóksala stúdenta, 1985). Pp. 8–10.

Chase, Martin. "Anonymous, *Lilja* 'Lily'." In >> *Poetry on Christian Subjects* (2007). Vol. 2, pp. 595–604.

Eirikr Magnusson, ed. and trans. *Lilja (The Lily): An Icelandic Religious Poem of the Fourteenth Century* (London and Edinburgh: Williams and Norgate, 1870). Pp. 29, 31, 33, 35, and 37.

Pilcher, Charles Venn. *Icelandic Christian Classics: The Lay of the Sun, the Lily, the Passion-Hymns, the Millennial Hymn* (Melbourne: Oxford University Press, 1950). Pp. 28–9.

French translations:

de Rivière, Philpin, ed. *Le chantre du Lilja Eystein Ásgrímsson ou le skalde de la Saintevierge au quatorzième siècle en Islande avec traduction du poème en vers francais* (Rome: Sacred Congregation for the Propagation of the Faith, 1833). Pp. 42–5.

Taillè, Michel, ed. and trans. *Le Lis: Poème religieux islandais ("Lilja") écrit au XIVe siècle par Frère Eysteinn Asgrimsson. Texts original, présentation, traduction et commentaire*. Cahiers du Centre de linguistique et de littérature religieuses 3 (Angers: Université Catholique de l'Ouest, 1989). Pp. 57, 59, 61, 63, 65, 67, 69, and 71.

German translations:

Baumgartner, Alexander, trans. *Die Lilie: Isländische Mariendichtung aus dem 14. Jahrhundert* (Freiburg im Breisgau: Herder, 1884). Pp. 48–50.

Lange, Wolfgang. *Christliche Skaldendichtung*. Kleine Vandenhoeck-Reihe 54 (Göttingen: Vandenhoeck and Ruprecht, 1958). Pp. 61–3.

Meissner, Rudolf, trans. *Die Lilie: Dichtung von Eysteinn Ásgrímsson* (Bonn and Leipzig: Kurt Schroeder, 1922). Pp. 12–15.

Studach, J.L., trans. *Schwedische Volksarfe* (Stockholm: Rumstedt, 1826).
Pp. 190–3.
Latin translations:
de Rivière, Philpin, ed. *Le chantre du Lilja Eystein Ásgrímsson ou le skalde de la Saintevierge au 14. siècle an Islande avec traduction du poème en vers francais* (Rome: Sacred Congregation for the Propagaion of the Faith, 1833). Pp. 117, 119, and 121.
Eirikr Magnusson, ed. and trans. *Lilium: poêma Islandicum quod ad Matrem Dei celebrandam cecinit Eysteinn Ásgrímsson A.D. 1350* (Vienna: Rospini, 1859). Pp. 24–6.
[n.e.]. *Lilja. Le Lis, poême islandais en l'honneur de la Mère de Dieu par Eystein Ásgrímsson* (Copenhagen: Berling, 1858). Pp. 21, 23, and 25.
Páll Halsson, ed. and trans. *Lilie. Det er Det Gammelt Islandske Rim* (Stock. Papp fol. no. 23, 1656).
– ed. and trans. *Eysteins Asgrimssonar Lilia, cum versione latina & lectionibus variantibus edita* (Copenhagen: [n. p.], 1773). Pp. 17, 19, and 21.
Norwegian translations:
Næss, Leonard, trans. *"Lilja."* In *Norrøne kristenkvæde*. Ed. Olaf Hanssen (Oslo: Detnorske samlaget, 1928). Pp. 70–2.
Orgland, Ivar, trans. *Islandske Dikt. Frå Sólarljóð til opplysningstid (13. hundreåret–1835)* (Reykjavík: Fonna, 1977). Pp. 151–3.
Paasche, Fredrik, trans. *Lilja: Et kvad til guds moder* (Kristiania [Oslo]: Aschehoug, 1915). Pp. 60–3.
Ødegård, Knut, trans. *Lilja* (Oslo: Tiden Norsk Forlag, 1980). Pp. 43–9.
Swedish translation:
Åkerblom, Axel, trans. *Lilja: Den nordiska medeltidens förnämsta religiösa dikt af den isländske munken Eystein Ásgrímsson* (Lund: Gleerup, 1916). Pp. 17–19.
Literature:
Anna Sigurðardóttir. *Allt hafði annan róm áður í páfadóm: Nunnuklaustrin tvö á Íslandi á miðöldum og brot úr kristnisögu* (Reykjavík: Kvennasögusafn Íslands, 1988). Pp. 214, 359, and 361–3.
Anon. "Den Oldnordisk-islandske Afdeling." Annual Report for 1847. *Antiquarisk Tidsskrift* 1846–8 (Copenhagen: Sally B. Salomon, 1847). Pp. 154–72, esp. p. 165.
Ármann Jakobsson. "The Homer of the North, or: Who Was Sigurður the Blind?" *European Journal of Scandinavian Studies* 44 (2014): 4–19, esp. pp. 5–7 and 14.
Ásdís Egilsdóttir, Gunnar Harðarson, and Svanhildur Óskarsdóttir, ed. *Maríukver. Sögur og kvæði af heilagri guðsmóður frá fyrri tíð* (Reykjavík: Hið íslenska bókmenntafélag, 1996). P. xxxv.

Attwood, Katrina. "Intertextual Aspects of the Twelfth-Century Christian *Drápur*." *Saga-Book* 24 (1996): 221–39, esp. p. 221.
– "Christian Poetry." In *A Companion to Old Norse–Icelandic Literature and Culture*. Ed. Rory McTurk (Oxford: Blackwell, 2005). Pp. 43–63, esp. pp. 49 and 59–61.
Bekker-Nielsen, Hans. "Mariadigtning." *KLNM* 11 (1966). Cols. 379–80, esp. col. 379.
Carpenter, William H., ed. *Nikolásdrápa Halls prests: An Icelandic Poem from circa A.D. 1400* (Halle: Karras, 1881). Pp. 1, 3, and 5.
Chase, Martin. "Christian Poetry: West Norse." In >> *Medieval Scandinavia: An Encyclopedia*. (1993). Pp. 73–7, esp. pp. 75–6.
– "Devotional Poetry at the End of the Middle Ages in Iceland." In >> *Eddic, Skaldic, and Beyond: Poetic Variety in Medieval Iceland*. Ed. Martin Chase (2014). Pp. 136–49, esp. pp. 136–7, 139, and 145.
Clunies Ross, Margaret. >> *A History of Old Norse Poetry and Poetics* (2005). Pp. 33, 206, 215, 217, 220, 227–30, and 233.
Cormack, Margaret. >> *The Saints in Iceland* (1994). P. 128.
Einar Sigurbjörnsson. "Maríukveðskapur á mótum kaþólsku og lúthersku." In >> *Til heiðurs og hugbótar* (2003). Pp. 113–29, esp. pp. 115–16.
Faulkes, Anthony. "Edda." *Gripla* 2 (1977): 32–9, esp. p. 34n11.
Fidjestøl, Bjarne. "Skaldic Verse." In >> *Medieval Scandinavia: An Encyclopedia* (1993). Pp. 592–4, esp. p. 592.
Finnur Jónsson. >> *Bókmentasaga Íslendinga fram undir siðabót* (1904–5). Pp. 461 and 464.
– >> *Den oldnorske og oldislandske Litteraturs Historie* (1920–4). Vol. 3, pp. 10–13 and 125.
Foote, Peter. "Latin Rhetoric and Icelandic Poetry: Some Contacts." In *Aurvandilstá: Norse Studies*. Ed. Michael Barnes, Hans Bekker-Nielsen, and Gerd Wolfgang Weber. Viking Collection 2 (Odense: Odense University Press, 1984). Pp. 249–70.
Frank, Roberta. "Skaldic Poeetry." In *Old Norse–Icelandic Literature: A Critical Guide*. Ed. Carol J. Clover and John Lindow. Islandica 45 (Ithaca and London: Cornell University Press, 1985). Pp. 157–96, esp. pp. 157 and 180.
Guðbrandur Jónsson. "Arngrímur ábóti Brandsson og bróðir Eysteinn Ásgrímsson." *Saga* 1 (1949–53): 394–469.
Guðrún Nordal. *Tools of Literacy: The Role of Skaldic Verse in Icelandic Textual Culture of the Twelfth and Thirteenth Centuries* (Toronto: University of Toronto Press, 2001). Pp. 45, 211, 376n16, 377n20, and 381n41.

– "Handrit, prentaðar bækur og pápísk kvæði á siðskiptaöld." In >> *Til heiðurs og hugbótar* (2003). Pp. 131–43, esp. pp. 140–1.

– "Á mörkum tveggja tíma: Kaþólskt kvæðahandrit með hendi siðbótarmanns, Gísl biskups Jónssonar." *Gripla* 16 (2005): 209–28, esp. pp. 220 and 225.

– "Helgubók. Kvæðasafn á mörkum kaþólsku og lútersku." In *Handrit úr förum Árna Magnússonar*. Ed. Svanhildur Óskarsdóttir, Matthew Driscoll, and Sigurður Svavarsson (Copenhagen: Den Arnamagnæanske Samling, Nordisk Forkningsinstitut; Reykjavík: Stofnun Árna Magnússonar í íslenskum fræðum; and Reykjavík: Bókaútgáfan Opna, 2013). P. 127.

– "Helgubók." In *Góssið hans Árna: Minningar heimsins í íslenskum handritum*. Ed. Jóhanna Katrín Friðriksdóttir (Reykjavík: Stofnun Árna Magnússonar í íslenskum fræðum, 2014). Pp. 21–35, esp. pp. 27–8 and 30.

Gunnar Finnbogason. "Var bróðir Eysteinn í Þykkvabæ höfundur Lilju?" In *Á góðu dægri: Afmæliskveðja til Sigurðar Nordals 14. sept. 1951 frá yngstu nemendum hans*. Ed. Ragnar Jónsson (Reykjavík: Helgafell, 1951). Pp. 82–93.

Hallberg, Peter. *Old Icelandic Poetry: Eddic Lay and Skaldic Verse.* Trans. Paul Schach and Sonja Lindgrenson (Lincoln: University of Nebraska Press, 1975). Pp. 177–80 and 183.

Hammerich, Fr. *De Episk-kristelige Oldkvad hos de gotiske Folk* (Copenhagen: Gyldendal, 1875). P. 141.

Haugen, Odd Einar. "Nicodemus, Gospel of." In >> *Medieval Scandinavia: An Encyclopedia.* (1993). Pp. 430–2, esp. p. 431.

Hill, Thomas D. "Eve's Light Answer: Lilja, Stanzas 16–17." *Mediaeval Scandinavia* 2 (1969): 129–31.

– "Number and Pattern in *Lilja*." *JEGP* 69 (1970): 561–7.

– "Lilja." In >> *Medieval Scandinavia: An Encyclopedia* (1993). Pp. 391–2.

Holtsmark, Anne. "Líknarbraut." *KLNM* 10 (1965). Cols. 553–4, esp. col. 554.

Jakob Benediktsson. "Helgendigte." *KLNM* 6 (1961). Cols. 318–21, esp. col. 320.

– "Kristdigte." *KLNM* 9 (1964). Cols. 292–4, esp. col. 292.

– "Lilja." *KLNM* 10 (1965). Cols. 555–7.

– "Religiøs digtning." *KLNM* 14 (1969). Cols. 37–40, esp. col. 39.

– >> "Helgikvæði." In *Hugtök og heiti í bókmenntafræði* (1983). Pp. 115–17, esp. p. 116.

Jón Helgason. "Nokkur íslenzk handrit frá 16. öld." *Skírnir* 106 (1932): 143–68.

– *Norrøn Litteraturhistorie* (Copenhagen: Levin and Munksgaard, 1934). Pp. 219 and 227.

– >> "Norges og Islands digtning." In *Litteraturhistorie B: Norge og Island* (1953). Pp. 3–179, esp. pp. 19, 102, and 161–4.

– *Gamall kveðskapur* (Copenhagen: Hið íslenzka fræðafélag, 1979). P. 73.

Jón Þórarinsson. *Íslensk tónlistarsaga 1000–1800* (Reykjavík: Tónlistarsafn Íslands, 2012). Pp. 171, 249, 253, 309, 313, 318, and 320.

Jón Þorkelsson. "Islandske håndskrifter i England og Skotland." *ANF* 8 (1892): 199–237, esp. pp. 205–6.

Jónas Kristjánsson. >> *Eddas and Sagas: Iceland's Medieval Literature* (1988). Pp. 87–8 and 385–8.

– "Bókmenntasaga." In *Saga Íslands* 5. Ed. Sigurður Líndal (Reykjavík: Hið íslenzka bókmenntafélag, Sögufélagið, 1990). Pp. 219–84, esp. pp. 272–4.

Kahle, Bernhard. *Die Sprache der Skalden auf Grund der Binnen- und Endreime* (Strassburg: Karl J. Trübner, 1892).

– "Das Christentum in der altwestnordischen Dichtung." *ANF* 13 (1901): 1–40 and 97–160, esp. pp. 18, 27, 99–101, 103–6, 118, 122–32, 134, 136–40, 148–51, and 153–6.

Kock, E.A. "Liljukvistur." *Studia Neophilologica* 15 (1942): 141–56, esp. p. 143.

Kristján Árnason. "On the Principles of Nordic Rhyme and Alliteration." *ANF* 122 (2007): 79–114, esp. pp. 103–4.

Kuhn, Hans. *Das Dróttkvætt* (Heidelberg: Carl Winter Universitätsverlag, 1983). Pp. 330 and 340–1.

Lange, Wolfgang. >> *Studien zur christlichen Dichtung der Nordgermanen 1000–1200* (1958). Pp. 96, 211, 218, 223, 253, and 273–4.

Lie, Hallvard. "Skaldestil-studier." *Mm* (1952): 1–92, esp. pp. 78–9 and 91.

Lindow, John. "Narrative and the Nature of Skaldic Poetry." *ANF* 97 (1982): 94–121, esp. pp. 102 and 119.

Mogk, Eugen. >> *Geschichte der norwegisch-isländischen Literatur* (1904). Pp. 714 and 719.

Møller, Arne. *Islands Lovsang gennem Tusind Aar* (Copenhagen: Gyldendal, 1923). Pp. 135–48.

Noreen, Erik. *Studier i fornvästnordisk diktning* 2. Uppsala Universitets Årsskrift 1922 (Uppsala: Akademiska bokhandeln, 1922). P. 30.

Orgland, Ivar. "Stefán frá Hvítadal og *Heilög kirkja*. Ei samanlikning med mellomalderkvadet *Lilja*." In *Festschrift für Oskar Bandle: Zum 60. Geburtstag am 11. Januar 1986*. Ed. Hans-Peter Naumann with Magnus von Platen and Stefan Sonderegger. Beiträge zur nordischen Philologie 15 (Basel and Frankfurt am Main: Helbing and Lichtenhahn, 1986). Pp. 233–44.

Paasche, Fredrik. >> *Kristendom og kvad* (1914). Pp. 5, 65, 134, and 174.

– *Norges og Islands litteratur inntil utgangen av middelalderen*. Rev. ed. by Anne Holtsmark (Oslo: Aschehoug, 1947). Pp. 177, 430, 534, and 539.

Páll Eggert Ólason. *Menn og menntir siðskiptaaldarinnar á Íslandi*. Vol. 1 (Reykjavík: Guðm. Gamalíelsson, 1919). P. 55.

– *Menn og menntir siðskiptaaldarinnar á Íslandi*. Vol. 4 (Reykjavík: Ársæll Árnason, 1926). Pp. 55 and 641.

Pétur Sigurðsson. "Vísnabók Guðbrands biskups." In *Iðunn: Tímarit til skemtunar, nytsemdar og fróðleiks*. Vol. 8. Ed. Magnús Jónsson (Reykjavík: Gutenberg, 1923–4). Pp. 61–87, esp. p. 62.

Schneider, Hermann. *Geschichte der norwegischen und isländischen Literatur* (Bonn: Universitätsverlag, 1948). P. 28.

Schorn, Brittany. "Divine Semantics: Terminology for the Human and the Divine in Old Norse Poetry." *Scripta Islandica* 64 (2013): 67–97, esp. pp. 90–1.

Schottmann, Hans. >> *Die isländische Mariendichtung* (1973). Pp. 30, 32, 54, 56, 64–6, 70–2, 88–90, 92–3, 97, 104–5, 107–10, 114, 119n3, 120–1, 124, 126, 130, 134, 136, 139, 188–272, 279, 282, 285, 289–90, 292–5, 299–301, 303, 307, 311–17, 322, 324, 326–8, 332, 334, 336, 400, 481, 493, 506–10, 512, 524, 530, 538n28, 543, 549–51, 554, and 556.

See, Klaus von. *Skaldendichtung: Eine Einführung* (Munich and Zürich: Artemis Verlag, 1980). Pp. 78–80.

Stéfan Einarsson. "Íslenzk helgikvæði á miðöldum." *Tímarit Þjóðræknisfélags Íslendinga* 36 (1955): 43–63, esp. pp. 43–4, 46, 48–52, and 62.

– *Íslensk bókmenntasaga 874–1960* (Reykjavík: Oddi, 1961). Pp. 81–3 and 86–9.

Sverrir Tómasson. "Hvenær var Tristrams sögu snúið?" *Gripla* 2 (1977): 47–78, esp. p. 61.

– "Kristnar trúarbókmenntir í óbundnu máli." In >> *Íslensk Bókmenntasaga* 1 (1992). Pp. 421–79, esp. p. 485.

– "Erlendur vísdómur og forn fræði." In >> *Íslensk Bókmenntasaga* 1 (1992). Pp. 519–70, esp. pp. 552 and 542.

– "'Nikulám skulu vér heiðra hér …'." In >> *Til heiðurs og hugbótar* (2003). Pp. 79–92, esp. p. 79.

Tate, George S. "The Cross as Ladder: *Geisli* 5–16 and *Líknarbraut* 34." *Mediaeval Scandinavia* 11 (1978–9): 258–64.

Vésteinn Ólason. "Kveðskaparhefð í upphafi ritaldar." In >> *Íslensk Bókmenntasaga* 1 (1992). Pp. 47–72, esp. pp. 70–1.

– "Dróttkvæði." In >> *Íslensk Bókmenntasaga* 1 (1992). Pp. 191–262, esp. p. 258.

– "Kristileg trúarkvæði til loka 13. aldar." In >> *Íslensk Bókmenntasaga* 1 (1992). Pp. 483–515, esp. pp. 490, 497, 511, and 514.

– "Old Icelandic Poetry." In *A History of Icelandic Literature*. Ed. Daisy
Neijmann. Histories of Scandinavian Literature 5 (Lincoln: University
of Nebraska Press, 2006). Pp. 1–64, esp. pp. 48–51.

Viðar Pálsson. "Pagan Mythology in Christian Society." *Gripla* 19 (2008):
123–58, esp. p. 153.

Wrightson, Kellinde. "Changing Attitudes to Old Icelandic Marian Poetry."
In *Old Norse Studies in the New World: A Collection of Essays to Celebrate
the Jubilee of the Teaching of Old Norse at the University of Sydney
1943–1993*. Ed. Geraldine Barnes, Margaret Clunies Ross, and Judy Quinn
(Sydney: Department of English, University of Sydney, 1994). Pp. 138–53,
esp. pp. 138–9.

Wolf, Kirsten, "The Influence of the *Evangelium Nicodemi* on Norse Literature:
A Survey." In *The Medieval* Gospel of Nicodemus: *Texts, Intertexts,
and Contexts in Western Europe*. Ed. Zbigniew Izydorczyk (Tempe, AZ;
Medieval and Renaissance Texts and Studies, 1997). Pp. 261–86, esp.
pp. 271–2 and 276–8.

64. Heilagra meyja drápa

A fourteenth-century poem about holy maidens. Stz. 1–10 treat Mary the
Blessed Virgin, her mother Saint Anne, and the Virgin's half-sisters, Mary, wife
of Alphaeus, and Mary, wife of Zebedee.

Incipit: "Heyrðu ómælds himna veldis herra guð."

Manuscripts:
See Agatha note (p. 13).

Editions:
Finnur Jónsson, ed. >> *Den norsk-islandske skjaldedigtning* (1912–15).
Vol. AII, pp. 526–8 and Vol. BII, pp. 582–5.

Jón Þorkelsson. >> *Om Digtingen på Island* (1888). P. 87 (stz. 1 only).

Kock, Ernst Albin, ed. >> *Notationes Norrœnæ* (1923–44). §§1838, 1839,
1840, 2970A, 2970B, 2971A, 2972, 3389A, 3389B, 3389C, and 3390.

– ed. >> *Den norsk-islandske skaldediktningen* (1946–50). Vol. 2, pp. 321–3.

Wolf, Kirsten, ed. "Anonymous, *Heilagra meyja drápa* 'Drápa about Holy
Maidens." In >> *Poetry on Christian Subjects* (2007). Vol. 2, pp. 892–8.

Danish translation:
Finnur Jónsson, ed. >> *Den norsk-islandske skjaldedigtning* (1912–15).
Vol. BII, pp. 582–5.

English translation:
Wolf, Kirsten, ed. "Anonymous, *Heilagra meyja drápa* 'Drápa about Holy
Maidens'." In >> *Poetry on Christian Subjects* (2007). Vol. 2, pp. 892–8.

65. Gjörði í einu

A poetic rendering of biblical stories composed between 1400 and 1550. The poem is also known as *Liljukvistur*. Stz. 15–23, 43–50, and 71–2 concern Mary the Blessed Virgin.

Incipit: "Gjörði í einu orði hreinu."

Manuscripts:
See Elizabeth 1 note (p. 82).
Edition:
Jón Helgason, ed. >> *Íslenzk miðaldakvæði* (1936–8). Vol. 1.2, pp. 161–2, 165–6, and 169.
German translation:
Kock, E.A. "Liljukvistur." *Studia Neophilologica* 15 (1942): 141–56, esp. pp. 146–7, 151–2, and 156.

66. Píslardrápa

A fragmentary passion poem composed ca. 1400–1550. Stz. 10, 15–16, 29, and 41 treat Mary the Blessed Virgin, and the chorus praises her.

Incipit: "Postuli einn með prýði hæsta."

Manuscripts:
See John the Evangelist 10 note (p. 133).
Edition:
Jón Helgason, ed. >> *Íslenzk miðaldakvæði* (1936–8). Vol. 1.2. Pp. 60 and 62–3.

67. Kristsbálkur

A late medieval (ca. 1400–1550) poem in praise of Jesus Christ based on oral tradition. Stz. 2, 18–26, 34–6, 64, and 70 concern Mary the Blessed Virgin.

Incipit: "Hæstur drottinn heiðri þig loptinn."

Manuscripts:
See Anne 6 note (p. 36).
Edition:
Jón Helgason, ed. >> *Íslenzk miðaldakvæði* (1936–8). Vol. 1.2, pp. 144, 146–8, and 152–3.

68. Heyr mig himins og láða

A fragmentary poem from ca. 1500 about the events surrounding Christ's birth and childhood. Stz. 5–19 concern Mary the Blessed Virgin.
  Incipit: "Heyr mig himins og láða."

Manuscript:
See Anne 10 note (p. 38).
Edition:
Jón Helgason, ed. >> *Íslenzk miðaldakvæði* (1936–8). Vol. 1.2, pp. 86–8.

69. Máríublóm

An early sixteenth-century poem in praise of Jesus Christ attributed to the priest Hallur Ögmundarson (d. ca. 1540). Stz. 13–14, 16, 25, 29, 35–7, 40, and 45–7 concern Mary the Blessed Virgin.
  Incipit: "Heyr mig Jesús hjálparinn mætr."

Manuscripts:
See Bernard of Clairvaux note (p. 51).
Editions:
Jón Helgason, ed. >> *Íslenzk miðaldakvæði* (1936–8). Vol. 1.2, pp. 175–81.
Jón Þorkelsson, ed. >> *Kvæðasafn* (1922–7). Pp. 357–8, 360, and 365.

70. Náð

An early sixteenth-century poem in honour of Saint Anne and her daughter Mary the Blessed Virgin ascribed to the priest Hallur Ögmundarson (d. ca. 1540).
  Incipit: "Heyr mildingur allra alda."

Manuscripts:
See Anne 1 note (p. 34).
Editions:
Carpenter, William H., ed. *Nikolásdrápa Halls prests: An Icelandic Poem from circa A.D. 1400* (Halle: Karras, 1881). P. 6 (stz. 1).
Jón Helgason, ed. >> *Íslenzk miðaldakvæði* (1936–8). Vol. 2, pp. 4–26.
Jón Þorkelsson. >> *Om Digtningen på Island* (1888). Pp. 54 (stz. 1^{1-2}) and 320 (stz. 1, 103, and 107^{7-8}).
Jón Þorkelsson, ed. >> *Kvæðasafn* (1922–7). Pp. 327–53.

71. Blómarós

A poem praising Jesus Christ and relating various biblical stories composed
ca. 1400–1550. Jón Helgason argues that it is probably from 1550 or the first
decade thereafter during the transition from Catholicism to Protestantism.
Stz. 63–113, 170–1, 183, 207–8, and 235 concern Mary the Blessed Virgin.
   Incipit: "Heyr guð faðir á himna hæðum."

Manuscripts:
See Elizabeth 6 note (p. 85).
Edition:
Jón Helgason, ed. >> *Íslenzk miðaldakvæði* (1936–8). Vol. 1.2, pp. 76–83,
   91–2, 96, and 99.

MARY OF EGYPT   April 2

Heilagra meyja drápa

A fourteenth-century poem about holy maidens. Stz. 14–16 treat Saint Mary of
Egypt.
   Incipit: "Heyrðu ómælds himna veldis herra guð."

Manuscripts:
See Agatha note (p. 13).
Editions:
Finnur Jónsson, ed. >> *Den norsk-islandske skjaldedigtning* (1912–15).
   Vol. AII, pp. 529–30 and vol. BII, pp. 585–6.
Kock, Ernst Albin, ed. >> *Notationes Norrænæ* (1923–44). §3391A.
 – ed. >> *Den norsk-islandske skaldediktningen* (1946–50). Vol. 2, pp. 323–4.
Wolf, Kirsten, ed. "Anonymous, *Heilagra meyja drápa* 'Drápa about Holy
   Maidens'." In >> *Poetry on Christian Subjects* (2007). Vol. 2, pp. 900–2.
Danish translation:
Finnur Jónsson, ed. *Den norsk-islandske skjaldedigtning* (1912–15). Vol. BII,
   p. 586.
English translation:
Wolf, Kirsten, ed. "Anonymous, *Heilagra meyja drápa* 'Drápa about Holy
   Maidens'." In >> *Poetry on Christian Subjects* (2007). Vol. 2, pp. 900–2.

MARY MAGDALEN   July 22

1. Vísur af Máríu Magdalene II

A poetic rendering composed between 1300 and 1550 of the composite legend
of Saints Mary Magdalen and Martha.
   Incipit: "Ágætt óðar efni."

Manuscripts:
AM 713 4to (ca. 1500–50), AM 920 4to (ca. 1800–1900), and Lbs 2166 4to
   (ca. 1885–1920).

Editions:
Jón Helgason, ed. >> *Íslenzk miðaldakvæði* (1936–8). Vol. 2, pp. 391–401.
   Based on AM 713 4to with variants from AM 920 4to and Lbs 2166 4to
   and C.R. Unger's edition of *Marthe saga ok Marie Magdalene* in *Heilagra
   manna søgur: Fortællinger og legender om hellige mænd og kvinder*, 2
   vols. (Christiania [Oslo]: Bentzen, 1877).
Jón Þorkelsson. >> *Om Digtningen på Island* (1888). P. 91 (stz. 1).
   Based on AM 713 4to and AM 920 4to.

Literature:
Bekker-Nielsen, Hans. "Maria Magdalena." *KLNM* 11 (1966). Cols. 410–11,
   esp. col. 410.
Bjarni Þorsteinsson, ed. *Íslenzk þjóðlög* (Copenhagen: Møller, 1906–9). P. 545.
Finnur Jónsson. >> *Den oldnorske og oldislandske Litteraturs Historie*
   (1920–4). Vol. 3, p. 126.
Foote, Peter, ed. *Lives of Saints. Perg. fol. nr. 2 in the Royal Library,
   Stockholm.* EIM 4 (Copenhagen: Rosenkilde and Bagger, 1962). P. 26.
Guðrún Nordal. "Handrit, prentaðar bækur og pápísk kvæði á siðskiptaöld."
   In >> *Til heiðurs og hugbótar* (2003). Pp. 131–43, esp. pp. 139–40.
Hálfdan Einarsson. *Sciagraphia historiæ literariæ islandicæ* (Copenhagen:
   Sander and Schröder, 1777). P. 58.
Jakob Benediktsson. "Helgendigte." *KLNM* 6 (1961). Cols. 318–21, esp.
   col. 320.
Jón Helgason. >> "Norges og Islands digtning." In *Litteraturhistorie B:
   Norge og Island* (1953). Pp. 3–179, esp. pp. 163–4.
Mogk, Eugen. >> *Geschichte der norwegisch-isländischen Literatur* (1904).
   P. 719.
Schottmann, Hans. >> *Die isländische Mariendichtung* (1973). P. 57n27.
Soffía Ófeigsdóttir. "*Veroníkukvæði.*" BA thesis. University of Iceland, 1986.
   P. 66.

Stéfan Einarsson. "Íslenzk helgikvæði á miðöldum." *Tímarit Þjóðræknisfélags Íslendinga* 36 (1955): 43–63, esp. p. 55.
– *Íslensk bókmenntasaga 874–1960* (Reykjavík: Oddi, 1961). P. 92.
Vésteinn Ólason. "Kveðskapur frá síðmiðöldum." In >> *Íslensk Bókmenntasaga* 2 (1993). Pp. 283–378, esp. pp. 316–17.
Wolf, Kirsten, ed. >> *Heilagra meyja sögur* (2003). Pp. liii–lv.
NOTE:
The poem contains material about other saints, especially Saints Lazarus and Martha. See the entries for the two saints.

2. Vísur af Máríu Magdalene I

A late medieval (ca. 1400–1550) poem in praise of Saint Mary Magdalen. Incipit: "Vil ég þér vísur vanda."

Manuscripts:
AM 713 4to (ca. 1500–50), AM 920 4to (ca. 1800–1900), and Lbs 2166 4to (ca. 1885–1920).
Editions:
Jón Helgason, ed. >> *Íslenzk miðaldakvæði* (1936–8). Vol. 2, pp. 386–9. Edition of AM 713 4to.
– ed. *Handritaspjall* (Reykjavík: Mál og menning, 1958). P. 65 (stz. 13–14). Facsimile of AM 713 4to.
Jón Þorkelsson. >> *Om Digtningen på Island* (1888). Pp. 91 (stz. 1^{1-2}) and 321 (stz. 1–2).
Edition of AM 713 4to and AM 920 4to.
Literature:
Bekker-Nielsen, Hans. "Maria Magdalena." *KLNM* 11 (1966). Cols. 410–11, esp. col. 410.
Finnur Jónsson. >> *Den oldnorske og oldislandske Litteraturs Historie* (1920–4). Vol. 3, p. 126.
Foote, Peter, ed. *Lives of Saints. Perg. fol. nr. 2 in the Royal Library, Stockholm.* EIM 4 (Copenhagen: Rosenkilde and Bagger, 1962). P. 26.
Guðrún Nordal. "Handrit, prentaðar bækur og pápísk kvæði á siðskiptaöld." In >> *Til heiðurs og hugbótar* (2003). Pp. 131–43, esp. pp. 139–40.
Hálfdan Einarsson. *Sciagraphia historiæ literariæ islandicæ* (Copenhagen: Sander and Schröder, 1777). P. 58.
Jakob Benediktsson. "Helgendigte." *KLNM* 6 (1961). Cols. 318–21, esp. col. 320.

Jón Helgason. >> "Norges og Islands digtning." In *Litteraturhistorie B:
   Norge og Island* (1953). Pp. 3–179, esp. pp. 163–4.
Mogk, Eugen. >> *Geschichte der norwegisch-isländischen Literatur* (1904).
   P. 719.
Schottmann, Hans. >> *Die isländische Mariendichtung* (1973). P. 26.
Soffía Ófeigsdóttir. "*Veroníkukvæði.*" BA thesis. University of Iceland, 1986.
   P. 66.
Stéfan Einarsson. "Íslenzk helgikvæði á miðöldum." *Tímarit Þjóðræknisfélags
   Íslendinga* 36 (1955): 43–63, esp. p. 55.
– *Íslensk bókmenntasaga 874–1960* (Reykjavík: Oddi, 1961). P. 92.
Sverrir Tómasson. "'Nikulám skulu vér heiðra hér …'." In >> *Til heiðurs og
   hugbótar* (2003). Pp. 79–92, esp. p. 92n39.
Vésteinn Ólason. "Kveðskapur frá síðmiðöldum." In >> *Íslensk
   Bókmenntasaga* 2 (1993). Pp. 283–378, esp. pp. 316–17.
Wolf, Kirsten, ed. >> *Heilagra meyja sögur* (2003). P. lv.
– ed. >> *Saga heilagrar Önnu* (2001). P. xliv.

NOTE:

The poem contains material about other saints, especially Saints Lazarus and
Martha, but also Saint Anne. See the entries for the individual saints.

3. Iðrunardiktur

A poem about Saint Mary Magdalen's repentence attributed to Jón Þorsteinsson
píslarvottur (1570–1627).
   Incipit: "Heyr þú mína hjartans bæn."

Manuscripts:
AM 148 8vo (ca. 1650–1700), JS 588 4to (ca. 1800–1900), Lbs 1485 8vo
   (ca. 1700), Lbs 2366 8vo (ca. 1770), and NKS 139a 4to (ca. 1700–50).
Editions:
Jón Helgason, ed. >> *Kvæðabók úr Vigur: AM 148, 8vo* (1955). Fol.
   236v–238r.
   Facsimile of AM 148 8vo.
Jón Þorkelsson. >> *Om Digtningen på Island* (1888). Pp. 91 (stz. 1) and 454
   (stz. 1¹).
   Edition of AM 148 8vo (p. 91) and NKS 139a 4to (p. 454).
Literature:
Páll Eggert Ólason. *Menn og menntir siðskiptaaldarinnar á Íslandi.* Vol. 4
   (Reykjavík: Ársæll Árnason, 1926). P. 652.

Soffía Ófeigsdóttir. *"Veroníkukvæði."* BA thesis. University of Iceland, 1986.
P. 66.

4. Harmsól

A twelfth-century praise-poem addressed to Christ by Gamli. Stz. 52 treats
Saint Mary Magdalen.
Incipit: "Hár stillir, lúk heilli."

Manuscripts:
See Mary the Blessed Virgin 61 (p. 226).
Editions:
*Attwood, Katrina, ed. "The Poems of MS AM 757a 4to: An Edition and
Contextual Study." PhD dissertation, University of Leeds, 1996.
– ed. "Gamli kanóki, *Harmsól* 'Sun of Sorrow'." In >> *Poetry on Christian
Subjects* (2007). Vol. 1, p. 119.
*Black, Elizabeth L. *"Harmsól*: An Edition." BLitt thesis, University of
Oxford, 1971.
Finnur Jónsson, ed. >> *Den norsk-islandske skjaldedigtning* (1912–15).
Vol. AI, p. 569 and vol. BI, p. 561.
– ed. *Carmina scaldica: udvalg af norske og islandske skjaldekvad.* 2nd rev.
ed. (Copenhagen: Gad, 1923). P. 85.
Kempff, Hjalmar, ed. *Kaniken Gamles "Harmsol" (Sol i Sorgen): Isländskt
andligt qväde från medeltiden, öfversättning och förklaringar* (Uppsala:
Edquist and Berglund, 1867). Pp. 15–16.
Based on Sveinbjörn Egilsson's edition (1844).
Kock, Ernst Albin, ed. >> *Notationes Norrœnæ* (1923–44). §1209.
– ed. >> *Den norsk-islandske skaldedigtningen* (1946–50). Vol. 1, p. 271.
Rydberg, Hugo, ed. *Die geistlichen Drápur und Dróttkvættfragmente des
Cod. AM 757 4to* (Copenhagen: Møller, 1907). P. 29.
Sveinbjörn Egilsson, ed. *Fjøgur gømul kvæði. Boðsrit til að hlusta á
þá opinberu yfirheyrslu í Bessastaða Skóla þann 22–29 mai 1844*
(Viðeyjarklaustur: Helgi Helgason, 1844). Pp. 29–30.
Danish translation:
Finnur Jónsson, ed. >> *Den norsk-islandske skjaldedigtning* (1912–15).
Vol. BI, p. 561.
English translation:
Attwood, Katrina, ed. "Gamli kanóki, *Harmsól* 'Sun of Sorrow'." In >>
Poetry on Christian Subjects (2007). Vol. 1, p. 119.

Norwegian translation:
Audne, Kr., trans. "*Harmsól.*" In *Norrøne kristenkvæde*. Ed. Olaf Hanssen (Oslo: Det norske samlaget, 1928). P. 34.

Swedish translation:
Kempff, Hjalmar, ed. *Kaniken Gamles "Harmsol" (Sol i Sorgen): Isländskt andligt qväde från medeltiden, öfversättning och förklaringar* (Uppsala: Edquist and Berglund, 1867). Pp. 15–16.

5. Drápa af Máríugrát

A fourteenth-century poem about Mary the Blessed Virgin's lament to Saint Augustine about her sorrows and her enumeration to a monk of her five joys. Stz. 12 mentions Saint Mary Magdalen.

Incipit: "Orðin gef þú mjög til mærðar, minn lausnari, skáldi þínu."

Manuscripts:
See Mary the Blessed Virgin 9 note (p. 176).

Editions:
Finnur Jónsson, ed. >> *Den norsk-islandske skjaldedigtning* (1912–15). Vol. AII, pp. 474–5 and vol. BII, p. 508.

Gade, Kari Ellen, ed. "Anonymous, *Drápa af Máríugrát* 'Drápa about the Lament of Mary'." In >> *Poetry on Christian Subjects* (2007). Vol. 2, p. 768.

Kahle, Bernhard, ed. >> *Isländische geistliche Dichtungen des ausgehenden Mittelalters* (1898). P. 58.

Kock, Ernst Albin, ed. >> *Den norsk-isländska skaldediktningen* (1946–50). Vol. 2, p. 278.

Sperber, Hans, ed. >> *Sechs isländische Gedichte legendarischen Inhalts* (1911). Pp. 32–3.

Wrightson, Kellinde, ed. >> *Fourteenth-Century Icelandic Verse on the Virgin Mary* (2001). P. 6.

Danish translation:
Finnur Jónsson, ed. >> *Den norsk-islandske skjaldedigtning* (1912–15). Vol. BII, p. 58.

English translations:
Gade, Kari Ellen, ed. "Anonymous, *Drápa af Máríugrát* 'Drápa about the Lament of Mary'." In >> *Poetry on Christian Subjects* (2007). Vol. 2, p. 768.

Wrightson, Kellinde, ed. >> *Fourteenth-Century Icelandic Verse on the Virgin Mary* (2001). P. 6.

6. Heilagra meyja drápa

A fourteenth-century poem about holy maidens. Stz. 11–13 treat Saint Mary Magdalen.
   Incipit: "Heyrðu ómælds himna veldis herra guð."

Manuscripts:
See Agatha note (p. 13).
Editions:
Finnur Jónsson, ed. >> *Den norsk-islandske skjaldedigtning* (1912–15).
   Vol. AII, p. 529 and vol. BII, p. 585.
Kock, Ernst Albin, ed. >> *Den norsk-islandske skaldediktningen* (1946–50).
   Vol. 2, p. 323.
Wolf, Kirsten, ed. "Anonymous, *Heilagra meyja drápa* 'Drápa about Holy
   Maidens'." In >> *Poetry on Christian Subjects* (2007). Vol. 2, pp. 898–900.
Danish translation:
Finnur Jónsson, ed. >> *Den norsk-islandske skjaldedigtning* (1912–15).
   Vol. BII, p. 585.
English translation:
Wolf, Kirsten, ed. "Anonymous, *Heilagra meyja drápa* 'Drápa about Holy
   Maidens'." In >> *Poetry on Christian Subjects* (2007). Vol. 2, pp. 899–900.

7. Gjörði í einu

A poetic rendering of biblical stories composed between 1400 and 1550. The
poem is also known as *Liljukvistur*. Stz. 58 mentions Saint Mary Magdalen.
   Incipit: "Gjörði í einu orði hreinu."

Manuscripts:
See Elizabeth 1 note (p. 83).
Edition:
Jón Helgason, ed. >> *Íslenzk miðaldakvæði* (1936–8). Vol. 1.2, p. 167.
German translation:
Kock, E.A. "Liljukvistur." *Studia Neophilologica* 15 (1942): 141–56, esp. p. 154.

8. Krossþulur

A poem about Christ and the Holy Cross composed ca. 1400–1550. Stz. 19–22
and additional stz. 1 (redaction B only) concern Saint Mary Magdalen.
   Incipit: "Það er upphaflegt."

Manuscripts:
See Cross, the Holy 3 note (p. 68).
Edition:
Jón Helgason, ed. >> *Íslenzk miðaldakvæði* (1936–8). Vol. 1.2, pp. 243 and
    246.

9. Gimsteinn

An early sixteenth-century poem about the cross-tree ascribed to the priest
Hallur Ögmundarson (d. ca. 1540). Stz. 61 mentions Saint Mary Magdalen.
    Incipit: "Heyr mig ilmanda hjartans yndi."

Manuscripts:
See Cross, the Holy 7 note (p. 73).
Editions:
Jón Helgason, ed. >> *Íslenzk miðaldakvæði* (1936–8). Vol. 1.2, pp. 317–18.
Jón Þorkelsson, ed. >> *Kvæðasafn* (1922–7). P. 312.

10. Blómarós

A poem praising Jesus Christ and relating various biblical stories composed
ca. 1400–1550. Jón Helgason argues that is is probably from 1550 or the first
decade thereafter during the transition from Catholicism to Protestantism. Stz.
126 and 217–20 concern Saint Mary Magdalen.
    Incipit: "Heyr guð faðir á himna hæðum."

Manuscripts:
See Elizabeth 6 note (p. 85).
Edition:
Jón Helgason, ed. >> *Íslenzk miðaldakvæði* (1936–8). Vol. 1.2,
    pp. 85 and 97.

11. Kvennadans

A poem in praise of famous women composed in 1619 by Magnús Ólafsson á
Laufás and extant in two versions of varying length. Saint Mary Magdalen is
treated in stz. 76 as well as in two additional stz. included before stz. 73 in the
margins of ÍB 105 4to and in JS 477 8vo.
    Incipit: "Mér er geðs þó ment sé rýr."

Manuscripts:
A: Lbs 221 4to (ca. 1760–70), Lbs 1698 4to (ca. 1620–50), Lbs 2129 4to
   (1886), Lbs 1014 8vo (1821–3), and Lbs 2157 8vo (ca. 1770);
B: ÍB 105 4to (1758–68), JS 267 4to (ca. 1700–1900), JS 154 8vo (ca. 1780),
   JS 471 8vo (ca. 1675–1900), JS 477 8vo (ca. 1675–1900), JS 480 8vo
   (ca. 1675–1900), JS 492 8vo (ca. 1675–1900), Lbs 378 fol. (ca. 1847–51),
   Lbs 1293 4to (1845–57), Lbs 1587 4to (1829), Lbs 2783 4to (1801), Lbs
   172 8vo (ca. 1850–70), Lbs 269 8vo (ca. 1850–70), Lbs 1059 8vo (1793),
   Lbs 1600 8vo (ca. 1700–1850), Lbs 1988 8vo (ca. 1790 and later), and Lbs
   2138 8vo (ca. 1700–1900).

Edition:
Faulkes, Anthony. *Magnúsarkver: The Writings of Magnús Ólafsson of
   Laufás* (Reykjavík: Stofnun Árna Magnússonar á Íslandi, 1993). Pp. 39
   and 69.
   Edition of Lbs 1698 4to with variants and additions from ÍB 105 4to, JS
   267 4to, JS 471 8vo, Lbs 221 4to, Lbs 1600 8vo, and Lbs 2157 8vo. The
   two additional stz. on p. 69 are based on JS 477 8vo.

Literature:
Aðalheiður Guðmundsdóttir. "DFS 67." *Opuscula* 9. Bibliotheca
   Arnamagnæana 42 (Copenhagen: Munksgaard, 2003). P. 238.
Jón Þorkelsson. >> *Om Digtningen på Island* (1888). P. 469.
Margrét Eggertsdóttir. "'Í blíðum faðmi brúðgumans': Hlutur kvenna í
   trúarlegum kveðskap á sautjándu og átjándu öld." In *Konur og kristsmenn:
   Þættir úr kristnisögu Íslands*. Ed. Inga Huld Hákonardóttir (Reykjavík:
   Háskólaútgáfan, 1956). Pp. 165–89, esp. pp. 170–3 and 188.
– "From Reformation to Enlightenment." Trans. Joe Allard. In *A History
   of Icelandic Literature*. Ed. Daisy Neijmann. Histories of Scandinavian
   Literature 5 (Lincoln: University of Nebraska Press, 2006). Pp. 174–250,
   esp. p. 206.
– *Icelandic Baroque: Poetic Art and Erudition in the Works of Hallgrímur
   Pétursson*. Trans. Andrew Wawn (Ithaca: Cornell University Press, 2014).
   Pp. 125–6.

12. Sprundahrós

A poem from the late eighteenth or early nineteenth century in praise of virtu-
ous women from the Bible and history, attributed alternatively to Jón Jónsson
að Kvíabekk (1739–85) and Ingjaldur Jónsson að Múla (1739–1832). Saint
Mary Magdalen is treated in stz. 6.

Incipit: "Margt er gjört að gamni sín."

Manuscript:
ÍB 815 8vo (ca. 1600–1900), JS 255 4to (1841), JS 589 4to (1841).
Edition:
Jón Árnason and Ólafur Davíðsson, ed. *Íslenzkar gátur, skemtanir, vikivakar og þulur.* 4 vols. (Copenhagen: Møller, 1887–1903). Vol. 3, p. 342 (refrain only).
Literature:
Hughes, Shaun D. "Late Secular Poetry." In *A Companion to Old Norse–Icelandic Literature and Culture.* Ed. Rory McTurk (Oxford: Blackwell, 2005). Pp. 205–22, esp. p. 217.

MATTHEW   September 21

1. Allra postola minnisvísur

A fourteenth-century poem about all the apostles. Saint Matthew is treated in stz. 10.
Incipit: "Pétr er páfi drottins prísaðr gleðivísum."

Manuscript:
See Andrew the Apostle 10 note (p. 30).
Editions:
Finnur Jónsson, ed. >> *Den norsk-islandske skjaldedigtning* (1912–15). Vol. AII, p. 511 and vol. BII, p. 561.
Kock, Ernst Albin, ed. >> *Notationes Norrænæ* (1923–44). §§1761 and 3376B.
– ed. >> *Den norsk-isländska skaldediktningen* (1946–50). Vol. 2, pp. 307–8.
McDougall, Ian, ed. "Anonymous, *Allra postula minnisvísur* 'Celebratory Vísur* about All the Apostles'." In >> *Poetry on Christian Subjects* (2007). Vol. 2, p. 866.
Danish translation:
Finnur Jónsson, ed. >> *Den norsk-islandske skjaldedigtning* (1912–15). Vol. BII, p. 561.
English translation:
McDougall, Ian, ed. "Anonymous, *Allra postula minnisvísur* 'Celebratory Vísur* about All the Apostles'." In >> *Poetry on Christian Subjects* (2007). Vol. 2, p. 866.

2. Tólf postula kvæði

A late medieval (ca. 1400–1550) celebratory poem about all the apostles. Saint
Matthew is treated in stz. 10.
   Incipit: "Sankti Pétur sannur páfi í Róma."

Manuscripts:
See Andrew the Apostle 11 note (p. 31).
Edition:
Jón Helgason, ed. >> *Íslenzk miðaldakvæði* (1936–8). Vol. 2, p. 277.

3. Rósa

An early sixteenth-century cosmological poem with an emphasis on the life of
Mary the Blessed Virgin attributed to Sigurður blindur. Stz. 6 mentions Saint
Matthew.
   Incipit: "Faðir og son á hæstum hæðum."

Manuscripts:
See Mary the Blessed Virgin 48 note (p. 212).
Editions:
Jón Helgason, ed. >> *Íslenzk miðaldakvæði* (1936–8). Vol. 1.2, p. 7.
Jón Þorkelsson, ed. >> *Kvæðasafn* (1922–7). P. 264.
Norwegian translation:
Orgland, Ivar, trans. and Anne-Lise Knoff, illus. *Rósa. Sigurður blindi í
   Fagradal* (Oslo: Solum, 1989). P. 20.

4. Postulavísur

A poem about all the apostles composed in 1629 by Guðmundur Erlendsson í
Felli (1595–1670). Stz. 2–22 and 32 concern Saint Matthew.
   Incipit: "Herrans hér postula."

Manuscripts:
See Andrew the Apostle 14 note (p. 32).

5. Postularaun

A poem in praise of all the apostles composed by Guðmundur Bergþórsson
(1657–1705). Stz. 49–55 concern Saint Matthew.
   Incipit: "Hér skal eina hróðar grein."

Manuscripts:
See Ananias note (p. 20).

MATTHIAS   February 24

1. Allra postola minnisvísur

A fourteenth-century poem about all the apostles. Saint Matthias is treated in stz. 12.
   Incipit: "Pétr er páfi drottins prísaðr gleðivísum."

Manuscript:
See Andrew the Apostle 10 note (p. 30).
Editions:
Finnur Jónsson, ed. >> *Den norsk-islandske skjaldedigtning* (1912–15).
   Vol. AII, p. 511 and vol. BII, p. 562.
Kock, Ernst Albin, ed. >> *Den norsk-isländska skaldediktningen* (1946–50).
   Vol. 2, p. 308.
McDougall, Ian, ed. "Anonymous, *Allra postula minnisvísur* 'Celebratory
   Vísur about All the Apostles'." In >> *Poetry on Christian Subjects* (2007).
   Vol. 2, p. 870.
Danish translation:
Finnur Jónsson, ed. >> *Den norsk-islandske skjaldedigtning* (1912–15).
   Vol. BII, p. 562.
English translation:
McDougall, Ian, ed. "Anonymous, *Allra postula minnisvísur* 'Celebratory
   Vísur about All the Apostles'." In >> *Poetry on Christian Subjects* (2007).
   Vol. 2, p. 870.

2. Tólf postula kvæði

A late medieval (ca. 1400–1550) celebratory poem about all the apostles. Saint Matthias is treated in stz. 12.
   Incipit: "Sankti Pétur sannur páfi í Róma."

Manuscripts:
See Andrew the Apostle 11 note (p. 31).
Edition:
Jón Helgason, ed. >> *Íslenzk miðaldakvæði* (1936–8). Vol. 2, p. 277.

3. Andréasdiktur II

A late medieval (ca. 1400–1550) poem about the life of Saint Andrew the Apostle based on oral tradition. Stz. 5 mentions Saint Matthias.
   Incipit: "Timens veit ég tíma rýra (að skýra)."

Manuscripts:
See Andrew the Apostle 3 note (p. 24).
Edition:
Jón Helgason, ed. >> *Íslenzk miðaldakvæði* (1936–8). Vol. 2, p. 298.

4. Postulavísur

A poem about all the apostles composed in 1629 by Guðmundur Erlendsson í Felli (1595–1670). Stz. 27 and 33 concern Saint Matthias.
   Incipit: "Herrans hér postula."

Manuscripts:
See Andrew the Apostle 14 note (p. 32).

5. Postularaun

A poem in praise of all the apostles composed by Guðmundur Bergþórsson (1657–1705). Stz. 78 mentions Saint Matthias.
   Incipit: "Hér skal eina hróðar grein."

Manuscripts:
See Ananias note (p. 20).

MAURICE   September 22

Heilagra manna drápa

A fourteenth-century poem about holy men. Stz. 25–6 treat Saint Maurice.
   Incipit: "... mildings f ... um dyrnar þustu ... særa."

Manuscripts:
See Blase note (p. 52).

Editions:
Finnur Jónsson, ed. >> *Den norsk-islandske skjaldedigtning* (1912–15).
   Vol. AII, p. 516 and vol. BII, pp. 568–9.
Kahle, Bernhard, ed. >> *Isländische geistliche Dichtungen des ausgehenden
   Mittelalters* (1898). P. 96.
Kock, Ernst Albin, ed. >> *Den norsk-islandske skaldediktningen* (1946–50).
   Vol. 2, p. 312.
Wolf, Kirsten, ed. "Anonymous, *Heilagra manna drápa* '*Drápa* about Holy
   Men'." In >> *Poetry on Christian Subjects* (2007). Vol. 2, pp. 889–90.
Danish translation:
Finnur Jónsson, ed. >> *Den norsk-islandske skjaldedigtning* (1912–15).
   Vol. BII, pp. 568–9.
English translation:
Wolf, Kirsten, ed. "Anonymous, *Heilagra manna drápa* '*Drápa* about Holy
   Men'." In >> *Poetry on Christian Subjects* (2007). Vol. 2, pp. 889–90.

MICHAEL THE ARCHANGEL   September 29

1. Michaelskvæði

A fragmentary *helmingr* on Saint Michael's role in the Last Judgment by
Arnórr Þórðarson (d. ca. 1075).
   Incipit: "Mikjáll vegr þats misgǫrt þykkir."

Manuscripts:
AM 242 fol. (*Codex Wormianus*) (ca. 1350), AM 756 4to (ca. 1400–1500),
   AM 757a 4to (ca. 1400), DG 11 (*Codex Upsaliensis*) (ca. 1300–50), GKS
   2367 4to (*Codex Regius*) (ca. 1300–50), and Traj 1374 (*Codex Trajectinus*)
   (ca. 1595).
Editions:
Eeden, Willem van, Jr, ed. *De Codex Trajectinus van de Snorra Edda*
   (Leiden: Eduard Ijdo, 1913). P. 81.
   Edition of Traj 1374.
Faulkes, Anthony, ed. *Codex Trajectinus: The Utrech Manuscript of the Prose
   Edda*. EIM 15 (Copenhagen: Rosenkilde and Bagger, 1985).
   Facsimile of Traj 1374.
– ed. *Edda: Skáldskaparmál*. 2 vols. (University College London: Viking
   Society for Northern Research, 1998). Vol. 1, p. 35.

Edition of GKS 2367 4to with variants from AM 242 fol. and Traj 1374.

Finnur Jónsson, ed. >> *Den norsk-islandske skjaldedigtning* (1912–15).
Vol. AI, p. 353 and vol. BII, p. 326.
Editon of GKS 2367 4to with variants from AM 242 fol., AM 757a 4to,
DG 11, and Traj 1374.

– ed. *Edda Snorra Sturlusonar. Codex Wormianus AM 242, fol.* (Copenhagen
and Kristiania [Oslo]: Gyldendal, 1924). P. 70.

– ed. *Edda Snorra Sturlusonar* (Copenhagen: Gyldendal, 1931). P. 115.
Edition of GKS 2367 4to with variants from AM 242 fol., AM 748b 4to I,
AM 748 4to II, AM 757a 4to, DG 11, and Traj 1374.

Heimir Pálsson, ed. >> *Snorri Sturluson. The Uppsala Edda* (2012). P. 152.
Edition of DG 11.

Heusler, Andreas, ed. *Codex Regius of the Elder Edda.* CCI 10 (Copenhagen:
Munksgaard, 1937).
Facsimile of GKS 2367 4to.

Jón Sigurðsson et al., ed. *Edda Snorra Sturlusonar: Edda Snorronis
Sturlaei.* 3 vols. (Copenhagen: Legatum Arnamagnaeanum, 1848–87;
rpt. Osnabrück: Zeller, 1966). Vol. 1, p. 320 and vol. 2, pp. 314 and 527.
Vol. 1, p. 320: edition of GKS 2367 4to with variants from AM 242 4to,
AM 756 4to, AM 757a 4to, and DG 11; vol. 2, p. 314: edition of DG 11;
and vol. 3: edition of AM 757a 4to.

Kock, Ernst Albin, ed. >> *Den norsk-islandske skaldediktningen* (1946–50).
Vol. 1, p. 165.

Sigurður Nordal, ed. *Codex Wormianus (The Younger Edda). MS No. 242 fol.
in The Arnamagnean Collection in the University Library of Copenhagen.*
CCI 2 (Copenhagen: Levin and Munksgaard, 1931).
Facsimile.

Wessén, Elias, ed. *Codex Regius of the Younger Edda. MS No. 2367 4to in
the Old Royal Collection in the Royal Library of Copenhagen.* CCI 14
(Copenhagen: Einar Munksgaard, 1940).
Facsimile of GKS 2367 4to.

Whaley, Diana, ed. *The Poetry of Arnórr jarlaskáld: An Edition and Study*
(Turnhout: Brepols, 1998). Pp. 134 and 312.
Edition of GKS 2367 4to with variants from AM 242 fol. and Traj 1374.

Modern Icelandic language edition:

Árni Björnsson, ed. *Snorra Edda* (Reykjavík: Iðunn, 1975). P. 147.

Danish translation:

Finnur Jónsson, ed. >> *Den norsk-islandske skjaldedigtning* (1912–15).
Vol. BII, p. 326.

English translations:

Faulkes, Anthony, trans. *Snorri Sturluson:* Edda (London: Dent, 1987). P. 90.

Heimir Pálsson, ed. >> *Snorri Sturluson. The Uppsala Edda* (2012). P. 153.

Whaley, Diana, ed. *The Poetry of Arnórr jarlaskáld: An Edition and Study* (Turnhout: Brepols, 1998). Pp. 134 and 312.

German translation:

Krause, Arnulf, trans. *Die Edda des Snorri Sturluson.* Reclams Universital-Bibliothek 782 (Stuttgart: Reclam, 1997). P. 130.

Latin translation:

Jón Sigurðsson et al. *Edda Snorra Sturlusonar: Edda Snorronis Sturlaei.* 3 vols. (Copenhagen: Legatum Arnamagnaeanum, 1848–87; rpt. Osnabrück: Zeller, 1966). Vol. 1, p. 321.

Literature:

Attwood, Katrina. "Christian Poetry." In *A Companion to Old Norse–Icelandic Literature and Culture.* Ed. Rory McTurk (Oxford: Blackwell, 2005). Pp. 43–63, esp. pp. 48–9.

Chase, Martin. "Christian Poetry: West Norse." In >> *Medieval Scandinavia: An Encyclopedia* (1993). Pp. 73–6, esp. p. 74.

Edwards, Diana. "Christian and Pagan References in Eleventh-Century Norse Poetry: The Case of Arnórr Jarlaskáld." *Saga-Book* 21 (1982–3): 34–53, esp. p. 40.

Fidjestøl, Bjarne. *Det norrøne fyrstediktet* (Øvre Ervik: Alvheim and Eide, 1982). P. 128.2.

Finnur Jónsson. >> *Den oldnorske og oldislandske Litteraturs Historie* (1920–4). Vol. 1, p. 611.

Kahle, Bernhard. *Die Sprache der Skalden auf Grund der Binnen- und Endreime* (Strassburg: Karl J. Trübner, 1892).

Konráð Gíslason. "Om helrim i förste og tredje linie af regelmæssigt 'drottkvætt' og 'hrynhenda'." *Indbydelsesskrift til Kjøbenhavns Universitets Aarsfest til Erindring om Kirkens Reformation* (Copenhagen: Schultz, 1877). Pp. 1–60, esp. pp. 8 and 20.

Lange, Wolfgang. >> *Studien zur christlichen Dichtung der Nordgermanen 1000–1200* (1958). Pp. 70–4.

Paasche, Fredrik. >> *Kristendom og kvad* (1914). Pp. 42–3 and 47.

Sverrir Tómasson. "Trúarbókmenntir í lausu máli á síðmiðöld." In >> *Íslensk Bókmenntasaga* 2 (1993). Pp. 249–82, esp. p. 255.

Vries, Jan de. >> *Altnordische Literaturgeschichte* (1964–7). Vol. 1, p. 269.

2. Michaelsflokkur

An early sixteenth-century poem about Saint Michael ascribed to the priest
Hallur Ögmundarson (d. ca. 1540).
  Incipit: "Óðar gef þú upphaf."

Manuscripts:
AM 622 4to (ca. 1549), AM 710d 4to (ca. 1700–25), AM 714 4to (ca. 1600),
  and AM 1032 4to (ca. 1700–25).
Editions:
*Jón Sigurðsson et al. *Edda Snorra Sturlusonar: Edda Snorronis Sturlaei.* 3
  vols. (Copenhagen: Legatum Arnamagnaeanum, 1848–87; rpt. Osnabrück:
  Zeller, 1966). Vol. 1, p. 320 and vol. 2, pp. 210–11 (stz. 14 and 16).
Jón Þorkelsson. >> *Om Digtningen på Island* (1888). Pp. 86 (stz. 1^{1-2}) and
  317 (stz. 1 and 66).
  Based on AM 622 4to, AM 710d 4to, AM 714 4to, and AM 1032 4to.
Jón Þorkelsson, ed. >> *Kvæðasafn* (1922–7). Pp. 370–85.
  Based on AM 622 4to with variants from AM 710d 4to and AM 714 4to.
Literature:
Björn K. Þórólfsson. "Kvantitetsomvæltningen i islandsk." *ANF* 45 (1929):
  35–81, esp. pp. 40 and 45–7.
Carpenter, William H., ed. *Nikolásdrápa Halls prests: An Icelandic Poem
  from circa A.D. 1400* (Halle: Karras, 1881). Pp. 3–6.
Chase, Martin. "Devotional Poetry at the End of the Middle Ages in Iceland."
  In >> *Eddic, Skaldic, and Beyond: Poetic Variety in Medieval Iceland.*
  Ed. Martin Chase (2014). Pp. 136–49, esp. p. 149.
Finnur Jónsson. >> *Bókmentasaga Íslendinga fram undir siðabót* (1904–5).
  P. 463.
– >> *Den oldnorske og oldislandske Litteraturs Historie* (1920–4). Vol. 3,
  p. 128.
Guðrún Nordal. "Handrit, prentaðar bækur og pápísk kvæði á siðskiptaöld."
  In >> *Til heiðurs og hugbótar* (2003). Pp. 131–43, esp. pp. 140–1.
– "Á mörkum tveggja tíma: Kaþólskt kvæðahandrit með hendi siðbótarmanns,
  Gísla biskups Jónssonar." *Gripla* 16 (2005): 209–28, esp. pp. 219–20.
– "Helgubók." In *Góssið hans Árna: Minningar heimsins í íslenskum
  handritum.* Ed. Jóhanna Katrín Friðriksdóttir (Reykjavík: Stofnun Árna
  Magnússonar í íslenskum fræðum, 2014). Pp. 21–35, esp. p. 30.
Mogk, Eugen. >> *Geschichte der norwegisch-isländischen Literatur* (1904).
  P. 719.

Paasche, Fredrik. >> *Kristendom og kvad* (1914). Pp. 35 and 44.

Schottmann, Hans. >> *Die isländische Mariendichtung* (1973). Pp. 384–5, 394, and 485.

Vésteinn Ólason. "Kveðskapur frá síðmiðöldum." In >> *Íslensk Bókmenntasaga* 2 (1993). Pp. 283–378, esp. pp. 306 and 318–20.

NOTE:

The poem contains material about Saints Ambrose, Augustine, Gregory the Great, Isidore of Seville, and John the Baptist. See the entries for the individual saints.

NICHOLAS   December 6

1. Nikulásdrápa

A fragment of a thirteenth-century poem in honour of Saint Nicholas. Incipit: "Ǫll þing boða engla."

Manuscript:

AM 242 fol. (*Codex Wormianus*) (ca. 1350).

Editions:

Björn Magnússon Ólsen, ed. *Den Tredje og Fjærde Grammatiske Afhandling i Snorres Edda Tilligemed de Grammatiske Afhandlingers Prolog og To Andre Tillæg.* STUAGNL 12 (Copenhagen: Knudtzon, 1884). P. 129.

Finnur Jónsson, ed. >> *Den norsk-islandske skjaldedigtning* (1912–15). Vol. AII, p. 160 and vol. BII, pp. 174–5.

Jón Sigurðsson et al., ed. *Edda Snorra Sturlusonar: Edda Snorronis Sturlaei.* 3 vols. (Copenhagen: Legatum Arnamagnaeanum, 1848–87; rpt. Osnabrück: Zeller, 1966). Vol. 2, p. 208.

Kock, Ernst Albin, ed. >> *Notationes Norrœnæ* (1923–44). §2334.

– ed. >> *Den norsk-isländska skaldediktningen* (1946–50). Vol. 2, pp. 91–2.

Sigurður Nordal, ed. *Codex Wormianus (The Younger Edda). MS No. 242 fol. in The Arnamagnean Collection in the University Library of Copenhagen.* CCI 2 (Copenhagen: Levin and Munksgaard, 1931). Facsimile.

Danish translation:

Finnur Jónsson, ed. >> *Den norsk-islandske skjaldedigtning* (1912–15). Vol. BII, pp. 174–5.

Latin translation:
Jón Sigurðsson et al., ed. *Edda Snorra Sturlusonar: Edda Snorronis Sturlaei.*
  3 vols. (Copenhagen: Legatum Arnamagnaeanum, 1848–87; rpt. Osnabrück:
  Zeller 1966). Vol. 2, pp. 209 and 211.
Literature:
Carpenter, William H., ed. *Nikolásdrápa Halls prests: An Icelandic Poem
  from circa A.D. 1400* (Halle: Karras, 1881). Pp. 7–8.
Cormack, Margaret. >> *The Saints in Iceland* (1994). Pp. 42 and 137.
Finnur Jónsson. >> *Den oldnorske og oldislandske Litteraturs Historie*
  (1920–4). Vol. 2, p. 122.
Foote, Peter, ed. *Lives of Saints. Perg. fol. nr. 2 in the Royal Library,
  Stockholm.* EIM 4 (Copenhagen: Rosenkilde and Bagger, 1962). P. 21.
Guðrún Nordal. *Tools of Literacy: The Role of Skaldic Verse in Icelandic
  Textual Culture of the Twelfth and Thirteenth Centuries* (Toronto:
  University of Toronto Press, 2001). Pp. 87, 256, and 258.
– "Helgubók." In *Góssið hans Árna: Minningar heimsins í íslenskum
  handritum.* Ed. Jóhanna Katrín Friðriksdóttir (Reykjavík: Stofnun Árna
  Magnússonar í íslenskum fræðum, 2014). Pp. 21–35, esp. p. 30.
Jakob Benediktsson. >> "Helgikvæði." In *Hugtök og heiti í bókmenntafræði*
  (1983). Pp. 115–17, esp. p. 116.
Jón Þorkelsson. >> *Om Digtningen på Island* (1888). P. 81.
Mogk, Eugen. >> *Geschichte der norwegisch-isländischen Literatur* (1904).
  P. 719.
Stéfan Einarsson. "Íslenzk helgikvæði á miðöldum." *Tímarit Þjóðræknisfélags
  Íslendinga* 36 (1955): 43–63, esp. p. 46.
– *Íslensk bókmenntasaga 874–1960* (Reykjavík: Oddi, 1961). P. 83.
Sverrir Tómasson, "Íslenskar Nikulás sögur." In *Helgastaðabók. Nikulás
  saga. Perg. 4to nr. 16 Konungsbókhlöðu í Stokkhólmi.* Introduction
  by Selma Jónsdóttir, Stefán Karlsson, and Sverrir Tómasson. Íslensk
  miðaldahandrit: Manuscripta Islandica medii aevi 2 (Reykjavík: Lögberg,
  1982). Pp. 11–41, esp. p. 25n9.
Vesteinn Ólason. "Old Icelandic Poetry." In *A History of Icelandic Literature.*
  Ed. Daisy Neijmann. Histories of Scandinavian Literature 5 (Lincoln:
  University of Nebraska Press, 2006). Pp. 1–64, esp. p. 48.

2. Nikulásvísur I

A short poem in honour of Saint Nicholas composed between 1300 and 1550.
  Incipit: "Nikulám skulu vér heiðra hér."

Manuscripts:
AM 640 4to (ca. 1450–1500) and JS 399a–b 4to (ca. 1700–1900).
Editions:
Jón Helgason, ed. >> *Íslenzk miðaldakvæði* (1936–8). Vol. 2, pp. 402–3.
   Edition of AM 640 4to.
Stéfan Einarsson. "Íslenzk helgikvæði á miðöldum." *Tímarit Þjóðræknisfélags*
   Íslendinga 36 (1955): 43–63, esp. pp. 58–9.
Sverrir Tómasson. "'Bið fyrir mér dandikall.' Ærlækjarbók." In *Góssið hans*
   Árna: Minningar heimsins í íslenskum handritum. Ed. Jóhanna Katrín
   Friðriksdóttir (Reykjavík: Stofnun Árna Magnússonar í íslenskum fræðum,
   2014). Pp. 63–77, esp. p. 68.
   Facsimile of AM 640 4to, fol. 56v.
Literature:
Finnur Jónsson. >> *Den oldnorske og oldislandske Litteraturs Historie*
   (1920–4). Vol. 3, p. 126.
Foote, Peter, ed. *Lives of Saints. Perg. fol. nr. 2 in the Royal Library,*
   Stockholm. EIM 4 (Copenhagen: Rosenkilde and Bagger, 1962). P. 21.
Hálfdan Einarsson. *Sciagraphia historiæ literariæ islandicæ* (Copenhagen:
   Sander and Schröder, 1777). P. 58.
Jakob Benediktsson. "Helgendigte." *KLNM* 6 (1961). Cols. 318–21, esp.
   col. 320.
Jón Helgason. >> "Norges og Islands digtning." In *Litteraturhistorie B:*
   Norge og Island (1953). Pp. 3–179, esp. pp. 163–4.
Jón Þorkelsson. >> *Om Digtningen på Island* (1888). P. 25.
Sigfús Blöndal. "St. Nikulás og dýrkun hans, sérstaklega á Íslandi." *Skírnir*
   123 (1949): 69–97, esp. p. 81.
Sverrir Tómasson, "Íslenskar Nikulás sögur." In *Helgastaðabók. Nikulás*
   saga. Perg. 4to nr. 16 Konungsbókhlöðu í Stokkhólmi. Introduction
   by Selma Jónsdóttir, Stefán Karlsson, and Sverrir Tómasson. Íslensk
   miðaldahandrit: Manuscripta Islandica medii aevi 2 (Reykjavík: Lögberg,
   1982). Pp. 11–41, esp. p. 25n9.
– "Erlendur vísdómur og forn fræði." In >> *Íslensk Bókmenntasaga* 1 (1992).
   Pp. 519–71, esp. p. 566.
– "'Nikulám skulu vér heiðra hér …'." In >> *Til heiðurs og hugbótar* (2003).
   Pp. 79–92, esp. p. 91.
Sverrir Tómasson, Bragi Halldórsson, and Einar Sigurbjörnsson, ed. *Heilagra*
   karla sögur. Íslensk trúarrit 3 (Reykjavík: Bókmenntafræðistofnun Háskóla
   Íslands, 2007). P. lvii.

Vésteinn Ólason. "Kveðskapur frá síðmiðöldum." In >> *Íslensk Bókmenntasaga* 2 (1993). Pp. 283–378, esp. p. 317.

3. Nikulásvísur II

A fragment of a poem in honour of Saint Nicholas from ca. 1400–1550. Incipit: "Engla guð sá allt má vinna."

Manuscripts:
Lbs 2166 4to (ca. 1885–1920) and Stock. Perg. 4to no. 16 (ca. 1375–1400).
Editions:
Jón Helgason, ed. >> *Íslenzk miðaldakvæði* (1936–8). Vol. 2, pp. 403–5.
Edition of Stock. Perg. 4to no. 16.
Jón Þorkelsson, ed. *Småstykker 1–16* (Copenhagen: Møller, 1884–91).
Pp. 293–6.
Edition of Stock. Perg. 4to no. 16.
Literature:
Finnur Jónsson. >> *Den oldnorske og oldislandske Litteraturs Historie*
(1920–4). Vol. 3, p. 126.
Foote, Peter, ed. *Lives of Saints. Perg. fol. nr. 2 in the Royal Library,
Stockholm.* EIM 4 (Copenhagen: Rosenkilde and Bagger, 1962). P. 21.
Hálfdan Einarsson. *Sciagraphia historiæ literariæ islandicæ* (Copenhagen:
Sander and Schröder, 1777). P. 58.
Jakob Benediktsson. "Helgendigte." *KLNM* 6 (1961). Cols. 318–21, esp.
col. 320.
Jón Helgason. >> "Norges og Islands digtning." In *Litteraturhistorie B:
Norge og Island* (1953). Pp. 3–179, esp. pp. 163–4.
Jón Torfason and Kristján Eiríksson, ed. >> *Vísnabók Guðbrands* (2000).
P. xxxix.
Sigfús Blöndal. "St. Nikulás og dýrkun hans, sérstaklega á Íslandi." *Skírnir*
123 (1949): 69–97, esp. p. 81.
Sverrir Tómasson. "Íslenskar Nikulás sögur." In *Helgastaðabók. Nikulás
saga. Perg. 4to nr. 16 Konungsbókhlöðu í Stokkhólmi.* Introduction
by Selma Jónsdóttir, Stefán Karlsson, and Sverrir Tómasson. Íslensk
miðaldahandrit: Manuscripta Islandica medii aevi 2 (Reykjavík: Lögberg,
1982). Pp. 11–41, esp. p. 25n9.
Vésteinn Ólason. "Kveðskapur frá síðmiðöldum." In >> *Íslensk Bókmenntasaga*
2 (1993). Pp. 283–378, esp. p. 317.

4. Nikulásdiktur

A late medieval (ca. 1400–1550) poem in honour of Saint Nicholas.
Incipit: "Dyrdar fullr drottinn minn dugi þú mér."

Manuscripts:
A: AM 710a 4to (ca. 1700–25), AM 721 4to (ca. 1500–50), JS 581 4to
   (ca. 1600–1900), Lbs 2166 4to (ca. 1885–1920), Lbs 201 8vo (ca. 1850–70);
B: AM 717a 4to (ca. 1700–25), AM 717h 4to (ca. 1650–1700), AM 150 8vo
   (ca. 1650–1700); BLAdd 4892 (ca. 1700–1800), BLAdd 11.179 (ca. 1700–
   1800), Bor 6 (20647) (ca. 1700–1800), ÍB 36 4to (ca. 1750–1800), JS
   256 4to (1840–5), JS 260 4to (1796), JS 514 4to (1865–6), JS 581 4to
   (ca. 1600–1900), JS 112 8vo (ca. 1700–1800), JS 487 8vo (ca. 1675–1900),
   JS 494 8vo (ca. 1675–1900), Lbs 512 4to (ca. 1700–50), Lbs 936 4to
   (ca. 1880), Lbs 953 4to (ca. 1760), Lbs 2166 4to (ca. 1885–1920), Lbs 754
   8vo (ca. 1700–1900), and Stock. Papp. fol. no. 64 (ca. 1650–1700).

Editions:
Carpenter, William H., ed. *Nikolásdrápa Halls prests: An Icelandic Poem
   from circa A.D. 1400* (Halle: Karras, 1881). P. 6 (stz. 1 only).
   Edition of AM 721 4to.
Jón Helgason, ed. >> *Íslenzk miðaldakvæði* (1936–8). Vol. 2, pp. 408–13.
   Based on AM 721 4to with variants from AM 150 8vo, AM 717a 4to, and
   AM 717h 4to.
Jón Þorkelsson. >> *Om Digtningen på Island* (1888). P. 81 (stz. 1).
   Based on AM 710a 4to, AM 717a 4to, AM 717h 4to, AM 721 4to, Bor 6
   (20647), ÍB 36 4to, JS 260 4to, Lbs 201 8vo, and Stock. Papp. fol. no. 64.

Literature:
Anon. "Den Oldnordisk-islandske Afdeling." Annual Report for 1846.
   Antiquarisk Tidsskrift 1846–8 (Copenhagen: Sally B. Salomon, 1847).
   Pp. 39–49, esp. p. 41.
Finnur Jónsson. >> *Den oldnorske og oldislandske Litteraturs Historie*
   (1920–4). Vol. 3, p. 126.
Foote, Peter, ed. *Lives of Saints. Perg. fol. nr. 2 in the Royal Library,
   Stockholm.* EIM 4 (Copenhagen: Rosenkilde and Bagger, 1962). P. 21.
Hálfdan Einarsson. *Sciagraphia historiæ literariæ islandicæ* (Copenhagen:
   Sander and Schröder, 1777). P. 58.
Jakob Benediktsson. "Helgendigte." *KLNM* 6 (1961). Cols. 318–21, esp.
   col. 320.
Jón Helgason. >> "Norges og Islands digtning." In *Litteraturhistorie B:
   Norge og Island* (1953). Pp. 3–179, esp. pp. 163–4.

Jón Þorkelsson. "Islandske håndskrifter i England og Skotland." *ANF* 8 (1892): 199–237, esp. p. 205.

Kock, E.A. "Anteckningar till Íslenzk Miðaldakvæði." *ANF* 61 (1946): 1–125, esp. pp. 103–4.

Sigfús Blöndal. "St. Nikulás og dýrkun hans, sérstaklega á Íslandi." *Skírnir* 123 (1949): 69–97, esp. p. 81.

Sverrir Tómasson. "Íslenskar Nikulás sögur." In *Helgastaðabók. Nikulás saga. Perg. 4to nr. 16 Konungsbókhlöðu í Stokkhólmi.* Introduction by Selma Jónsdóttir, Stefán Karlsson, and Sverrir Tómasson. Íslensk miðaldahandrit: Manuscripta Islandica medii aevi 2 (Reykjavík: Lögberg, 1982). Pp. 11–41, esp. p. 25n9.

Vésteinn Ólason. "Kveðskapur frá síðmiðöldum." In >> *Íslensk Bókmenntasaga* 2 (1993). Pp. 283–378, esp. p. 317.

5. Nikulásdrápa

An early sixteenth-century poem in honour of Saint Nicholas ascribed to the priest Hallur Ögmundarson (d. ca. 1540).

Incipit: "Í nafni guðs vil ég upphaf efna."

Manuscripts:
Adv 21.8.14 (ca. 1750–75), AM 622 4to (ca. 1549), AM 710e 4to (ca. 1700–25), BLAdd 11.191 (ca. 1750–1800), Bor 102 (20743) (ca. 1800), JS 260 4to (1796), JS 399a–b 4to (ca. 1700–1900), JS 581 4to (ca. 1600–1900), JS 514 8vo (ca. 1675–1900), Lbs 444 4to (ca. 1820–50), and Lbs 201 8vo (ca. 1850–70).

Editions:
Carpenter, William H., ed. *Nikolásdrápa Halls prests: An Icelandic Poem from circa A.D. 1400* (Halle: Karras, 1881). Pp. 13–32.
    Edition of AM 622 4to.

Jón Helgason, ed. >> *Íslenzk miðaldakvæði* (1936–8). Vol. 2, pp. 417–33.
    Based on AM 622 4to with variants from Adv 21.8.14 and JS 399a–b 4to.

Jón Þorkelsson, ed. >> *Kvæðasafn* (1922–7). Pp. 385–405.
    Edition of AM 622 4to.

Literature:
Anon. "Den Oldnordisk-islandske Afdeling." Annual Report for 1847. *Antiquarisk Tidsskrift* 1846–8 (Copenhagen: Sally B. Salomon, 1847). Pp. 154–72, esp. p. 165.

Ármann Jakobsson. "The Homer of the North, or: Who Was Sigurður the Blind?" *European Journal of Scandinavian Studies* 44 (2014): 4–19, esp. p. 5.

Björn K. Þórólfsson, "Kvantitetsomvæltningen i islandsk." *ANF* 45 (1929): 35–81, esp. pp. 40, 42, and 44.

Faulkes, Anthony. "Edda." *Gripla* 2 (1977): 32–9, esp. p. 34n11.

Finnur Jónsson. >> *Bókmentasaga Íslendinga fram undir siðabót* (1904–5). P. 463.

– >> *Den oldnorske og oldislandske Litteraturs Historie* (1920–4). Vol. 3, p. 128.

Foote, Peter, ed. *Lives of Saints. Perg. fol. nr. 2 in the Royal Library, Stockholm.* EIM 4 (Copenhagen: Rosenkilde and Bagger, 1962). P. 21.

Guðrún Nordal. "Handrit, prentaðar bækur og pápísk kvæði á siðskiptaöld." In >> *Til heiðurs og hugbótar* (2003). Pp. 131–43, esp. pp. 140–1.

– "Á mörkum tveggja tíma: Kaþólskt kvæðahandrit með hendi siðbótarmanns, Gísla biskups Jónssonar." *Gripla* 16 (2005): 209–28, esp. pp. 219–20.

Jakob Benediktsson. "Helgendigte." *KLNM* 6 (1961). Cols. 318–21, esp. cols. 319–20.

Finnur Jónsson. >> *Den oldnorske og oldislandske Litteraturs Historie* (1920–4). Vol. 3, p. 126.

Jón Þorkelsson. >> *Om Digtningen på Island* (1888). Pp. 315–16 and 319.

Páll Eggert Ólason. *Menn og menntir siðskiptaaldarinnar á Íslandi.* Vol. 2 (Reykjavík: Guðm. Gamalíelsson, 1922). P. 119.

Schottmann, Hans. >> *Die isländische Mariendichtung* (1973). Pp. 54n19, 206–7, and 485.

Sigfús Blöndal. "St. Nikulás og dýrkun hans, sérstaklega á Íslandi." *Skírnir* 123 (1949): 69–97, esp. pp. 75–6, 81, and 84.

Sverrir Tómasson, "Íslenskar Nikulás sögur." In *Helgastaðabók. Nikulás saga. Perg. 4to nr. 16 Konungsbókhlöðu í Stokkhólmi.* Introduction by Selma Jónsdóttir, Stefán Karlsson, and Sverrir Tómasson. Íslensk miðaldahandrit: Manuscripta Islandica medii aevi 2 (Reykjavík: Lögberg, 1982). Pp. 11–41, esp. p. 25n9.

Vésteinn Ólason. "Kveðskapur frá síðmiðöldum." In >> *Íslensk Bókmenntasaga* 2 (1993). Pp. 283–378, esp. pp. 301, 306, and 317.

NOTE:

The poem contains material about Saints Augustine, Elizabeth, Eugenia, John the Baptist, and Zachariah. See the entries for the individual saints.

NICODEMUS   August 31

1. Gimsteinn

An early sixteenth-century poem about the cross-tree ascribed to the priest Hallur Ögmundarson (d. ca. 1540). Stz. 64 mentions Saint Nicodemus.
   Incipit: "Heyr mig ilmanda hjartans yndi."

Manuscripts:
See Cross, the Holy 7 note (p. 73).
Editions
Jón Helgason, ed. >> *Íslenzk miðaldakvæði* (1936–8). Vol. 1.2, p. 318.
Jón Þorkelsson, ed. >> *Kvæðasafn* (1922–7). P. 312.

2. Niðurstigningsvísur

A poetic rendering of the story of Christ's descent to hell composed ca. 1525 by Bishop Jón Arason (1484–1550). Stz. 11 mentions Saint Nicodemus.
   Incipit: "Djarflig er mér diktan."

Manuscripts:
See Anne 13 note (p. 43).
Editions:
Finnur Jónsson, ed. >> *Jón Arasons religiøse digte* (1918). P. 61.
Jón Helgason, ed. >> *Íslenzk miðaldakvæði* (1936–8). Vol. 1.2, p. 225.
[Jón Sigurðsson and Guðbrandur Vigfússon, ed.] >> *Biskupa sögur* (1858–78).
   Vol. 2, p. 549.

OLAV OF NORWAY   July 29

1. Róðudrápa

An eleventh-century fragment of a poem by Þórðr Særeksson (Sjáreksson) commemorating the battle in Helgeå, where the allies Óláfr Haraldsson and the Swedish king Ǫnundr Óláfsson fought against King Canute the Great.
   Incipit: "Átti Egða dróttinn Ǫleifr þrimu stála."

Manuscripts (these include):
AM 35 fol. (ca. 1675–1700), AM 38 fol. (*Jöfraskinna*) (ca. 1675–1700), AM
   61 fol. (ca. 1400–50), AM 68 fol. (ca. 1300–50), AM 73a fol. (ca. 1700),

AM 75c fol. (ca. 1325), AM 303 4to (ca. 1675–1700), AM 321 4to
(ca. 1650–1700), AM 325 4to V (ca. 1300–20), AM 325 4to VII (ca. 1250–
1300), AM 325 2 4to IX (ca. 1300–25), AM 325 1 4to XI (ca. 1300–25),
DG 8 (ca. 1225–50), GKS 1005 fol. (*Flateyjarbók*) (ca. 1387–95), GKS
1008 fol. (*Tómasskinna*) (ca. 1400–1500), Lbs fragm 82 fol. (ca. 1260),
Stock. Perg. 4to no. 2 (ca. 1250–1450), Stock. Perg. fol. no. 1 (*Bergsbók*)
(ca. 1400–25), Stock. Perg. 4to no. 4 (ca. 1320–40), and Thott 972 fol.
(ca. 1700).

Editions (these include):

Bjarni Aðalbjarnarson, ed. >> *Heimskringla* (1941–51). Vol. 2, p. 281.
   Manuscripts used are AM 35 fol., AM 36 fol., AM 37 fol., AM 38 fol.,
   AM 39 fol., AM 42 fol., AM 45 fol., AM 47 fol., AM 63 fol., AM 66 fol.,
   AM 70 fol., AM 325 1 4to VIII, AM 325 1 4to XI, AM 325 2 4to IX, AM
   1056 4to, GKS 1010 fol., Stock. Papp. fol. no. 18, Stock. Perg. fol. no. 1,
   Stock. Perg. fol. no. 9 II, Stock. Perg. fol. no. 18, Stock. Perg. 4to no. 2,
   and UppsUB R 685.

Bjarni Einarsson, ed. *Ágrip af Nóregs konunga sǫgum. Fagrskinna – Nóregs
   konungatal.* Íslenzk fornrit 29 (Reykjavík: Hið íslenzka fornritafélag,
   1985). P. 187.
   Edition of OsloUB 371 with emendations and supplements from AM 51
   fol., AM 52 fol., AM 301 4to, AM 302 4to, AM 303 4to, and NRA 51.

Finnur Jónsson, ed. >> *Heimskringla* (1893–1900). Vol. 2, p. 366.
   Edition of AM 35 fol., AM 36 fol., AM 37 fol., AM 38 fol., AM 63 fol.,
   and AM 325 1 4to XI with variants from AM 37 fol., AM 38 fol., AM 39
   fol., AM 45 fol., AM 47 fol., AM 70 fol., AM 325 1 4to VIII, AM 325 2 4to
   IX, AM 325 1 4to XI, Lbs fragm 82, OsloUB 521 fol., Stock. Papp. fol. no.
   18, Stock. Perg. fol. no. 9 II, and Stock. Perg. 4to no. 36 II.

Finnur Jónsson, ed. *De bevarede Brudstykker af Skindbøgerne Kringla og
   Jöfraskinna i fototypisk gengivelse.* STUAGNL 24 (Copenhagen: Møller,
   1895).
   Facsimile of AM 35 fol., AM 36 fol., AM 38 fol., and AM 63 fol.

– ed. *Fagrskinna: Nóregs kononga tal.* STUAGNL 30 (Copenhagen: Møller,
   1902–3). P. 165.
   Edition of AM 303 4to, NRA 51, and OsloUB 371 fol. with variants from
   AM 51 fol., AM 52 fol., AM 301 4to, AM 302 4to, and AM 303 4to.

– ed. *Snorri Sturluson: Heimskringla. Nóregs konunga sǫgur* (Copenhagen:
   Gad, 1911; rpt. Oslo: Universitetsforlaget, 1966). P. 345.
   Edition of AM 35 fol., AM 36 fol., AM 37 fol., AM 38 fol., AM 39 fol.,
   AM 45 fol., and AM 63 fol.

– ed >> *Den norsk-islandske skjaldedigtning* (1912–15). Vol. AI, p. 329 and
   vol. BI, p. 303.

Edition of AM 35 fol. with variants from AM 38 fol., AM 61 fol., AM 68 fol., AM 73a fol., AM 75c fol., AM 303 4to, AM 325 4to V, AM 325 4to VII, AM 325 2 4to IX, AM 325 1 4to XI, DG 8, GKS 1005 fol., GKS 1008 fol., and Stock. Perg. fol. no. 1.

– ed. *Flateyjarbók (Codex Flateyensis): MS no. 1005 fol. in the Old Royal Collection in the Royal Library of Copenhagen.* CCI 1 (Copenhagen: Levin and Munksgaard, 1930).

Facsimile of GKS 1005 fol.

Gade, Kari Ellen, ed. "*Róðudrápa.*" In >> *Poetry from the Kings' Sagas 1* (2012). Vol. 1, p. 243.

Edition of Lbs fragm 82 with variants from AM 35 fol., AM 38 fol., AM 61 fol., AM 68 fol., AM 73a fol., AM 75c fol., AM 303 4to, AM 321 4to, AM 325 4to V, AM 325 4to VII, AM 325 2 4to IX, AM 325 1 4to XI, DG 8, GKS 1005 fol., GKS 1008 fol., Stock. Perg. fol. no. 1, and Stock. Perg. 4to no. 4.

Gudbrand Vigfusson and C.R. Unger, ed. >> *Flateyjarbók* (1860–8). Vol. 2, p. 281.

Edition of GKS 1005 fol.

Heinrichs, Anne, Doris Janshen, Elke Radicke, and Harmut Röhn, ed. *Olafs saga hins helga. Die "Legendarishe Saga" über Olaf den Heiligen (Hs. Delagard. saml. nr 8*^{II}*)* (Heidelberg: Carl Winter Universitätsverlag, 1982). P. 146.

Edition of DG 8.

Holtsmark, Anne, ed. *Legendarisk Olavssaga.* CCN, Quarto serie 2 (Oslo: Selskabet til utgivelse av gamle norske håndskrifter, 1956).

Facsimile of DG 8.

Johnsen, Oscar Albert, ed. *Olafs saga hins helga efter pergamenthåndskrift i Uppsala Universitetsbibliotek, Delagardieske samling nr. 8*^{II}. Det norske historiske kildeskriftfond skrifter 47 (Kristiania [Oslo]: Dybwad, 1922). P. 61.

Edition of DG 8.

Johnsen, Oscar Albert, and Jón Helgason, ed. *Saga Óláfs konungs hins helga* (1941). Vol. 1, p. 438.

Edition of Stock. Perg. 4to no. 2 with emendations and variants from Stock. Perg. fol. no. 1, AM 61 fol., AM 68 fol., AM 71 fol., AM 73a fol., AM 73b fol., AM 75a fol., AM 75b fol., AM 75c fol., AM 75e 1 fol., AM 75 e 2 fol., AM 75 e 3 fol., AM 75e 4 fol., AM 76a fol., AM 325 fol. VI, AM 321 4to, AM 325 4to V, AM 325 4to VII, AM 325 2 a 4to, AM 325 2 b 4to XI, AM 325 2 c 4to XI, AM 325 2 d 4to XI, AM 325 2 e 4to XI, AM 325 2 f 4to XI, AM 325 2 g 4to XI, AM 325 2 h 4to XI, AM 325 2 i 4to XI, AM 325 2 k 4to XI, AM 325 2 l 4to XI, AM 325 2 m 4to XI, AM 325 2 n

4to XI, AM 325 2 o 4to XI, AM 325 2 p 4to XI, AM 325 3 4to XI, AM 904
4to, AM 921 4to II, BLAdd 11.242, GKS 1005 fol., GKS 1008 fol., Stock.
Perg. fol. no. 1, and Stock. Perg. 4to no. 4.

Keyser, R., and C.R. Unger, ed. *Óláfs saga hins Helga. En kort Saga om
Kong Olaf den Hellige fra anden Halvdeel af det tolfte Aarhundrede*
(Christiania [Oslo]: Feilberg and Landmark, 1849. P. 50.
Edition of DG 8.

Kock, Ernst Albin, ed. >> *Den norsk-isländska skaldediktningen* (1946–50).
Vol.1, p. 154.

Lindblad, Gustaf, ed. *Bergsbók. Perg. Fol. nr. 1 in the Royal Library,
Stockholm*. EIM 5 (Copenhagen: Rosenkilde and Bagger, 1963).
Facsimile of Stock. Perg. fol. no. 1.

Loth, Agnete, ed. *Thomasskinna. Gl. Kgl. Saml. 1008 fol. in The Royal
Library, Copenhagen*. EIM 6 (Copenhagen: Rosenkilde and Bagger, 1964).
Facsimile of GKS 1008 fol.

Munch, P.A., and C.R. Unger, ed. *Fagrskinna. Kortfattet norsk Konge-Saga*
(Christiania [Oslo]: Malling, 1847). P. 82.
Edition of AM 303 4to with variants from AM 51 fol., AM 52 fol., AM 301
4to, AM 302 4to, and NRA 51.

Munch, P.A. and C.R. Unger, ed. *Saga Olafs konungs ens helga. Udförligere
saga om kong Olaf den hellige* (Christiania [Oslo]: Carl C. Werner, 1853).
P. 165.
Edition of Stock. Perg. 4to no. 4.

Schöning, Gerhard, et al., ed. *Heimskringla edr Noregs konunga-sögur af Snorra
Sturlusyni*. 3 vols. (Copenhagen: Stein, 1777–1826). Vol. 2, pp. 272–3.
Edition of GKS 1005 fol.

Sigurður Nordal et al., ed. *Flateyjarbók*. 4 vols. (Akranes: Flateyjarútgáfan,
1944–5). Vol. 2, p. 385.
Edition of GKS 1005 fol.

Unger, C.R., ed. *Heimskringla eller Norges Kongesagaer af Snorre
Sturlassøn* (Christiania [Oslo]: Brøgger and Christie, 1868). P. 422.
Edition of AM 35 fol., AM 36 fol., AM 37 fol., AM 38 fol., AM 45 fol.,
and AM 47 fol.

Modern Icelandic language edition:

Bergljót Kristjánsdóttir, Bragi Halldórsson, Jón Torfason, and Örnólfur
Thorsson, ed. *Heimskringla*. 3 vols. (Reykjavík: Mál og menning, 1991).
Vol. 2, p. 457.

Danish translations:

Finnur Jónsson, ed. >> *Den norsk-islandske skjaldedigtning* (1912–15).
Vol. BI, p. 303.

Schöning, Gerhard, et al., ed. *Heimskringla edr Noregs konunga-sögur af Snorra Sturlusyni.* 3 vols. (Copenhagen: Stein, 1777–1826). Vol. 2, pp. 272–3.

English translations:

Finlay, Alison, and Anthony Faulkes, trans. *Snorri Sturluson: Heimskringla.* Vol. 2. *Óláfr Haraldsson (the Saint)* (University College London: Viking Society for Northern Research, 2014). P. 189.

Gade Kari Ellen, ed. "*Róðudrápa.*" In >> *Poetry from the Kings' Sagas 1* (2012). Vol. 1, p. 243.

Hollander, Lee M., trans. *Heimskringla: History of the Kings of Norway by Snorri Sturluson.* The American-Scandinavian Foundation (Austin: University of Texas Press, 1964). Pp. 442–3.

Scholz, Joyce, and Paul Schach. *The Legendary Saga of King Olaf Haraldsson. Including Fragments from the Oldest Saga of Olaf the Saint.* Ed. Susanne M. Arthur and Kirsten Wolf. WITS 2, no. 14 (Madison: Department of Scandinavian Studies University of Wisconsin–Madison, 2014). P. 68.

German translations:

Heinrichs, Anne, Doris Janshen, Elke Radicke, and Harmut Röhn, ed. *Olafs saga hins helga. Die "Legendarishe Saga" über Olaf den Heiligen (Hs. Delagard. saml. nr 8^{II})* (Heidelberg: Carl Winter Universitätsverlag, 1982). P. 147.

Hube, Hans-Jürgen, trans. *Snorri Sturluson "Heimskringla": Sagen der nordischen Könige* (Wiesbaden: Marix Verlag, 2006). P. 383.

Niedner, Felix, trans. *Snorris Köningsbuch (Heimskringla).* Thule: Altnordische Dichtung und Prosa 2, Reihe 14–16. 3 vols. (Jena: Diedrichs, 1922–3). Vol. 2, p. 285.

Latin translation:

Schöning, Gerhard, et al., ed. *Heimskringla edr Noregs konunga-sögur af Snorra Sturlusyni.* 3 vols. (Copenhagen: Stein, 1777–1826). Vol. 2, p. 272.

Norwegian translations:

Aall, Jacob, trans. *Snorre Sturlesons norske kongers sagaer.* 2 vols. (Christiania [Oslo]: Guldberg and Dzwonkowski, 1838–9). Vol. 1, p. 308.

Steinar Schjøtt, Hallvard Magerøy, Halvdan Koht, Gunnar Pedersen, and Kr. Audne, trans. *Norges konge soger.* Ed. Finn Hødnebø and Hallvard Magerøy. 4 vols. (Oslo: Det Norske Samlaget, 1979). Vol. 2, p. 48.

Literature:

Bjarni Þorsteinsson, ed. *Íslenzk þjóðlög* (Copenhagen: Møller, 1906–9). P. 125.

Fidjestøl, Bjarne. "'Have You Heard a Poem Worth More?' A Note on the Economic Background of Early Skaldic Praise-Poetry." In Bjarne Fidjestøl.

Selected Papers. Ed. Odd Einar Haugen and Else Mundal. Trans. Peter
Foote. Viking Collection 9 (Odense: Odense University Press, 1997).
Pp. 117–32, esp. pp. 125–6.

Finnur Jónsson. >> *Den oldnorske og oldislandske Litteraturs Historie*
(1920–4). Vol. 1, pp. 603–4.

Mogk, Eugen. >> *Geschichte der norwegisch-isländischen Literatur* (1904).
P. 686.

Vries, Jan de. >> *Altnordische Literaturgeschichte* (1964–7). Vol. 1, p. 260.

2. Erfidrápa Óláfs helga

A poem in praise of King and Saint Óláfr Haraldsson by Sighvatr Þórðarson
(d. ca. 1045).

Incipit: "Tólf frák tekna elfar tálaust viðu bála."

Manuscripts (these include):

AM 36 fol. (ca. 1675–1700), AM 38 fol. (*Jöfraskinna*) (ca. 1675–1700),
  AM 39 fol. (ca. 1300), AM 45 fol. (*Codex Frisianus*) (ca. 1300–25), AM
  47 fol. (*Eirspennill*) (ca. 1300–25), AM 61 fol. (ca. 1400–50), AM 63
  fol. (ca. 1675–1700), AM 68 fol. (ca. 1300–50), AM 73a fol. (ca. 1700),
  AM 75c fol. (ca. 1325), AM 75e 4 fol. (ca. 1350–1400), AM 242 fol.
  (*Codex Wormianus*) (ca. 1350), AM 321 4to (ca. 1650–1700), AM 325
  4to V (ca. 1300–20), AM 325 4to VI (ca. 1350–1400), AM 325 4to VII
  (ca. 1250–1300), AM 325 2 g 4to XI (ca. 1300), AM 325 2 n 4to XI
  (1275–1300), AM 748b 4to I (ca. 1300–25), AM 761b 4to (ca. 1600–25),
  DG 11 (*Codex Upsaliensis*) (ca. 1300–25), GKS 1005 fol. (*Flateyjarbók*)
  (ca. 1387–95), GKS 1008 fol. (*Tómasskinna*) (ca. 1400–1500), GKS 2367
  4to (*Codex Regius*) (ca. 1300–50), GKS 2368 4to (ca. 1600–1700), Lbs
  fragm 82 fol. (ca. 1260), Stock. Papp. fol. no. 18 (ca. 1650–1700), Stock.
  Perg. fol. no. 1 (*Bergsbók*) (ca. 1400–25), Stock. Perg. 4to no. 2 (ca. 1250–
  1450), Stock. Perg. 4to no. 4 (ca. 1320–40), Thott 972 fol. (ca. 1700), Traj
  1374 (*Codex Trajectinus*) (ca. 1595), and UppsUB R 686 (ca. 1600–1700).

Editions (these include):

Bjarni Aðalbjarnarson, ed. >> *Heimskringla* (1941–51). Vol. 2, pp. 267–8,
  329–30, 366–7, 377, 379–84, 386, 393–4, 406, 409–10 and vol. 3, pp. 20–1.
  Manuscripts used are AM 35 fol., AM 36 fol., AM 37 fol., AM 38 fol., AM
  39 fol., AM 42 fol., AM 45 fol., AM 47 fol., AM 63 fol., AM 66 fol., AM
  70 fol., AM 325 1 4to VIII, AM 325 1 4to XI, AM 325 2 4to IX, AM 1056
  4to, GKS 1010 fol, Stock. Papp. fol. no. 18, Stock. Perg. fol. no. 1, Stock.
  Perg. fol. no. 9 II, Stock. Perg. fol. no. 18, Stock. Perg. 4to no. 2, and
  UppsUB R 685.

Björn Magnússon Ólsen, ed. *Den tredje og fjærde grammatiske Afhandling i Snorres Edda tilligemed de grammatisker Afhandlingers Prolog og to andre Tillæg*. STUAGNL 12 (Copenhagen: Knudtzon, 1884). P. 90.
Edition of AM 748b 4to with variants from AM 242 fol., AM 757b 4to, and AM 757a 4to.

Eeden, Willem van, Jr, ed. *De Codex Trajectinus van de Snorra Edda* (Leiden: Eduard Ijdo, 1913). P. 111.
Edition of Traj 1374.

Faulkes, Anthony, ed. *Edda Magnúsar Ólafssonar (Laufás Edda)*. Vol. 1 of *Two Versions of Snorra Edda from the 17th Century* (Reykjavík: Stofnun Árna Magnússonar, 1977–9). P. 365.
Edition of AM 758b 4to I with reconstructions of the lacunae and variants from AM 164 8vo, Stock. Papp. 4to no. 10, and Thott 1494 4to.

– ed. *Codex Trajectinus: The Utrech Manuscript of the Prose Edda*. EIM 15 (Copenhagen: Rosenkilde and Bagger, 1985).
Facsimile of Traj 1374.

– ed. *Snorri Sturluson: Edda. Skáldskaparmál*. 2 vols. (University College London: Viking Society for Northern Research, 1998). Vol. 1, pp. 77–8 (stz. 28).
Edition of GKS 2367 4to with emendations and variants from AM 242 fol., AM 748v 4to I, AM 748 4to II, AM 757a 4to, DG 11, and Traj 1374.

Finnur Jónsson, ed. *Codex Frisianus. En Samling af norske Konge-Sagaer* (Christiania [Oslo]: Malling, 1871). P. 174.
Edition of AM 45 fol.

– ed. >> *Heimskringla* (1893–1900). Vol. 2, pp. 347, 421–32, 469–70, 485, 488–95, 504–5, 519, 522–3, vol. 3, pp. 22–3, and vol. 4, pp. 141, 159–60, 165–71, 173–4, 176–7, and 186–7.
Edition of AM 35 fol., AM 36 fol., AM 37 fol., AM 38 fol., AM 63 fol., and AM 325 1 4to XI with variants from AM 37 fol., AM 38 fol., AM 39 fol., AM 45 fol., AM 47 fol., AM 70 fol., AM 325 1 4to VIII, AM 325 2 4to IX, AM 325 1 4to XI, Lbs fragm 82, OsloUB 521 fol., Stock. Papp. fol. no. 18, Stock. Perg. fol. no. 9 II, and Stock. Perg. 4to no. 36 II.

– ed. *De bevarede Brudstykker af Skindbøgerne Kringla og Jöfraskinna i fototypisk gengivelse*. STUAGNL 24 (Copenhagen: Møller, 1895).
Facsimile of AM 35 fol., AM 36 fol., AM 38 fol., and AM 63 fol.

– ed. *Snorri Sturluson: Heimskringla. Nóregs konunga sǫgur* (Copenhagen: Gad, 1911; rpt. Oslo: Universitetsforlaget, 1966). Pp. 338, 371, 392–3, 399–403, 407, 416, and 428.
Edition of AM 35 fol., AM 36 fol., AM 37 fol., AM 38 fol., AM 39 fol. AM 45 fol., and AM 63 fol.

– ed. >> *Den norsk-islandske skjaldedigtning* (1912–15). Vol. AI, pp. 257–65 and vol. BI, pp. 239–45.

Stz. 1: edition of UppsUB R 686 with variants from Johann Peringskiöld's edition (*Heims Kringla, eller Snorre Sturlusons Nordländske konunga sagor*, 2 vols. [Stockholm: Literis Wankiwianis, 1697]); stz. 2: based on Gudgrand Vigfusson and C.R. Unger's edition of *Flateyjarbók* (1860–8); stz. 3: edition of AM 36 fol. with variants from AM 38 fol., AM 68 fol., AM 61 fol., AM 73a fol., AM 75c fol., AM 325 4to V, AM 325 4to VII, GKS 1005 fol., GKS 1008 fol. Stock. Perg. fol. no. 1, Stock. Perg. 4to no. 2, and Stock. Perg. 4to no. 4; stz. 4–5: edition of AM 36 fol. with variants from AM 38 fol., AM 61 fol., AM 68 fol., AM 73a fol., AM 325 4to V, AM 325 4to VII, AM 325 2 g 4to XI, GKS 1005 fol., GKS 1008 fol., Stock. Perg. fol. no. 1, Stock. Perg. 4to no. 2, and Stock. Perg. 4to no. 4; stz. 6: edition of AM 36 fol. with variants from AM 61 fol., AM 68 fol., AM 73a fol., AM 325 fol. V, AM 325 fol. VII, AM 325 2 g 4to XI, GKS 1005 fol., GKS 1008 fol., Stock. Perg. fol. no. 1, Stock. Perg. 4to no. 2, and Stock. Perg. 4to no. 4; stz. 7: edition of AM 36 fol. with variants from AM 38 fol., AM 61 fol., AM 68 fol., AM 73a fol., AM 75c 4 fol., AM 325 fol. V, AM 325 fol. VII, GKS 1005 fol., GKS 1008 fol., Stock. Perg. fol. no. 1, Stock. Perg. 4to no. 2, and Stock. Perg. 4to no. 4; stz. 8: edition of AM 36 fol. with variants from AM 38 fol., AM 61 fol., AM 68 fol., AM 73a fol., AM 325 fol. V, AM 325 fol. VII, GKS 1005 fol., GKS 1008 fol., Stock. Perg. fol. no. 1, Stock. Perg. 4to no. 2, and Stock. Perg. 4to no. 4; stz. 9: edition of AM 36 fol. with variants from AM 38 fol., AM 61 fol., AM 325 fol. VIII, GKS 1005 fol., GKS 1008 fol., Stock. Perg. fol. no. 1, Stock. Perg. 4to no. 2, and Stock. Perg. 4to no. 4; stz. 10–11: edition of AM 36 fol. with variants from AM 38 fol., AM 61 fol., AM 73a fol., AM 325 4to V, AM 325 4to VII, GKS 1005 fol., GKS 1008 fol., Stock. Perg. 4to no. 2, and Stock. Perg. 4to no. 4; stz. 12–13: edition of AM 36 fol. with variants from AM 38 fol., AM 61 fol., AM 325 4to V, AM 325 4to VII, GKS 1005 fol., GKS 1008 fol., Stock. Perg. 4to no. 2, and Stock. Perg. 4to no. 4; stz. 14: edition of AM 36 fol. with variants from AM 38 fol., AM 61 fol., AM 73a fol., AM 325 4to V, AM 325 4to VII, GKS 1005 fol., GKS 1008 fol., Stock. Perg. 4to no. 2, and Stock. Perg. 4to no. 4; stz. 15: edition of AM 36 fol. with variants from AM 38 fol., AM 61 fol., AM 73a fol., AM 242 fol., AM 325 4to V, AM 325 4to VII, GKS 1005 fol., GKS 1008 fol., Stock. Perg. 4to no. 2, and Stock. Perg. 4to no. 4; stz. 16–17: edition of AM 36 fol. with variants from AM 38 fol., AM 61fol., AM 73a fol., AM 325 4to V, AM 325 4to VII, GKS 1005 fol., GKS 1008 fol., Stock. Perg. 4to no. 2, and Stock. Perg. 4to no. 4; stz. 18–20: edition of AM 36 fol. with variants from AM 38 fol., AM 61 fol., AM 73a fol., AM 325 4to V, AM 325 4to VII, GKS 1005 fol., GKS 1008 fol., Stock. Perg. fol. no. 1, Stock. Perg. 4to no. 2, and Stock. Perg. 4to no. 4; stz. 21–2: edition of AM 36 fol. with variants from AM 38 fol., AM 61 fol., AM 73a fol., AM 325 4to V, AM 325 4to VII, GKS 1005 fol., GKS 1008 fol., Stock. Perg. fol. no. 1, and Stock. Perg. 4to no. 2; stz. 23: edition of AM 36 fol. with variants from AM 39 fol., AM 61 fol., AM 73a fol., AM 325 4toV, AM 325 4to VI, GKS 1005 fol., GKS 1008 fol., Stock. Perg. fol. no. 1, Stock. Perg. 4to no. 2, and Stock. Perg. 4to no. 4; stz. 24–5: edition of AM 36 fol. with variants from AM 38 fol., AM 39 fol., AM 45 fol., AM 47 fol., AM 61 fol., AM 73a fol., AM 325 4to V, AM 325 4to VI, AM 325 4to VII, AM 468 4to, GKS 1005 fol., GKS 1008 fol., Stock. Perg. fol. no. 1, Stock. Perg. 4to no. 2, and Stock. Perg. 4to no. 4; stz. 26: edition of AM 242 fol. with variants from AM 748b 4to I; stz. 27: edition of AM 325 4to V with variants from AM 61 fol., AM 73a fol., AM 325 4to VI, AM 325 4to VII, GKS 1005 fol., GKS 1008 fol., Stock. Perg. fol. no. 1, Stock. Perg. 4to no. 2, and Stock. Perg. 4to no. 4; stz. 28: edition of GKS 2367 4to with variants from AM 242 fol., AM 748b 4to I, DG 11, and Traj 1374.

– ed. *Eirspennill – Am 47 fol. – Nóregs konunga sǫgur. Magnús góði – Hákon gamli* (Christiania [Oslo]: Den Norske historiske kildeskriftskommission, 1916). P. 14.
Edition of AM 47 fol.

– ed. *Edda Snorra Sturlusonar: Codex Wormianus AM 242, fol.* (Copenhagen and Kristiania [Oslo]: Gyldendal, 1924). P. 85.
Edition of AM 242 fol.

– ed. *Óláfr Þórðarson: Málhljóða- og málskrúðsrit: Grammatisk-retorisk afhandling*. Det kgl. Danske Videnskabernes Selskab. Historisk-filologiske Meddelelser 13.2 (Copenhagen: Høst, 1927). P. 65.
Edition of AM 748 4to with variants from AM 242 fol. and AM 757 4to.

– ed. *Flateyjarbók (Codex Flateyensis): MS no. 1005 fol. in the Old Royal Collection in the Royal Library of Copenhagen*. CCI 1 (Copenhagen: Levin and Munksgaard, 1930).
Facsimile of GKS 1005 fol.

– ed. *Edda Snorra Sturlusonar* (Copenhagen: Gyldendal, 1931). P. 159.
Edition of GKS 2367 4to with variants from AM 242 fol., AM 748b 4to I, AM 748 4to II, AM 757a 4to, DG 11, and Traj 1374.

Gudbrand Vigfusson and C.R. Unger, ed. >> *Flateyjarbók* (1860–8). Vol. 2, pp. 68, 275, 316, 346, 352, 354–7, 366, 371, 374, 376, and 379.
Edition of GKS 1005 fol.

Gudbrand Vigfússon and F. York Powell, ed. *Corpus Poeticum Boreale: The Poetry of the Old Northern Tongue from the Earliest Times to the Thirteenth Century*. 2 vols. (Oxford: Clarendon Press, 1883). Vol. 2, pp. 138–42.
Edition of Stock. Perg. fol. no. 1 with emendations from GKS 1005 fol.

Halldór Hermannsson, ed. *Codex Frisianus (Sagas of the Kings of Norway)*. CCI 4 (Copenhagen: Levin and Munksgaard, 1932).
Facsimile of AM 45 fol.

Heimir Pálsson, ed. >> *Snorri Sturluson. The Uppsala Edda* (2012). P. 192.
Edition of DG 11.

Jesch, Judith, ed. "*Erfidrápa Óláfs helga*." In >> *Poetry from the Kings' Sagas 1* (2012). Vol. 1, pp. 665–97.
Stz. 1: edition of UppsUB R 686 with variants from Johann Peringskiöld's edition (*Heims Kringla, eller Snorre Sturlusons Nordländske konunga sagor,* 2 vols. [Stockholm: Literis Wankiwianis, 1697]); stz. 2: edition of GKS 1005 fol. with variants from AM 761b 4to; stz. 3: edition of AM 36 fol. with variants from AM 38 fol., AM 61 fol., AM 68 fol., AM 73a fol., AM 73b fol., AM 75c fol., AM 321 4to, AM 325 4to V, AM 325 4to VII, GKS 1005 fol., GKS 1008 fol., Stock. Perg. 4to no. 2, and Stock. Perg. 4to no. 4; stz. 4: edition of AM 36 fol. with variants from AM 38 fol., AM 61 fol., AM 68 fol., AM 73a fol., AM 321 4to, AM 325 4to V, AM 325 4to VII, AM 325 2 g 4to XI, GKS 1005 fol., GKS 1008 fol., Stock. Papp. fol. no. 18, Stock. Perg. fol. no. 1, Stock. Perg. 4to no. 2, and Stock. Perg. 4to no. 4; stz. 5: edition of AM 36 fol. with variants from AM 61 fol., AM 68 fol., AM 73a fol., AM 321 4to, AM 325 4to V, AM 325 4to VII, AM 325 2 g 4to XI, GKS 1005 fol., GKS 1008 fol., Stock. Perg. fol. no. 1, Stock. Perg. 4to no. 2, and Stock. Perg. 4to no. 4; stz. 6: edition of AM 36 fol. with variants from AM 61 fol., AM 68 fol., AM 73a fol., AM 321 4to, AM 325 4to V, AM 325 4to VII, AM 325 2 g 4to XI, GKS 1005 fol., GKS 1008 fol., Stock. Perg. fol. no. 1, Stock. Perg. 4to no. 2, and Stock. Perg. 4to no. 4; stz. 7: edition of AM 36 fol. with variants from AM 38 fol., AM 61 fol., AM 68 fol., AM 73a fol., AM 75e 4 fol., AM 325 4to V, AM 325 4to VII, GKS 1005 fol., GKS 1008 fol., Stock. Perg. fol. no. 1, Stock. Perg. 4to no. 2, and Stock. Perg. 4to no. 4; stz. 8: edition of AM 36 fol. with variants from AM 38 fol., AM 61 fol., AM 68 fol., AM 73a fol., AM 325 4to V, AM 325 4to VII, GKS 1005 fol., GKS 1008 fol., Stock. Perg. fol. no. 1, Stock. Perg. 4to no. 2, and Stock. Perg. 4to no. 4; stz. 9: edition of AM 36 fol. with variants from AM 38 fol., AM 61 fol., AM 321 4to, AM 325 4to VII, GKS 1005 fol., GKS 1008 fol., Stock. Perg. fol. no. 1, Stock. Perg. 4to no. 2, and Stock. Perg. 4to no. 4; stz. 10: edition of AM 36 fol. with variants from AM 38 fol., AM 61 fol., AM 73a fol., AM 321 4to, AM 325 4to V,

AM 325 4to VII, GKS 1005 fol., GKS 1008 fol., Stock. Perg. 4to no. 2, and Stock. Perg. 4to no. 4; stz. 11: edition of AM 36 fol. with variants from AM 38 fol., AM 73a fol., AM 321 4to, AM 325 4to V, AM 325 4to VII, GKS 1005 fol., GKS 1008 fol., Stock. Perg. 4to no. 2, and Stock. Perg. 4to no. 4; stz. 12–14: edition of AM 36 fol. with variants from AM 38 fol., AM 61 fol., AM 321 4to, AM 325 4to V, AM 325 4to VII, GKS 1005 fol., GKS 1008 fol., Stock. Perg. 4to no. 2, and Stock. Perg. 4to no. 4; stz. 15: edition of AM 36 fol. with variants from AM 38 fol., AM 61 fol., AM 73a fol., AM 242 fol., AM 325 4to V, AM 325 4to VII, GKS 1005 fol., GKS 1008 fol., Stock. Perg. 4to no. 2, and Stock. Perg. 4to no. 4; stz. 16: edition of AM 36 fol. with variants from AM 38 fol., AM 61 fol., AM 73a fol., AM 321 4to, AM 625 4to V, AM 625 4to VII, GKS 1005 fol., GKS 1008 fol., Stock. Perg. 4to no. 2, and Stock. Perg. 4to no. 4; stz. 17: edition of AM 36 fol. with variants form AM 38 fol., AM 61 fol., AM 73a fol., AM 325 4to V, AM 325 4to VII, GKS 1005 fol., GKS 1008 fol., Stock. Perg. 4to no. 2, and Stock. Perg. 4to no. 4; stz. 18: edition of AM 36 fol. with variants from AM 38 fol., AM 73a fol., AM 321 4to, AM 325 4to V, AM 325 4to VII, GKS 1005 fol., GKS 1008 fol., Stock. Perg. fol. no. 1, Stock. Perg. 4to no. 2, and Stock. Perg. 4to no. 4; stz 19: edition of AM 36 fol. with variants from AM 38 fol., AM 61 fol., AM 73a fol., AM 321 4to, AM 325 4to V, AM 325 4to VII, GKS 1005 fol., GKS 1008 fol., Stock. Perg. fol. no. 1, and Stock. Perg. 4to no. 4; stz. 20: edition of AM 36 fol. with variants from AM 38 fol., AM 61 fol., AM 73a fol., AM 321 4to, AM 325 4to V, AM 325 4to VII, GKS 1005 fol., GKS 1008 fol. Stock. Perg. fol. no. 1, Stock. Perg. 4to no. 2, and Stock. Perg. 4to no. 4; stz. 21–2: edition of AM 36 fol. with variants from AM 61 fol., AM 73a fol., AM 321 4to, AM 325 4to V, AM 325 4to VI, AM 325 4to VII, AM 325 2 g 4to XI, GKS 1005 fol., GKS 1008 fol., Stock. Perg. fol. no 1, and Stock. Perg. 4to no. 2; stz. 23: edition of AM 36 fol. with variants from AM 39 fol., AM 61 fol., AM 73a fol., AM 32 4to, AM 325 4to V, AM 325 4to VI, GKS 1005 fol., GKS 1008 fol., Stock. Perg. fol. no. 1, Stock. Perg. 4to no. 2, and Stock. Perg. 4to no. 4; stz. 24: edition of AM 63 fol. with variants from AM 38 fol., AM 45 fol., AM 47 fol., AM 61 fol., AM 73a fol., AM 321 4to, AM 325 4to V, AM 325 4to VI, AM 325 4to VII, GKS 1005 fol., GKS 1008 fol., Stock. Perg. fol. no. 1, Stock. Perg. 4to no. 2, and Stock. Perg. 4to no. 4; stz. 25: edition of AM 63 fol. with variants from AM 38 fol., AM 39 fol., AM 45 fol., AM 47 fol., AM 61 fol., AM 73a fol., AM 321 4to, AM 325 4to V, AM 325 4to VI, AM 325 4to VII, GKS 1005 fol., GKS 1008 fol., Stock. Perg. fol. no. 1, Stock. Perg. 4to no. 2, and Stock. Perg. 4to no. 4; stz. 26: edition of AM 748b 4to I with variants from AM 242 fol.; stz. 27: edition of Stock. Perg. 4to no. 2 with variants from AM 61 fol., AM 73a fol., AM 321 4to, AM 325 4to V, AM 325 4to VI, GKS 1005 fol., GKS 1008 fol., Stock. Perg. fol. no. 1, and Stock. Perg. 4to no. 4; stz. 28: edition of GKS 2367 4to with variants from AM 242 fol., AM 748b 4to I, DG 11, GKS 2368 4to, and Traj 1374.

Johnsen, Oscar Albert, and Jón Helgason, ed. >> *Saga Óláfs konungs hins helga* (1941). Vol. 1, pp. 422, 501–2, 553–4, 567, 569–75, 586–7, 603, 609, and 616–17, and vol. 2, pp. 768 and 1086.
Edition of Stock. Perg. 4to no. 2 with emendations and variants from Stock. Perg. fol. no. 1, AM 61 fol., AM 68 fol., AM 71 fol., AM 73a fol., AM 73b fol., AM 75a fol., AM 75b fol., AM 75c fol., AM 75e 1 fol., AM 75 e 2 fol., AM 75 e 3 fol., AM 75e 4 fol., AM 76a fol., AM 325 fol. VI, AM 321 4to, AM 325 4to V, AM 325 4to VII, AM 325 2 a 4to XI, AM 325 2 b 4to XI, AM 325 2 c 4to XI, AM 325 2 d 4to XI, AM 325 2 e 4to XI, AM 325 2 f 4to XI, AM 325 2 g 4to XI, AM 325 2 h 4to XI, AM 325 2 i 4to XI, AM 325 2 k 4to XI, AM 325 2 l 4to XI, AM 325 2 m 4to XI, AM 325 2 n 4to XI, AM 325 2 o 4to XI, AM 325 2 p 4to XI, AM 325 3 4to XI, AM 904 4to, AM 921 4to II, BLAdd 11.242, GKS 1005 fol., GKS 1008 fol., Stock. Perg. fol. no. 1, and Stock. Perg. 4to no. 4.

Jón Helgason, ed. *Skjaldevers*. Nordisk filologi. Tekster og lærebøger til universitetsbrug. A: Tekster (Copenhagen: Ejnar Munksgaard; Oslo: Dreyers forlag; Stockholm: Svenska Bokförlaget, 1968). P. 49.

Jón Sigurðsson et al., ed. *Edda Snorra Sturlusonar: Edda Snorronis Sturlaei*. 3 vols. (Copenhagen: Legatum Arnamagnaeanum, 1848–87, rpt. Osnabrüch: Zeller, 1966). Vol. 1, p. 450 and vol. 2, pp. 140, 497, 334, and 445.
Stz. 15: edition of AM 242 fol.; stz. 26: edition of AM 748b 4to with variants from AM 242 fol., AM 757b 4to, and AM 757a 4to; stz. 28: edition of DG 11 and edition of GKS 3267 4to with variants from AM 748b 4to I and UppsUB R 686.

Jón Skaptason. "Material for an Edition and Translation of the Poems of Sighvat Þórðarson." PhD dissertation, State University of New York at Stony Brook, 1983. Pp. 156–82.
Edition of UppsUB R 686 with variants and emendations from Johann Peringskiöld's edition (*Heims Kringla, eller Snorre Sturlusons Nordländske konunga sagor*, 2 vols. [Stockholm: Literis Wankiwianis, 1697]) and Thott 972 fol.; stz. 2: edition (with corrections) of GKS 1005 fol.; stz. 3: edition of AM 36 fol. with variants and emendations from AM 38 fol., AM 61 fol., AM 68 fol., AM 73a fol., AM 75c fol., AM 321 4to, AM 325 4to V, AM 325 4to VII, GKS 1005 fol., GKS 1008 fol., Stock. Perg. fol. no. 1, Stock. Perg. 4to no. 2, and Stock. Perg. 4to no. 4; stz. 4: edition of AM 36 fol. with variants and emendations from AM 38 fol., AM 61 fol., AM 68 fol.,

AM 73a fol., AM 321 4to, AM 325 4to V, AM 325 4to VII, AM 325 2 g 4to XI, GKS 1005 fol., GKS 1008 fol., Stock. Perg. fol. no. 1, Stock. Perg. 4to no. 2, and Stock. Perg. 4to no. 4; stz. 5: edition of AM 36 fol. with variants and emendations from AM 61 fol., AM 68 fol., AM 73a fol., AM 321 4to, AM 325 4to V, AM 325 4to VII, AM 325 2 g 4to XI, GKS 1005 fol., GKS 1008 fol., Stock. Perg. fol. no. 1, Stock. Perg. 4to no. 2, and Stock. Perg. 4to no. 4; stz. 6: edition of AM 36 fol. with variants and emendations from AM 61 fol., AM 68 fol., AM 73a fol., AM 321 4to, AM 325 4to V, AM 325 4to VII, AM 325 2 g 4to XI, GKS 1005 fol., GKS 1008 fol., Stock. Perg. fol. no. 1, Stock. Perg. 4to no. 2, and Stock. Perg. 4to no. 4; stz. 7: edition of AM 36 fol. with variants and emendations from AM 38 fol., AM 61 fol., AM 68 fol., AM 73a fol., AM 75e 4 fol., AM 325 4to V, AM 325 4to VII, GKS 1005 fol., GKS 1008 fol., Stock. Perg. fol. no. 1, and Stock. Perg. 4to no. 2; stz. 8: edition of AM 36 fol. with variants and emendations from AM 38 fol., AM 61 fol., AM 68 fol., AM 73a fol., AM 75e 4 fol., AM 325 4to V, AM 325 4to VII, GKS 1005 fol., GKS 1008 fol., Stock. Perg. fol. no. 1, Stock. Perg. 4to no. 2, and Stock. Perg. 4to no. 4; stz. 9: edition of AM 36 fol. with variants and emendations from AM 38 fol., AM 61 fol., AM 321 4to, AM 325 4to VII, GKS 1005 fol., GKS 1008 fol., Stock. Perg. 4to no. 2, and Stock. Perg. 4to no. 4; stz. 10–11: edition of AM 36 fol. with variants and emendations from AM 38 fol., AM 61 fol., AM 73a fol., AM 321 4to, AM 325 4to V, AM 325 4to VII, GKS 1005 fol., GKS 1008 fol., Stock. Perg. 4to no. 2, and Stock. Perg. 4to no. 4; stz. 12: edition of AM 36 fol. with variants and emendations from AM 61 fol., AM 321 4to, AM 325 4to V, AM 325 4to VII, GKS 1005 fol., GKS 1008 fol., Stock. Perg. 4to no. 2, and Stock. Perg. 4to no. 4; stz. 13: edition of AM 36 fol. with variants and emendations from AM 38 fol., AM 61 fol., AM 321 4to, AM 325 4to V, AM 325 4to VII, GKS 1005 fol., GKS 1008 fol., Stock. Perg. 4to no. 2, and Stock. Perg. 4to no. 4; stz. 14: edition of AM 36 fol. with variants and emendations from AM 38 fol., AM 61 fol., AM 73a fol., AM 321 4to, AM 325 4to V, AM 325 4to VII, GKS 1005 fol., GKS 1008 fol., Stock. Perg. 4to no. 2, and Stock. Perg. 4to no. 4; stz. 15: edition of AM 36 fol. with variants and emendations from AM 38 fol., AM 61 fol., AM 73a fol., AM 242 fol., AM 321 4to, AM 325 4to V, AM 325 4to VII, GKS 1005 fol., GKS 1008 fol., Stock. Perg. 4to no. 2, and Stock. Perg. 4to no. 4; stz. 16: edition of AM 36 fol. with variants and emendations from AM 38 fol., AM 61 fol., AM 321 4to, AM 325 4to VII, GKS 1005 fol., GKS 1008 fol., and Stock. Perg. 4to no. 2; stz. 17: edition of AM 36 fol. with variants and emendations from AM 38 fol., AM 61 fol., AM 73a fol., AM 321 4to, AM 325 4to V, AM 325 4to VII, GKS 1005 fol., GKS 1008 fol., Stock. Perg.

4to no. 2, and Stock. Perg. 4to no. 4; stz. 18–20: edition of AM 36 fol. with variants and emendations from AM 38 fol., AM 61 fol., AM 73a fol., AM 321 4to, AM 325 4to V, AM 325 4to VII, GKS 1005 fol., GKS 1008 fol., Stock. Perg. fol. no. 1, Stock. Perg. 4to no. 2, and Stock. Perg. 4to no. 4; stz. 21: edition of AM 36 fol. with variants and emendations from AM 38 fol., AM 61 fol., AM 73a fol., AM 321 4to, AM 325 4to V, AM 325 4to VI, AM 325 4to VII, AM 325 2 n 4to XI, GKS 1005 fol., GKS 1008 fol., Stock. Perg. fol. no. 1, and Stock. Perg. 4to no. 2; stz. 22: edition of AM 36 fol. with variants and emendations from AM 61 fol., AM 38 fol., AM 73a fol., AM 321 4to, AM 325 4to V, AM 325 4to VI, AM 325 4toVII, AM 325 2 n 4to XI, GKS 1005 fol., GKS 1008 fol., Stock. Perg. fol. no. 1, and Stock. Perg. 4to no. 2; stz. 23: edition of AM 36 fol. with variants and emendations from AM 39 fol., AM 61 fol., AM 73a fol., AM 321 4to, AM 325 4to V, AM 325 4to VI, GKS 1005 fol., GKS 1008 fol., Stock. Perg. fol. no. 1, Stock. Perg. 4to no. 2, and Stock. Perg. 4to no. 4; stz. 24: edition of AM 36 fol. with variants and emendations from AM 38 fol., AM 39 fol., AM 45 fol., AM 47 fol., AM 61 fol., AM 73a fol., AM 321 4to, AM 325 4to V, AM 325 4to VI, AM 325 4to VII, GKS 1005 fol., GKS 1008 fol., Stock. Perg. fol. no. 1, Stock. Perg. 4to no. 2, and Stock. Perg. 4to no. 4; stz. 25: edition of AM 36 fol. with variants and emendations from AM 38 fol., AM 39 fol., AM 47 fol., AM 61 fol., AM 73a fol., AM 321 4to, AM 325 4to V, AM 325 4to VI, AM 325 4to VII, GKS 1005 fol., GKS 1008 fol., Stock. Perg. fol. no. 1, Stock. Perg. 4to no. 2, and Stock. Perg. 4to no. 4; stz. 26: edition of AM 242 fol. with variants and emendations from AM 61 fol., AM 73a fol., AM 321 4to, AM 325 4to V, AM 325 4to VI, AM 325 4to VII, GKS 1005 fol., GKS 1008 fol., Stock. Perg. fol. no. 1, Stock. Perg. 4to no. 2, and Stock. Perg. 4to no. 4; stz. 27: edition of GKS 2367 4to with variants from AM 242 fol., AM 748b 4to I, Traj 1374, and UppsUB R 686; stz. 28: edition of GKS 2367 4to with variants and emendations from AM 242 fol. and AM 748b 4to I.

Kock, Ernst Albin. >> *Notationes Norrœna* (1923–44). §§620, 656, 657, 658, 659, 660, 661, 662, 663, 664, 665, 666, 667, 668, 819B, 826, 1115, 1116, 1117, 1118, 1121, 1825, 1853A, 1853F, 1870, 1871, 1879, 1936B, 1956, 2247A, 2261, 2312, 2478, 2479, 2480D, 2480E, 2777, 2988C, 3068, and 3069A.

Kock, Ernst Albin, ed. >> *Den norsk-isländska skaldediktningen* (1946–50). Vol. 1, pp. 124–7.

Krömmelbein, Thomas, ed. and trans. *Óláfr Þórðarson Hvítaskáld. Dritte grammatische Abhandlung*. Studia nordica 3 (Oslo: Novus, 1998). P. 172. Based on Björn Magnússon Ólsen's edition (1884).

Lindblad, Gustaf, ed. *Bergsbók. Perg. Fol. nr. 1 in the Royal Library, Stockholm.* EIM 5 (Copenhagen: Rosenkilde and Bagger, 1963). Facsimile of Stock. Perg. fol. no. 1.

Loth, Agnete, ed. *Thomasskinna. Gl. Kgl. Saml. 1008 fol. in The Royal Library, Copenhagen.* EIM 6 (Copenhagen: Rosenkilde and Bagger, 1964). Facsimile of GKS 1008 fol.

Munch, P.A., and C.R. Unger, ed. *Saga Olafs konungs ens helga. Udförligere saga om kong Olaf den hellige* (Christiania [Oslo]: Carl C. Werner, 1853). Pp. 190, 210, 215–19, 223, 230, 232–3, and 235–6. Edition of Stock. Perg. 4to no. 4.

Schöning, Gerhard, et al., ed. *Heimskringla edr Noregs konunga-sögur af Snorra Sturlusyni.* 3 vols. (Copenhagen: Stein, 1777–1826). Vol. 2, pp. 261, 316, 352, 363, 365–70, 378, 390–1, 393–4, and vol. 3, pp. 14–15. Edition of GKS 1005 fol.

Sigurður Nordal, ed. *Codex Wormianus (The Younger Edda). Ms No. 242 fol. in The Arnamagnean Collection in the University Library of Copenhagen.* CCI 2 (Copenhagen: Levin and Munksgaard, 1931). Facsimile of AM 242 fol.

Sigurður Nordal et al., ed. *Flateyjarbók.* 4 vols. (Akranes: Flateyjarútgáfan, 1944–5). Vol. 2, pp. 143, 377, 669, 424, 257–8, 465, 467–70, 480, 489, 492, and 494. Edition of GKS 1005 fol.

Unger, C.R., ed. *Heimskringla eller Norges Kongesagaer af Snorre Sturlassøn* (Christiania [Oslo]: Brøgger and Christie, 1868). Pp. 414, 453, 480, 488, 490–3, 499, 508, 510, and 523. Edition of AM 35 fol., AM 36 fol., AM 37 fol., AM 38 fol., AM 45 fol., and AM 47 fol.

Unger, C.R., and A.C. Drolsum, ed. *Codex Frisianus. En Samling af norske Konge-Sager.* Norske historiske kildeskriftfonds skrifter 9 (Christiania [Oslo]: Malling, [1869]–1871]. P. 174. Edition of AM 45 fol.

Wessén, Elias, ed. *Codex Regius of the Younger Edda. MS No. 2367 4to in the Old Royal Collection in the Royal Library of Copenhagen.* CCI 14 (Copenhagen: Einar Munksgaard, 1940). Facsimile of GKS 2368.

Modern Icelandic language editions:

Árni Björnsson, ed. *Snorra Edda* (Reykjavík: Iðunn, 1975). P. 207.

Bergljót Kristjánsdóttir, Bragi Halldórsson, Jón Torfason, and Örnólfur Thorsson, ed. *Heimskringla.* 3 vols. (Reykjavík: Mál og menning,1991). Vol. 2, pp. 447, 493, 520–1, 528–34, 540, 552, 549, and 568–9.

Danish translations:

Finnur Jónsson, ed. >> *Den norsk-islandske skjaldedigtning* (1912–15). Vol. BI, pp. 239–45.

Petersen, Sv. Aa. *Vikinger og vikingeaand: Sighvat Thordssøn og hans skjaldskab* (Copenhagen: Ejnar Munksgaard, 1946). Pp. 128–39.

Schöning, Gerhard, et al., ed. *Heimskringla edr Noregs konunga-sögur af Snorra Sturlusyni.* 3 vols. (Copenhagen: Stein, 1777–1826). Vol. 2, pp. 261, 316, 352, 363, 365–70, 378, 390–1, 393–4, and vol. 3, pp. 14–15.

English translations:

Faulkes, Anthony, trans. *Snorri Sturluson: Edda* (London: Dent, 1987). P. 127.

Finlay, Alison, and Anthony Faulkes, trans. *Snorri Sturluson: Heimskringla.* Vol. 2. *Óláfr Haraldsson (the Saint)* (University College London: Viking Society for Northern Research, 2014). Pp. 180, 221, 245, 252–7, 263, 271, and 271.

Gudbrand Vigfússon and F. York Powell, ed. *Corpus Poeticum Boreale: The Poetry of the Old Northern Tongue from the Earliest Times to the Thirteenth Century.* 2 vols. (Oxford: Clarendon Press, 1883). Vol. 2, pp. 138–42.

Heimir Pálsson, ed. >> *Snorri Sturluson. The Uppsala Edda* (2012). P. 194.

Hollander, Lee M., trans. *Heimskringla: History of the Kings of Norway by Snorri Sturluson.* The American-Scandinavian Foundation (Austin: University of Texas Press, 1964). Pp. 433–4, 475–6, 502–3, 511–16, 521, 530, 533, and 548.

– trans. *The Skalds: A Selection of Their Poems with Introduction and Notes* (Ann Arbor: University of Michigan Press, 1968). P. 175.

Jesch, Judith, ed. "*Erfidrápa Óláfs helga.*" In >> *Poetry from the Kings' Sagas 1* (2012). Vol. 1, pp. 665–97.

Jón Skaptason. "Material for an Edition and Translation of the Poems of Sighvat Þórðarson." PhD dissertation, State University of New York at Stony Brook, 1983. Pp. 156–82.

Laing, Samuel, trans. *Snorri Sturluson. Heimskringla: Sagas of the Norse Kings.* Rev. ed. Peter Foote (London: Dent, 1961). Vol 2, pp. 135–6.

– *Snorri Sturluson. Heimskringla: The Olaf Sagas.* Revised with an Introduction and Notes by Jacqueline Simpson. 2 vols. (London: Dent; New York: Dutton, 1964). Vol. 2, pp. 302, 339, 363–4, 372–5, 376, 381, 390, and 392.

Lindow, John. "St Olaf and the Skalds." In *Sanctity in the North: Saints, Lives, and Cults in Medieval Scandinavia.* Ed. Thomas A. DuBois (Toronto: University of Toronto Press, 2008). Pp. 103–27, esp. pp. 124–7.

German translations:

Hube, Hans-Jürgen, trans. *Snorri Sturluson "Heimskringla": Sagen der nordischen Könige* (Wiesbaden: Marix Verlag, 2006). Pp. 376, 410, 433, 439, 441–4, 449, 457–8, and 470.

Krause, Arnulf, trans. *Die Edda des Snorri Sturluson.* Reclams Universital-Bibliothek 782 (Stuttgart: Reclam, 1997). P. 192.

Krömmelbein, Thomas, ed. and trans. *Óláfr Þórðarson Hvítaskáld. Dritte grammatische Abhandlung.* Studia nordica 3 (Oslo: Novus, 1998). P. 172.

Niedner, Felix, trans. *Snorris Köningsbuch (Heimskringla).* Thule: Altnordische Dichtung und Prosa 2, Reihe 14–16. 3 vols. (Jena: Diedrichs, 1922–3). Vol. 2, pp. 273, 325–6, 359–60, 369, 371–5, 383, 394, 396–7, and vol. 3, p. 32.

Latin translations:

Jón Sigurðsson et al., ed. *Edda Snorra Sturlusonar: Edda Snorronis Sturlaei.* 3 vols. (Copenhagen: Legatum Arnamagnaeanum, 1848–87, rpt. Osnabrück: Zeller, 1966). Vol. 2, pp. 141 and 451.

Schöning, Gerhard, et al., ed. *Heimskringla edr Noregs konunga-sögur af Snorra Sturlusyni.* 3 vols. (Copenhagen: Stein, 1777–1826). Vol. 2, pp. 261, 316, 352, 363, 365–70, 378, 390–1, 393–4, and vol. 3, pp. 14–15.

Norwegian translations:

Aall, Jacob, trans. *Snorre Sturlesons norske kongers sagaer.* 2 vols. (Christiania [Oslo]: Guldberg and Dzwonkowski, 1838–9). Vol. 1, pp. 302, 329, 344–5, 350–3, 356, 361–2, and vol. 2, p. 8.

Flo, R.L. "Sigvat skald og hans samtid." *Syn og segn* 8 (1902): 178–90, esp. pp. 184–5.

Steinar Schjøtt, Hallvard Magerøy, Halvdan Koht, Gunnar Pedersen, and Kr. Audne, trans. *Norges konge soger.* Ed. Finn Hødnebø and Hallvard Magerøy. 4 vols. (Oslo: Det Norske Samlaget, 1979). Vol. 2, pp. 40, 75–6, 97, 103–6, 111, 117, 119, and 131.

Tveiten, Hallvard, trans. *Norrøne Skaldekvad. Frå norrønt i nynorsk gjendikting* (Oslo: J. Saabye, 1966). Pp. 94–7.

Literature:

Attwood, Katrina. "Christian Poetry." In *A Companion to Old Norse–Icelandic Literature and Culture.* Ed. Rory McTurk (Oxford: Blackwell, 2005). Pp. 43–63, esp. pp. 45–8 and 51.

Bekker-Nielsen, Hans, Thorkil Damsgaard Olsen, and Ole Widding. >> *Norrøn fortællekunst* (1965). P. 46.

Bjarni Þorsteinsson, ed. *Íslenzk þjóðlög* (Copenhagen: Møller, 1906–9). P. 125.

Chase, Martin. "*Concatenatio* as a Structural Element in the Christian *Drápur.*" In *The Sixth International Saga Conference 28/7–2/8 1985.*

280   Olav of Norway

Workshop Papers. 2 vols. ([Copenhagen]: Det arnamagnæanske Institut, 1985). Pp. 115–29, esp. p. 123.

– "Christian Poetry: West Norse." In >> *Medieval Scandinavia: An Encyclopedia* (1993). Pp. 73–6, esp. p. 74.

Clunies Ross, Margaret. >> *A History of Old Norse Poetry and Poetics* (2005). P. 49.

– "*Reginnaglar.*" In *News from Other Worlds: Studies in Nordic Folklore, Mythology and Culture in Honor of John F. Lindow*. Ed. Merrill Kaplan and Timothy R.Tangherlini (Berkeley: North Pinehurst Press, 2012). Pp. 3–21, esp. pp. 5 and 7.

Cormack, Margaret. >> *The Saints in Iceland* (1994). Pp. 142–3.

Cornell, Henrik. "Et bidrag til Liljas genesis." *Edda* 21 (1924): 140–4.

Edwards, Diana. "Christian and Pagan References in Eleventh-Century Norse Poetry: The Case of Arnórr Jarlaskáld." *Saga-Book* 21 (1982–3): 34–53, esp. pp. 34, 36, 39, and 43.

Fidjestøl, Bjarne. "Kongetruskap og gullets makt." *Mm* (1975): 4–11, esp. p. 10.

– "Pagan Beliefs and Christian Impact: The Contribution of Scaldic Studies." In *Viking Revaluations*. Ed. Anthony Faulkes and Richard Perkins (University College London: Viking Society for Northern Research, 1993). Pp. 100–20, esp. pp. 104–5, 109–11, and 116–17.

– "'Have You Heard a Poem Worth More?' A Note on the Economic Background of Early Skaldic Praise-Poetry." In Bjarne Fidjestøl. *Selected Papers*. Ed. Odd Einar Haugen and Else Mundal. Trans. Peter Foote. Viking Collection 9 (Odense: Odense University Press, 1997). Pp. 117–32, esp. p. 125.

Finnur Jónsson. "Kenningers ledomstilling og tmesis." *ANF* 59 (1933): 1–23, esp. p. 19.

– *Sigvat skjald Tordsson. Et Livsbillede*. Studier fra Sprog- og Oldtidsforskning udgivne af det Philologisk-Historiske Samfund 49 (Copenhagen: Kleins forlag, 1901). Pp. 29–30.

– >> *Den oldnorske og oldislandske Litteraturs Historie* (1920–4). Vol. 1, pp. 594–5.

Frank, Roberta. *Old Norse Court Poetry: The* Dróttkvætt *Stanza*. Islandica 42 (Ithaca: Cornell University Press, 1998). Pp. 129–30.

Friesen, Otto v. "Sighvat skald och solförmörkelsen år 1030." *Uppsala Universitets Årsskrift* 2 (1924): 1–16.

Gering, Hugo. "Beiträge zur Kritik und Erklärung skaldischer Dichtungen." *Zeitschrift für deutsche Philologie* 44 (1912): 133–48, esp. p. 146.

Guðrún Nordal. *Tools of Literacy: The Role of Skaldic Verse in Icelandic Textual Culture of the Twelfth and Thirteenth Centuries* (Toronto: University of Toronto Press, 2001). Pp. 383n47 and 387n69.

Heinrichs, Anne. "Óláfs saga helga." In >> *Medieval Scandinavia: An Encyclopedia* (1993). Pp. 447–8, esp. p. 447.

Hellberg, Staffan. "Om inskjutna satser i skaldediktningen." *Mm* (1981): 1–24, esp. pp. 16 and 19–20.

Hollander, Lee M. "Sigvat Thordson and His Poetry." *Scandinavian Studies* 16 (1940–1): 43– 67, esp. p. 66.

– "The Role of the Verb in Skaldic Poetry." *APS* 20 (1949): 267–76, esp. pp. 273–4.

Holm-Olsen, Ludvig, and Kjell Heggelund. *Norges Litteratur Historie. Fra Runene til Norske Selskab.* Ed. Edvard Beyer (Oslo: Cappelen, 1974). P. 244.

Holtsmark, Anne. "Sankt Olavs liv og mirakler." In *Festskrift til Francis Bull på 50 årsdagen* (Oslo: Gyldendal, 1937). Pp. 121–33, esp. pp. 122–3. Rpt. in Anne Holtsmark. *Studier i norrøn diktning* (Oslo: Gyldendal, 1956). Pp. 15–24, esp. p. 16.

– "Uppreistarsaga." *Mm* (1958): 93–7, esp. pp. 93 and 97.

– "Lovkvad." *KLNM* 10 (1965). Cols. 700–4, esp. col. 702.

– "Olavslegenden." *KLNM* 12 (1967). Cols. 584–8, esp. col. 585.

Jakob Benediktsson. "Religiøs digtning." *KLNM* 14 (1969). Cols. 37–40, esp. col. 37.

Jón Helgason. *Norrøn Litteraturhistorie* (Copenhagen: Levin and Munksgaard, 1934). Pp. 81 and 225.

– >> "Norges og Islands digtning." In *Litteraturhistorie B: Norge og Island* (1953). Pp. 3–179, esp. p. 124.

Jónas Kristjánsson. >> *Eddas and Sagas: Iceland's Medieval Literature* (1988). Pp. 106 and 308.

Kahle, Bernhard. *Die Sprache der Skalden auf Grund der Binnen- und Endreime* (Strassburg: Karl J. Trübner, 1892).

– "Das Christentum in der altwestnordischen Dichtung." *ANF* 13 (1901): 1–40 and 97–160, esp. p. 154.

Kristensen, Marius. "Skjaldenes mytologi." *APS* 5 (1930): 67–92, esp. p. 68.

Kuhn, Hans. *Das Dróttkvætt* (Heidelberg: Carl Winter Universitätsverlag, 1983). P. 301.

Lange, Wolfgang. >> *Studien zur christlichen Dichtung der Nordgermanen 1000–1200* (1958). Pp. 39, 62, 112, 119, and 139–41.

Lassen, Annette. "Øjets sprog: En undersøgelse af blikkets og blindhedens symbolværdi i den norrøne litteratur." *Mm* (2001): 113–34, esp. pp. 114–15.

Lie, Hallvard. "Skaldestil-studier." *Mm* (1952): 1–92, esp. p. 88n1.

– "Sigvatr Þórðarson." *KLNM* 15 (1970). Cols. 231–8, esp. col. 237.

Lindow, John. "Narrative and the Nature of Skaldic Poetry." *ANF* 97 (1982): 94–121, esp. pp. 97n15 and 101.

– "St Olaf and the Skalds." In *Sanctity in the North: Saints, Lives, and Cults in Medieval Scandinavia*. Ed. Thomas A. DuBois (Toronto: University of Toronto Press, 2008). Pp. 103–27, esp. pp. 117–21.

Mogk, Eugen. >> *Geschichte der norwegisch-isländischen Literatur* (1904). P. 683.

Naumann, Hans-Peter. "Nordische Kreuzzugsdichtung." In *Festschrift für Oskar Bandle: Zum 60. Geburtstag am 11. Januar 1986*. Ed. Hans-Peter Naumann with Magnus von Platen and Stefan Sonderegger. Beiträge zur nordischen Philologie 15 (Basel and Frankfurt am Main: Helbing and Lichtenhahn, 1986), Pp. 175–89, esp. p. 179.

Niedner, Felix. "Könige und Skalden in der Heimskringla." *Internationale Monatsschrift für Wissenschaft, Kunst und Technik* 14 (1920): 246–366, esp. pp. 344–55.

Noreen, Erik. *Studier i fornvästnordisk diktnning* 2. Uppsala Universitets Årsskrift 1922 (Uppsala: Akademiska bokhandeln, 1922). Pp. 21 and 23–5

Paasche, Fredrik. >> *Kristendom og kvad* (1914). Pp. 15, 21, 29–30, and 73.

– "Sigvat Tordssøn. Et skaldeportræt." *Edda* 8 (1917): 57–86.

– *Norges og Islands litteratur inntil utgangen av middelalderen*. Rev. ed. by Anne Holtsmark (Oslo: Aschehoug, 1947). Pp. 257–8.

Phelpstead, Carl. *Holy Vikings: Saints' Lives in the Old Icelandic Kings' Sagas* (Tempe, AZ: ACMRS, 2007). Pp. 20, 125, 127, and 154.

Piebenga, Gryt Anne. "Miracles, Collections of." In >> *Medieval Scandinavia: An Encyclopedia* (1993). Pp. 413–14, esp. p. 414.

Poole, Russell. "Sighvatr Þórðarson." In >> *Medieval Scandinavia: An Encyclopedia* (1993). Pp. 580–1, esp. p. 581.

– "The 'Conversion Verses' of Hallfreðr vandræðaskáld." *Mm* (2002): 15–37, esp. pp. 18–19 and 26.

See, Klaus von. "Skaldenstrophe und Sagaprosa. Ein Beitrag zum Problem der mündlichen Überlieferung in der altnordischen Literatur." *Mediaeval Scandinavia* 10 (1977): 58–82, esp. pp. 65–6

Sverrir Tómasson. "Kristnar trúarbókmenntir í óbundnu máli." In >> *Íslensk Bókmenntasaga* 1 (1992). Pp. 419–79, esp. p. 452.

Turville-Petre, G. *Origins of Icelandic Literature* (Oxford: Clarendon Press, 1967). Pp. 144–6.

– *Scaldic Poetry* (Oxford: Clarendon Press, 1976). Pp. 83–5.

Vésteinn Ólason. "Dróttkvæði." In >> *Íslensk Bókmenntasaga* 1 (1992). Pp. 191–262, esp. p. 219.

Vries, Jan de. "Über Arnórr Jarlaskáld." *ANF* 67 (1952): 156–75, esp. pp. 161–2.

– >> *Altnordische Literaturgeschichte* (1964–7). Vol. 1, pp. 99n1, 246–7, 255–8, and vol. 2, pp. 20–1 and 51.

3. Glælognskviða

An eleventh-century poem in praise of King and Saint Óláfr Haraldsson by
Þórarinn loftunga.
Incipit: "Þats dullaust, hvé Danir gerðu dyggva fǫr."

Manuscripts (these include):
AM 36 fol. (ca. 1675–1700), AM 39 fol. (ca. 1300), AM 47 fol. (*Eirspennill*)
(ca. 1300–25), AM 52 fol. (ca. 1675–1700), AM 61 fol. (ca. 1400–50), AM
63 fol. (ca. 1675–1700), AM 73a fol. (ca. 1700), AM 301 4to (ca. 1700),
AM 303 4to (*Fagrskinna*) (ca. 1675–1700), AM 321 4to (ca. 1650–1700),
AM 325 4to V (ca. 1300–20), AM 325 4to VI (ca. 1350–1400), AM 325
4to VII (ca. 1250–1300), AM 325 2 n 4to XI (ca. 1275–1300), GKS 1005
fol. (*Flateyjarbók*) (ca. 1387–95), GKS 1008 fol. (*Tómasskinna*) (ca. 1400–
1500), Oslo UB 371 fol. (1657–1707), Stock. Papp. fol. no. 64 (ca. 1650–
1700), Stock. Perg. fol. no. 1 (*Bergsbók*) (ca. 1400–25), Stock. Perg. fol.
no. 9 II (ca. 1300–25), Stock. Perg. 4to no. 2 (ca. 1250–1450), and Stock.
Perg. 4to no. 4 (ca. 1320–40).

Editions (these include):
Bjarni Aðalbjarnarson, ed. >> *Heimskringla* (1941–51). Vol. 2, pp. 399 and
406–8.
   Manuscripts used are AM 35 fol., AM 36 fol., AM 37 fol., AM 38 fol.,
   AM 39 fol., AM 42 fol., AM 45 fol., AM 47 fol., AM 63 fol., AM 66 fol.,
   AM 70 fol., AM 325 1 4to VIII, AM 325 1 4to XI, AM 325 2 4to IX, AM
   1056 4to, GKS 1010 fol., Stock. Papp. fol. no. 18, Stock. Perg. fol. no. 1,
   Stock. Perg. fol. no. 9 II, Stock. Perg. fol. no. 18, Stock. Perg. 4to no. 2,
   and UppsUB R 685.
Bjarni Einarsson, ed. *Ágrip af Nóregs konunga sǫgum. Fagrskinna–Nóregs
   konungatal.* Íslenzk fornrit 29 (Reykjavík: Hið íslenzka fornritafélag,
   1985). P. 201.
   Edition of OsloUB 371 with emendations and supplements from AM 51
   fol., AM 52 fol., AM 301 4to, AM 302 4to, AM 303 4to, and NRA 51.
Dietrich, Franz Eduard Christoph. *Altnordisches Lesebuch. Aus der
   skandinavischen Poesie und Prosa bis zum XIV. Jahrhundert* (Leipzig: F.A.
   Brockhaus, 1864). Cols. 69–70.
Finnur Jónsson, ed. *Heimskringla* (1893–1900). Vol. 2, pp. 520–1 and vol. 4,
   pp. 173–6.
   Edition of AM 35 fol., AM 36 fol., AM 37 fol., AM 38 fol., AM 63 fol.,
   and AM 325 1 4to XI with variants from AM 37 fol., AM 38 fol., AM 39
   fol., AM 45 fol., AM 47 fol., AM 70 fol., AM 325 1 4to VIII, AM 325 2 IX

4to, AM 325 1 4to XI, Lbs fragm 82, OsloUB 521 fol., Stock. Papp. fol. no. 18, Stock. Perg. fol. no. 9 II, and Stock. Perg. 4to no. 36 II.

– ed. *De bevarede Brudstykker af Skindbøgerne Kringla og Jöfraskinna i fototypisk gengivelse.* STUAGNL 24 (Copenhagen: Møller, 1895). Facsimile of AM 35 fol., AM 36 fol., AM 38 fol., and AM 63 fol.

– ed. *Fagrskinna: Nóregs kononga tal.* STUAGNL 30 (Copenhagen: Møller, 1902–3). Pp. 183–4.
Edition of AM 303 4to, NRA 51, and OsloUB 371 fol. with variants from AM 51 fol., AM 52 fol., AM 301 4to, AM 302 4to, and AM 303 4to.

– ed. *Snorri Sturluson: Heimskringla. Nóregs konunga sǫgur* (Copenhagen: Gad, 1911; rpt. Oslo: Universitetsforlaget, 1966). Pp. 411 and 415–16.
Edition of AM 35 fol., AM 36 fol., AM 37 fol., AM 38 fol., AM 39 fol., AM 45 fol., and AM 63 fol.

– ed. >> *Den norsk-islandske skjaldedigtning* (1912–15). Vol. AI, pp. 324–7 and vol. BI, pp. 300–1.
Stz. 1: edition of AM 36 fol. with variants from AM 47 fol., AM 61 fol., AM 73a fol., AM 325 4to V, AM 325 4to VI, GKS 1005 fol., GKS 1008 fol., Stock. Perg. fol. no. 1, Stock. Perg. 4to no. 2, and Stock. Perg. 4to no. 4; stz. 2: edition of AM 36 fol. with variants from AM 39 fol., AM 61 fol., AM 73a fol., AM 325 4to V, AM 325 4to VI, AM 325 4to VII, GKS 1005 fol., GKS 1008 fol., Stock. Perg. fol. no. 1, Stock. Perg. 4to no. 2, and Stock. Perg. 4to no. 4; stz. 3: edition of AM 36 fol. with variants from AM 39 fol., AM 61 fol., AM 73a fol., AM 325 4to V, AM 325 4to VI, AM 325 4to VII, GKS 1005 fol., GKS 1008 fol., Stock. Perg. fol. no. 1, and Stock. Perg. 4to no. 2; stz. 4: edition of AM 36 fol., with variants from AM 39 fol., AM 61 fol., AM 73a fol., AM 325 4to V, AM 325 4to VII, GKS 1005 fol., GKS 1008 fol., Stock. Perg. fol. no. 1, and Stock. Perg. 4to no. 2; stz. 5–7: edition of AM 36 fol. with variants from AM 39 fol., AM 61 fol., AM 73a fol., AM 325 4to V, AM 325 4to VI, AM 325 4to VII, GKS 1005 fol., GKS 1008 fol., Stock. Perg. fol. no 1, and Stock. Perg. 4to no. 2; stz. 8: edition of AM 36 fol. with variants from AM 39 fol., AM 61 fol., AM 325 4to VI, AM 325 4to VII, GKS 1005 fol., GKS 1008 fol., and Stock. Perg. 4to no. 2; stz. 9: edition of AM 36 fol. with variants from AM 39 fol., Stock. Perg. 4to no. 2, AM 47 fol., AM AM 61 fol., AM 73a fol., AM 325 4to V, AM 325 4to VI, AM 325 4to VII, GKS 1005 fol., GKS 1008 fol., and Stock. Perg. fol. no. 1.

– ed. *Eirspennill – Am 47 fol. – Nóregs konunga sǫgur. Magnús góði – Hákon gamli* (Christiania [Oslo]: Den Norske historiske kildeskrifts-kommission, 1916). Pp. 1 and 3.
Edition of AM 47 fol.

– ed. *Carmina scaldica: udvalg af norske og islandske skjaldekvad* (Copenhagen: Gad, 1923). Pp. 46–7.
Based on Finnur Jónsson's edition (1912–15).
– ed. *Carmina scaldica: udvalg af norske og islandske skjaldekvad.* 2nd rev. ed. (Copenhagen: Gad, 1929). Pp. 48–9.
Based on Finnur Jónsson's edition (1912–15).
– ed. *Flateyjarbók (Codex Flateyensis): MS no. 1005 fol. in the Old Royal Collection in the Royal Library of Copenhagen.* CCI 1 (Copenhagen: Levin and Munksgaard, 1930).
Facsimile of GKS 1005 fol.
Gudbrand Vigfusson and C.R. Unger, ed. >> *Flateyjarbók* (1860–8). Vol. 2, pp. 369 and 377.
Edition of GKS 1005 fol.
Johnsen, Oscar Albert and Jón Helgason, ed. *Saga Óláfs konungs hins helga* (1941). Vol. 1, pp. 594 and 603–4.
Edition of Stock. Perg. 4to no. 2 with emendations and variants from Stock. Perg. fol. no. 1, AM 61 fol., AM 68 fol., AM 71 fol., AM 73a fol., AM 73b fol., AM 75a fol., AM 75b fol., AM 75c fol., AM 75e 1 fol., AM 75 e 2 fol., AM 75 e 3 fol., AM 75e 4 fol., AM 76a fol., AM 325 fol. VI, AM 321 4to, AM 325 4to V, AM 325 4to VII, AM 325 2 a 4to XI, AM 325 2 b 4to XI, AM 325 2 c 4to XI, AM 325 2 d 4to XI, AM 325 2 e 4to XI, AM 325 2 f 4to XI, AM 325 2 g 4to XI, AM 325 2 h 4to XI, AM 325 2 i 4to XI, AM 325 2 k 4to XI, AM 325 2 l 4to XI, AM 325 2 m 4to XI, AM 325 2 n 4to XI, AM 325 2 o 4to XI, AM 325 2 p 4to XI, AM 325 3 4to XI, AM 904 4to, AM 921 4to II, BLAdd 11.242, GKS 1005 fol., GKS 1008 fol., Stock. Perg. fol. no. 1, and Stock. Perg. 4to no. 4.
Kock, Ernst Albin, ed. >> *Notationes Norrœna* (1923–44). §§965, 1130, 2017, and 2988I.
– ed. >> *Den norsk-isländska skaldediktningen* (1946–50). Vol. 1, pp. 152–3.
Lindblad, Gustaf, ed. *Bergsbók. Perg. Fol. nr. 1 in the Royal Library, Stockholm.* EIM 5 (Copenhagen: Rosenkilde and Bagger, 1963).
Facsimile of Stock. Perg. fol. no. 1.
Loth, Agnete, ed. *Thomasskinna. Gl. Kgl. Saml. 1008 fol. in The Royal Library, Copenhagen.* EIM 6 (Copenhagen: Rosenkilde and Bagger, 1964).
Facsimile of GKS 1008 fol.
Magerøy, Hallvard, ed. *Glælognskviða av Toraren Lovtunge.* Bidrag til nordisk filologi av studerende ved Universitetet i Oslo 12 (Oslo: Aschehoug, 1948). Pp. 16–18.
Based on Finnur Jónsson's edition (1912–15) and Oscar Albert Johnsen and Jón Helgason's edition (1941).

Munch, P.A., and C.R. Unger, ed. *Saga Olafs konungs ens helga. Udförligere saga om kong Olaf den hellige* (Christiania [Oslo]: Carl C. Werner, 1853). Pp. 226 and 230.
Edition of Stock. Perg. 4to no. 4.

Munch, P.A., and C.R. Unger, ed. *Fagrskinna. Kortfattet norsk Konge-Saga* (Christiania [Oslo]: Malling, 1847). Pp. 90–1.
Edition of AM 303 4to with variants from AM 51 fol., AM 52 fol., AM 301 4to, AM 302 4to, and NRA 51.

Schöning, Gerhard, et al., ed. *Heimskringla edr Noregs konunga-sögur af Snorra Sturlusyni.* 3 vols. (Copenhagen: Stein, 1777–1826). Vol. 2, pp. 383–4 and 391–3.
Edition of GKS 1005 fol.

Sigurður Nordal et al., ed. *Flateyjarbók.* 4 vols. (Akranes: Flateyjarútgáfan, 1944–5). Vol. 2, pp. 484 and 492.
Edition of GKS 1005 fol.

Townend, Matthew, ed. *"Glælognskviða."* In >> *Poetry from the Kings' Sagas 1* (2012). Vol. 1, pp. 865–75.
Stz. 1: edition of AM 36 fol. with variants from AM 47 fol., AM 61 fol., AM 303 4to, AM 321 4to, AM 325 4to V, AM 325 4to VI, GKS 1005 fol., GKS 1008 fol., Stock. Perg. fol. no. 1, Stock. Perg. 4to no. 2, and Stock. Perg. 4to no. 4; stz. 2: edition of AM 36 fol. with variants from AM 39 fol., AM 61 fol., AM 321 4to, AM 325 4to VI, AM 325 4to VII, GKS 1005 fol., GKS 1008 fol., Stock. Perg. fol. no. 1, Stock. Perg. 4to no. 2, and Stock. Perg. 4to no. 4; stz. 3: edition of AM 36 fol. with variants from AM 39 fol., AM 61 fol., AM 321 4to, AM 325 4to V, AM 325 4to VI, AM 325 4to VII, GKS 1005 fol., GKS 1008 fol., Stock. Perg. fol. no. 1, and Stock. Perg. 4to no. 2; stz. 4: edition of AM 36 fol. with variants from AM 39 fol., AM 61 fol., AM 325 4to V, AM 325 4to VII, GKS 1005 fol., GKS 1008 fol., Stock. Perg. fol. no. 1, and Stock. Perg. 4to no. 2; stz. 5: edition of AM 36 fol. with variants from AM 39 fol., AM 61 fol., AM 321 4to, AM 325 4to V, AM 325 4to VI, AM 325 4to VII, AM 325 2 n 4to XI, GKS 1005 fol., GKS 1008 fol., Stock. Perg. fol. no. 1, and Stock. Perg. 4to no. 2; stz. 6: edition of AM 36 fol. with variants from AM 61 fol., AM 321 4to, AM 325 4to V, AM 325 4to VI, AM 325 4to VII, AM 325 2 n 4to XI, GKS 1005 fol., GKS 1008 fol., Stock. Perg. fol. no. 1, and Stock. Perg. 4to no. 2; stz. 7: edition of AM 36 fol. with variants from AM 61 fol., AM 321 4to, AM 325 4to V, AM 325 4to VI, AM 325 4to VII, AM 325 2 n 4to XI, GKS 1005 fol., GKS 1008 fol., Stock. Perg. fol. no. 1, and Stock. Perg. 4to no. 2; stz. 8: edition of AM 36 fol. with variants from AM 39 fol., AM 61 fol., AM 321 4to, AM 325 4to VI, AM 325 4to VII, AM 325 2 n 4to XI, GKS 1005 fol., GKS

1008 fol., and Stock. Perg. 4to no. 2; edition of AM 36 fol. with variants
from AM 39 fol., AM 47 fol., AM 61 fol., AM 321 4to, AM 325 4to V, AM
325 4to VI, AM 325 4to VII, AM 325 2 n 4to XI, GKS 1005 fol., GKS
1008 fol., Stock. Perg. fol. no. 1, and Stock. Perg. 4to no. 2.

Unger, C.R., ed. *Heimskringla eller Norges Kongesagaer af Snorre
Sturlassøn* (Christiania [Oslo]: Brøgger and Christie, 1868). Pp. 503
and 509.

Edition of AM 35 fol., AM 36 fol., AM 37 fol., AM 38 fol., AM 45 fol.,
and AM 47 fol.

Modern Icelandic language edition:

Bergljót Kristjánsdóttir, Bragi Halldórsson, Jón Torfason, and Örnólfur
Thorsson, ed. *Heimskringla*. 3 vols. (Reykjavík: Mál og menning, 1991).
Vol. 2, pp. 544 and 549–51.

Danish translations:

Finnur Jónsson, ed. >> *Den norsk-islandske skjaldedigtning* (1912–15).
Vol. BI, pp. 300–1.

Schöning, Gerhard, et al., ed. *Heimskringla edr Noregs konunga-sögur
af Snorra Sturlusyni*. 3 vols. (Copenhagen: Stein, 1777–1826). Vol. 2,
pp. 383–4 and 391–3.

English translations:

Finlay, Alison, and Anthony Faulkes, trans. *Snorri Sturluson: Heimskringla*.
Vol. 2. *Óláfr Haraldsson (the Saint)* (University College London: Viking
Society for Northern Research, 2014). Pp. 267 and 271–3.

Hollander, Lee M., trans. *Heimskringla: History of the Kings of Norway
by Snorri Sturluson*. The American-Scandinavian Foundation (Austin:
University of Texas Press, 1964). Pp. 525 and 531–2.

Laing, Samuel, trans. *Snorri Sturluson. Heimskringla: The Olaf Sagas*.
Revised with an Introduction and Notes by Jacqueline Simpson. 2 vols.
(London: Dent; New York: Dutton, 1964). Vol. 2, pp. 385 and 390–1.

Lindow, John. "St Olaf and the Skalds." In *Sanctity in the North: Saints,
Lives, and Cults in Medieval Scandinavia*. Ed. Thomas A. DuBois
(Toronto: University of Toronto Press, 2008). Pp. 103–27, esp. pp. 122–3.

Townend. Matthew. "Knútr and the Cult of St. Óláfr: Poetry and Patronage in
Eleventh-Century Norway and England." *Viking and Medieval Scandianvia*
1 (2005): 251–79, esp. pp. 258–60.

Townend, Matthew, ed. "*Glælognskviða*." In >> *Poetry from the Kings' Sagas
1* (2012). Vol. 1, pp. 865–75.

German translations:

Hube, Hans-Jürgen, trans. *Snorri Sturluson "Heimskringla": Sagen der
nordischen Könige* (Wiesbaden: Marix Verlag, 2006). Pp. 452 and 457.

Lange, Wolfgang. *Christliche Skaldendichtung* (Göttingen: Vandenhoeck and Ruprecht, 1958). Pp. 14–15.

Niedner, Felix, trans. *Snorris Köningsbuch (Heimskringla)*. Thule: Altnordische Dichtung und Prosa 2, Reihe 14–16. 3 vols. (Jena: Diedrichs, 1922–3). Vol. 2, pp. 388 and 395–6.

Latin translation:

Schöning, Gerhard, et al., ed. *Heimskringla edr Noregs konunga-sögur af Snorra Sturlusyni*. 3 vols. (Copenhagen: Stein, 1777–1826). Vol. 2, pp. 384 and 391–3.

Norwegian translations:

Aall, Jacob, trans. *Snorre Sturlesons norske kongers sagaer*. 2 vols. (Christiania [Oslo]: Guldberg and Dzwonkowski, 1838–9). Vol. 1, pp. 358 and 362.

Steinar Schjøtt, Hallvard Magerøy, Halvdan Koht, Gunnar Pedersen, and Kr. Audne, trans. *Norges konge soger*. Ed. Finn Hødnebø and Hallvard Magerøy. 4 vols. (Oslo: Det Norske Samlaget, 1979). Vol. 2, pp. 114 and 118.

Tveiten, Hallvard, trans. *Norrøne Skaldekvad. Frå norrønt i nynorsk gjendikting* (Oslo: J. Saabye, 1966). Pp. 110–11.

Literature:

Attwood, Katrina. "Christian Poetry." In *A Companion to Old Norse– Icelandic Literature and Culture*. Ed. Rory McTurk (Oxford: Blackwell, 2005). Pp. 43–63, esp. pp. 47 and 51.

Bekker-Nielsen, Hans, Thorkil Damsgaard Olsen, and Ole Widding. >> *Norrøn fortællekunst* (1965). P. 46.

Bjarni Þorsteinsson, ed. *Íslenzk þjóðlög* (Copenhagen: Møller, 1906–9). P. 125.

Chase, Martin. "Christian Poetry: West Norse." In >> *Medieval Scandinavia: An Encyclopedia* (1993). Pp. 73–6, esp. p. 74.

Clunies Ross, Margaret. >> *A History of Old Norse Poetry and Poetics* (2005). Pp. 33, 38n15, and 49.

– "Reginnaglar." In *News from Other Worlds: Studies in Nordic Folklore, Mythology and Culture in Honor of John F. Lindow*. Ed. Merrill Kaplan and Timothy R. Tangherlini (Berkeley: North Pinehurst Press, 2012). Pp. 3–21.

Cormack, Margaret. >> *The Saints in Iceland* (1994). P.142.

Edwards, Diana. "Christian and Pagan References in Eleventh-Century Norse Poetry: The Case of Arnórr Jarlaskáld." *Saga-Book* 21 (1982–3): 34–53, esp. pp. 36 and 40.

Fidjestøl, Bjarne. "Pagan Beliefs and Christian Impact: The Contribution of Scaldic Studies." In *Viking Revaluations*. Ed. Anthony Faulkes and

Richard Perkins (University College London: Viking Society for Northern
Research, 1993). Pp. 100–20, esp. pp. 105–10.

Finnur Jónsson. >> *Den oldnorske og oldislandske Litteraturs Historie*
(1920–4). Vol. 1, pp. 602–3.

Heinrichs, Anne. "Óláfs saga helga." In >> *Medieval Scandinavia: An
Encyclopedia* (1993). Pp. 447–8, esp. p. 447.

Hellberg, Staffan. "Kring tilkomsten av *Glælognskviða.*" *AFN* 99 (1984): 14–48.

Holtsmark, Anne. "Sankt Olavs liv og mirakler." In *Festskrift til Francis Bull
på 50 årsdagen* (Oslo: Gyldendal, 1937). Pp. 121–33, esp. p. 122. Rpt.
in Anne Holtsmark, *Studier i norrøn diktning* (Oslo: Gyldendal, 1956).
Pp. 15–24, esp. p. 16.

– "Glælognskviða." *KLNM* 5 (1960). Cols. 361–2.

– "Olavslegenden." *KLNM* 12 (1967). Cols. 584–8, esp. cols. 584–5.

Jakob Benediktsson. "Religiøs digtning." *KLNM* 14 (1969). Cols. 37–40, esp.
col. 37.

Jón Helgason. >> "Norges og Islands digtning." In *Litteraturhistorie B:
Norge og Island* (1953). Pp. 3–179, esp. pp. 17 and 126.

Lange, Wolfgang. >> *Studien zur christlichen Dichtung der Nordgermanen
1000–1200* (1958). Pp. 112–20, 127, and 285.

Lindow, John. "St Olaf and the Skalds." In *Sanctity in the North: Saints,
Lives, and Cults in Medieval Scandinavia.* Ed. Thomas A. DuBois
(Toronto: University of Toronto Press, 2008). Pp. 103–27, esp. pp. 112–13
and 121.

Malcolm, Mary. "Þórarinn loftunga" In >> *Medieval Scandinavia: An
Encyclopedia* (1993). Pp. 580–1.

Mogk, Eugen. >> *Geschichte der norwegisch-isländischen Literatur* (1904).
Pp. 659 and 686.

Olsen, Karin. "Metaphorical Density in Old English and Old Norse Poetry."
ANF 117 (2002): 171–95, esp. p. 182.

Paasche, Fredrik. >> *Kristendom og kvad* (1914). Pp. 14–15, 19, and 22.

– *Norges og Islands litteratur inntil utgangen av middelalderen.* Rev. ed. by
Anne Holtsmark (Oslo: Aschehoug, 1947). Pp. 255, 257, and 267.

Phelpstead, Carl. *Holy Vikings: Saints' Lives in the Old Icelandic Kings'
Sagas* (Tempe, AZ: ACMRS, 2007). Pp. 20, 125, and 134.

Piebenga, Gryt Anne. "Miracles, Collections of." In >> *Medieval
Scandinavia: An Encyclopedia* (1993). Pp. 413–14, esp. p. 414.

Poole, Russell. "Crossing the Language Divide: Anglo-Scandinavian
Language and Literature." In *Cambridge History of Early Medieval
English Literature.* Ed. Clare A. Lees (Cambridge: Cambridge University
Press, 2012). Pp. 579–606, esp. p. 602.

Sverrir Tómasson. "Kristnar trúarbókmenntir í óbundnu máli." In >> *Íslensk Bókmenntasaga* (1992). Pp. 419–79, esp. p. 452.

Townend, Matthew. "Like Father, Like Son? *Glælognskviða* and the Anglo-Danish Cult of Saints." In *Scandinavian and Christian Europe in the Middle Ages. Papers of the 12th International Saga Conference. Bonn/Germany, 28th July–2nd August 2003*. Ed. Rudolf Simek and Judith Meurer (Bonn: Hausdruckerei der Universität Bonn, 2003). Pp. 471–82.

– "Knútr and the Cult of St. Óláfr: Poetry and Patronage in Eleventh-Century Norway and England." *Viking and Medieval Scandianvia* 1 (2005): 251–79.

Turville-Petre, G. *Origins of Icelandic Literature* (Oxford: Clarendon Press, 1967). Pp. 143–4.

Vésteinn Ólason. "Kristileg trúarkvæði til loka 13. aldar." In >> *Íslensk Bókmenntasaga* 1 (1992). Pp. 483–515, esp. pp. 487.

Vries, Jan de. >> *Altnordische Literaturgeschichte* (1964–7). Vol. 2, pp. 250–1 and vol. 2, p. 88.

Whaley, Diana. *Heimskringla: An Introduction* (University College London: Viking Society for Northern Research, 1991). P. 76.

4. Geisli

A twelfth-century poem about King and Saint Óláfr Haraldsson composed by Einarr Skúlason probably in 1153.

Incipit: "Eins má óð ok bœnir."

Manuscripts (these include):
Adv 21.2.9 (ca. 1700–1800), Adv 21.8.14 (ca. 1750–75), AM 39 fol. (ca. 1300), AM 47 fol. (*Eirspennill*) (ca. 1300–25), AM 63 fol. (ca. 1675–1700), AM 66 fol. (*Hulda*) (ca. 1350–75), AM 72 fol. (ca. 1675–1700), AM 73a fol. (ca. 1700), AM 242 fol. (*Codex Wormianus*) (ca. 1350), AM 748b 4to I (ca. 1300–25), AM 1009 4to (ca. 1700), Bor 102 (20743) (ca. 1800), DG 11 (*Codex Upsaliensis*) (ca. 1300–25), DKNVSB 3 4to (ca. 1750), GKS 1005 fol. (*Flateyjarbók*) (ca. 1387–95), GKS 1008 fol. (*Tómasskinna*) (ca. 1400–1500), GKS 1010 fol. (*Hrokkinskinna*) (ca. 1400–50), GKS 2365 4to (*Codex Regius*) (ca. 1270), JS 260 4to (1796), JS 406 4to (ca. 1800–1900), Lbs 444 4to (ca. 1820–50), Oslo UB 262 fol. (ca. 1750–1800), Stock. Perg. fol. no. 1 (*Bergsbók*) (ca. 1400–25), Stock. Perg. 4to no. 2 (ca. 1250–1450), Stock. Perg. 4to no. 4 (ca. 1320–40), Thott 1498 4to (ca. 1750–1800), and Traj 1374 (*Codex Trajectinus*) (ca. 1595).

Editions:

Bjarni Aðalbjarnarson, ed. >> *Heimskringla* (1979). Vol. 3, pp. 271–2.
  Manuscripts used are AM 35 fol., AM 36 fol., AM 37 fol., AM 38 fol.,
  AM 39 fol., AM 42 fol., AM 45 fol., AM 47 fol., AM 63 fol., AM 66 fol.,
  AM 70 fol., AM 325 1 4to VIII, AM 325 1 4to XI, AM 325 2 4to IX, AM
  1056 4to, GKS 1010 fol, Stock. Papp. fol. no. 18, Stock. Perg. fol., no. 1,
  Stock. Perg. fol. no. 9 II, Stock. Perg. fol. no. 18, Stock. Perg. 4to no. 2,
  and UppsUB R 685.

Björn Magnússon Ólsen, ed. *Den tredje og fjærde grammatiske Afhandling
  i Snorres Edda tilligemed de grammatisker Afhandlingers Prolog og to
  andre Tillæg.* STUAGNL 12 (Copenhagen: Knudtzon, 1884). P. 112.
  Edition of AM 748b 4to with variants from AM 242 fol., AM 757b 4to,
  and AM 757a 4to.

Cederschiöld, G, ed. *Geisli eða Óláfs Drápa ens Helga er Einarr orti
  Skúlason. Eftir "Bergsboken" Utgifven.* Lunds Universitets Årsskrift 10
  (Lund: Berling, 1874). Pp. 1–10.
  Edition of Stock. Perg. fol. no. 1.

*Chase, Martin, ed. "Einar Skúlason's *Geisli*: A Critical Edition." PhD
  dissertation, University of Toronto, 1981.

– ed. *Einarr Skúlason's* Geisli. *A Critical Edition* (Toronto: University of
  Toronto Press, 2005). Pp. 51–121.
  Edition of GKS 1005 fol. (stz. 1–30 and 34–71) and Stock. Perg. fol. no. 1
  (stz. 31–3) with variants from AM 39 fol., AM 47 fol., AM 63 fol., AM 66
  fol., AM 73a fol., AM 242 fol., AM 748 4to I, DG 11, GKS 1005 fol., GKS
  1008 fol., GKS 1010 fol., GKS 2365 4to, Stock. Perg. fol. no. 1, Stock.
  Perg. 4to no. 2, Stock. Perg. 4to no. 4, and Traj 1374.

– ed. "Einarr Skúlason, *Geisli* 'Light-beam'." In >> *Poetry on Christian
  Subjects* (2007). Vol. 1, pp. 7–65.
  Edition of GKS 1005 fol. (stz. 1–30 and 34–71) and Stock. Perg. fol. no. 1
  (stz. 31–3) with variants from AM 39 fol., AM 47 fol., AM 63 fol., AM 66
  fol., AM 73a fol., AM 242 fol., AM 748 4to I, DG 11, GKS 1005 fol., GKS
  1008 fol., GKS 1010 fol., GKS 2365 4to, Stock. Perg. fol. no. 1, Stock.
  Perg. 4to no. 2, Stock. Perg. 4to no. 4, and Traj 1374.

Eeden, Willem van, Jr, ed. *De Codex Trajectinus van de Snorra Edda*
  (Leiden: Eduard Ijdo, 1913). P. 111.
  Edition of Traj 1374.

Faulkes, Anthony, ed. *Codex Trajectinus: The Utrecht Manuscript of the
  Prose Edda.* EIM 15 (Copenhagen: Rosenkilde and Bagger, 1985).
  Facsimile of Traj 1374.

– ed. *Snorri Sturluson: Edda. Skáldskaparmál.* 2 vols. (University College
London: Viking Society for Northern Research, 1998). Vol. 1, p. 78.
Edition of GKS 2367 4to with emendations and variants from AM 242 fol.,
AM 748 4to I, AM 748 4to II, AM 757a 4to, DG 11, and Traj 1374.

Finnur Jónsson, ed. >> *Heimskringla* (1893–1900). Vol. 3, p. 308.
Edition of AM 35 fol., AM 36 fol., AM 37 fol., AM 38 fol., AM 63 fol.,
and AM 325 1 4to XI with variants from AM 37 fol., AM 38 fol., AM 39
fol., AM 45 fol., AM 47 fol., AM 70 fol., AM 325 1 4to VIII, AM 325 2 4to
IX, AM 325 1 4to XI, Lbs fragm 82, OsloUB 521 fol., Stock. Papp. fol.
no. 18, Stock. Perg. fol. no. 9 II, and Stock. Perg. 4to no. 36 II.

– ed. *De bevarede Brudstykker af Skindbøgerne Kringla og Jöfraskinna i
fototypisk gengivelse.* STUAGNL 24 (Copenhagen: Møller, 1895).
Facsimile of AM 35 fol., AM 36 fol., AM 38 fol., and AM 63 fol.

– ed. *Snorri Sturluson: Heimskringla. Nóregs konunga sǫgur* (Copenhagen:
Gad, 1911; rpt. Oslo: Universitetsforlaget, 1966). P. 551.
Edition of AM 35 fol., AM 36 fol., AM 37 fol., AM 38 fol., AM 39 fol.,
AM 45 fol., and AM 63 fol.

– ed. >> *Den norsk-islandske skjaldedigtning* (1912–15). Vol. AI, pp. 459–73
and vol. BI, pp. 427–45.
Edition of GKS 1005 fol. (stz. 1–30 and 34–71) and Stock. Perg. fol. no. 1
(stz. 31–3).

– ed. *Eirspennill – Am 47 fol. – Nóregs konunga sǫgur. Magnús
góði – Hákon gamli* (Christiania [Oslo]: Den Norske historiske
kildeskriftskommission, 1916). P. 161.
Edition of AM 47 fol.

– ed. *Edda Snorra Sturlusonar. Codex Wormianus AM 242, fol.* (Copenhagen
and Kristiania [Oslo]: Gyldendal, 1924). Pp. 85 and 112.
Edition of AM 242 fol.

– ed. *Flateyjarbók (Codex Flateyensis): MS. No. 1005 fol. in the Old Royal
Collection in the Royal Library of Copenhagen.* CCI 1 (Copenhagen:
Levin and Munksgaard, 1930).
Facsimile of GKS 1005 fol.

– ed. *Edda Snorra Sturlusonar* (Copenhagen: Gyldendal, 1931). P. 159.
Edition of GKS 2367 4to with variants from AM 242 fol., AM 748b 4to I,
AM 748 4to II, AM 757a 4to, DG 11, and Traj 1374.

Gudbrand Vigfússon and F. York Powell, ed. *Corpus Poeticum Boreale:
The Poetry of the Old Northern Tongue from the Earliest Times to the
Thirteenth Century.* 2 vols. (Oxford: Clarendon Press, 1883). Vol. 2,
pp. 284–94.
Edition of Stock. Perg. fol. no. 1 with emendations from GKS 1005 fol.

Gudbrand Vigfússon and C.R. Unger, ed. >> *Flateyjarbók* (1860–8). Vol. 1, pp. 1–7.
Edition of GKS 1005 fol.

Heimir Pálsson, ed. >> *Snorri Sturluson. The Uppsala Edda* (2012). P. 194.
Edition of DG 11.

Heusler, Andreas, ed. *Codex Regius of the Elder Edda*. CCI 10 (Copenhagen: Munksgaard, 1937).
Facsimile of GKS 2365 4to.

Johnsen, Oscar Albert, and Jón Helgason, ed. >> *Saga Óláfs konungs hins helga* (1941). Vol. 1, p. 648.
Edition of Stock. Perg. 4to no. 2 with emendations and variants from Stock. Perg. fol. no. 1, AM 61 fol., AM 68 fol., AM 71 fol., AM 73a fol., AM 73b fol., AM 75a fol., AM 75b fol., AM 75c fol., AM 75e 1 fol., AM 75e 2 fol., AM 75e 3 fol., AM 75e 4 fol., AM 76a fol., AM 325 fol. VI, AM 321 4to, AM 325 4to V, AM 325 4to VII, AM 325 2 a 4to XI, AM 325 2 b 4to XI, AM 325 2 c 4to XI, AM 325 2 d 4to XI, AM 325 2 e 4to XI, AM 325 2 f 4to XI, AM 325 2 g 4to XI, AM 325 2 h 4to XI, AM 325 2 i 4to XI, AM 325 2 k 4to XI, AM 325 2 l 4to XI, AM 325 2 m 4to XI, AM 325 2 n 4to XI, AM 325 2 o 4to XI, AM 325 2 p 4to XI, AM 325 3 4to XI, AM 904 4to, AM 921 4to II, BLAdd 11.242, GKS 1005 fol., GKS 1008 fol., Stock. Perg. fol. no. 1, and Stock. Perg. 4to no. 4.

Kock, Ernst Albin, ed. >> *Notationes Norrœna* (1923–44). §§924, 925, 926, 927, 928, 929, 930, 931, 932, 933, 934, 935, 936, 937, 938, 939, 940, 941, 942, 943, 944, 945, 946, 948, 949, 950, 951, 952, 953, 1161B, 1204D, 1794, 1853B, 2051, 2052, 2053, 2054, 2055, 2056, 2247D, 2271, 2315A, 2536, 2537, 2791, 2792, 3106, 3281, and 3396T.

– ed. >> *Den norsk-isländska skaldediktningen* (1946–50). Vol. 1, pp. 211–19.

Krömmelbein, Thomas, ed. and trans. *Óláfr Þórðarson Hvítaskáld. Dritte grammatische Abhandlung*. Studia nordica 3 (Oslo: Novus, 1998). P. 228.
Based on Björn Magnússon Ólsen's edition (1884).

Lindblad, Gustaf, ed. *Bergsbók. Perg. Fol. Nr. 1, Royal Library, Stockholm*. EIM (Copenhagen: Rosenkilde and Bagger, 1963).
Facsimile of Stock. Perg. fol. no. 1.

Loth, Agnete, ed. *Thomasskinna. Gl. Kgl. Saml. 1008 fol. in The Royal Library, Copenhagen*. EIM 6 (Copenhagen: Rosenkilde and Bagger, 1964).
Facsimile of GKS 1008 fol.

Munch, P.A., and C.R. Unger, ed. *Saga Olafs konungs ens helga. Udförligere saga om kong Olaf den hellige* (Christiania [Oslo]: Carl C. Werner, 1853). P. 248.
Edition of Stock. Perg. 4to no. 4.

Schöning, Gerhard, et al., ed. *Heimskringla edr Noregs konunga-sögur af Snorra Sturlusyni.* 3 vols. (Copenhagen: Stein, 1777–1826). Vol. 3, pp. 287 and 461–80.
Edition of GKS 1005 fol.

Sigurður Nordal, ed. *Codex Wormianus (The Younger Edda). MS No. 242 fol. in The Arnamagnean Collection in the University Library of Copenhagen.* CCI 2 (Copenhagen: Levin and Munksgaard, 1931).
Facsimile of AM 242 fol.

Sigurður Nordal et al., ed. *Flateyjarbók.* 4 vols. (Akranes: Flateyjarútgáfan, 1944–5). Vol. 1, pp. 1–7.
Edition of GKS 1005 fol.

Unger, C.R., ed. *Heimskringla eller Norges Kongesagaer af Snorre Sturlassøn* (Christiania [Oslo]: Brøgger and Christie, 1868). P. 696.
Edition of AM 35 fol., AM 36 fol., AM 37 fol., AM 38 fol., AM 45 fol., and AM 47 fol.

Wenneberg, Lars, ed. *Geisli. Einarr Skúlason orti. Öfversätning med Anmärkningar* (Lund: Håkan Ohlssons Boktryckeri, 1874). Pp. 1–47.
Based primarily on *Fornmannasögur.*

Wessén, Elias, ed. *Codex Regius of the Younger Edda. MS No. 2367 4to in the Old Royal Collection in the Royal Library of Copenhagen.* CCI 14 (Copenhagen: Einar Munksgaard, 1940).
Facsimile of GKS 2367.

– ed. *Fragments of the Elder and the Younger Edda. AM 748 I and II 4to.* CCI 17 (Copenhagen: Einar Munksgaard, 1945).
Facsimile of AM 748 4to I and AM 648 4to II.

Wisén, Theodor. *Úrval af norrænum fornkvæðum handa hinum bókmennta-iðkendum* (Lund: Berling, 1870). Pp. 65–72.

Wisén, Theodor, ed. *Carmina Norrœna. Ex Reliquiis Vestustioris Norrœnæ Poësis. Selecta, Regognita, Commentariis et Glossario Instructa.* 2 vols. (Lund: Ohlsson, 1886–9). Vol. 1, pp. 53–62.
Based on G. Cederschiöld's edition (1874).

Modern Icelandic language editions:

Árni Björnsson, ed. *Snorra Edda* (Reykjavík: Iðunn, 1975). P. 208.

Bergljót Kristjánsdóttir, Bragi Halldórsson, Jón Torfason, and Örnólfur Thorsson, ed. *Heimskringla.* 3 vols. (Reykjavík: Mál og menning, 1991). Vol. 2, p. 742.

Danish translations:

Finnur Jónsson, ed. >> *Den norsk-islandske skjaldedigtning* (1912–15). Vol. BI, pp. 427–45.

Schöning, Gerhard, et al., ed. *Heimskringla edr Noregs konunga-sögur af Snorra Sturlusyni.* 3 vols. (Copenhagen: Stein, 1777–1826). Vol. 3, pp. 287 and 461–80.

English translations:

Chase, Martin, ed. *Einarr Skúlason's* Geisli. *A Critical Edition* (Toronto: University of Toronto Press, 2005). Pp. 51–121.

– ed. "Einarr Skúlason, *Geisli* 'Light-beam'." In >> *Poetry on Christian Subjects* (2007). Vol. 1, pp. 7–65.

Faulkes, Anthony, trans. *Snorri Sturluson:* Edda (London: Dent 1987). P. 127.

Gudbrand Vigfússon and F. York Powell, ed. *Corpus Poeticum Boreale: The Poetry of the Old Northern Tongue from the Earliest Times to the Thirteenth Century.* 2 vols. (Oxford: Clarendon Press, 1883). Vol. 2, pp. 284–94.

Heimir Pálsson, ed. >> *Snorri Sturluson. The Uppsala Edda* (2012). P. 195.

Hollander, Lee M., trans. *Heimskringla: History of the Kings of Norway by Snorri Sturluson.* The American-Scandinavian Foundation (Austin: University of Texas Press, 1964). P. 711.

Laing, Samuel, trans. *Snorri Sturluson. Heimskringla: Sagas of the Norse Kings.* Rev. ed. Peter Foote (London: Dent, 1961). Vol. 2, p. 314.

German translations:

Hube, Hans-Jürgen, trans. *Snorri Sturluson "Heimskringla": Sagen der nordischen Könige* (Wiesbaden: Marix Verlag, 2006). P. 604.

Krause, Arnulf, trans. *Die Edda des Snorri Sturluson.* Reclams Universital-Bibliothek 782 (Stuttgart: Reclam, 1997). P. 192.

Krömmelbein, Thomas, ed. and trans. *Óláfr Þórðarson Hvítaskáld. Dritte grammatische Abhandlung.* Studia nordica 3 (Oslo: Novus, 1998). P. 229.

Lange, Wolfgang. *Christliche Skaldendichtung* (Göttingen: Vandenhoeck and Ruprecht, 1958). P. 29.

Niedner, Felix, trans. *Snorris Köningsbuch (Heimskringla).* Thule: Altnordische Dichtung und Prosa 2, Reihe 14–16. 3 vols. (Jena: Diedrichs, 1922–3). Vol. 3, p. 236.

Latin translation:

Schöning, Gerhard, et al., ed. *Heimskringla edr Noregs konunga-sögur af Snorra Sturlusyni.* 3 vols. (Copenhagen: Stein, 1777–1826). Vol. 3, pp. 287 and 461–80.

Norwegian translations:

Aall, Jacob, trans. *Snorre Sturlesons norske kongers sagaer.* 2 vols. (Christiania [Oslo]: Guldberg and Dzwonkowski, 1838–9). Vol. 2, p. 134.

Eggen, Erik, trans. *"Geisli."* In *Norrøne kristenkvæde.* Ed. Olaf Hanssen (Oslo: Det norske samlaget, 1928). Pp. 13–23.

Steinar Schjøtt, Hallvard Magerøy, Halvdan Koht, Gunnar Pedersen, and
Kr. Audne, trans. *Norges konge soger*. Ed. Finn Hødnebø and Hallvard
Magerøy. 4 vols. (Oslo: Det Norske Samlaget, 1979). Vol. 2, p. 260.

*Ødegård, Knut, trans. *Einarr Skúlason: Geisli* (Trondheim: Tapir Akademisk
Forlag, 2003).

Swedish translation:

Wenneberg, Lars, ed. *Geisli. Einarr Skúlason orti. Öfversätning med
Anmärkningar* (Lund: Håkan Ohlssons Boktryckeri, 1874). Pp. 1–47.

Literature:

Abram, Christopher. "Einarr Skúlason, Snorri Sturluson, and the Post-Pagan
Mythological Kennings." In >> *Eddic, Skaldic, and Beyond*. Ed. Martin
Chase (2014). Pp. 44–61, esp. pp. 48, 50, and 58–60.

Attwood, Katrina. "Intertextual Aspects of the Twelfth-Century Christian
Drápur." *Saga-Book* 24 (1996): 221–39.

– "Leiðarvísan and the 'Sunday Letter' Tradition in Scandinavia." In >> *Til
heiðurs og hugbótar* (2003). Pp. 53–78, esp. p. 54.

– "Christian Poetry." In *A Companion to Old Norse–Icelandic Literature
and Culture*. Ed. Rory McTurk (Oxford: Blackwell, 2005). Pp. 43–63, esp.
pp. 50–2.

Bekker-Nielsen, Hans, Thorkil Damsgaard Olsen, and Ole Widding. >>
Norrøn fortællekunst (1965). P. 46.

Bjarni Einarsson. "Geisli." *KLNM* 5 (1960). Cols. 230–2.

Bjarni Þorsteinsson, ed. *Íslenzk þjóðlög* (Copenhagen: Møller, 1906–9).
P. 125.

Chase, Martin. "*Concatenatio* as a Structural Element in the Christian
Drápur." In *The Sixth International Saga Conference 28/7–2/8 1985.
Workshop Papers*. 2 vols. ([Copenhagen]: Det arnamagnæanske Institut,
1985). Vol. 1, pp. 115–29, esp. pp. 118–21 and 124–5.

– "Christian Poetry: West Norse." In >> *Medieval Scandinavia: An
Encyclopedia* (1993). Pp. 73–6, esp. p. 75.

– "Einarr Skúlason." In >> *Medieval Scandinavia: An Encyclopedia* (1993).
P. 159.

– "Framir kynnask vátta mál: The Christian Background of Einarr Skúlason's
Geisli." In >> *Til heiðurs og hugbótar* (2003). Pp. 11–32.

– "The Refracted Beam: Einarr Skúlason's Liturgical Theology." In *Verbal
Encounters: Anglo-Saxon and Old Norse Studies for Roberta Frank*. Ed.
Antonina Harbus and Russell Poole (Toronto: University of Toronto Press,
2005). Pp. 203–21.

Clover, Carol J. "Skaldic Sensibility." *ANF* 93 (1978): 63–81, esp. p. 67.

Clunies Ross, Margaret. >> *A History of Old Norse Poetry and Poetics* (2005). Pp. 33, 35–6, 49, 124, 130–2n19, 133n20, 193, and 231.
– *"Reginnaglar."* In *News from Other Worlds: Studies in Nordic Folklore, Mythology and Culture in Honor of John F. Lindow*. Ed. Merrill Kaplan and Timothy R.Tangherlini (Berkeley: North Pinehurst Press, 2012). Pp. 3–21, esp. p. 5.
Cormack, Margaret. >> *The Saints in Iceland* (1994). Pp. 42 and 142–3.
– "Sagas of Saints." In *Old Icelandic Literature and Society*. Ed. Margaret Clunies Ross (Cambridge: Cambridge University Press, 2000). Pp. 302–18, esp. pp. 311–12.
– "Poetry, Paganism and the Sagas of Icelandic Bishops." In >> *Til heiðurs og hugbótar* (2003). Pp. 33–51, esp. pp. 33 and 45.
Edsman, Carl-Martin. "Solsymbolik." *KLNM* 16 (1971). Cols. 421–6, esp. col. 424.
Edwards, Diana. "Christian and Pagan References in Eleventh-Century Norse Poetry: The Case of Arnórr Jarlaskáld." *Saga-Book* 21 (1982–3): 34–53, esp. p. 445.
Ekrem, Inger. "Om *Passio Olavis* tilblivelse og eventuelle forbindelse med *Historia Norwegie.*" In *Olavslegenden og den latinske historieskrivning i 1100-tallets Norge*. Ed. Inger Ekrem, Lars Boje Mortensen, and Karen Skovgaard-Petersen (Copenhagen: Museum Tusculanum, 2000). Pp. 108–56, esp. pp. 150–1.
Fidjestøl, Bjarne. "Skaldic Verse." In >> *Medieval Scandinavia: An Encyclopedia* (1993). Pp. 592–4, esp. p. 593.
– "'Have You Heard a Poem Worth More?' A Note on the Economic Background of Early Skaldic Praise-Poetry." In Bjarne Fidjestøl. *Selected Papers*. Ed. Odd Einar Haugen and Else Mundal. Trans. Peter Foote. Viking Collection 9 (Odense: Odense University Press, 1997). Pp. 117–32, esp. pp. 122 and 125.
Finnur Jónsson. >> *Den oldnorske og oldislandske Litteraturs Historie* (1920–4). Vol. 2, pp. 21 and 65–9.
– "Kenningrs ledomstilling og tmesis." *ANF* 59 (1933): 1–23, esp. p. 20.
Frank, Roberta. *Old Norse Court Poetry: The* Dróttkvætt *Stanza*. Islandica 42 (Ithaca: Cornell University Press, 1978). Pp. 30 and 139.
Gísli Sigurðsson. "Óláfr Þórðarson hvítaskáld and Oral Poetry in the West of Iceland *c.* 1250: The Evidence of References to Poetry in *The Third Grammatical Treatise.*" In *Old Icelandic Literature and Society*. Ed. Margaret Clunies Ross (Cambridge: Cambridge University Press, 2000). Pp. 96–115, esp. pp. 101–2 and 104.

Gjerløw, Lilli. "Olav den hellige: Liturgi." *KLNM* 12 (1967). Cols. 561–7, esp. col. 561.

Guðrún Nordal. *Tools of Literacy: The Role of Skaldic Verse in Icelandic Textual Culture of the Twelfth and Thirteenth Centuries* (Toronto: University of Toronto Press, 2001). Pp. 8, 28, 40, 78, 251, 276, 286, 293, 313, 318, 336, 340, 342, 376n14, 377n20, 378n23 and n64.

Hallberg, Peter. *Old Icelandic Poetry: Eddic Lay and Skaldic Verse.* Trans. Paul Schach and Sonja Lindgrenson (Lincoln: University of Nebraska Press, 1975). P. 169.

Haugen, Odd Einar. "Nicodemus, Gospel of." In >> *Medieval Scandinavia: An Encyclopedia* (1993). Pp. 430–2, esp. p. 431.

Heinrichs, Anne. "Óláfs saga helga." In >> *Medieval Scandinavia: An Encyclopedia* (1993). Pp. 447–8, esp. p. 447.

Holm-Olsen, Ludvig, and Kjell Heggelund. *Norges Litteratur Historie. Fra Runene til Norske Selskab.* Ed. Edvard Beyer (Oslo: Cappelen, 1974). Pp. 247–8.

Holtsmark, Anne. "Sankt Olavs liv og mirakler." In *Festskrift til Francis Bull på 50 årsdagen* (Oslo: Gyldendal, 1937). Pp. 121–33, esp. pp. 123–4, 127–8, and 131–2. Rpt. in Anne Holtsmark, *Studier i norrøn diktning* (Oslo: Gyldendal, 1956). Pp. 15–24, esp. pp. 17–20 and 23.

– "Líknarbraut." *KLNM* 10 (1965). Cols. 553–4, esp. col. 554.

– "Lovkvad." *KLNM* 10 (1965). Cols. 700–4, esp. col. 702.

– "Olavslegenden." *KLNM* 12 (1967). Cols. 584–8, esp. col. 585.

Jakob Beneditksson. "Helgendigte." *KLNM* 6 (1961). Cols. 318–21, esp. cols. 318–19.

– "Religiøs digtning." *KLNM* 14 (1969). Cols. 37–40, esp. col. 37.

– "*Hafgerðingadrápa.*" In *Specvlvm Norroenvm: Norse Studies in Memory of Gabriel Turville-Petre.* Ed. Ursula Dronke, Guðrún P. Helgadóttir, Gerd Wolfgang Weber, and Hans Bekker-Nielsen (Odense: Odense University Press, 1981). Pp. 27–32, esp. p. 31.

– >> "Helgikvæði." In *Hugtök og heiti í bókmenntafræði* (1983). Pp. 115–17, esp. p. 116.

Jón Helgason. *Norrøn Litteraturhistorie* (Copenhagen: Levin and Munksgaard, 1934). Pp. 85 and 87–8.

– >> "Norges og Islands digtning." In *Litteraturhistorie B: Norge og Island* (1953). Pp. 3–179, esp. pp. 103, 110, and 154.

Jónas Kristjánsson. >> *Eddas and Sagas: Iceland's Medieval Literature* (1988). Pp. 109 and 112.

Jørgensen, Jon Gunnar. "Passio Olavii og Snorre." In *Olavslegenden og den latinske historieskrivning i 1100-tallets Norge.* Ed. Inger Ekrem, Lars

Boje Mortensen, and Karen Skovgaard-Petersen (Copenhagen: Museum Tusculanum, 2000). Pp. 157–69, esp. pp. 161–2.

Kahle, Bernhard. *Die Sprache der Skalden auf Grund der Binnen- und Endreime* (Strassburg: Karl J. Trübner, 1892).

– "Das Christentum in der altwestnordischen Dichtung." *ANF* 13 (1901): 1–40 and 97–160, esp. pp. 11, 20, 27–31, 98, 103, 107, 109–11, 113–15, 117–18, 123–31, 133–4, 136–40, 144–7, and 152–4.

Konráð Gíslason. "Om helrim i förste og tredje linie af regelmæssigt 'drottkvætt' og 'hrynhenda'." *Indbydelsesskrift til Kjøbenhavns Universitets Aarsfest til Erindring om Kirkens Reformation* (Copenhagen: Schultz, 1877). Pp. 1–60, esp. pp. 16–17, 22–3, 26–7, 29, 31, and 59–60.

Kristján Árnason. "On the Principles of Nordic Rhyme and Alliteration." *ANF* 122 (2007): 79–114, esp. pp. 99, 103, and 106.

Kuhn, Hans. *Das Dróttkvætt* (Heidelberg: Carl Winter Universitätsverlag, 1983). Pp. 255 and 313–16.

Lange, Wolfgang. >> *Studien zur christlichen Dichtung der Nordgermanen 1000–1200* (1958). Pp. 14, 98, 107, 110–12, 120–6, 218, and 269–70.

Lindow, John. "Narrative and the Nature of Skaldic Poetry." *ANF* 97 (1982): 94–121, esp. pp. 102 and 110.

– "St Olaf and the Skalds." In *Sanctity in the North: Saints, Lives, and Cults in Medieval Scandinavia*. Ed. Thomas A. DuBois (Toronto: University of Toronto Press, 2008). Pp. 103–27, esp. p. 120.

Marold, Edith. "Das Gottesbild der christlichen Skaldik." In *The Sixth International Saga Conference 28/7–2/8 1985. Workshop Papers*. 2 vols. ([Copenhagen]: Det arnamagnæanske Institut, 1985). Vol. 2, pp. 717–49, esp. pp. 731–3, 736, and 747–8.

Mogk, Eugen. >> *Geschichte der norwegisch-isländischen Literatur* (1904). Pp. 603, 680, and 692.

Mortensen, Lars Boje. "Olav den Helliges mirakler i det 12. årh.: streng tekstkontrol eller fri fabuleren?" In *Olavslegenden og den latinske historieskrivning i 1100-tallets Norge*. Ed. Inger Ekrem, Lars Boje Mortensen, and Karen Skovgaard-Petersen (Copenhagen: Museum Tusculanum, 2000). Pp. 89–107, esp. pp. 95 and 97.

Møller, Arne. *Islands Lovsang gennem Tusind Aar* (Copenhagen: Gyldendal, 1923). Pp. 11–17.

Naumann, Hans-Peter. "Nordische Kreuzzugsdichtung." In *Festschrift für Oskar Bandle: Zum 60. Geburtstag am 11. Januar 1986*. Ed. Hans-Peter Naumann with Magnus von Platen and Stefan Sonderegger. Beiträge zur nordischen Philologie 15 (Basel and Frankfurt am Main: Helbing and Lichtenhahn, 1986). Pp. 175–89, esp. p. 188.

Noreen, Erik. *Studier i fornvästnordisk diktnning* 2. Uppsala Universitets
Årsskrift 1922 (Uppsala: Akademiska bokhandeln, 1922). Pp. 27–8.

Olsen, Karin. "Metaphorical Density in Old English and Old Norse Poetry."
ANF 117 (2002): 171–95, esp. pp. 182–3.

Paasche, Fredrik. >> *Kristendom og kvad* (1914). Pp. 5, 32, 72–83, 91, 97,
105–8, 137, and 171–2.

– *Norges og Islands litteratur inntil utgangen av middelalderen*. Rev. ed. by
Anne Holtsmark (Oslo: Aschehoug, 1947). Pp. 268, 311–12, 335, and 494.

Phelpstead, Carl. *Holy Vikings: Saints' Lives in the Old Icelandic Kings'
Sagas* (Tempe, AZ: ACMRS, 2007). Pp. 20, 125–6.

Piebenga, Gryt Anne. "Miracles, Collections of." In >> *Medieval
Scandinavia: An Encyclopedia* (1993). Pp. 413–14, esp. p. 414.

Schneider, Hermann. *Geschichte der norwegischen und isländischen
Literatur* (Bonn: Universitätsverlag, 1948). P. 28.

Schottmann, Hans. >> *Die isländische Mariendichtung* (1973). Pp. 39–42,
122, 191, 205, 207–8, 213–15, 249, and 397–8.

See, Klaus von. *Skaldendichtung: Eine Einführung* (Munich and Zürich:
Artemis Verlag, 1980). Pp. 42–3 and 58–9.

Sigurður Líndal. "Upphaf kristni og kirkju." In *Saga Íslands* 5. Ed. Sigurður
Líndal (Reykjavík: Hið íslenzka bókmenntafélag, Sögufélagið, 1974). Pp.
227–86, esp. p. 270.

Skard, Vemund. "Harmsól, Plácítusdrápa og Leiðarvísan." *ANF* 68 (1953):
97–108, esp. p. 100.

Stéfan Einarsson. "Íslenzk helgikvæði á miðöldum." *Tímarit Þjóðræknisfélags
Íslendinga* 36 (1955): 43–63, esp. pp. 44–6.

– *Íslensk bókmenntasaga 874–1960* (Reykjavík: Oddi, 1961). Pp. 82–3.

Sverrir Tómasson. "Hvenær var Tristrams sögu snúið?" *Gripla* 2 (1977):
47–78, esp. p. 61.

– "Kristnar trúarbókmenntir í óbundnu máli." In >> *Íslensk Bókmenntasaga*
1 (1992). Pp. 421–79, esp. p. 452.

– Bragi Halldórsson and Einar Sigurbjörnsson, ed. *Heilagra karla sögur*.
Íslensk trúarrit 3 (Reykjavík: Bókmenntafræðistofnun Háskóla Íslands,
2007). P. 203.

Tate, George Sheldon. "The Cross as Ladder: *Geisli* 5–16 and *Líknarbraut*
34." *Mediaeval Scandinavia* 11 (1978–9): 258–64.

Turville-Petre, G. *Origins of Icelandic Literature* (Oxford: Clarendon Press,
1967). Pp. 156–8, 179, and 181.

Vésteinn Ólason. "Dróttkvæði." In >> *Íslensk Bókmenntasaga* 1 (1992).
Pp. 191–262, esp. p. 258.

– "Kristileg trúarkvæði til loka 13. aldar." In >> *Íslensk Bókmenntasaga* 1
(1992). Pp. 483–515, esp. pp. 488–93, 495, 497, and 515.

– "Kveðskapur frá síðmiðöldum." In >> *Íslensk Bókmenntasaga* 2 (1993). Pp. 283–378, esp. pp. 292 and 208.

– "Old Icelandic Poetry." In *A History of Icelandic Literature*. Ed. Daisy Neijmann. Histories of Scandinavian Literature 5 (Lincoln: University of Nebraska Press, 2006). Pp. 1–64, esp. p. 44.

Vries, Jan de. "Über Arnórr Jarlaskáld." *ANF* 67 (1952): 156–75, esp. p. 173.

– >> *Altnordische Literaturgeschichte* (1964–7). Vol. 1, pp. 119, and vol. 2, pp. 16, 19–23, 41, 43, 53, 55, 58, 229, and 239.

Weber, Gerd Wolfgang. "Saint Óláfr's Sword: Einarr Skúlason's *Geisli* and Its Trondheim Performance AD 1153 – A Turning Point in Norwego-Icelandic Skaldic Poetry." In *Sagas and the Norwegian Experience/ Sagaene og Noreg. 10th International Saga Conference, Trondheim, 3.–9. August 1977* (Trondheim: NTNU, 1997). Pp. 655–61.

Whaley, Diana. *Heimskringla: An Introduction* (University College London: Viking Society for Northern Research, 1991). Pp. 38, 46, and 121–2.

Wolf, Kirsten. "The Influence of the *Evangelium Nicodemi* on Norse Literature: A Survey." In *The Medieval* Gospel of Nicodemus: *Texts, Intertexts, and Contexts in Western Europe*. Ed. Zbigniew Izydorczyk (Tempe, AZ; Medieval and Renaissance Texts and Studies, 1997). Pp. 261–86, esp. p. 277.

5. Óláfs ríma Haraldssonar

A mid-fourteenth-century poem in praise of King and Saint Óláfr Haraldsson by Einarr Gilsson (d. 1369).

Incipit: "Óláfr kongr ǫrr ok fríðr."

Manuscripts:
AM 1009 4to (ca. 1700), GKS 1005 fol. (*Flateyjarbók*) (ca. 1387–95), JS 24 fol. (ca. 1845), JS 57 4to (ca. 1760–1822), JS 83 8vo (ca. 1800–25), Lbs 438 4to (ca. 1800–1900), Lbs 201 8vo (ca. 1850–70), NKS 1705 4to (ca. 1750–1800), Rask 23 (1794), Stock. Papp. 4to no. 9 (ca. 1650), and Thott 1500 4to (ca. 1750–1800).

Editions:
Finnur Jónsson, ed. >> *Rímnasafn* 35 (1905–15). Vol. 1, pp. 1–9. Edition of GKS 1005 fol.

– ed. *Flateyjarbók (Codex Flateyensis): MS. No. 1005 fol. in the Old Royal Collection in the Royal Library of Copenhagen*. CCI 1 (Copenhagen: Levin and Munksgaard, 1930). Facsimile of GKS 1005 fol.

Finnur Sigmundsson. >> *Rímnatal.* 2 vols. (1966). Vol. 1, p. 367 (introductory verse).

Guðbrandr Vigfússon and C.R. Unger, ed. >> *Flateyjarbók* (1860–8). Vol. 1, pp. 8–11.
Edition of GKS 1005 fol.

Sigurður Nordal et al., ed. *Flateyjarbók.* 4 vols. (Akranes: Flateyjarútgáfan, 1944–5). Vol. 1, pp. 7–10.
Edition of GKS 1005 fol.

Sveinbjörn Beinteinsson, ed. *Rímnasafnið: Sýnisbók rímna frá 14. öld til nútímans* (Reykjavík: Helgafell, 1966) (stz. 1–2).

Literature:

Bjarni Þorsteinsson, ed. *Íslenzk þjóðlög* (Copenhagen: Møller, 1906–9). P. 805.

Björn K. Þórólfsson. *Rímur fyrir 1600.* Safn fræðafjelagsins 9 (Copenhagen: Møller, 1934). Pp. 1, 22, 24, 46, 48–9, 51, 103, 210, 234, 237, 259, 289, 298–9, and 519.

Chase, Martin. "Introduction." In >> *Eddic, Skaldic, and Beyond: Poetic Variety in Medieval Iceland.* Ed. Martin Chase (2014). Pp. 1–15, esp. p. 6.

Clunies Ross, Margaret. "Christian Skaldic Rhetoric in Einarr Gilsson's *Selkolluvísur.*" In *Scandinavian and Christian Europe in the Middle Ages. Papers of the 12th International Saga Conference. Bonn/Germany, 28th July–2nd August 2003.* Ed. Rudolf Simek and Judith Meurer (Bonn: Hausdruckerei der Universität Bonn, 2003). Pp. 90–8, esp. p. 90.

– >> *A History of Old Norse Poetry and Poetics* (2005). Pp. 5, 12, and 213.

Cormack, Margaret. >> *The Saints in Iceland* (1994). Pp. 42 and 142.

Fidjestøl, Bjarne. "Skaldic Verse." In >> *Medieval Scandinavia: An Encyclopedia* (1993). Pp. 592–4, esp. p. 592.

Finnur Jónsson. >> *Bókmentasaga Íslendinga fram undir siðabót* (1904–5). P. 462.

– >> *Den oldnorske og oldislandske Litteraturs Historie* (1920–4). Vol. 3, pp. 13–14, 25, and 43.

Guðrún Nordal. *Tools of Literacy: The Role of Skaldic Verse in Icelandic Textual Culture of the Twelfth and Thirteenth Centuries* (Toronto: University of Toronto Press, 2001). P. 318.

Hughes, Shaun. "Late Secular Poetry." In *A Companion to Old Norse–Icelandic Literature and Culture.* Ed. Rory McTurk (Oxford: Blackwell, 2005). Pp. 205–22, esp. p. 206.

Jón Árnason and Ólafur Davíðsson, ed. *Íslenzkar gátur, skemtanir, vikivakar og þulur.* 4 vols. (Copenhagen: Møller, 1887–1903). Vol. 2, p. 207.

Jón Helgason. >> "Norges og Islands digtning." In *Litteraturhistorie B: Norge og Island* (1953). Pp. 3–179, esp. pp. 168–70.

Jón Þorkelsson. >> *Om Digtningen på Island* (1888). P. 122.

Jónas Kristjánsson. >> *Eddas and Sagas: Iceland's Medieval Literature* (1988). Pp. 370, 378, and 380.

Jorgensen, Peter A. "Rímur." In >> *Medieval Scandinavia: An Encyclopedia* (1993). Pp. 536–7, esp. p. 536.

Kahle, Bernhard. "Das Christentum in der altwestnordischen Dichtung." *ANF* 13 (1901): 1–40 and 97–160, esp. pp. 113, 132, and 155.

Konráð Gíslason. "Om helrim i förste og tredje linie af regelmæssigt 'drottkvætt' og 'hrynhenda'." *Indbydelsesskrift til Kjøbenhavns Universitets Aarsfest til Erindring om Kirkens Reformation* (Copenhagen: Schultz, 1877). Pp. 1–60, esp. p. 52.

Mogk, Eugen. >> *Geschichte der norwegisch-isländischen Literatur* (1904). Pp. 603, 716, and 722–5.

Ólafur Halldórsson. "Rímur." *KLNM* 14 (1969). Cols. 319–24, esp. col. 323.

Orgland, Ivar, trans. *Islandske Dikt. Frå Sólarljóð til opplysningstid (13. hundreåret–1835)* (Reykjavík: Fonna, 1977). P. 50.

Poole, R.G. *Viking Poems on War and Peace: A Study in Skaldic Narrative* (Toronto: University of Toronto Press, 1991). P. 30.

Rokkjær, Carl C. "Rímur og folkeviser." *APS* 26 (1964): 100–8, esp. p. 103.

Vésteinn Ólason. "Kveðið um Ólaf helga." *Skírnir* 157 (1983): 48–63.

– "Kveðskapur frá síðmiðöldum." In >> *Íslensk Bókmenntasaga* 2 (1993). Pp. 283–378, esp. pp. 322–3, 328, 330, 335–8, and 350.

– "Old Icelandic Poetry." In *A History of Icelandic Literature*. Ed. Daisy Neijmann. Histories of Scandinavian Literature 5 (Lincoln: University of Nebraska Press, 2006). Pp. 1–64, esp. pp. 56 and 58.

6. Óláfs rímur

Two anonymous and fragmentary *rímur* about King and Saint Óláfr Haraldsson and based on *Rauðúlfs þáttr*.

Incipit: "Vaskir gjörðu virðar fyrr."

Manuscript:
Stock. Perg. 4to no. 23 (ca. 1500–50).

Editions:
Finnur Jónsson, ed. *Rímnasafn. Samling af de ældste islandske Rimer*. 2 vols. STUAGNL 35 (Copenhagen: Møller, 1905–15). Vol. 1, pp. 215–21.

Finnur Sigmundsson. >> *Rímnatal*. 2 vols. (1966). Vol. 1, p. 367 (introductory verse and refrain).

Jón Þorkelsson. >> *Om Digtningen på Island* (1888). P. 142 (I.1–3).

Literature:

Björn K. Þórólfsson. *Rímur fyrir 1600.* Safn fræðafjelagsins 9 (Copenhagen: Møller, 1934). Pp. 234, 464–5, and 523.

Finnur Jónsson. >> *Bókmentasaga Íslendinga fram undir siðabót* (1904–5). P. 462.

Mogk, Eugen. >> *Geschichte der norwegisch-isländischen Literatur* (1904). P. 725.

7. Óláfsvísur I

A late medieval (ca. 1400–1550) poem in praise of King and Saint Óláfr Haraldsson.
   Incipit: "Mjöður af mærðar blandi."

Manuscripts:

AM 710i 4to (ca. 1700–25), AM 714 4to (ca. 1600), JS 399a–b 4to (ca. 1700–1900), JS 581 4to (ca. 1600–1900), Lbs 2166 4to (ca. 1885–1920), and Lbs 201 8vo (ca. 1850–70).

Editions:

Jón Helgason, ed. >> *Íslenzk miðaldakvæði* (1936–8). Vol. 2, pp. 434–6.
   Based on AM 714 4to with variants from AM 710i 4to and JS 399a–b 4to.

Jón Þorkelsson. >> *Om Digtningen på Island* (1888). P. 29 (stz. 1 and 18).
   Based on AM 710i 4to, AM 714 4to, and Lbs 201 8vo.

Literature:

Anon. "Den Oldnordisk-islandske Afdeling." Annual Report for 1846.
   Antiquarisk Tidsskrift 1846–8 (Copenhagen: Sally B. Salomon, 1847). Pp. 39–49, esp. p. 41.

Bjarni Þorsteinsson, ed. *Íslenzk þjóðlög* (Copenhagen: Møller, 1906–9). P. 125.

Finnur Jónsson. >> *Den oldnorske og oldislandske Litteraturs Historie* (1920–4). Vol. 3, p. 126.

Hálfdan Einarsson. *Sciagraphia historiæ literariæ islandicæ* (Copenhagen: Sander and Schröder, 1777). P. 58.

Jakob Benediktsson. "Helgendigte." *KLNM* 6 (1961). Cols. 318–21, esp. col. 320.

Jón Helgason. >> "Norges og Islands digtning." In *Litteraturhistorie B: Norge og Island* (1953). Pp. 3–179, esp. pp. 163–4.

Jónas Kristjánsson. >> *Eddas and Sagas: Iceland's Medieval Literature* (1988). P. 380.

Kock, E.A. "Anteckningar till Íslenzk Miðaldakvæði." *ANF* 61 (1946): 1–125, esp. pp. 106–9.

Mogk, Eugen. >> *Geschichte der norwegisch-isländischen Literatur* (1904).
P. 718

Vésteinn Ólason. "Kveðskapur frá síðmiðöldum." In >> *Íslensk Bókmenntasaga* 2 (1993). Pp. 285–378, esp. pp. 317–18.

8. Óláfsvísur II

A poem from ca. 1400–1550 in praise of King and Saint Óláfr Haraldsson. Incipit: "Guð faðir og son það líf og ljós."

Manuscripts:

A: Stock. Perg. fol. no. 1 (*Bergsbók*) (ca. 1400–25);

B: AM 713 4to (ca. 1500–50), JS 399a–b 4to (ca. 1700–1900), and Lbs 1486b 4to (ca. 1860–78);

C: AM 713 4to (ca. 1500–50), AM 717a 4to (ca. 1700–25), AM 953 4to (ca. 1700–25), and AM 150 8vo (ca. 1650–1700).

Editions:

Jón Helgason, ed. >> *Íslenzk miðaldakvæði* (1936–8). Vol. 2, pp. 438–41. Based on Stock. Perg. fol. no. 1 with variants and emendations from AM 713 4to, AM 717a 4to, AM 953 4to, and AM 150 8vo.

Jón Þorkelsson. >> *Om Digtningen på Island* (1888). P. 29 (stz. 1). Based on AM 713 4to, AM 717a 4to, and AM 150 8vo.

Literature:

Anon. "Den Oldnordisk-islandske Afdeling." Annual Report for 1846. *Antiquarisk Tidsskrift* 1846–8 (Copenhagen: Sally B. Salomon, 1847). Pp. 39–49, esp. p. 41.

Bjarni Þorsteinsson, ed. *Íslenzk þjóðlög* (Copenhagen: Møller, 1906–9). P. 125.

Finnur Jónsson. >> *Den oldnorske og oldislandske Litteraturs Historie* (1920–4). Vol. 3, p. 126.

Guðrún Nordal. "Handrit, prentaðar bækur og pápísk kvæði á siðskiptaöld." In >> *Til heiðurs og hugbótar* (2003). Pp. 131–43, esp. pp. 139–40.

Hálfdan Einarsson. *Sciagraphia historiæ literariæ islandicæ* (Copenhagen: Sander and Schröder, 1777). P. 58.

Jakob Benediktsson. "Helgendigte." *KLNM* 6 (1961). Cols. 318–21, esp. col. 320.

Jón Helgason. "Nokkur íslenzk handrit frá 16. öld." *Skírnir* 106 (1932): 143–68.

– >> "Norges og Islands digtning." In *Litteraturhistorie B: Norge og Island* (1953). Pp. 3–179, esp. pp. 163–4.

Mogk, Eugen. >> *Geschichte der norwegisch-isländischen Literatur* (1904). P. 718.

Sverrir Tómasson. "Hvenær var Tristrams sögu snúið?" *Gripla* 2 (1977):
    47–78, esp. p. 61n66.
Vésteinn Ólason. "Kveðskapur frá síðmiðöldum." In >> *Íslensk
    Bókmenntasaga* 2 (1993). Pp. 283–378, esp. pp. 317–18.

9. Óláfsvísur III

A late medieval (ca. 1400–1550) poem in praise of King and Saint Óláfr
Haraldsson.
   Incipit: "Herlegt fólk og hæverskar þjóðir."

Manuscripts:
AM 710g 4to (ca. 1700–25), AM 713 4to (ca. 1500–50), JS 399a–b 4to
    (ca. 1700–1900), JS 581 4to (ca. 1600–1900), Lbs 2166 4to (ca. 1885–
    1920), and Lbs 201 8vo (ca. 1850–70).
Editions:
Jón Helgason, ed. >> *Íslenzk miðaldakvæði* (1936–8). Vol. 2, pp. 442–4.
    Edition of AM 713 4to.
Jón Þorkelsson. >> *Om Digtningen på Island* (1888). P. 30 (stz. 1).
    Based on AM 710g 4to, AM 713 4to, and Lbs 201 8vo.
Literature:
Bjarni Þorsteinsson, ed. *Íslenzk þjóðlög* (Copenhagen: Møller, 1906–9). P. 125.
Finnur Jónsson. >> *Den oldnorske og oldislandske Litteraturs Historie*
    (1920–4). Vol. 3, p. 126.
Guðrún Nordal. "Handrit, prentaðar bækur og pápísk kvæði á siðskiptaöld."
    In >> *Til heiðurs og hugbótar* (2003). Pp. 131–43, esp. pp. 139–40.
Hálfdan Einarsson. *Sciagraphia historiæ literariæ islandicæ* (Copenhagen:
    Sander and Schröder, 1777). P. 58.
Jakob Benediktsson. "Helgendigte." *KLNM* 6 (1961). Cols. 318–21, esp.
    col. 320.
Jón Helgason. "Nokkur íslenzk handrit frá 16. öld." *Skírnir* 106 (1932):
    143–68.
– >> "Norges og Islands digtning." In *Litteraturhistorie B: Norge og Island*
    (1953). Pp. 3–179, esp. pp. 163–4.
Kock, E.A. "Anteckningar till Íslenzk Miðaldakvæði." *ANF* 61 (1946): 1–125,
    esp. pp. 109–10.
Mogk, Eugen. >> *Geschichte der norwegisch-isländischen Literatur* (1904).
    P. 718.
Vésteinn Ólason. "Kveðskapur frá síðmiðöldum." In >> *Íslensk
    Bókmenntasaga* 2 (1993). Pp. 283–378, esp. p. 318.

10. Óláfsvísur IV

A late medieval (ca. 1400–1550) poem in praise of King and Saint Óláfr Haraldsson.
Incipit: "Herra Óláf hjálpari Nóregs landa."

Manuscripts:
A: AM 710h 4to (ca. 1700–25), AM 721 4to (ca. 1500–50), JS 581 4to (ca. 1600–1900), and Lbs 201 8vo (1850–70);
B: AM 720a 4to I (ca. 1500) and Lbs 2030 4to (ca. 1880–1900);
C: AM 716c 4to (ca. 1700), AM 717a 4to (ca. 1700–25), AM 717b 4to (ca. 1600–1700), AM 717c 4to (1678), AM 717d α 4to (ca. 1700), AM 717h 4to (ca. 1650–1700), AM 719b 4to (ca. 1700), AM 148 8vo (ca. 1650–1700), AM 150 8vo (ca. 1650–1700), AM 166a 8vo (ca. 1600–1700), BLAdd 4892 (ca. 1700–1800), BLAdd 11.179 (ca. 1700–1800), Bor 6 (20647) (ca. 1700–1800), Bor 75 (20716) (ca. 1700–1800), ÍB 36 4to (ca. 1750–1800), ÍB 37 8vo (ca. 1840), ÍB 340 8vo (1821–37), JS 256 4to (1840–5), JS 260 4to (1796), JS 399a–b 4to (ca. 1700–1900), JS 514 8vo (ca. 1675–1900), JS 112 8vo (ca. 1700–1800), JS 487 8vo (ca. 1675–1900), JS 494 8vo (ca. 1675–1900), Lbs 512 4to (ca. 1700–50), Lbs 936 4to (ca. 1880), Lbs 953 4to (ca. 1760), Lbs 1750 4to (ca. 1850–65), Lbs 2033 4to (ca. 1880–1920), Lbs 494 8vo (ca. 1700), Lbs 754 8vo (ca. 1700–1900), Lbs 956 8vo (ca. 1600–1800), Lbs 1331 8vo (ca. 1700–1900), Lbs 2345 8vo (ca. 1775–1800), NKS 1894 4to (ca. 1700–1800), Rask 88a (ca. 1700), Stock. Papp. fol. no. 64 (ca. 1650–1700), and Stock. Papp. fol. no. 97 (ca. 1700–50).

Editions:
Jón Helgason, ed. >> *Íslenzk miðaldakvæði* (1936–8). Vol. 2, pp. 455–9.
Based on AM 721 4to with emendations and variants from AM 717a 4to, AM 717b 4to, AM 717c 4to, AM 717d α 4to, AM 717h 4to, AM 720a 4to I, AM 148 8vo, AM 150 8vo, AM 166a 8vo, Lbs 956 8vo, and Rask 88a.
– ed. >> *Kvæðabók úr Vigur: AM 148, 8vo* (1955). Fol. 308r–310r.
Facsimile of AM 148 8vo.
Jón Þorkelsson. >> *Om Digtningen på Island* (1888). P. 30 (stz. 1[1]) and 310 (stz. 1 and 8).
Based primarily on Lbs 2033 4to, and somewhat on AM 717h 4to I.
Jón Þorkelsson, ed. >> *Kvæðasafn* (1922–7). Pp. 222–7.
Based on AM 721 4to and AM 720a 4to I with emendations from Stock. Papp. fol. no. 64.

Literature:

Ármann Jakobsson. "The Homer of the North, or: Who Was Sigurður the
  Blind?" *European Journal of Scandinavian Studies* 44 (2014): 4–19, esp.
  p. 10n8.
Finnur Jónsson. >> *Bókmentasaga Íslendinga fram undir siðabót* (1904–5).
  P. 463.
– >> *Den oldnorske og oldislandske Litteraturs Historie* (1920–4). Vol. 3,
  pp. 126–7.
Hálfdan Einarsson. *Sciagraphia historiæ literariæ islandicæ* (Copenhagen:
  Sander and Schröder, 1777). P. 58.
Jakob Benediktsson. "Helgendigte." *KLNM* 6 (1961). Cols. 318–21, esp.
  col. 320.
Jón Helgason. >> "Norges og Islands digtning." In *Litteraturhistorie B:
  Norge og Island* (1953). Pp. 3–179, esp. pp. 163–4.
Jón Þorkelsson. "Islandske håndskrifter i England og Skotland." *ANF* 8
  (1892): 199–237, esp. p. 206.
Jónas Kristjánsson. >> *Eddas and Sagas: Iceland's Medieval Literature*
  (1988). P. 398.
Kock, E.A. "Anteckningar till Íslenzk Miðaldakvæði." *ANF* 61 (1946): 1–125,
  esp. pp. 35 and 111–13.
Mogk, Eugen. >> *Geschichte der norwegisch-isländischen Literatur* (1904).
  P. 718.
Páll Eggert Ólason. *Menn og menntir siðskiptaaldarinnar á Íslandi.* Vol. 4
  (Reykjavík: Ársæll Árnason, 1926). P. 442.
Schottmann, Hans. >> *Die isländische Mariendichtung* (1973). P. 82n12.
Stefán Einarsson. "Íslenzk helgikvæði á miðöldum." *Tímarit Þjóðræknisfélags
  Íslendinga* 36 (1954): 43–63, esp. p. 53.
Vésteinn Ólason. "Kveðskapur frá síðmiðöldum." In >> *Íslensk
  Bókmenntasaga* 2 (1993). Pp. 283–378, esp. pp. 318–19.
– "Old Icelandic Poetry." In *A History of Icelandic Literature.* Ed. Daisy
  Neijmann. Histories of Scandinavian Literature 5 (Lincoln: University of
  Nebraska Press, 2006). Pp. 1–64, esp. p. 53.

11. Óláfsvísur

A poem about King and Saint Óláfr Haraldsson based on saga tradition and no
older than the mid-sixteenth century.

Incipit: "Ólafur kóngur Haraldsson."

Manuscript:
AM 319 4to (ca. 1700).

Editions:
Einar Ól. Sveinsson, Páll Eggert Ólason, and Arnór Sigurjónsson, ed. *Íslands
     þúsund ár: Kvæðasafn*. 3 vols. (Reykjavík: Helgafell, 1947). Vol. 3,
     pp. 98–103.
Grundtvig, Svend, and Jón Sigurðsson, ed. *Íslenzk fornkvæði*. 2 vols.
     (Copenhagen: Berling and Møller, 1859–85). Vol. 2, pp. 142–7.
Jón Þorkelsson. >> *Om Digtningen på Island* (1888). P. 28 (stz. 1).
     Based on Grundtvig and Jón Sigurðsson's edition (1859–85).
Vésteinn Ólason, ed. *Sagnadansar* (Reykjavík: Prentsmiðja Hafnarfjarðar,
     1979). Pp. 298–301.
Norwegian translation:
Orgland, Ivar, trans. *Islandske Dikt. Frå Sólarljóð til opplysningstid (13.
     hundreåret–1835)* (Reykjavík: Fonna, 1977). Pp. 215–19.
Literature:
Björn K. Þórólfsson. *Rímur fyrir 1600*. Safn fræðafjelagsins 9 (Copenhagen:
     Møller, 1934). P. 49.
Hálfdan Einarsson. *Sciagraphia historiæ literariæ islandicæ* (Copenhagen:
     Sander and Schröder, 1777). P. 58.
Mogk, Eugen. >> *Geschichte der norwegisch-isländischen Literatur* (1904).
     P. 718.
Stefán Einarsson. *Íslensk bókmenntasaga 874–1960* (Reykjavík: Oddi, 1961).
     P. 116.
Vésteinn Ólason. "Kveðskapur frá síðmiðöldum." In >> *Íslensk Bókmenntasaga*
     2 (1993). Pp. 283–378, esp. pp. 365–6.
– "Old Icelandic Poetry." In *A History of Icelandic Literature*. Ed. Daisy
     Neijmann. Histories of Scandinavian Literature 5 (Lincoln: University
     of Nebraska Press, 2006). Pp. 1–64, esp. p. 53.

12. Syndavísur

A poem composed during the Catholic era. Stz. 37 mentions King and Saint
Óláfr Haraldsson.
     Incipit: "María drottning mild og skær."

Manuscripts:
AM 713 4to (ca. 1500–50), AM 920 4to (ca. 1800–1900), AM 1032
     4to (ca. 1700–25), JS 399a–b 4to (ca. 1700–1900), and Lbs 2166 4to
     (ca. 1885–1920).
Edition:
Jón Þorkelsson. >> *Om Digtningen på Island* (1888). P. 97 (stz. 1, 39$^{1-2}$,
     and 40$^{5-7}$).

Based on AM 713 4to, AM 920 4to, and AM 1032 4to.

Literature:

Chase, Martin. "Devotional Poetry at the End of the Middle Ages in Iceland."
In >> *Eddic, Skaldic, and Beyond: Poetic Variety in Medieval Iceland.* Ed.
Martin Chase (2014). Pp. 136–49, esp. p. 148.

PAUL THE APOSTLE   June 29

1. Pálsvísur

A fragment of a poem in honour of Saint Paul composed in the late medieval
(ca. 1400–1550) period.
    Incipit: " … herrann fer er hjálpin skæði."

Manuscripts:

AM 720a 4to VII (ca. 1500), AM 920 4to (ca. 1800–1900), Lbs 1486b 4to
    (ca. 1860–78), and Lbs 2166 4to (ca. 1885–1920).

Editions:

Jón Helgason, ed. >> *Íslenzk miðaldakvæði* (1936–8). Vol. 2, pp. 284–5.
    Based on AM 720a 4to VII with variants from Lbs 1486b 4to and Lbs 2166
    4to.

Jón Þorkelsson. >> *Om Digtningen på Island* (1888). P. 66 (stz. 1$^{3-5}$ and 8).
    Based on AM 720a 4to VII and AM 920 4to.

Literature:

Bekker-Nielsen, Hans. "Paulus: Norrøn tradition." *KLNM* 13 (1968). Cols.
    153–4, esp. col. 153.

Finnur Jónsson. >> *Bókmentasaga Íslendinga fram undir siðabót* (1904–5).
    P. 461.

– >> *Den oldnorske og oldislandske Litteraturs Historie* (1920–4). Vol. 3,
    p. 126.

Hálfdan Einarsson. *Sciagraphia historiæ literariæ islandicæ* (Copenhagen:
    Sander and Schröder, 1777). P. 58.

Jakob Benediktsson. "Helgendigte." *KLNM* 6 (1961). Cols. 318–21, esp.
    col. 320.

Kock, E.A. "Antecknignar till Íslenzk Míðaldakvæði." *ANF* 61 (1946):
    1–125, esp. pp. 80–1.

Stéfan Einarsson. "Íslenzk helgikvæði á miðöldum." *Tímarit Þjóðræknisfélags
    Íslendinga* 36 (1954): 43–63, esp. p. 54.

– *Íslensk bókmenntasaga 874–1960* (Reykjavík: Oddi, 1961). P. 91.

Vésteinn Ólason. "Kveðskapur frá síðmiðöldum." In >> *Íslensk Bókmenntasaga*
2 (1993). Pp. 283–378, esp. p. 315.

2. Pálsdiktur

A late medieval (ca. 1400–1550) poem in honour of Saint Paul.
Incipit: "Bið ég að styrki málsnilld mína."

Manuscripts:
A: AM 717a 4to (ca. 1700–25), AM 150 8vo (ca. 1650–1700), and Lbs 2166
4to (ca. 1885–1920);
B: AM 717h 4to (ca. 1650–1700), BLAdd 11.179 (ca. 1700–1800), JS 256
4to (1840–5), JS 260 4to (1796), JS 112 8vo (ca. 1700–1800), JS 514 8vo
(ca. 1675–1900), Lbs 953 4to (ca. 1760), Lbs 2166 4to (ca. 1885–1920),
Lbs 201 8vo (ca. 1850–70), Lbs 2345 8vo (ca. 1775–1800), and Stock.
Papp. fol. no. 64 (ca. 1650–1700).
Editions:
Jón Helgason, ed. >> *Íslenzk miðaldakvæði* (1936–8). Vol. 2, pp. 287–91.
Based on AM 150 8vo with variants from AM 717a 4to and AM 717h 4to.
Jón Þorkelsson. >> *Om Digtningen på Island* (1888). P. 66 (stz. 1).
Based on AM 717a 4to, AM 717h 4to, AM 150 8vo, JS 260 4to, Lbs 201
8vo, and Stock. Papp. fol. no. 64.
Literature:
Anon. "Den Oldnordisk-islandske Afdeling." Annual Report for 1846.
Antiquarisk Tidsskrift 1846–8 (Copenhagen: Sally B. Salomon, 1847).
Pp. 39–49, esp. p. 41.
Bekker-Nielsen, Hans. "Paulus: Norrøn tradition." *KLNM* 13 (1968). Cols.
153–4, esp. col. 153.
Finnur Jónsson. >> *Bókmentasaga Íslendinga fram undir siðabót* (1904–5).
P. 461.
– >> *Den oldnorske og oldislandske Litteraturs Historie* (1920–4). Vol. 3,
p. 126.
Hálfdan Einarsson. *Sciagraphia historiæ literariæ islandicæ* (Copenhagen:
Sander and Schröder, 1777). P. 58.
Jakob Benediktsson. "Helgendigte." *KLNM* 6 (1961). Cols. 318–21, esp.
col. 320.
Kock, E.A. "Anteckningar till Íslenzk Miðaldakvæði." *ANF* 61 (1946): 1–125,
esp. pp. 42–3 and 80–1.
Stéfan Einarsson. "Íslenzk helgikvæði á miðöldum." *Tímarit Þjóðræknisfélags
Íslendinga* 36 (1955): 43–63, esp. p. 54.

– *Íslensk bókmenntasaga 874–1960* (Reykjavík: Oddi, 1961). P. 91.

Vésteinn Ólason. "Kveðskapur frá síðmiðöldum." In >> *Íslensk Bókmenntasaga* 2 (1993). Pp. 283–378, esp. p. 315.

NOTE:

The poem contains material about Saint Anne. See her entry.

3. Rímur af Páli postula

Fourteen *rímur* about Saint Paul written by Eiríkur Hallsson í Höfða (1614–98).

Incipit: "Meistari dyggða menntafróð."

Manuscript:

Lbs 528 8vo (ca. 1720).

Edition:

Finnur Sigmundsson. >> *Rímnatal.* 2 vols. (1966). Vol. 1, pp. 375–6 (preface, introductory verse, refrain, and conclusion).

4. Allra postola minnisvísur

A fourteenth-century poem about all the apostles. Saint Paul is treated in stz. 2.

Incipit: "Pétr er páfi drottins prísaðr gleðivísum."

Manuscript:

See Andrew the Apostle 10 note (p. 30).

Editions:

Finnur Jónsson, ed. >> *Den norsk-islandske skjaldedigtning* (1912–15). Vol. AII, p. 509 and vol. BII, p. 559.

Kock, Ernst Albin, ed. >> *Den norsk-isländska skaldediktningen* (1946–50). Vol. 2, p. 306.

McDougall, Ian, ed. "Anonymous, *Allra postula minnisvísur* 'Celebratory Vísur about All the Apostles'." In >> *Poetry on Christian Subjects* (2007). Vol. 2, p. 855.

Danish translation:

Finnur Jónsson, ed. >> *Den norsk-islandske skjaldedigtning* (1912–15). Vol. BII, p. 559.

English translation:

McDougall, Ian, ed. "Anonymous, *Allra postula minnisvísur* 'Celebratory Vísur about All the Apostles'." In >> *Poetry on Christian Subjects* (2007). Vol. 2, p. 855.

5. Tólf postula kvæði

A late medieval (ca. 1400–1550) celebratory poem about all the apostles. Saint Paul is treated in stz. 2.

Incipit: "Sankti Pétur sannur páfi í Róma."

Manuscripts:
See Andrew the Apostle 11 note (p. 31).
Edition:
Jón Helgason, ed. >> *Íslenzk miðaldakvæði* (1936–8). Vol. 2, p. 274.

6. Rósa

An early sixteenth-century cosmological poem with an emphasis on the life of Mary the Blessed Virgin attributed to Sigurður blindur. Stz. 6 mentions Saint Paul.

Incipit: "Faðir og son á hæstum hæðum."

Manuscripts:
See Mary the Blessed Virgin 48 note (p. 212).
Editions:
Jón Helgason, ed. >> *Íslenzk miðaldakvæði* (1936–8). Vol. 1.2, p. 7.
Jón Þorkelsson, ed. >> *Kvæðasafn* (1922–7). P. 264.
Norwegian translation:
*Orgland, Ivar. *Rósa* (Oslo: Solum, 1989).

7. Huggunarvísur fyrir þá sem syrgja eftir ástmenn sína

A poem of comfort for those grieving loved ones composed ca. 1600 by Einar Sigurðsson í Eydölum (1539–1626). It draws in part on 1 Corinthians. Stz. 6 and 11 mention Saint Paul.

Incipit: "Hvör sem eftir ástmann þreyr."

Editions:
Guðbrandur Þorláksson, ed. >> *Ein ny wiisna bok* (1612). P. 107.
Jón Torfason and Kristján Eiríksson, ed. >> *Vísnabók Guðbrands* (2000).
   P. 126.
Jón Þorkelsson. >> *Om Digtningen på Island* (1888). P. 443 (stz. 1).
   Based on *Ein ny wiisna bok* (1612).

Literature:
Pétur Sigurðsson. "Vísnabók Guðbrands biskups." In *Iðunn: Tímarit til skemtunar, nytsemdar og fróðleiks*. Vol. 8. Ed. Magnús Jónsson (Reykjavík: Gutenberg, 1923–4). Pp. 61–87, esp. pp. 72–3.

8. Píslarminning

A poem about Christ's passion composed ca. 1600 by Einar Sigurðsson í Eydölum (1539–1626). Saint Paul is mentioned in stz. 1.
    Incipit: "Hinn helgi Paulus hefur það kent."

Manuscripts:
See John the Evangelist 23 note (p. 140).
Editions:
Guðbrandur Þorláksson, ed. >> *Ein ny wiisna bok* (1612). P. 90.
Jón Torfason and Kristján Eiríksson, ed. >> *Vísnabók Guðbrands* (2000).
    P. 106.
Jón Þorkelsson. >> *Om Digtningen på Island* (1888). Pp. 96 (stz. 1^{1-2}) and
    442 (stz. 1).

9. Vísur um sanna iðran og ávöxtu hennar

A poem composed ca. 1600 by Einar Sigurðsson í Eydölum encouraging Christian people to obey Saint Paul's teachings in the letters to the Romans and the Ephesians. Saint Paul is mentioned in stz. 1–2.
    Incipit: "Postulinn drottins Páll með orðum blíðum."

Manuscript:
AM 720a 4to XI (ca. 1600–1700).
Editions:
Guðbrandur Þorláksson, ed. >> *Ein ny wiisna bok* (1612). P. 97.
Jón Torfason and Kristján Eiríksson, ed. >> *Vísnabók Guðbrands* (2000).
    P. 113.
Jón Þorkelsson. >> *Om Digtningen på Island* (1888). P. 442 (stz. 1).
    Based on *Ein ny wiisna bok* (1612).
Literature:
Björn Þorleifsson. "Kvantitetsomvæltningen i islandsk." *ANF* 45 (1929):
    35–81, esp. p. 55.

10. Postulavísur

A poem about all the apostles composed in 1629 by Guðmundur Erlendsson í
Felli (1595–1670). Stz. 28–30 and 34–8 concern Saint Paul.
   Incipit: "Herrans hér postula."

Manuscripts:
See Andrew the Apostle 14 note (p. 32).

11. Postularaun

A poem in praise of all the apostles composed by Guðmundur Bergþórsson
(1657–1705). Stz. 21 and 81–4 concern Saint Paul.
   Incipit: "Hér skal eina hróðar grein."

Manuscripts:
See Ananias note (p. 20).

PERPETUA   March 7

1. Pétrsdrápa

A fourteenth-century poem in honour of Saint Peter. Stz. 12 mentions Saint
Perpetua.
   Incipit: "Orð satt upphafs gjörði eitt næst stafi hæsta."

Manuscripts:
See Peter the Apostle 1 note (p. 318).
Editions:
Finnur Jónsson, ed. >> *Den norsk-islandske skjaldedigtning* (1912–15).
   Vol. AII, p. 502 and vol. BII, p. 548.
Kahle, Bernhard, ed. >> *Isländische geistliche Dichtungen des ausgehenden*
   Mittelalters (1898). Pp. 80–1.
Kock, Ernst Albin, ed. >> *Den norsk-isländska skaldediktningen* (1946–50).
   Vol. 2, p. 300.
McDougall, David, ed. "Anonymous, *Pétrsdrápa* 'Drápa about S. Peter'."
   In >> *Poetry on Christian Subjects* (2007). Vol. 2, p. 805.

Danish translation:
Finnur Jónsson, ed. >> *Den norsk-islandske skjaldedigtning* (1912–15).
  Vol. BII, p. 548.
English translation:
McDougall, David, ed. "Anonymous, *Pétrsdrápa* '*Drápa* about S. Peter'."
  In >> *Poetry on Christian Subjects* (2007). Vol. 2, p. 805.

PETER THE APOSTLE   June 29

1. Pétrsdrápa

A fourteenth-century poem in honour of Saint Peter.
  Incipit: "Orð satt upphafs gjörði eitt næst stafi hæsta."

Manuscripts:
AM 621 4to (ca. 1450–1500) and AM 920 4to (ca. 1800–1900).
Editions:
Finnur Jónsson, ed. >> *Den norsk-islandske skjaldedigtning* (1912–15).
  Vol. AII, pp. 500–50 and vol. BII, pp. 545–58.
  Edition of AM 621 4to.
Jón Þorkelsson. >> *Om Digtningen på Island* (1888). P. 40.
  Edition of AM 621 4to (stz. 1 only).
Kahle, Bernhard, ed. >> *Isländische geistliche Dichtungen des ausgehenden
  Mittelalters* (1898). Pp. 78–90.
  Edition of AM 621 4to.
Kock, Ernst Albin, ed. >> *Notationes Norrœna* (1923–44). §§58B, 1707,
  1708, 1709, 1710, 1711, 1712A, 1712B, 1712C, 1713, 1714, 1715, 1716,
  1717, 1718, 1719, 1720, 1721, 1722, 1723, 1724, 1725, 1726, 1727, 1728,
  1729, 1730, 1731, 1732, 1733, 1734, 1735, 1736, 1737, 1738, 1739, 1740,
  1741, 1742, 1743, 1744, 1745, 1746, 1747, 1748, 1749, 1750, 1751, 1752,
  1753, 1754, 1755, 2774, 2831, 2873, 2874, 2875, 2876, 2877, 2878, 2879,
  2880, 2881, 2882, 2883, 2884, 2885, 2997C, 3371, 3372, 3373, 3374,
  3375, 3397, and 3397L.
– ed. >> *Den norsk-isländska skaldediktningen* (1946–50). Vol. 2,
  pp. 299–305.
Konráð Gíslason. *Fire og fyrretyve for en stor deel forhen utrykte prøver
  af oldnordisk sprog og literatur* (Copenhagen: Gyldendal, 1860). P. 557
  (extract only).
  Edition of AM 621 4to.

McDougall, David, ed. "Anonymous, *Pétrsdrápa* 'Drápa about S. Peter'."
In >> *Poetry on Christian Subjects* (2007). Vol. 2, pp. 797–844.
Edition of AM 621 4to.

Wisén, Theodor. *Úrval af norrænum fornkvæðum handa hinum bókmennta-iðkendum* (Lund: Berling, 1870). P. 47 (extract only).

Danish translation:
Finnur Jónsson, ed. >> *Den norsk-islandske skjaldedigtning* (1912–15).
Vol. BII, pp. 545–57.

English translation:
McDougall, David, ed. "Anonymous, *Pétrsdrápa* 'Drápa about S. Peter'."
In >> *Poetry on Christian Subjects* (2007). Vol. 2, pp. 797–844.

Literature:
Bekker-Nielsen, Hans. "Petrus, apostel: Norrøn tradition." *KLNM* 13 (1968).
Cols. 261–3, esp. col. 262.

Cormack, Margaret. >> *The Saints in Iceland* (1994). P. 41n60.

– "Poetry, Paganism and the Sagas of Icelandic Bishops." In >> *Til heiðurs og hugbótar* (2003). Pp. 33–51, esp. p. 50.

Finnur Jónsson. >> *Den oldnorske og oldislandske Litteraturs Historie* (1920–4). Vol. 3, pp. 17–18.

Gade, Kari Ellen. *The Structure of Old Norse Dróttkvætt Poetry*. Islandica 49 (Ithaca and London: Cornell University Press, 1995). P. 244.

Guðrún Nordal. *Tools of Literacy: The Role of Skaldic Verse in Icelandic Textual Culture of the Twelfth and Thirteenth Centuries* (Toronto: University of Toronto Press, 2001). Pp. 377n20 and 386n66.

Jakob Benediktsson. "Helgendigte." *KLNM* 6 (1961). Cols. 318–21, esp. col. 320.

Kahle, Bernhard. "Das Christentum in der altwestnordischen Dichtung." *ANF* 13 (1901): 1–40 and 97–160, esp. pp. 27, 31–2, 100–3, 105–8, 111, 113–16, 122, 124, 128–40, 147, and 150–2.

Mogk, Eugen. >> *Geschichte der norwegisch-isländischen Literatur* (1904). P. 718.

Poole, R.G. *Viking Poems on War and Peace: A Study in Skaldic Narrative* (Toronto: University of Toronto Press, 1991). P. 32.

Schottmann, Hans. >> *Die isländische Mariendichtung* (1973). Pp. 33, 207, 238n8, and 255–6.

Stéfan Einarsson. "Íslenzk helgikvæði á miðöldum." *Tímarit Þjóðræknisfélags Íslendinga* 36 (1955): 43–63, esp. p. 49.

– *Íslensk bókmenntasaga 874–1960* (Reykjavík: Oddi, 1961). P. 86.

Sverrir Tómasson. "'Nikulám skulu vér heiðra hér …'." In >> *Til heiðurs og hugbótar* (2003). Pp. 79–92, esp. p. 89.

Vésteinn Ólason. "Kveðskapur frá síðmiðöldum." In >> *Íslensk Bókmenntasaga* 2 (1993). Pp. 283–378, esp. p. 315.
– "Old Icelandic Poetry." In *A History of Icelandic Literature*. Ed. Daisy Neijmann. Histories of Scandinavian Literature 5 (Lincoln: University of Nebraska Press, 2006). Pp. 1–64, esp. p. 48.

NOTE:
The poem contains material about Saints Andrew, Perpetua, Petronilla, and Simon. See their entries.

2. Pétursvísur

A late medieval (ca. 1400–1550) poem in honour of Saint Peter.
   Incipit: "Þér vil ég vísur færa."

Manuscripts:
AM 713 4to (ca. 1500–50) and Lbs 2166 4to (ca. 1885–1920).

Editions:
Jón Helgason, ed. >> *Íslenzk miðaldakvæði* (1936–8). Vol. 2, pp. 278–80. Edition of AM 713 4to.
Jón Þorkelsson. >> *Om Digtningen på Island* (1888). P. 64 (stz. 1). Based on AM 713 4to.

Literature:
Bekker-Nielsen, Hans. "Petrus, apostel: Norrøn tradition." *KLNM* 13 (1968). Cols. 261–3, esp. col. 262.
Finnur Jónsson. >> *Bókmentasaga Íslendinga fram undir siðabót* (1904–5). P. 461.
– >> *Den oldnorske og oldislandske Litteraturs Historie* (1920–4). Vol. 3, p. 126.
Guðrún Nordal. "Handrit, prentaðar bækur og pápísk kvæði á siðskiptaöld." In >> *Til heiðurs og hugbótar* (2003). Pp. 131–43, esp. pp. 139–40.
Hálfdan Einarsson. *Sciagraphia historiæ literariæ islandicæ* (Copenhagen: Sander and Schröder, 1777). P. 58.
Jakob Benediktsson. "Helgendigte." *KLNM* 6 (1961). Cols. 318–21, esp. col. 320.
Jón Helgason. "Nokkur íslenzk handrit frá 16. öld." *Skírnir* 106 (1932): 143–68.
Kock, E.A. "Anteckningar till Íslenzk Miðaldakvæði." *ANF* 61 (1946): 1–125, esp. p. 79.
Schottman, Hans. >> *Die isländische Mariendichtung* (1973). P. 29n27.

Stéfan Einarsson. "Íslenzk helgikvæði á miðöldum." *Tímarit Þjóðræknisfélags Íslendinga* 36 (1954): 43–63, esp. p. 54.
– *Íslensk bókmenntasaga 874–1960* (Reykjavík: Oddi, 1961). P. 91.
Vésteinn Ólason. "Kveðskapur frá síðmiðöldum." In >> *Íslensk Bókmenntasaga* 2 (1993). Pp. 283–378, esp. p. 315.

3. Pétursdiktur

A late medieval (ca. 1400–1550) poem in honour of Saint Peter.
Incipit: "Postulann skulum vér prísa leita."

Manuscripts:
AM 721 4to (ca. 1500–50), AM 1032 4to (ca. 1700–25), JS 399a–b 4to (ca. 1700–1900), and Lbs 2166 4to (ca. 1885–1920).

Editions:
Jón Helgason, ed. >> *Íslenzk miðaldakvæði* (1936–8). Vol. 2, pp. 278–80.
Based on AM 721 4to with variants from AM 1032 4to and JS 399a–b 4to.
Jón Þorkelsson. >> *Om Digtningen på Island* (1888). P. 64 (stz. 1).
Based on AM 721 4to and AM 1032 4to.

Literature:
Bekker-Nielsen, Hans. "Petrus, apostel: Norrøn tradition." *KLNM* 13 (1968). Cols. 261–3, esp. col. 262.
Finnur Jónsson. >> *Bókmentasaga Íslendinga fram undir siðabót* (1904–5). P. 461.
– >> *Den oldnorske og oldislandske Litteraturs Historie* (1920–4). Vol. 3, p. 126.
Hálfdan Einarsson. *Sciagraphia historiæ literariæ islandicæ* (Copenhagen: Sander and Schröder, 1777). P. 58.
Jakob Benediktsson. "Helgendigte." *KLNM* 6 (1961). Cols. 318–21, esp. col. 320.
Kock, E.A. "Anteckningar till Íslenzk Miðaldakvæði." *ANF* 61 (1946): 1–125, esp. pp. 79–80.
Stéfan Einarsson. "Íslenzk helgikvæði á miðöldum." *Tímarit Þjóðræknisfélags Íslendinga* 36 (1955): 43–63, esp. p. 54.
– *Íslensk bókmenntasaga 874–1960* (Reykjavík: Oddi, 1961). P. 91.
Vésteinn Ólason. "Kveðskapur frá síðmiðöldum." In >> *Íslensk Bókmenntasaga* 2 (1993). Pp. 283–378, esp. p. 315.

4. Harmsól

A twelfth-century praise-poem addressed to Christ by Gamli. Saint Peter is
treated in stz. 50–1.
    Incipit: "Hár stillir, lúk heilli."

Manuscripts:
See Mary the Blessed Virgin 61 note (p. 226).
Editions:
*Attwood, Katrina, ed. "The Poems of MS AM 757a 4to: An Edition and
    Contextual Study." PhD dissertation, University of Leeds, 1996.
– ed. "Gamli kanóki, *Harmsól* 'Sun of Sorrow'." In >> *Poetry on Christian
    Subjects* (2007). Vol. 1, pp. 117–18.
*Black, Elizabeth L. "*Harmsól*: An Edition." BLitt thesis, University of
    Oxford, 1971.
Finnur Jónsson, ed. >> *Den norsk-islandske skjaldedigtning* (1912–15).
    Vol. AI, p. 569 and vol. BI, p. 561.
– ed. *Carmina scaldica: udvalg af norske og islandske skjaldekvad.* 2nd rev.
    ed. (Copenhagen: Gad, 1923). P. 85.
Kempff, Hjalmar, ed. *Kaniken Gamles "Harmsol" (Sol i Sorgen): Isländskt
    andligt qväde från medeltiden, öfversättning och förklaringar* (Uppsala:
    Edquist and Berglund, 1867). P. 15.
Kock, Ernst Albin, ed. >> *Den norsk-islandske skaldediktningen* (1946–50).
    Vol. 1, p. 272.
Rydberg, Hugo, ed. *Die geistlichen Drápur und Dróttkvættfragmente des
    Cod. AM 757 4to* (Copenhagen: Møller, 1907). Pp. 28–9.
Sveinbjörn Egilsson, ed. *Fjøgur gømul kvæði. Boðsrit til að hlusta á
    þá opinberu yfirheyrslu í Bessastaða Skóla þann 22–29 mai 1844*
    (Viðeyjarklaustur: Helgi Helgason, 1844). P. 29.
Danish translation:
Finnur Jónsson, ed. >> *Den norsk-islandske skjaldedigtning* (1912–15).
    Vol. BI, p. 561.
English translation:
Attwood, Katrina, ed. "Gamli kanóki, *Harmsól* 'Sun of Sorrow'." In >>
    Poetry on Christian Subjects (2007). Vol. 1, pp. 117–18.
Norwegian translation:
Audne, Kr., trans. "*Harmsól.*" In *Norrøne kristenkvæde.* Ed. Olaf Hanssen
    (Oslo: Det norske samlaget, 1928). P. 34.

Swedish translation:
Kempff, Hjalmar, ed. *Kaniken Gamles "Harmsol" (Sol i Sorgen): Isländskt andligt qväde från medeltiden, öfversättning och förklaringar* (Uppsala: Edquist and Berglund, 1867). P. 15.

5. Allra postola minnisvísur

A fourteenth-century poem about all the apostles. Saint Peter is treated in stz. 1. Incipit: "Pétr er páfi drottins prísaðr gleðivísum."

Manuscript:
See Andrew the Apostle 10 note (p. 30).
Editions:
Finnur Jónsson, ed. >> *Den norsk-islandske skjaldedigtning* (1912–15). Vol. AII, p. 509 and vol. BII, p. 559.
Kock, Ernst Albin, ed. >> *Den norsk-isländska skaldediktningen* (1946–50). Vol. 2, p. 306.
McDougall, Ian, ed. "Anonymous, *Allra postula minnisvísur* 'Celebratory *Vísur* about All the Apostles'." In >> *Poetry on Christian Subjects* (2007). Vol. 2, p. 854.
Danish translation:
Finnur Jónsson, ed. >> *Den norsk-islandske skjaldedigtning* (1912–15). Vol. BII, p. 559.
English translation:
McDougall, Ian, ed. "Anonymous, *Allra postula minnisvísur* 'Celebratory *Vísur* about All the Apostles'." In >> *Poetry on Christian Subjects* (2007). Vol. 2, p. 854.

6. Pétursdiktur

A Marian miracle poem from ca. 1300–1550 about a monk at Saint Peter's Church in Cologne who fathered a child and died without last rites, but was brought back to life through the aid of Saint Peter and Mary the Blessed Virgin (cf. C.R. Unger, ed., *Mariu saga: Legender om Jomfru Maria og hendes jertegn* [Christiania (Oslo): Brögger and Christie, 1871], pp. 860–2).
    Incipit: "Máríu ertu mild og skær."

Manuscripts:
See Mary the Blessed Virgin 11 note (p. 177).

Editions:
Jón Helgason, ed. >> *Íslenzk miðaldakvæði* (1936–8). Vol. 2, pp. 123–7.
Jón Þorkelsson. >> *Om Digtningen på Island* (1888). P. 49 (stz. 1).

7. Boðunarvísur

A poem in honour of Mary the Blessed Virgin composed ca. 1300–1550. Stz. 19
mentions Saint Peter.
   Incipit: "Ave dýrust drósa."

Manuscripts:
See Mary the Blessed Virgin 19 note (p. 184).
Edition:
Jón Helgason, ed. >> *Íslenzk miðaldakvæði* (1936–8). Vol. 2, p. 31.

8. Tólf postula kvæði

A late medieval (ca. 1400–1550) celebratory poem about all the apostles. Saint
Peter is treated in stz. 1 and 3.
   Incipit: "Sankti Pétur sannur páfi í Róma."

Manuscripts:
See Andrew the Apostle 11 note (p. 31).
Editions:
Jón Helgason, ed. >> *Íslenzk miðaldakvæði* (1936–8). Vol. 2, pp. 274–5.
Jón Þorkelsson. >> *Om Digtningen på Island* (1888). P. 62 (stz. 1).

9. Píslardrápa

A fragmentary passion poem composed ca. 1400–1550. Stz. 1 mentions Saint
Peter.
   Incipit: "Postuli einn með prýði hæsta."

Manuscripts:
See John the Evangelist 10 note (p. 133).
Editions:
Jón Helgason, ed. >> *Íslenzk miðaldakvæði* (1936–8). Vol. 1.2, p. 59.
Jón Þorkelsson. >> *Om Digtningen på Island* (1888). P. 96 (stz. 1, 28^5, and 47.

10. Andréasdiktur I

A poem about the life and martyrdom of Saint Andrew probably composed ca.
1400–1550. Saint Peter is mentioned in stz. 22.
   Incipit: "Miskun þín hinn mildi guð."

Manuscripts:
See Andrew the Apostle 2 note (p. 23).
Edition:
Jón Helgason, ed. >> *Íslenzk miðaldakvæði* (1936–8). Vol. 2, p. 295.

11. Andréasdiktur II

A late medieval (ca. 1400–1550) poem about the life of Saint Andrew based on
oral tradition. Stz. 1 mentions Saint Peter.
   Incipit: "Timens veit ég tíma rýra (að skýra)."

Manuscripts:
See Andrew the Apostle 3 note (p. 24).
Edition:
Jón Helgason, ed. >> *Íslenzk miðaldakvæði* (1936–8). Vol. 2, p. 298.

12. Rósa

An early sixteenth-century cosmological poem with an emphasis on the life of
Mary the Blessed Virgin attributed to Sigurður blindur. Stz. 6 mentions Saint
Peter.
   Incipit: "Faðir og son á hæstum hæðum."

Manuscripts:
See Mary the Blessed Virgin 48 note (p. 212).
Editions:
Jón Helgason, ed. >> *Íslenzk miðaldakvæði* (1936–8). Vol. 1.2, p. 7.
Jón Þorkelsson, ed. >> *Kvæðasafn* (1922–7). P. 264.
Norwegian translation:
Orgland, Ivar, trans. and Anne-Lise Knoff, illus. *Rósa. Sigurður blindi í*
   Fagradal (Oslo: Solum, 1989). P. 20.

13. Gimsteinn

An early sixteenth-century poem about the cross-tree ascribed to the priest
Hallur Ögmundarson (d. ca. 1540). Stz. 31 concerns Saint Peter.
   Incipit: "Heyr mig ilmanda hjartans yndi."

Manuscripts:
See Cross, the Holy 7 note (p. 73).
Editions:
Jón Helgason, ed. >> *Íslenzk miðaldakvæði* (1936–8). Vol. 1.2, p. 311.
Jón Þorkelsson, ed. >> *Kvæðasafn* (1922–7). P. 305.

14. Náð

An early sixteenth-century poem in honour of Saint Anne and her daughter
Mary the Blessed Virgin ascribed to the priest Hallur Ögmundarson (d. ca.
1540). Stz. 8 mentions Saint Peter.
   Incipit: "Heyr mildingur allra alda."

Manuscripts:
See Anne 1 note (p. 34).
Editions:
Jón Helgason, ed. >> *Íslenzk miðaldakvæði* (1936–8). Vol. 2, p. 5.
Jón Þorkelsson, ed. >> *Kvæðasafn* (1922–7). P. 329.

15. Krossvísur I

A poem about Christ and the Holy Cross composed ca. 1525 by Bishop Jón
Arason (1484–1550). Stz. 12 mentions Saint Peter.
   Incipit: "Dýrðarfullur drottinn minn."

Manuscripts:
See Cross, the Holy 8 note (p. 75).
Editions:
Finnur Jónsson, ed. >> *Jón Arasons religiøse digte* (1918). P. 71.
Jón Helgason, ed. >> *Íslenzk miðaldakvæði* (1936–8). Vol. 1.2, p. 255.
[Jón Sigurðsson and Guðbrandur Vigfússon, ed.] >> *Biskupa sögur*
   (1858–78). Vol. 2, pp. 560–1.
*Peringskiöld, J.F. >> *Fragmentum runicopapisticum* (1721).

16. Niðurstigningsvísur

A poetic rendering of the story of Christ's descent to hell, composed ca. 1525 by Bishop Jón Arason (1484–1550). Stz. 14 mentions Saint Peter.
   Incipit: "Djarflig er mér diktan."

Manuscripts:
See Anne 13 note (p. 43).
Editions:
Finnur Jónsson, ed. >> *Jón Arasons religiøse digte* (1918). P. 62.
Jón Helgason, ed. >> *Íslenzk miðaldakvæði* (1936–8). Vol. 1.2, p. 226.
[Jón Sigurðsson and Guðbrandur Vigfússon, ed.] >> *Biskupa sögur* (1858–78).
   Vol. 2, p. 550.

17. Ein ágæt minning herrans Jesú Kristi pínu

A passion poem composed ca. 1600 by Arngrímur Jónsson lærði (1568–1648). Stz. 19 mentions Saint Peter.
   Incipit: "Mér er í hug að minnast."

Manuscript:
SÁM 48 (1730).
Editions:
Guðbrandur Þorláksson, ed. >> *Ein ny wiisna bok* (1612). P. 266.
Jón Torfason and Kristján Eiríksson, ed. >> *Vísnabók Guðbrands* (2000). P. 300.
Literature:
Jón Þorkelsson, ed. >> *Om Digtningen på Island* (1888). Pp. 96 and 474.
Pétur Sigurðsson. "Vísnabók Guðbrands biskups." In *Iðunn: Tímarit til skemtunar, nytsemdar og fróðleiks*. Vol. 8. Ed. Magnús Jónsson (Reykjavík: Gutenberg, 1923–4). Pp. 61–87, esp. p. 80.
NOTE:
The poem contains material about Saint Simeon the Righteous. See his entry.

18. Postulavísur

A poem about all the apostles composed in 1629 by Guðmundur Erlendsson í Felli (1595–1670). Stz. 3–8 and 29 concern Saint Peter.
   Incipit: "Herrans hér postula."

Manuscripts:
See Andrew the Apostle 14 note (p. 32).

19. Postularaun

A poem in praise of all the apostles composed by Guðmundur Bergþórsson (1657–1705). Stz. 15–21 and 23 concern Saint Peter.
Incipit: "Hér skal eina hróðar grein."

Manuscripts:
See Ananias note (p. 20).

PETRONILLA   May 31

1. Pétrsdrápa

A fourteenth-century poem in honour of Saint Peter. Stz. 12 mentions Saint Petronilla.
Incipit: "Orð satt upphafs gjörði eitt næst stafi hæsta."

Manuscripts:
See Peter the Apostle 1 note (p. 318).
Editions:
Finnur Jónsson, ed. >> *Den norsk-islandske skjaldedigtning* (1912–15).
Vol. AII, p. 502 and vol. BII, p. 548.
Kahle, Bernhard, ed. >> *Isländische geistliche Dichtungen des ausgehenden Mittelalters* (1898). Pp. 80–1.
Kock, Ernst Albin, ed. >> *Den norsk-isländska skaldediktningen* (1946–50).
Vol. 2, p. 300.
McDougall, David, ed. "Anonymous, *Pétrsdrápa* 'Drápa about S. Peter'."
In >> *Poetry on Christian Subjects* (2007). Vol. 2, p. 805.
Danish translation:
Finnur Jónsson, ed. >> *Den norsk-islandske skjaldedigtning* (1912–15).
Vol. BII, p. 548.
English translation:
McDougall, David, ed. "Anonymous, *Pétrsdrápa* 'Drápa about S. Peter'."
In >> *Poetry on Christian Subjects* (2007). Vol. 2, p. 805.

2. Heilagra meyja drápa

A fourteenth-century poem about holy maidens. Stz. 55 treats Saint Petronilla.
Incipit: "Heyrðu ómælds himna veldis herra guð."

Manuscripts:
See Agatha note (p. 13).
Editions:
Finnur Jónsson, ed. >> *Den norsk-islandske skjaldedigtning* (1912–15).
   Vol. AII, p. 538 and vol. BII, pp. 595–6
Kock, Ernst Albin, ed. >> *Notationes Norrænæ* (1923–44). §3376B.
– ed. >> *Den norsk-islandske skaldediktningen* (1946–50). Vol. 2, p. 330.
Wolf, Kirsten, ed. "Anonymous, *Heilagra meyja drápa* '*Drápa* about Holy
   Maidens'." In >> *Poetry on Christian Subjects* (2007). Vol. 2, p. 926.
Danish translation:
Finnur Jónsson, ed. >> *Den norsk-islandske skjaldedigtning* (1912–15).
   Vol. BII, p. 596.
English translation:
Wolf, Kirsten, ed. "Anonymous, *Heilagra meyja drápa* '*Drápa* about Holy
   Maidens'." In >> *Poetry on Christian Subjects.* (2007). Vol. 2, p. 926.

PHILIP THE APOSTLE   May 1

1. Allra postola minnisvísur

A fourteenth-century poem about all the apostles. Saint Philip is treated in stz.
7.
   Incipit: "Pétr er páfi drottins prísaðr gleðivísum."

Manuscript:
See Andrew the Apostle 10 note (p. 30).
Editions:
Finnur Jónsson, ed. >>*Den norsk-islandske skjaldedigtning* (1912–15).
   Vol. AII, p. 510 and vol. BII, pp. 560–1.
Kock, Ernst Albin, ed. >> *Den norsk-isländska skaldediktningen* (1946–50).
   Vol. 2, p. 307.
McDougall, Ian, ed. "Anonymous, *Allra postula minnisvísur* 'Celebratory
   Vísur about All the Apostles'." In >> *Poetry on Christian Subjects* (2007).
   Vol. 2, p. 861.
Danish translation:
Finnur Jónsson, ed. >> *Den norsk-islandske skjaldedigtning* (1912–15).
   Vol. BII, pp. 560–1.

English translation:
McDougall, Ian, ed. "Anonymous, *Allra postula minnisvísur* 'Celebratory
    Vísur about All the Apostles'." In >> *Poetry on Christian Subjects* (2007).
    Vol. 2, p. 862.

2. Tólf postula kvæði

A late medieval (ca. 1400–1550) celebratory poem about all the apostles. Saint
Philip is treated in stz. 5.
    Incipit: "Sankti Pétur sannur páfi í Róma."

Manuscripts:
See Andrew the Apostle 11 note (p. 31).
Edition:
Jón Helgason, ed. >> *Íslenzk miðaldakvæði* (1936–8). Vol. 2, p. 275.

3. Rósa

An early sixteenth-century cosmological poem with an emphasis on the life of
Mary the Blessed Virgin attributed to Sigurður blindur. Stz. 6 mentions Saint
Philip.
    Incipit: "Faðir og son á hæstum hæðum."

Manuscripts:
See Mary the Blessed Virgin 48 note (p. 212).
Editions:
Jón Helgason, ed. >> *Íslenzk miðaldakvæði* (1936–8). Vol. 1.2, p. 7.
Jón Þorkelsson, ed. >> *Kvæðasafn* (1922–7). P. 264.
Norwegian translation:
Orgland, Ivar, trans. and Anne-Lise Knoff, illus. *Rósa. Sigurður blindi í
    Fagradal* (Oslo: Solum, 1989). P. 20.

4. Postulavísur

A poem about all the apostles composed in 1629 by Guðmundur Erlendsson í
Felli (1595–1670). Stz. 15, 22, and 30 concern Saint Philip.
    Incipit: "Herrans hér postula."

Manuscripts:
See Andrew the Apostle 14 note (p. 32).

5. Postularaun

A poem in praise of all the apostles composed by Guðmundur Bergþórsson (1657–1705). Stz. 37–8 and 51 concern Saint Philip.
Incipit: "Hér skal eina hróðar grein."

Manuscripts:
See Ananias note (p. 20).

PRAXIS   July 21

Heilagra meyja drápa

A fourteenth-century poem about holy maidens. Stz. 57 mentions Saint Praxis.
Incipit: "Heyrðu ómælds himna veldis herra guð."

Manuscripts:
See Agatha note (p. 13).
Editions:
Finnur Jónsson, ed. >> *Den norsk-islandske skjaldedigtning* (1912–15).
Vol. AII, p. 538 and vol. BII, p. 596.
Kock, Ernst Albin, ed. >> *Notationes Norrænæ* (1923–44). §§2970B and 2971B.
– ed. >> *Den norsk-islandske skaldediktningen* (1946–50). Vol. 2, p. 330.
Wolf, Kirsten, ed. "Anonymous, *Heilagra meyja drápa* '*Drápa* about Holy Maidens'." In >> *Poetry on Christian Subjects* (2007). Vol. 2, p. 927.
Danish translation:
Finnur Jónsson, ed. >> *Den norsk-islandske skjaldedigtning* (1912–15).
Vol. BII, p. 596.
English translation:
Wolf, Kirsten, ed. "Anonymous, *Heilagra meyja drápa* '*Drápa* about Holy Maidens'." In >> *Poetry on Christian Subjects* (2007). Vol. 2, p. 927.

PRISCA   January 18

Heilagra meyja drápa

A fourteenth-century poem about holy maidens. Stz. 57 mentions Saint Prisca.
Incipit: "Heyrðu ómælds himna veldis herra guð."

Manuscripts:
See Agatha note (p. 13).
Editions:
Finnur Jónsson, ed. >> *Den norsk-islandske skjaldedigtning* (1912–15).
   Vol. AII, p. 538 and vol. BII, p. 596.
Kock, Ernst Albin, ed. >> *Notationes Norrœnæ* (1923–44). §§2970B and
   2971B.
– ed. >> *Den norsk-islandske skaldediktningen* (1946–50). Vol. 2, p. 330.
Wolf, Kirsten, ed. "Anonymous, *Heilagra meyja drápa* 'Drápa about Holy
   Maidens'." In >> *Poetry on Christian Subjects* (2007). Vol. 2, p. 927.
Danish translation:
Finnur Jónsson, ed. >> *Den norsk-islandske skjaldedigtning* (1912–15).
   Vol. BII, p. 596.
English translation:
Wolf, Kirsten, ed. "Anonymous, *Heilagra meyja drápa* 'Drápa about Holy
   Maidens'." In >> *Poetry on Christian Subjects* (2007). Vol. 2, p. 927.

PUSINA   April 23

Heilagra meyja drápa

A fourteenth-century poem about holy maidens. Stz. 57 mentions Saint Pusina.
   Incipit: "Heyrðu ómælds himna veldis herra guð."

Manuscripts:
See Agatha note (p. 13).
Editions:
Finnur Jónsson, ed. >> *Den norsk-islandske skjaldedigtning* (1912–15).
   Vol. AII, p. 538 and vol. BII, p. 596.
Kock, Ernst Albin, ed. >> *Notationes Norrœnæ* (1923–44). §§2970B and
   2971B.
– ed. >> *Den norsk-islandske skaldediktningen* (1946–50). Vol. 2, p. 330.
Wolf, Kirsten, ed. "Anonymous, *Heilagra meyja drápa* 'Drápa about Holy
   Maidens." In >> *Poetry on Christian Subjects* (2007). Vol. 2, p. 927.
Danish translation:
Finnur Jónsson, ed. >> *Den norsk-islandske skjaldedigtning* (1912–15).
   Vol. BII, p. 596.
English translation:
Wolf, Kirsten, ed. "Anonymous, *Heilagra meyja drápa* 'Drápa about Holy
   Maidens." In >> *Poetry on Christian Subjects* (2007). Vol. 2, p. 927.

PUTENTIANA   May 19

Heilagra meyja drápa

A fourteenth-century poem about holy maidens. Stz. 57 mentions Saint Putentiana.
Incipit: "Heyrðu ómælds himna veldis herra guð."

Manuscripts:
See Agatha note (p. 13).
Editions:
Finnur Jónsson, ed. >>*Den norsk-islandske skjaldedigtning* (1912–15).
Vol. AII, p. 538 and vol. BII, p. 596.
Kock, Ernst Albin, ed. >> *Notationes Norrœnæ* (1923–44). §§2970B and 2971B.
– ed. >> *Den norsk-islandske skaldediktningen* (1946–50). Vol. 2, p. 330.
Wolf, Kirsten, ed. "Anonymous, *Heilagra meyja drápa* 'Drápa about Holy
Maidens." In >> *Poetry on Christian Subjects* (2007). Vol. 2, p. 927.
Danish translation:
Finnur Jónsson, ed. >> *Den norsk-islandske skjaldedigtning* (1912–15).
Vol. BII, p. 596.
English translation:
Wolf, Kirsten, ed. "Anonymous, *Heilagra meyja drápa* 'Drápa about Holy
Maidens." In >> *Poetry on Christian Subjects* (2007). Vol. 2, p. 927.

SABINA   August 29

Heilagra meyja drápa

A fourteenth-century poem about holy maidens. Stz. 57 mentions Saint Sabina.
Incipit: "Heyrðu ómælds himna veldis herra guð."

Manuscripts:
See Agatha note (p. 13).
Editions:
Finnur Jónsson, ed. >> *Den norsk-islandske skjaldedigtning* (1912–15).
Vol. AII, p. 538 and vol. BII, p. 596.
Kock, Ernst Albin, ed. >> *Notationes Norrœnæ* (1923–44). §§2970B and 2971B.
– ed. >> *Den norsk-islandske skaldediktningen* (1946–50). Vol. 2, p. 330.
Wolf, Kirsten, ed. "Anonymous, *Heilagra meyja drápa* 'Drápa about Holy
Maidens'." In >> *Poetry on Christian Subjects* (2007). Vol. 2, p. 927.

Danish translation:
Finnur Jónsson, ed. >> *Den norsk-islandske skjaldedigtning* (1912–15).
   Vol. BII, p. 596.
English translation:
Wolf, Kirsten, ed. "Anonymous, *Heilagra meyja drápa* 'Drápa about Holy
   Maidens'." In >> *Poetry on Christian Subjects* (2007). Vol. 2, p. 927.

SCHOLASTICA   February 10

Heilagra meyja drápa

A fourteenth-century poem about holy maidens. Stz. 56 treats Saint Scholastica.
   Incipit: "Heyrðu ómælds himna veldis herra guð."

Manuscripts:
See Agatha note (p. 13).
Editions:
Finnur Jónsson, ed. >> *Den norsk-islandske skjaldedigtning* (1912–15).
   Vol. AII, p. 538 and vol. BII, p. 596
Kock, Ernst Albin, ed. >> *Notationes Norrænæ* (1923–44). §§2970C, 2971D,
   and 2979.
– ed. >> *Den norsk-islandske skaldediktningen* (1946–50). Vol. 2, p. 330.
Wolf, Kirsten, ed. "Anonymous, *Heilagra meyja drápa* 'Drápa about Holy
   Maidens'." In >> *Poetry on Christian Subjects* (2007). Vol. 2, p. 926.
Danish translation:
Finnur Jónsson, ed. >> *Den norsk-islandske skjaldedigtning* (1912–15).
   Vol. BII, p. 596.
English translation:
Wolf, Kirsten, ed. "Anonymous, *Heilagra meyja drápa* 'Drápa about Holy
   Maidens'." In >> *Poetry on Christian Subjects* (2007). Vol. 2, p. 926.

SEVEN SLEEPERS   July 27

Rímur af sjö sofendum

Four *rímur* about the Seven Sleepers of Ephesus composed in 1765 by
Guðmundur Björnsson (1712–1784).
   Incipit: "Upp skal setja einföld ljóð."

Manuscripts:
JS 477 8vo (ca. 1675–1900), Lbs 625 4to (ca. 1800–10), Lbs 1197 4to
(ca. 1750–1800), Lbs 2324 4to (1882–93), Lbs 2344 4to (1871–3), Lbs
5169 4to (ca. 1900), Lbs 319 8vo (1793), Lbs 784 8vo (1896), Lbs 1117
8vo (ca. 1850), Lbs 3839 8vo (1877), Lbs 4540 8vo (ca. 1800–1900), and
Lbs 4860 8vo (ca. 1800–1900).

Edition:
Finnur Sigmundsson, ed. >> *Rímnatal* (1966). Vol. 1, p. 434 (introductory stz.
and refrain).

SIMEON THE RIGHTEOUS   February 3

1. Drápa af Máríugrát

A fourteenth-century poem about Mary the Blessed Virgin's lament to Saint
Augustine about her sorrows and her enumeration to a monk of her five joys.
Stz. 6 mentions Saint Simeon the Righteous.
   Incipit: "Orðin gef þú mjög til mærðar, minn lausnari, skáldi þínu."

Manuscripts:
See Mary the Blessed Virgin 9 note (p. 176).
Editions:
Finnur Jónsson, ed. >> *Den norsk-islandske skjaldedigtning* (1912–15).
   Vol. AII, p. 473 and vol. BII, pp. 506–7.
Gade, Kari Ellen, ed. "Anonymous, *Drápa af Máríugrát* 'Drápa about the
   Lament of Mary'." In >> *Poetry on Christian Subjects* (2007). Vol. 2,
   p. 763.
Kahle, Bernhard, ed. >> *Isländische geistliche Dichtungen des ausgehenden
   Mittelalters* (1898). Pp. 56–7.
Kock, Ernst Albin, ed. >> *Notationes Norrœna* (1923–44). §§1663, 1664D,
   1666, 2680A, 2683, and 3354B.
– ed. >> *Den norsk-isländska skaldediktningen* (1946–50). Vol. 2, pp. 276–8.
Sperber, Hans, ed. >> *Sechs isländische Gedichte legendarischen Inhalts*
   (1911). P. 31.
Wrightson, Kellinde, ed. >> *Fourteenth-Century Icelandic Verse on the Virgin
   Mary* (2001). P. 3.
Danish translation:
Finnur Jónsson, ed. >> *Den norsk-islandske skjaldedigtning* (1912–15).
   Vol. BII, pp. 506–7.

English translations:
Gade, Kari Ellen, ed. "Anonymous, *Drápa af Máríugrát* 'Drápa about the Lament of Mary'." In >> *Poetry on Christian Subjects* (2007). Vol. 2, p. 763.
Wrightson, Kellinde, ed. >> *Fourteenth-Century Icelandic Verse on the Virgin Mary* (2001). P. 3.

2. Gjörði í einu

A poetic rendering of biblical stories composed between 1400 and 1550. The poem is also known as *Liljukvistur*. Stz. 28 mentions Saint Simeon the Righteous.
  Incipit: "Gjörði í einu orði hreinu."

Manuscripts:
See Elizabeth 1 note (p. 83).
Edition:
Jón Helgason, ed. >> *Íslenzk miðaldakvæði* (1936–8). Vol. 1.2, p. 162.
German translation:
Kock, E.A. "Liljukvistur." *Studia Neophilologica* 15 (1942): 141–56, esp. p. 149.

3. Bjóða vil ég þér bragsins smíð

A poem in praise of Mary the Blessed Virgin from ca. 1400–1550. The text is probably based on oral tradition. Stz. 20 mentions Saint Simeon the Righteous.
  Incipit: "Bjóða vil ég þér bragsins smíð."

Manuscripts:
See Mary the Blessed Virgin 36 note (p. 199).
Edition:
Jón Helgason, ed. >> *Íslenzk miðaldakvæði* (1936–8). Vol. 2, p. 56.

4. Máríugrátur

A poem in honour of Mary the Blessed Virgin from ca. 1400–1550. Stz. 8 mentions Saint Simeon the Righteous.
  Incipit: "Blómstrið brúða og kvenna."

Manuscripts:
See Mary the Blessed Virgin 37 note (p. 201).

Edition:
Jón Helgason, ed. >> *Íslenzk miðaldakvæði* (1936–8). Vol. 2, pp. 60–3.
Modern Icelandic language edition:
Ásdís Egilsdóttir, Gunnar Harðarson, and Svanhildur Óskarsdóttir, ed.
  Maríukver: Söur og kvæði af heilagri guðsmóður frá fyrri tíð (Reykjavík:
  Hið íslenska bókmenntafélag, 1996). P. 156.

5. Heyr mig himins og láða

A fragmentary poem from ca. 1500 about the events surrounding Christ's birth
and childhood. Stz. 12 mentions Saint Simeon the Righteous.
  Incipit: "Heyr mig himins og láða."

Manuscript:
See Anne 10 note (p. 38).
Edition:
Jón Helgason, ed. >> *Íslenzk miðaldakvæði* (1936–8). Vol. 1.2, p. 187.

6. Rósa

An early sixteenth-century cosmological poem with an emphasis on the life of
Mary the Blessed Virgin attributed to Sigurður blindur. Stz. 110 mentions Saint
Simeon the Righteous.
  Incipit: "Faðir og son á hæstum hæðum."

Manuscripts:
See Mary the Blessed Virgin 48 note (p. 212).
Editions:
Jón Helgason, ed. >> *Íslenzk miðaldakvæði* (1936–8). Vol. 1.2, p. 30.
Jón Þorkelsson, ed. >> *Kvæðasafn* (1922–7). P. 288.
Norwegian translation:
Orgland, Ivar, trans. and Anne-Lise Knoff, illus. *Rósa. Sigurður blindi í
  Fagradal* (Oslo: Solum, 1989). P. 58.

7. Milska

A early sixteenth-century poem about the life of Mary the Blessed Virgin. Stz.
36 mentions Saint Simeon the Righteous.
  Incipit: "Faðir vor Kristur friður hinn hæsti."

Manuscripts:
See Mary the Blessed Virgin 49 note (p. 214).
Edition:
Jón Helgason, ed. >> *Íslenzk miðaldakvæði* (1936–8). Vol. 1.2, p. 46.
Modern Icelandic language edition:
Jón Sigurðsson, ed. *Milska* (Reykjavík: Listahátíð í Reykjavík, 1994). P. [13].
Norwegian translations:
Orgland, Ivar. *Milska* (Reykjavík: Listahátíð í Reykjavík, 1994). P. [13].
Orgland, Ivar, trans. and Anne-Lise Knoff, illus. *Milska: Eit Maria-kvad frå islandsk seinmellomalder* (Oslo: Solum, 1993). P. 38.

8. Sælust sjóvar stjarna

An early sixteenth-century poem in praise of Mary the Blessed Virgin attributed to the priest Hallur Ögmundarson (d. ca. 1540). Stz. 9 mentions Saint Simeon the Righteous.

Manuscripts:
See Mary the Blessed Virgin 50 note (p. 214).
Editions:
Jón Helgason, ed. >> *Íslenzk miðaldakvæði* (1936–8). Vol. 2, pp. 64–6.
Jón Þorkelsson, ed. >> *Kvæðasafn* (1922–7). P. 368.

9. Píslargrátur

A poetic rendering of the passion of Christ composed ca. 1525 by Bishop Jón Arason (1484–1550). Stz. 34 mentions Saint Simeon the Righteous.
   Incipit: "Faðir vor Kristur í friðinum hæsta."

Manuscripts:
See John the Evangelist 22 note (p. 139).
Editions:
Finnur Jónsson, ed. >> *Jón Arasons religiøse digte* (1918). P. 33.
Guðbrandur Þorláksson, ed. >> *Ein ny wiisna bok* (1612). P. 259.
Jón Helgason, ed. >> *Íslenzk miðaldakvæði* (1936–8). Vol. 1.2, p. 203.
[Jón Sigurðsson and Guðbrandur Vigfússon, ed.] >> *Biskupa sögur* (1858–78). Vol. 2, p. 517.
Jón Torfason and Kristján Eiríksson, ed. >> *Vísnabók Guðbrands* (2000). P. 202.

10. Blómarós

A poem praising Jesus Christ and relating various biblical stories composed ca. 1400–1550. Jón Helgason argues that it is probably from 1550 or the first decade thereafter during the transition from Catholicism to Protestantism. Stz. 106 mentions Saint Simeon the Righteous.

   Incipit: "Heyr guð faðir á himna hæðum."

Manuscripts:
See Elizabeth 6 note (p. 85).
Edition:
Jón Helgason, ed. >> *Íslenzk miðaldakvæði* (1936–8). Vol. 1.2, p. 82.

11. Máríuvísur

A poem in praise of Mary the Blessed Virgin composed ca. 1600 by Einar Sigurðsson í Eydölum (1539–1626). Stz. 33 mentions Saint Simeon the Righteous.

   Incipit: "Mjúkast vilda ég mærðarvers."

Manuscripts:
See Mary the Blessed Virgin 55 note (p. 220).
Editions:
Guðbrandur Þorláksson, ed. >> *Ein ny wiisna bok* (1612). P. 96.
Jón Torfason and Kristján Eiríksson, ed. >> *Vísnabók Guðbrands* (2000).
   P. 112.

12. Máríuævi eða Lífssaga helgustu guðs móður

A poem about the life of Mary the Blessed Virgin composed ca. 1600 by the priest Ólafur Guðmundsson (ca. 1537–1609). Stz. 23 mentions Saint Simeon the Righteous.

   Incipit: "Ég vil jómfrú eina."

Manuscript:
See Mary the Blessed Virgin 57 note (p. 221).
Editions:
Guðbrandur Þorláksson, ed. >> *Ein ny wiisna bok* (1612). P. 304.
Jón Torfason and Kristján Eiríksson, ed. >> *Vísnabók Guðbrands* (2000).
   Pp. 342.

13. Ein ágæt minning herrans Jesú Kristi pínu

A passion poem from ca. 1600 by Arngímur Jónsson lærði (1568–1648). Stz.
32 mentions Saint Simeon the Righteous.
   Incipit: "Mér er í hug að minnast."

Manuscripts:
See Peter 17 note (p. 325).
Editions:
Guðbrandur Þorláksson, ed. >> *Ein ny wiisna bok* (1612). P. 267.
Jón Torfason and Kristján Eiríksson, ed. >> *Vísnabók Guðbrands* (2000). P. 301.

SIMON   October 28

1. Pétrsdrápa

A fourteenth-century poem in honour of Saint Peter. Stz. 11 and 23–4 mention
Saint Simon.
   Incipit: "Orð satt upphafs gjörði eitt næst stafi hæsta."

Manuscripts:
See Peter the Apostle 1 note (p. 318).
Editions:
Finnur Jónsson, ed. >> *Den norsk-islandske skjaldedigtning* (1912–15).
   Vol. AII, pp. 502 and 504–5 and vol. BII, pp. 547 and 550–1.
Kahle, Bernhard, ed. >> *Isländische geistliche Dichtungen des ausgehenden
   Mittelalters* (1898). Pp. 80 and 83.
Kock, Ernst Albin, ed. >> *Notationes Norrœna* (1923–44). §§1712B, 1724,
   1725, 2876, and 2997C.
– ed. >> *Den norsk-isländska skaldediktningen* (1946–50). Vol. 2, pp. 300
   and 302.
McDougall, David, ed. "Anonymous, *Pétrsdrápa* 'Drápa about S. Peter'."
   In >> *Poetry on Christian Subjects* (2007). Vol. 2, pp. 804, 815, and 817.
Danish translation:
Finnur Jónsson, ed. >> *Den norsk-islandske skjaldedigtning* (1912–25).
   Vol BII, pp. 547 and 550–1.
English translation:
McDougall, David, ed. "Anonymous, *Pétrsdrápa* 'Drápa about S. Peter'." In
   >> *Poetry on Christian Subjects* (2007). Vol. 2, pp. 805, 815, and 817.

2. Allra postola minnisvísur

A fourteenth-century poem about all the apostles. Saint Simon is treated in stz. 11.
   Incipit: "Pétr er páfi drottins prísaðr gleðivísum."

Manuscript:
See Andrew the Apostle 10 note (p. 30).
Editions:
Finnur Jónsson, ed. >> *Den norsk-islandske skjaldedigtning* (1912–15).
   Vol. AII, p. 511 and vol. BII, pp. 561–2.
Kock, Ernst Albin, ed. >> *Den norsk-isländska skaldediktningen* (1946–50).
   Vol. 2, p. 308.
McDougall, Ian, ed. "Anonymous, *Allra postula minnisvísur* 'Celebratory
   Vísur about All the Apostles'." In >> *Poetry on Christian Subjects* (2007).
   Vol. 2, p. 867.
Danish translation:
Finnur Jónsson, ed. >> *Den norsk-islandske skjaldedigtning* (1912–15).
   Vol. BII, pp. 561–2.
English translation:
McDougall, Ian, ed. "Anonymous, *Allra postula minnisvísur* 'Celebratory
   Vísur about All the Apostles'." In >> *Poetry on Christian Subjects* (2007).
   Vol. 2, p. 867.

3. Tólf postula kvæði

A late medieval (ca. 1400–1550) celebratory poem about all the apostles. Saint
Simon is treated in stz. 11.
   Incipit: "Sankti Pétur sannur páfi í Róma."

Manuscripts:
See Andrew the Apostle 11 note (p. 31).
Edition:
Jón Helgason, ed. >> *Íslenzk miðaldakvæði* (1936–8). Vol. 2, p. 277.

4. Rósa

An early sixteenth-century cosmological poem with an emphasis on the life of
Mary the Blessed Virgin attributed to Sigurður blindur. Stz. 6 mentions Saint
Simon.
   Incipit: "Faðir og son á hæstum hæðum."

Manuscripts:
See Mary the Blessed Virgin 48 note (p. 212).
Editions:
Jón Helgason, ed. >> *Íslenzk miðaldakvæði* (1936–8). Vol. 1.2, p. 7.
Jón Þorkelsson, ed. >> *Kvæðasafn* (1922–7). P. 264.
Norwegian translation:
Orgland, Ivar, trans. and Anne-Lise Knoff, illus. *Rósa. Sigurður blindi í*
   Fagradal (Oslo: Solum, 1989). P. 20.

5. Náð

An early sixteenth-century poem in honour of Saint Anne and her daughter
Mary the Blessed Virgin ascribed to the priest Hallur Ögmundarson (d. ca.
1540). Stz. 76 mentions Saint Simon.
   Incipit: "Heyr mildingur allra alda."

Manuscripts:
See Anne 1 note (p. 34).
Editions:
Jón Helgason, ed. >> *Íslenzk miðaldakvæði* (1936–8). Vol. 2, p. 19.
Jón Þorkelsson, ed. >> *Kvæðasafn* (1922–7). P. 345.

6. Postulavísur

A poem about all the apostles composed in 1629 by Guðmundur Erlendsson í
Felli (1595–1670). Stz. 24 and 32 concern Simon.
   Incipit: "Herrans hér postula."

Manuscripts:
See Andrew the Apostle 14 note (p. 32).

7. Postularaun

A poem in praise of all the apostles composed by Guðmundur Bergþórsson
(1657–1705). Saint Simon is treated in stz. 62–6 (where he is conflated with
Saint Simeon of Jerusalem [February 19]) and 67.
   Incipit: " Hér skal eina hróðar grein."

Manuscripts:
See Ananias note (p. 20).

STEPHEN THE DEACON   December 26

1. Fyrirlát mér jungfrúin hreina

A poem about Christ and the Holy Cross probably composed in Norway ca.
1400–1550. Stz. 7–8 treat Saint Stephen.
   Incipit: "Fyrirlát mér jungfrúin hreina."

Manuscripts:
See Cross, the Holy 6 note (p. 71).
Edition:
Jón Helgason, ed. >> *Íslenzk miðaldakvæði* (1936–8). Vol. 1.2, pp. 269–70.

2. Gimsteinn

An early sixteenth-century poem about the cross-tree ascribed to the priest
Hallur Ögmundarson (d. ca. 1540). Stz. 89 mentions Saint Stephen.
   Incipit: "Heyr mig ilmanda hjartans yndi."

Manuscripts:
See Cross, the Holy 7 note (p. 73).
Editions:
Jón Helgason, ed. >> *Íslenzk miðaldakvæði* (1936–8). Vol. 1.2, p. 324.
Jón Þorkelsson, ed. >> *Kvæðasafn* (1922–7), P. 318.

SUNNIVA AND COMPANIONS   July 8

Heilagra meyja drápa

A fourteenth-century poem about holy maidens. Stz. 53 treats Saint Sunniva.
   Incipit: "Heyrðu ómælds himna veldis herra guð."

Manuscripts:
See Agatha note (p. 13).
Editions:
Finnur Jónsson, ed. >> *Den norsk-islandske skjaldedigtning* (1912–15).
   Vol. AII, p. 537 and vol. BII, p. 595
Kock, Ernst Albin, ed. >> *Notationes Norrænæ* (1923–44). §§1849 and
   3397N.

– ed. >> *Den norsk-islandske skaldediktningen* (1946–50). Vol. 2, p. 330.

Wolf, Kirsten, ed. "Anonymous, *Heilagra meyja drápa* 'Drápa about Holy Maidens'." In >> *Poetry on Christian Subjects* (2007). Vol. 2, p. 924.

Danish translation:

Finnur Jónsson, ed. >> *Den norsk-islandske skjaldedigtning* (1912–15). Vol. BII, p. 595.

English translation:

Wolf, Kirsten, ed. "Anonymous, *Heilagra meyja drápa* 'Drápa about Holy Maidens'." In >> *Poetry on Christian Subjects* (2007). Vol. 2, p. 924.

THOMAS THE APOSTLE   December 21

1. Thómasdiktur

A fragment of a poem in honour of Saint Thomas composed between 1300 and 1550.

Incipit: "Vil ég hins bjarta blóma."

Manuscripts:

AM 720a 4to VII (ca. 1500), AM 920 4to (ca. 1800–1900), Lbs 1486b 4to (ca. 1860–78), and Lbs 2166 4to (ca. 1885–1920).

Editions:

Jón Helgason, ed. >> *Íslenzk miðaldakvæði* (1936–8). Vol. 2, pp. 317–18. Edition of AM 720a 4to VII.

Jón Þorkelsson, ed. >> *Om Digtningen på Island* (1888). P. 67 (stz. 1 and 10[1–2]).

Based on AM 720a 4to VII and AM 920 4to.

Literature:

Finnur Jónsson. >> *Den oldnorske og oldislandske Litteraturs Historie* (1920–4). Vol. 3, p. 126.

Jakob Benediktsson. "Helgendigte." *KLNM* 6 (1961). Cols. 318–21, esp. col. 320.

Kock, E.A. "Anteckningar till Íslenzk Miðaldakvæði." *ANF* 61 (1946): 1–125, esp. p . 89.

Stéfan Einarsson. "Íslenzk helgikvæði á miðöldum." *Tímarit Þjóðræknisfélags Íslendinga* 36 (1955): 43–63, esp. p. 54.

– *Íslensk bókmenntasaga 874–1960* (Reykjavík: Oddi, 1961). P. 91.

Vésteinn Ólason. "Kveðskapur frá síðmiðöldum." In >> *Íslensk Bókmenntasaga* 2 (1993). Pp. 283–378, esp. p. 315.

2. Allra postola minnisvísur

A fourteenth-century poem about all the apostles. Saint Thomas is treated in stz. 6.
   Incipit: "Pétr er páfi drottins prísaðr gleðivísum."

Manuscript:
See Andrew the Apostle 10 note (p. 30).
Editions:
Finnur Jónsson, ed. >> *Den norsk-islandske skjaldedigtning* (1912–15).
   Vol. AII, p. 510 and vol. BII, p. 560.
Kock, Ernst Albin, ed. >> *Notationes Norrœnæ* (1923–44). §§2983 and 3376A.
– ed. >> *Den norsk-isländska skaldediktningen* (1946–50). Vol. 2, p. 307.
McDougall, Ian, ed. "Anonymous, *Allra postula minnisvísur* 'Celebratory
   Vísur about All the Apostles'." In >> *Poetry on Christian Subjects* (2007).
   Vol. 2, p. 860.
Danish translation:
Finnur Jónsson, ed. >> *Den norsk-islandske skjaldedigtning* (1912–15).
   Vol. BII, p. 560.
English translation:
McDougall, Ian, ed. "Anonymous, *Allra postula minnisvísur* 'Celebratory
   Vísur about All the Apostles'." In >> *Poetry on Christian Subjects* (2007).
   Vol. 2, p. 860.

3. Tólf postula kvæði

A late medieval (ca. 1400–1550) celebratory poem about all the apostles. Saint
Thomas is treated in stz. 7.
   Incipit: "Sankti Pétur sannur páfi í Róma."

Manuscripts:
See Andrew the Apostle 11 note (p. 31).
Editions:
Jón Helgason, ed. >> *Íslenzk miðaldakvæði* (1936–8). Vol. 2, p. 276.
Jón Þorkelsson. >> *Om Digtningen på Island* (1888). P. 62.

4. Rósa

An early sixteenth-century cosmological poem with an emphasis on the life of
Mary the Blessed Virgin attributed to Sigurður blindur. Stz. 6 mentions Saint
Thomas.
   Incipit: "Faðir og son á hæstum hæðum."

Manuscripts:
See Mary the Blessed Virgin 48 note (p. 212).
Editions:
Jón Helgason, ed. >> *Íslenzk miðaldakvæði* (1936–8). Vol. 1.2, p. 7.
Jón Þorkelsson, ed. >> *Kvæðasafn* (1922–7). P. 264.
Norwegian translation:
Orgland, Ivar, trans. and Anne-Lise Knoff, illus. *Rósa. Sigurður blindi í
    Fagradal* (Oslo: Solum, 1989). P. 20.

5. Blómarós

A poem praising Jesus Christ and relating various biblical stories composed
ca. 1400–1550. Jón Helgason argues that it is probably from 1550 or the first
decade thereafter during the transition from Catholicism to Protestantism.
Stz. 225–6 treat Saint Thomas.
    Incipit: "Heyr guð faðir á himna hæðum."

Manuscripts:
See Elizabeth 6 note (p. 85).
Edition:
Jón Helgason, ed. >> *Íslenzk miðaldakvæði* (1936–8). Vol. 1.2, p. 98.

6. Postulavísur

A poem about all the apostles composed in 1629 by Guðmundur Erlendsson í
Felli (1595–1670). Stz. 18–19 and 31 concern Saint Thomas.
    Incipit: "Herrans hér postula."

Manuscripts:
See Andrew the Apostle 14 note (p. 32).

7. Postularaun

A poem in praise of all the apostles composed by Guðmundur Bergþórsson
(1657–1705). Stz. 44–8 concern Saint Thomas.
    Incipit: "Hér skal eina hróðar grein."

Manuscripts:
See Ananias note (p. 20).

THOMAS BECKET   December 29

1. Thómasdrápa

A fragment of a poem in honour of Saint Thomas Becket by Óláfr Þórðarson hvítaskáld (d. 1259).
   Incipit: "Þér fremizk því med tíri."

Manuscript:
AM 242 fol. (*Codex Wormianus*) (ca. 1350).
Editions:
Björn Magnússon Ólsen, ed. *Den tredje og fjærde grammatiske afhandling i Snorres Edda tilligemed de grammatiske afhandlingers prolog og to andre tillæg.* STUAGNL 12 (Copenhagen: Knudtzon, 1884). P. 127.
Finnur Jónsson, ed. >> *Den norsk-islandske skjaldedigtning* (1912–15). Vol. AII, p. 97 and vol. BII, p. 109.
Jón Sigurðsson et al., ed. *Edda Snorra Sturlusonar: Edda Snorronis Sturlaei.* 3 vols. (Copenhagen: Legatum Arnamagnaeanum, 1848–87; rpt. Osnabrück: Zeller, 1966). Vol. 2, p. 204.
Kock, Ernst Albin, ed. >> *Den norsk-isländska skaldediktningen* (1946–50). Vol. 2, p. 58.
Sigurður Nordal, ed. *Codex Wormianus (The Younger Edda). MS No. 242 fol. in The Arnamagnean Collection in the University Library of Copenhagen.* CCI 2 (Copenhagen: Levin and Munksgaard, 1931). Facsimile.
Danish translation:
Finnur Jónsson, ed. >> *Den norsk-islandske skjaldedigtning* (1912–15). Vol. BII, p. 109.
Latin translation:
Jón Sigurðsson et al., ed. *Edda Snorra Sturlusonar: Edda Snorronis Sturlaei.* 3 vols. (Copenhagen: Legatum Arnamagnaeanum, 1848–87; rpt. Osnabrück: Zeller, 1966). Vol. 2, p. 205.
Literature:
Cormack, Margaret. >> *The Saints in Iceland* (1994). Pp. 42 and 157.
Eiríkr Magnússon, ed. *Thómas saga erkibyskups: A Life of Archbishop Thomas Becket in Icelandic.* 2 vols. Rolls Series 65.2 (London: Eyre and Spottiswoode, 1875–83). Vol. 2, pp. xxii–xxiii.
Finnur Jónsson. >> *Den oldnorske og oldislandske Litteraturs Historie* (1920–4). Vol. 2, p. 95.

Foote, Peter, ed. *Lives of Saints. Perg. fol. nr. 2 in the Royal Library, Stockholm.* EIM 4 (Copenhagen: Rosenkilde and Bagger, 1962). P. 20.

Jakob Benediktsson. "Helgendigte." *KLNM* 6 (1961). Cols. 218–21, esp. cols. 218–19.

– >> "Helgikvæði." In *Hugtök og heiti í bókmenntafræði* (1983). Pp. 115– 17, esp. p. 116.

Kahle, Bernhard. *Die Sprache der Skalden auf Grund der Binnen- und Endreime* (Strassburg: Karl J. Trübner, 1892).

Paasche, Fredrik. >> *Kristendom og kvad* (1914). P. 125.

Stéfan Einarsson. "Íslenzk helgikvæði á miðöldum." *Tímarit Þjóðræknisfélags Íslendinga* 36 (1955): 43–63, esp. p. 46.

– *Íslensk bókmenntasaga 874–1960* (Reykjavík: Oddi, 1961). P. 83.

Vries, Jan de. >> *Altnordische Literaturgeschichte* (1964–7). Vol. 2, p. 85.

2. Thómas diktur erkibiskups

A late medieval (ca. 1400–1550) poem in honour of Saint Thomas Becket based on oral tradition.

Incipit: "Hæstur heilagur andi."

Manuscripts:
AM 713 4to (ca. 1500–50), AM 920 4to (ca. 1800–1900), and Lbs 2166 4to (ca. 1885–1920).

Editions:
Eiríkr Magnússon, ed. *Thómas saga erkibyskups: A Life of Archbishop Thomas Becket in Icelandic.* Rolls Series 65.2 (London: Eyre and Spottiswoode, 1875–83). Vol. 2, pp. 289–93.
Edition of AM 713 4to.

Jón Helgason, ed. >> *Íslenzk miðaldakvæði* (1936–8). Vol. 2, pp. 460–2.
Edition of AM 713 4to.

Jón Þorkelsson. >> *Om Digtningen på Island* (1888). P. 82 (stz. 1).
Based on AM 713 4to and AM 920 4to.

Literature:
Bekker-Nielsen, Hans. "Thómas saga erkibiskups." *KLNM* 18 (1974). Cols. 249–51, esp. col. 250.

Finnur Jónsson. >> *Den oldnorske og oldislandske Litteraturs Historie* (1920–4). Vol. 3, p. 126.

Foote, Peter, ed. *Lives of Saints. Perg. fol. nr. 2 in the Royal Library, Stockholm.* EIM 4 (Copenhagen: Rosenkilde and Bagger, 1962). P. 20.

Guðrún Nordal. "Handrit, prentaðar bækur og pápísk kvæði á siðskiptaöld." In >> *Til heiðurs og hugbótar* (2003). Pp. 131–43, esp. pp. 139–40.

Jakob Benediktsson. "Helgendigte." *KLNM* 6 (1961). Cols. 318–21, esp. col. 320.

Jón Helgason. "Nokkur íslenzk handrit frá 16. öld." *Skírnir* 106 (1932): 143–68.

– >> "Norges og Islands digtning." In *Litteraturhistorie B: Norge og Island* (1953). Pp. 3–179, esp. pp. 163–4.

Mogk, Eugen. >> *Geschichte der norwegisch-isländischen Literatur* (1904). P. 719.

Schottman, Hans. >> *Die isländische Mariendichtung* (1973). P. 82n12.

Stéfan Einarsson. "Íslenzk helgikvæði á miðöldum." *Tímarit Þjóðræknisfélags Íslendinga* 36 (1955): 43–63, esp. p. 55.

– *Íslensk bókmenntasaga 874–1960* (Reykjavík: Oddi, 1961). P. 92.

Vésteinn Ólason. "Kveðskapur frá síðmiðöldum." In >> *Íslensk Bókmenntasaga* 2 (1993). Pp. 83–378, esp. p. 317.

3. Heilagra manna drápa

A fourteenth-century poem about holy men. Stz. 1–4 treat Saint Thomas Becket.

Incipit: "... mildings f ... um dyrnar þustu ... særa."

Manuscripts:
See Blase note (p. 52).

Editions:
Finnur Jónsson, ed. >> *Den norsk-islandske skjaldedigtning* (1912–15). Vol. AII, pp. 511–12 and vol. BII, pp. 562–3.

Kahle, Bernhard, ed. >> *Isländische geistliche Dichtungen des ausgehenden Mittelalters* (1898). Pp. 90–1.

Kock, Ernst Albin, ed. >> *Notationes Norrænæ* (1923–44). §§1541, 1757, 1764, 1765, 1766, 2889, 2890, and 3377.

– ed. >> *Den norsk-islandske skaldediktningen* (1946–50). Vol. 2, p. 308.

Wolf, Kirsten, ed. "Anonymous, *Heilagra manna drápa* 'Drápa about Holy Men." In >> *Poetry on Christian Subjects* (2007). Vol. 2, pp. 872–6.

Danish translation:
Finnur Jónsson, ed. >> *Den norsk-islandske skjaldedigtning* (1912–15). Vol. BII, p. 563.

English translation:
Wolf, Kirsten, ed. "Anonymous, *Heilagra manna drápa* 'Drápa about Holy Men'." In >> *Poetry on Christian Subjects* (2007). Vol. 2, pp. 872–6.

URSULA AND COMPANIONS   October 21

1. Úrsúlukvæði

A poem about Saint Ursula and her companions composed ca. 1700. It is also
known as *Annálskvæði af 11000 meyjum*. It appears to be based on a chapter in
Kirjalax saga in which Ursula is mentioned.
   Incipit: "Það skal upphaf óðarbands."

Manuscripts:
Eink 1-5 (ca. 1850–1950), Eink 210-23 (ca. 1855), ÍB 183 4to (ca. 1750),
   JS 265 4to (ca. 1860), JS 588 4to (ca. 1800–1900), JS 84 8vo (ca. 1700–
   1900, missing stz.14⁴–21⁴), JS 234 8vo (ca. 1700–1800), JS 259 8vo
   (ca. 1800–50), JS 515 8vo (ca. 1675–1900), Kvennasögusafn Íslands
   box 27 (ca. 1980), Lbs 2286 4to (1879–1905), Lbs 2344 4to (1871–3),
   Lbs 201 8vo (ca. 1850–70), Lbs 269 8vo (ca. 1850–70), Lbs 1368 8vo
   (ca. 1750–1900), Lbs 1742 8vo (ca. 1845), Lbs 2166 8vo (ca. 1860 and
   1897), Lbs 2538 8vo (ca. 1700–1900), Lbs 2941 8vo (1884–6), Lbs 3238
   8vo (ca. 1800), Lbs 3714 8vo (ca. 1800–50), Lbs 3982 8vo (ca. 1800–50),
   Lbs 4059 8vo (1898), SÁM 85/355 EF (1969), SÁM 85/357 EF (1969),
   SÁM 85/413 EF (1970), and SÁM 87/1140 EF (1970).

Editions:
Anna Sigurðardóttir. *Allt hafði annan róm áður í páfadóm: Nunnuklaustrin
   tvö á Íslandi á miðöldum og brot úr kristnisögu* (Reykjavík:
   Kvennasögusafn Íslands, 1988). Pp. 353–6.
   Based on Sigríður Einarsdóttir's (1901–1989) handwritten copy in
   Kvennasögusafn Íslands box 27.
Finnur Karlsson. "Úrsúlukvæði." In *Fimm kvæði um heilaga menn:
   Agnesarkvæði, Dórotheukvæði, Laurentíuskvæði, Margrétarkvæði,
   Úrsúlukvæði*. Unpublished manuscript at Landsbókasafn, 1981. Pp. 15–22.
   Edition of JS 84 8vo with additions to the lacuna from Lbs 1368 8vo.
Jón Þorkelsson. >> *Om Digtningen på Island* (1888). P. 93 (stz. 1).
   Based on ÍB 183 4to and Lbs 201 8vo.

Literature:
Bjarni Þorsteinsson, ed. *Íslenzk þjóðlög* (Copenhagen: Møller, 1906–9). P. 496.
Jón Þórarinsson. *Íslensk tónlistarsaga 1000–1800* (Reykjavík: Tónlistarsafn
   Íslands, 2012). P. 368.
Soffía Ófeigsdóttir. "*Veroníkukvæði*." BA thesis. University of Iceland, 1986.
   P. 66.

2. Heilagra meyja drápa

A fourteenth-century poem about holy maidens. Stz. 54 treats Saint Ursula.
   Incipit: "Heyrðu ómælds himna veldis herra guð."

Manuscripts:
See Agatha note (p. 13).
Editions:
Finnur Jónsson, ed. >> *Den norsk-islandske skjaldedigtning* (1912–15).
   Vol. AII, p. 537 and vol. BII, p. 595.
Kock, Ernst Albin, ed. >> *Notationes Norrœnæ* (1923–44). §§2764 and 2970B
   – ed. >> *Den norsk-islandske skaldediktningen* (1946–50). Vol. 2, p. 330.
Wolf, Kirsten, ed. "Anonymous, *Heilagra meyja drápa* 'Drápa about Holy
   Maidens." In >> *Poetry on Christian Subjects* (2007). Vol. 2, p. 925.
Danish translation:
Finnur Jónsson, ed. >> *Den norsk-islandske skjaldedigtning* (1912–15).
   Vol. BII, p. 595.
English translation:
Wolf, Kirsten, ed. "Anonymous, *Heilagra meyja drápa* 'Drápa about Holy
   Maidens'." In >> *Poetry on Christian Subjects* (2007). Vol. 2, p. 925.

VERONICA   July 12

Verónikukvæði

A poem from ca. 1725 about Saint Veronica (and to a greater extent the dream
of Pilate's wife and the destruction of Jerusalem). It is attributed to Þorvaldur
Magnússon (d. 1747).
   Incipit: "Kveð ég um kvinnu eina."

Manuscripts:
Eink 74-3 (ca. 1784–1872), Eink 330-34 (ca. 1865–1931), Eink 379-12
   (ca. 1670–1740), G-9/5 (1882), G-13/29 (ca. 1800–1900), G-13/32
   (ca. 1800–1900), G-32/5 (ca. 1892–1971), G-40/270 (ca. 1700–1900),
   G-62/2 (1845–8), HSk 203 4to (1887–8), HSk 862 4to (ca. 1878–1926),
   Hsk 117 8vo (1828), ÍB 183 4to (ca. 1750), ÍB 29 8vo (ca. 1800–1900),
   ÍB 33 8vo (ca. 1800–1900), ÍB 212 8vo (1853–5), ÍB 278a 8vo (ca. 1700–
   1900), ÍB 291 8vo (1854), ÍB 388 8vo (ca. 1700–1900), ÍB 534 8vo

(ca. 1780), ÍB 657 8vo (ca. 1750–1900), ÍB 681 8vo (ca. 1770–90), ÍB 811
8vo (ca. 1800–1900), ÍB 816 8vo (ca. 1600–1900), ÍBR 58 4to (ca. 1800–
1900), ÍBR 30 8vo (ca. 1700–1900), ÍBR 32 8vo (ca. 1700–1850), ÍBR 74
8vo (1852), ÍBR 112 8vo (ca. 1830), ÍBR 113 8vo (ca. 1700–1800), ÍBR
152 8vo (1735–6 and later), ÍBR 159 8vo (ca. 1700–1800), JS 201 4to
(ca. 1837–50), JS 265 4to (ca. 1860), JS 286 4to (ca. 1800–50), JS 582 4to
(ca. 1600–1900), JS 120 8vo (ca. 1787–97), JS 237 8vo (ca. 1700–1900),
JS 244 8vo (ca. 1800–20), JS 259 8vo (ca. 1800–50), JS 284 8vo (ca. 1850),
JS 313 8vo (ca. 1700–1850), JS 416 8vo (ca. 1700–1900), JS 470 8vo
(ca. 1675–1900), JS 480 8vo (ca. 1675–1900), JS 481 8vo (ca. 1675–1900),
JS 484 8vo (ca. 1675–1900), JS 495 8vo (ca. 1675–1900), JS 499 8vo
(ca. 1675–1900), JS 508 8vo (ca. 1675–1900), JS 510 8vo (ca. 1675–1900),
JS 515 8vo (ca. 1675–1900), JS 518 8vo (ca. 1675–1900), Lbs 480 fol.
(ca. 1800–2000), Lbs 565 4to (ca. 1860), Lbs 1218 4to (1856–9), Lbs 1293
4to (ca. 1845–57), Lbs 1459 4to (ca. 1700–1900), Lbs 1756 4to (ca. 1800–
25), Lbs 2125 4to (1865–1912), Lbs 2286 4to (1879–1905), Lbs 2344 4to
(1871–3), Lbs 4174 4to (ca. 1800–2000), Lbs 5177 4to (ca. 1800–1900),
Lbs 201 8vo (ca. 1850–70), Lbs 270 8vo (ca. 1850–70), Lbs 318 8vo
(1851), Lbs 448 8vo (ca. 1850), Lbs 556 8vo (ca. 1700–1900), Lbs 676 8vo
(1842), Lbs 1014 8vo (1821–3), Lbs 1032 8vo (ca. 1800 and 1880), Lbs
1070 8vo (1748), Lbs 1098 8vo (ca. 1800–1900), Lbs 1160 8vo (ca. 1870),
Lbs 1170 8vo (ca. 1770 and 1850), Lbs 1228 8vo (ca. 1780), Lbs 1545 8vo
(ca. 1850), Lbs 1567 8vo (ca. 1800–1900), Lbs 1571 8vo (ca. 1780 and ca.
1810), Lbs 1600 8vo (ca. 1700–1850), Lbs 1766 8vo (ca. 1800–50), Lbs
1779 8vo (ca. 1700–1900), Lbs 1787 8vo (ca. 1700–1800), Lbs 1812c 8vo
(ca. 1700–1900), Lbs 1922 8vo (ca. 1800), Lbs 1987 8vo (1781 and later),
Lbs 1988 8vo (ca. 1790 and later), Lbs 2475 8vo (ca. 1800–50), Lbs 2930
8vo (1788), Lbs 2937 8vo (ca. 1800–2000), Lbs 2941 8vo (1884–6), Lbs
2974 8vo (ca. 1800–1900), Lbs 3169 8vo (ca. 1850–1900), Lbs 3238 8vo
(ca. 1800), Lbs 3241 8vo (ca. 1800–2000), Lbs 3388 8vo (ca. 1800–50),
Lbs 3630 8vo (ca. 1750–1850), Lbs 3668 8vo (ca. 1800–2000), Lbs
3713 8vo (ca. 1750–1900), Lbs 3714 8vo (ca. 1800–50), Lbs 3790 8vo
(ca. 1800–50), Lbs 3907 8vo (ca. 1800–1900), Lbs 3909 8vo (ca. 1800–
1900), Lbs 3920 8vo (ca. 1900), Lbs 3970 8vo (ca. 1800–2000), Lbs 3976
8vo (ca. 1850–1900), Lbs 3982 8vo (ca. 1800–50), Lbs 4041 8vo (1882,
1885, and 1904), Lbs 4156 8vo (ca. 1800–1900), Lbs 4240 8vo (ca. 1850–
1900), Lbs 4255 8vo (ca. 1850–1900), Lbs 4411 8vo (1878–9), Rask 110
(ca. 1700–1800), SÁM 8 (ca. 1840–50), SÁM 39 (ca. 1890–1910), SÁM
08/4206 ST (1903–12), SÁM 85/300A EF (1965), SÁM 85/354 EF (1969),
SÁM 86/794 EF (1963), SÁM 87/1028 EF (1903–12), SÁM 87/1130 EF/U
(1957), SÁM 92/3171 EF (1964), and SÁM 92/3269 EF (1967).

Editions:

Bjarni Halldórsson. *"Veroníkukvæði." Lesbók Morgunblaðsins.* Vol. 42. July 2, 1967. P. 10.

Jón Þorkelsson. >> *Om Digtningen på Island* (1888). Pp. 93–4 (stz. 1).
Based on ÍB 183 4to, ÍB 29 8vo, ÍB 33 8vo, ÍB 212 8vo, ÍB 278a 8vo, ÍB 291 8vo, ÍB 388 8vo, ÍB 534 8vo, ÍB 657 8vo, ÍB 681 8vo, ÍBR 58 4to, ÍBR 74 8vo, ÍBR 112 8vo, ÍBR 152 8vo, and Lbs 201 8vo.

Parsons, Katelin Marit, and Guðmundur Steinn Gunnarsson. "A Saint in Saskatchewan." In *Geislubaugar: Fægður Margaret Cormack sextugri 23. ágúst 2012* (Reykjavík: Menningar- og Minningarsjóður Mette Magnussen, 2012). P. 52 (stz. 13–15).
Based on Ingibjörg Hóseasdóttir's *kvæðabók* housed in a private collection in Mozart, Saskatchewan, Canada.

Soffía Ófeigsdóttir. *"Veroníkukvæði."* BA thesis. University of Iceland, 1986. Pp. 46–52.
Based on Lbs 1070 8vo with additional stz. from ÍB 33 8vo, ÍB 388 8vo, ÍB 816 8vo, JS 244 8vo, JS 284 8vo, JS 481 8vo, Lbs 1756 4to, Lbs 2125 4to, Lbs 1014 8vo, Lbs 1170 8vo, and Lbs 1545 8vo.

Literature:

Bjarni Þorsteinsson, ed. *Íslenzk þjóðlög* (Copenhagen: Møller, 1906). P. 598.

Jón Árnason and Ólafur Davíðsson, ed. *Íslenzkar gátur, skemtanir, vikivakar og þulur.* 4 vols. (Copenhagen: Møller, 1887–1903). Vol. 3, p. 152.

Jón Þórarinsson. *Íslensk tónlistarsaga 1000–1800* (Reykjavík: Tónlistarsafn Íslands, 2012). P. 368.

ZACHARIAH   September 23

1. Bjóða vil ég þér bragsins smíð

A poem in praise of Mary the Blessed Virgin from ca. 1400–1550. The text is probably based on oral tradition. Stz. 4–5 concern Saint Zachariah's relationship to his wife, Saint Elizabeth, and his son, Saint John the Baptist.
Incipit: "Bjóða vil ég þér bragsins smíð."

Manuscripts:
See Mary the Blessed Virgin 36 note (p. 199).

Edition:
Jón Helgason, ed. >> *Íslenzk miðaldakvæði* (1936–8). Vol. 2, p. 54.

2. Nikulásdrápa

An early sixteenth-century poem in honour of Saint Nicholas ascribed to the priest Hallur Ögmundarson (d. ca. 1540). Stz. 16 mentions Saint Zachariah.
   Incipit: "Í nafni guðs vil ég upphaf efna."

Manuscripts:
See Nicholas 5 note (p. 262).
Editions:
Carpenter, William H., ed. *Nikolásdrápa Halls prests: An Icelandic Poem from circa A.D. 1400* (Halle: Karras, 1881). P. 16.
Jón Helgason, ed. >> *Íslenzk miðaldakvæði* (1936–8). Vol. 2, p. 420.
Jón Þorkelsson, ed. >> *Kvæðasafn* (1922–7). P. 389.
Literature:
Björn K. Þórólfsson. "Kvantitetsomvæltningen i islandsk" *ANF* 45 (1929): 35–81, esp. p. 42.

3. Postularaun

A poem in praise of all the apostles composed by Guðmundur Bergþórsson (1657–1705). Stz. 6 mentions Saint Zachariah.
   Incipit: "Hér skal eina hróðar grein."

Manuscripts:
See Ananias note (p. 20).
Literature:
Jón Þorkelsson. >> *Om Digtningen på Island* (1888). P. 63.

Index of Manuscripts

Toronto Old Norse and Icelandic Series

General Editor
Andy Orchard

Editorial Board
Robert E. Bjork
Roberta Frank

1 *Einarr Skulason's* Geisli*: A Critical Edition* edited and translated
by Martin Chase
2 *Anglo-Saxon England in Icelandic Medieval Texts* by Magnus Fjalldal
3 *Sanctity in the North: Saints, Lives, and Cults in Medieval Scandinavia*
edited by Thomas DuBois
4 *Snorri Sturluson and the* Edda*: The Conversion of Cultural Capital
in Medieval Scandinavia* by Kevin J. Wanner
5 *Myths, Legends, and Heroes: Essays on Old Norse and Old English
Literature in Honour of John McKinnell* edited by Daniel Anlezark
6 *The Legends of the Saints in Old Norse–Icelandic Prose* by Kirsten Wolf
7 *Essays on Eddic Poetry* by John McKinnell
8 *Into the Ocean: Vikings, Irish, and Environmental Change in Iceland
and the North* by Kristjan Ahronson
9 *Egil, the Viking Poet: New Approaches to* Egil's Saga edited by Laurence
de Looze, Jón Karl Helgason, Russell Poole, and Torfi H. Tulinius
10 *The Saints in Old Norse and Early Modern Icelandic Poetry* by Kirsten
Wolf and Natalie M. Van Deusen